Apart from John Calvin, who preached 200 sermons (an English translation appeared in 1583), I am not sure I can think of a volume of 74 sermonic expositions on Deuteronomy that comes remotely close to this great achievement. I studied Deuteronomy in a seminary class and over forty years later, I still haven't found the courage to preach through the book. Dr. Kelly's exceptional preaching skills and insightful application make this a page turner. The importance of Deuteronomy, both in Moses' time and later in the reforms of King Josiah make it uniquely important for our time. Dr. Kelly will inspire a host of preachers to take up Deuteronomy and preach it. If God spares, I will be among them.

Derek W. H. Thomas
Senior Minister, First Presbyterian Church, Columbia, South Carolina
Chancellor's Professor, Reformed Theological Seminary
Teaching Fellow, Ligonier Ministries

Anyone who says that Deuteronomy is not practical for real life evidently never heard Douglas Kelly preach it. Here, faithfully proclaimed, is the book of the Bible to which Christ turned three times in a row when tempted by the devil, applied to our homes and hearts. Highly recommended!

Joel R. Beeke
President, Puritan Reformed Theological Seminary, Grand Rapids, Michigan

Deuteronomy is one of the lesser-known books of the Bible to the church, and so Dr. Kelly's exposition is a welcome contribution. Dr. Kelly drills down into the word of God to tap into the well of biblical truth. His exposition flows with the living water of the gospel that equips for every good work—he points the church to Christ so we can seek the grace of God for salvation and godly living.

J. V. Fesko
Harriet Barbour Professor of Systematic and Historical Theology, Reformed Theological Seminary, Jackson, Mississippi

Douglas Kelly has produced an excellent, lucid exposition of Deuteronomy. He presents the message of the book in a clear and accessible way. Free from jargon and technicalities, while yet informed by scholarly discussion, this should be of great value for pastors and lay readers alike.

Robert Letham
Professor of Systematic and Historical Theology, Union School of Theology, Wales

DEUTERONOMY

A MENTOR EXPOSITORY COMMENTARY

DOUGLAS F. KELLY

MENTOR

Unless otherwise stated Scripture quotations are taken from the *King James Version*.

Scripture quotations marked 'NIV' are taken from *The Holy Bible, New International Version*®, NIV® Copyright © 1973, 1978, 1984, 2011 by Biblica, Inc.™ Used by permission. All rights reserved worldwide.

Copyright © Douglas F. Kelly 2021

Hardback ISBN 978-1-5271-0639-0

10 9 8 7 6 5 4 3 2 1

Published in 2022
in the
Mentor Imprint
by
Christian Focus Publications Ltd.,
Geanies House, Fearn, Ross-shire,
IV20 1TW, Scotland, Great Britain

www.christianfocus.com

Cover design by dufiart.com
Printed by Bell & Bain, Glasgow

All rights reserved. No part of this publication may be reproduced, stored in a retrieval system, or transmitted, in any form, by any means, electronic, mechanical, photocopying, recording or otherwise without the prior permission of the publisher or a licence permitting restricted copying. In the U.K. such licences are issued by the Copyright Licensing Agency, 4 Battlebridge Lane, London, SE1 2HX. www.cla.co.uk

Contents

Author's Foreword 9
Thanks 13

1 How Do We Face the Future?
   Deuteronomy 1:1-8 15

2 Representative Government is a Divine Blessing
   Deuteronomy 1:9-18 25

3 The High Stakes of Trusting in God
   Deuteronomy 1:19-33 31

4 The Price of Disobedience
   Deuteronomy 1:34-46 37

5 The God of the Second Chance
   Deuteronomy 2:1-15 43

6 Take Possession of What I Gave You
   Deuteronomy 2:16-37 49

7 The Future is At Least as Good as the Past
   Deuteronomy 3:1-22 55

8 The Patience of Unanswered Prayer
   Deuteronomy 3:23-29 59

9 Which Way the Western World
   Deuteronomy 4:1-8 65

10 True Spiritual Worship
    Deuteronomy 4:9-14 71

11 What the Transcendence of God Requires
    Deuteronomy 4:15-24 77

12 A Secure Future
    Deuteronomy 4:25-31 83

13 Remembrance Gives Hope
    Deuteronomy 4:32-40 89

14 The Cities of Refuge
    Deuteronomy 4:41-43 95

15 Three Uses of God's Moral Law
    Deuteronomy 4:44-49 99

16 A Second Beginning
    Deuteronomy 5 107

17 First Things First
    Deuteronomy 6:1-3 113

18 The *Shema*
    Deuteronomy 6:3-9 119

19 A Thankful Spirit
    Deuteronomy 6:10-15 125

20 What to Teach the Children
    Deuteronomy 6:16-25 129

21 Obedience in the Promised Land
    Deuteronomy 7:1-11 133

22 The Returns of Love
    Deuteronomy 7:12-26 141

23 Obedience is the Ground of Blessing
    Deuteronomy 8:1-10 147

24 The Curse of the Covenant
    Deuteronomy 8:11-20 153

25	The Necessity of Intercession *Deuteronomy 9* 159		43	How to Guide Your Life: The Word of God *Deuteronomy 18* 275
26	God's Grace in Action *Deuteronomy 10:1–11* 165		44	The Law of Retaliation *Deuteronomy 19* 281
27	A Circumcised Heart *Deuteronomy 10:12–22* 171		45	Holy War *Deuteronomy 20* 287
28	The Blessings and Cursings of Grace *Deuteronomy 11* 179		46	The Sacredness of Life *Deuteronomy 21* 293
29	The Second Commandment *Deuteronomy 12:1–11* 185		47	The Broadness and Beauty of God's Law *Deuteronomy 22:1–12* 299
30	Practical Help in Old Testament Worship *Deuteronomy 12:12–32* 191		48	Holiness of God in Engagement and Marriage *Deuteronomy 22:13–29* 305
31	God's Name and Exclusive Worship *Deuteronomy 13* 197		49	Holiness in Unexpected Places *Deuteronomy 22:30–23:14* 311
32	Clean and Unclean Animals *Deuteronomy 14:1–21* 203		50	God Turns Curses into Blessings *Deuteronomy 23:3–6* 319
33	The Tithe *Deuteronomy 14:22–29* 209		51	Instead of Stealing, Give *Deuteronomy 23:15–25* 325
34	The Sabbath and Poverty *Deuteronomy 15:1–11* 215		52	The Far Reach of the Eighth Commandment *Deuteronomy 24:1–7* 331
35	The Sabbath and Freedom from Slavery *Deuteronomy 15:12–18* 221		53	No False Witness *Deuteronomy 24:8–16* 337
36	Consecration *Deuteronomy 15:19–23* 227		54	How to Treat the Disadvantaged (Part I) *Deuteronomy 24:17–22* 343
37	The Passover *Deuteronomy 16:1–8* 233		55	How to Treat the Disadvantaged (Part II) *Deuteronomy 24:17–22* 347
38	The Feasts of Firstfruits and Tabernacles *Deuteronomy 16:9–15* 241		56	Fair Punishment *Deuteronomy 25:1–3* 353
39	God's Authority in the Courts *Deuteronomy 16:16–20* 249		57	Never Covet *Deuteronomy 25:4–19* 359
40	Integrity in Worship and Judgment *Deuteronomy 16:21–17:7* 255		58	Tithing of First Fruits *Deuteronomy 26:1–15* 365
41	The Foundation of Justice *Deuteronomy 17:8–13* 261		59	The Covenant Confirmed *Deuteronomy 26:16–19* 371
42	The King of Israel *Deuteronomy 17:14–20* 267			

Contents

60 Curses of the Covenant
Deuteronomy 27   377

61 Blessings of Covenant Obedience
Deuteronomy 28:1–14   383

62 Covenant Curses
Deuteronomy 28:15–29:1   389

63 Take the Covenant Oath
Deuteronomy 29:2–15   395

64 Idols Destroy, But God Saves
Deuteronomy 29:16–29   403

65 Success Can Follow Failure
Deuteronomy 30:1–10   409

66 The Truth is Not Hard to Find
Deuteronomy 30:11–20   415

67 The Future is Secure
Deuteronomy 31:1–13   421

68 Don't Make It Happen
Deuteronomy 31:14–30   427

69 The Song of Moses
Deuteronomy 31:30–32:4   433

70 Remember the One Who Blesses
Deuteronomy 32:5–14   439

71 The High Cost of Forgetting God
Deuteronomy 32:15–25   445

72 Hope for a Sinful People
Deuteronomy 32:26–52   451

73 The Blessings of Moses
Deuteronomy 33:1–29   459

74 Death Has Lost Its Sting
Deuteronomy 34:1–12   467

Subject Index   475

Scripture Index   483

This book is dedicated to my two close friends of Dillon, South Carolina, both of whom are Presbyterian elders: James A. Atkins and Michael N. Brown, M. D.

'… there is a friend that sticketh closer than a brother' (Prov. 18:24).

Author's Foreword

Deuteronomy (or 'Second Law') consists of Moses' explication of the practical meaning of the Ten Commandments, given as the children of Israel were gathered on the banks of Jordan, before Joshua led them over into the Promised Land, shortly after Moses would be called to 'his long home.' After many failures in the wilderness, Israel was facing a new opportunity to show the glory of God among the nations.

These thirty-four chapters could accurately be summarized as 'the splendor of living God's way.' They were called to a life based on the sheer grace of the Sovereign God, where—by His constant help—they could demonstrate the beautiful qualities (or 'attributes' of the Holy One of Israel). While it is certainly a 'second reading of the Law', it is anything but an external or hard legalism. It is the life of a community of faith, living 'face to face' with the loving and holy God of the Covenant of Grace (ch. 17), made long ago with their fathers, and now renewed in power with this generation, and indeed, for all to come, to the end of time.

This Triune God is always in control of the nations (ch. 7), and of the very cosmos itself, yet He has the most tender regard for His chosen people. For that reason, He calls them to share in His holiness in a relationship of love and joy, if only they will keep looking to Him in faith and obedience. His grace is wondrously free, but it has its profound requirements, which can be fulfilled only by those who have been subject to that spiritual circumcision which occurs with the new heart. Without that 'new birth' it is impossible for us 'to see', which is necessary for us to share in the splendor of the divine life (ch. 64).

But given the putting forth of the divine power 'that makes us willing' (Ps. 110:3), (chs 14 and 28) we are then enabled to live life in a fallen world that will show in every relationship, just who God is, and how beautiful His character is. That is the true goal of life (ch. 73), and it extends into an eternity of bliss, in which failure and defeat are no more, and 'death has lost its sting' (ch. 78). Moses asks us to come with him!

True love of God always seeks obedience, as Jesus taught us (John 15:15), and while the demands are high, the merciful grace of pardon is ever available, and we find Him to be 'the God of the second chance' throughout the struggles of our life (chs 13 and 78). The 'city of refuge' is not far off (ch. 15), and our Mediator always stands in for us, where otherwise, we would be cut off from the life of God, and from all hope (ch. 17).

This God of all grace, with whom it is our indescribable privilege to live 'face to face' (chs 17, 78), rightly summons us to live as His own children. His love and grace to us, and election of us to be His, call us to 'walk in the light, as he is in the light,' and that can mean nothing less than for His holy character to serve as the wholesome structure of our life on earth (ch. 60). Therefore, Moses expounds the principles of the Ten Commandments throughout Deuteronomy, saying: 'This is the way, walk ye in it' (Isa. 30:21). It is a walk in the immediate presence of God, who 'has put his law in our inward parts, and has written it in our hearts' in the New Covenant (ch. 14), so that 'he is our God and we are his people' (Jer. 31:33).

To disobey Him, or, at its worst, to put anything else before Him (idolatry) is a denial of who we are in Christ, our Mediator (chs 14 and 17), and, if persisted in, to move outside the camp of faith, where we must experience the high cost of forgetting Him who loved us, and drew us with cords of love (chs 25 and 72). Yet as Psalm 130:3 promises: 'There is forgiveness with thee, that thou mayest be feared' (or as John Owen translates, 'that thou mayest be worshiped'), (ch. 73).

Although, in the holy camp (the community of faith), we do live 'face to face' with this gracious God, we must—in His name and power—also face many an enemy, and thus we have to 'wrestle with principalities and powers', yet it is not an equal struggle, for victory is guaranteed for those who fight in His Name (chs 7 and 8). All through, He keeps us as the precious 'apple of his eye' (ch. 71).

These expositions look at the disastrous theological misunderstanding of 'antinomianism', as well as 'legalism' (chs 16 and 27), and commends what the church has long termed 'the three-fold use of the Law' (ch. 18). In a number of places, it shows that while major aspects of the Mosaic Law no longer pertain to the church and the modern state, it is always to be taken seriously, in terms of what the Westminster Assembly called its 'general equity' as a healthy guide for every aspect of societal life (chs 18, 35, 37, 42, etc.).

Moses knew that the power to keep the law does not come from the law itself, but from the grace of God, in whose presence we live (chs 42 and 60). God's grace never destroys the law, but magnifies the One from whose character it shines out (ch. 27). And for those who are seeking to follow him, God has a wonderful way of turning the curses of a hateful world against them into blessings (ch. 51).

Therefore, the eye of His people is to be upon Him, not upon their adversaries or difficult circumstances (ch. 8). As we are increasingly taken up with God, to our surprise, we may unexpectedly discover the grace to exemplify something that the world desperately needs to see: consecration (chs 18 and 37). When the unexpected happens, they will glorify Him, not us (ch. 73).

Everything is based upon this solid foundation of triumphant divine grace; a grace that as an integral aspect of it, provides a healthy structure for living in every society, Moses takes us in many directions, showing the truth of Psalm 119:96— 'Thy commandment is exceeding broad.' Behind all holy requirements is the spirituality of God (ch. 11) and His transcendence (ch. 12). The Oneness of the Triune God, and His infinite love is conveyed in the Shema (Deut. 6:4–5; see ch. 19).

Thus, the gracious One who made the world, controls it, and redeems it, properly calls us to live in terms of His character within it. Hence, Moses calls God's people to pure worship of the Holy One of Israel, whose own words set the terms for how He is to be recognized and praised (chs 68, 30, 31, 38, 41, etc.).

God's transcendence, and ever present control of all reality, is why 'his commandment is exceeding broad'. On that basis, Moses calls us to observe the sabbath principle (chs 34, 35, 36); to honor Him by tithing (chs 34, 59); to teaching our children in his fear (ch. 21), to compassionate, practical help to the poor (ch. 55, 56), to principles of just war (ch. 46), to legitimate civil power, and limitations of it (ch. 43), to proper legal retaliation, without personal vengeance (chs 45, 51), to legitimate enjoyment of creational life (ch. 46), to prohibition of man-stealing (ch. 53), to protection of a run-away slave (ch. 52), to honest talk, mercy in lending, and timely payment of bills (ch. 54). Spiritual meditation and daily Scripture reading are also expounded (ch. 75), as are landmarkers (ch. 45), the occult (ch. 44), and the three pilgrim festivals (ch. 38).

The ethical matters above have been generally an accepted part of the broad Christian tradition, as well as that of Judaism, over the ages. However, Moses takes us in some other directions that are rather less familiar to us, other than transvestism, which is increasingly known amongst us (ch. 45). However, we usually hear little of such things as nesting birds, mixture of species, and tassels on garments (ch. 48), or of clean and unclean animals (ch. 33). Certainly, over the years, there has been some discussion of laws of consanguinity (as concerns marriage), incest and personal sanitation (ch. 50).

In sum, the paths of righteousness are pointed out to us by God's servant, Moses, and as we seek to follow them, as empowered by the Spirit (ch. 60), rays of the splendor of God's glory will be shining out in an otherwise darkened world. For what else could happen, since we are in intimate touch thereby with Him who is Light?

These expositions of Deuteronomy were delivered in Reedy Creek Presbyterian Church, Minturn, South Carolina, during 2008 and 2009. Hence, this volume of expositions is the second in the Reedy Creek Series (the first was the Exposition of Revelation).

Thanks

My thanks to the Lord for the blessing of his Word and Spirit, as I have sought to explicate the teaching of Moses in Deuteronomy. Also I am profoundly grateful to Mrs. Karl (Linda) Rudolph of Greenville, South Carolina, for having typed all these expositions, gratis, out of love for the Lord. And I thank my good wife, Caroline, for all her assistance with computer issues, and for other encouragements. I am grateful to the session of Reedy Creek Presbyterian Church (T. Curt McSwain, Clerk of Session) for their help in providing for the beginning of the process of printing these messages. Also I am thankful for the staff of Christian Focus Publications, in seeing through this volume.

Douglas F. Kelly,
Carthage, South Carolina

1

How Do We Face the Future?

Deuteronomy 1:1-8

Deuteronomy is the right book to help us think about facing the future. Every human being, Christian or not, must think about what the future will be like. It is always unknown, uncertain, and sometimes dangerous. Particularly as believers, how do we face our own future? Such a question every day takes us to the cusp of the unknown.

But there are particular junctures in our life when it comes powerfully before us. How do we decide what kind of job to take, where to go to college, whom we marry, or how many children to have? All of us must face the unknown.

Deuteronomy was delivered by Moses while Israel was facing an unknown future. They had been under his leadership for forty years in the wilderness. By the Lord's work through him, Moses had led them out of slavery in Egypt. Now we find them here on the verge of the River Jordan and God has said, 'You have been here long enough; it is time for you to cross over the river.'

This crossing would be challenging, even to the faith of the strongest person, especially because Moses could not go into the land with them. The Lord would remove the strong, competent leader whom they knew and trusted. However, in the wilderness, for the most part, except on a few occasions (as with the Amalekites), they didn't have to face many enemies.

It will be different for the children of Israel after crossing the Jordan River. They must face 'battle royal' time after time, and they must do so without Moses. There were hostile cities to be conquered, and powerful tribes to be forced out. They already knew enough to realize that their future, in the plan of God, must include warfare, danger, slaughter, and sometimes death.

So how did they face this kind of future? What Moses says in Deuteronomy is a wonderful key to all our futures, and we do well to take it to heart, whether we knowingly face danger or not.

Four Reasons to Study Deuteronomy

because 'all scripture is inspired by god'

Any part of the sixty six books of the Bible should be studied, because, 'All Scripture is inspired by God [or God-breathed], and is profitable for reproof, for instruction' (2 Tim. 3:16).

Many ministers worldwide were influenced by the Rev. William Still from Aberdeen Scotland.

He wrote a book for students over sixty years ago entitled *The Work of the Pastor*. His essential point is that the main work of the pastor is to take his people through different parts of the Bible, by expounding each text. One has to balance different parts of the Old Testament and New Testament, and one must vary in one's preaching Law, Prophets, Wisdom, History, Gospel, Epistle, and the future. He holds that if the preacher does not give his congregation all parts of the whole Bible, they will not grow in Christ-like character in certain areas because each part assists different aspects of the believer's character. The Holy Spirit uses each text to change, strengthen, and transform us. Sitting under the preaching of the whole counsel of God's Word over time, even though we don't feel it ourselves, will cause others to perceive that we've been with the Lord; that we're becoming more like Him. All Scripture accomplishes this goal of transformation of the life because it is directly inspired by God, who uses it to make his people more like his Son. That transforming process includes Deuteronomy, which is reason enough to study it closely.

The Old Testament was Written for Our Learning

Romans 15:4 says that 'whatsoever things were written aforetime were written for our learning, that we through patience and comfort of the Scriptures might have hope.' By 'written aforetime', he means the Old Testament, because the New Testament had not yet been fully written.

A. W. Pink once remarked that it is an Old Testament characteristic that it often puts into the concrete many New Testament doctrines. For instance, some of the sharp difficulties that God's saints in the Old Testament era went through, are not fundamentally different from hardships we face. When we see that they got through these trials with God's help, then we cry out: I too can get through it! Studying the Old Testament strengthens us in hope—and who needs anything more than hope?

Through Moses, God attaches special blessings to the study and practice of Deuteronomy.

One finds several promises of blessing for studying and seeking to practice. For instance:

> And it shall come to pass, if thou shalt hearken diligently unto the voice of the LORD thy God, to observe and to do all his commandments which I command thee this day, that the LORD thy God will set thee on high above all nations of the earth: And all these blessings shall come on thee, and overtake thee, if thou shalt hearken unto the voice of the LORD thy God. (Deut. 28:1–2)

So through Moses God is saying that your life, and the life of a nation, can be different if many in it will hearken to these words.

In Deuteronomy 29:9, we find a similar kind of promise; 29:14–15 makes rich promises as well, not just to the children of Israel, some 1,400 years before Christ, as they were standing near Jordan, but for their spiritual descendants, such as us: 'Neither with you only do I make this covenant and this oath; But with him that standeth here with us this day before the LORD our God, and also with him that is not here with us this day:' We were born 3,400 years later, and He still covenants with us, if we are in the faith. Similarly, in Deuteronomy 30:9-10, the principle is that your heart is given to God; it is not merely attention to rules (even good ones), but Moses tells us here that we are to live face to face with God. That is the heart of the Covenant that He sets forth (though it is never without powerful rules).

Deuteronomy 32:44–47 promises even more blessings, which believers can take as their own.

Jesus used Deuteronomy to overcome the devil

A fourth reason to study Deuteronomy is this: our Lord Jesus Christ, after His baptism and at the beginning of His public ministry, went out into the wilderness to be tempted. While He is there, Satan attacks Him in all his fury, and tempts Him to do wrong. But how did Jesus find strength to overcome the devil? The Lord Jesus Christ in His humanity, made use of three passages from Deuteronomy to deal with the evil one's three temptations. He quotes Deuteronomy 8:3:

> And when the tempter came to him, he said, 'If thou be the Son of God, command that these stones be made bread'. But he answered and said, 'It is written, Man shall not live by bread alone, but by every word that proceedeth out of the mouth of God'. (Matt. 4:3–4)

The devil then takes Him up on the wing of the temple (Matt.4:5-7) and essentially says, 'You can show off and make a tremendous media impact if You jump down and show that God can protect you.' Jesus answered him from Deuteronomy 6:16: 'Ye shall not tempt the LORD your God, as ye tempted him in Massah'.

The third temptation is in Matthew 4:8–10 and Christ's response to the devil again is from Deuteronomy (Deut. 6:13). So I believe you will agree that if Jesus felt the need of Deuteronomy to help Him in His hour of trial, surely it can help us in the difficulties of our lives.

Authorship of Deuteronomy

The heading of your Bibles calls Deuteronomy 'the fifth book of Moses,' which I believe is correct. It is believed that Moses wrote the first five books of the Bible, although he may well have used, particularly in Genesis, sources going as far back as Adam and Noah, although we don't know for certain how he got his sources. But we do know that Moses was inspired to write the first five books, including this fifth book, Deuteronomy. It says in verse 1, 'These be the words which Moses spake.'

In the nineteenth century there was a deeply influential movement of secularization called 'Higher Criticism'. For the most part it began in Germany, and then it spread through Britain to the USA, and to many of the universities, seminaries, and colleges. 'Higher Criticism' was an aspect of 'Modernism', and as such, it sought to undercut traditional authorities, especially the authority of Scripture, with particular disregard for the Old Testament. The 'higher critics' argued that Moses could not have written this book.

In the early phase of the higher critical movement, an argument was made that writing did not exist in the time of Moses—but evidence in no way supports this idea. In fact, we now know from plenty of documentary evidence that writing was thousands of years before Moses, so higher criticism had to drop that one as an argument against Mosaic authorship.

Although this argument fell through, these critics didn't give up. They then took another approach, arguing that Deuteronomy was put together long after the time of Moses from disparate sources and that these sources were cobbled together, producing a book that has no clear structure or focus.

Recent archeological support

However, in the twentieth century, a considerable amount of archeological and documentary scholarship based on research done in the Middle

East between the two world wars has found several treaties from the time of Moses and vindicated the likelihood of the Mosaic authorship of Deuteronomy. These treaties, dating back to the middle of the second millennium BC, were found on clay tablets and sometimes dried parchments and were written by the ruling powers of the ancient Near East at that time, particularly by a huge, powerful group known as the Hittites. We have a treasure of these Hittite writings that originated at precisely the same time Moses would have lived.

SUZERAINTY TREATIES

Interestingly, these Hittite treaties, known as suzerainty treaties, are structured in much the same way as Deuteronomy. In Hittite culture, a suzerain was a mighty king, and when this mighty king sent in his generals to take over another subject country, he would make a treaty or covenant with them. The ancient Hittite treaties from the time of Moses begin with a preamble, much like Deuteronomy 1:1–8. This preamble serves to identify the high king or suzerain, and then it moves on to a review of the history of the relationship between the Suzerain and the people with whom he was entering into a treaty. Next, the treaty moves to the stipulations or requirements of the covenant, and then the sanctions, that is, blessings for obedience, cursing for disobedience, and then to a statement that this covenant will be displayed publicly. Deuteronomy takes that precise form. So therefore, there is every reason to believe historically, in documentary terms, that Deuteronomy was written by Moses in the same way that treaties were made by the Hittites, by the Assyrians and by others in this time and to accept this historically as authentic; it fits in with the way things were done in Moses' lifetime—that is, the middle of the second millennium before Christ.

In addition to such excellent archeological evidence, the New Testament quotes portions of Deuteronomy and clearly ascribes them to the hand of Moses. For instance, Luke 20:28 quotes Deuteronomy 25:5 and says 'Moses wrote'. Considering that early Jews and Christians considered these to be the words of Moses, we too should accept the Mosaic authorship of Deuteronomy.

THE OUTLINE OF DEUTERONOMY

Does Deuteronomy have an outline, that is, a structure? At one time in the nineteenth century, critics argued that Deuteronomy did not make sense as one document; it seemed to be thrown together, with no sort of form or structure.

And yet, as we have already seen, it seems to be clear based on Hittite suzerainty treaties, and this helps us to see that this fifth book of Moses follows a very intentional structure. Specifically, much of the book follows the order of the Ten Commandments given in Deuteronomy 5, which parallels the first time they are given in Exodus 20.

In fact, so central to Deuteronomy is this second giving of the Ten Commandments, that the name of the book itself literally means 'second law' (from the Greek *deuteros* meaning 'second' and *nomos* meaning 'law'). Yet why give the Law again, when Exodus 20 has already presented it in a most glorious manner?

What Moses is doing here is explaining the spirit behind the Ten Commandments, and also providing illustrations of how you carry them out in normal, everyday life. We must understand that Deuteronomy is not a new giving of the law, as though it is adding something different. It's the same law as Exodus 20, given on Mt. Sinai, but it's the second reading. In this second reading, Moses gives careful explication of what it means, thereby showing its spiritual depths, and its practical ramifications. This is similar to what Jesus does in Matthew 5 in the Sermon on the Mount. He expounds the law by showing the spiritual depth and inner connectedness it requires, and how it goes into the deep places of human life and daily living. It would be safe to say that in some ways, Deuteronomy is similar in spirit to Christ's Sermon on the Mount—though of course it's not exactly the same.

Dr. John Currid brings out this outline of Deuteronomy in his recent commentary.

1. 1:1–8 is a preamble (like second millennium B.C. suzerainty treaties)
2. 1:9–4:43 is a review of the history of the relationship between Jehovah and Israel from Abraham to the plains of Moab.
3. 4:44–26:19 gives the stipulations of the covenant; a reiteration of the Ten Commandments and a practical exposition of what each of them will mean for life in the promised land. This longest section of Deuteronomy follows the order of the Decalogue:
   a. 4:44–5:33 giving the setting and proclamation of the ten commandments
   b. 6:1–11:32 constitute a commentary on the first commandments, opening with the Shema (6:4)
   c. 12:1–31 commentary on the second commandment, calling for eradication of pagan cults
   d. 12:32–14:21 commentary concerning taking God's name in vain, thus condemning false prophets
   e. 14:22–16:17 Sabbath law and festal calendar of Israel (based on Sabbath principle)
   f. 16:18–18:22 the fifth commandment: parental authority and authority of hierarchical structures
   g. 19:1–22:12 the sixth commandment: no killing, warfare and punishment for capital offences
   h. 22:13–23:14 the seventh commandment: no adultery, and laws against other forms of sexual impurity
   i. 23:15–24:7 the eighth commandment: stealing and other property violations
   j. 24:8–16 the ninth commandment: no false witness: pledges and vows made to one's neighbor; keeping one's word
   k. 24:17–26:19 the tenth commandment: do not covet; restriction of violations against rights and privileges of others
4. 27:1–29:1 The blessings and curses of the covenant
5. 27:1–4 A statement of display (to erect stones and write on them the covenant words)
6. 29:2–30:20 An oath of allegiance of the vassal to the covenant
7. 31:1–32:47 Three witnesses to the covenant: the law itself, the song of Moses and Joshua, and heaven and earth.

As you can see, it is clear from our knowledge of the structure of Hittite treaties, that we must reject the idea that Deuteronomy has no structure as the critics once thought. Rather, we now know that it is written with an identifiable and intentional structure

THE PREAMBLE TO DEUTERONOMY 1:1-8
Now that we have uncovered the background and context of the book, let us consider Deuteronomy 1:1–8. Just as in ancient Hittite suzerainty treaties, this covenant document starts off with a preamble, somewhat like the Constitution of the United States of America begins with a preamble.

Moses starts off in verse 1 by identifying himself as the spokesman of the Lord. Next, in verses 3 and 6–8, he makes clear that it is God Almighty, the great king and covenant Lord, who is speaking through His servant Moses. In doing so, Moses specifies the precise time of the second reading of the law and the place where it was done. These verses give us precise details as to the immediate history when it was written.

First, the time was at the end of the forty years of wandering, just before the people of Israel would cross over Jordan into the Promised Land. Verse 3 says it was the fortieth year, the eleventh month, the first day of the month. That's being very precise; clearly this was not a mythological dream, but a precise, historical, datable matter.

Second, the place of the second reading of the law is, according to verse 5, what we call today Transjordan, east of the Jordan River in the ancient territory of Moab. Thus, the people of God were on the verge of the greatest movement they have made since they came out of slavery in Egypt and crossed over the Red Sea some forty years before. And while they were still God's people, most of that generation which left Egypt had died out, and the group Moses is leading here is a new generation, with a few exceptions. Hence, they are preparing to cross into the Promised Land that God would give them!

However, to gain it, they would face a tremendous amount of fighting and risk their lives on the high places of the field. Naturally, any normal human, even those with faith, facing those kinds of battles would become quite sober, and probably have a bad feeling in the pit of their stomach. And so Moses is writing this book to encourage them, as Paul says, 'that you might have hope through the Scriptures' (Rom. 15:4). They need encouragement as they face an unknown, and warlike future. To do so, he gives them this encouragement by turning their hearts and minds to who God is, and to what His covenant promises are like for His people.

As he does so, he reminds them they are in the line of the patriarchs whom God chose and blesses: Abraham, Isaac, and Jacob. As they went through their difficulties, they found that God is still just as big as He was in the time of Abraham, Isaac, and Jacob, and indeed, as He was when they came through the Red Sea. Moses is saying afresh, if you will look to Him, it will give you all the encouragement you need to face severe testing and physical battles, and that you will be fighting for your lives and your children. Only faith in this God of the covenant will get you through. They will not have Moses with them after this; God will take him home, and bury him, so they go forward without the comfort of this tremendous leader and shepherd.

Sometime back, we attended the wedding of a young man, who within days was to be sent to Iraq as an army officer. I decided that I would write a letter and hand it to him. In that letter, I wrote out by hand Psalm 121, and asked him to memorize it before he goes to Iraq.

> I will lift up mine eyes unto the hills,
> from whence cometh my help.
> My help cometh from the Lord,
> which made heaven and earth.
> He will not suffer thy foot to be moved:
> he that keepeth thee will not slumber.
> Behold, he that keepeth Israel
> shall neither slumber nor sleep.

I could think of nothing better that I could do for a young man, just married, who would soon endure such trials, than give him Psalm 121. His greatest hope is to lift up his eyes to the Lord who made heaven and earth as he faces every battle and some of the severe challenges of life.

Notice two points in 1:1-8 First, Moses tells them to look by faith at who God is. And secondly, he tells them to look at the land that God has promised to give them. These two points are a summary way of saying, your future can be a very good one, if only you will keep your hand in My hand.

Looking by faith at who God is, is the big picture. In Deuteronomy 1:6, Moses calls Him, Jehovah our God. We don't know exactly how the word translated *Jehovah* or *Jah-*veh [or *Yahweh*] was pronounced, but it was given to Moses in Exodus 3:14 at the burning bush. In this account, the Lord has just told Moses to go into Egypt and tell Pharaoh to 'let My people go.' In response, Moses tells God that it will be a very hard thing, and for help in doing so, he asks God, 'What's your name?' God responds, 'I am that I am', which basically means, 'I depend on nothing; I am always existent; everything else depends on me. Pharaoh depends on me. The Red Sea depends on me. You go down there and tell him I am that I am has sent you, and says, let the slaves go free.' The word given to Moses at the burning bush encouraged him to do the impossible.

Much later, as a million of the children of Israel were standing on the banks of the Jordan River, he gives them the same name that God gave to him. What a wonderful encouragement to the people as they literally stand on the edge of some extremely difficult, onerous days! He reminds them that it is the Lord God, *Jehovah*, or *Jah-veh* who told them to go and, and that God Himself will go ahead of them.

God has several names in the Bible. The one for the Creator of the whole world is usually *Elohim*. It speaks of God's mighty, creative force. But the one He specially reserves for His people, both to the Jews in the Old Testament and Christians in the New Testament, is usually *Jehovah*, and it's a covenant name, a name of grace. When God gives you that name, it says you are included in the grace that I have shown to the unworthy; I have called you to be Mine, and I am dealing with you graciously in a special way, in a salvational way, so the name Jehovah is a name reserved to His covenant people. That's how Moses names Him again, as they are standing on the banks of the river, needing Him so much, since they will not have Moses with them as their leader anymore. They are going to have to face hostile Amorites, Canaanites (Deut. 1:7), but Moses wants them to know that the Almighty Creator is more than sufficient because whatever enemy you must face, it is less than God. They were called on to remember that.

Earlier I mentioned Psalm 121, verse 1, 'I will lift up mine eyes unto the hills, from whence cometh my help. My help cometh from the LORD, which made heaven and earth'. Another wonderful psalm, Psalm 141:7–8, contemplates a terrible situation. One thinks of the various terrorist attacks on innocent people in different countries, where bodies are blown apart by bombs, or crowds run into by cars or trucks: 'Our bones are scattered at the grave's mouth, as when one cutteth and cleaveth wood upon the earth'. And now verse 8, (and this is what is happening in Deuteronomy): 'But my eyes are unto Thee, O God the LORD. In Thee is my trust. Leave not my soul destitute'. I don't believe any minister, priest, or whoever, is called upon to explain why God lets some of these terrible things happen, because we really don't know. But we are called on to remember the suffering, and to remind ourselves to turn to God (Ps. 141:8). Moses says that turning to God will keep you from being totally devastated by awful things.

Or think of Ezekiel 37:1–3 where the Lord leads the prophet Ezekiel down to this valley of bleached bones. What Ezekiel saw there was like a huge army that had been destroyed ages before, where the bones are bleached and sticking up in the shining, sparkling desert sands. God asks Ezekiel, 'Son of man, can these bones live?' It's impossible. But not if God is there. And Ezekiel gives a very brilliant answer. Oh, that you and I could give such an answer when we face challenges we don't know how we're going to get through! Ezekiel says, 'O Lord, Thou knowest'. He does not give an answer from the realm of his human common sense. He knows that dead bones that are disassembled don't live. But then he remembers that God is in it, the Maker of heaven and earth, *Jehovah,* is in it. And the bones come together and are clothed with flesh, and then God breathed into them the breath of life. That is the value of looking to God!

In the New Testament, we see a similar movement. You may be facing difficulty, an unknown future, where everything seems to have gone wrong, but call to mind what happened in Mark 9:20–24. They brought to Jesus a desperately ill child. Immediately when Jesus saw him, the evil spirit caused the boy to have fits: 'And he fell on the ground and wallowed, foaming at the mouth'. This was apparently something like epilepsy, in addition to being deaf and dumb. Jesus asked His father, how long is it since this came to him? and he answered, 'Of a child. Oft times it would cast him into the fire and into the waters to destroy him, but if Thou canst do anything, have compassion on us, and help us. Jesus said unto him, If thou canst believe, all things are possible to him that believeth'. Notice the honesty of this father in his concern for his very handicapped child: 'And straightway the father of the child cried out, and said with tears, Lord, I believe; help thou mine unbelief'. I'm not where I ought to be; yet I'm looking with faith, and I do believe, as far as I can. Help me anyway. And God did.

Never contemplate your future without thinking of how powerful and gracious God is. That's what you've got to do every day, particularly before certain turning points in your life: think about how great, how mighty, how good, how gracious, how condescending, how loving, your God is, who is in absolute control of all things you have to face. Some of these things make you afraid, but God is bigger than they. Think of Him. Think of how faithful He is to fulfill every promise He makes to His people. He has never failed yet; He's never lied one time. I consider the key here to be Romans 8:32, 'He that spared not his own Son, but delivered him up for us all, how shall he not with him also freely give us all things?'

If God gave you Jesus, that took care of your biggest need! Sins to be cleansed, hell to be conquered, gates of heaven to be opened, everything you need to be a transformed person, in renewed image of God, like Christ. God gave you these stupendous gifts on the cross; God gave you all this when He gave you Jesus! That's the big gift; if He gave you the big thing, He will also give you lesser things. For instance, if somebody asks his father, 'Could you lend me $1,000?' and the father agrees. Then at some later time the son or daughter wouldn't mind asking, 'Could I have $5?' Of course, He would give it! If God gave you the big one, His Son, surely He is going to take care of your future next week. Why not? Hereby Paul, in Romans 8:32, points us in the same direction that Moses was pointing in Deuteronomy.

Then briefly, the second point of this preamble is, look by faith at what God has promised to give His people. Look by faith; exercise faith in what God said He would do. That helps it to become real. Now with the Old Testament people of Israel, at this stage of their history, it was particularly the

Promised Land, a specific territory. Even though it was a particular piece of real estate, Abraham, and others, knew that that land represented a better country on the other side, to which they were eventually going.

To us Christian believers today, you could say that the Promised Land represents the rest of our remaining years on earth, however many they be, which by grace are to be characterized by a spiritual union with Christ—we are one with Christ; He is in us and we are in Him, by the invisible bonds of the Holy Spirit. That's all we need. That is our place of security and rest. We are one with Christ in a real sense, and beyond that, and as part of that, glory and eternal life follow.

How different we all are, alike in many ways, but we have very different backgrounds and challenges in our lives, and so the rest of the time that we live on this earth will be different for each one of us. But, what will be the same, what really matters for all of us who have faith, is that Psalm 23 will always be true of us; the Psalm of the Shepherd, 'The Lord is my Shepherd, I shall not want', I shall not lack, for the presence of the Good Shepherd with all of His graces will meet me in my time of need tomorrow, and on every tomorrow. And it's interesting to note that in the Hebrew text, Psalm 23:1, says, 'Jehovah is my Shepherd—'I am that I am' is my Shepherd'. David says that the same one that Moses met at the burning bush, and of whom Moses reminds the people, 'this is your God, the I am that I am, the all-sufficient, gracious Jehovah, that's who your shepherd is' is precisely the one of whom David is singing in Psalm 23:1. Then, during His Incarnation, Jesus shows us how He is the fullness of the Good Shepherd, as in John 10.

In sum, what Moses says to the wilderness Israelites in verse 8, can in a real sense be said of all who are God's people: 'Behold, I have set the land before you: go in and possess it'. The literal translation of 'behold', and some of you have a more modern English version, is simply the Hebrew word 'see', I have set the land before you. This verb, the imperative 'see', is important because in the ancient Near East, the legal transaction conveying a piece of property from one person to another, was concluded by taking the person who had bought the property or inherited it, and making him look at it, and literally walk on it. Once they had looked at it, then they had the legal authority in the presence of the elders of the community, to go in and possess the land. To 'see', concluded a real estate transaction. So God is saying, 'look,' 'see' the things that I have promised you through Christ, through My grace. Then by faith go in and occupy, take possession of it. That is our future. Take possession of what God has promised. See it, and by faith occupy it in union with Him.

In closing, I remember reading the history of the International Fellowship of Evangelical Students. Just before the outbreak of World War II (in 1939), they were having a meeting, I believe in London, of university students from various countries. The students from Germany were meeting for the last time they were able to travel to the British Isles. War was imminent; Hitler was believed to be preparing to invade Poland, and it was known that communications would soon be cut off. Christian students from Germany were in London, but also Scottish, English, Welsh and Irish students were there. As they were leaving, they hugged one another, knowing that terrible things were going to happen, and they wouldn't see each other for a long time as Christians, maybe never, or maybe even meet on the battlefields of northern Europe. And so before they left they stood and sang this wonderful hymn to the tune of Be Still My Soul:

Deuteronomy

We rest on Thee, our Shield and our Defender!
We go not forth alone against the foe;
Strong in Thy strength, safe in Thy keeping tender,
We rest on Thee, and in Thy Name we go.

2

Representative Government is a Divine Blessing

Deuteronomy 1:9–18

Holy Scripture covers every aspect of life, not just personal salvation. It also sets before God's people how they are to conduct their corporate lives in society, in accordance with God's will. Deuteronomy chapter one shows us that representative government by elders is a divine blessing.

We consider four points on this subject:

1. Government by elders is a blessing from God.
2. Who set up government by elders?
3. What did these elders do?
4. What personal qualifications enabled them to be chosen as an elder or a judge?

GOVERNMENT BY REPRESENTATIVE ELDERS IS A BLESSING FROM GOD

Why would Moses start talking about elders or representative government just before the people pass over the River Jordan into the Promised Land, the place of great danger?

This book follows the movement of the Near Eastern ancient suzerainty treaties or covenants. In our last message, we saw that typical Hittite and Assyrian covenants or treaties start with a preamble. The preamble identifies the sovereign overlord and then gives a historical review about the relationship between the overlord and his subjects. The review is to remind them that they ought to be grateful to the overlord, and thus conduct themselves in terms of his character.

Specifically, Moses is saying in Deuteronomy 1:9–18, that the representative government by elders in Israel is the sign of God's blessing in their history. This kind of government will be a mainstay for His people, and they are reminded of it before they have to face great conflict.

In other words, they should be grateful to God for representative government in their past history in the wilderness. And they ought to continue to live with the same form of government when they cross over into the Promised Land, if they expect to receive God's blessing. To follow the elders, as appointed by God, will be to follow God Himself, and thus to experience God's continued blessing.

Let me say a brief word here about the high value of remembering our history. One of the foundational problems of our modern Western education is that many of our schools do not teach history, but rather, social studies. There is a place for social studies, but something is lost if you don't teach straight history, for here is great value in remembering your history.

The Psalms of David are filled with this kind

of thing. For instance, Psalm 78:5-8 give you the value of communicating your spiritual history to your children and grandchildren. Failure to do so will result in serious problems for them, as Psalm 78:8 shows: 'and might not be as their fathers, a stubborn and rebellious generation; a generation that set not their heart aright, and whose spirit was not steadfast with God.'

The Psalm goes on to describe blessings for a family where you communicate the truths of what God has done for that family. While no one comes from a perfect family, there is great value for the next generation in telling them about the experiences their ancestors have gone through.

Another Psalm (143) is about the value of remembering your history, not so much for our children, as it is for us. What should you do when you get down in your spirit, and you feel terrible? David is saying that when you're down, thinking of God's past deliverances in your own life will often bring you out. We see how David feels in Psalm 143:3-6. I guess we've all joined him in that dark place from time to time. Can a good Christian ever feel desolate and overwhelmed? Of course they can! But there's a way out. It is found in verse 5: 'I remember the days of old; I meditate on all thy works; I muse on the work of thy hands'. Think about what God has done, how wonderful God is in His doings in our own past! 'I stretch forth my hands unto thee'. He is saying, Lord, do it again! Can you say that with him? 'My soul thirsteth after thee, as a thirsty land. Selah'. And then verse 9: 'Deliver me, O LORD, from mine enemies: I flee unto thee to hide me.'

In this regard, I want to say a word about the value of being past sixty years old. Certainly, life past sixty has some disadvantages. Your body may not be so agile; you may feel arthritis in a place or two, a few pains; your reaction time perhaps is getting a bit slower; your eyes are probably not so sharp as they were when you were twenty, and that kind of thing. But that is more than counterbalanced by this great advantage, that you can only have with five or six decades of life experience. The little aches and pains and the general slowing down are more than compensated by this tremendous advantage, namely, that just like the Psalmist, just like Moses in Deuteronomy 1, you remember your history so much better, because you've got more to remember! There is a rich world of experience present in your mind to take around with you everywhere you go.

It is a great advantage that you remember more clearly and vividly as you get older, the things that matter the most, and it means that you can make better decisions on all kinds of things than you ever could when younger (at least as a general rule). This remembrance makes life more serene—you get less upset—and it enables you to be a tower of strength, at least to a few other people, when that is needed.

I'm talking about the ordinary people of God, not just ordained ministers. Preachers are usually no better, no worse. Along this line of the value of memory, let me add here for all believers the value of having a Bible reading program to get you through the Bible once a year. There are several good reasons to do so, such as: 'The entrance of Thy Word giveth light,' (Ps. 119:130).

As you read the Bible year by year, you remember more of it, and a certain atmosphere develops inside your mind. As events take place around you, you automatically think: 'Such and such a verse from the Bible that I recently read, helps me make more sense of what's happening to me, and what's happening to other people. In a certain sense, every Christian life is meant to be a merging of Bible principles and spiritual history with our own life experience in our family and world. Daily reading in the Word of God keeps shining bright light on our pathway through a complex world.

Remembering God's Word as we mature is particularly required by God in those who will be the representative elders of the people. In Old and New Testaments, some maturity was always required; no novice should be ordained to leadership (1 Tim. 3:6). Without years of experience in life, as well as by assimilating ever more of the Word of God, a person lifted up too quickly to leadership can well be puffed up with pride. That's why good government, whether in the church or the state, always requires a certain maturity in the people to whom the government is entrusted, namely some years' experience in life, and some years in learning about God's truth, before power should be handed over to them. At this early stage of their spiritual experience, their focus tends to be on self, not on others.

Who Set Up Government by Representative Elders?

The setting up of elders in Deuteronomy 1 is clarified by looking at events in Exodus 18 and Numbers 11. Together, they are all talking about the same thing: Moses' choosing seventy elders upon whom the Spirit would come to help him govern perhaps as many as a million people.

Some scholars have suggested a discrepancy in the Bible on this point. Some critics say: that in Deuteronomy 1, Moses speaks as though government by elders were his idea. But in Exodus 18, we are told it was the idea of his father-in-law Jethro. Then in Numbers 11, God Himself is said to be the one who commanded the appointment of elders to help govern the flock of the Lord. So which is right?

All three are true at the same time. The Spirit of God always works through consecrated humans to formulate certain plans that come directly from God Himself. There's no contradiction; that's how God works. For instance, the Holy Spirit inspired the writing of Scripture; men wrote the Scriptures. But the Spirit of God was inspiring them to put down what God wanted (see 2 Peter 1:21). God is behind it, but humans think of it, and there is no contradiction between the two whatsoever.

In Jethro, Moses had a very fine father-in-law. Have you ever thought that at least some times, God might actually speak through your in-laws? I'll just leave that question with you. Maybe not all the time, but possibly some of the time? Ultimately, spiritual and civil government by representative elders is a divine appointment. It is God's way, to work through the thoughts of Jethro and Moses to accomplish His plan of setting up elders in Israel. This type of representative government was a blessing of God in Old and New Testament Churches.

Of course, any system of government by humans is going to have some bad leaders in it, or some who maybe go bad after they get into it. But that does not remove the fact that a proper structure of governing is absolutely necessary in the church and in the nation. As for the church, without some kind of legitimate leadership, even though it's imperfect, the church would become a place of confusion, heresy, and corruption, and the gospel would be lost. Particularly, an accountability structure is essential to prevent all kinds of abuse of doctrine and power.

That is because we are all descendants of fallen Adam, so there is a tendency in us to self-centered action that is easily dismissive of the needs and rights of others. Indeed, one could go so far as to say that life would not be livable on earth without some kind of government. Hence, God set up judges and elders in Israel as one of His great blessings to His people.

What Did These Elders Do?

Deuteronomy 1:16, and elsewhere in the books of Moses, shows us the way these officers, or elders, were organized: captains over thousands, captains over hundreds, fifties and tens; reflecting a military capacity. In the United States and in most modern governments, we have a professional standing army, but Israel did not; it was a citizen's army that had to be ready to come to action in short order, if they were attacked. They were organized in thousands, hundreds, fifties, and tens, like a kind of militia, organized from the top, with generals, down to the bottom, with corporals and privates, so they could function on the battlefield in a regular, sensible, effective way. Hence, the elders at this stage could serve as military officers of different ranks in an orderly fashion to save the country.

These same men also regularly served as civil judges of various levels, so they could adjudicate disputes of everyday life: property, settlement of inheritance, marriage issues, fights, and sometimes murders. In this capacity, these elders also served as spiritual, pastoral counselors. Pastoral counseling is not a modern invention after 1950. You read about it in the Reformers, in their own way, and in the Middle Ages they had books of how to counsel people in certain needs and sins, and somewhat like that, these elders were to serve as pastoral counselors, administering the healing hand of the Good Shepherd of Israel to the flock.

Personal Qualifications to Serve as Elder or Judge

We learn about these qualifications particularly in Deuteronomy 1: 13 and 17. In Deuteronomy 1:13, God tells Moses to choose out 'men of wisdom and understanding, known among your tribe', meaning, don't choose somebody unless they have a reasonably good testimony in the community. And other places in the five books of Moses would indicate that the people had a veto over the elders that were chosen, and possibly the people could even nominate somebody to be chosen to serve as a judge, an officer, an elder.

So what valuable personal qualities were required for this leadership role? It says here, 'men of wisdom and understanding'. Some translations say, and rightly so, 'men who are wise and discreet'. That is to say, such people are divinely gifted with spiritual insight into the revealed will of God and thus they are able to be of service.

Moses often says, 'Meditate in the book of God; meditate in His law; meditate in His Word.' They have done that. And thus they have a practical discretion in dealing with difficult people. Sometimes they have to go to a higher captain, or a higher elder, and so forth, and get some help, but they already have a practical discretion to deal with a difficult situation without panicking or over-reacting. The book of Proverbs is full of this kind of practical, Godly discretion, and how wonderful it is to have in a family, not to mention the church and the state, that kind of wisdom and discretion, which comes from long years of poring over the Word of God, and thereby seeking Him, which helps to make our lives as livable, pleasant, noble, and happy as can be in a fallen world.

Recently, I pulled out the Bible that belonged to my father, which his great grandmother, a wonderful Christian woman, gave him upon his graduation from high school in 1925, in Moore County, North Carolina, In the flyleaf of this Bible my great grandmother Blue had written these good words from Proverbs 3:17 to her grandson: 'Remember that wisdom's ways are the ways of pleasantness, and all her paths are peace.' I thought of that over the years that father showed me this Bible. May God give us such officers and leaders!

They were also to be chosen on the basis of substantial moral purity: not perfection, for it doesn't exist, but basic moral honesty and spiritual insight. Deuteronomy 1:17 goes on to say that in cases where the leaders of God's people, whether in church or state, must judge controversies between different persons, both of whom say they're right, then the elders are not to show partiality, either on the basis of whether they like the person, or whether one is more socially distinguished than the other. True elders must always resist the temptation either to favor the rich or to favor the poor.

One time in the USA, it probably was the tendency to assume that the rich must be right. More recently, there seems to be a tendency to assume that the poor will be right. But the Hebrew text literally says that a judge is 'not to recognize a face'. 'Face' is the closest the Hebrew comes to 'person'. Outside the United States Supreme Court in Washington, there is a statue of Lady Justice holding the balances in her hand, with her eyes blindfolded, which is a way of saying that justice is blind as to personality or social distinction. In principle, this means that everybody is equal before the same law, according to God's appointed way.

That is why our fathers said we are to have 'a government of laws, not of men'. That is easier said than done. Is it ever possible for Lady Justice to be blindfolded before social distinctions and other differences? Yes, it is possible, although hard. To achieve that, Moses reminds us in Deuteronomy 1:17 that leaders: whether elders, officers, judges, police, or military, are to keep God in mind every time they look at a controversy, and then render a decision: think about God! If this were brought back into the countries of the West, how much healing we would have; how much bitterness and anger and grief would dissipate in a short time! Notice this clause in Deuteronomy 1:17: 'for the judgment is God's.' When you try to deal with a controversy, even an unofficial one between people, you've got to remember that the judgment is God's. I must do this for God, and I must blot out my personal prejudices, to be just. When that's the case, you're going to have potential healing in all sorts of situations.

Such God-centered leadership is a Divine blessing where exercised, to enable us to live with some safety on earth, and most of all to prepare for heaven, where we will be with the One who blessed us with elders, who were in fellowship with the Good Shepherd. God is a God of order. Where you see some measure of good order on earth, it reflects God's presence and serves as a sort of stair-step up to a better country.

3

The High Stakes of Trusting in God

Deuteronomy 1:19–33

This passage brings before us in vivid fashion, the high stakes involved in whether or not we trust in God. Of course, we do not know exactly why big difficulties suddenly come into our lives. But God does give us help to deal with them. For instance, in this passage, we see how quickly a situation can turn from apparently being just fine, to one in which we are suddenly facing terrible troubles that can quickly change everything in our experience.

Why does this sort of change occur in God's providence for His people? I believe one main reason is that when we suddenly come up against severe trials, we learn something of great value that we cannot realize when it is easy to trust in God. Often in difficulties, we find out how wonderful, and how faithful, and how great He is! As Lamentations 3:23 says: 'Great is Thy faithfulness'. We have a way of learning that far more profoundly than we do in easy circumstances. At such points of pressure, we find out that it is God who carries us through. Then we know deep inside that all of it was worthwhile, because we found God faithful when it was not easy for us.

That's how it was when the children of Israel were massed on the banks of the River Jordan, some forty years after they had come out of Egypt, and were going into the Promised Land, although they knew it would involve fighting and difficulty. The question was: will we trust God and move by faith, as He has said, into this difficulty, believing that through Him we can conquer?

From ancient times, the experience of the children of Israel has always been understood, in certain respects, to be a parable of our Christian lives. God lets us get to the banks of different Jordans, as it were, where we face hard things. Then the question arises: will we trust in God enough to move in through it, believing that He is more than sufficient for the testings that we must go through, in order to be faithful to Him?

We note four points in this text:

1. God's past blessings during difficulties (19–21).
2. The spies are selected to search out the new land, to figure out how great the difficulties are (22–23).
3. A divided report (24–28).
4. The firm promise of God given once again, as they face these difficulties (29–33).

God's Blessing During Their Great Difficulties (1:19-21)

These chosen people already knew how good God had been to them, and therefore that He had the right to demand their loyalty and obedience in the difficulties to come. We are reminded of how God got them out of Egypt, the strongest country in the world. God sent the ten plagues and then got them to the edge of the Red Sea, and opened the Red Sea, miraculously getting the children of Israel through it.

After that, He led them through the great and terrible wilderness where there were many dangers (Deut. 8:15). They had been through times that would have killed any group of people, if God had not been in the situation, orchestrating it. So they needed to remember this as an encouragement for what they must now face.

When God loves you, He doesn't pamper you in cotton wool, and remove all difficulties from your life. It is His normal way to let you face the severe difficulties of spiritual growth that test you to the bottom of your heart. Through it all, what God is trying to teach you is this: 'Trust in Me.'

Sometimes we, at a worship service, may affirm the Apostles' Creed, or say that we believe the Bible, or perhaps the Westminster Confession of Faith, or the Thirty-Nine Articles. That is good as far as it goes, but we have to remember that God is working, so that we may appropriate those truths about God in our hearts. When we have done so, we can, with a certain amount of courage, face the trials that He has set before. Thereby, God is setting everything up, so that we will heed Him when He says: Trust in Me! This is happening, as it were, behind the scenes, throughout all our lives in its different stages. The Lord is saying to us now, in whatever difficulty we face, whether it be severe illness or financial hardship, 'remember how I got you through this in the past; and thus you can handle it with faith in Me; I will handle it for you if you will trust me, and move out across that river'.

Common sense seems to say to us, that it depends on how difficult things are, as to whether or not we can get through them. But passages like Deuteronomy 1:19-33 show us that it is not the severity of the current difficulties we must face that shall limit our success; rather, it is the greatness of God, and His exquisite care for us, if we actually trust in Him to enable us to handle anything that He calls on us to go through. As Israel stood on the banks of the River, Moses reminded them that what God had brought them through in the past was worse than what they were facing now, but still, He got them through it. So why should they fear or give up now? If only they would stop and think what God had already brought them through? Don't you think I can do it again? Therefore, God is saying to a people facing major testing, you must trust me afresh.

In this regard, let us think about what the Western world is facing with the plague of terrorism. Without underrating this evil, it is not the worst thing that Western countries have ever had to face. Serious as it is for our generation, it is salutary to remember that our forefathers came through far worse than that in the past; God got them through it.

This is no time to lose our courage and back down from harsh opposition.

One could think of severe difficulties in Great Britain during the Civil Wars of the 1640s, or during the Nazi bombing of London, three hundred years later. We could think of critical challenges in North America during the War for Independence, or the earlier wars with the Yemassee Indians in South Carolina, when the British population of the East Coast stood a good chance of being wiped out. I doubt that our people who are alive today, ever went through such a situation as that. Even if terrorists get into this country, and do much damage, in my view it won't be nearly as bad as what our fourth great grandparents were facing in the Tuscarora and Yemassee wars, and during the French and Indian conflict of the early 1700s. Or how could it compare with the Vikings coming into Britain in the Middle Ages? But God got our people through it all in those very hard times.

People as old as I am can easily remember the worst years of the Cold War in the 1950s, when the USA and Russia had nuclear missiles facing each other. Of course, we could not have known then, that about forty years later, the Soviet Union would collapse, largely bloodlessly. As a later part of that stand-off, in my first year at the University of North Carolina, we faced the Cuban Missile Crisis. We wondered: how can we get out of this one? And yet, the gracious God of our fathers got us through it. And indeed, at the same time, He preserved the massive population of Russia from destruction. We need to remember such things.

So I am saying that these situations in the past were worse than anything we see now. If, like our fathers, we trust God, He has charge of every bomb, and of those who use them, for as Proverbs 21:1 says: 'the king's heart is in the hand of the LORD, as the rivers of water; He turneth whithersoever He will'. God is in charge of the whole situation.

Who knows how we will be able to overcome present terrorist challenges, immensely complicated by the internal political divisions amongst ourselves? But God is on the throne. 'He that keepeth Israel shall neither slumber nor sleep', as Psalm 121:4 reminds us. If we trust in Him, God will get our people through it. In sum, this first point reminds us that God's past blessings during difficulties must always be remembered, to encourage us to face unknown times and personal dangers that lie ahead.

The Selection of the Spies (1:22-23)

It is normal military procedure to send in spies, to find out what they can about the country, and about the strength of the people with whom they will be in conflict. Some commentators have claimed that Israel didn't have faith when they sent in spies. But a careful look at the situation will show that this is untrue. Moses, the spiritual man of God Himself, approved of sending in spies, and chose out twelve, one from each tribe. What could be wrong with that? On the contrary, God is a God who will let you look at difficulties quite realistically. I'm not aware that God has ever asked you to bury your head in the sand and pretend that there's no bad, no evil, no death, no trouble. God doesn't do that. He said, look at it in the face! It will be difficult, BUT look up to me; I'm greater; trust in me! You can get through it. So the spies went into the land of Canaan, the Promised Land, and then came back.

A Divided Report (1:24-28)

Most of the spies were terrified, and did not want to attack, but there was a minority report, brought in from Joshua and Caleb. These two faithful men said: 'it's a beautiful land, with huge grapes (they brought some back); it is a land flowing with milk and honey, as the Lord promised. Yes, there are war-like tribes, but because God is so great and His promises so firm, let's go in; we can take it! Let's trust God.' That was the minority report of Joshua and Caleb.

But at the same time, the ten other spies gave an extremely different report that must have sent chills through the bones of the pilgrim people of

Israel. These ten distrusted the Lord when they saw how difficult the task was.

It is easy enough, in our arm-chairs, to criticize these frightened ten spies, but we didn't see those giants, those Anakim (like Goliath). Archaeology has demonstrated that there were certain tribes characterized by giantism. These huge and powerful people also had strong walls. No doubt it was an exaggeration to say that the walls went up to heaven, but they were imposing and frightening.

Notice that God did not shield their eyes from looking at the difficulty; that was not his way. But what He said was, Trust in Me, in the face of those difficulties. It makes you think of the book of Daniel, chapter 3, when the three Hebrew children were cast into the fiery furnace by King Nebuchadnezzar, for refusing to worship him. The circumstances were impossible, humanly speaking that is, but God got them through, and they kept trusting in Him.

It was the same with Daniel, who was cast into the den of lions (Dan. 6). Daniel knew the punishment was coming, but would not bend his knees to anyone but God Almighty. He did not know what God would do in that den of lions, but he wasn't going to disobey God. He went into the place of death trusting, and God shut the mouths of the lions and preserved His servant. It says elsewhere in Daniel, they that 'know their God shall be strong, and do exploits' (Dan. 11:32).

Christians in our time, who are facing possibly fatal challenges from the powers of evil, will be given a chance 'to do exploits'; to stand up in the face of danger and difficulty, for the right and for God, as so many tried and true saints in the past have stood up. If we will trust in God in bad situations, then we too shall be able to do exploits, as God's providence sees fit.

THE FIRM PROMISE OF GOD IS GIVEN AGAIN IN TIMES OF DIFFICULTY (1:29-33)

Let us note two brief points here: first, a renewed promise (29-31). Here is what the mighty, majestic God of heaven says, as He stoops down like a caring father or a tender mother: 'I will carry you in My arms in the future, as I have in the past. Why do you think I'm going to drop my child then? He will be in my arms, as he keeps trusting' (See also Isaiah 40:27-31).

Secondly, if the firm promise of God that He makes to take you through difficulties is going to work in your life, you have got to participate by trusting Him, especially when it does not feel good.

We know that Israel could have entered into rest, and not have had to wander forty years, if they had trusted (Ps. 95:8-11; cf. Heb. 4:1-2).

What does it mean 'not mixed with faith'? I am no cook, but I know that someone making a cake puts in the dry measures: flour, sugar, and other ingredients. But to have the cake rise, the cook has to pour in the wet measures: milk, a pound of butter, vanilla, etc. and then stir it all together. If the cook does not mix in the wet measures with the dry ingredients, there will be no cake. This brings out the point that for the firm promises of God to become real to you, they must be mixed with something that comes from you. Of course, God gives it to you, for faith is a gift (Eph. 2:8-9). Still, you've got to bring your faith. When God says, I'll do this, I'll get you through this difficulty, He means that you've got to trust Him, and that involves adding in your faith (even though that faith is a divine gift).

Yes, the Scriptures show that He gives you the faith, but you still must choose to bring it forward, and mix it into the lump in question, saying God will carry me in His arms through this, as He has in the past. On the contrary, you can say it's too dangerous, it's too scary, I don't want to be involved. And you will fail. The promises of God are given us in order that they may be trusted by us personally. That is the test for every one of us, whether we're going to make it or not through the hard times. Will we trust in God? Similarly, Moses says, if you don't trust the Lord, because you're not trusting, you're going to lose.

We can overdo some things, but we can never trust God too much. I don't believe there is a man or woman who will come to the end of their life and say, 'Oh dear; I trusted God too much!' But we will say, with the hymn, 'O for grace to trust him more!'

Probably most of our personal failures, when we went down and tasted bitter defeat, finally have come from our having failed to trust God; when we failed to remember what He did for us in the past. In the once-popular gospel hymn 'Tell me the Old, Old Story', there is this line:

Tell me the old, old story,
for I forget so soon,
the early dew of morning
has passed away at noon.

How soon we forget the past mercy of God, especially when we face another round of testing! It is indeed like the dew has gone away under the noontime sun, for we feel dry and weak, and don't know what to do. But through it all, God says, I have set up the world in such a way that for you to advance spiritually and personally, you've got to trust in me.

Does this run contrary to the sovereignty of God, which affirms that God will get everything accomplished that He wishes? Not for a moment! Look at Ephesians 1:11, 'God worketh all things after the counsel of His will'. In light of that, we are to remember that God has set up the world with us in His image, thus with human personalities; He has set it up, so that His program marches forward as His people mingle their faith with His promises, especially when they face difficulties.

You might object: how is God going to get His will done if people sometimes don't trust Him, as the Israelites failed to do? The answer to that is this: there are mysteries that I wouldn't be able to explain, but I can tell you this much: if you don't trust God in this difficulty, somebody else will do so. God knows exactly how to get His purposes accomplished. But He gives you and me a chance to move forward in His army, as His pilgrim people. And thus, He says, trust me, and I can do important things through you, if only you'll trust.

By the same token, you might object and say: well, what if some Christians don't mingle their faith, and the cake doesn't rise, as it were. What then? God will raise up somebody else to trust. He never leaves Himself without a witness. Jesus once said, if these children were not praising me, God could cause the very stones to cry out! What happens if we don't trust doesn't mean that we have defeated the purposes of God, and that is impossible. What it does mean, is that we miss out on the blessing of victory, after which we will receive yet more grace, and then more struggle, and greater victory, greater glory, with more growth, and then yet more struggle, yet greater victory, and even greater growth; bringing honor to God, and touching many people we know, or perhaps do not know.

God gives each one of us this opportunity in the difficulties that He permits to come into our lives. He says to us, what He said through Moses to the people of Israel on the banks of the Jordan: Trust me in this; I have carried you in my arms in the past; I won't drop you, if only you keep believing, and face it with courage. I will give you all the strength and indeed, all the courage you need. And you'll be glad you did, and you'll have a part in advancing My holy purposes. Let it be so with each of us.

4

THE PRICE OF DISOBEDIENCE

Deuteronomy 1:34-46

This solemn passage brings before us quite realistically the price of disobedience to the promises of God. About 100 years ago a famous preacher, G. Campbell Morgan, of Westminster Chapel in London, often said: 'Obedience is the ground of blessing.' Of course with Campbell Morgan, we know that the grace of God is behind everything, even obedience, and with it, the electing love of God from eternity. But that does not remove the fact that this passage and many another, demonstrate that obedience is the basis for further blessing in our life, while disobedience, which is grounded in distrust of God, and refusal to obey His promises, is the basis of much defeat and unnecessary grief.

We note two points in this text:

1. The refusal of Israel to trust God's promises at this juncture in their history.
2. The consequences of distrust.

THE REFUSAL OF ISRAEL TO TRUST GOD'S PROMISE (1:34-35)

We read in Deuteronomy 1:28 that the people were very distressed when the spies came back, at which time, ten of the twelve brought a negative report about the impossibility of conquering the Promised Land. The Anakim were a tribe of giants, and apparently from them, came 400 years later, Goliath and others. Numbers 13-14, give us much more detail on this negative report so that the people, near the banks of the Jordan, were so discouraged, that they refused to go in or to trust God's promise that He would be with them, and that if He were with them, all would be well.

So once again, forty years after this event, they are massed on the banks of River Jordan, and Moses, who will not be able to go in with them, because of a sin he had committed at the rock (Num. 20:7-13), is reminding them of how they failed to enter the land through distrust of God's promises forty years earlier. This means that now is the time to do better than your forefathers; believe God, take Him at His Word, even though you cannot see how He's going to help. Trust Him, and then you can take that land, and you can prosper and be victorious.

In this passage, Israel had come again in Moses' time to the point where they had to make a decision. The first time, it was either trust God, or trust the unbelieving spies. To which one will you give the most credit? God who says that He is able to work in such a way that difficulties will supernaturally melt away if you believe in Him, or the spies, who bring the common sense, man-of-the-street report that these giants, with huge walled cities, well fortified, cannot be conquered by us? It was decision time again: will we go with what God says, at a time when we cannot see how He is going to be with us, and how He will cause our difficulties to melt away? Or, will we insist on seeing everything before we obey?

1 John says, 'this is the victory that overcomes the world, even our faith'. Our Christian lives have been set up by God, somewhat like the experience of Israel in the Old Testament, so that we will come to many junctures and turning points, where we can vividly imagine the great difficulties of being obedient to God. God is then saying, will you trust me, when you cannot see my provision for next week or next year? Or, do you insist on seeing everything ahead of time, and unless you do, you will refuse to trust Me?

Let me say a word about the difficulty of faith in such circumstances, when we face considerable challenges, including physical dangers. In such cases, we do not know how it is going to work out. But what matters is that God has given His people certain promises, He says, hold on to them, step out in faith, but I'm not going to show you yet how it will work out. Instead, I want you to trust in me, especially when you cannot see the way ahead. Of course, that is easier said than done.

We can see how this operates in Hebrews 11:1, which defines faith as 'the substance of things hoped for, the evidence of things not seen'. Hebrews 11, time after time, connects faith with not seeing. You remember how Abraham went out 'not knowing' whither he went; God just said, leave home and come! He couldn't see it yet. And Moses' parents, Amram and Jocebed, who had this beautiful child, at a time when Pharaoh wanted the baby boys killed, hid their little boy in a basket of reeds in the river. They didn't know what was ahead, but they had faith in God, to risk their lives in preserving the life of this little son, whom God had provided them. They definitely could not see the future, yet they obeyed.

Later Moses himself, when he came to manhood, (having been raised in the opulent palace of Pharaoh, with all the riches and treasures of wealthy Egypt), had to face a choice based on things he could not yet see. 'Moses chose to suffer affliction with the people of God rather than to enjoy the riches of Egypt' (Heb. 11:25). He couldn't see what was ahead; he couldn't see how God would deliver the slaves out of Egypt, and take them into a wonderful place. But he obeyed when he could not see. That is faith.

You and I cannot expect that God is going to show us exactly how He is going to provide for us. I used to wonder at one stage, when we had five children in Christian school, with some of them going off to college, and so much money to be paid, how in the world would we ever get through it. At that time of pressure, I was asking myself, why is it like this? And then the answer became clear: you've got to learn to trust Me; you preach to other people Sunday by Sunday, and you teach in classes to trust God. So why do you think I'm going to let you by any easier than anybody else to whom you are preaching, without your having to learn when it's painful and when you can't see, that I am faithful and that My promises are sufficient? The message was: trust Me.

When trials come into your life, what you can see very clearly are the enemies, the hang-ups, the difficulties, as the spies saw the Anakim, the giants, and their cities. But what you ordinarily cannot see is the only thing that matters, for it alone will show you how to get through all this: 'Faith is the evidence of things not seen'. What you don't normally see is God supernaturally intervening, either with His holy angels, or through the Holy

Spirit, or some other way, getting His hand into this world, into your circumstances, and working it out and causing enemies to melt, to become irrelevant, to be moved away. We don't see such things yet, and God has set it up that way, because He wants us to learn to trust Him; He wants us to love Him enough to do what He says before He shows us precisely how it is going to work out. Otherwise we don't love God for Himself; we're using Him as sort of a water boy, at our convenience; God will not be dealt with that way! He wants to see that we love Him. We love Him when we trust Him, even though we do not see yet what He is going to do.

We come back to Campbell Morgan's statement, 'obedience is the ground of blessing'. Our God is always in complete control of absolutely everything. He works 'all things after the counsel of His will' (Eph. 1:11). That much is clear.

But at the same time, God has set up this world and organized our lives, where He gives us many opportunities to say, Lord, I don't see what is coming, but I trust you. I believe that you love your people, that you're involved in our lives and that you will take care of me. God does not force you to exercise faith. If He did, it would not be a love relationship. God made us in His image, and so He wants us to love Him, as He loves us, person to person. You wouldn't have a love relationship if you were forcing the other person. Part of being created in the image of God is that you have a choice. I know that we are totally depraved and that the Holy Spirit renews our will, so that we truly can trust and obey. Then along our pilgrim way, we've got to decide at many points, whether we're going to default to merely human common sense, which dictates that we will doubt, unless we see with our physical eyes. In that state, we will to listen to those who say that it cannot work out.

Or, when we get into a tight place, we can say, Lord, I don't know what's going to happen, but I know I trust You, and as far as I am able, I am going to step out in faith on what you say. Then that love relationship is strengthened; God is transmuting our own character, so that He can do far more through us than would have been the case if we were puppets and had been manipulated with no choice, but externally forced to trust God.

Many times in our life, God says, I'm not showing you what will happen to you next week; instead, I want you to trust Me. That means, laying yourself down on the altar, including your physical life if necessary, and saying, Lord, You deserve it; I'm giving this to You.

In other words, God is more interested in developing this relationship of love in the salvation experience, to prepare us for service here and for joy in heaven, than automatically making it easy for us on earth. Yes, the Lord gives us much ease, and much joy! But He does not always insulate our lives, nor keep us from having to trust Him in the dark.

An old hymn says:

> When we in darkness walk,
> nor feel the heavenly flame,
> then is the time to trust our God,
> and lean upon His name.

God is more interested in developing this relationship, in changing us, than in making it easy; I suppose that is why He let the ten spies come back with that negative report, and still lets the equivalent of the ten, unbelieving spies talk to us, from time to time. But when that happens, we have to decide: Do I feel like God is big enough, good enough, true enough, that I can literally lay everything on the altar and step out in obedience?

The Consequences of Unbelief (1:35–46)

Deuteronomy 1:35–36 tells us that an entire generation, everybody with two exceptions, Caleb and Joshua, everyone that was over twenty years old would have to die in the wilderness, before this vast people could move over Jordan to take the Promised Land.

It does not necessarily mean that all of these people lost their salvation, but they did miss out on something wonderful. That generation did lose much blessing in this life, because they wouldn't trust. It meant that they would have to die in the wilderness, never seeing that Promised Land. Yet through the grace of God, the children of their own body, would be given a second chance.

We read in verses 41 and following that they foolishly said: we should have obeyed God, once they learned that they were going to die in the wilderness, and thus would not get into the Promised Land. So they decided, let us go into the hill country of the Amorites, defeat them, and then we'll start taking the land anyway. They were saying, sin does not have consequences, at least not for us; we're special. We find it hard to accept that we'll have to go back and die in the wilderness. Surely, as many people as we are, we can do it. So let us go up and begin a victorious assault on the pagans (i.e., the Amorites).

God said to them, don't do it! While I forgive your sin, I do not remove all of its consequences. But they seem to be saying, not only do you forgive us, but you must remove the consequences of sin. Yet God doesn't always do that. He forgave David, but He certainly let him experience for the rest of his time on earth, the consequences of a broken, disastrous family life.

I don't doubt, for I have seen it, that God will forgive someone who has seriously abused alcohol for forty or fifty years, and near the end, had cirrhosis of the liver. Yes, God will forgive them, if they believe in Jesus. I have prayed with them, and offered them the gospel. Still, it is not likely that God will restore their liver; in most cases, He does not remove the consequences, although there are mysteries in His providence, and so sometimes, He may do so. Or somebody may have committed serious sexual misbehavior which God says is wrong, and they get AIDS, and are near the end of the line. Again, I don't have any doubt that if they repent of their sin and ask Jesus to save them, He will save them. But it's not likely that He would necessarily restore their immune system, although He can do miracles when He wants to. Even so, in most cases, although He may save a person, He will leave some of the consequences of their sin. This shows us that God is holy, and that Jesus' death was very precious and honored God in our salvation, but it does not always include removing the physical consequences of our sins.

And so it was with the Israelites; they had specifically refused to accept the promises of God, when they could have done so. Instead, they said, we accept the report of the unbelieving ten spies, For that reason, God says, you are not going in, and they foolishly replied: Oh, but we can enter in anyway, for we don't feel it's proper for God to leave us with the consequences of sin. But of course, they found out; they were massively, bitterly defeated (1:44–45).

Now in the New Testament, this specific lesson must be very important in the mind of God, for it is talked about in 1 Corinthians 10 and Hebrews 3.

1 Corinthians 10:5–6, says of the experience in the wilderness: 'But with many of them God was not well pleased: for they were overthrown in the wilderness. Now these things were our examples, to the intent we should not lust after evil things, as they also lusted.' I take it that 'evil things' would refer to thinking that we can take hold of the world, and enjoy what is in it, apart from

God. In that sense, even while we are going on in disobedience to God, acting as though there is not a God, we foolishly think we can handle these matters very well. And so *'evil things'* are what you get, when you live without reference to God and His holiness, His promises of salvation and His will. Thus, things that would otherwise be good: like fruitful fields, stately homes, abounding vineyards, olive yards, and dripping winepresses, can become evil things, if we think we're going to get the best apart from the Lord. That's how St. Paul interprets this passage from Deuteronomy.

Hebrews 3:15–19 takes us back to the same pivotal event because it gives us the principles of spiritual life, by which we are able to overcome the world, namely, to believe God, when it's hard to see. Hebrews 3:15–19 cites Psalm 95, which also speaks of the same event:

> ¹⁵While it is said, [Psalm 95] To day if ye will hear his voice, harden not your hearts, as in the provocation [the provocation in the wilderness, where they said we accept the report of the ten doubting spies, not of Caleb and Joshua]. ¹⁶For some, when they had heard, did provoke: [that means provoke God; when you don't believe, when you reject the promises, you're provoking God—that's the seriousness of it] howbeit not all that came out of Egypt by Moses. ¹⁷But with whom was he grieved forty years? was it not with them that had sinned, whose carcasses fell in the wilderness? [They'd have to die before their children and grandchildren could take the land]. ¹⁸And to whom sware he that they should not enter into his rest, [and he warns them in Deuteronomy 1 that they can't have this rest, this peace, this joy, because you specifically refused to obey] but to them that believed not? ¹⁹So we see that they could not enter in because of unbelief.

Later, Hebrews 4:9–10 makes clear the principle that we can have true rest and peace of spirit, no matter what the circumstances, when we trust in the God whom we do not see, instead of self and world, which we do see. That's the only way for true rest of heart, true serenity of spirit: trust in Him whom you do not see, hear His Word, rather than trust in your common sense perception of how you can work it out through manipulating the things you can see, and believe that you can handle.

A question that I guess comes to our minds as Christians is that Israel had all these privileges: the fiery, cloudy pillar—they saw it. And God got them through the Red Sea. He was camping over the tabernacle: it was fire and warmth at night, and it was shade and cool and refreshment in the day time; they literally didn't see God, but they saw the evidence of His presence—miracles—and yet, when they got in a pinch, they did not believe that He would do what He said He would do. Now if that's the case, we might ask this question. Can I make it with my frail, little faith? How in the world could I make it, if they couldn't? It is not a bad question to say to ourselves: I wonder if I can face the challenges that are very painful, and step out on the mere Word of God, going against the common sense perception of what might happen?

It is all important that we note that following the story of the rebellion in the wilderness, Hebrews provides a discussion of the great High Priest whom we have in heaven. Certainly Moses had interceded on earth for the people to be forgiven, and God heard him. But a greater than Moses is interceding for us, and is in the seat of power in the heavenly realm (Heb. 4:14–16):

> ¹⁴Seeing then that we have a great high priest, that is passed into the heavens, Jesus the Son of God, let us

hold fast our profession. ¹⁵For we have not an high priest which cannot be touched with the feeling of our infirmities; but was in all points tempted like as we are, yet without sin.

He knows when we're tempted to throw in the towel, saying Lord, it's too hard, I don't believe I can do this. But Jesus knows how oppressed we sometimes feel, and how totally, utterly weak we know we are.

What is the solution? 'Let us therefore come boldly unto the throne of grace, that we may obtain mercy, and find grace to help in time of need.' Grace means that God is dealing with you infinitely better than what you deserve. Even though your faith is as small as a grain of mustard seed, if you keep coming to Him, and looking to the throne, He will get you through it; He will fight your battles for you. When you don't see Him in the field, He is there preparing the way.

We have got to keep our eyes and hearts focused on our great High Priest, who is praying for us. In fellowship by faith with Him, truly, all will be well.

> But we never can prove
> the delights of His love,
> until all on the altar we lay...

That is God's call to us; with His Holy Spirit's help and the grace whom Christ sends down from His heavenly sanctuary, we can do it.

5

The God of the Second Chance

Deuteronomy 2:1–15

This passage illustrates a great principle of the Bible, that God is the God of the second chance. That's a great joy to know. Before we speak about the second chance, we must speak about the first chance—chance in the sense of opportunity. How about the first opportunity that Israel had? It would be dependent upon whether or not they believed God would fulfill His promise. That is always the right way to take advantage of a real opportunity that will bring blessing. We do not need to see how He will provide ahead of time; in fact, hoping to do so can be counter-productive. He will not show you the details of how it works out ahead of time, but it is sufficient for Him to give you a true opportunity to take the right step, without being able to see very far ahead.

In Hebrews 11:11, a woman of faith is our example: a woman from whom all those children of Israel descended; but they did not do what their grandmother had done, and that was their problem the first time. They did not follow Sarah, Abraham's wife, who is described in this verse (11:11): 'through faith also, Sarah herself received strength to conceive seed, and was delivered of a child when she was past age.' She was 90 years old; it was a miracle!

If it hadn't been for that miracle, those Israelites would not have been standing by the Jordan, hearing God say, I'll get you in if you believe Me like your grandmother believed Me! Then listen to this: she was delivered of a child when she was past age, (and here's the key for all of us, if we're going to get anywhere for God): 'because she judged Him faithful who had promised'. Sarah is our example. She judged Him faithful, who had promised, so she had this miracle child, Isaac, and from him over a million people, 500 or 600 years later, were standing on the banks of the Jordan.

We are also told that Abraham 'considered not his own body', but the promises of God. He was 100, past normal reproduction age. But that wasn't the issue; it was what God said He would do. Abraham, along with Sarah, judged Him faithful who had promised. The question that we face in our lives many times is this: do we judge God to be faithful to fulfill what He has said in His Word He will do for believers, including ourselves?

The heroes of the faith in Hebrews 11 faced in many cases worse trials than we do, but they triumphed; they became heroes and heroines, truly victorious, because they judged God to be faithful who had promised that He would look after them, and enable them to win the victory.

The painful period of which Moses reminds the children of Israel, as they stand the second time on the banks of Jordan, had occurred about 38 years prior; a whole generation of Israelites had refused to believe that God was either big enough, or possibly good enough, to carry out His Word and thus they missed a tremendous opportunity.

As far as I can tell, God will give many of us a chance of getting into a situation where it's too big for us to handle; we don't have the resources to cope with it. Believe it or not, it is God's gift to us! So it's never the combination of difficult circumstances looming before us that holds us back. How about Sarah, age 90 and Abraham, age 100, and the children of Israel at the Red Sea? It's not the circumstances that we can blame for our failures. Rather, it is this: we do not follow Sarah and Abraham in the way they judged God, who has promised to be faithful to carry out precisely what He said He would do.

From this text let us look at God's faithfulness for three different groups:

1. The Edomites;
2. The Moabites;
3. The unbelieving Israelites.

God's Faithfulness to The Edomites (2:1–8)

God's central promises were to the Israelites, that is, to the descendants of Abraham through Jacob, whose name was changed to Israel. As Jesus later answered the woman at the well of Samaria, who asked where should they worship: Mount Gerizim or Mount Zion, he answered that salvation is of the Jews. That is, the Messiah, who is the world's Savior, is a descendant of, Abraham, Jacob, and Judah.

But at the same time, God also imparted covenant blessings, a large land, and certain natural and national blessings to other descendants of Abraham, who, like the Edomites, were not of the Messianic line; salvation does not come through them, but they did share in certain real blessings by virtue of their descent from faithful Abraham.

Moses specifically mentions the Edomites; they were the children of Esau, the older brother whom Jacob tricked, and then had to flee the country, so the brother wouldn't kill him for what he had done to him. Indeed, Jacob and his mother, Rebekah, tricked Isaac into giving the major blessing to Jacob, instead of it going to the older son, the firstborn Esau, as was the proper custom. Still, Isaac did reserve a smaller, yet definite blessing, for Esau (Gen. 27:38–40).

Since Isaac was a true prophet, the Lord Himself was involved in this smaller, yet definite blessing that Isaac put on his older son Esau. And for that reason, God had secured the hilly country of Edom to those descendants of Esau for the last five or six hundred years. Hence, when the children of Israel are passing near Edom, or at least, through one corner of it, God reminds them that their distant cousins are still under covenant protection, so they are not to fight with the Edomites, because they are the descendants of Isaac. They are not to attempt to take even an inch of their ground. God will continue to honor His promise of a secure land to these descendants of Esau. Why would God do that? Why, 500 or 600 years later, is God still saying, it's their land; don't try to take it? Because God is faithful, even to those outside the major Messianic line. If God makes a promise to them, He will keep it to the utmost. That's who God is. He's not fickle.

God's Faithfulness to The Moabites (2:8–12)

Once again, they are passing through Moab, one of the countries they have to go near to get to the Promised Land, after they left Egypt and had wandered about in the wilderness for so long. God, through Moses, tells Israel not to meddle with the Moabites whose land is nearby, where they will cross over the Jordan. That is because the Moabites, and also a neighboring nation, the Ammonites, were descendants of Abraham's nephew Lot through incestuous relations with his daughters, after the destruction of Sodom.

In spite of their forefather's sin in this matter, (incest), the blessing of God in some definite sense, still rested upon the Moabites and the Ammonites, who were cousins of the children of Israel. God wanted them to have their land and to keep it, and He told the Israelites to respect them, and to give them wide berth because, in verse 9, he says, 'I have given it to them for a possession'. Because the God of the covenant is faithful to His every promise, He still looks after the Moabites 500 or more years after the time of Abraham and Lot. God will not let His own Messianic, chosen people do them the slightest harm, or take any of their property. God had made some promises to Lot about his descendants, and God was still keeping those promises six centuries later. Truly, God is faithful; He never breaks a promise. This is unlike the politicians in most of our countries, who generally cannot be counted on to keep their word, if they find it inconvenient.

God's Faithfulness to The Disobedient Israelites (2:13–15)

There are two points here: God was faithful to this people in a negative sense, and in a positive sense.

The first point is that God carried out the punishment He had announced. It took thirty-eight years for that disbelieving generation, who refused to go into the Promised Land by faith, to die off and be buried in the wilderness. God said it would have to happen before they could get into the Promised Land, as a chastisement for their disbelief. It is always a serious matter to disbelieve the God who has been so kind and good to you.

The New Testament book of Jude speaks of this event: 'I will therefore put you in remembrance, though ye once knew this, how that the Lord having saved the people out of the land of Egypt, afterward destroyed them that believed not' (v. 5). The worst issue of not trusting God's promises when we don't see the way ahead, is this: they missed an opportunity to honor the Lord and to show how great He was among the nations.

Our Lord Jesus Christ not long before He died, uttered the great High Priestly prayer in John 17, as He was consecrating Himself before He went to Gethsemane and Calvary; He prayed: 'Father, I have glorified Thee; I have finished the work which Thou gavest Me to do'. But when the wilderness children of Israel died, they could not, in any sense, say that.

To live and die, feeling that in some imperfect, but nonetheless sincere manner, we have sought to please God, is the most supreme pleasure that any human could have on this earth. That is the only thing that matters about our life: not job, money, fame, health, houses, lands; we must leave all that anyway but have I lived, and will I die, sincerely seeking to bring pleasure to the heart of Jesus?

One of my many great-aunts, a number of years ago, near the end of her life, was weeping with joy that for all her weak points, she had sincerely sought to love Christ and serve Him. She was simply full of joy as she faced what seemed to be at that time, the end. She had sought to bring pleasure to the heart of Jesus, and she was one happy woman, as she faced the valley of the shadow of death in her 80s. That supreme pleasure is open for all us, if we want it, to know that we have sought to please Jesus.

Secondly, God gave the children of the disbelieving generation, a second chance. God took good care of the disobedient parents, and of the children, through 38 more years of wilderness wandering, sustaining them by His mercy, until the door of divine opportunity would be opened by an invisible hand, the second time. How kind and how longsuffering God is to us, even when we've been out of line and deserve nothing but His punishment! Deuteronomy 2:7 says, 'These forty years the LORD thy God hath been with thee, and thou hast lacked nothing'. He had fed them with manna from heaven; he had given them water out of the rock; he had sheltered them with the glory cloud, and protected them with angel hosts. Indeed, Deuteronomy 8:4 specifies that 'Thy raiment waxed not old upon thee [their clothes didn't wear out]; neither did thy foot swell these forty years'. God truly intervened in such a supernatural way that they could keep going until He could give them, or at least their children, this second chance.

So now the God of second chances sets before this new generation an open door. You might wonder: if I had parents who were disobedient, will God bless me? Of course He will!—if you accept what He offers this second time, to a new generation. Moses preaches these facts to this new generation, so that unlike their disbelieving fathers and mothers, they can enter the Promised Land, with hearts full of belief that God is faithful to do everything He promised. Psalm 78:5–8 is a wonderful meditation on this.

The Lord says to this new generation: it can be different with you! I believe God is saying to our increasingly apostate countries across the world that it could be different. The sins of your parents do not have to take you down in the same direction. If you look to me, with Sarah, and judge me to be faithful, who has made these promises, it can be different; it can be better.

It may be one of the advantages of the grace of Christ in the New Testament, that God will give us a second chance, in the *same* generation, if we truly repent and believe. In other words, it doesn't just have to be our children to whom God will give a second chance, but to ourselves, in the same lifetime. This means that the same people who give way to murmuring, complaining, failing to walk by faith, going along with the sinful crowd, not wanting to be different from the popular multitude, but following a multitude to do evil; these same people can later, in their own life, have an open door set before them, one more time.

It was so with Simon Peter. He denied the Lord Jesus Christ three times. But he was given an opportunity to repent, which he did, and was given a glorious ministry; Paul offered the same opportunity to the Galatians and to the Corinthians who were out of line, to come back to the blessing of the Lord. In Revelation 2:5, the risen Christ offers a second chance to the church people at Ephesus, who had lost their first love and gone worldly and cold towards God, 'Repent and do the first works'. Get back to the place of consecration, and I'll bless you. God offers the same to us today who have failed Him in the past.

Jesus' parable in Matthew 21:28–31 teaches the same principle, that you can be given a second chance. Publicans and harlots had violated many of the basic principles of true godliness, and Jesus set before them, as John the Baptist had, an opened door, and many of them humbled themselves and went into it. Many of the Pharisees, who had the outward form, but denied the reality in their lives, refused to humble themselves, and to go through the door in humility. But Jesus says, those who take the second chance will be blessed by God, if they humble themselves in believing Him.

I've lived long enough to think back over forty years of ministry, and think about people I've known along the way. Some of them, as far as I could tell, largely wasted the most productive period of their lives through selfishness or worldliness. Maybe they were barely Christians, but you'd hardly know it. Yet I have seen God's Holy Spirit get hold of these people, who had wasted many years in worldliness, and seen them set on fire for the glory of God for the last fifteen or twenty years of their lives and accomplish great things!

I remember a man, possibly in his 70s, no doubt a believer, but who was generally proud and self-sufficient, and treated harshly anybody who disagreed with him. At an evangelistic meeting, the Holy Spirit of God got hold of him, and it was evident to all that he was profoundly changed, and on fire for the Lord for the rest of his time on earth; maybe twenty years. He gladly took advantage of a second chance. He got back to the place, I would assume, of his first consecration, and deemed that God was faithful, and worth giving everything to.

Earlier, I referred you to Jude 5 about the children of Israel refusing to trust God. But then verses 20–21 give us the way out; we are shown how to take advantage of a second chance: 'But ye, beloved, building up yourselves on your most holy faith, praying in the Holy Ghost, Keep yourselves in the love of God, looking for the mercy of our Lord Jesus Christ unto eternal life'. And so, Moses called that generation of the children of Israel to a new surrender, and God also comes to us and offers us a new surrender. If we accept it, we could say with the hymn writer,

All to Jesus I surrender;
all to Him I freely give.
I will gladly serve and love Him;
in His presence live, daily live…

That is the only way to happiness; no matter how much we have wasted the past, no matter how much time we lost, let us now look to the future; let us surrender everything that is left, and great things will lie ahead, for whatever time God leaves us down here.

6

Take Possession of What I Gave You

Deuteronomy 2:16–37

This last half of Deuteronomy 2, in a sense, gives us the dynamic of what faith is like and how faith works. One can find many definitions of faith. One is in Hebrews 11, 'faith is the substance of things hoped for, the evidence of things not seen', and that fits in well with this. What God is doing in this chapter of Deuteronomy follows from the fact that He had given them the Promised Land. Then He commands: 'go in and possess it'. That's the struggle of faith, in the Old Testament and the New Testament, Christian era. God says, I have done so and so according to My character and upon the assurance of the promises of My Word, now you live on that basis. But we tend to say, 'we don't see it yet.' That's the struggle. Whether you win or you fail, depends upon your acting on the basis of what God has promised, even before you are able, physically, to see it. That's true faith.

Let us note three points in these verses:

1. God controls the destiny of nations and peoples.
2. The struggle of faith.
3. Is holy war ever right?

God Controls the Destiny of Nations and Peoples (2:16–23)

This part of Deuteronomy shows us the beginning of the occupation of the Promised Land. Israel is standing at the same place their ancestors had stood forty years before, when they had disbelieved the promises of God and thus wandered forty more years in the wilderness. That generation had died out except for Caleb, Joshua, and Moses. Now God brings them back to the river and says, 'Believe My promise, and begin to occupy this land that I have already given you'. This means that they will have to take a huge step of obedient faith, which will involve them in many years of military conflict.

Before the people go into battle, facing great danger, Moses takes them down to basic spiritual principles about the life of faith.

This differs from modern secular political planning, which relies on a common-sense assessment of military and economic capacity, as well as motivations of national leaders. Nobody could reasonably deny that there is a necessary place for this, but as far as the obedience of faith is concerned, the Bible gives us a very different picture: it presents a God who is directly controlling the destiny and movements of people (though usually hidden from our human eyes).

Let us consider four things under point one: first, God specifically told Israel to spare the Ammonites. Those were the descendants of Lot, the nephew of Abraham, the father of the faithful. Because of Lot's relationship to Abraham, and I assume Lot had some kind of relationship to God, God would have mercy for generations on his descendants. So God forbids Israel from attacking the descendants of Lot; respect them; they're still under His care.

It was the same with the Moabites and the descendants of Esau. For all his sins, Esau had some kind of relationship to God and to Abraham, Isaac, and Jacob, so God said: 'I am going to give protection and land to your descendants for many generations.' Again, here we see a God, who disposes the nations in accordance with His covenant promises. He said: 'when you go through the land of Moab, pay them for the water and for the food, and do the same when you go through the land of the Ammonites.'

Secondly, God told Israel, 'but I do want you to attack and take over the land of the pagan Amorites', for they had no covenant relationship to the Lord. We will come back to that later.

Thirdly, God tells them what land Israel is not to take and specifically tells them what land they are to take.

Fourthly, God through Moses reminds the Israel of the pre-history of that region and of how much God had already done generations beforehand to get everything ready for His people to have the victory (v. 20, 23); and how God disposed several races of giants, so that Moab and Ammon could take the land.

This also amplifies the principle that God is in complete control, even among pagan tribes. His wise and far-reaching providence gets things ready for the time when His people will be told to move in, illustrated by God using the Caphtorim (or Philistines); they had been involved in the great movement of sea peoples from Greece, and specifically from the island of Crete. They had come in; and, though pagans, had been used by God, to displace that tough race of giants, to make it possible for the children of Esau and of Lot to get their property.

God is always at work preparing things for the future of His people. God did not give up control in the Old Testament, nor on the day of Pentecost. He still reigns and rules supreme in all that is happening in world politics, economics, culture, and military (though we cannot see it at the time), working invisibly to get things the way He wants them, so His people can move in with His truth and grace and holiness.

That's who God is: 'Jesus Christ, the same yesterday, today, and for ever'. 'He fainteth not, nor groweth weary with the passing of years'. God is eternally in control. The British could think of how God brought a fierce hurricane that devasted the Spanish Armada in 1588. The ancestors of the Americans, a relatively small group of English colonists from the Mayflower, who came to New England in 1620 and founded the Massachusetts Bay Colony, were able to survive only because something remarkable had taken place some six months before they arrived at Plymouth Rock. Until six months earlier, there had been a very large, hostile Indian tribe, but a plague had gone through and decimated nearly everybody in that very unfriendly tribe. If it hadn't been for that plague six months before the Pilgrims landed, the large hostile tribe would have killed all the pilgrims. But God had sent a plague.

However, another tribe was very friendly, who had not experienced the plague. Also, in God's strange providence, the Pilgrims found an

Indian named Squanto. Somehow the Spanish had picked him up and sold him into slavery, and he had got to England as a slave, and was there long enough to learn English. We don't know exactly how, but he escaped from England, and got back to Spain, and then all the way back to Massachusetts. Wonderfully for the Pilgrim Fathers, Squanto served as a translator for them in the 1620 settlement of Massachusetts. Looking back, Christians would see that God was preparing the continent of America to be settled by Christians, and He used the plague to get it ready, as He had used the Philistines to remove the giants so Moab and Edom could come in.

The teaching of Scripture, including this passage, is that God is in charge of what He is allowing to happen. In addition to Ephesians 1:11, we can look at Job 12:23, where Job says, 'He [God] increaseth the nations and destroyeth them; He enlargeth the nations, and straiteneth them again'. And in Deuteronomy 32:8, 'When the Most High divided to the nations their inheritance, when He separated the sons of Adam, He set the bounds of the people according to the number of the children of Israel'.

This total control is also found in the New Testament, in Acts 17:26-27: 'And hath made of one blood all nations of men for to dwell on all the face of the earth, and hath determined the times before appointed and the bounds of their habitation…' Such divine determination of what transpires among the nations is nearly always mysterious, and we have to be careful not to claim to know more than we know! Yet, on the basis of what the Scriptures say, we get the point that this movement of peoples; bringing down some tribes and nations, and lifting up others, directly related to God's gracious plan to give room to people who can be used to live out and speak forth His truth, with its grace and healing power, in a way that could not have happened if He had left the pagans in undisputed control.

This does not mean that God does not love the pagans. If we could see far enough (and down here, we cannot), we would realize that God has plans of grace for these people that could not work out if they were left undisturbed in the pagan state. It is divine love that displaces them for a time; not His hatred.

It is good for us to remember this as we see God allowing massive movements of peoples in Europe and America. Some of these people hate His gospel at this stage, but as God orchestrates many a movement, that can change!

While much of what the famous nineteenth-century historian of American history, Josiah Bancroft, wrote is outdated, he raises an important question: why was it that the North American continent was not really settled until after the Spanish Armada's defeat in 1588? Bancroft argues that it was providential that once Spain lost a great deal of its power, it was unable to control the settlement of the North American continent. He suggests that this was precisely the time when the English were able to move in and establish a colony in 1607, at Jamestown, Virginia, and then in Massachusetts in 1620. He argued that it was in the plan of God that the North American continent be settled by Protestant, Puritan people who had been revived, and believed the gospel, so that gospel-believing people could take the land, and in later generations become a tremendous missionary-sending agency to the entire world. Many scholars would fiercely disagree with Bancroft's reading of the historical situation, but it makes sense with what God was doing in the settlement of this continent.

I am not very knowledgeable about the history of Korea, but scholars tell me that for some reason, Buddhism had largely lost its power not long before the Christian missionaries began arriving in that country. That may be one reason why Korea is now the largest Christian country in Southeastern Asia.

So God is able to use all sorts of events, even plagues and battles, to advance His gospel. However, we can discern but very little of this during the time it is happening, and it is never wise to think of ourselves as favored above all others, because *'pride goeth before a fall.'*

The Struggle of Faith (2:24-25).
The heart of this struggle is based on God's having said: 'I have given ... take possession'. It is commented on in Psalm 95, which is picked up in Hebrews 4, 'strive to enter into His rest'. 'There remains a rest for the people of God', now work hard to get in it! I have given you that land, therefore get out and fight for it, and you'll find that it's already yours. That's the struggle of faith.

Authentic faith, in the Old and New Testament, never means that if you believe hard enough, you can have something without any effort on your part. Not so! That's not biblical faith.

One of the things that God does to make it possible for His people to take over, is that He puts the fear of the Israelites on those pagan nations. Verse 25 makes it clear: 'This day will I begin to put the dread of thee and the fear of thee upon the nations that are under the whole heaven who shall hear report of thee and shall tremble and be in anguish because of thee'. And similarly in Exodus 15:14-15.

One of the signs that a nation cannot stand, is when its people become cowardly so that they are not ready to fight for what they used to believe. That's a sure sign of impending defeat when the pressure comes. A careful study of the fall of the Roman Empire shows that the Romans still greatly outnumbered the barbarians who came to the gates of Rome. William Carroll Bark, in his famous book, charts it out. Fear and trembling had taken hold of the Romans, to such a degree that they were unwilling to fight and just gave up. The highest value of many of them did not go beyond 'let us eat, drink, and be merry, for tomorrow we die'. The surest way to wreck a nation is to get its people so materialistic and pleasure and leisure oriented, they don't believe anything, and are profoundly unlike their fathers and grandfathers. When they believe nothing, they will fall for everything, and they will not hazard their lives on the high places of the field.

Now the Amorites are the ones about whom God said, you shall go in and take their property, but do not interfere with the Ammonites and the Moabites, they're under My protection; but go and take the Amorites under King Sihon. First, Moses sent a message to Sihon (v. 26-29): 'Let us go through; we'll do like we did to Moab; we'll pay for the water, we'll pay for the bread and we'll stay on the highway.'

But Sihon made a suicidal move. He attacked the people of God (v. 30-31); God had hardened His heart, like He had Pharaoh's heart forty years earlier, and thus he made a bad military decision and was crushed.

A. W. Pink used to say that 'when God works, He works at both ends of the line', and that is the case when He tells us to do something and we go there in obedience. All we can see is our own end of the line, and it may frighten us to be instructed by the Lord, to go here, or go there, or talk to somebody. But God is already working, speaking to that person, getting them ready. Hence, God tells Moses and His people to go through the country of the pagan Amorites, (Gilead,) whom God has worked to make them carry out a foolish military decision to attack the people of God, sending a spirit of fear and a spirit of hardness. This results, in verses 32–33, in a victorious battle; 'and this is the victory that overcometh the world, even our faith' (1 John 5:4). They won. It says something significant: they not only killed the king, they killed his sons. They were the life insurance for the future, but the whole dynasty, the royal house, was wiped out in one fell swoop. Verses 34–35 show that in accordance with God's command, they did a total house cleaning of the nation, wiping out everything but the animals and the spoils.

It is important to notice here a contrast between faith and unbelief. God said, I'm going to give it to you; it's already yours. Deuteronomy 2:35 says: 'God gave us everything'. What a contrast to some forty years earlier, when this same people refused to go, when 'ye murmured in your tents' (Deut. 1:27-37).

On the earlier occasion, Israel disbelieved. They said, That nation is too strong; God hates us; we're going to lose everything. But forty years later, when the unbelievers had died out, their children had more faith, and were able to say, God has given us everything.

This struggle of faith is much like what we find in the New Testament teaching. Over the years, I have appreciated learning from Dr. Martin Lloyd-Jones that the way of sanctification is this: God tells you what you are in Christ, and then He says: now be that! In the first eleven chapters of Romans, we are given the wonderful doctrines of God's grace and election. Immediately afterward, we are told in Romans 12:1–2 that as we think about who we are in Christ, we are to be transformed by it; we are to step out in faith. In other words, God says: here's what you are in Christ; here's what I've done for every believer; I have included them in the death of Christ to cleanse their sins; I have included them in the resurrection of Christ to give them His continuing resurrection power; now be that! Act like that in your marriage, in your job, in church; be what I have made you! Hence, the New Testament position on sanctification and on victorious living, is in many ways, closely related to how the people of God moved into the Promised Land.

Is Holy War Ever Right?

To put it another way, does God have the right to clean out a wicked, immoral, degenerate nation? Is it right even for God to do it? That's the question. Not many people in this relativistic day, where everybody's got a little good and everybody's got a little bad, will be willing to say that it is. Let me respond to this concern.

Psalm 24:1: 'The earth belongs unto the LORD and the fullness thereof'. God owns the earth. Acts 17 states that He has appointed the bounds of the nations, and so He pulls one down, and sets up another, in accordance with His holy character and perfect will. In Genesis 15:7 God's will had been announced long before Israel was to have the land of the Amorites. God had set it aside for them, but it wasn't moving time yet. And when God says it's moving time, He who owns the whole world has the inherent right to change the inhabitants, to move one group out and another in. After all, He created the heavens and the earth out of nothing, and controls them. He is the final owner, and has the right to dispose of it as He sees fit. And He always does everything in accordance with His goodness and His wisdom.

A second observation about holy war: archeology tells us and ancient literary studies tell us that the Canaanites, of whom the Amorites were a part, were morally, profoundly degenerate, past the point of no return. You can look in Genesis 15:16, 'for the iniquity of the Amorites is not yet full'. God gave them time for repentance, and yet they got worse and worse. One could look at Leviticus 18, and Deuteronomy 18, where it lists the wicked practices that had taken root and taken control of the Amorites: incest, adultery, child sacrifice, temple prostitution, and unnatural sexual activity. God gave them a long time to repent, but from what we read in Genesis 15, they refused.

In light of that long-term refusal, the Lord had the right to pick out His people Israel as an avenging rod upon them to clean them out. You might object: but is that fair? Well, if God did it, it's fair. Many generations later, the same Israel, that is, their descendants, would be cleaned out by the Assyrians and then the Babylonians as an avenging rod of God. So if the Lord uses His people to clean out one degenerate group, they need to be careful not to become proud and immoral, because He will send somebody in to clean them out.

That is one serious reason why, even though America does have much Christian history, as does Great Britain; we should never be so foolish as to take refuge in it; especially if our own generation is proudly violating the Word of God. To have had Puritan forefathers is insufficient, if we no longer manifest their faith and obedience. In fact, godly ancestors will cause us to undergo heavier judgment than those who were never anything but pagans! If we become as degenerate as the Amorites were, and as the Israelites later became, God will raise up somebody to clean us out, because His holy character has not changed.

In Deuteronomy 2, God largely used physical weapons, although He did employ the emotional, such as in sending fear. In the church, we have primarily spiritual weapons (2 Cor. 10:3–5), and God says they're mighty—capable of 'pulling down' strongholds. *If* my people will once again believe me and act on it, a bad situation will change.

7

The Future is At Least as Good as the Past

Deuteronomy 3:1–22

This passage about the conquest of land in accordance with the blessing of God, teaches us a very important principle that is always true in the lives of the people of God: the future is at least as good as the past, if we walk in faith. A famous Catholic scholar in nineteenth-century Germany, Baron von Hugel, said: 'The secrets that God keeps are at least as good as the ones He reveals.'

Scripture says you know not what a day may bring forth. It's a secret hidden with God. 'The secret things belong to our God but the things that are revealed unto us and to our children, that we may do them' (Deut. 29:29). The future is a secret. But the future will be at least as good as the past, if we trust in the Lord.

To see how this works out, let us look at three points in this chapter:

1. The purpose of chapter 3 within the book;
2. When God is in the battle, giants turn into pygmies;
3. Not to fear is a command of God.

The Purpose of Deuteronomy 3

This chapter is part of the historical prologue to the covenant of God with Israel. In Moses' time, they renewed the covenant that the Lord had made with His people. Now God is saying, I have set before you this wonderful country, and I want you to consider what I've done for you in the past, before you cross Jordan and go in to take all that land. I want you to remind yourself that the future is going to be at least as good—indeed, better than what I've done for you in the past, if you have obedient faith in Me.

Here we see Moses reminding Israel, before facing major warfare, of how faithful God is to His promises. They are to remember that He is the one with whom they are in covenant. Moses reminds them of how the rich lands east of the Jordan (Gilead) had been easily conquered from strong, warlike people, because God had been with them, and they moved in obedience to His promise.

Now God will do the same thing for them when they cross that river, *if* they keep trusting in Him and obeying Him. The purpose of chapter 3 is to recall how faithful God is, and that we are to be obedient without question.

When God Is in the Battle, Giants Can Turn Into Pygmies (3:1–11)

God never hides from us the fact that there are

giants out there, whom at times we have to face. There were scary advantages held by the pagans. —the giants, the high-walled cities, the king who was an actual giant, around 13 feet tall—that had kept the people of Israel from 'taking a chance' and crossing the river forty years earlier.

They trusted the report of the ten disbelieving spies, who said '*the cities are great and walled up to heaven*', and giants live in them (Deut. 1:28). Caleb and Joshua, on the contrary said: 'Yes, there are giants; yes, there are high walled cities; but God said He would give those things to us if we trust Him; let's go!' So the majority of the nation focused only on the difficulties and refused to obey God and take Him at his word.

But then that generation had died out, except for Caleb and Joshua. Their children, in the mercy of God, had a different spirit. Sometimes people say nothing ever changes; that's not true! Things do change. Families change. People's attitudes can change. In the wilderness, as the older generation of Israel died out, the younger one seems to have developed a renewed faith, presumably through worship in the tabernacle, and the proclamation of the Word. Wonderful attitudinal changes occurred, and evidently, they must have begun to think: God is great; God is good; let us follow Him. The text does not specifically say it, but I believe it is a fair reading of a change that had occurred.

Just before they went over, Moses says, 'You have taken this very rich land of Gilead, with only a few hours of intense struggle; God gave it to you. Your fathers didn't believe, but you have believed, and in a few hours you got what your forefathers didn't get in forty years.' The difference is not giants, or high walls, for they were still problems. Instead, one generation said, 'We don't believe God will intervene and do anything. It all depends on us; therefore, we can't win and we're not going to take a chance; we will not obey Him.'

But another generation, worked upon by the Spirit of God, were far more prepared to look out of self and up to the Lord. That attitudinal shift made the difference. Faith in God is what gave them the victory. It wasn't that the pagans had been weakened, but the people of God themselves had been strengthened and had exercised faith; and they realized how strong God is; that is what enables us to march forward into victory.

An old commentator once said this about the unbelief of the earlier generation of the Israelites: 'He that despairs, degrades the Deity and seems to intimate that God is insufficient.'

Yes, King Og was a giant, and a descendant of the Rephaim, a very tall, strong race of people. He was the last figure of that race of giants(Deut. 2:11). Now here's the point: not that the giants weren't there, but active faith in the Word of God made Og's strength melt into that of a pygmy.

In our own time, think of what happened in East Germany, in 1989. The Berlin Wall was still up. President Reagan had told the Russians when he visited Berlin in 1987, 'Take down this wall,' but they did not, and missiles pointed in our direction. But the people of God started prayer meetings in Leipzig, filling a huge Lutheran Church. Word spread to East Berlin, where they soon filled up a huge church, and then spread into the town square. Eventually, the East German army was commanded to shoot the prayer meeting, with thousands in the streets, but refused to obey orders; they wouldn't shoot their own people. The next day the wall came down. The government had lost its authority. Most newspapers in America have not reported these details, especially that the coming down of the wall in 1989 was in response to prayer meetings by the people of God, when another mighty giant was shrunk to a pygmy.

Listen to Psalm 37:20: 'But the wicked shall perish and the enemies of the Lord shall be as the fat of lambs; they shall consume into smoke'. Many of the Puritans, after the 1588 destruction of the Spanish Armada by hurricane force winds and waves, issued medallions, on which they inscribed a verse from the Psalms: 'The Lord destroyed them with the breath of His mouth'.

Most of us remember that the Berlin Wall came down and hastened the rapidly declining might of once powerful Marxism. But at present, we face something that actually might be harder to handle than Marxism: aggressive, wealthy, fervent Islam, that has an intense hatred of Christianity and the West. And at the same time, we have a weak-kneed, modernist Christianity, that is no longer sure what it believes, and is not necessarily willing to stand up for anything. So how are we going to face the future?

Deuteronomy would say: active faith in God and His promises, and ready obedience to Him is all it will take to turn the tide. Truly fervent faith would be shown by attendance at weekly congregational prayer meetings. But I don't know of very many churches that have a regular Wednesday night prayer meeting, including the supposedly conservative Presbyterian Church in America. Recently, I asked one of my former students, now in active ministry: 'Do you have a prayer meeting?' A little bit embarrassed, he mumbled, 'Well, people are not used to that.'

My answer comes from the book of James: 'Ye have not because ye ask not.' When you ask about liberalism and immoralism in the United States and Europe, and the moving in of aggressive Islam, what are we going to do? Well, if you do not have a prayer meeting, who has any right to complain that there's no power for godliness sufficient to roll back evil? As long as we don't pray, and don't believe that God will help us to do right, we're going to be like the first generation of the Israelites, wandering in the wilderness, and letting giants and high walls go unchallenged, as though God were not sufficient for this situation.

But there is a better choice: if the true believing churches would renew prayer meetings, and give their all to live devout lives, based on faith in God's Word, things could be different, perhaps more quickly than we dare to hope! The major issue before the Western world today is whether we will be like the disbelieving generation that wandered fruitlessly for forty years because they would not take God at His Word; or will we be like that later generation which decided that since God is real, He is worthy of all trusting?

NOT TO FEAR IS A DIVINE COMMAND (3:22)
Why should we not fear when we face such a scary future? Moses gives us a reason not to live fearful lives: 'The LORD your God, He shall fight for you'. That's the reason! God is in it! (v. 22).

The church once again is brought into difficult straits in Western culture, to where we've got to decide, does God exist or not? Is His Word true or not? If it be true, will we step out in faith on it? That's the issue. We can also think of our own little lives, and the walls and giants that make us afraid: health, financial, jobs, broken relationships, personal sins we cannot handle, false friends, bitter enemies; who among us does not see the equivalent of walls and giants to make us at times wish to crawl into a hole and hide?

Sometime we may feel like the man in the parable of Jesus, who took that one talent and buried it in the dirt. That was the story of the first generation that came out of Egypt. Maybe it's been our story for a number of years. But we could, right now, decide to change from defeat to victory, from nothingness to something great, and start by taking God literally at His written Word, not like the liberals. God has spoken! It is our honor to take Him at His Word, and then everything will open for us, as God sees fit. When we take Him at His Word, and step out on it, especially when we don't see the future, we may say with all the saints: 'Lord, I don't need to see it, you've told me enough; I leave the future with you. I'm going to step out now on your Word, and with your help, do, the best I can what you have told me to do.' Then every giant that God wishes to be removed from our lives, will shrink down to a pygmy.

Do you remember the movie, *Honey, I Shrunk the Kids?* It was a silly little movie, but in a very different way, if we believe in God enough to obey Him, when it involves us facing hard difficulties, all kinds of things can be shrunken down into pygmy size that can be trampled underfoot.

In Mark 9:23–24, a distressed father with a demon-possessed child—his 'giant'—came to Jesus for help. 'Jesus said unto him, if thou canst believe, all things are possible to him that believeth. And straightway the father of the child cried out and said with tears, Lord, I believe, help Thou mine unbelief.'

God give us the grace to be among the meek who, with the second generation of Israel, took God at His holy Word.

8

The Patience of Unanswered Prayer

Deuteronomy 3:23–29

This text brings before us a subject of great importance. It is mentioned in the fourth verse of the hymn, Spirit of God,

> Teach me to feel that Thou art always nigh;
> teach me the struggles of the soul to bear,
> to check the rising doubt, the rebel sigh;
> teach me the patience of unanswered prayer.

All Christians have experienced what George Croly calls 'unanswered prayer'. It comes into focus here near the end of the earthly pilgrimage of the prophet Moses. In the truest sense, the prayer was answered, but the answer was 'No.' Sometimes God says 'No.' Then, indeed, the Lord adds this: 'Do not speak to me any more about this.'

Let us notice four points:

1. What kind of prayer was denied to Moses?
2. God's no to prayer may not be His final word;
3. If no is said, you can still be a blessing to many, and
4. The source of patience in times of unanswered prayer.

What Kind of Prayer Was Denied to Moses? (3:21–26)

Four minor points help us answer this question.

First, surely it was a sincere, loving, believing, heart-felt prayer on the part of Moses. He says in verses 25, 'O Lord, please let me go over Jordan and get into the Promised Land'. The meaning of the Hebrew is 'I pleaded with God.' It's a strong verb in Hebrew, rather like the Greek verb Paul uses in 2 Corinthians 5:2: 'Now then we are ambassadors for Christ, as though God did beseech you'—that means, please do it, we pray you—'by us: we pray you in Christ's stead, be ye reconciled to God'.

I remember when I was teaching in Jackson, Mississippi, taking a question from a student who seemed rather full of himself, and especially wanted to impress the class with his high Calvinist credentials. He said something like this: 'Well, I believe God has planned who will be saved, who will be lost, so I don't need to worry about that in my preaching; all I have got to do is announce the fact that if you believe you'll go to heaven and if you don't believe you'll go to hell and that's that, and leave it that way.'

I immediately discerned the heart of his problem—pride. I said to him: 'Why don't you tell that to the Apostle Paul? To the Paul who said in Acts 20:31, "For the space of three years I ceased not to warn everyone night and day with tears." Where are your tears for the lost? You cannot preach effectively to people unless you give them your heart, unless you care what happens to them.'

Of course, God is sovereign in salvation, as in everything else. But true Bible-believers, including Calvin himself (in whose writings we constantly see it), plead with, care for and weep over, the lost.

In my early ministry at Raeford, North Carolina, each Sunday morning, before service at the main church, I preached at a little country chapel. There was a fine and godly farm family there, who truly cared for the lost. Their heart-felt concern was shown when, during an evangelistic meeting by Presbyterian Evangelistic Fellowship, they were able to deal with a young army officer, who had served in many parts of the world, and seemed to feel that he was above the people (though he had married a local girl years before).

This officer came under serious conviction one night during the preaching by the visiting evangelist, but was hesitant to make a move. The next day, this humble and Christ-like farm wife went to the officer and said to him, 'If you don't give your heart to Christ and ask Him to save you from your sins, you're going to die and go to hell.' She was literally weeping as she did so. She added, 'You may not have much longer, and you'd better do it now, and follow the Spirit's calling.' Her testimony broke through to him, and a night or two later, he wanted to testify in church. I have never forgotten the testimony. He said something like this: 'Yes, I was proud and self-sufficient, but the tears of Mrs. So-and-so got through to me.'

Moses' prayer would have been one with tears, warm and fervent, not cold, formal, mechanical, or external. In that sense, even though it was not answered positively, it was a model prayer for all of us. So there's nothing wrong with his prayer on that basis.

Secondly, the thing he asked God for was surely based on Holy Scripture, because he knew what God had promised his ancestor, Abraham, in Genesis 17:7–8. Moses takes a scriptural promise and says, 'Lord, make it real!' That's true prayer.

Charles H. Spurgeon and A.W. Pink often said that 'Prayer is pleading the promises of God.' I remember how that impinged upon me when we were in Jackson, Mississippi. We needed to do something about housing; we were in a very little place, with not enough room for all those children. Naturally, we asked some of the strong Christians to pray for this matter. A dear old lady, Mrs. Anna Ware, from First Presbyterian Church, took my hand one day and squeezed it and said, 'Douglas, plead the promises; plead the promises.' And that's what we did. And by and by, God worked a wonder. So Moses is pleading the promises; surely, nobody would criticize that part of his prayer; you will do well if you follow it.

The third observation about this kind of prayer—a noble prayer, if there ever was one, in the league of Daniel, Samuel, David, and Noah— is this: it did not work, because Moses' request was contrary to God's specific word given him forty years earlier. It all goes back to the painful event of Kadesh-barnea, where the first generation refused to believe God when they heard the bad report of the ten spies, and said we're not going to go into the Promised Land; it's too dangerous. Moses had recalled it in Deuteronomy 1:37, 'Also the Lord was angry with me for your sakes, saying, 'Thou shalt not go in thither'.'

Now this rebellious event, which caused an entire generation to die, also involved Moses, though for a different transgression. Numbers 20 explains why God's refusal to Moses had to be maintained forty years later. If Moses had taken God at His word, and spoken to the rock, rather than hitting it with the rod (which, after all, had divided the Red Sea), he would have been able, no doubt, to go into the land. But God said no, I cannot let you go into the land, because you didn't honor Me in front of the people before that mysterious rock. Maybe Moses somehow felt that God would relent. But it was not to be, so God says: 'Speak no more to Me of this matter' (Deut. 3:26).

The fourth characteristic of Moses' prayer is that it was patient. And that is the most honorable example for all of us to follow, all our days. His patience is indicated when in verse 24, he terms himself, 'Your servant.' He rests on God's sovereignty, saying 'You are God overall and I rest on that; I am only Your servant'. That is a patient spirit.

I learned the heart of that when I spent the summers from age five till I finished university, working on the old family farm in Moore County, North Carolina. The matriarch of the family, my great-aunt, came in and prayed with me every night, and also taught me the Shorter Catechism. She emphasized the patience required in true prayer: that whatever specific help we ask, we are always to be submissive and patient. That means we say: 'Lord, you know best; your will be done.'

We hear that in Moses' prayer. 'Yes, Lord, I wish you would let me go in the Promised Land; nevertheless, I am Your servant and I know You're in charge and I want You to be in charge'. That is a patient prayer. Therefore, when God says, 'No, don't mention it again,' Moses patiently accepts; he also faithfully instructs Joshua to be the leader into the Promised Land as God commanded, even though God didn't give him the desire of his heart.

Nowhere in Deuteronomy, nor anywhere else in the Bible I am aware of, gives the slightest hint that Moses was angry with God for saying 'No,' or that he tried to punish God by not giving his full obedience. On the contrary, Moses' spirit was like the spirit of the Lord Jesus Christ in the Garden of Gethsemane, when Jesus said, 'Lord, if You could let this cup pass, please do it; nevertheless, not My will, but Thine be done'.

Significantly, looking in the Gospels, only a short time before Gethsemane, Jesus had been at the Mount of Transfiguration, and Moses and Elijah were speaking with Him. I wonder if the heavenly Father sent Moses to speak to Christ just before He went to Gethsemane, maybe to help Him be willing to accept the Father's 'No' to the passing of the cup? And I wonder, did not the pre-incarnate Christ (Christ always existed from eternity to eternity with the Father, sometimes showing up in the history of Israel or various purposes) come to Moses 1,400 years before at the burning bush, to help Moses be willing to say, 'Not my will but Thine be done.' I have never read anything on this specifically, but Hebrews 11:26 may speak to it: 'Moses esteemed the reproaches of Christ greater treasure than the wealth of Egypt.' Christ helped Moses get things right, and maybe Moses helped Christ too. If true, then one could say reverently, that the favor was returned!

This mysterious and wonderfully invisible working of providence is why we can afford to be patient with God, when we're asking for something. God takes His time. God knows exactly what He is doing with our little lives; it may well be some things we go through now, will make a difference in the holy kingdom, as it did with Moses 1,400 years before the incarnation of Christ. So we can be patient with the Lord when He says to us, 'No, not now.'

God's 'No' to True Prayer May Not Be His Final Word (3:27)

There may well be something beyond God's initial 'No' to His beloved child as it was for Moses. Immediately afterwards, God took him up on a mountain so that he could see the Promised Land—north, south, east, and west. His view from the mountain was like a Divinely set-up telescope, through which he could see with perfect clarity.

We have noted earlier that in the ancient Near East, one of the legal ways of conveying a piece of property was not only on a manuscript or a clay tablet, but the person who was buying the property would be taken to look at it and stand on it, which confirmed the deal. So when God says, Moses, I'm going to let you look at the property, He is really saying, it is yours; although I won't let you put your foot in it, I will nonetheless let you put your eyes on it. 'Get thee up into the top of Pisgah, and lift up thine eyes westward, and northward, and southward, and eastward, and behold it with thine eyes: for thou shalt not go over this Jordan' (Deut. 3:27). And then we're given a little more information later (Deut. 34: 1–4).

Since we must always interpret Scripture by Scripture, we must move on in the sacred texts some 1,400 years later, to discover how it all turned out for Moses. God was still not through with him. It is as though centuries later, the Lord says, 'Yes, I'm taking you over'. Literally, Moses puts his feet (now in his spiritual body) on the Land. 'Moses, I'm taking you down from heaven for a little while to this Mount of Transfiguration, with Elijah, and I want you to meet with your Lord Jesus, and talk to Him before He goes to Gethsemane and Calvary'.

The Gospels give an account of the Mount of Transfiguration, where Jesus was with Moses and Elijah when they 'spake with Him of the exodus which He should accomplish in Jerusalem'. Perhaps Moses was saying, 'Lord, I went through the little exodus out of Egypt; now you have got to lead your people through the big exodus that is soon to occur at Jerusalem, on Calvary; all that I did depends on your going through the big exodus'. So, God did, in His own time, let Moses stand in the Promised Land.

The Rev. Jim Philip of Holyrood Abbey Church in Edinburgh wrote on this passage: 'Does not this [meaning Moses' getting into the land 1,400 years later] whisper to us that what is denied to us here in this life, because of the disciplines of grace, may be granted to us and wonderfully fulfilled for us in the life to come?'

Many things you wanted, which God wouldn't let you have, you may well receive them in far greater measure one day, 'where there is no night'. Never be disappointed with God for His temporal 'Noes', until you have entered the beauties of eternity with its ten million 'yeses'.

John Calvin mentions this in *The Institutes of the Christian Religion,* Book III, chapter 20, section 52, speaks about unanswered prayer, or denial of our request:

> Even if God grants our prayer, He does not always respond to the exact form of our request, but rather seems to hold us in suspense. Nevertheless in a remarkable way He eventually shows us our prayers have not been in vain. This is what John's words mean: And if we know that He hears us, whatever we ask, we know that we have the petitions we have asked of Him, 1 John 5:15. Now this may seem to be rather a repetitive collection of words, but the assertion in fact is extremely practical because it tells us that God, even when He does not comply with our wishes, is still attentive and kindly disposed towards our prayers. This means that any

hope based upon His Word will never disappoint us. So believers need to be patient, sustained by faith in this truth, since they could not stand for very long, if they did not rely upon it.

The famous nineteenth-century Presbyterian preacher of New Orleans, Benjamin Morgan Palmer, quoted Calvin and expanded what he said, some three hundred years later: 'Those things which we have been pleading for with the Lord that we don't get in this earthly life are not ultimately denied to us. Instead, God gives us the true underlying intention of our prayer which was whatever the Holy Spirit was asking for inside of us.' Moses got it in a different way, and we will get what God has for us also, but often in a different way from what we had in mind.

If No Is Said to You, You Can Still Be a Blessing to Many

People to whom God has said 'No' can be a great positive blessing in the lives of others, and that is brought out in verse 28: 'But charge Joshua and encourage him and strengthen him'. God is saying to Moses, 'No, I can't give you this; but I want you to think about and get involved in the future of the kingdom of heaven; it's far bigger than the current thing you're exercised about.'

Likewise, God calls us to strengthen others even when He says no to us in something. We can still strengthen them, because as they are blessed, in the future years and into eternity, we too will be blessed, whether we received all that we were asking for or not in this earthly experience. And so we see in 1 Corinthians 3:3–8.

The Source of Patience in Times of Unanswered Prayer

How are you going to get it? It hurts when somebody says 'no' to you—most of all God! How are we going to be patient and bear it up and cheerfully go on serving and strengthening others? Here's the answer: look at the bigger picture. Get your eyes beyond your own little life and your own little corner. Look at the big picture of what God is doing, of which your life is certainly a part. Of course, Moses would have thought of Israel getting into the Promised Land, although he couldn't go with them. But why was their going into the land so important for the larger plan of salvation? The main reason God got them into that Promised Land was so that the Jews would be there, and 'salvation is of the Jews', as Jesus said. The most important reason was so that Messiah could be born there, as Micah prophesied.

That's the big event of history: Israel goes into Canaan, and takes it, so there will be a birth-place and home for Messiah to fulfill Old Testament prophecies. Was Moses left out? Of course not! Just before the momentous events of Gethsemane and Calvary, God sends Moses from the other realm to meet with Jesus the Messiah and to encourage Him. Surely for Moses to get up on the Mount of Transfiguration was a greater blessing than if the Lord had let him put his feet on the unconquered land of Canaan. So he got it; 1,400 years later. How beautifully his patience was rewarded!

We must look at the New Testament commentary on the Old Testament saints—Hebrews 11—to trace the source of this patience. Hebrews comments that not only Moses (Heb. 11:26), but all who died in faith, shared that forward look:

> For they that say such things declare plainly that they seek a country. And truly if they had been mindful of that country from whence they came out, they might have had opportunity to have

returned. But now they desire a better country, that is, an heavenly; wherefore God is not ashamed to be called their God; for He hath prepared for them a city.

Verses 39–40 refer to all the Old Testament saints who died before Jesus was on earth: 'And these all, having obtained a good report through faith, received not the promise; God having provided some better thing for us, that they without us should not be made perfect'. Finally, Moses would say to us: 'For here have we no continuing city; but we seek one to come' (Heb. 13:14). That is the source of all the patience of all the children of God to whom God says, 'No, dear child; not this; not now.'

Hence, the source of patience is looking at the bigger picture: the coming of the heavenly Jerusalem, and the beautiful things that God has in store for all of His saints. So Moses found that God's initial denial of him would finally end up in a great positive 'Yes!'—not this, but something better.

You might think well, I would like to have married so-and-so; but she would not do it. God did not open his or her heart. Or, I would like to have had children, but that didn't come about. Or I would wish to have had a high achievement in my job or profession; I tried hard, but things never came together. Or think of the refusal of divine healing of relatives: maybe somebody kin to us had a lifelong disability that we would have wished to see removed by God; but He didn't. Or God removed by death some loved one for whom we were praying to the Lord to leave a while longer, and the Lord said no. To be a Christian in this world is to experience more than once God's refusals, and in all of these, he would have us exercise the patience of unanswered prayer. You know that you are doing so, when you say, Lord, I don't know whether You will give this or not; Your will be done; but I'm available, whatever You want me to do in the future. That's our response; when God says 'No,' you say 'Lord, I'm available, whatever I can do that would make a difference.'

Years ago, Elisabeth Elliot gave her testimony at the First Presbyterian Church of Jackson. She talked about her experience after the Auca Indians had killed her husband. She and a small daughter were encamped, not far from where the Auca Indian tribe lived, who had just killed her husband. I don't have any doubt that she would have prayed for her husband that morning, when he was going up into dangerous territory. But God did not answer that prayer from a faithful woman of God. He let her husband get killed. When she found out her husband was dead, she said, 'Lord, I am available. I'll stay here with my daughter, and do what I can until you show me otherwise.' That's the patience of unanswered prayer.

Later, God would wonderfully work in the hearts of the Auca Indians; one of the Indians who had stabbed her husband to death gave his Christian testimony at the Urbana University Missionary Fellowship. After the killing of the missionaries, much of that tribe had been saved. Moses, and Elisabeth Elliot instruct us to say: 'Lord, teach me the patience of unanswered prayer.' Every denial of God to us has a larger, more positive meaning in the life of that heavenly city which we are seeking.

9

Which Way the Western World
Deuteronomy 4:1–8

This passage does not directly speak of the Western World, or the Third World, or any modern entity. It deals with a situation roughly 1,400 years before Christ. Yet there are certain spiritual, historical principles in it that apply across the ages. Hence, let us consider three points:

1. The right use of history (Deut. 4:1, 3–4).
2. The right use of the Word of God (Deut. 4:2).
3. The right way to live (Deut. 4: 1 and 5–8) and the honour God's people win among pagan nations.

The Right Use of History (4:1, 3–4)

Chapter 4 begins a new section of Deuteronomy, relating this great discourse by Moses on the plains of Moab. Hebrew scholars tell us that the first word, 'Now', 'now therefore', indicates that Moses is concluding this first major discourse and is getting ready to apply to their consciences the historical events he has mentioned in the first three chapters.

Moses has rehearsed the big stories of the previous forty years, and now he says: 'This is what it's going to mean as you enter the Promised Land; I have told you all this (in the first three chapters), to keep you from making the same mistakes, so I can put you on the high road to success.

One commentator said that Moses was speaking to a generation of young men in the plains of Moab, because, except for Moses, Caleb and Joshua, most of the people of Israel were under 40 years old and none over 60. Because of that judgment, Moses is speaking to a generation who did not have the knowledge of history that an older generation would have had. Therefore, Moses knows that they need to learn lessons, particularly out of their recent history, so they can successfully handle the future.

Moses picks out one event from the past forty years to warn these young believers what, above all else, they must avoid. A terrible thing had happened many years earlier in the valley of Bethpeor, not too far from where they were camped. Moses said, if you want to go in and conquer that land, don't be repeating the disastrous sin of what happened in the valley of Bethpeor (Num. 25:1–5, 9).

The New Testament says that the prophet, Balaam, sought to please the king of Moab by cursing the Israelites. But Balaam every time he tried to curse them, the Holy Ghost would get hold of him so that he would, against his own will, begin blessing them. However, Balaam was a devious man. He thought of a way to corrupt the Israelites. He had the King of Moab send out several thousand half-naked young women, to allure the young men of Israel to commit fornication with them.

To understand the background, we must add that in that part of the world at that time, there were fertility cults, for the worship of idols was connected with sexual orgies. It was believed that performing immoral sexual practices—strictly forbidden by Scripture—would make the land rich, crops abound, and the animals reproduce abundantly. Given the weakness of human nature, the plot worked, so that thousands of Israelite men went out and got involved with these young women, which was not only a question of personal immorality, but also involved worship of the false god Baalpeor, before whom they bowed down in idolatrous orgy.

Moses could have taken many lessons out of the forty years' experience in the wilderness, but this is the one he wanted to emphasize. It was: be sure not to turn your back on the true God, so as to join yourselves to idols and their prostitutes, for that is to invite utter destruction.

Twenty-four thousand Israelites were slain in judgment after this orgy: the priests put a good many of the leaders to death, followed by a plague from God on the whole nation, so that 24,700 were wiped out. Truly, 'the wages of sin is death'. What Israel had done was to violate the first and greatest commandment, as Jesus taught us: 'Thou shalt love the Lord thy God with all thy heart, mind, soul and strength, and Him only shalt thou serve'. It was like committing adultery on their true husband, friend, Savior, and Lord. Such immorality and gross disloyalty required the death penalty. Otherwise, the holiness of their Covenant God would have been publicly besmirched.

Some people will wonder, 'Isn't this a bit harsh?' Well, here's the answer. If we saw how beautiful, pure, shining and splendid is the burning holiness of God, we would immediately perceive how just and necessary the destruction of these people was, in order to spare the rest of the nation. Our God truly is a consuming fire. Thus, this nation was warned, that their heartfelt loyalty to the holiness of God is the only way to life and peace. They will be able to cross over the river to a victorious life in the Promised Land, only insofar as they worship the true God alone and seek to live in His holy law. That is the right way to live, as Moses clearly instructed them.

The Right Use of God's Word (4:2)

Old and New Testaments tell us that we may never add to or take anything from the written Word of God, for instance, here in 4:2. That's very definite and strict, and accords with the last chapter of the last book of the Bible: 'And if any man shall take away from the words of the book of this prophecy, God shall take away His part out of the book of life and out of the holy city and from the things which are written in the book' (Rev. 22:19).

Why is it so serious to tamper with the written Word of God, whether in the days of Moses, or what was given as the last book of Scripture by the apostle John? 'All Scripture is inspired', says 2 Timothy 3:16. The Greek word is θεόπνευστος, meaning all Scripture is God-breathed: that is, every word in the Bible is breathed out by the Spirit of God. It is a product of the creative breath of God Himself, working through the prophets, apostles and wise men to have it accurately written down. Peter tells us that 'holy men of old spoke as they were carried along by the Spirit'. Thus, the Bible comes from God; it bears His attributes of absolute truth and holiness. To tamper with it, is to put oneself above the God who gave the Bible. Can you see what an arrogant, blasphemous thing that is to do? To say, I don't agree with all the Bible; I'll take some parts of it, and other parts I will not accept, and change it a little bit to fit the times, is to put yourself above God. That is to follow a false god of our own devising.

Moses was very far-seeing. I don't know how far he could see into the future, but it must have been a long way, because what he's saying is what our formerly Christian nations need to hear. To tamper with the Word of God will eventually result in disaster for those who do it. Let me give you two illustrations to show how they determine the bad shape the world is in today.

The first is the rise of Islam. Tampering with the Word of God is what Mohammed did. He took certain bits and pieces of Old and New Testament, and at the same time, rejected much of it, and added many things in. Thereby, he put a different interpretation on the bits of Holy Scripture that he took, and put them into the Koran. For instance, he denied the Holy Trinity, and thus the full deity of Jesus Christ.

He says in the Koran, that God is not a Father, and does not have a Son. He denied salvation by the grace of God, and put in its place a kind of works-righteousness. In sum, Islam is a religion that's based on the most serious tampering with the Word of God.

And then the second illustration I want to give you of tampering with the Word of God is what we call 'the European Enlightenment', about 200 years ago. 'The Enlightenment' has done far more damage among us than Islam. It begat a movement that we now call Modernism. The Modernists were basically rejecting traditional Christianity, wanting to start over and have something better. To achieve this, these people denied the truth of a great deal of Holy Scripture. For example, they said even if there is a God, still He is not able to intervene in the world; He is remote; He does not have all power. He cannot change the world. It's sometimes known as Deism.

The best answer to the question, Why Modernism? was given by a conservative Roman Catholic, E. Michael Jones. He wrote *Modern Degenerates: Sexual Degeneracy of the Modern West*. In it, he argues you can take only one of two approaches to truth: first, you can conform your desires to the truth. That means you accept the Lordship of God totally. Or second, you can conform the truth to your desires, and that means you change the parts of the Bible you don't like, that keep you from living self-centered, immoral lives.

E. Michael Jones teaches that the Modernist Movement has sought to conform God's truth to its lustful desires for illicit sexual activity, so it will not feel guilty for immoral lives. This has been deeply influential in the main-line churches across the West, not unlike what occurred in the time of Moses, in the valley of Bethpeor. If Jones is right, the reason the Modernists have tampered with the Word of God and denied Scriptural truth is so they can commit adultery, homosexuality, and the rest, without feeling guilty. That is what has weakened us before the enemy of men's souls.

Is God any less holy now than He was in roughly the year 1400 B.C.? If He dealt in the most serious way with His people who turned their back on His Word, and committed adultery and idolatry, why would you think we are going to get by with it anymore than the children of Israel did?

On the contrary, Moses is saying to these young people of Israel that to be saved, to know God, to possess eternal life, means bowing down in humble submission to every written Word of God. In that way lies life, peace and victory. The right use of the Word of God is the only hope for the future. If we would have a movement in America and in the British Isles back to submission to the Word of God, we would have massive changes for the better, and the enemy would be confounded. But will that happen?

The Right Way to Live (4:6–8)

It may not be so complicated as we think. Could the reason why some people want to make it complicated is that it requires total personal obedience? Is it because it requires taking a stand? Let us note two points under the right way to live. First, the nearness of God, and second, the honor His people win among the pagan nations, when they live in the near presence of God.

Those who, from the heart, seek to obey His Word will be unlike the rebels at Bethpeor, who saw the naked Moabite women and bowed down to their idols for a few moments' pleasure. Rather, they will be like the large majority of Israel, who refused to get into adultery and idolatry because God was '*nigh unto them*' (verse 7); God was close to the ones who obeyed Him, when the others were disobeying.

'Everybody else is doing it!' is used as a reason for premarital sexuality and other things. You could have said that in the valley of Bethpeor, but most of Israel did not. You cannot have God filling your life with His presence and blessing, and, at the same time, besmirch His holiness.

Psalm 148:14 says that God exalts the horn of His people, the praise of all His saints, even of the children of Israel, 'a people near unto Him. Praise ye the Lord'. Notice that description. No matter what is happening in the culture around you, you can still have God near unto you, and you have all that is ever worth having.

The nearness of God is the opposite of pagan, modernist deism, which puts God way up there, us down here, and the natural world a closed machine that even God cannot get into. Here's how it really is: the majestic, transcendent God who inhabits eternity, who created all things out of nothing in six days, by the Word of His power, the mighty One who inhabits the throne of splendor, literally comes down into this world of nature and personalities and bodies and draws very near to us, person to person, spirit to spirit, to the humblest human, who seeks to trust and obey this God. God Himself comes down into your life!

Romans 10:6–9, (which refers to Deut. 30) puts it thus: God has done everything necessary to get so close to us; He's in your body and in your soul, through the activity of Christ, who left His throne of splendor and came into this world as one of us; He was a sacrificial Lamb, without ever ceasing to be God, and did everything necessary to remove every barrier between this holy transcendent God and us, sinful human persons. Jesus came and put everything right for those who will receive it.

Ephesians 2:13 speaks of this nearness: 'But now in Christ Jesus ye who sometimes were far off in Christ Jesus are made nigh by the blood of Christ'. Jesus has paid for every one of our sins which separated you and me from a holy God, in the shedding of His blood; and in His rising from the dead He has raised us with Him into nearness to God. Christian life is basically nearness to God, and that means walking in His holiness as best we can. We do have some sins to confess every day. But the very nearness of God drives us to want to be more holy and to confess our sins and keep coming back.

Now the greatest part of eternal life, while we are on earth, is the nearness of God to us.

Romans 8:14–17 tells us that God has sent the Spirit of adoption into our hearts, causing us to cry out *'Abba Father'*. The Holy Spirit comes from the throne, from the Father and from Jesus, into our innermost beings, making us know that God is our Father and helping us pray. That's what makes life worth living! And then the heaven of heavens will be, that we're going to be even closer to the throne of God than we were while on earth, as Revelation 21:3 shows:

> And I heard a great voice out of heaven saying, Behold, the tabernacle of God is with men, and he will dwell with them, and they shall be his people, and God himself shall be with them, and be their God.

A grand old gospel hymn sings out:

> Nearer, still nearer, while life shall last
> 'Til safe in glory my anchor is cast.
> Through endless ages, ever I'll be
> Nearer, my Savior, still nearer to Thee.

This is the only way worth living: an immediate fellowship with God in the Holy Spirit and the prelude to our life in eternity. Not to experience nearness of God means that your life is finally not worth living. 'It is a tale told by an idiot, full of sound and fury, signifying nothing' (Macbeth, Act 5, Scene 5).

The Honor God's People Win Among the Pagan Nations

It would be well to develop how being near to God means that your life follows wise principles, and those tend to bring, in the long run, certain blessings, of families and communities, and sometimes entire nations. That happened in Israel, when King Solomon in his wisdom and glory attracted people from all over the world, such as the Queen of Sheba. Godliness tends to win approval, even among the pagans.

We close with this question: which way are the once Christian nations of the world going? If we continue in our sexual immorality, systematic unbelief and exclusion of Christianity from the public square, the nations will have to experience something like Baalpeor: a plague, the wiping out of large numbers. But I hope and pray that it is still not too late. If the churches in half-dead nations will pray hard, maybe we could see a third Great Awakening in the twenty-first century. The first Great Awakening was in the 1730s and 1740s. God used George Whitefield, John Wesley, Jonathan Edwards, Samuel Davies, Howell Harris, and others to transform Britain and the American Colonies. Then things slipped back, and after that, what we call the Second Great Awakening broke out, roughly from the 1780s to the 1830s. Vast numbers of those who became our leaders were converted, as the Holy Spirit was poured out on Britain and these young states. The hour is late, but we could still be praying for a third great outpouring of the Holy Spirit in the United States, Britain, and the rest. Let us set our hearts to be near unto God, and everything else will be well.

10

TRUE SPIRITUAL WORSHIP

Deuteronomy 4:9–14

Moses considered true spiritual worship of utmost importance. The spirituality of God is crucial here. It is what matters most for time and for eternity. The text brings before us two major points: (1) lasting safety for us and for our children lies in remembering how God reveals Himself, in particular, His spirituality, and (2) How God shows us who He is?

LASTING SAFETY FOR US AND OUR CHILDREN LIES IN REMEMBERING THE SPIRITUALITY OF GOD (4:9–12)

A literal translation of the Hebrew of verse 9 is this: 'Guard yourself <u>for</u> yourself'. That is to say, 'keep your heart with all diligence, for out of it are the issues of life', as it says in Proverbs 4:23; and in a line from a hymn: 'Principalities and powers, lurking in unseen array, watch for thine unguarded hours, watch and pray'.

In Ephesians 6:12, the apostle Paul talks about spiritual warfare and armor. He describes how God gives us particular armor—helmet of salvation, gospel shoes, and so forth—to help us through a difficult, sinful world, where we are attacked and tempted from many directions. But all of the defensive armor that Paul so wonderfully describes in Ephesians 6 is summarized here in Deuteronomy 4 under one defensive weapon: 'guarding yourself' by keeping in mind how God reveals Himself.

Here in Deuteronomy 4, the whole thing is boiled down into one suit of armor consisting of holy light, coming down upon you from God Almighty, covering every aspect of your personality and being your going in, your coming out, and giving you a divine protection.

Now here is how you keep this armor of light upon you in a dark world: remember how God reveals Himself, what kind of God He is; and live your life walking in the light of that knowledge, and thereby having divine protection from wickedness and evil.

Deuteronomy 4 and Ephesians 6 assume that to do so is a difficult work, for there are things out there that wish to destroy you. The evil one is generally hidden behind the world system with which we have to cope, wishing to get us off the tracks and get our mind away from who God is, so that he can remove the armor of light and come at us.

He did that in the Garden of Eden with our first parents, Adam and Eve. God had told them what to do and what not to do; and so the evil one came in the form of a serpent to get them out from under the armor of light by posing a question: 'Yea, hath God said …? Follow me, not God.' As they gave in, the armor of light was gone, and we still pay the price as their descendants in being born into sin, struggling with it all our days, and facing physical death, and judgment beyond.

Ever since the fall of our first parents, there is a perverseness in us. One of the main ways it manifests itself is that we tend to resist the high spiritual road that God gives us to walk on, resisting the spirituality of God and seeking a lower, flesh-pleasing way to exercise religion. The devil never stops trying to pull us down from worshiping the spirituality of God, down to fleshly, humanistic, self-serving religion. When we go down we lose the armor of light, but when we come back up, we can regain it.

Now the destiny of individual human souls turns on whether or not they remember, and are true to, the way God reveals Himself; or, whether they take the easy way out, the way the devil tempted our first parents, 'Yea, hath God said..?', thus treading the route of the world, the flesh, and the devil.

How Does God Show Us Who He Is? (4:13-14)

As Moses has made clear, God does not reveal Himself through idols. The great question arises: How then <u>does</u> He reveal Himself? How <u>does</u> He show us who He is?

God reveals Himself through the spoken Word and the Holy Spirit, never in images or physical shapes, similitudes, idols, sun, moon, stars, animals, or whatever. Here, we remember the second commandment: *'Thou shalt not make unto thee any graven image'*. The only way to keep ourselves and our families from the moral and cultural degradation that inevitably follows every kind of idolatry is keeping in mind God's pure, holy spirituality. That's the most practical thing you can ever do.

Notice in verse 12: 'And the LORD spake unto you out of the midst of the fire [at Mt. Sinai]: ye heard the voice of the words, but saw no similitude; only ye heard a voice'. God reveals Himself to Israel and then to the Church, not in pictures, or images, or idols, but through His Word, through a voice, and that voice for us today is given in the written Word of God. Let us think about that truth negatively and then positively.

Negatively, the true God does not reveal Himself through forms or idols. John Calvin is clear and helpful here.

> Meanwhile, since this brute stupidity gripped the whole world to pant after visible figures of God and thus to form gods of wood, stone, gold, silver or other dead and corruptible matter, we must cling to this principle: God's glory is corrupted by an impious falsehood whenever any form is attached to Him. Therefore in the law, after claimed for Himself alone the glory of deity, when He would teach that the worship He approves or repudiates, God soon adds 'You shall not make for yourself a graven image or any likeness' (*Institutes of the Christian Religion*, Book 1, chapter 11).

Calvin goes on later to say: 'God's majesty is sullied by an absurd fiction when the incorporeal is made to resemble corporal matter; the invisible made to resemble a visible likeness; the spirit an inanimate object; the immeasurable a puny bit of wood, stone or gold'.

Paul also reasons in the same way in Acts 17: 'Since we are the offspring of God, we ought not to judge the deity to be like gold and silver or stone carved by the art or devising of man'. From this it is clear, that every statue man erects, or every image he paints to represent God, simply displeases God as something dishonorable to His majesty.

Why do you think that an otherwise intelligent and able people, such as the Indians and Chinese, ancient Philistines, erected idols and bowed down to them? Here is what Calvin would answer:

> Daily experience teaches the flesh is always uneasy until it has obtained some figment like itself in which it may fondly find solace as in the image of God. In almost every age since the beginning of the world, men, in order that they might obey this blind desire, have set up symbols in which they believed God appeared before their bodily eyes.

Calvin says in another place that the mind of man is a perpetual factory of idols. We make idols, if we don't keep in mind the spirituality of God.

Why do we do it? I think Calvin is right: flesh is uneasy with the spirituality of God, with the purity and holiness and greatness, the nearness and the transcendence of God—that makes people uneasy. The real God makes people nervous and scared, particularly when they don't remember the gospel. And so they say, let's have a god who is easier to handle, a god who is more like us, and then we may be able to live our lives rather more pleasantly. Here is another reference from the Rev. William Still from Aberdeen, as to reason why idolatry is so widespread:

> To worship an inanimate object is so unsatisfying to intellectual creatures that their worship must engage their active powers in some form of self-expression. Since sticks and stones do not make any moral demands, the self-expression becomes more and more carnal and gives at last entrance to demon spirits whose office it is to invade empty personalities and find rest in them to the destruction of those personalities.

In other words, he is saying that if you reject the spirituality of God, you can form another god, who is not spiritual, and who does not make major moral demands upon you. Take the example of the protection of the lives of the unborn. Now if you have a humanistic god, who did not absolutely say 'Thou shalt not kill', but instead, if you get a god who is there to make you feel comfortable, where you don't have to spend time and money on unwanted babies, then you can get rid of them. It is that kind of thing.

Modernist theology doesn't bow down before physical idols. They take aspects of God that they find acceptable, such as God is loving; but they remove other aspects that they find unacceptable, such as God is holy—and particularly, God demands your moral obedience, and will bring you into judgment for what you do with your life, and how you treat other people.

In place of that, Modernists say, God helps you actualize the self-life, helps you be happy, whatever it takes. Now the kind of god that Modernism offers is an idol; he doesn't exist; he's a phony god. He will not get you through the hour of death; he will not sustain you through the awful, final assize, the last judgment. Much of the Western world comforts itself by worshiping a self-serving idol, which will do them absolutely no good. That's the negative: God does not reveal Himself in forms or idols, including kinds of religion and philosophy and theology that does not accept how God does describe Himself.

But then the positive: how God <u>does</u> reveal Himself; how you <u>can</u> know God. And there lies safety, happiness and lasting joy. God reveals Himself in His spoken Word, and by means of the Holy Spirit. Notice verse 12: 'Ye heard the voice of the words'. Verse 13 mentions the Ten Commandments, and verse 14 mentions statutes and judgments, which means the other parts of the five books of Moses. God has revealed the words in the Bible to instruct us about who He is; the most important thing to know is who God is. You can get the rest of it right, if you know that. And He has given us that in His holy Word, as to who He is, and what He will do; in Old and New Testaments, and supremely we have who God is, in the way He reveals Himself, in the Lord Jesus Christ. 'And the Word became flesh and dwelt among us, full of grace and truth' (John 1:14). On Mt. Sinai they get God's true law, showing His spirituality, and His holy requirements; but they can never live up to it. On Mt. Calvary, God comes down in the flesh and personality of His Son, and dies for our sin and is raised from the empty tomb to do everything we can't do, to give us eternal life in the saving knowledge of God.

In John 14 Philip said to Jesus, 'Lord, show us the Father, and it sufficeth us'. And Jesus answered; 'Philip, have you been with me so long a time, and do you not know that he that hath seen Me, hath seen the Father?' H. R. Mackintosh, used to say, 'It is in the face of Jesus that we have seen most fully the heart of the Father revealed.' God reveals Himself in His written Word, and above all else, the written Word is fulfilled and exemplified and carried out in the life of the eternal Son of God in the flesh, the Lord Jesus Christ. So He reveals Himself in the Word, but you won't get anywhere with the Word, unless the Holy Spirit breathes upon it and makes it real to you. That is one of the things that the apostle Paul prays about, for the Holy Spirit to come down in the Word, and make it real; otherwise you don't know God.

In other words, if you're going to church where the minister is a conservative, and at least formally believes the Bible, but the service is dead as a doornail, what is wrong? It is simply because the Holy Spirit did not breathe upon the Word, and make it alive. I can't resist telling a story my wife brought up yesterday. Cousin Sally McRae Bennett, who was a long-time faithful member here and I'm sure taught most of you in Sunday School, came back from church one Sunday, and asked her cook how the service had gone at his church. He replied that the minister read from the Bible, and supposedly preached, but 'the Spirit never rose up from the page'. Now that's the problem. Unless the Holy Spirit comes down and blesses the Word, and makes it real, the words fall to the ground.

It's seen in Ephesians 1:16–19, where Paul prays for the church at Ephesus, and for all of God's people; and any preacher worth his salt has always prayed this for his people, and for himself:

> … making mention of you in my prayers; That the God of our Lord Jesus Christ, the Father of glory, may give unto you the spirit of wisdom and revelation in the knowledge of him: The eyes of your understanding being enlightened; that ye may know what is the hope of his calling, and what the riches of the glory of his inheritance in the saints, and what is the <u>exceeding</u> greatness of his power to us-ward who believe, according to the working of his mighty power which He wrought in Christ when He raised Him from the dead.

Like Paul we need to need to pray in every sermon: 'Lord, come down with the same power that was being exercised when the body of your Son was raised from the physical death into spiritual resurrection of the body; come down in the same power that raised up Jesus and do Your work through this Word, that they can know who You really are. For as Jesus taught, "God is Spirit".'

Let me conclude with three brief points from this lesson about true spiritual worship. The first point is the simplicity of true worship. Neither our Puritan ancestors nor the Calvinists were perfect;

we know that. But one thing they had that was right, that transformed the world, and we're still benefiting from it, is that they were profoundly convinced of the simplicity of worship (hence the word 'Puritan' meaning to purify all elements of medieval worship that obscure the gospel, and let God be seen as God).

That is why, in a traditional Puritan Presbyterian church, and others in various denominations, the architecture is very simple. There is a chasteness, an austerity in Puritan church architecture: plain, white, often clear windows, and in the middle of the church is a pulpit with a Bible on it.

Some of you have been to St. Giles Cathedral in Edinburgh, once a Medieval Roman Catholic cathedral before the Reformers took it and made it Presbyterian. One thing you find on the outside and on the inside, are empty niches and little stubs of stone in those niches. The Calvinists went in, convinced that the second commandment is true—*no graven images*—and chopped out all the idols, in hopes of making the worship more pure. The same thing happened in the Cathedral of Saint John in Lyon. Whether that is always necessary, I cannot say. But they were attempting to make the point that God is Spirit, and must be worshiped as such.

Secondly, in addition to simplicity of architecture, these Reformed Christians tried to institute Bible-centered worship (not of the Bible, but of the Holy Trinity). Moses says in this text, 'you heard His voice'; God reveals Himself by the voice, by the explication of His Word; God walks down upon His explained, preached, believed Word, and transforms you with His own presence and life.

Thirdly, is the importance of praying, in prayer meetings and in personal prayer, for the Holy Spirit to bless the Word. God reveals Himself primarily through the Word. We must always guard plenty of time in the service for preaching the Word. But that won't work by itself. As Cousin Sally's cook said, the Spirit will never rise from the page! You will go home maybe worse than when you came in, unless the Holy Spirit is there in power, with resurrection might, in the preached Word.

The Rev. James Philip of Holyrood Abbey Church in Edinburgh, wrote about the importance of a church praying, if the Word is to do its work in revealing the spirituality of God:

> Utterance is something more than eloquence. It is burning words, fraught with spiritual power to change lives. This Paul indicates comes through prayer and a battle has to be fought with the powers of darkness before such an unction can be bestowed upon a preacher. Nor is it his battle alone; it is also the congregation's. It lies in their hands and in their prayers for him to put the sharp, cutting edge in his ministry. Who can doubt that this is the greatest need of the proclamation of the gospel today? It is prayer, intelligent, focused, concentrated, persistent prayer that turns orthodox truth into Spirit-charged life-giving dynamic.

May it be so.

11

What the Transcendence of God Requires

Deuteronomy 4:15–24

Moses clearly says that God is a consuming fire. To put it another way, Moses is telling them that the major thing he wants them to remember when they go into that new country, is the transcendence of God, the true spirituality of God. If they will remember that our God is a consuming, holy fire, they and their children can be blessed, indeed.

Now this passage sets before us what the transcendent purity of God requires of us, His people. Although spoken by Moses, maybe 3,400 years ago, it is the same today. That is in line with how the book of Hebrews speaks of 'Jesus Christ, the same yesterday, today, and for ever'.

Our God changes not—the book of Isaiah's full of it—God's holiness, His purity, and His existence, both in beautiful, wonderful love, and as a pure, consuming fire, have never changed in the slightest. Moses taught that we must always deal with who God is in order to be properly related to Him.

We look at four points from this text: (1) God's revelation of His purity (Deut. 4:15); (2) how we remember our history (Deut. 4:20–23); (3) what we are to remember, and (4) a holy warning (Deut. 4:23–24).

God's Revelation of His Purity (4:15)

The answer in the child's catechism to the question 'What is God?' is this: 'God is a Spirit and hath not a body like men.' We humans live in a world of bodies, and bodies are good; they are made by God, and joined with our spirits and somehow together, they make us truly human. Certainly, the connection between Spirit and body is a mystery, and I cannot explore it here. All I will say is that the concept that only the material is real is disastrously wrong, not least because God Himself is Spirit, and His creative activity lies behind all material things. In Genesis 1, God creates all things out of nothing, by the Word of His power. God always was: Father, Son, and Holy Spirit, dwelling in love and purity and consuming fire—so bright and beautiful! Thus, material things had a beginning. For countless eons of eons before there was a created order, before there were sun, moon, stars, galaxies, planets, there were no bodies: neither luminous bodies in the heavens, nor terrestrial bodies of earth, nor physical bodies of animals, plants or men and women, but God always was. God is a most pure spirit, and He transcends His creation.

The basis, in my opinion, of modernism and liberal theology that has destroyed so many churches is to think that God is not bigger than His creation, that He is bound and limited by nature. But God is transcendent; He always was, and then at a certain point several thousand years ago, He brings this wonderful cosmos into being. Yet God remains a pure, holy, burning, bright, beautiful, spiritual reality—even more real than the material. Material things decay after the fall of Adam, and go back into the dust. That can be stated scientifically, in terms of the second law of thermodynamics: things decay, things break down, they are no longer there; but the most pure, holy, bright, glorious spirit God is always there, always the same. So He's more real than anything else.

When God shows us who He is, He teaches us something about Himself by using the created order, such as the sun, the moon, and the stars, which do declare His glory; they tell us about God's handiwork (Psalms 8 & 19: Genesis 1, etc.). But when God reveals who He Himself is, it is not primarily by using elements from the created order (though He does so on Mt. Sinai). Deuteronomy 4:15 is saying that at Mt. Sinai the holy fire of God that set that whole mountain alight with frightening flames that mounted up to the skies, they also heard a voice.

God speaks in order to communicate; He doesn't show Himself by means of animals or stars or anything else. God, who is Spirit, has a voice, He has a mind, a prime personality, and speaks words from the mountain. He's a most pure spirit. He is a real person, indeed, three Persons in one. Jesus Christ is the *logos,* the Word; and before His incarnation, that Word comes from the mountain where Moses was.

If you should go to Mount Sinai today, you will not see the holy flames leaping up to heaven that Moses saw, and you will not hear God's voice speaking. But you are no loser, for you have it in the Book! We can get in touch with who God is through the Words of the Book, and the Book hasn't changed. According to the second commandment, no graven image of any animal is allowable in the church or in Christian worship.

By contrast, in ancient Egypt, they worshiped the sun god, Amun Ra; in Mesopotamia, where Abraham came from, they worshiped the lunar god, god of the moon. The Philistines worshiped a fish god, Dagon. But such impure worship is forbidden in Deuteronomy 4:16–18. Then Deuteronomy 4:19 forbids worship of any of the elements of nature. It is clear that these created things are not God; He made them for His glory.

You might think, why should we be preaching against ancient Egyptian religion or modern religion in India, for we are not involved in these things. But the modern West may not be so far from it as you think! In a famous essay entitled 'The Humanist Frame' (1966), Sir Julian Huxley says that we must reject 'the God hypothesis.' But when somebody rejects the transcendent God, they make a substitute. In the essay (page 113 of my edition), Huxley says that what man should worship is the universe 'seen as a unitary and evolutionary process.' Like Huxley, some form of the evolutionary process is about the only god vast numbers of people have: that things are evolving, that we are part of it; we hope it's going to get better, and perhaps that explains everything else. That may be why some people become so upset if you raise scientific arguments against evolution: you are criticizing the only god they have!

One of the things my wife and I discussed when our first child was two or three years old, was how we should place him in a school which taught that God is Creator, and did not base everything on evolution. Many of us think that evolution is questionable scientifically, and certainly the teaching of Scripture about God's transcendence and purity does not fit with the evolutionary process.

God's Demand For Purity in Our Worship and Thinking (4:16 and 19)

This passage is dealing with what you think about; it is also important in the New Testament, where we are instructed 'whatsoever things are true, honest, just, pure, lovely, of good report, think on these things' (Phil. 4:8). This section of Deuteronomy 4 is very important for how we think; specifically that we are to remember that God is a pure, transcendent Spirit.

What You Are to Remember (4:20–23)

Here Moses says that it's very important that you remember your history as the people of God, where you've come from and where you are going. He adds that God brought the children of Israel, out of the iron furnace, from the horrid oppression of Egypt as slaves, being beaten and abused; but God got them out; don't ever forget it!

That is the reason why the feast of the Passover was instituted to be celebrated every spring by the Jewish people, so that they would always remember that God had brought them out of slavery, by blood and by power. Similarly, the feast of the Passover for the church in the New Testament was fulfilled in the Lord's Supper. God has said that we should regularly celebrate the Lord's Supper. Thereby, we remember, in the Lord's Supper, what the Jewish people remember in the Passover, that God has redeemed us out of our sinful, self-destructiveness, out of ego-centrism. In Old and New Testaments, remembrance is very important.

Then Moses speaks about how the Lord divided the world among the nations, and allotted them with certain boundaries (see also Acts of the Apostles). I think it means that when the world was destroyed by the flood—which Noah and his three sons and their wives survived—it was from the three sons of Noah: Shem, Ham, and Japheth, all the nations of the world come (see Genesis 10 and elsewhere).

God was preparing the world for redemption, which would come out of Jerusalem in the fullness of time. The point made here (verse 20) is that God chose a particular nation as His inheritance, the Jews. He chose Abraham and the seed of Abraham, Isaac and Jacob, and later the seed of David. God chose them, among all others, to be the line of salvation to the rest of the nations. He would bless them in a particular way, and eventually would send His own beloved Son to be a Jew, while remaining God, to fulfill all of the Old Testament and to do for us, as Gentiles and as Jews, what we could never do for ourselves.

Let us think about how God's people are His inheritance; inheritance is something that we value and pass down over the generations: rings, gold coins, and things of great sentiment; we treasure such things. You and I take care of land; if we are wise, we would put gold coins or beautiful things in a safe place. But God's treasure is His people.

God, a most pure Spirit, seated in glory on the rainbow-circled throne, below which stretch out the streets of gold, treasures something far more than all the gold, one little humble sinner: one penitent man or woman who says 'God, be merciful to me, a sinner.'

Truly God is different from ourselves! We fallen humans have a tendency to love things and use people, but God treasures His people above all created things, no matter how beautiful to our eyes! God's merciful dealing with His often recalcitrant people demonstrates to what a degree they are His highest treasure.

A Holy Warning (4:22–24)

In a sense, what happened to Moses constituted the first warning, when God said to him, I'll let you look over the Promised Land, but you can't go in; you're going to have to die in the wilderness. Why did Moses remind them of that? It was a graphic way of saying, if you don't keep in mind the spirituality, the transcendence of the holiness of God, and make that the center of your thinking and worship, you will not be able to keep the land; the land will be taken from you; it will spew you out.

Moses attaches a reason to this warning: 'The Lord thy God is a consuming fire, even a jealous God', verse 24. Now that is exactly quoted in Hebrews 12, especially verse 19, is quoting exactly from Deuteronomy 4: 'For our God is a consuming fire'. And before that they had been given the commandment, 'Serve God acceptably with reverent and godly fear'. Hebrews takes us back to Mt. Sinai, and adds one thing, that Jesus is the mediator (verse 24). Moses in a sense was a mediator, but an imperfect one; he couldn't go into the land. Jesus is the perfect mediator; He bears in His own body our sins on the tree, and He leads us into the land. The Son of God becomes flesh, while remaining God; He dies for our sin, is raised in a new body to give us eternal life. The reason we should be serving God with reverence and godly fear is appended in Hebrews 12:29, as it was in Deuteronomy 4:24: 'God is a consuming fire'.

You can think of God as a consuming fire in two different ways, and both would be right. First, you can think of God's purity, holiness, and beauty being expressed in this fire, a fire that doesn't destroy. Exodus 3 speaks of Moses seeing the burning bush, and yet the bush was not consumed. Thus, God's pure, holy fire can be rightly thought of in terms of the beauty of His spotless character, which is non-consuming for those who worship Him in reverence and in godly fear.

A hymn by Frederick W. Faber expresses the holy fire that doesn't consume, but purifies you and lifts you up, like the burning bush.

> My God, how wonderful Thou art,
> Thy majesty, how bright;
> How beautiful Thy mercy seat
> In depths of burning light!
>
> How dread are Thy eternal years,
> O everlasting Lord,
> By prostrate spirits day and night
> Incessantly adored!
>
> O how I fear Thee, living God,
> With deepest and tenderest fears;
> And worship Thee with trembling hope,
> And penitential tears!
>
> Yet, I may love Thee, too, O Lord,
> Almighty as Thou art;
> For Thou hast stooped to ask of me
> The love of my poor heart!
>
> How beautiful, how beautiful,
> The sight of Thee must be;
> Thine endless wisdom, boundless power,
> And aweful purity.

In the book of Revelation, chapter 8, the angel takes fire from the altar and puts incense in the censer, and sprinkles it over the prayers of His people. This is a way of expressing that the holy fire comes down in our prayers, to purify, to make them beautiful and fragrant, so that the fire of God gets into them, causing them to reach all the way to heaven. God's character is revealed as a purifying fire.

Another aspect is that He is a consuming fire. At one time Nadab and Abihu took 'strange fire' and in response, devouring fire went out from God, and burned them up. God is a consuming fire to that which is contrary to His character. He must eventually burn up that which is ungodly and hateful to Him, and destructive to human life.

Notice Revelation 19:20: 'And the beast was taken, and with him the false prophet that wrought miracles before him, with which he deceived them that had received the mark of the beast, and them that worshiped his image. These both were cast alive into a lake of fire burning with brimstone'. In Matthew 25, the words of Jesus warn us to flee from the wrath to come. Hell is real, and goes on for those who reject God and reject the gospel, and will not serve God in reverence and godly fear, preferring idols instead. According to Revelation 19:20, they give God no choice, but to cast them into the lake of fire.

And the lake of fire burns on, because God's purity is eternal. Heaven is maintained in its wondrous integrity because of the purity and holiness of God. Hell is maintained in its awful reality for those who keep bowing to idols instead of the one pure God. Hell is maintained eternally by the same holiness of God. If we realize today that we have a choice; what a blessed people we are!

12

A SECURE FUTURE

Deuteronomy 4:25–31

This passage speaks of a secure future. As far as the general life and wellbeing of the people of God in this world goes, God tells us through Moses that they, and their children, can be secure in the Promised Land for many ages. He doesn't say they won't be without trials. But He does say they will have general security for them and their families in spite of the trials, on one condition. We must note here that what the land meant to Israel in the Old Testament, the general blessings of the true Christian life mean to us in the New Testament. There is a definite way that we and our children can enjoy security for the future. What is it?

We consider five points: first, avoid the evil: Deuteronomy 4:25; second, the consequences of giving in to evil, verses 26–28; third, the time of our greatest danger, verse 25; fourth, the sure way back to the place of blessing: 4:29–30; fifth, why God really will let us back in, 4:31.

What Is Necessary for a Secure Future (4:25)

God says that for a secure future, we must avoid 'the evil' (written in Hebrew with the article 'the': i.e., 'the evil.') and identified in verse 25 as idolatry. The main enemy to our future and security is not the stock market, or who's going to be elected president, or the wars: those things are all important, but those are not the main enemy. There's one main enemy, as Moses points out; it is replacing God in our thinking and in our affections, with an idol—that's the worst thing that can ever happen; that will destroy your future more quickly than anything else.

John Calvin often said that the mind of man is a constant idol-factory. You go through history, philosophy, and religion, and one of the signs of the fallen version of Adam, and of us his descendants, is that our minds tend to become a factory that turn out idols, something else to replace God, at a considerable rate.

It first started in the Garden of Eden, at the beginning of human history, when the devil said to our first parents: 'if you will follow my program, then don't listen to God, and you shall be as God, knowing good and evil.' That's when it started, and the idol factory work that we all are tempted with, has never slowed down, except in times of revival.

The nineteenth-century German commentator Franz Delitzsch, wrote that the more the human mind grows corrupt and loses its sense of the presence of God, the worse kinds of idols it produces, thereby destroying its future. Delitzsch said: 'What Moses threatens here follows from the eternal laws of Divine government. The more refined idolatry of image worship leads to coarser and coarser forms, in which the whole nature of idol worship is manifested in all its pitiableness.' Then he adds,

> When once the God of revelation is forsaken, the God of imagination must also soon be given up, and make way for still lower powers that perfectly accord with the I, the ego exalted upon the throne, and in the time of pretended 'illumination' or enlightenment to atheism or materialism also.

That downward spiral seems to be the story of the Western world, especially since eighteenth-century Deism which said, 'yes, there's a God somewhere out there, but He can't interfere with this world'. And then it went downward from Deism to atheism in the nineteenth century, at which time Darwin said that the world explains itself by evolution; you don't need a Creator. To this day, many look to evolutionary, naturalistic processes as being the nearest thing you could have to some kind of god. That is one of the reasons our culture is in the state of disintegration morally it is in now.

Professor Herb Schlossberg, in his book *Idols for Destruction,* quotes Hosea 8:4, that they chose them idols for their destruction. He says that if you replace God with something that is not God, it will in due season destroy you. He says that the Eastern world Buddhists and Hindus bow themselves down to stone statues, but in the Western world, we don't do that. But we have other kinds of idols that are equally destructive and abhorrent to God, such as idols of the mind, or idols of nature, or idols of history. Ultimately, Professor Schlossberg states an idol is anything that replaces God in your mind, imagination or affections. Anything other than God that motivates you, that you think is most important of all, is an idol!

With time we might also consider Romans 1 and Psalm 14:1: 'The fool hath said in his heart there is no God.'

The Consequences of Giving into the Evil (4:26–28)

Hosea 8 tells us that when you replace God with something other than God, you lose everything. Moses told Israel, if you give in to idolatry of pagan nations, you will lose the Promised Land; and you'll be deported in grievous ways.

For us Christians, since the New Testament, it hasn't been that we would lose one particular country, but the blessings of walking in the favor of God, in the light of His countenance, with His peace and His joy. We lose the only things that make life worth living.

Moses calls upon nature to witness—hills, rocks, streams, trees, and skies—because God made nature, and the country is part of it. In one of the covenant treaties with a conquered people, Marcellus—a Hittite king about the time of Moses—says, if you're not faithful to the terms of this covenant, I call on nature itself to witness against you. If we break the covenant with the God who made nature, nature itself will witness against us. You will see more of that in Deuteronomy 28.

The book of Judges (5:20) says that *'the stars in their courses fought against Sisera'.* The very elements of nature worked against this terrible pagan, who oppressed the people of God, so that massive torrents of rain descended, and bogged down his chariots. Thus, the people of God were blessed to overcome him. But nature can also work against Israel, if it is unfaithful. Amos shows how God lifts the hand of common grace from off the seasons and the crops, when God's people turn to idolatry. The same thing is made clear here in Deuteronomy 4:26: 'I call heaven and earth to witness against you this day, that you shall soon utterly perish from off the land whereunto ye go over Jordan to possess it; ye shall not prolong your days upon it, but shall utterly be destroyed'.

III. The Time of Greatest Danger (4:25)

Moses implies that it will be most difficult for the children of Israel when they came into the land. If we say that the youth of Israel occurred during their forty years in the wilderness, then perhaps when they marched into the Land of Promise, they entered something like middle age, perhaps the time of greatest danger; when we have been successful and things have gone well with us and our family, we face the greatest temptation to turn from God to our favorite idols, foolishly thinking that our own cleverness has got us where we are, and that even if we compromise, we're still always going to be blessed.

I think over my long life that I have heard far more sermons dealing with the sins of youth than with those of middle age. But middle life is far more dangerous and it was so with King David. When he was a young man, persecuted by Saul, he generally did well spiritually. But after success and honor as king, he got into middle life and committed horrendous sins. A.W. Pink said that every servant of God should take this prayer from Psalm 119:117, and make it his own: 'Hold Thou me up and I shall be safe'.

After Israel settled in the Promised Land, the temptation to be like the rest of the pagan world would be far greater than when they were having to fight their way in; having to exercise faith and crying to their faithful God every day, 'Lord, help us!' as they faced Amorites, Canaanites, and Philistines. However, once they became established, that's when temptation hit them the worst. And I would say it is still that way with most of us.

The Way Back to the Place of Blessing (4:29-30)

After all seemed lost, after Israel was deported to Babylon, and over a century before that, the northern kingdom had been deported to Assyria, God still offered them (that is, the southern kingdom) a way back: 'If thou seek Him with all thy heart and with all thy soul' (4:29); that is the key: sincerity, desperation of purpose, humiliation for our sin, and recognizing that we did wrong, calling them what God calls them, and saying, 'Lord, be merciful to me!'

God never requires perfection to get back to the place of rest; nobody could. He requires sincere purpose of heart, 'a broken and a contrite heart, O God, Thou wilt not despise' (Ps. 51:17). Jeremiah 29 speaks about what would happen after they were deported to Babylon for their idolatry: 'For thus says the Lord, that after seventy years be accomplished at Babylon I will visit you and perform My good word toward you, in causing you to return to this place'—the Promised Land—to come back to the place of rest. And God says: 'Then shall ye call upon Me, and ye shall go and pray unto Me, and I will hearken unto you. And ye shall seek Me and find Me when ye shall search for Me with all your heart' (29:12-14). That remains a promise to this day. God will never go back on it.

The apostle Paul says in Ephesians 2:11, 'wherefore remember': remember what God did in your salvation, taking your sins in Christ, and raising you with Him, seating you with Christ in heavenly places, according to His eternal, gracious purpose: wherefore, remember all that, says Paul, and you can get back to the place of blessing, better than ever.

Why God Will Let Us Back In (4:31)

If you apologize to somebody whom you offended, you don't know how they will react. But we know what God will do and say if we apologize with all our hearts to Him: He will take us back in every time. Why? 'God is not a man that He should lie'. God is different from us. At times, we may not show mercy to somebody who sinfully hurt us, but God will always show mercy.

How is he so different from us, that he will take offensive people back in? Verse 31 says that 'He is compassionate'. God is a compassionate God. One commentator said that compassion is a deep, emotional attachment—not just a superficial legal thing on a document that doesn't enter into the wellsprings and the deepest part of your personality. God's whole being and affection yearns over His people. God has a deep, emotional attachment to his people, like a mother who yearns over an erring child; or the father who, seeing his prodigal and repenting son coming down the road, gathers up his robes and goes running out to greet him.

It is very important to remember when you confess daily sin, that God has a deep emotional attachment, deeper than any loving parent or any child of the womb. I saw a reflection of this one day in the Charlotte airport, where a little group of extended family, eight or ten people, greeted an obviously embarrassed relative, who was getting off the plane. They had a homemade sign which said: 'Welcome home.' The young woman whom they were greeting, was weeping. When she saw the sign, 'Welcome Home', she literally broke down, and her family broke down weeping with her. I don't know what the story was: had she been off to have an illegitimate child? Or maybe drug rehab; or maybe in prison? It was evident that her family believed she might feel they wouldn't receive her, and so there they were, a humble knot of people with a sign, 'Welcome Home.'

I thought on that day, I have seen a beam of the mercy of God from this family, taking back a daughter who had no doubt painfully embarrassed them. And I thought, yes! God is like that with us all!

We see the mercy of God, I suppose, most clearly in what Jesus did for us. 'Seeing then that we have a great high priest that has passed into the heavens, Jesus the Son of God, let us hold fast our profession. For we have not an high priest which cannot be touched with the feeling of our infirmities' (Heb. 4:14–16). Compassion is a deep, emotional attachment. God feels what we're going through. You say, He's too great! No, you haven't understood God. This is why He takes you back, for our Saviour 'was in all points tempted like as we are, yet without sin. Let us therefore come boldly unto the throne of grace that we may obtain mercy and find grace to help in time of need'.

One illustration of how Jesus takes somebody in, is found in Luke 23:39–43:

And one of the malefactors which were hanged railed on him, saying, 'If thou be Christ, save thyself and us.' But the other answering rebuked him, saying, 'Dost not thou fear God, seeing thou art in the same condemnation? And we indeed justly; for we receive the due reward of our deeds: but this man hath done nothing amiss.' And he said unto Jesus, 'Lord, remember me when thou comest into thy kingdom.' And Jesus said unto him, 'Verily I say unto thee, Today shalt thou be with me in paradise'.

One assumes he was there for something serious, like murder, and he admits it. But he asked Jesus for mercy. Jesus immediately took him back into the favor of God, and into the Father's presence; that's the mercy of God.

We come back to the earlier question: How can we secure our future and that of our dear children? Moses says that the people of God have a perverse way of turning aside to idols, and ultimately the real idol is the self-life that hounds us the most. But does our human perversity leave us without hope for the future? Moses points us past our own sins and failures, and calls us to rest upon the sheer mercy and compassion of God.

As Hosea took back his adulterous wife, if we will repent and believe afresh, this gracious, holy, pure, loving God promises that He will take us back. In repenting and turning we find rest and security. And so we can sing with old Isaac Watts the lovely hymn,

> 'O God, our help in ages past,
> our hope for years to come;
> our shelter from the stormy blast;
> and our eternal home.'

13

REMEMBRANCE GIVES HOPE

Deuteronomy 4:32–40

In this wonderful and encouraging passage we have this major thought: remembrance always gives us hope. In the book of Lamentations, after the prophecy of Jeremiah, when the people have been taken captive, we find this wonderful verse: 'This I recall to mind [and Jeremiah is recounting how God has been in charge of everything and is still their God]; therefore have I hope' (Lam. 3:21). To remember who God is, and what He has done for His people, is the ground of boundless hope and truest optimism, and the motivation of a holy life. To forget what God has done for us is the surest way to discouragement and spiritual depression. So God says that there will be hope, if you remember!

I note just two points from this passage. First: what Israel is to remember as it soon enters the Promised Land (verses 32-39). Second: holy memory shapes holy lives (verse 40).

WHAT ISRAEL IS TO REMEMBER AS IT ENTERS THE PROMISED LAND

In 4:32–39, Moses makes it plain, and the Holy Spirit through him, that what Israel remembers will determine whether their future life goes well with them, and their children, or not. That thought is taught not only in verse 40, but throughout the passage. Moses tells this pilgrim people specifically to remember three things as the key to a happy future in the Promised Land:

We are to keep in our minds, first, how God has revealed Himself, as we see in verses 33 and 36. The one true God has literally spoken, so that we can hear Him and know His will directly. God is not silent, not absent, not a dark mystery keeping you from knowing what He expects. No, God has spoken in human words that you can get hold of. 'Know therefore this day, and consider it in thine heart, that the LORD he is God in heaven above, and upon the earth beneath: there is none else' (verse 39). And in verse 33: 'Did ever people hear the voice of God speaking out of the midst of the fire, as thou hast heard, and live?'

I remember when I was in high school in Lumberton, North Carolina, having a friend, who was from a difficult family background. He began to go somewhat off the rails spiritually, and he started talking about astrology, which was unusual in Lumberton, a pretty fundamental Christian community. One day I asked him to show me the magazine he was reading on astrology. I looked in it, and it said, 'We look in the stars, so we know the will of God.' I quickly said to him, 'That's ridiculous! God gives us His will in His book, you know that!'

Well then, later, he started talking about palmistry, and certain lifelines, etc. Again, I said, show me the magazine. It claimed that you could find out what your future would be, if you learned how to read lines on the palms of your hands. I said to him, 'That is the silliest thing I have heard of! If both your hands were cut off in an accident, you still have a future! God talks about your future in the Bible; you know better than that.'

When I came to Dillon 34 years ago, as far as I remember, we did not see fortune-teller parlors around Dillon. Now they are there, with big neon signs, 'Madame So-and-so will solve your problems and tell you your future'. This is a deception of the devil. It's as though God has not spoken clearly in His Word! Isaiah speaks about it:

> And when they should say unto you, seek unto them that have familiar spirits, and unto wizards that peep and that mutter, should not a people seek unto their God? for the living to the dead? To the law and to the testimony: if they speak not according to this word, it is because there is no light in them (Isa. 8:19–20).

God has clearly spoken in His Word what His will is. At Mt. Sinai all aflame with a holy fire, God has a voice; God is personal; not a black hole or a mysterious, impersonal force. We do not go beyond Him to know what is right, and what is our future.

John 1:1 says, 'In the beginning was the Word.' We know that by 'the Word', John means the Son of God, the Lord Jesus Christ. From all eternity, the Father speaks His Word, and the Word, the Son, speaks back to Him in the Holy Spirit; so in God is Word. It goes back to the fact that personal relationship involves words. God is our heavenly Father. Through grace we're His children, and a father communicates to his children. And the main communication of God is His Son in the flesh (and all of Holy Scripture accurately points to Him).

God speaks. To go to an astrologer, palm reader or 'new age' thing is to give the devil immediate access to you. On the contrary, God speaks in this holy book, and we can understand it, as we see in Psalm 19:7–8: 'The law of the LORD is perfect, converting the soul: the testimony of the LORD is sure, making wise the simple. The statutes of the LORD are right, rejoicing the heart: the commandment of the LORD is pure, enlightening the eyes'.

Those other ways, instead of enlightening the eyes, darken the heart, and only lead you into destruction. Sad to say, the boy to whom I was testifying, in later years, took his own life. Getting involved in those things did not enlighten his eyes, or lift up his heart.

So God has spoken in the Old Testament: Moses, the holy prophets, and then He sends His Son in the flesh, the Lord Jesus Christ, and the Son sends the Holy Spirit to endow the holy apostles to write the New Testament.

In the middle verse of the Bible, if you take the Bible and count the verses—so I am told by scholars—the very middle verse of the whole Bible, between Genesis 1 and Revelation 22 is this: 'Wherewithal shall a young man cleanse his ways? By taking heed thereto according to Thy Word' (Ps. 119:9). Jesus says in John 6:63: 'The Words that I speak unto you, they are spirit and they are life'. God is still revealing Himself in the same Holy Word—still conveying spirit and life through the Bible, as it is received in faith in the Holy Spirit.

In Romans 10:9, you will discover what that Word does for you, if you receive it. It promises that 'If thou shalt confess with thy mouth that Jesus is Lord and believe in thine heart that God has raised Him from the dead, thou shalt be saved'. Salvation involves commitment to the pure revelation, and especially to the Lord Jesus Christ whom it sets forth. It includes Sinai, the Sermon on the Mount, the epistles and all the rest of the Bible, for it is all the Word of God.

The second thing to remember is how God has delivered His people (verses 34 and 38). The miracle of the exodus is summarized in this clause: 'God took a nation from the midst of another nation'.

To take a nation, whole and entire, from the midst of another powerful nation that doesn't want them to leave is a miracle! It was hard to do, but not too hard for God, who did it through the devastating series of ten plagues. The last plague was the destroying Angel of Death, passing over all the houses and killing the firstborn. God told the holy nation of Israel to put blood on the doorposts, so that the destroying Angel of Death would pass them by. After that, the Red Sea cooperated by the power of God! Israel passed through dry-shod, and the Egyptians were drowned: a nation from the midst of a nation. Israel's deliverance was, and is, a miracle.

This principle, that God takes a new nation out of an old nation, applies to what has been happening since the coming of Christ, and His establishment of the church. It is not exactly the same, but there are connections.

According to 1 Corinthians 6:9–11 as lost sinners, connected to fallen Adam, we were taken out of him and grafted into Christ, the second Adam (see also Romans 5 and 11). The people in Corinth, saved, justified, filled with the Holy Spirit, had been in the category of fornicators, idolaters, adulterers, effeminate or homosexual, abusers, thieves, drunkards, and the rest of it; 'such were some of you; but ye are washed, but ye are sanctified, but ye are justified in the name of the Lord Jesus, and by the Spirit of our God'. God does a miracle any time somebody comes from a sinful, fallen human race; God takes them out like He took Israel out of Egypt, under the blood and through the Red Sea—salvation is always a miracle—never forget it.

Or look at 2 Peter 2:9: 'The Lord knoweth how to deliver the godly out of temptation and reserve the unjust unto the Day of Judgment to be punished.' God knows how to deliver. He's still in that business while we've got the church. Or go to 1 Peter 2:9–10, that's us! Out of darkness into His marvelous light. We were no people until the holy presence of Jesus Christ came upon us.

Now the Greek word for church is *ecclesia*, and it means 'called out.' The church is called out from the sinful nation, and this indicates that God prepares a holy nation by miraculous deliverance. Remember that, say both Moses, and Paul.

The third thing is to remember the electing love of God. 'And because he loved thy fathers, therefore he chose their seed after them, and brought thee out in his sight with his mighty power out of Egypt' (Deut. 4:37). The basis of the mystery of election—God choosing sinners from among others to be made saints through Christ—is always the wondrous, infinite, tender love of God. There is no explanation of it; that is all we can say.

Electing love was the basis of Israel. They were slaves, they were in bad shape humanly speaking; but God's heart yearned upon them and chose them. And Pharaoh and all his army and all the host of hell could not keep Israel from being delivered. And it's the same with us who know Christ.

I sometimes wonder why I would be a Christian. A while ago, a very intelligent man, who came from a kind of pagan background, asked me, 'Why is it that you are a Christian and I am not?' I answered that I couldn't exactly say, except I know that God by His providence put me in a believing family. All I can conclude is this: 'because He loved thy fathers'.

That same electing love, 'because he loved thy fathers', is the basis of the Christian church, which is the fulfillment of Israel; in continuity with Israel; it's not a split between us, but rather an opening up to all the nations of the world, every people, tribe, nation and tongue. I would say to anybody that wishes to be saved, the electing love of God is the basis of everything as expounded in Ephesians 1:3–6:

That's the basis of Israel and of the Christian church. Remember those things, and you'll always have grounds for solid hope. Remember how God revealed Himself; remember how He has delivered His people; remember the Father's electing love.

Holy Memory Shapes Holy Lives

Verse 40 teaches that holy memory shapes holy lives: 'Thou shalt keep therefore His statutes and His commandments which I command thee this day, that it may go well with thee and with thy children after thee, that thou mayest prolong thy days upon the earth which the Lord thy God giveth thee forever'. Keep in mind where you came from, who God is, and where you're going, and your life gets cleaned up, and has a certain purity and a sparkle about it that comes from above.

Reverend James Philip of Holyrood Abbey Church in Edinburgh, wrote, in reference to Deuteronomy 4 and Ephesians 2:11-13:

It is this that is emphasized so clearly in Paul's words in Ephesians 2:11, Wherefore remember; and this we may add is the purpose and function of a continuing ministry of the Word in the Christian church today. But how better could we recollect the mighty acts of God in our redemption than by going over the Word that expounds and enfolds them over and over again, joined with continual wonder and awe from the realization of the greatness of God's love in Christ. This is the best way to remember, being much in the whole counsel of God, delighting in its riches, meditating on His ways, until our whole souls are kindled and fired by a passion to walk in obedience to His will all the days of our lives.

Holy memory, the kind of memory that the Word is talking about keeps you pure in times of temptation; and also encourages you to live a life of good works: the negative and the positive.

I remember a wonderful seminary professor I had many years ago who was once moderator of the old Southern Presbyterian Church—an excellent man—and he told us one day about when he had been a chaplain in the United States Army, during the invasion of Normandy. He remained there for a while with the army, and could have had opportunity to do certain things that were against the will of God, certain sins of the flesh, that presumably nobody would have known about. The thing that kept him true was the thought of the purity of his mother, who lived in North Carolina. You might say, well, I don't feel my mother or father were good models. Well, think of the purity of Christ and you will not be able to do these things that the flesh is pulling you down to do.

The Red Horse, one of the best novels of the twentieth century, is by a wonderful Christian man in Northern Italy, Eugenio Corti, whom we visited once in his home in Milan. He went through World War II, and was in the frozen horrors of Siberia. His novel takes you through all that, and after the breakup of Italy, Nazism, Fascism, takes us down to the 1970s. In these decades, he is following the characters and stories of three young men, who were in the University of Milan when they were called up to the Italian army. There is a very moving passage in it after they have been through all of this, when Italy is rebuilding and Europe is facing its problems in the early 1970s.

The hero of the novel had a very difficult marriage, to say the least, and several years later, he fell for a beautiful young woman whom he had almost married 30 years before. Many years later, he made arrangements to have a meeting with this still-beautiful woman whose husband was dead. Thinking about Christ and about his own boys who were in their late teens, keen Christians and working in a particular election to try to get some local Christians elected, he thought, 'I can't do this! Think of Christ and think of my sons' respect for me; no, I won't do this.' Well, holy memory will keep you pure in times of testing when nothing else in the world will work. That's the negative side of this text, and it has great power for good.

And then the positive: holy memory encourages us to be active all the days of our lives, even when we're tired, in doing good works. Notice two areas from Ephesians chapter 6 where holy memory will enable us to be active in doing good, when otherwise it might be hard for us.

The first area is the family. Ephesians 6 says for children to obey their parents 'in the Lord; honor thy father and mother which is the first commandment with promise'. What it is saying is, children, remember your relationship with the Lord that overarches your relationship with your parents, and that will help you relate to your parents in a godly way. And fathers, 'provoke not your children to wrath, but bring them up in the nurture and admonition'—of what?—'of the Lord'. Fathers be careful not to discourage your children. Probably most fathers would be like me in wishing we had done a better job. Nonetheless, at whatever stage of family life, bring up children in a way that will not discourage them. Remember that they are 'in the Lord', and you are 'in the Lord', and He is the focus of what you are trying to teach and admonish and accomplish. That provides the high goal and the power for a good family life.

And then in the work place, in verses 5-9: 'servants, be obedient to them that are your masters'. These days people are very uneasy if the word 'servant' is used, particularly given the American background of slavery. But to think of some worker as a kind of servant does not necessarily have to be, in every case, negative or demeaning. After all, we are all under authority of somebody else, and in that sense, if in no other, we function as a kind of servant. It doesn't mean that your bosses are better than you, but that you are bound to do your work very well.

Notice that we are to do our work: 'in singleness of heart as unto Christ'. It is simple; it is profound. Throughout the work day, we are seeking to keep Christ in view. That is saying a great deal!

You might not particularly like very much the company where you work, or the school where you teach, or whatever; but you're not finally doing it for them—you're doing it for Christ. And that has a way of causing absolute excellence, whether we are trash collectors or school teachers, or farmers, or work on an assembly line, or cleaning houses—remember Christ is in the house, the assembly, in the school, and we are doing it as unto Christ. Now some days you would like to stay in bed, and not show up for work. But you do show up, not only to draw your salary, but because you know that Christ will be there, and He expects you to do your best. It's for Him!

Verse 6 tells us it is to be *from the heart* and explains that doing the will of God from the heart means sincerely seeking to do the very best you can. That makes for wonderful school teachers, wonderful students, wonderful house cleaners. How encouraging it is every time a cheerful worker shows up; it's beautiful! And in verse 5 this thing is '*unto Christ*'. We do it therefore from the heart, unto Him. Let me give you a poem from a seventeenth-century poet, George Herbert:

'A servant with this clause
Makes drudgery divine:
Who sweeps a room, as for Thy laws
Makes that and th' action fine.'

Sweeping for Jesus—yes indeed!

And a few lines from a poem by the great Puritan poet John Milton, Sonnet 7, *How Soon hath Time*:

Yet be it less or more, or soon or slow,
It shall be still in strictest measure even
To that same lot, however mean or high,
Toward which Time leads me, and the will of Heaven;
All is, if I have grace to use it so,
As ever in my great Taskmaster's eye.

Isn't that wonderful? Everything worth doing in our studying, speaking, work, serving, visitation, we remember as ever in my great Taskmaster's eye. And that lies behind the transforming of life, for we remember that we're His, and that it's for Him. We, at the same time, remember where we're going, and how He revealed Himself, and how He has delivered His people. Those holy memories have a supernatural way of shaping a holy life, and that is the chief testimony and power of the Christian church, anywhere in the world, to convert the lost and to make life worth living.

14

The Cities of Refuge

Deuteronomy 4:41–43

Cities of Refuge Set up by Moses

God, through Moses, appoints for the people of Israel as they are standing on the banks of the Jordan before going into the Promised Land 'The Cities of Refuge'.

Anyone would know by experience that there comes a time in life—of serious trouble, of the consequences of failures, of sins—when we need a place of refuge.

David, in Psalm 71:3, says that he wants to go to a place of refuge whereto he may continually resort, a feeling that every person, especially at particular junctures in life that are bad, or hard, or hurtful, strongly desires.

In the Law of Moses, these cities were a merciful provision in Old Testament law for manslaughter—that is, for those who accidentally killed. Now nearly all ancient cultures—some up to the present time—have a custom of 'blood vengeance.' That is, if somebody in your family got killed, it was felt to be the duty of the next male person, who was kin to the killed person, to seek them out for vengeance and to take their life. Scholars say that there was no such provision for manslaughter in any of the ancient Middle Eastern nations that surrounded Israel. Israel, and Israel alone, had these cities.

We may note that, without the Old Testament law given through Moses on which the law codes of Western Europe, and the United States of America are founded, our progress and prosperity for these last 2,000 years would have been totally impossible; but now we're looking only at the cities of refuge, what they meant in Moses' time and afterwards; and secondly, what they would really mean for us today.

What the Cities of Refuge Provided in the Old Testament Economy

If, in Israel, someone accidentally killed another person, provision is made of six cities throughout Israel, three on the east side of Jordan placed strategically, during the time of Moses, and three on the west side—in the north, south and middle—when Joshua had led the people of Israel over Jordan. At least one city would be no more than a day's walk. The person concerned was instructed to hasten to the closest city so that the avenger of blood would not be able to kill them.

Once they got to one of those cities, a trial took place, run by the Levites, the teaching, ministering tribe in the Old Testament [Moses and Aaron were Levites;], who were scattered throughout Israel in order to teach the law of God and to be judges as 'decentralized' scholars. They knew Scripture, and knew how to render fair judgment. The person who fled to the city, would meet with them; and they and the lay elders of the city would hear the avenger's case.

If the Levites decided that the man really was a murderer, and had been lying in wait in order to do so, a decision would be made to turn the murderer over to the avenger of blood. But if the Levites, after careful scrutiny, decided that it had been an accidental killing, then the elders and the Levites would say, 'You can stay in this city; you must not go out, and here you will be safe until the death of the current High Priest. When he dies, you will be free to go home again, and the avenger of blood cannot touch you and your future will be secure' (see Num. 35:25)

In sum, cities of refuge would be an early instance of what we call due process of law, ultimately going back to Moses, making our society safe and happy.

The Meaning of Cities of Refuge for Us Today

What do the cities of refuge mean for us today? Times have changed, and our situation, our culture, is very different, so that the meaning is somewhat different. In Moses' time and in ours, the will of God graciously makes provision for those who find themselves in trouble. In Moses' time and now, God's plan provides refuge for the endangered and the troubled. And that refuge has some kind of connection with the ministry and death of the high priest.

According to Numbers 35:25, the death of the anointed high priest, the successor of Aaron, makes it possible for the accused to go home free, with a clean slate and a future full of hope. In this sense, there is a close similarity between ancient Israel and modern Christianity, in that the death of the High Priest takes care of their condemnation.

However, because we're in different cultures and times, there are vast differences between the Mosaic cities of refuge, and the universal refuge that God makes available to all people today who ask Him for it.

Physical Location

The first major difference between Moses' cities of refuge and our need for refuge today is that of physical location. At least since the time of the deportation of the Jewish people to Babylon, about 586 B.C. and maybe long before that, these cities of refuge have no longer served this purpose. Where then is the refuge? It is no longer in a physical location; it is in a relationship to a Divinely ordained Person. In the Old Testament days, the Aaronic high priests were chosen human persons descended from Aaron, who at the end of a life of service, like all of us humans, had to die. Then the captives were set free; that was the provision for then.

In our generation, we are called to take refuge in a great High Priest, who died 'once for all', and then came back victoriously alive from the dead. Saints are not perfect people because they need intercession; they are sinners, but this great High Priest is able to put them right with God so they can be called holy, or saints, in that sense.

> By so much was Jesus made a surety of a better testament. [or 'covenant'.] And they truly [the Aaronic order of high priests] were many priests, because they were not suffered to continue by reason of death:. But this man, [Christ,] because he continueth ever, hath an unchangeable priesthood. Wherefore he is able also to save them to the uttermost that come unto God by him, seeing he ever liveth to make intercession for them. (Heb. 7:22-25)

The epistle to the Hebrews tells us about the final and great High Priest, who, in His person and work, replaces the cities of refuge by His own death and resurrection, so that He becomes, if we will receive it, our own lasting refuge. It says that the high priest was anointed with the holy oil—making him the priest in the succession of Aaron—and called *Mashiyach* from where we get the English word 'Messiah.' In the Greek translation of the Hebrew Old Testament, known as the Septuagint, *Mashiyach* is translated with *Christos*, from the Greek word 'to anoint' or 'to pour oil on'. And so *Mashiyach*, Messiah, and *Christos*, or Christ, reveal how the Old Testament high priests have their life and work fulfilled in this one, who comes and continues to do what they so nobly began:

> But Christ being come an high priest of good things to come, by a greater and more perfect tabernacle, not made with hands, [that is Christ's human nature]; Neither by the blood of goats and calves, but by his own blood he entered in once into the holy place, having obtained eternal redemption for us (Heb. 9:11-12).

… then Hebrews 10:11–12:

> By the which will [of God] we are sanctified through the offering of the body of Jesus Christ once for all. And every priest standeth daily ministering and offering oftentimes the same sacrifices, which can never take away sins But this man, after he had offered one sacrifice for sins for ever [death on the cross], sat down on the right hand of God.

In other words, Old Testament sacrifice covered sins temporarily, but something was needed to take them away eternally—the precious blood of Christ.

The wonderful news is that God has done absolutely everything to deal with our sins, our debt, and our corruption as fallen people. On the basis of which, God gives us an invitation in Hebrews 4:14–16, which recalls, and infinitely surpasses, the six ancient cities of refuge; this greater and lasting refuge is refuge in Christ. We are invited to come to it by faith:

> Seeing then that we have a great high priest, that is passed into the heavens, Jesus the Son of God, let us hold fast our profession. For we have not an high priest which cannot be touched with the feeling of our infirmities; but was in all points tempted like as we are, yet without sin. Let us therefore come boldly unto the throne of grace [as they ran to the cities of refuge in Moses' time, now the Lord says let's come boldly to the throne of grace—run to it!], that we may obtain mercy, and find grace to help in time of need.

In sum, that's the first difference: it was once a physical location, and now it is in a relationship by faith to the High Priest, the final High Priest that God has provided.

Difference in types of sinners

Here is the second major difference between the Mosaic cities of refuge and the place of refuge that God provides for us. In Deuteronomy and Numbers, the escape to the cities of refuge was only for a person who had not intended to commit murder and had no murderous intent.

But how different with the great High Priest! By the infinitely worthy virtue of His holy life, the shedding of His blood, His glorious resurrection and outpoured Spirit, God is able to give us refuge from all condemnation, and forgive us of our sins, even when we are willfully guilty. He shelters us even when we cannot say, 'I didn't mean to do it! It was a mere accident, a combination of circumstances!'

This refuge in Christ is for those who are willfully guilty, who have done wrong, and are worthy of death! The Father says, 'My Son has paid the penalty for your sins and taken your death upon Him; come into this place of refuge, and you shall find absolute pardon and eternal security.'

The woman taken in adultery (John 8) found the great High Priest and He gave her eternal pardon for her sin. He said 'Go and sin no more.' In other words, He imputed the power of a transformed life to live above that kind of thing. The woman at the well of Samaria whom Jesus met in the middle of the day, had five ex-husbands and a live-in boyfriend at that time. Jesus offers her the refuge from the consequences of her sin, and she drinks of the living waters of the gospel, is restored, and becomes a witness in her own town. Simon Peter was forgiven of his betrayal of Jesus, and was joyfully restored to a fruitful ministry. The very people who put to death Christ on the cross of Calvary are offered a place of refuge, as Jesus prays, 'Father, forgive them, for they know not what they do'.

In other words, no matter how much we fail others and God, no matter how guilty we are inside and outside, the door of grace, the city of refuge, is open for forgiveness from every sin; full pardon and eternal help and a heavenly home are freely available to us, if only we will come to the place of refuge. It is a decision we ourselves have to make.

We conclude with two brief readings from 1 John 1:9 and 2:1–2:

> If we confess our sins He is faithful and just to forgive us our sins and to cleanse us from all unrighteousness. If any man sin we have an advocate with the Father, Jesus Christ he righteous, and He is the propitiation [that word means 'mercy seat,' as on the Ark of the Covenant] for our sins, turning away all the wrath of God against us.

Thus, at the mercy seat, we find the smile of God; and not only for our sins only, but also for the sins of the whole world; the door is universally open to whosoever wishes to come. And so the real issue is not, do I need a place of refuge, (we all do), but will I come to it and seek Him?

Let us close with a little poem, written at the end of World War I, by Edward Shillito; (I found it in Archbishop of Canterbury William Temple's readings of John's Gospel). Edward Shillito had lived through the horror of trench warfare in the battlefields of northern France in the first World War, where men were blown to pieces, left to be eaten by rats and vermin. Many wondered, where was God? I think an answer was provided out of that terrible experience, in a poem he wrote, which, to my mind, shows exactly what the city of refuge could mean to me and you:

> If we have never sought, we seek Thee now:
> Thine eyes burn through the dark, our only stars;
> We must have sight of thorn-pricks on Thy brow,
> We must have Thee, O Jesus of the Scars.
> The heavens frighten us; they are too calm;
> In all the universe we have no place.
> Our wounds are hurting us; where is the balm?
> Lord Jesus, by Thy Scars, we claim Thy grace.
> The other gods were strong; but Thou wast weak;
> They rode, but Thou didst stumble to a throne;
> But to our wounds only God's wounds can speak,
> And not a god has wounds, but Thou alone.

And that is why He is our everlasting place of refuge; as David says in Psalm 71:3: 'My place of refuge whereunto I may continually resort'.

15

Three Uses of God's Moral Law

Deuteronomy 4:44–49

This brief but significant passage sets before us the significance of the law of God to the well-being of the people of Israel and, after the New Testament, of all Christian people. We shall look at the three uses of God's moral law. We must think of how Moses' exposition of the law of God was to be the foundation for their life in the Promised Land, and then, how much does the law of God pertain to us as a Christian people in the modern world?

Now if you should write a book entitled *How to be Happy in Today's World,* (or *How to Achieve a Successful life*), you would almost certainly sell a great many copies, if marketed well. However, if you write on what is the place of God's law in the life of the Christian today, you are not likely to sell very many books, even amongst Christians. Popular or not, the truth is if you try to be happy, if you try to have a successful life, but avoid the significance of the character of God expressed in His law, you're taking a short cut which will lead you into a swamp of moccasins and quicksands, ending in destruction not happiness. Therefore when we speak of the place of the holy character and the holy law of God in the Christian life, we are speaking of the only way any man or woman can ever achieve spiritual success, and experience a life of holiness and joy.

Notice two major points from this text. The first is the structure of Deuteronomy; and the second the place of God's moral law in the spiritual life of the believer.

The Structure of Deuteronomy

You already know that Deuteronomy is a Greek word, two words really, *deuteros, nomos,* meaning the second law, or explication by Moses on what God's law means for the life of the people in the world. And this text shows how real all of this is, specifying where they were standing when they heard Moses preach, and naming the kings they defeated on the east side of Jordan; it's the real world, it's the world of conflict; a world where you have got to exercise faith; and it shows how we are to live in the context of a fallen world. It teaches us that the spiritual law is the most practical thing to enable you to handle your conflicts, and to reach the place where God has called you.

Here is its structure: Chapters 1:1–4:43, which are introductory to this second giving of the law. And then the next part is 4:44–26:19—the very heart of the book. In this major portion, Moses shows how the future life of the people of God in the Promised Land must be based on the character of God, that is on a right relationship to who God really is, and without which you cannot live a true and a happy life. This relationship is expressed in the divine law, the details of which and what it means for a true and a happy life we'll be looking at for many weeks to come.

We come now to the second part of the message: namely, the place of God's moral law in the spiritual life. What is the place of all this that Moses is talking about in the life of the true believer?

Returning to last Sunday's message, let us recall chapter 4:39-40:

> Know therefore this day and consider it in thine heart, that the Lord He is God in heaven above and upon the earth beneath; there is none else. Thou shalt therefore keep His statutes and His commandments which I command thee this day [Why?] that it may go well with thee and with thy children after thee; [I want my children to amount to something right. Moses says, and God says to him, now look at what the law really means for you and for them] that thou mayest prolong thy days upon the earth which the Lord thy God giveth thee for ever.

And then verse 44, the beginning of this text: 'And this is the law'.

Why is the law of God so important in Holy Scripture and therefore, in true Christianity? If The texts dealing with God's law in Old and New Testaments comprise a tremendous percentage of the Holy Bible. In space alone, it is very significant. But why?

The law of God is the expression of the very heart of God. It shows us God's holy character in every relationship of life. The Ten Commandments, expounded from the end of chapter 4 to the end of chapter 26, are like letters of uncreated light shining in the darkness of human confusion. What a blessing! Now Jesus too of course is the <u>fullest</u> expression of the heart of God; in His face we see God's heart.

No doubt, the law is complicated! But Jesus, who came out from the heart of God, tells us that the law of God can be summarized into two parts. First, love God above everything else; second, love your neighbor as yourself. It is said, 'Love is the fulfilling of the law' (Rom. 13:10). God is love. Love to God and to our fellow man is the fulfillment of all the righteous requirements of God, the foundation of any life that will count for time and count for eternity.

If you have been to Edinburgh, you may remember that if you go down the High Street, running from Edinburgh Castle down to Holyrood Palace—the queen's residence whenever she is in Edinburgh—part of way down is St Giles Cathedral and several yards further down is John Knox's house, the place where the great Scottish reformer died. On the outside of the house you can see this verse plastered onto the outside wall: 'Love God above all and your neighbor as yourself.'

These two parts are in the Westminster Confession of Faith, Chapter 19 says that there are three kinds of law in all of the Bible (already identified by Medieval scholars, like Thomas Aquinas): civil law that pertained to the life of Israel as a theocracy; ceremonial law giving us the Levitical system, with the shedding of blood and purging of sin, and all the holiness requirements; and the moral law— basically the Ten Commandments—'to love God above all and your neighbor as yourself'.

Now the civil law has in many ways been fulfilled, in that we are not a theocracy. After the history of Israel ends, in the New Testament, we are in a different situation where God's Word goes to all the nations. The civil law does not precisely pertain to modern states and kingdoms, only insofar as the confession says, to 'the general equity' of it, that is, certain principles of justice which we would wish to carry out are still in force. But the details of the civil law have been fulfilled and surpassed in the Christian revelation. The ceremonial law has been fulfilled and surpassed in Jesus' shedding of blood; we don't have animal sacrifices with the sprinkling of blood and water on the people and so forth, because Jesus took that to its completion, doing everything that was required to fulfill the ceremonial law in His death on the cross and His bodily resurrection. What remains is the moral law: to love God and to love our fellow man.

So then, in what sense is the Christian believer still under the law? He and she is not under it in its civil use, other than to general principle of fair equity, but not to detail; he and she is not under it as far as its ceremonial use: we don't go to the temple with its blood sacrifices, for Jesus did all that in our place. But we are under the law insofar as it expresses who God is: God created us in His image, and He said 'Live this way!' I redeem you not to live against My character, but I redeem you, and bring you out of sin into holiness, so that you can express who I really am.

I would say, the most demanding thing for a parent, and the most privileged thing, is to express who God is in their lives. How much grace, and how much of the Holy Spirit we need to do it! The greatest thing you can do for your children is to live in a Christ-like manner. You know we're not up to it, but the Holy Spirit helps us. Thus, the moral law is still the way we're to live the life of redemption.

It is necessary to mention here a false idea in many Christian circles, known as 'antinomianism' ('anti' is Greek for against; 'nomos' is law = 'against the law'). That is, some people say that the law is bad, and that even the moral law has no relationship to us whatsoever. And that if you're under grace, you have to be against the law.

How much damage this defective position has done. Antinomian Christians have lived on its basis and said: 'I'm under grace; I don't have to conform to any Divine requirement whatsoever'.

Years ago, when I lived in Jackson, Mississippi, I hired a man, who was also a preacher, to paint the house. I found out only later that he would regularly say to customers, 'I need $100 to get some more paint' and then wouldn't show up and never finished the job. Yet at the same time, he was preaching. One day I confronted him, and said, 'Look here, you're a preacher; you say you're an evangelical believer in the Bible. How can you steal from people?' 'It's not stealing,' he said, 'the Holy Spirit didn't lead me to come back.' 'Oh yes,' I replied, 'you've broken your word and you have stolen, and I'm told you have done it in other places.' He said, 'Well look here, what you're talking about is the law. That does not pertain to me; I'm saved and I feel saved, so I don't have to carry through those things.' I replied, 'I can't be sure, but I believe you have false assurance. A sinner can be on the way to hell; read Matthew 25 when you go home, and you will see that some people who wind up in hell, thought they were saved for sure, and would be in heaven, but then they died and went to hell. If so, you have a false assurance, because if you're not concerned in your life to honor God in your business and financial relationships, you are by no means saved, and I beg of you to repent.' Well, I never heard any more from him.

Antinomianism, has denuded much of the modern Christian church of its holiness and has made unbelievers cynical about our message. Who's going to believe you if you say you need to be right with Jesus, you need to get saved by the one who is holy, and yet you steal from people? You lie to them? You won't keep your commitments? So many unbelievers feel under no pressure whatsoever to become a Christian, because Christians are, from all they have seen, notably unholy. It makes the work of preaching the gospel very difficult, and it's based on a tragic misunderstanding of the place of God's law in our life.

Let me add this: we all can speak of evangelism, and we certainly ought to; we are called to be soul-winners in our own way. Of course, keeping the moral law, is not in and of itself evangelism; but it is a necessary foundation for evangelism. If we deny the moral law of God in the way we live, nobody can take seriously our message.

I have sadly noticed that in some cases, not a single one of the children of some ministers have themselves ever accepted the Christian faith. How can this be? Although one hates to say it, it is possible for a minister who preaches well, to effectively deny who God is, in how he relates to his wife and children. At those points, he is antinomian: he denies God's command to him to love his wife, and not provoke his children. In that way he may well run off his own children from the faith.

So, if you believe the Bible, it cannot ever be right to think that a spiritual person—one who has the Holy Spirit and is in union with the Lord Jesus Christ—could live contrary to the character of God? How could you be in the family and deny everything the family stands for in your living? Since 'God is love' (1 John 4:8), we are called to live in love. Since God is light—Jesus says 'I am the light of the world' (John 8:12)—we are called to walk in the light, not in darkness, not to live in selfishness, or lack integrity in our business. Jesus said: 'He that hath My commandments, and keepeth them, he it is that loveth Me' (John 14:21). That shows where antinomianism is contrary to the clear teaching of our Savior.

Fairness requires me to say that over long years, I have observed that many Christians who have been taught (in their church or study Bibles) unsound views of the relationship of law and grace, and thereby wrongly concluded that grace discounts the law, actually seem to me to live lives that, from all I can tell, honour the Lord. I would conclude that their lives are better than their theology: a most happy inconsistency!

Be that as it may, a sign of true regeneration by the Holy Spirit is that the saved man or woman is sensitive to moral issues, and cares about, and is thoughtful of, the character of God and the will of God in their lives. That goes with salvation, not perfection; you cannot reach perfection any one day in this life. Only Jesus had that, and we will have it in glory. But you are given a deep desire in the heart to please God, and when you know that you have displeased, Him you are grieved, and you come back and repent and seek His strength to do better. These things always go with a true conversion.

The Place of the Moral in
The Life of The Believer

We have already looked at how the Westminster Confession of Faith spoke of three kinds of law. The great Reformer, John Calvin, does the same; he teaches that the civil and ceremonial aspects of the law have been fulfilled in Christ, and then expands three purposes of *the moral law*.

Calvin says (in his *Institutes of the Christian Religion* II. vii) that the moral law has three purposes.

(1) To show God's righteousness and point to man's sin

According to his understanding, the first use of the moral law shows God's righteousness, and therefore, in light of it, man's sin. Thereby, it points sinners to salvation in Christ, showing who God is, as at the beginning of the Ten Commandments in Exodus 20: 'I am the Lord Thy God'. And in Leviticus 19:2: 'I the Lord am holy, therefore be ye holy' (quoted in 1 Peter 1:16).

Calvin calls the law 'a mirror' in which we see who we really are, and thus we come to realize that we need forgiveness, which only Christ can provide. He often quotes Romans 3:20: 'For by the law is the knowledge of sin'. He says: 'For since all of us are proved to be transgressors, the more clearly it reveals God's righteousness, conversely the more it uncovers our iniquity. The more surely it confirms the reward of life and salvation as dependent upon righteousness, the more certain it renders the destruction of the wicked' (*Institutes* II. vii. 7).

It is a sovereign grace, given to the elect, that they have their pride broken in seeing their sin, and then turn to the righteousness provided by God in Christ. Galatians 3:24 says that the law is a tutor to lead us to Christ.; like an ancient Greek tutor who would pick up the child from his mother and take him by hand safely to the school house.

The law is condemning when it shows us what we're like. Not to crush us into the dirt, but to say—look! You're not right! You can't do it right! You haven't done it right! Here is a place you can go to be forgiven and to receive eternal life and lasting glory. Some of the old Puritans call this 'the killing work of the law,' 'the dispensation of death'. It kills that which keeps us back from coming to Christ—our foolish, self-centered pride. It doesn't destroy the personality; God doesn't do that. But it kills the pride of life and says, 'Look: here is who God is; here is what He made you to be; you're not up to it!' When that happens, the arrogance and pride that was given us in the fall of Adam is slain, and then we can go to the right place to get help.

Dr. D. James Kennedy, a famous preacher in Florida, and a great Christian statesman, died a few years ago. I remember hearing him speak years ago on the killing work of the law, and how it is a tutor to lead us to Christ. He had been the top dance instructor in the Arthur Murray Studios, in all the United States; he had a tremendous salary back in the early 1950s. On one occasion, he had been at a dance, drinking and carrying on most of the night. He woke up not feeling well with a hangover and feeling depressed, so he just happened to flip on the radio. He heard the great preacher of the Tenth Presbyterian Church in Philadelphia, Dr. Donald Gray Barnhouse issuing this question to all the radio congregation, of which D. James Kennedy was a part. His question changed D. James Kennedy's life, and was in fact the basis of the whole Evangelism Explosion program that has reached so many millions for Jesus throughout the world.

Barnhouse asked, 'If you died tonight and stood before God, what reason would you give to God to let you in His heaven?' Kennedy was sober enough to think a little bit, and he first thought, well, I guess I'm not a bad person; I don't kill people, I don't hate people, I haven't been in jail, so I reckon I'm pretty good, and I'd maybe tell God that I've tried to do more or less right, although Kennedy said the thought came to him that he had a hangover that morning. Anyway, maybe he will let me into heaven.

And then Donald Gray Barnhouse demolished every argument for saving ourselves, showing that our righteousness is as filthy rags, and that the self taints everything we do, and that we cannot save ourselves by 'being good', because we 'mess it up' one way or another every time. Hence God will not let us into heaven on any such basis.

Then Barnhouse took him to the next point of the sermon: 'How would you get in heaven?' He explained that it is through the perfect righteousness of Christ, who died for sinners, to fulfill the law in their place, and to pay the penalty for all their sins. Then God sends down the Holy Spirit to transform them.

So D. James Kennedy knew the killing work of the law as our tutor, and, though he has left us, there must be many a soul in heaven, waiting to thank him for his preaching on television, and most of all for the Evangelism Explosion.

Listen to Psalm 78:34: 'When He slew them, then they sought Him; and they returned and inquired early after God'. The law can wield the sword of the Spirit, as it brings all the often painful issues of the offended law of God, and, as it were, sticks in you, thereby slaying your pride, and your self-righteousness. Then you realize how serious is your situation, and you cry out: 'I can't do it!'

This slaying, however, is different from all others. Instead of forever removing your life, it has power in it to raise you up! Then, in the words of Scripture, 'you return to Him and seek Him early'! In this slaying and raising up, you find the grace of God!

Note that the law itself does not give us power to obey it: that would be legalism. Only the Holy Spirit gives you the power to walk pleasingly in the paths of the law. And so Jesus says, 'Abide in Me, bring forth much fruit' (John 15). The power to keep the law is not in the law, it's in the Spirit, who unites us to Christ, our holy substitute who lived out the law and lives it out for His people.

Another word on the killing work of the law: we were thinking last Sunday about the six Cities of Refuge that were set up by Moses. Isn't Moses' preaching in Deuteronomy remarkable? Even before Moses outlines the moral law of God, the Lord has already provided a way of escape, a City of Refuge, for those who break the law!

Now do you see the significance of chapter 4 coming before chapter 5 in Deuteronomy? It is a picture of the grace of God being the foundation of all moral law. The law is not given you in a context of law; the law is given you in a context of God's grace. It is wonderful, if you think of it! Refuge from sin, by God's grace, is provided, even before the sins are specified in the following chapters. What a gracious God we have!

The Cities of Refuge for involuntary murder are just a shadowy picture, a forecasting, of the total refuge from every kind of sin, involuntary sins and those that Moses calls *'sins with a high hand,'* those we did willfully and knowingly. Those cities are not available anymore. This refuge is now in the Lord Jesus Christ; He, in our stead, lived a totally holy life, and paid the full penalty for any and every sin through His death, power, and through His resurrection. In Him, we have a place of strongest refuge, that can easily survive any testing!

Romans 4:23–25, which speaks of Abraham, and how he was made righteous, helps explain this refuge: *'Now it was not written for his sake alone, that it was imputed to him* [the righteousness of Christ was accounted to him]; *but for us also'* [for us modern people, for us Gentiles, saying 'here's the City of Refuge! Come to it, when you see what you're like!', *'to whom it'* [the righteousness of God, the full holiness of Christ and with Barnhouse and Kennedy, the opening of the gates of heaven] *'shall be imputed, if we believe on him that raised up Jesus our Lord from the dead; who was delivered for our offences, and was raised again for our justification'.*

In Greek, the preposition that we normally translate 'for' means 'on account of'. Jesus was delivered 'on account of' our sins. My sins put Him on the cross; He was delivered because Douglas Kelly is a sinner—and the rest of us. And the same preposition, 'He was raised for our justification', signifies 'on account of' our justification. When God raised Jesus from the dead, He is saying: 'My Son paid for all the sins of all who ever believe; therefore I raised Jesus, and when I raised Jesus, you will always be eternally, totally pardoned, if you stand in Him by faith: it is "on account of him".'

(2) To restrain sin in society

Calvin saw a second use of the moral law, and that was to restrain sin in society at large, even among non-believers. This function (in Scripture, and on man's conscience, as Romans 2 teaches us) makes life in a fallen society possible. Calvin writes: 'All who are still unregenerate feel…that they are not drawn to obey the law voluntarily, but impelled by a violent fear, do so against their own will and despite their opposition to it. With this constrained and forced righteousness is necessary for the public community of men, for whose tranquility the Lord herein provided…' (*Institutes* II. vii. 10).

(3) A positive guide to the Christian Life

But above all the other uses of the moral law, Calvin mentions its third use as a positive guide for the Christian life. Contrary to antinomianism, the moral law that instructs us to love God above all, and our neighbors as ourself, is a positive guide to help us walk in the Spirit, walk in the light, by which we express who Jesus really is.

Calvin's *Institutes*, Book II, Chapter 7, Sections 12 and following, show that even believers have need of the moral law to guide them. In their hearts, the Spirit of God already lives and reigns, as Jeremiah 31:33 and Hebrews 10:16 show us. They have been moved and quickened through the directing of the Spirit, so that they long to obey God; and yet these same people still profit by the law, by contemplating what God requires in these various situations.

How much specific guidance for believers there is in Holy Scripture! For instance, think of Romans chapters 1–11: that's the basic doctrine of salvation, God's holiness in the atonement of His Son making the way for us. And then think of Romans chapters 12–16, which you might call the duty—how this salvation works out in our daily lives. There we're told about integrity and kindness and goodness and purity towards wife and children, in business and our duties with the state and so forth.

How well I remember when we had our first child, the large number of books we were buying, in order to read all we could on child rearing, because we really wanted to do it right, and realized that we did not know exactly how to do it. As much as I read, looking back, I cannot honestly say that I managed to get it right every time. But at least, my wife and I were trying to see what Christian parents would do, in bringing up a son in the nurture and admonition of the Lord. It would have been very foolish not to have looked into the Word of God to seek out the best way to raise a child. You do not always meet the goal, but you do have a beautiful goal in mind!

Similarly with premarital counseling. I still sometimes perform marriages, and I never do it without having to talk about what it is to be married. Again, I'm not feeling that I have the perfect marriage, but I know that both of us have wanted to do it in God's way, as best we could, without ever fully achieving it, of course. Let us say that an engaged couple comes to you, wanting to get married. They are in love, and that is good! But if you don't help them, they might violate some of the most basic principles of Christian living for a man and wife, unless they are shown in the law of God what it means to be a Christian husband, and a Christian wife.

I always take them to Ephesians chapter 5, where the love of Christ for His church is the model of how a husband is to love his wife self-sacrificially. That, in principle, takes care of a great deal of it, but not all of it. The wife is to remember that as the church submits to her Lord, who gave Himself for her, so the Christian wife is to submit, in the Lord, not outside the Lord, to her husband. There are many particularities of carrying that out, and it involves a life-long seeking the face of God in prayer, for a successful marriage.

To come anywhere near this, we constantly need the Holy Spirit! How can we have Him? Jesus says in Luke 11 that the Holy Spirit is given in answer to prayer.

In conclusion, let us remember a wonderful old line from the Church of England liturgy. When the Ten Commandments are being read, there is a prayer following, that is repeated, commandment after commandment: 'O Lord, incline our hearts to keep this law'. When that cry is answered, then the world will begin to see a little bit of who Jesus is, and be softened up to hear the message of the gospel. That is what the third use of the moral law: a positive guide to the Christian life means. Lord, make it so for us! Amen.

16

A SECOND BEGINNING

Deuteronomy 5:1–33

We could think of this fifth chapter of Deuteronomy as 'A Second Beginning' or a second chance or opportunity: when you didn't do well the first time, God gives another opportunity. Who of us would be here if that were not the case? So the first thing I want to look at is Deuteronomy 5:1–6.

A SECOND BEGINNING (5:1–6)

We remember from Exodus 20 that the people of Israel were given the beautiful law of God on Sinai, and then committed idolatry and immorality, and the majority had to die in the wilderness. Then God gave their descendants a second chance, about forty years later. Let us think today of the God of the second chance, the God who gives us a new opportunity.

There comes to mind a Christian family I know well in Charlotte. They have been, and still are, influential in the kingdom of God, and have raised wonderful children. Yet they had a very unsuccessful beginning. This man and his wife both graduated from a conservative Christian college and were church members, but he later said he wasn't even converted at that time. There they were, married, with a very responsible job and well off, and everything that would seem to be necessary for happiness. But then this man went out and committed adultery in a continuing pattern. Naturally his wife had to divorce him.

She had, I believe, the responsibility of four young sons. To say the least, it looked like it was a disaster; everything was ruined and lost. Indeed, the woman was the daughter of a very fine, conservative minister. I wonder how her father would have felt when that happened? No doubt, this good man prayed. And then the God of the Covenant extended His grace, and gave the erring husband and his ex-wife, a new opportunity, which has continued into their being fruitfully used, and very happy in the work of the kingdom of God.

Deuteronomy 5 is not exactly a repetition, but is rather close to Exodus 20. Although the generation to whom the Ten Commandments were given had committed sin, and therefore had to be judged and die before being allowed into the Promised Land, nevertheless they had their own children. God speaks again, to this new generation, the very same covenant law and promises, giving them a new opportunity to regain lost ground.

We notice an interesting phrase here in verse 3, 'The Lord made not this covenant with our fathers'; he is speaking of the giving of the law at Mt. Sinai. That phrase, 'not with our fathers' if traced out in Hebrew as used elsewhere in the books of Moses, means by 'our fathers' the patriarchs: Abraham, Isaac, and Jacob.

Now the covenant was the same, in that it was gracious; God saves by grace, and requires holy living as a response to His grace. But there was a difference, particularly when God gives this fuller expression of the covenant of grace in the Ten Commandments; it is in the context of saying, you are going into the Promised Land to inhabit it permanently, and this is the way I want you to live in that land. This is the constitution of the land. Whereas when Abraham, Isaac, and Jacob dwelt in tents, they were sojourners or pilgrims, at times, in what became the Promised Land, but they could not inhabit it permanently. This phase of the covenant was with their descendants, not with them.

Hence God says something like 'Now I am ready to take you in and give you this wonderful country, a land flowing with milk and honey, and here's the basis on which you are to live all your relationships'. In the work of God, even though all our fathers were sinful, even if they were saints, they stand in solidarity together before God. 'Forty years ago, I showed you the right way to live, even though you were not yet born. Today, forty years later, I am reminding you of what it is.' And we, some 3,400 years later, although not there physically either, we <u>were</u> there, because we are part of the people of God and stand face to face with Him, to live on the basis of His grace and His holy love. There is a solidarity in this covenant, in which God, in His mercy and longsuffering, offers to a people whose parents were severely in the wrong, a second opportunity.

In the broken marriage I mentioned, by God's grace, a particular man got hold of this erring ex-husband—who knew in his head about the gospel, but had kept it out of his heart—and evangelized him; the Holy Spirit brought him to genuine repentance and true conversion. Then this man humbled himself to his wife, his parents-in-law, and his sons, and they actually had another marriage in the church. His wife forgave him; God forgave him; his sons and in-laws forgave him. Since that time he has lived on the basis of God's holy law.

In his prophecy, Hosea compares Israel to his ex-wife who became a prostitute to idolatry and immorality, breaking God's law with a high hand. Hosea goes after her, and God's grace works so that he brings her back and restores her. The law is given in the context of a marriage. It's not legalism, but a way to relate lovingly and honestly to one another before the face of God. When one is restored, it doesn't mean you are free to keep doing the things that broke the marriage. No! You are given a new heart, and because of it, you want to please God and, by the same token, please the one to whom you are married. God's grace therefore, does not mean that you become licentious, but far more sensitive, thoughtful, careful, kind, and good. That is the wholesome fruit of a divinely given second opportunity.

The Covenant Law in the Context of Personal Relationship to God (5:2,6,24)

Sometimes you may think of the law of God like the 15 regulations nailed up on the gates of a state park. If you break this one or that one, the ranger will get you. Maybe the rules are good, but at times, it does seem like you are being imposed upon, and it doesn't give you a good feeling to have all those regulations frowning down upon you, lest you make some minor mistake, such as letting your dog loose!

God's law is not that way. It's never to beat you down. In the context of a marriage, it's a love relationship, a personal relationship with Him. Notice how God identifies Himself in verse 2: 'The Lord our God made a covenant with us, His people'. The covenant is a way to save us, by which we can live with God and with one another. Verse 4 says, 'The Lord talked with you face to face.' We, in Christianity, serve a God to whom we can be 'face to face'—in closest, personal relationship. 'Face to face' in Hebrew is the word for 'countenance.'

The concept we have of person, or personality, can be traced through the New Testament back to the Old Testament, where you find the concept of 'face'. God has a face, and the fact that we have personality means that we are created in His image to live 'face to face' with Him. He says that He delivered Israel from bondage to evil powers, and thus, He is a God who makes a difference in our lives in getting us out of a mess too big for us to handle. As a Christian, you can look back and know that He, who is the supreme Person, delivers you, a created person and in certain respects like Him.

'I am the Lord thy God' takes us back to Genesis 1: 'In the beginning, God created the heavens and the earth'. The Father speaks worlds into existence. He issues a 'word' and the light shines; the 'Word' is the Son, and then the Spirit moves upon the water. So, even though the mystery of the Holy Trinity is not yet fully revealed, there are already certain intimations of the Father, the Son, and the Holy Spirit. In the New Testament we learn that God is a Trinity.

His revealed law is like a transcript of the purity, and loving, holy relationship within the Trinity. We read in Ephesians 3:14 and 15: 'Father, for whom the family in heaven and on earth is named'. The fact that we have fatherhood, and fathers, mothers, children, and grandchildren in families, is an analogy of the Trinity: God has made us to live in families, in personal relationship, because that's how He lives in His own supreme way.

That's why loneliness can be truly destructive, because God made us to be in fellowship with Him and with one another. This personal relationship can be boiled down to one word, 'love.' 'God is love' (1 John 4:8). Jesus summarizes the law, and we saw it last week, 'Thou shalt love the Lord thy God with all thy heart, soul, mind and strength; thou shalt love thy neighbor as thyself'. All the Ten Commandments lead you to this underlying foundation: love to God, love to others. To be the Lord's, we must live in accordance with the character of the One who created us, and then when we sinned, He saved us, and in redeeming us, restored us to love Him, and to love others. That is what face to face with God means.

The fallen husband in Charlotte, who by grace got it right with his wife, probably would say that for the first time they are 'face to face'. Impossible if he had gone and started committing adultery. We cannot live face to face with God, and engage in stealing or gossip or hatred or adultery. The prophets often say 'your sins have hidden God's face from you.'

In one sense, that's the point of the Aaronic benediction given to us in the Old Testament, which the High Priest put on the people, after the sacrifice for sin: 'The Lord bless thee and keep thee; the Lord lift up His countenance upon thee and give you peace'. 'Countenance' means 'face.' With the sacrifice for sin that you have received, and the blood sprinkled on you, through faith, God's smile returns to you. The Lord lift up His countenance upon you; the light of His face shines upon you, and He gives you peace.

Shalom, in Hebrew, includes everything worth having. It is the peace of God, as the New Testament says, that passes all understanding. Thus, forgiveness means, we can be 'face to face' with God.

On the human level it is like when we're out with somebody; we don't look in their face. If somebody speaks ill of you, and sees you on the street, they may turn their face away, unable to look you in the face. But once you and they have forgiveness, you're back, face to face.

The wonderful thing about forgiveness is that we can now live—no matter what we've done in the past, no matter how many moral laws we've broken—through the atonement of Christ, the sprinkling of the blood, and His resurrection, 'face to face' with Him, which is the basis for us being face to face with every person with whom it is possible.

A Mediator Brings Us Face to Face With God

A mediator is somebody who stands in-between, sometimes called 'umpire,' as in the book of Job: 'neither is there any daysman betwixt us, that might lay his hand upon us both' (Job 9:33). Jesus is the daysman, the umpire, the mediator, that stands betwixt us and God.

Moses was in some sense foreshadowing Jesus Christ as the Mediator, who lets us get into the presence of God without being smitten and slain for our sin. It's clear in verses 4–5 and 28, that the people were terrified when the holiness of God breaks out in fire ('God is a consuming fire'); the fire sets ablaze Mt. Sinai, with a terrifying presence. And the people said, 'Moses, we know we're sinful and that God is holy, and we're going to be slain, if we stand before this burning holiness; we're terrified. How about standing between us and the Lord—and we'll do what He says, if you will only represent us and we don't have to be face to face; we're afraid it will be the end of us'(Deut. 5:25–27).

In His matchless grace, God makes a way for people to be related to Him in His holiness, and yet not be smitten into destruction. God knew that we sinners need someone to represent us before Him. Jesus Christ is this Mediator; Moses foreshadowed Him; Christ fulfills it. 'There is one God and one Mediator between God, the man Christ Jesus' (1 Tim. 2:5). In Hebrews 8:6, 'Jesus Christ is the Mediator of a better covenant' in which He does everything to represent us, and to fulfill our side of the bargain, and then conveys us the Holy Spirit to live it out.

You can say this: Moses is representing sinful people on Sinai; Jesus represents us on another mountain, Mt. Calvary. Moses received the pattern of the tabernacle and sacrificial offerings and the holy law on Sinai; Jesus IS the perfect sacrifice for sins on Mt. Calvary: 'Christ through the eternal Spirit offered Himself without spot to God' (Heb. 9:14). Moses could offer sacrifices but Jesus offers Himself! Jesus is all that God will ever require for you to be right with Him.

You might say, I don't feel assurance of salvation; I don't know whether I'm saved or not or able to do enough to get into heaven. But 'Jesus paid it all—all to Him I owe; sin had left a crimson stain; He washed it white as snow'. Jesus, in His holy living and dying and rising, has done everything to represent me to God. I need add nothing to what Jesus did—just receive Jesus, by humble faith. 1 Peter 3:18 is beautifully commented on by Andrew Murray in more than one of his devotional books; he emphasizes that 'Jesus died to bring us near to God'. Everybody who is saved here, knows exactly what I'm talking about: that to be a Christian by faith in Jesus, is to know, personally, experimentally, directly, the smile of God upon you. You already know it without some preacher having to tell you. Along this thought here are two hymns I often think of:

Jesus, I am resting, resting, in the joy of what Thou art;
I am finding out the greatness of Thy loving heart.
Thou hast bid me gaze upon Thee, as Thy beauty fills my soul,
for by Thy transforming power, Thou hast made me whole.
Ever lift Thy face upon me as I work and wait for Thee;
resting 'neath Thy smile, Lord Jesus, earth's dark shadows flee.
Brightness of my Father's glory, sunshine of my Father's face,
keep me ever trusting, resting, fill me with Thy grace.
~ Jean Sophia Pigott, 1876

Loved with everlasting love, led by grace that love to know,
Spirit breathing from above, Thou hast taught me it is so.
O this full and perfect peace, O this presence all divine;
in a love that cannot cease, I am His and He is mine.
Heav'n above is deeper blue, earth around is sweeter green;
Something lives in every hue, Christless eyes had never seen.
Birds with gladder songs o'er flow, flow'rs with richer beauties shine,
since I know, as now I know, I am His and He is mine.
~ George W. Robinson, 1890

Now that is the normal Christian life, and there is nothing that you could have, or could ever achieve, that would be one millionth the value of having the smile of God upon you by day and by night.

That's what happens in revival. You will see it in a recent book about the Lewis revival, *Sounds from Heaven*, about the revival on the Isle of Lewis from 1949–1952. At that time, there was a remarkable outpouring of the Spirit on Lewis; it is said by witnesses that you could almost cut the presence of God with a knife. The power of God changed many things in what was a formally Presbyterian island. Large numbers of its inhabitants were brought face to face with God; they received the smile of God upon them.

'The consciousness of the presence of the Lord was the outstanding characteristic of the revival in Lewis in 1949,' according to Duncan Campbell, a preacher, who was mightily used in this revival. Large numbers were converted and apparently some supernatural things happened.

But the major benefit was the awareness of God laying hold of that community. Revival is God-consciousness everywhere you go in the community. According to the book, Agnes Morrison says, 'Whatever we were doing or wherever we were, we were conscious of the presence of God. We had no desire to go to sleep, even though we had so little sleep, we were not tired.' Marian Morrison, described the presence of God as 'a canopy overhead.' She says, 'Everywhere I went I was conscious of God.' Kenny MacDonald says, 'Wherever you went you could not get away from the presence of the Lord.' Christie Maggie said, 'God was everywhere in the very atmosphere, whether they were godly or godless, people knew that God was there.' And John M. Smith says, 'If I were to tell you the outstanding characteristic of this 1949–52 revival, it is this: there was a universal consciousness of the presence of God.'

Not only in unusual times of revival, but in the regular life of a Spirit-filled Church, God shines His face, and there follows the most profound repentance, cleaning up of lives and restoring of relationships, and yielding to God for Christian service; giving Him everything He deserves.

To Live Before the Mediator Is to Keep God's Law From the Heart

When Jesus saves you, He gives you a new heart: Jeremiah 31 and Hebrews 8 say He writes the law in the heart—He puts in you the deepest desire to want to please God. You don't always live up to it.

I remember Rev. William Still saying to the Christian Union of Edinburgh University: 'We don't contemplate the law to be holy, at least that's not the main thing we contemplate. We contemplate the face of Jesus. We look on Jesus and then we really will seek to fulfill the will of the Father in the moral law. "But we all, with unveiled face beholding, as in a mirror the glory of the Lord, are changed into the same image from glory to glory, even as by the Spirit of the Lord" (2 Cor. 3:18).'

Ephesians 1–3 are about election in Christ and the church: in other words, the face of the Savior. Chapters 4–6 tell how you walk in the light of His face. The first three chapters contain the doctrine; the last three, the duty. Herein you see the face of Jesus, and in its light, you perceive how to treat your wife: that is, as Christ loved the church; and wives perceive how to submit to husbands in the Lord. It is all illumined by the face of Jesus! And in your work, the light of that same face shows you that it means to let no man steal any more, but work hard enough to have some extra money to give to poor people, as in Ephesians 4:28. In other words, 'yes, keep the law, but go beyond the strict requirements, and think of what God really wants as you relate to other people, and walk in His requirements, so that you do even more. As Jesus said to the Pharisees, 'what do ye more than others?' True believers, in the light of the face of God, are enabled to see and to do more than others!

The rest of Deuteronomy 5 is the Ten Commandments. You could say that Deuteronomy 6-11 explicate what the first commandment practically means. Then the second commandment is in Deuteronomy 12; the third in chapters 13 and 14; the fourth in 14 and 15; the fifth in 16 and 18; the sixth is in chapters 19–22; the seventh in chapter 23; the eighth and ninth in chapter 24; the tenth in the latter part of 24 through chapter 26.

As we look at these commandments, we will find who God is! That's what He's called us to be, face to face with Him. That's what it means to live in a way that as God said to Moses, 'O, that it might go well with you and with your children'.

> Trust and Obey, for there's no other way,
> To be happy in Jesus, but to trust and obey.

An old Puritan, Samuel Bolton, said, 'The law sends us to the gospel, to learn how to be saved, because the law cannot save us. And the gospel sends us back to the law to learn how to live.' Thus, when we are living in the presence of Jesus the Mediator, who brings us to the Father, face to face, we really do desire to please Him. And so we can say with Psalm 119:97, 'O how I love Thy law; it is my meditation all the day'. And with 1 John 5:3, 'For Thy commandments are not grievous; they are not burdensome'. Indeed, the commandments of the gospel, instead of being a burden, a cross to bear us down, actually give us wings to rise and fly, through the supernatural empowerment of the Holy Spirit! Amen.

17

First Things First

Deuteronomy 6:1–3

We might call these first three verses of chapter 6, 'First Things First.' A person whose motivations are clear, and whose life is well organized, puts first things first—a major advantage in a complicated situation.

Think of it this way: if your house were on fire, what would you take out first, the old family Bible or something else? Or, in a different context, what if a competent doctor told you that you probably had six weeks at the most to live? What would you rank first as the most important that you had to do to get ready?

Or, barring crises, since we are nearly all very busy, what do we consider to be of first importance in the usage of our limited time?

Many years ago in seminary, I was visiting one of my great aunts. At that time, I had a large number of things to do in a short time. But especially, I needed to go down to Lumberton and take my father to the doctor. Another relative had some errands that she wanted me to run at the same time; so what would I do? I remember Great Aunt Ethel saying, 'Douglas, you put first things first; your father is first. And then these other errands are all right, but they would have to come in second place when you have the chance.' That was a good lesson for me; if many demands are upon me, more than I can do, I must figure out what are the first things I am going to do with my limited time and limited money.

What does God Himself put first in the Ten Commandments? We saw last week that everything between chapters 5 and 26 of Deuteronomy is an exposition of the Ten Commandments, making them very practical and showing how they encompass all of our life: our business life, family life, national life—every relationship.

In Deuteronomy, 5:7, we are shown what the Lord put first in the Holy Law: 'Thou shalt have none other gods before me'. All of Deuteronomy 6:1—11:32, is an exposition of this first commandment, where God states first: 'Put Me first!' The inspired writer takes five whole chapters expounding what it means to put God first.

Now let me ask you this: what does Jesus put first? We who are here trusting Jesus as our personal Lord and our Savior, are relying on Him in death, and of course, we are also relying on Him in our daily life. So what does our one and only Lord and Savior put first? In Matthew 22:36–38, Jesus quotes this passage from Deuteronomy. One of the religious lawyers had asked:

Master, which is the great commandment in the law? Jesus said unto Him, 'Thou shalt love the Lord thy God with all thy heart, and with all thy soul, and with all thy mind, for this is the first and great commandment. And the second is like unto it. Thou shalt love thy neighbor as thyself. On these two commandments hangeth all the law and the prophets.'

'The law and the prophets' means that the whole Old Testament is an outworking of the primary truth, based upon the foundation of love: God first, and then your neighbor as yourself. Jesus is very clear about what is first.

Let us note briefly two points in what we're told in Deuteronomy 6:1-3: the covenant law, and a bountiful land.

The Covenant Law

Verse 1a: 'Now these are the commandments, the statutes, and the judgments which the Lord your God commanded to teach you', and the second clause in verse 2: 'to keep all His statutes and His commandments which I command thee, thou and thy sons'—your grandchildren—are parallel phrases in the Hebrew: commandments, statutes, judgments. That means the entire body of covenant law, the whole Old Testament legal corpus, is encompassed in this. This is what I want you to teach your children: that's their hope; that's their life, these commandments, statutes, judgments—the covenant law.

Let's put that in more familiar terms as Christians: it is the idea of consecration. In the Old Testament the High Priest was consecrated or set apart; he put on the sacred robes as appointed by God, and then anointing oil was poured on his head, as symbolic of the Holy Spirit. Then he had the divinely given authority to go into the holiest place of all once a year, there to confess the sins of the people and to bring out the benediction of God to the people—consecration.

The High Priest's consecration foreshadows that of our great High Priest, the Lord Jesus Christ. Because of our relation to Him by faith, we're told in Leviticus and in 1 Peter that we are a kingdom of priests, a holy nation, that God consecrates not only the Old Testament priests and the New Testament ministers and elders and deacons, but all His people—all believers. He has consecrated them, set them apart, anointed them to His service.

Frances Ridley Havergal, a nineteenth-century English lady, wrote a hymn that summarizes what Deuteronomy 6:1-2 says about the statutes, law, commandments, and judgments. In other words, I'm not the focus of my life; God is. A great psychological and emotional liberation, available for the redeemed, is to get out of the prison of focusing on the self-life and be set free, like a bird out of a cage, soaring up to heaven. That liberation is directly connected to putting God first and then others. After that, the legitimate needs of self will be happily taken care of; ironically, precisely when you don't concentrate on the self. This is the idea of consecration.

Once you see the beauty of consecration, you will never think that it is any kind of externalist legalism. God saves you through the blood of the innocent substitute; the Mosaic system not only gave you the law, the way you are to live, but also gave the lambs, bulls, goats and rams to be slain, morning and evening, and the sprinkling of the blood on the mercy seat. In the Old Testament and the New Testament, God saves us by the blood, and 'without the shedding of blood, there is no remission of sin' (Heb. 9:22).

So, in many passages related to the law, there is the shedding of blood, that God cleanses our sin by His grace. But then something wonderful happens in the cleansing of sin when you believe in the blood and appropriate it by faith. There is a change in the heart. I think that is the only way a person can break out of the prison of self, for you are looking to someone else to do it; not yourself!

Some years ago, a young woman studying at seminary, was so focused on self, that she could not seriously look at anything else. In class, I was told that every one of her questions only referred to how something would affect her; she simply could not look at the larger reality. More than one of us prayed for God to get her out of the prison of self, perhaps the hardest prison to escape, to experience the grace and power of God, so that it would break this awful psychological and emotional bondage, that she would seek God, trust in the blood and have a changed heart that would make her think about the Lord and others.

This liberation happens when the Holy Spirit renews the heart; we call it regeneration, new birth, which only God can bring; you can ask God to help you, and He will. Jeremiah 31 conveys this liberation of soul as a central promise in the new covenant: 'I will put my Spirit in your heart'. Ezekiel 36:26 promises that God will take the heart of stone within you, and turn it into a heart of flesh, on which he will write his law. In other words, in the new birth, in true Christianity, the Holy Spirit invisibly, omnipotently comes inside of us, in a way we don't understand, and frees us from the bondage of self, making us want to please God, to wish to do things His way.

But don't we fail God? Yes, of course we do. Nobody perfectly lives up to the holy standard that they really desire for themselves. But our desire is, as Christ said, '... to do the will of him that sent Me'; 'Not My will, but thine be done'.

In spite of every failure, we have this part that wishes to please God and to do right, a sign of regeneration of the Holy Spirit and indication that God has written his law in our heart. When we do fail, we come to him and confess our sins, knowing he is faithful and just to forgive us and to strengthen us for new obedience. That's the covenant law, with the reality that when you're saved, the Holy Spirit puts the desire that God should be first and then others.

No matter how much religious talk there is, when people see a Christian put others first in the name of the Lord, before selfish interest, it makes an impact. That's something they cannot argue with, for the basic promise of the New Covenant means that the Holy Spirit has changed us.

A Bountiful Land

These verses portray a bountiful land: 'that it may be well with thee, and that ye may increase mightily, as the Lord God of thy fathers hath promised thee, in the land that floweth with milk and honey' (6:3, a life blessed, with increase of children, and a land flowing with milk and honey).

Looking at the Middle East today, you see that Palestine is very arid. But—I am told by experts—that certain archeological and climatological studies show that 3,000 years ago, the weather was very different; it was like a lush garden. Researchers dug, and found things that only grow in the tropics and require a great deal of water. So at one time, about the time of Moses and Joshua, it was one of the most beautiful, rich garden spots of the entire world. To them, God said, 'I'm going to give you that, and you are going to have the opportunity to live for me, and your life can be blessed.'

In our relationship with God, when first things are first, everything else in our life, even how our children will turn out, will be determined in accordance with the gracious will of God. So in verse 3 we are told something important (and we will pick it up next time, in verse 4): 'Hear

O Israel!' the Hebrew *shema;* everything starts with this. If you are to make a change with a renewed heart, free from control by the self-life, experiencing the blessing God wants to give you, it is all to begin with a listening ear, an open heart, a willing mind.

You and I cannot be renewed without the Holy Spirit, because it requires a miracle to get close enough to God, so that you hear His Word and think His thoughts. Blessedly, God does such miracles, and one of them is that the Holy Spirit comes inside us to set us free!

Think of the gospel hymn: 'Open mine eyes that I may see, glimpses of truth Thou hast for me'; open my heart, open my ears. This is close to the phrase from Psalm 40, quoted by Christ in the New Testament: 'Mine ears hast thou opened'.

You might say, 'I don't know how to get my ears opened; it seems as though nothing is working. I can't seem to hear "the music of the spheres"; I can't hear the heavenly psalms; I'd like to, but I can't.' Here's the answer: Jesus is the ear-opener. He takes our Adamic human nature—without sin, of course, although as a true human, He is fully able to represent us, and as the great High Priest, He listens to God; He opens the ear. On this basis, we can pray, 'Lord, your Son opens the ears of all His people; come, open my ears and give me a receptive, humble, willing spirit.' First things first: God is first.

As you study the history of the last 250 years of Western culture in Europe, Britain and America, it is hard not to perceive a huge, wilful 'stopping up' of the ears of millions, as Secularism replaces biblical faith for masses of people, especially, those the most privileged. I have argued elsewhere that this is a primary reason why so many have rejected strong scientific arguments in favour of creation.

But no matter how secularistic our culture in the West seems to be, things could profoundly change for the better, so that multitudes scrape the wax out of their ears!

What do we need to do first? The answer is not hard to understand, although much harder to do. Jesus says, first of all, love God with everything you've got. God Himself said through Moses, 'Thou shalt have no other gods before Me'. Listen! Hear God! Get in touch with Him! Trust in His salvation; follow Him—and everything changes

We see the glorious light and sound involved in that change in the experience of Jonathan Edwards, often considered, even by atheists, to have been the greatest philosopher and theologian, who ever lived in North America. At the beginning of a great revival as a young man, one day in the woods, meditating (in 1737), he wrote in his memoirs:

> I felt an ardency of soul to be, what I know not otherwise how to express, emptied and annihilated; to lie in the dust, and to be full of Christ alone; to love him with a holy and pure love; to trust in him; to live upon him; to serve and follow him; and to be perfectly sanctified and made pure, with a divine and heavenly purity. I have many times had a sense of the glory of the third person in the Trinity, in his office of Sanctifier; in his holy operations, communicating divine light and life to the soul. God, in the communications of his Holy Spirit, has appeared as an infinite fountain of divine glory and sweetness; being full, and sufficient to fill and satisfy the soul; pouring forth itself in sweet communications; like the sun in its glory, sweetly and pleasantly diffusing light and life.

From a self-enclosed, alienated, unhappy, imprisoned existence with ears and heart closed to God, when the Holy Spirit brings Christ to us, we can have something like Jonathan Edwards had. A hymn says:

Now none but Christ can satisfy;
none other Name for me!
There's love, and life, and lasting joy,
Lord Jesus, found in Thee.

First things first! And in the unfolding of God's good providence, everything else will come out just right.

18

The *Shema*

Deuteronomy 6:3–9

Proverbs 23:26 says, 'My son, give me thy heart' (and a hymn is written from it which I will quote later). 'Heart to heart' sonship is what this famous passage is about: 'Hear, O Israel: The Lord our God—the Lord is one'.

This is true biblical religion at its deepest foundation. As God's sons and daughters, we give Him our heart. Adam failed to do so, as did Israel. So God sent His own Son in human flesh in our place, to be that Son, who gave God His heart, and in so doing, lived out the response, 'Hear, O Israel; the Lord our God, the Lord is one'. And in Him, we do it! Jesus, unlike Adam or Israel in the wilderness, said, 'My meat is to do the will of Him that sent me; I must work the works of Him that sent Me while it is day', and in Gethsemane, 'Not My will, but Thine be done', and, quoting Psalm 40:8, 'I delight to do Thy will, O My God'.

Deuteronomy 6:3–9, especially verses 4 and 5, is the background for the central confession of true Christianity that we find in Romans 10:9. In Hebrew it reads: *Sh'ma Yis'ra'eil Adonai Eloheinu Adonai echad*. That is the basis of true godliness; the gate to heaven. It is known in English by the Hebrew word *shema* meaning 'hear' or 'listen.'

Let us note four things about it: (1) God is first; (2) this God is One in being but three Persons; (3) this God deserves our heart and (4) this God in the shema is the basis of all true education, holy living on earth and joy in heaven.

But when the Pharisees had heard that He had put the Sadducees to silence they were gathered together. And one of them which was a lawyer asked him a question, tempting Him, and saying: Master, which is the great commandment in the law? Jesus said unto him, [quoting Deuteronomy 6:4-5] Thou shalt love the Lord thy God with all thy heart, and with all thy soul, and with all thy mind. This is the first and great commandment. And the second is like unto it, thou shalt love thy neighbor as thyself. On these two commandments hang all the law and the prophets (Matt. 22:34–38).

All the Old Testament is caught up in the command to love God first, from the heart, and then love to everybody else around us.

This same priority of God first in the heart is the basis of evangelical Christianity. Romans 10:9, relates the first confession of the Christian church, long before the Nicene Creed, Apostles' Creed or any others. It is simply, 'Jesus Christ is Lord.' Romans 10:9-10 says, 'That if thou shalt confess with thy mouth the Lord Jesus and shalt believe in thine heart that God hath raised Him from the dead, thou shalt be saved. For with the heart man believeth unto righteousness and with the mouth confession is made unto salvation.' '... if thou shalt confess with thy mouth the Lord Jesus', literally means that Jesus is Jehovah, God Almighty. This word "Lord", used in 6:4-5, in the Greek translation (known as LXX) is *Kurios*, which means 'sovereign master'. Often in the New Testament, *Kurios* is applied to the Person of our Lord Jesus Christ. Therefore, Jesus is included in the One whom Israel is confessing as God. 'God first' is the confession of Old Testament, and is clarified in the confession of the New Testament, that Jesus is Lord.

That is why John, in 1 John 5:21, warns us: 'Little children keep yourselves from idols'; don't put anything first but God. When we put other things before God, tragic things happen, such as the growing plague of abortion.

Probably the biggest crisis facing the governments in the next 50 years is exactly that: depopulation of the wealthy countries because of abortion, and those with a different religion who may, by and by, take power. Well, it is the just result of our sins of not putting God first. The hour is late for the West; it would take a major renewal of faith in the Lord, and deep repentance for things to change, but that is not impossible, for we say with the Apostle's Creed: 'I believe in the Holy Ghost!'

THIS ONE GOD EXISTS IN THREE PERSONS

This God is one being who exists in three Persons—the mystery of the Trinity. The Trinity is not clearly taught in Deuteronomy 6:4-6, but what it says is consistent with what we find elsewhere in the Bible, especially in the New Testament: this one God exists as Father, Son, and Holy Spirit. As B. B. Warfield said: 'God did not clearly reveal the Trinity in words, until He revealed the persons of the Trinity in the coming of redemption.' The inspired words of the New Testament, plainly showing that the one God exists in three persons, were given after the Son and the Holy Spirit had come from the Father.

Yet, even before the New Testament, there are already some foreshadowings of God's three-in-onenesss. For example, in Hebrew, there are two Hebrew words for 'one'. One is *yachid*, and the other is *echad*. *Yachid* means absolute numerical one—no diversity. The word *echad* means oneness of unity—one being, but with a rich diversity of life—and is used here in Deuteronomy 6: 'Hear O Israel, the Lord our God, the Lord is *echad*'. There's a unity in His being, but a rich personal life in which there is Father, out of that one Being; Son, out of that one Being; and Holy Spirit out of that one Being. And we see this in the way the New Testament applies the word *Lord,* or *Kurios,* or *Yahweh,* to all three Persons of the Trinity.

In the Gospel of John, you read, 'I am the bread of life; I am the way, the truth, and the life; I am the resurrection and the life'—I AM is the word for God that was given to Moses at the burning bush. 'My Name is I AM, Jehovah, or Yahweh', and it is the very word used here in Deuteronomy 6. Jesus is the *I AM*; He is Jehovah God, as is said in Romans 10:9, that if thou shalt confess with thy mouth that Jesus is God, is Jehovah, is Yahweh, is the one God, thou shalt be saved—not by confessing that Jesus was a good person, who lived a long time ago, and who left us an example. You have got to believe and be willing to take a public stand that He is the fullest expression of God in the flesh.

The same words are applied to the Holy Spirit, as in 2 Corinthians 3:17: 'The Lord is that Spirit', the Spirit is Jehovah, the Spirit is Almighty God.

Hence, you have Father in the One God, Son in the One God, Spirit in the One God.

Richard of Saint Victor, a Scottish theologian who taught in France in the twelfth century, said it all goes back to 'God is love' (1 John 4:8). It takes more than one person to have and to share love, because as 1 Corinthians 13 says, 'love seeketh not its own'; it is overflowing, outgoing, and generous, and thus desires to have it sent back in response. God is that kind of love. So God has never been a solitary individual; God has always existed in a rich inner life of three co-equal, fully divine Persons: Father, Son, and Holy Spirit. 'Hear O Israel, the Lord our God, the Lord is one' is the basis of everything. Confess that first, and all the rest will work out right.

God Deserves Our Heart

We started out by citing Proverbs 23: 'My son, my daughter, give Me thy heart'. And this is particularly seen in Deuteronomy 6:5-6 and 8-9. Heart, in the Bible, is something like 'center of the personality,' who we really are in the deepest wellsprings of our being. The word 'soul' in Deuteronomy 6:5 literally means breath: love God with each and every breath you take. Some of you know the gospel hymn, 'Then shall my latest breath whisper Thy name; this be the parting cry, my heart shall raise.' Or Charles Wesley's:

> Happy if with my latest breath
> I might but gasp Thy name;
> preach Thee in life and cry in death,
> 'Behold, behold the Lamb.

Loving God involves at least two things: first, it is a matter of the intellect, grasping at least a little bit of the infinite truth that God is Father, Son, and Holy Spirit. It doesn't take a great deal, but the thief on the cross at least could say, 'Lord, [O God] remember me, when Thou comest into Thy kingdom'. By necessity, it involves the intellect, but it is also a matter of the feelings. You cannot see God, as He is, and not feel it very deeply. It's impossible to have a saving grasp of this God without having something profound happen in your feelings, in your deepest affections and motivations as a person.

We see this sometimes on a human level. When young people fall in love, there's a tendency, in many cases, for their selfishness to be broken open, and by loving one another, they are set free to love others. Sometimes it may be that way with a couple having a baby, when self-centered sufficiency may be broken open by true love, and their attitude towards the public changes.

Presbyterian theologian, Robert L. Dabney, in the last year of his life, 1898, in his blindness and with help, wrote one last book, *The Practical Philosophy*. Dabney was a traditional Calvinist of highly intellectual standing, always emphasizing the truth; and yet he says: 'When you get down to the bottom of it, it is the feelings that make the man. It is the feelings, the affections, that determine who we really are.' Now that is what is meant by 'My son, give Me thy heart'; or 'Thou shalt love the Lord thy God with all thy heart and soul and might'.

Similarly, in his book, *Charity and its Fruits*—a series of sermons, preached in his church in Massachusetts in 1737—Jonathan Edwards says there are two different kinds of faith in God. One is with the heart or the soul and affections, which is what the saints and angels have, and the other kind is what the devils have (for James says 'they believe in God and tremble'):

> It is not only necessary that we should know God and have a sense of His greatness [the devils have that; they're scared of Him] but we must, as saints, also have

a sense of His excellence and loveliness. The devils and damned spirits see a great deal of God's greatness, wisdom, omnipotence. God makes them feel it in His dealings with them. However, they are unwilling to know anything beyond that about Him. They have no humility, nor will they ever have, because, though they see and feel God's greatness, yet they see and feel nothing of His loveliness.

He goes on to say that without seeing the loveliness, the beauty of God, thus loving Him with all the heart and soul, one cannot truly claim to be saved. A medieval hymn says:

Jesus, thou Joy of loving hearts,
Thou Fount of truth, Thou Life of men;
from the best bliss that earth imparts,
we turn, unfilled, to Thee again.

J. S. Bach's wonderful piece of music: 'Jesu, Joy of man's desiring' expresses it exactly. You almost have to get to music to convey what it means.

Two things are mentioned in 6:6–9, concerning how we express this heart-devotion.

First, verse 6, God is in our constant thoughts. It means intellectual content, who this God is: Father, Son and Holy Spirit, gracious loving God, Jesus in our place, Jesus crucified, Jesus risen, Holy Spirit present with us. Psalm 16:8 says 'I have set the Lord always before me; because He is at my right hand, I shall not be moved'. And Psalm 121:1: 'I to the hills will lift mine eyes from whence will come my aid; my safety cometh from the Lord, Who heaven and earth hath made'. Lift up the eyes! God needs to be a great deal in our actual thought-life.

Secondly, verses 8–9, thoughts of God control the use we make of our eyes and our hands. I take these two things to be figurative, although some orthodox Jews have taken them literally, with leather cups on their hands, and phylacteries between their eyes. Not wishing to debate this point, it appears to me that 'to bind these words, the *shema*, between your eyes and put them on your hands and on your doorposts', is to say that you are to use your eyes, as you seek to see everything that you see in this normal physical world—who God is, and what he's called you to be in Christ. Looking at things in that way, you will perceive that you are His, and that He is your God. To keep that in mind is the best way to handle temptations: remembering that I am the Lord's; He is my God, and I am His child.

John Calvin's *Institutes,* Book 3, expresses well the point of the *shema* : 'We are not our own; we are the Lord's. Let us therefore not set it as our goal to seek what is expedient for us according to the flesh. We are not our own. Insofar as we can, let us therefore forget ourselves and all that is ours. Conversely we are God's; let us therefore live for Him and die for Him. We are God's; let His wisdom and will therefore rule all our actions.' Think of the hymn:

> Take my hands and let them move
> at the impulse of Thy love;
> take my feet and let them be
> swift and beautiful for Thee.

The *Shema* is the Basis of All True Christian Education

Deuteronomy 6:7 gives two ways for Christian education to happen, both in a family and in a more formal teaching situation. First, we convey who God is, formally in classical teaching, and secondly, we convey who God is, casually in the responses and attitudes of our normal life.

Formal teaching is required (verse 7 uses the word 'diligently') involving having our children memorize passages of the Bible or maybe teaching them the Shorter Catechism or Child's Catechism; taking them to Sunday School; taking them to Church; or if possible, having them in a Christian school. This is formal teaching of who God is, and of who they are.

Secondly, we are to be involved in casual teaching, in other words, the informal influence of our life, as those children live with us day by day. 'When thou sittest; when thou walkest, lieth down, risest up' is saying to let God be so important in your deepest affection all through the day, that your children, even little children, will sense there is somebody very, very precious to you above everyone else, and it is God.

How careful we should be as parents! Your children will perceive whom you love, even if that love changed from years past. And they're likely to follow what they see you really loving. They probably will think it would work for them too.

The greatest casual influence on our families would be living with an attitude of calm, quiet confidence in God, so that no matter what happens, we calmly refer everything to His gracious will. I believe I got that from my family. That may be what Paul meant in Philippians 4:11–13: 'I have learned in whatsoever state I am therewith to be content'—a calm content because your affections for the One who has charge of everything penetrates the consciousness of those who happen to live with you.

Think again of Proverbs 23, 'My son, give me thy heart'. It was once turned into a gospel song:

> Give me thy heart, says the Father above;
> No gift so precious to Him as your love.
> Softly He whispers wherever thou art,
> Gratefully trust Me and give Me thy heart.
> Give me thy heart says the Savior of men,
> Calling in mercy again and again;
> Turn now from sin and from evil depart;
> Have I not died for thee? Give me thy heart.
> Give me thy heart says the Spirit Divine;
> All that thou hast to My keeping resign;
> Grace more abounding is Mine to impart;
> Make full surrender and give Me thy heart.
> Give Me thy heart, Give Me thy heart;
> Hear the soft whisper wherever thou art.
> From this dark world He would draw thee part,
> Speaking so tenderly, Give Me thy heart.

Thus says God the Father, Son and Holy Ghost. And may we respond, 'Lord, we offer our hearts to Thee.' Amen.

19

A Thankful Spirit

Deuteronomy 6:10–15

This passage calls for a thankful spirit. In Medieval Europe, there was a legend, that there was something called the philosopher's stone. Anything that the stone touched would turn to gold. Of course, it is a legend. But it may not be totally useless, for William Law, the devotional writer who influenced John Wesley and others, takes the legend and draws a spiritual lesson from it. In *A Serious Call to a Devout and Holy Life,* he asks: 'Would you like to know who is the happiest person in all the world? It is he that has a constantly thankful spirit. A constantly thankful spirit is like the philosopher's stone in that it turns everything it touches into happiness.'

This Christian virtue of thankfulness is spoken of throughout Scripture, and where it is mentioned, it tends to bring joy and holy light into the soul, no matter what may be happening on the outside, as in this passage. Note two points: first, what God gives us (verses 10–11), and then secondly, what we are to give back to God (verses 12–15).

What God Gives Us (6:10–11)

In addition to the unspeakable blessing of eternal life in the spiritual realm, which was already being signified in Israel by the divinely appointed ceremonies in the tabernacle and the temple, something else is added. Moses is talking about how God provides everything else we need to make life on earth possible and pleasant. In the case of Israel, they had been brought out of slavery into freedom of the wilderness, but it was a barren wilderness, and they had to dwell in tents that could be jerked up in a moment and moved somewhere else.

Moses is speaking to them before Joshua leads them across the Jordan into the Promised Land, where they will change their tents for stone houses, with fine wells for water, excellent gardens, vineyards and olive trees, to sustain their physical needs—all that was necessary for a happy life—so that they didn't just get by, but really enjoyed their life in the Promised Land.

This was not only true for the ancient Israelites, but is also still true for many of us, whether we live in America, Britain, or wherever. We need to remember it. We did not build the houses in which we live, in most cases; we did not dig the wells, or make the water pipes from which we drink, nor did we usually clear the fields where we farm, nor plant the orchards and vineyards. God provided all these good things for us, by means of ancestors or in other ways.

As we read Isaiah 65:24: 'Before they call I will answer; and while they are yet speaking, I will hear', most of the blessings of your life, God gave before you asked Him. He's that kind of God. For Israel, God sovereignly gave them the possessions of the Canaanites. For most of us, He has passed down to us the heritage of our grandparents. Up in Moore County, North Carolina, my family still farms some of the fields that our third great grandfather cleared in the year 1790.

That is what Moses is saying here in verses 10–11. Look at them: 'houses full of all good things, which thou filledst not, and wells digged, which thou diggedst not, vineyards and olive trees, which thou plantedst not'. And we all live lives where most of what we have has been one way or another passed down to us (See also Neh. 9:25).

It is much the same in the teaching of the New Testament, although land is not the central focus of the blessings there. The Apostle Paul reminds us to have the same remembrance that everything we've got, God gave it, and that's the equivalent of the philosopher's stone turning things into gold in the realm of the Spirit. 'But who maketh thee to differ from another? And what hast thou that thou didst not receive? Now if thou didst receive it, why dost thou glory or boast as if thou hadst not received it?' (1 Cor. 4:7). Any combination of gifts and qualities and environment that you have been given came from God, and hence you are to give Him the thanks for it every time you use it.

In our modern economy, the illustrations here from Moses and Nehemiah may not seem relevant to us. We might well reply: I do not have any land, I have very little money; my grandparents had nothing to pass down to me. Well, you do have a normal mind; you have a certain amount of health; you have freedom of movement; you live in a free country; you've been brought up where the Bible is to a large degree believed; and God offers the same bright, beautiful future both to those who very little and to those who have the most. So, who among us does not have very strong reason to thank God—not least that we could know Christ and have assurance of eternal salvation and His presence to make it through?

We Are to Render Thanks to God for Everything (6:12–15)

There are many things you and I cannot do: As far as I know, you can't control the next presidential election; you're not going to be able to determine whether the New York Stock Exchange or the Footsie is up or down tomorrow. But here's something you can do, if you're God's child: you can determine to be thankful. And that turns all that it touches, says William Law, into spiritual gold.

Now the first part of Deuteronomy 6:12, puts this matter of thanksgiving in the negative: 'Beware, lest you forget the Lord', the opposite of thankfulness—to forget the Lord who has exhibited His love in what He has provided. Those of you who have children, when it was time for them to leave the family home, of what, if anything, did you warn them? Well, Moses, who is soon going to leave these people he has dealt with for forty years, warns them: 'Beware, lest you forget the Lord'.

Then verse 13 puts it positively, with three commands: fear the Lord, serve the Lord, swear by His name—that is, live your life on the basis of His integrity. Keep constantly in your mind how very much He has done for you, and you will become a thankful person.

There's an old English hymn by Joseph Hart:

How good is the God we adore;
Our faithful, unchangeable Friend!
His love is as great as His power,

And knows neither measure nor end.
'Tis Jesus the First and the Last,
Whose Spirit shall guide us safe home;
We'll praise Him for all that is past,
And trust Him for all that's to come.

In the matter of remembering the goodness of God, I have to go back to the First Presbyterian kindergarten of Lumberton, North Carolina, about the age of five. We had a little recess in the morning, when the ladies brought in trays of little Dixie cups filled with orange juice; and when they handed it out they said: 'Now, before you drink the orange juice, let's sing 'God is great, God is good'.

Many years later, as a grown man, I was on an airplane. Oddly enough, they passed out Donald Duck orange juice and I almost started singing, 'God is great, God is good!' Some days it may not be so easy to do it, but think about Psalm 103. In the Highlands of Scotland where, for many of us, our ancestors lived, they take the sacrament of the Lord's Supper very seriously. Normally it's observed twice a year. After people have come forward to take the Lord's Supper, the whole congregation then is seated, and the presenter leads them in singing several verses from Psalm 103.

I have thought in the years since then, that if I could trace out in my life and were asked, 'What do you feel about your life?', what I'd like to respond is this, 'Let us sing Psalm 103.' The interesting thing about it is there is not one single petition for God to do anything for us. It's a psalm of what some of the old saints used to call 'unmingled praise':

Bless the Lord, O my soul,
and all that is within me, bless His holy name.
Bless the Lord O my soul and forget not all His benefits'

That's very Mosaic: forget not His benefits. Remember what you have today: you're not in a mental institution; you were able to walk here; you go home and you have something to eat; you probably have a roof over your head; you have some way of transportation; you have at least a few people who love you; and presumably you have on the inside, assurance of eternal salvation. Moses says to beware, when you have had all these things, lest you forget the Lord. 'Who forgiveth all thine iniquities; who healeth all thy diseases; who redeemeth thy life from destruction; who crowneth thee with loving-kindness and tender mercy; who satisfieth thy mouth with good things, so that thy youth is renewed like the eagle's'. If we're thankful, we can't be grumpy. Jonathan Edwards brings that out in *Charity and its Fruits* that in the same personality, at the same time, thankfulness and grumpiness simply cannot co-exist. If on some day, you or I realize we are getting a bit fussy or grumpy, it means that we are forgetting about God, that we have lost sight of the big picture and concentrated on some little annoyance that comes to everybody. We're not being thankful to God.

A lack of a thankful spirit might lead us away from a victorious Christian life faster than anything else. The old Puritans used to say that poverty and hardship are a test. But there's an even harder test to handle, they said; and that is prosperity and ease and excellent health and beauty. It is this latter test that most of us in Presbyterian circles in the United States are now facing, and have been for a long time—the difficult test of prosperity and success. Moses says it here, David in Psalm 103 and Paul in 1 Corinthians 4.

From such passages, we gather that the test of things going right is harder to handle than failure.

That is why Proverbs 30:8-9 pray a very wise prayer, 'Remove far from me vanity and lies; give me neither poverty nor riches; feed me with food convenient for me lest I be full and deny Thee and say, Who is the Lord? or lest I be poor and steal and take the name of my God in vain'. Now whether we, as it were, financially have much or little, the way to spiritual solidity and true joy is to be thankful to God for everything. Learn to send every mercy you receive back up to God in thankfulness, not ostentatiously before others, but silently in your spirit and enough in your family that your children would know where you think good things come from.

In verse 12 Moses warns us that the primary danger of being well off is that God's existence, providence and love get behind the hills of blessing, eclipsing God from our eyes and our conscience. We foolishly begin thinking that we deserve, and that our own cleverness and diligence—or superior background—provided these things. It's what I would call the Nebuchadnezzar syndrome. Preaching near July 4th, 1976, the 200th anniversary of the United States' independence, I decided that I would preach on what Nebuchadnezzar said in Daniel 4:28-32:, and draw a parallel with America.

There is Nebuchadnezzar, walking around this marvelous walled city with the hanging gardens of Babylon going up like a mountain; an amazing architectural wonder of the world! And Nebuchadnezzar said 'Is not this great Babylon, that I have built'—didn't I do it all? As a judgment, God took his mind from him for quite a time, and he dwelt in the fields like an animal; and then his mind returned, and he blessed God; he knew it was from God that Babylon had been erected. The Nebuchadnezzar syndrome: we need to avoid it like the plague.

Moses says the same thing chapter 32 of Deuteronomy, about the children of Israel,

> But Jeshurun [that is an affectionate name for Israel] waxed fat, and kicked; thou art waxed fat, thou art grown thick [that means you have had so much to eat, you are so privileged]; thou art covered with fatness; then he forsook God which made him and lightly esteemed the Rock of his salvation. ... Of the Rock that begat thee thou art unmindful, and hast forgotten God that formed thee (32:15, 18).

That is the surest way to lose it all: 'Beware, lest thou forget the Lord thy God'. Remember: be not forgetful of all His gracious benefits.

We can be people who cultivate a thankful spirit. There is a lot in life you cannot control, your health and many other issues. But there is something we are able to do. God in the Christian life gives us this privilege: to be thankful. 'In everything give thanks; for this is the will of God in Christ Jesus concerning you' (1 Thess. 5:18). It is something you've got to learn. St. Paul says in Philippians 4:11, 'I have learned, in whatsoever state I am, therewith to be content. I know both how to be abased, and I know how to abound'. The blessed Apostle Paul said that he had to learn: 'I have learned'. We are in the school of learning to be thankful, and as we do so, not forgetting the Lord, remembering to trace all these benefits back up to Him; then it turns into something like spiritual gold—into joy, into peace, into kindness, into love. God give us, with all of His giving, God give us a spirit of thankfulness. Amen.

20

What to Teach the Children

Deuteronomy 6:16–25

This section is as wonderful a summation as I know in all of Scripture of what to teach the children. To teach our children that God is always first is the greatest gift we can give them.

We saw previously that Deuteronomy chapters 6–11 are an exposition of the first and greatest commandment: 'Thou shalt have no other gods before me'. Six entire chapters are devoted to the foundational truth that God is first.

We also looked at the *Sh'ma Yis'ra'eil;* 'Hear, O Israel, the Lord our God, the Lord is one', in chapter 6. It is the basic confession of all biblical religion, and its New Testament form is 'Jesus Christ is Lord'. On this confessional foundation we live and die, and all will be well. This truth of all truths—God is first, this God is my God and none other—is what the first commandment is all about and gives us the primary educational content we must convey to our children above everything else.

Thus I want us to look at three points in this holy educational text: a warning, (v. 16); a promise (vv. 17–19); and what we are to teach the children (vv. 20–25).

A Warning (6:16)

Even before we start teaching the children, we are warned to avoid setting before them the worst possible example as parents. And what is it? Avoid whining at God. 'Ye shall not tempt the Lord your God, as in Massah'. Massah was an incident described in Exodus 17:1–7, where they didn't get the water; and Moses smites the rock as the unhappy people are fussing at Moses, and even worse, fussing at God. 'Who does He think He is, not providing us the water that we need?'

We should avoid the attitude that says to God, 'If you do not step in and help us immediately, why should we even follow You?' At Massah the children of Israel essentially said, 'we will consider that You are irrelevant unless You do our bidding immediately'.

With that kind of talk about God when things are hard, our children will get the impression that God is our servant, not our Master; and that we have the right to fuss at Him and even turn our backs on Him, if He does not meet our demands. Such an attitude is a denial of the sovereignty of God, a direct violation of the first commandment, and a vain attempt to replace almighty God with the demands of self. It leads to spiritual and physical disaster because it is a reversal of the Creator/creature distinction.

Now God tests us many times in our lives, when we have a decision to make in front of our children, our friends, our family: whether we will let God be God, and submit trustingly, or cut loose, as it were, and fuss at Him? Let us seek the grace in our daily prayers that our children, or family or friends will never see us fussing at God, demanding that He do our bidding—or else we despise Him. Let us even seek the grace before we need it, that on what may seem the worst day of our lives and in the jaws of the greatest unmet need, we would say: 'God is first. I implicitly submit and follow Him, even in this dark valley. I know that God is good and will make a way out of this for us when it suits Him, and I'll trust Him till then.' Happy children, happy relatives, who have such parents or kinfolk.

John Newton, the former slave trader who was gloriously converted, wrote the most famous hymn of all, *Amazing Grace*. But he also wrote other hymns, and I want to quote one verse from one of them—if our children could hear us sing this, what a blessing would come on them!

> The birds without barn or storehouse are fed;
> From them let us learn to trust for our bread.
> His saints, what is fitting shall ne'er be denied;
> So long as 'tis written, The Lord will provide.'
> -- but on His calendar, not ours.

A Promise (verses 17-19)

I will be brief on this point since I covered it previously: always be eager to keep the commandments of God, especially this first one; and eventually, in due season, everything will work out right for you and for yours. 'Do right and good in the sight of the Lord' means that we give our very hearts to keep the commandments, because we are in the direct sight of God, face to face with Him, always seeking to please Him. Thus, we are in company with Jesus who said, 'I do always those things which please My Father' (John 8:29).

It is no burden to keep the first commandment, for the face of God is shining on our pathway. True, we do not always directly <u>feel</u> it, but as Psalm 34:15 says, 'The eyes of the Lord are upon the righteous and His ears are open to their cry'. To keep the first commandment from the heart is not legalism but the heart-expression of the most tender personal relationship to the living God— His face upon me.

Now here's the promise: when we keep God first, He superintends our truest personal, earthly interests, as well as heavenly ones. Deuteronomy 6:18-19 says that God will give us the land to possess and will deal with our enemies who may be too strong for us. It is much like—even the summation of—the promise made to Abraham in Genesis 15:1: 'Fear not, Abraham, I am thy shield and thy exceeding great reward'. God promises to be a shield against our enemies when we put Him first, and to be our reward here on earth, and hereafter in glory.

When the water does not come as quickly as we could wish, the way it was at Massah, we can think of our own challenges. Remember that God says, 'Dear child, put Me first and I will take care of all your truest interests in ways you cannot even imagine'. For He is 'able to do exceeding abundantly above all we can think or ask' (Eph. 3:20).

We must put God first, humbly submitting soul and body to Him, and trusting Him at all times. When our children and our friends see us doing this, very great blessing will come upon them: the land—or its modern equivalent: the means of production, a job of some sort; strength for another day; victory over temptation; practical wisdom. God will provide even when we have not the slightest idea where any of it is coming from.

What to Teach Your Children (verses 20-25)

Living in a godly home will automatically raise certain questions in a child's mind: such as, why are you structuring this household in terms of these precise requirements of God? An immediate illustration would be Sabbath keeping. Why do we not go to the store or attend public events on Sunday? Why do we go to church twice every Sunday, if you have an evening service? God says to parents, take immediate advantage of this teaching opportunity. 'Then thou shalt say …' (v. 21). What should we say when children notice they are required to live differently from the secular society around them?

First, do not base the requirements of Christian family living upon your own authority, but directly upon God Himself. Say to your son or daughter, 'we are under God; we must do what He says in His Word. That's why we're going in a different direction from a lot of our neighbors'. That God-centered attitude will make it much easier for the children to accept certain limitations on their behavior, than if it only came from an opinion or strong arm of a parent. It is not that you are against them or forcing them; rather, it is that you are seeking to honor the One whom you are both under.

Second, teach them how good God has been to you, your family, and to all His people in past years. Verses 21–23 speak of the miraculous redemption of the slaves out of Egypt by the mighty hand of this covenant-keeping God, the same God who calls us to obey Him from the heart every day. During the Exodus, the blood of lambs was smeared on the doorposts of the Israelites to turn away the avenging Angel of Death. We too have been redeemed by blood. 'Forasmuch as ye know that ye were not redeemed with corruptible things, as silver and gold, from your vain conversation received by tradition from your fathers; but with the precious blood of Christ, as of a lamb without blemish and without spot' (1 Pet. 1:18-19). All the lambs were pointing to the Lamb slain, from the foundation of the world. The God who gave His beloved Son, the Son of His heart, to go through all He did on the cross of Calvary to save me, He is the one who says 'Put Me first and remember that I have redeemed you.'

In other words, the God we serve put our interest before Himself in the life, death, and resurrection of Jesus and has every right to ask us to put Him first in our living and in our dying. We are therefore to teach our children, and anybody else we can influence, that the first, last, and constant duty of every day is to do everything we do in the light of the face of God. That is the goal of life; the prime basis of all true education. 'God first' makes many complex things rather simple and it has a way of turning otherwise hard duty into the sweetest, purest joy.

21

Obedience in the Promised Land

Deuteronomy 7:1–11

This is a portion of the section from chapter 6 through chapter 11: an exposition of what the first commandment means, 'Thou shalt have no other gods before Me', in different areas of our life. This passage contemplates life in the Promised Land. They are on the verge of Jordan, and Moses' leadership is about to end; Joshua will lead them across the river. Moses makes it clear that the first thing they are to do in the land is to keep the first commandment.

No doubt this was relevant in 1400 BC for the people of Israel, but 3,400 years later, what relation does this text have to Christian people scattered across the globe?

The Apostle Paul, writing to the Christian church at Corinth—in a very different situation from ancient Israel—speaks about the experience of Israel coming out of Egypt, and what happened to them in the wilderness on their way to the Promised Land. Paul says, 'Now all these things happened unto them for examples; and they are written for our admonition upon whom the ends of the world are come' (1 Cor. 10:11).

'The ends of the world' means that Jesus fulfilled the Old Testament, the end of one economy and the beginning of another. Paul says, then, under divine inspiration, that the experience of Israel gives a very important example for how we are to live the Christian life during our experience on earth. So, the first commandment meant that the people of God, as they crossed into the Promised Land, were to be obedient in putting God first; therefore, never to allow an idol into their thinking and practice—the same for the people of God in every age, including today. We are shown much of our responsibility to honor God's first and greatest commandment from the experience of Israel.

This first commandment always calls us to be different from the pagan world around us, whether in Old Testament Israel, with those seven corrupt nations; whether in Corinth, with an immoral, corrupt society; or whether in modern Europe and America.

Let us notice two points that show how we are to be different from the secularism or paganism around us, in terms of the first commandment. The first point, in 7:1-8: God's holiness requires that His people reject and resist the sinful world system. The second point, in 7:9-11: this holy God who keeps covenant with His people requires us to keep covenant with Him.

God's Holiness Requires the Rejection of the Sinful World System of Our Day (7:1–8)

The basic point is that God is holy, as Isaiah 6:3 says 'Holy, holy, holy is the Lord of Hosts'. When He calls us to be His, we must then live our life on earth in terms of His holy character. That is to say, God's adopted sons and daughters must begin to take on the lineaments of the family character, which is holiness, or purity.

In the Old Testament, *kadosh*—the Hebrew word for holy—can be traced through the many places where it is used in the Old Testament. One could summarize that holiness means primarily two inter-related realities: first of all, holy or holiness means 'separated;' and secondly, it means 'shining, or brightness.'

Holiness means 'separated', that is to say, cut off from moral evil and cultural corruption. You must split with those things that are contrary to God's character in order to be His people and to live in face-to-face fellowship with the Lord. It has the negative aspect: 'cut off' from evil practices; but also the positive one: 'face-to-face' fellowship with the living God.

You might say, O dear, to be cut off from those things! But they're <u>nothing</u> compared to day and night, year after year, living one's life with the sense of the smile of God upon you. None of those paltry, sinful practices could for one moment compare with fellowship with the holy God. So, *kadosh*, or holy, means separation from moral evil. That's one side of the holiness to which God calls all His people, both in Old and in New Testament.

The second aspect of holiness is what we might call 'brightness', or 'shining out', something beautiful that is splendid, raying out from its center in the triune God. It is similar to what the Old Testament calls the glory cloud over the tabernacle, in Hebrew, often called *shekinah*. There is also a frequent word in Hebrew, *kabod*, often used where it means the glory was so bright it was shining directly from heaven; almost pressing down on that amazing tent. All through the night, it was giving a million people encamped in the wilderness a shining and comforting light; the very beauty of the presence of God.

Holiness as a 'shining out of the resplendent beauty of the Lord' is found in the New Testament, although stated in other terms there, as in the words of Jesus in the Sermon on the Mount. God wants His people to become bright with His holiness, for which He works in them in grace, and thereby shine out so that others see. Jesus says:

> Ye are the light of the world. A city that is set on a hill cannot be hid. Neither do men light a candle and put it under a bushel, but on a candlestick; and it gives light unto all that are in the house. Let your light so shine before men, that they may see your good works, and glorify your Father which is in heaven (Matthew 5:14–16).

One of the major components of holiness is not so much a physical shining out, but rather the quiet, but strong display of the sincerity, and the beauty of Christian character. Hence the eight beatitudes set forth the beautiful shining of spiritual integrity, where 'blessed' (or 'happy') are such as the poor in spirit, the pure in heart, and the peacemakers. Through them, God's people, observers may perceive the outshining of the holy character of God.

Then something wonderful happens that the world needs more than anything else: they see your good works, and they glorify—not you, you're not worthy of glory—but rather, your Father in heaven; He is the source, and He alone is to be glorified. Similarly, Paul speaks in Philippians 2:15 of this: 'That you may be blameless and harmless (that's wholly cut off from worldly practices), the sons of God without rebuke in the midst of a crooked and perverse nation, among whom ye shine as lights in the world in holding forth the word of life'. To shine with light in the world means, (parallel to the next verse, which talks about holding forth the word of life), that for the preaching to be in any sense credible, to be received in a sinful culture, there must be church people who are shining with light in the world. Pagan men and women can see something of God's light in the life of a person who is exhibiting the beatitudes. In God's good providence, this predisposes unbelievers to receive the preaching of the Word of God.

According to much evangelistic research, most people who were converted, and are then interviewed, say that they saw something in another person's life that was different from the rest of the world, and it put them to asking questions. They began wondering why worldly ways of living and thinking are insufficient and unclean, especially when they see a clean life and observe the mercies of God in another personality. More often than not, it prepared them to receive the gospel, the power of God to salvation in their lives.

Long before he became one of the first professors at Princeton Theological Seminary, Archibald Alexander had been converted in the Second Great Awakening in Hampden Sydney, Virginia, in the 1780s. He wrote many books on apologetics; that is, how to present the Christian faith intellectually to people who did not believe, including *Thoughts on Spiritual Experience*; he knew such an approach very well. But toward the end of his life, he realized that the thing that made people ready to be saved was a holy life seen in some sincere Christian.

Alexander gave an illustration of a leading lawyer in Philadelphia—an atheist and very proud of his intellect. Hard-nosed, he wouldn't set foot in church; he argued against Christianity, because of the existence of evil, and nobody could get anywhere with him. However, he lived in a boarding house where there was a very sincere, simple, young Christian lady. She read her Bible, went to church, and something about her was very different, with a certain sweetness and goodness. This lawyer, in his late 70s, noticed her life, and he humbled himself to talk to her and ask questions. This Christian woman with little education—but in a sense much education, because she knew the Lord—led this man to a glorious conversion. She showed forth the light of God; and this hard man saw it and received it. I believe it's God's program for expansion of the church that people who are unconvinced, have got to see the light of God on some normal human's face, and in their character, in order to be attracted out of moral darkness to the beauty and purity of God's salvation.

We're told a little more by Moses about the origin of holiness in human beings in verses 7–8, which will keep us from becoming proud if God has ever used us to reach another person. It is the truth of divine election of sinners, chosen to be made right with God through believing in His grace, that causes any and all holiness reflected in their lives.

Those who do become holy, were no better than anybody else in this sinful world system (v. 7). The Israel that was caused to reflect the beauty of divine holiness was a nation of slaves—a complaining, worrisome people—not chosen for their moral qualities, or worldly impressiveness. The Egyptians were the cultured, sophisticated, wealthy, educated ones in the world. Who could compare with them?

The Assyrians, the mightiest military machine in the world, were far more impressive than the Israelites. But God chose a nation of enslaved people to be His own holy, beautiful, triumphant people. Things miraculously turned around for Jonah, once he prayed towards Jerusalem and cried out: 'Salvation is of the Lord' (Jonah 2:9). The great fish spat up so that he came out alive.

Election shows us that, and yet some churches who say they are orthodox, will never preach election, simply because it is too worrying to let God be God. But nothing is more wonderful, or more liberating than admitting that God is God, and bowing down with praise before Him, even when all human explanations fail. Election depends upon who God is, not on who we are: that's the long and the short of it.

The New Testament fully backs the Old Testament on this point. For instance, in Ephesians 2:1-3: 'And you hath He quickened, who were dead in trespasses and sins'. We were as unimpressive as the Israelites, dead in trespasses and cut off from God, creatures of our lusts, unworthy, condemned, on the way to perdition; 'in time past, ye walked according to the course of this world, according to the prince of the power of the air [the devil], the spirit that now worketh in the children of disobedience': you say you see a lot of people under the influence of the devil; it's true, but think about your own past: 'among whom also we all had our conversation in times past, in the lusts of our flesh, fulfilling the desires of the flesh and of the mind; and were by nature the children of wrath, even as others'.

Everybody in the church who is saved, one way or another, comes from a background of corruption and spiritual deadness with the wrath of God upon them and unworthy—though some hide it much better than others, owing to education and culture. Ephesians 2:4, echoing Deuteronomy 7:7, says: 'But God, who is rich in mercy, for His great love wherewith He loved us'. Ephesians goes on to say that He chooses us in Christ, takes us down into death with Christ, purges us from our sins, and lifts us up into the resurrection life of Christ.

Deuteronomy 7 and Ephesians 2 are saying that our election to salvation is dependent on the love of God, not on something in us. It is wrong to think or to feel that I am a cut above the common herd, or the fact that I'm a believer today proves that I was at least a little better than—or not as bad as—somebody else. The fact that you're elected to believe and to obey goes back to who God is, not to who you are. You might say, why would I ever come to believe when others didn't? The answer is the love of God. Because God loved the fathers, the patriarchs of Israel, He chose their children. Because in all eternity God has loved us in Christ, all who would ever believe and be His, He calls us to know His love. The reason is not in us but in God; He works, so that, in fact, we do believe.

To have our lives centered on God, to live out the first commandment in the 'Promised Land'. As Calvin often said, 'the Promised Land' since the coming of Christ speaks of the Christian experience in this world, though, of course, not exactly the same. Yet, we are to live by many of the same principles in our land of Canaan—planet earth—after we are converted. To have our lives shine out with the holiness of God in Christ, is said in Deuteronomy 7:1-5 to involve two specific areas of obedience to God, : first, warfare against paganism and second, marriage only within the covenant.

First, to follow the Ten Commandments in the Land of Promise or Christian life on earth before we go above, means a constant warfare against paganism. There may be more differences than similarities between how Israel waged warfare against paganism, and how we Christians have to wage warfare.

Israel was a holy theocracy, limited to one specific land for several hundred years. To make it a holy land, God required Israel to clean out the pagan nations, destroying their sinful idols, and rejecting their morally corrupt customs. Because God made heaven and earth and they are His (Ps. 24:1), He has the moral right to dispose of the earth to whichever tribe He sees fit; and thus to call Israel to wage war against thoroughly degenerate nations.

The people of Israel would serve as God's sword of vengeance against cultures that had degenerated beneath what the image of God calls for in human life. Leviticus 18:6-24 describes the moral disqualification of the seven nations of people in Canaan, due to corrupt sexual misconduct, incest and other matters. Adding what the Apostle Paul says in Romans 1-2, it seems that degenerate sexual practices occur when a culture is about to burn out, when God has to clean house. That does happen from time to time.

God said to Abraham, in Genesis 15:16, that his descendants will take the Land of Promise 'when the iniquity of the Amorites is full'. God gave these people many opportunities to repent, between the time of Abraham and the time of Moses. But they only grew morally more corrupt. Then God said, 'It's enough!' and had them cleaned out. They were finally judged for going against the basic qualities of being in the image of God, against the natural law written on their hearts.

If Israel had not obeyed God at that point under Joshua, in clearing out those degenerate nations, then they could not have been a holy people, even for one generation, and the line of salvation to Christ would have been lost in paganism, centered on idolatry—the worst offense against the first and greatest commandment—and immoral sexual practices. Such nations thoroughly deserved the penalty they received at the hands of Israel.

That was how they waged holy warfare and resisted a corrupt world system. But it's different with us since New Testament times. The Christian church has to live in pagan nations, yet we are still called to be a holy people—that's the great strength of the church, to be a city set on a hill, to be salt, a light that cannot be hid and that will draw people. But we're not a governmental theocracy; we're not called to wipe out pagan populations. Rather, we are called and empowered to convert many of the pagans.

We read about that in Acts 15:19-20, at the apostolic council, dealing with pagans coming into the church; would they have to be made first into Jews, and then become Christians? The answer was no; while they are to respect the basic principles of the Law of Moses, the main obligation is that they have come to God through Christ, and that is sufficient for full salvation. The Apostolic Council says: 'Wherefore my sentence is, that we trouble not them, which from among the Gentiles are turned to God'; our warfare doesn't consist of killing people, but turning them to God, and it takes God's Spirit to do it. The Council adds 'that we write unto them that they abstain from pollution of idols and fornication'—and from what is mentioned in Leviticus and Deuteronomy 7—'from things strangled and from blood'. And, from Matthew 28 (the great commission): 'Go ye into all the world and preach the gospel; teaching them to observe all things whatsoever I have commanded you, baptizing them in the Name of the Father, of the Son and of the Holy Ghost'.

In other words, as a Christian church, we fight with spiritual weapons: the sword of the Spirit, which is the Word of God; the Holy Spirit to make the Word alive, active and fruitful; and 'the weapon of all prayer' (Ephesians 6).

God, who always speaks according to truth, says that these spiritual weapons are the mightiest of all, according to the apostle in 2 Corinthians 10:3-5: 'For though we walk in the flesh, we do not war after the flesh'. So, the warfare now for the church is different; it is not after the flesh, but rather than being less powerful, it is actually far more powerful, 'mighty through God to the pulling down of strongholds'.

These spiritual weapons, instead of being weak, actually overturned the Roman Empire! 'Casting down imaginations and every high things that exalteth itself against the knowledge of God and bringing into captivity every thought to the obedience of Christ.' (2 Cor. 10:5). So our warfare against wicked paganism is to live a holy life, to encourage the preaching of the gospel, to use the sword of the Spirit which is the Word of God. As someone said, the sword of the Spirit is the only sword you stick into a dead man, and he becomes a living man. That's how we fight; we back up every action with prayer.

In spite of these differences, there is strong similarity between Old Testament Israel and modern Christian people in what they must fight. In both Testaments, we are required to battle against idolatry and the immoral corruption of the paganism that always goes along with it. 'Love not the world, neither the things that are in the world' (1 John 2:15) and in the words of Jesus, 'No man can serve two masters' (Matt. 6:24). Particularly in this rich culture of the West, we must be on our guard never to bow down to the attractive idol of materialism, including unrestrained sexual pleasure that goes along with it. Material greed is perhaps the greatest threat to a true Christian testimony in Europe and America. Jesus says we cannot serve God and 'mammon', an old word for wealth; you cannot give your heart to both. To keep us on our guard against the idolatry of materialism and giving our heart and soul to worshiping money, Jesus asks: 'What shall it profit a man, if he shall gain the whole world, and lose his own soul?' (Mark 8:36). So we are to resist idolatry and moral corruption, so we can keep the first commandment, in the land of our Christian promise and salvation.

Secondly, because of the first commandment and God's priority in our life, we are to marry only within the covenant. And it is exactly the same for Old Testament Israel and New Testament and modern church, to marry only within the covenant, only within the faith. That is clearly laid down for us, though many disobey it. In my many years as a minister, I have performed many marriages, and I always require that both of them be believers, or at least say they are. Sometimes I honestly was not sure that either were believers, but they said they were, so I had to give them the benefit of the doubt.

Why does God require us not to marry outside the covenant, both in the time of Israel and today? To marry an unbeliever, makes it likely that this unbeliever may cause us to put something else in the place of God, that something else is more important than God. And it may involve us in taking part in their idolatry to keep the peace.

That is what finally brought down Israel. As you look in Chronicles, you find that Solomon's idolatrous wives stole his heart and he began sharing in the worship of their false gods; he let them set up idols in the palaces he built for them; and that's what ultimately brought down Israel. You might argue that's Solomon; that only pertains to the time of the Old Testament. But I must answer that it's the same with us Christians. Look at 2 Corinthians 6:14-18:

> Be ye not unequally yoked together with unbelievers; for what fellowship hath righteousness with unrighteousness? And what communion hath light with darkness? And what concord hath Christ with Belial? Or what part hath he that believeth with an infidel? And what agreement hath the temple of God with idols? For ye are the temple of the living God; as God hath said: I will dwell in them, and walk in them; and I will be their God and they shall be My people. Wherefore come out from among them and be ye separate, saith the Lord, and touch not the unclean thing; and I will receive you. And I will be a Father unto you, and ye shall be My sons and daughters, saith the Lord Almighty.

We Christians are never to marry outside the faith, because that is to be unequally yoked—belief with unbelief. It is forbidden. Why? I have known of people who wanted to marry a non-believer, and several church people have asked: what's wrong with it? They say that they feel great love for each other right now. I have no doubt they do.

But here is what's wrong: marriage is the closest of all human relationships. It is the tenderest possible tie between two human beings: nothing else is that close. It is a solid foundation of every other institution: church, state, school, business. There of all places, in marriage, we—husband and wife—must be heart to heart, looking in the same direction, believing together, loving together, honoring God together as our first priority—keeping the first commandment, with all of our heart, mind, soul, and strength; and raising up children who will see mother and father putting God first, and not split apart in their crucial priorities. Not to be at one in the faith does tragic things to people who disobey God in this most important human relationship, and we've all seen the years of grief that result from this disobedience to God in marrying outside the faith.

God Requires Us to Keep Covenant With Him (7:9-11)

The God who keeps covenant with us, requires us to keep covenant with Him. Here too it is the same with Old Testament Israel, who went into the Promised Land, as it is with the church in the 'Land of Canaan' in their earthly experience: we are to obey the Lord.

'If you love Me, keep My commandments' (John 14:15). To love God is to seek to obey God. To follow the first and the greatest commandment is to obey God by resisting the sinful pagan culture around us, including its materialism and sexual immorality, and marrying only in the faith. That way, in some real measure, we demonstrate the purity and brightness of the Holy One of Israel, of the God and Father of our Lord Jesus Christ.

In conclusion there is a simple, but stunning beauty in obedience! To avoid obeying the Lord, you can come up with all kind of reasons: such as the claim that grace keeps me from loving God enough to obey Him (and surely, that is its own answer!). After all is said and done, if the believer is honest before God, he will admit that to love God is to seek from the heart to obey Him, and that always takes us in very specific directions. It was so in the Land of Promise, and it is so in the land of salvation. God help us to be an obedient people: 'Trust and obey, for there's no other way, to be happy in Jesus, but to trust and obey'.

22

The Returns of Love

Deuteronomy 7:12–26

The great theme of this passage is found in the first clause of verse 13, where it speaks of God's good promise towards us: 'and He will love thee and bless thee'. We know that true human love always desires to have that love returned, so that it will be a true loving relationship. We're made to desire the returns of love, because God is love, and God made us in His image. Now, by the same token, this passage shows us that God Himself desires that His love be returned by us to Him. It is about the returns of love that God calls for from all His people. In addition, the passage shows us that true love involves obedience to God. Jesus says, 'If ye love Me, keep My commandments' (John 14:15). That's how we show love to God. And that sort of obedience is visited by wonderful encouragements and surprising good things that the Lord sends.

In particular, verse 13 says: 'and I will love thee'. That is what is before us in verses 12–26. There are four points: first, answering love, verses 12–13; second, what God returns to those who love Him, verses 13–24; third, the answer to fear, verses 18 and 21; and fourth, the duty of love, verses 25–26.

Answering Love (7:12–13)

First, answering love: 'He will love thee'—the mighty infinite God, believe it or not—and we tend to discount this because God is so great, which is why I am insisting on it. But that's the wrong way to look at it. It is correct to say that God is great, but it is profoundly incorrect to think that therefore, He is not interested in my little love. Nothing could be more wrong-headed.

The infinitely majestic God is intensely interested in being loved back by His people. When we answer God's divine love with our own responding love, weak and frail though it be, God is very interested in and very pleased with our little love, for verse 12 is saying that we answer back God's love by obeying Him; implying that He is on the lookout for this, our proper answer of love to God.

But does still God love us when we are unworthy, and when we are profoundly mean and unloving? Of course He does. 'We love Him because He first loved us' (1 John 4:19); and 'When we were without strength, in due time Christ died for the ungodly' (Rom. 5:8). He gave everything He had for those who were His enemies. So, thank heavens, God does love sinners. If He didn't, not one of us could possibly be here today.

Deuteronomy 7:13 sets before us the kind of love that God wants in answer to His unmerited, amazing love towards us. We might call it 'answering love.' If you don't love somebody back who loves you, you haven't got a relationship. God wants this relationship as seen in the words of Jesus: 'He that hath My commandments and keepeth them, he it is that loveth Me; and he that loveth Me shall be loved of My Father. And I will love Him and will manifest Myself to Him … If a man love Me he will keep My words; and my Father will love him, and we will come unto him and make our abode with him' (John 14:21–23).

Our lack of obedience, including mine, often prevents God from giving greater expressions of the wealth of His love for us. On the other hand, to answer the Lord's love by sincere attempts at obedience, opens the floodgates of even deeper expressions of God's love. The Psalmist speaks of this in Psalm 81:13–16:

> Oh that My people had hearkened unto Me,
> and Israel had walked in My ways!
> I should soon have subdued their enemies,
> and turned My hand against their adversaries.
> The haters of the Lord should have submitted themselves unto Him;
> Oh that My people had hearkened unto Me,
> and Israel had walked in My ways!
> I should soon have subdued their enemies,
> and turned My hand against their adversaries.
> The haters of the Lord should have submitted themselves unto Him; but their time should have endured for ever.
> He should have fed them also with the finest of the wheat
> and with honey out of the rock should I have satisfied thee.

God is pictured here as wishing to give us the very finest; but we often prevent it, by being cold towards Him, and not delighting in obeying Him. I often think of the little children's hymn, sung in the Church of Scotland:

> Savior, teach me day by day, love's sweet lesson to obey.
> Sweeter lesson cannot be; loving Him who first loved me.
> With a child's glad heart of love, at Thy bidding may I move;
> Prompt to serve and follow Thee, loving Him who first loved me.
> Love in loving finds employ in obedience all her joy;
> Ever new that joy will be, loving Him who first loved me.

Let me repeat it, because it's hard for us to take it in: the glorious, transcendent, majestic, sovereign God and ruler of the entire universe, the mightiest of all, vast and omnipotent His reign—He is actually interested and cares about our little love. God watches for the smallest signs of obedient love in a little boy or girl, or some poor widow in a rest home, whom nobody ever visits or cares what happens to her. Or somebody in jail who has sincerely repented; He, the mightiest of all, is pleased that somebody down in the jail loves Him. And it opens the gates of rich blessings to come, here and hereafter. Keep verse 13 in mind: 'He will love thee'. That is who God precisely is.

Last Sunday we were looking at the doctrine of election (verses 6–8); it's interesting that God choosing us to be His, is immediately followed by the fact that our life is to be laid out for Him and other people in obedient love. The simple connection of election and obedient love, teaches us that a true understanding of election never breeds pride, hardness of heart, and disobedience. but is a relationship of love giving rise to tender, thankful obedience to God and greatest kindness to others. Obedience does not cause election, for all are sinful; but election gives rise to heartfelt obedience.

In Luke 19, Zacchaeus—a short man, a crook who used the tax system to defraud everybody—climbs a sycamore tree to see Jesus. Jesus stops, looks up and says, 'Zacchaeus, come down from the tree; I would like to eat dinner at your house today'. Absolutely overwhelmed and thrilled, Zacchaeus went home and got ready the best food. Then he said to Jesus, who with His disciples was eating with him, 'Lord, I repent of how corrupt and dishonest I have been; and if I have defrauded any man, I will restore fourfold; I will put everything right, I'm going to pay it back'.

Now, Jesus didn't wait until this man showed penitence and obedience or elect him on the basis of what Zacchaeus had already done. Jesus loved him, elected him, and came to his place, and the man laid everything he ever had on the altar. That's how it is with election and responding love; that is the way God has set it up.

The Returns of Love (7:13-24)

Even somebody like Zacchaeus tries to show the Lord he loves Him. That normally follows, as we so often see, when a child gets converted; they want to do some little something that shows the Lord they love Him, which always brings further blessing, that will be appropriate for any individual in their own way. Three areas of blessing are mentioned here: fruitfulness, health, and victory.

First, fruitfulness in body, land, and flocks—reproduction of offspring, homeland, and economy (vv. 13-14). In other words, God takes care, not only of our souls, but also provides most generously for the needs of our bodily life. Some people don't agree with that; they don't think God has any interest in anything but the soul. But that can't be right. 'Beloved, I wish above all things that thou mayest prosper and be in health, even as thy soul prospers' (3 John 2). Yes, God's primary concern is our immortal soul that needs to be saved. John prays that their soul really prospers; but, at the same time, he asks that they might have from God the worldly prosperity and health that is best to enable them to do what God has for them.

We see this in Joseph, who loved and showed profound obedience to God, in that he would not commit sin with Potiphar's wife. For his pains he got put in jail. However, he kept loving God in jail, and eventually became the second most powerful man, Chief of Staff to Pharaoh. Joseph, who had been sold into slavery by his hateful brothers, lied about by Potiphar's wife, and thrown in prison, at the end of it all let his brothers know that he would not take it out on them, and saw it in the light of God: 'You meant it for evil, but the Lord meant it for good.'

Sometimes, for God to give us the greater blessings that obedient love will make possible, it may come as something that seems very painful, dark, and difficult to understand. But that is often the prelude to a larger blessing. It is interesting that Joseph called one of his sons Ephraim, which means 'fruitful.' Why? He said, 'because the Lord has made me fruitful in the land of my affliction'.

While driving a dear Christian lady home after Wednesday night prayer meeting in Charlotte recently, she said she came from a distinguished, but very difficult family; the mother abandoned them when she was a little girl. This later took a tremendous toll on this woman after she was married, with children. But she said Christians gathered around and the Holy Spirit helped her and she worked through it. And then she said she took the name of Joseph's son, Ephraim, as a spiritual promise: 'God has made me fruitful in the land of my affliction'. How fruitful, blessed and happy has been the life of this Christian woman, who is now somewhere in her 80s. She is an illustration of how God has promised fruitfulness to His people who seek to love Him.

Then health is mentioned: 'None of these diseases of Egypt shall be laid upon thee', perhaps meaning the plagues or maybe something broader; but at the very least, God will not lay the plagues that devastated Egypt upon His people, if they seek to obey Him. In addition to supernatural intervention, history shows that wherever Christianity has gone, healthy disciplines of life, medicine, and hospitals have always followed with a tremendous raising of the standard of health.

Then victory over enemies is promised as a blessing of fuller obedience to God. Before dealing with that, let me mention the problem that might arise, if you are following this text closely. If, as this text plainly says, God blesses the obedient with fruitfulness, health, and victory over the evil powers that oppress them, how is it, in the real world, that often we see some of the most godly men and women die young; noble Christian couples unable to have children; excellent men at times forced out of a job, for their refusal to take part in dishonesty and corruption. How then can we say that their obedience was divinely blessed?

Here, I think, we must hear what Paul says: 'For we walk by faith and not by sight' (2 Cor. 5:7). We've got to see this short earthly life in the light of eternity, or we will not understand what happens to us and to ours. We've got to walk by faith, not by sight; and to think of the panorama of an immortal existence that God has promised us. Indeed, 'we walk by faith not by sight', is preceded by something very important in 2 Corinthians 4:17–18:

For our light affliction which is but for a moment, worketh for us a far more exceeding and eternal weight of glory while we look not at the things which are seen, but at the things which are not seen. For the things which are seen are temporal, but the things which are not seen are eternal.

In other words, here's the case: sometimes the godly die early; they don't have children; they lose jobs. But the very honor of God is on the line to use them even more widely, and bless them, even more than if they had been granted such things; always looking at the experience of this life in the light of an endless eternity of bliss for all who love God. One day on the other side, (I believe this by faith), when we can look back on all this, including disappointments, we will thank the Lord for having withheld these blessings from us on earth, once we see all the increase of glory that came out of our disappointments and sufferings which were, after all, 'but for a moment'.

So, in the light of eternity, it is true that obedience is blessed, many times blessed here on earth, but always blessed in the world to come.

The Answer to Fear (7:18 and 21)

God has promised to obedient people that He will give them victory over ungodly enemies. But all enemies do look very scary, when we consider the limited strength that we have. To go back to Deuteronomy and to Moses, we know that Bronze Age Palestine was full of wealthy, fortified, strongly armed city-states.

If you only think of the enemy, fear can paralyze your ever taking any action, and can keep you from doing what God said He would bless. What then do you do when you are afraid? Yes, God has said, 'Do this'. But we respond, 'I'm scared! I don't see how I can get through it'.

How do you deal with this kind of fear? Verse 18 gives us the solution in one word, 'Remember'. Remember what the Lord did to Egypt, which, in logic, is an *a fortiori* argument: if God took care of powerful Egypt, 'how much more will He take care of these smaller city-states? God is saying, 'The battle is not yours; it is Mine.'

Verse 20 says God can send hornets against the enemy, His control is so total over every aspect of nature. I can also take you into places in Judges and elsewhere, to show you where this was done. He can use insects, weather, earthquakes, tidal waves, fires, or whatever, to defeat the devil's troops. So God says, 'remember, remember': your battles in the cause of truth are always my battles. That is the answer to fear.

Many fear the growing influence of Islam in Europe and in America. Yet I think the primary enemy we have is not Islam, but rather secular humanism, the left-wing modernism that hates biblical Christianity, and has been like a battering ram to beat down all the great pillars of Christian truth. What an appropriate time to recall here Deuteronomy 7, that God is saying, 'if my church will obey me, I will take care of their enemies'.

It seems to me that this passage is teaching obedience to the Lord from the heart, at all costs. If we will put God first, if we would repent of our own materialism, unbelief, and immorality where appropriate, God will send the hornets, figuratively speaking, to handle the enemy in ways we could never do. God might sting some of them with conviction of sin and they receive the gospel. Wouldn't that be best of all?

Remember that the gospel has triumphed over hatred and sin; that love is stronger than evil; that love is stronger than death. Remember this: God will do for us what we cannot do for ourselves. Let us not be depressed; God is on His throne. He was on His throne when Joseph, Daniel and Paul were in prison. But greater blessing followed them than before, when the Lord brought them out. I believe God can handle this situation if His church would do right, repent and go to her knees. He doesn't need my or anyone's advice how to control the future—and I wouldn't know what to tell him—but God will send blessing to His church, if we will put Him first. He can take care of the situation, convert many of the enemy: that would be my desire—to see them converted, to see them brought to Christ.

Ephesians 3:20 promises: 'He is able to do exceeding abundantly above all we can think or ask'. That's our God! He says, 'Put Me first; renew your vows of love and obedience to Me; seek to follow Me with all your heart; I will take care of your enemies, even when they're in your midst, and have great influence: whether the media, the government, schools, or whatever—I am easily able to send the hornet and do whatever I need to do'. In such times, trust in God.

THE DUTY OF LOVE: CLEAN YOUR HOUSE OF ALL IDOLS (VERSES 25–26).
To clean our house of all idols brings us back to the first and greatest commandment, 'Thou shalt have no other gods before Me, love the Lord your God with all your heart, mind, soul and strength'. Anything that you know that needs to be put right with mighty Jehovah; no longer bow down to any substitute; no longer give your heart to anything less than God; clean it out and see what God will do.

23

Obedience Is the Ground of Blessing

Deuteronomy 8:1–10

This passage, and the rest of Deuteronomy 8, indicates that once we have been saved by God's grace, then for the rest of our lives, obedience is the ground of blessing, and that obedience is never separate from the continued grace of God. Let us note four points out of these ten verses: first, we are elected to be obedient; second, we are trained in the experiences of life to be obedient; third, there are temptations to be disobedient that come to us; and fourth, blessing is tied to continued obedience to God.

We Are Elected Unto Obedience (8:1)

Deuteronomy 8:1 is preceded by Deuteronomy 7:6–7: 'For thou art an holy people unto the Lord thy God. The Lord thy God hath chosen thee to be a special people unto himself.' Election comes before obedience, but this gracious election always calls us to obedience. Obedience never causes election; it's the other way around, and verse 7 makes that clear.

We see here a certain tension of Scripture between two complementary truths: election (Deuteronomy 7), and obedience (Deuteronomy 8). That holy tension is where we are called to live as God's children. The New Testament, as well as the Old Testament, teaches that we are elected to holiness: 'According as He hath chosen us in Him [in Christ], before the foundation of the world, that we should be holy and without blame before Him in love' (Eph. 1:4). God elected us in Christ, and it is in our union with Christ that enables us to live a holy life. 'For we are His workmanship, created in Christ Jesus unto good works which God hath before ordained that we should walk in them' (Eph. 2:10); election unto good works; election unto obedience.

It is the same in 1 Peter 1:2: 'elect according to the foreknowledge of God the Father through sanctification of the Spirit unto obedience and sprinkling of the blood of Jesus Christ'. Believers are elect through what Jesus has done, and it is the Father and the Son who send down the Holy Spirit to indwell us, thus making it possible for us to live lives of obedience.

We Are Trained in the Experiences of Life to Be Obedient (8:2,5)

We can properly say that all of God's people are in educational training while on earth. God has an overarching purpose for all the days of our lives; He has elected us to be obedient, and then He providentially, in our experience, lets things happen, so that we will learn to be obedient, as we become further educated in His divine school. That providential training is seen in Deuteronomy 8:2 and 5:

> And thou shalt remember all the way which the LORD thy God led thee these forty years in the wilderness, to humble thee, and to prove thee, to know what was in thine heart, whether thou wouldest keep his commandments, or no. Thou shalt also consider in thine heart, that, as a man chasteneth his son, so the LORD thy God chasteneth thee.

The Lord's overarching plan is this: a good father trains his sons and daughters to be like him, to show the family likeness. God is doing that in every Christian life. Nothing is outside this great program. The Lord is using our talents, our heredity, our environment, our good points and our weak points, and our contacts to train us to be His and thereby to show His character. He has elected us that we would show the character of Christ, to be conformed to the image of Christ (Rom. 8:29), the final purpose of foreknowledge and predestination.

To make us like Christ is not unlike raising a child: 'the Lord chasteneth thee as a man chasteneth his son', that is to admonish, to correct, sometimes to apply the rod, but mostly to spend time to explain, to help, to live with, to play with, and to pour yourself into them, so that they will go in a definite direction. If they go out of line, you have to get them back into line with divine principles. Any decent father and mother does that with their children, and God does so with us.

We read in Proverbs 3:11–12 how God chastens all His children, and as quoted in Hebrews 12:11: 'No chastening for the present seemeth to be joyous, but rather grievous, yet afterward it yieldeth the peaceable fruit of righteousness to them that are exercised thereby'. In other words, to have been chastened by your father when needed is not pleasant, especially when the chastening had to involve a rod. And so, when God our heavenly Father lets us go through briar patches and times of illness, defeat, and disappointment and hurt, it is painful; it does not seem to be joyous.

Even if you're a good Christian, you cannot expect every day to be abounding in joy. But when some of our experiences are far from joyous, it greatly helps to remember that our heavenly Father is working with a specific program to get us where we need to be. This text indicates that these tough disciplines will yield the peaceable fruit of righteousness to those who have gone through it; we will know every hard trial was worth it. In the meantime, we are called to remember that God is always working so that we will come to an end of ourselves and depend on Him.

With that kind of maturity, which thinks less of self and more of God, obedience becomes second nature. That is, God calls you first to be His child, and an obedient life flows from that, not the other way around.

Deuteronomy 8:3 and 5, show how, in the wilderness, Israel had to learn to be dependent upon God; God was all they had. There were no grocery stores, no fields of wheat; it was a drought, barren, and terrible. Yet God provided water; God provided manna from the skies; God sent quails from the seashore; God gave them light by night; God gave them victory over the Amalekites. God was working to make Israel say, 'We depend on God for everything!' When that is the case, there is not the slightest question but to seek to obey Him out of gratitude for what He's done for you, and for who He is.

Yet to reach the point where we say, 'God is our hope; God is our confidence; God is our shield and exceeding great reward,' as Abraham would have said, requires some humbling and testing in our personal experiences. The middle of verse 2 it says: 'to humble thee'.

Many people (maybe most people, when at their worst) want a religious experience that exalts the self-life. The exaltation of proud flesh is what the devil offers, as he did to our first parents: 'You shall be as gods'.

On the contrary, the true church says, you must come to an end of yourself, and depend on God; submit, humble yourself in the sight of the Lord, and He will lift you up. That shows us what God is doing in the providential occurrences of our lives: He sends things to humble us. In the wilderness experience of Israel, no water, enemies like the Amalekites; snakes, as a way of driving His children to His bosom, so that His children would lean hard upon Him for everything.

God can make us learn to lean on Him through positive and negative experiences. I learned how it can work positively, when my family and I lived in the home of a wonderful medical doctor, a great Christian lady in Melbourne, Australia, in the summers of 1985 and 1986. She told us of a brother of hers, who was a cattle rancher in Queensland. The land up there is generally so dry that it can only support a few cattle on an entire acre; but he had thousands of cattle and was a very successful cattle rancher. He noticed that there are two ways you can keep your cattle at home. One way is to put up expensive fences around thousands of acres. But there's another way, the cheapest way, to keep your cattle near home: it is to provide wells, sometimes powered by windmills. With sources of water providing drink for cattle in different parts of the ranch, there is an exact number of miles beyond which the cattle will not stray. In that case, you don't need fences.

In a sense it's a picture of God dealing with us. He makes us unable to do something or to handle something; He sends enemies to drive us to the well, to the water of life, to Him, to Jesus. According to Deuteronomy 8:4–5, it takes times of hardship, humiliation, desperate need—and then we see instances of God's provisions, such as in verse 4: your clothing did not wear out for forty years, your feet did not swell, and the leather on your soles did not wear out, even though you walked hundreds and hundreds of miles; a miracle of God's renewal. God uses both the need and the enemies and the supernatural provisions providentially in our lives to get us to where we trust in Him, and know it comes from Him; hence we lean hard on His bosom. God has everything arranged in your experience to make you an obedient child.

We Face Temptations to Be Disobedient (8:10)

Like our first parents, we are tempted to be disobedient. One way this temptation comes to us is seen in verse 10: having eaten to your satisfaction, and having anything you want, you may well begin feeling: 'Maybe I deserve this; I have worked hard, and I know I have been more diligent than some people, and so it does seem appropriate that I'm in pretty good shape'

But God says that you'd have none of it, if He hadn't given it to you! Don't forget me when things are going well. Indeed, when things are going at their very best, be distrustful of yourself, and realize how quickly health and money can take wings and fly away, and leave you with nothing. Continue to have confidence in God; keep loving Him, and, knowing that everything depends on Him, seek to obey Him. When tempted to take the credit for your well-being, just say 'No! Everything depends on God; I'm not going to give way to feeling that I deserve it and that I can handle it and that I can make my own way, morally or any other way, without considering God.'

Continued Blessing Is Tied to Obedience to the Lord

Throughout this passage, especially verses 1, 4 and 10, when you've eaten and are full, remember that God did it and that he deserves the love and obedience of your heart. We cannot fail to see how this principle is picked up in the experience of Jesus in the New Testament.

Scholars have long noted that when Jesus went through the wilderness temptations, what the devil brought before Him were reflections of the very temptations that caused Israel to do so poorly in the wilderness. For instance, in Matthew 4, when Satan tempted Jesus concerning food while Jesus was fasting, the devil said, 'don't trust in God and wait on Him; why don't You yourself turn the stones into bread?' (verse 3), Jesus answers by quoting from Deuteronomy 8:3, that 'man doth not live by bread alone, but by every word that proceedeth out of the mouth of God' (verse 4).

So, continued blessing is tied to the obedience that trusts God for everything! Jesus had internalized this, and instead of murmuring in the hour of need—very hungry—he trusts in the Father. Jesus knows that God will provide at the right time, maybe not that day, but God must be implicitly trusted and submitted to until He knows it's the right time to give Jesus what He needs.

In terms of Deuteronomy 8, Jesus will be looking for something even more precious than wheat and bread, namely 'every word that proceedeth out of the mouth of God'. Jesus is saying, Lord, let me see it Your way; that will be my food, and that will help me hold on until you give me actual physical food; I want to see it your way, I want to go your way; that will be the sustenance of my life until you see fit to intervene physically.

Now see if we can understand a foundational truth about our salvation here, something that goes even beyond the holy example He set for us. It is profoundly true that Jesus answered Satan with the Word of God; that is the example He sets us. But there is something deeper; Jesus stood in for us when He received baptism at the hands of John the Baptist in the River Jordan; He underwent the baptism of repentance. John was shocked! He knew that Jesus was holy and sinless, and said: 'Lord, I need to be baptized by you, not you by me.' But Jesus said no, 'suffer it to be so for thus it becometh us to fulfill all righteousness'. Jesus is saying, I am identifying with sinners; sinners need to be baptized to show they are repentant for their sins. I am going to repent in their place. Now Jesus has never committed a sin. He was tempted, but He never gave in.

As our substitute and representative, Jesus goes into our place, into the place of all who ever believe in Him, and repents—for them! The innocent Lamb repents for the sinners, for the goats. All through Jesus' life, He is doing it for His people. It's not just that He dies for our sins—He does that, and that's the heart of the gospel, the innocent for the wicked, the holy for the guilty.

But Jesus does something else: He lives a holy life to be credited to my account. Jesus' death is credited to my account; thus I am forgiven and will get into heaven, and will get my prayers answered. But also, Jesus' holy life is credited to my account, and God the Father sees me in Jesus when Jesus (unlike Israel) is obeying in the wilderness, saying 'man shall not live by bread alone, but by every word that proceedeth from the mouth of God'.

Jesus does that as the Head of His church. He is the Head; the church is the body; where the Head goes, the body goes. We can see something of how this works in Romans 5:12-21: the first man, Adam, brought us by his sin into death, whereas the last Adam, Christ, by His obedience, brings us into eternal life. The first Adam makes us sinners; the last Adam makes us righteous. And that includes not only His dying, but His holy living and His overcoming the temptations. Indeed, Hebrews 5:7-9:

> Who in the days of His flesh, when He had offered up prayers and supplications with strong crying and tears unto Him that was able to save Him from death, and was heard in that He feared; though He were a Son, yet learned He obedience by the things which He suffered; and being made perfect, He became the author of eternal salvation unto all them that obey Him.

He was standing in for us, praying for us, living for us, overcoming sin for us, being baptized in repentance for us, shedding His blood for us, rising for us. And 'we are seated with Him in heavenly places' (Eph. 2:6). He has literally taken us up to the Holy seat in heaven with Him, it is so certain we are going to be there because the Head is there, the body is there, and that is how we have power in prayer.

If someone announced that he was going to preach next Sunday on obedience, do you think it would cut down on the attendance? Well, it ought not to, for after all, the call to obedience to the Lord is good news! But how can it be good news, I don't feel like I can be obedient. It's too hard.

In fact, God has provided His Son as the obedient One, the Holy One of Israel to stand in for sinners and do for them what they can never do for themselves—not only to die for their sins—yes that!—but to live an obedient life to the Father. In the obedience of Christ, the Father, sees us as having obeyed and having already been seated with Christ in heavenly places.

But let us think carefully here. Christ's obedience in our stead does not mean that we don't need to be obedient; for that would mean that we are unbelievers, if we have no desire to obey the Lord who saved us. But it does mean that because Christ has done it for us, the Holy Spirit takes of that obedient spirit of Christ and that victory of Christ, and works in us, so that our earthly experience is reflecting more and more of what we already have in Christ in heaven. And that is the wonder and indeed the miracle of the Christian life: obedience is the ground of every blessing, and indeed, that obedience is provided for us in Christ, who, as Hebrews says, is the Author and the Finisher of the faith. Stay in touch with Him, and our lives shall reflect more of what He has already won for us. Be it so.

24

The Curse of the Covenant

Deuteronomy 8:11–20

This rather clear, but solemn passage, brings before us something we don't hear preached about very much, but it's a crucial part of Scripture: namely, the curses of the covenant. Why don't we hear much preaching on the curses of the covenant, which are intertwined all through the Old and the New Testament? I believe it is because much of modern Christianity wants a god who is not really holy, who is indulgent of every kind of sin, and is honor-bound to save every person who ever lived at the end of their life.

Is that whom you meet in the Bible: the indulgent god, who never punishes sin, who has no curses in his covenant? Such a god is simply an idol of the fallen man's imagination, not the God of Holy Scripture, who is wonderful love—kind, merciful, as described all through. But He is also holy in the way He carries out His infinite love to us. That is to say, God is holy love—or loving holiness—because that is His character: love and holiness. His dealings with mankind involve both blessing and cursing, and a solid biblical belief has to speak to them both, to be faithful to Scripture and to who God really is.

Deuteronomy 8:1–10 emphasizes the blessings of faith and obedience, verses 11–20 emphasize the curses upon unbelief: disobedience, forgetfulness of God, and a life given over to self. Let us note two points in this text: first the primary cause of disobedience: and second, the constant hand of God in what happens to us.

First, the primary cause of disobedience. This passage of Scripture is clear and not difficult to understand, unlike some passages in Ezekiel or Revelation. But Deuteronomy 8 does raise a hard question: why do people who have been so pampered with blessings, go off the rail and misuse everything they've been given? Verse 11 gives us the primary reason—there are other reasons, 'Beware lest you forget the Lord your God'. That's the danger.

Near the close of the reign of Queen Victoria—a reign of immense accomplishments for England and the British Empire—pride at what they had accomplished would not be unexpected. While celebrating the sixtieth year of the Queen's reign, Rudyard Kipling was asked to write an appropriate poem. Although a wonderful poem, many people severely criticized Kipling for what he wrote. I guess it was too near the bone. The constant refrain through this wonderful poem is: 'Lord God of Hosts, be with us yet; lest we forget, lest we forget.'

God of our fathers, known of old,
Lord of our far-flung battle-line,
Beneath whose awful Hand we hold
Dominion over palm and pine
Lord God of Hosts, be with us yet,
Lest we forget lest we forget!

The tumult and the shouting dies;
The Captains and the Kings depart:
Still stands Thine ancient sacrifice,
An humble and a contrite heart.
Lord God of Hosts, be with us yet,
Lest we forget lest we forget!

Far-called, our navies melt away;
On dune and headland sinks the fire:
Lo, all our pomp of yesterday
Is one with Nineveh and Tyre!
Judge of the Nations, spare us yet,
Lest we forget lest we forget!

If, drunk with sight of power, we loose
Wild tongues that have not Thee in awe,
Such boastings as the Gentiles use,
Or lesser breeds without the Law
Lord God of Hosts, be with us yet,
Lest we forget lest we forget!

For heathen heart that puts her trust
In reeking tube and iron shard,
All valiant dust that builds on dust,
And guarding, calls not Thee to guard,
For frantic boast and foolish word
Thy mercy on Thy People, Lord!

Forget what? Forget the Sovereign, Triune God, whom Scotland and England had believed in and worshiped, who had given them everything they had. The same forgetfulness can be seen in many a church in America, which has also massively benefited from the Lord.

So when people, who had great privileges, become disobedient and live in an unchristian way, the reason is simply because they forgot the Lord their God, who gave their fathers all these benefits; they turned away from Him, and became focused on self.

Verses 12–14 show that after tremendous blessing, our primary temptation is to forget that God gave you these blessings, enabled you to do the work, to have the relationships and be there, who put you at the right place at the right time, and made these things wonderfully work out. Scripture and human experience show that when we're successful, the temptation is to forget that God did it. Beautiful houses, abundant crops, multiplied cattle, gold and silver, fine investments, and excellent savings gradually take first place in our hearts, and replace God. We foolishly ascribe the comforts we enjoy to our own power and cleverness. We say, 'I haven't done too badly, have I?'

Hosea speaks of this, reflecting on the history of Israel and the terrible things that had happened to them: 'According to their pasture, so were they filled; they were filled, and their heart was exalted; therefore they have forgotten Me' (Hos. 13:6).

Strange, isn't it! God answers our prayer, and the first thing we do when we get all this and everything is going right, is to forget God! It is THE temptation to believers in times of much blessing, such as described in verses 15-17

You see this when you study the history of an old family. Since I was a little boy, I was very interested in genealogy. I heard the older members of the family talk about people who lived 200 and 300 years ago. Some of our ancestors in the Carolinas, were well off from the beginning, but most came with very little, and had to struggle hard to make ends meet. By and by, they were blessed. But even while they had very little, they did have their Bibles and Catechisms: and above all else, large numbers of these emigrants had the treasure of a saving faith in Christ, and a willingness to work hard and be self-restrained. Eventually, they came to know major blessings.

But then they were faced with a new temptation, described in verse 17: 'And thou say in thine heart, My power and the might of my hands hath gotten me this wealth'. The United States of America, like Old Testament Israel, once it became established in wealth and safety and power, has generally turned away from God, and ascribed its success to human concepts, like democracy and our own inventiveness and abilities. Let me give you a trivial illustration.

A few years ago, I was with a high university official, who knew one of my sons, who was then serving in Africa. I asked this distinguished official to write Christmas greetings to my son on a card I had with me at this particular reception. He first wrote 'Merry Christmas' along with the boy's name; and then evidently thought better of it, and changed it to 'Holiday Greetings'. He is emblematic of many throughout our nation.

The fear of offending an atheist has caused large numbers to refuse to honor God. A country pays a heavy price for that. As a student in the 1960s, I could see the change coming: an embarrassment over traditional faith in God. It took another 20 years to see what it meant. So within about two decades—after our leadership had been turning its back on God—a number of the curses that always come to privileged countries, once they forget God, were unleashed in America.

I don't need to chronicle in any detail: it would be too depressing. But massive divorce; drugs in every class of society, destroying people's minds; pornography; legal abortion; many incompetent schools, and in our cities, gangs, who are franchised. Therefore, the need for security systems on our homes; general fear of strangers, so that people are scared to be friendly anymore; and now terrorism and strange foreign wars. Such griefs are curses of the covenant, for having forgotten the God, who called us, saved us, and who blessed our fathers so wonderfully from nothing to all this.

The Constant Hand of God Upon Us (8:11–20)

In this time of moral and social decline, it is encouraging to remember that the hand of God is always involved in everything that happens to us; God did not lose charge in the 1960s. Even when curses are falling upon us, we need to call to mind once more the great truth that has made us who we are: it is that God intervened to provide us with every blessing. But for several years, we have been on the verge of losing those blessings and—far worse— of dishonoring God Himself.

The three uses of the verb 'multiply' in verse 13 are passives not actives. Israel is not the subject of the verb; you didn't multiply your herd; you didn't multiply your silver and gold; you didn't multiply your houses. The herds were multiplied for you by God; the silver and gold, the investments that worked out, were multiplied for you by God; and everything you have, including your bodily health and your mind—that was multiplied for you by God.

The Christian Church is not the subject of this verb; we are the objects, the recipients; God has done the multiplying, not us. It's not about us primarily, it's about God. It's not from us; it's from God. That's the teaching of Deuteronomy 8:13.

How appropriate this is in these chapters of Deuteronomy, chapters 6–11, for, as I have told you, these chapters are an exposition of the first commandment, 'Thou shalt have no other gods before Me'. All these chapters are looking at what the first commandment means every way you turn.

So, in our thinking about our physical, societal, and economic standing, we must always think of God first. It is not natural, but it is supernatural; it is a biblical requirement that we focus our thinking, when we look at anything that is helpful, good, encouraging, necessary, to remember: it has come from the hand of God.

Jesus says in John 15: 5, 'Without me, ye can do nothing'. David says in Psalm 16:8, 'I have set the Lord always before me; because He is at my right hand I shall not be moved'. David is thinking, God is first. Similarly, in Deuteronomy 11:2, the eyes of God are on His people from the beginning of the year to the end of the year. We would have nothing; it would be a total disaster, if the eyes of the Lord were not constantly upon us, making good things happen. So God is always intervening to bless His people who do not forget Him.

Verses 19–20 speak of the curses of the covenant. This includes the chastisements, terrible things that occur to us when we forget God. There are serious consequences of not doing what David said, or not remembering what Jesus said, and especially when we turn to idolatry. It does not necessarily mean bowing down before a stone statue, few of us in America would do such a thing. Broadly, idolatry means giving first place in your affections to something instead of God. If we do, God will eventually cause us to perish as a people, unless we repent.

I think this means more than affirming the true statement that God lets us undergo the consequences of our sins. This text is saying more than that; it is saying that God directly intervenes to break us down as a people, so that we cannot comfortably continue in our proud self-sufficiency. His curse—when bad things happen, one after another—is meant to stir us up, and get us out of the place of sure and final judgment, so we will seek His face once again. God's curse is the only possibility of our getting back the blessing, and could be the prelude to good news.

God is intervening, both in the curses of the covenant among His people, and thereby, giving them a possibility of getting back to the place of blessing. We see this in Ezekiel 11:8-10

> Ye have feared the sword; and I will bring a sword upon you, saith the Lord God. And I will bring you out of the midst thereof (from Jerusalem) and deliver you into the hands of strangers, and will execute judgments upon you. Ye shall fall by the sword (i.e., Babylon) I will judge you.

You will know I did it.

Sometimes people say that the only kind of judgment God gives is just to let you take the consequences of your sin. I do believe it, but it's more. God intervenes in the judgments to make them happen and yet, in this is His mercy. It is the only way a once-blessed and now-sinful people can get anywhere. Taking the judgments to heart, can drive them back to the place of repentance.

Isaiah 26:8–9 says the same:

> Yea, in the way of thy judgments, O LORD, have we waited for thee; the desire of our soul is to thy name, and to the remembrance of thee. With my soul have I desired thee in the night; yea, with my spirit within me will I seek thee early; for when thy judgments are in the earth, the inhabitants of the world will learn righteousness.

When we forget righteousness, when we forget to be obedient, we become disobedient, and then the judgments come.

The great devotional writer, Andrew Murray, among much else, wrote *Waiting on God*. There's a little chapter in there for each day of the month, and for the 19th day he says: 'Mercy saves the sinner not in spite of, but by means of the very judgment that came upon his soul.' Think about that. Later he says: 'Judgment prepares the way and breaks out in wonderful mercy. It is written, "Zion shall be redeemed with judgment."' So, the most important thing for a people, for us as individuals, is to get back to the place of devotion where we remember that God gave us everything and to have Him take first place in our heart, and to interpret the things that come to break us down, whether it is nationally or personally.

We're told something else in Ezekiel 11:18-20 that is very encouraging. When things are bad, when the pagans begin taking over, what are you going to do? God says: 'And they shall come thither, and they shall take away all the detestable things thereof and all the abominations thereof from thence'. God can use His sworn enemies to begin cleaning up His people!

Then, after the painful cleansing by foreign agents, the way is cleared for something wonderful to happen, as Ezekiel 11:19-20 tells us:

> And I will give them one heart, and I will put a new spirit within you; and I will take the stony heart out of their flesh, and I will give them an heart of flesh; that they may walk in my statutes, and keep mine ordinances, and do them; and they shall be my people and I will be their God.

If God's erring people repent and remember Him, whatever the situation, God will intervene and they will have the blessing of a new heart. When you are self-centered and materialistic, the heart is hard like stone and it takes a miracle of grace— God intervenes and replaces the heart of stone with a heart of flesh that beats in accordance with His love, in response to His mercy, and believes and trusts and seeks to obey. This, in Jeremiah 31, is the New Covenant, whose central characteristic is that God writes His law on their hearts (called in John 3 the New Birth). As a result of that gracious impartation of new life, you do more that will please the Lord, and are very sorry when you don't, and will come back and repent. But often this comes after a period of the letting loose of the curses of God.

Finally, the fact that God will intervene gives us hope. Beware lest you forget the Lord your God in all these judgments; but in these judgments, if you will remember me again, there will be a little sanctuary, like Jonah had down in the whale's belly. He turned his face toward Jerusalem and began to pray. Then everything changes.

Remember! You can't control a lot of things; you can't control societal trends, but you can remember God, and call to mind that with humble faith in Him, things are going to work out. Psalm 111:4-10:

> He hath made his wonderful works to be remembered:
> the LORD is gracious and full of compassion.

You've got to remember that—you may feel like you are under judgment this moment; everything is going wrong. Remember this: the Lord is gracious and full of compassion towards you, more so than any human on earth ever could. Remember Him:

> He hath given meat unto them that fear him: he will ever be mindful of his covenant.

We're back to the covenant—the curses and the blessings!

He hath shewed his people the power of his works,
that he may give them the heritage of the heathen.
The works of his hands are verity and judgment; all
his commandments are sure.
They stand fast for ever and ever, and are done in
truth and uprightness.
He sent redemption unto his people:
he hath commanded his covenant for ever:
holy and reverend is his name.
The fear of the Lord is the beginning of wisdom:
a good understanding have all they that do his
commandments.

Remembering the Lord, you can be obedient, you can want to do His commandments, and then you will know that 'his praise endureth for ever'.

25

The Necessity of Intercession

Deuteronomy 9:1–29

Deuteronomy 9 sets before us the necessity of intercession; intercessory prayer is the only thing that keeps God's people from being destroyed, and keeping the enemy from wrecking what God has helped them establish.

The children of Israel were about to cross River Jordan and enter into frightening new challenges. Moses tells them that they are going to fight some very strong and big nations. One would be the Anakim—giants. Giantism sometimes occurs genetically in the human race—perhaps through inbreeding—with some people being eight and nine feet tall. The Anakim were well trained militarily and dwelt behind high walls.

Moses said to the soldiers of Israel, you've got to face them; but you can and will win, if you depend on God, and somebody's praying for you. Israel's dependence upon intercessory prayer was nothing new. But he reminds them of how very much they shall need intercession as they face a future that will involve many hard conflicts.

We note three points in this passage: first, the power of the enemy (verses 1–2); second, the power of God (verses 3–6 and 29); and third, the necessity of intercession (verses 7–28).

The Power of the Enemy (9:1–2).

Anakim were huge, frightening people, well armed, and able to crush their enemies like ants. Remember what the boastful Goliath said to Saul and to David. He was winning everything, it seems, by intimidation, until a teenage boy got in there, who sincerely believed in the Lord; then everything changed. Moses reminds them that they are going to have to do a great deal of fighting in order to take what God is giving them. Moses says, you've got to understand that the enemy is strong and you are weak.

Those of you who have served in the military might say, 'Whoever said that to an army?' Well, that's the watchword of God's army: the enemy is strong and we are weak! It seems to me that it's God's plan—all through the Bible and through history—to let His people see how weak they are in themselves, and how strong the enemy is. Being realistic about our own need, weakness and inabilities, in light of the power of the evil culture around us, is the only way even a saved man or woman is going to look to the Lord. Otherwise, we are going to depend upon ourselves.

The Christian army has to realize that we are weak and they are strong. Only then are we in a position to say, 'but I know somebody who is stronger', so let us look to Him, as King Jehoshaphat did (2 Chron. 20:12), calling the people to renewed faith and intercessory prayer. He said a wonderful thing that is often on my mind when I face difficulties: 'Neither know we what to do, but our eyes are upon thee'. In intercessory prayer, no matter how disadvantaged you are, you say 'I don't know what to do, Lord, but our eyes are upon you!'

The next morning Jehoshaphat gathered together the armies and did a strange thing: he called for the white robed Levitical choirs to come out of the temple, to stand before the army—in the front line—and told them to start praising the Lord. The Authorized Version says that the Lord God 'set ambushments'; that is, he destroyed the enemy when the praises went up. The devil was enraged, and although we don't know exactly how it happened, the enemy was destroyed, based on the intercessory prayer of the people.

Here, we cannot help but think of our modern Western nations, facing many challenges, some of them of our own making, as we have departed from faith in God and his Word: aggressive Secularism, rampant immoralism, the destructive drug culture, and not least, Islamic terrorism.

What a time to be like Moses and Jehoshaphat, who poured themselves out in intercession for Israel! Never has fervent intercession been more called for. But in our own ranks, we see precisely the opposite!

A number of years ago, an editorial in the *Wall Street Journal* (Friday, December 7, 2007) reflected on what one of the presidential candidates had said in giving his viewpoint on the history of how the secularists have taken America:

> The core of the Democratic Party shifted over time towards secular absolutism where any public engagement with religion is tantamount to its public establishment and maybe even repeal of the secularist enlightenment. The Supreme Court also took an active role in making the policy preferences of the secular left wing the law of the land, beginning in 1963 with the prohibition of prayer in public school.

Well, that is not what Moses said! That hostility to prayer in America is no different in Great Britain and Western Europe. The problem of all our Western nations is that we do not see that our greatest enemies are not on the outside, but on the inside. The most serious enemy is in our midst: a functional atheism that is trying to throw out the last remains of biblical Christianity from public life. In biblical terms, I fear our people, for a number of years, have already been in the throes of apostasy. That is far harder to handle than an enemy nation on the outside.

Humanly speaking the future looks bad, doesn't it? But that is just the point. Are we only keeping our eyes upon the human factors, or are we looking to God? Moses and Jehoshaphat would tell us that the direction we choose to look—that and that alone—will determine our future. Thus this first point reminds us of the power of the enemy and of our own weakness.

The Power of God (9:3–6, and 29)

The infinite power of God is no small matter, which we often forget as we look at the challenges of the world in our time. But Scripture is not hesitant to remind us of it! Deuteronomy 9:3 calls God 'a consuming fire', and it is said in other places of Scripture, 'It is a fearful thing to fall into the hands of the living God'. The God, who is a consuming fire, can easily destroy entire nations given over to wickedness. In verse 29, Moses reminds the people, soon to face battle, of the mighty power with which God brought Israel out of Egypt. It was a putting forth of divine, supernatural power that trounced a huge army and that got them through the Red Sea.

Now surely none of us thinks that the power of God has diminished since the time of the Exodus, or since the dawn of creation, or since the resurrection of the body of our Lord Jesus Christ! We humans age, and our powers diminish; now well past sixty, I see some of this decline in myself. But God does not diminish in His limitless wisdom, nor any of the power of His being with the passing of years; the passing of years is irrelevant to the God who inhabits eternity. Time is a little stitch inside eternity; God never changes or grows weak, and 'He fainteth not', says Isaiah. He can put forth His infinite, mighty, supernatural power any moment He deems right, and bring down nations and open seas, bringing one down and raising up another: that's who God is. Moses says to Israel, don't look too much at the giants; look at God far more. A giant is not even a termite or a flea on the back of a rat, compared to the matchless power of Almighty God.

We are still in the larger section of Deuteronomy (chapters 6-11), which is an exposition of the first commandment: 'Thou shalt have no other gods before Me.' In that light, Moses is saying something that still holds good today, as we regularly need to apply the first commandment; always, but especially when things are far too hard for us. When you face fearsome things, things too big to handle, that is precisely the time to apply the first commandment. We are to lift our eyes up to God by faith and bring Him into the picture. You may have some giants to face, even enemies within yourself, which are the worst by far, but it changes when you bring God into it.

I realize, of course, that actually we mere humans do not 'bring' God anywhere; He is always on the Throne, and when He puts forth His power, it is in accordance with His sovereign will. Yet it is also true that, 'According unto your faith, be it unto you', as Jesus said to the blind man whom He healed in Matthew 9:29. In a word, God's sovereign plan includes the faith responses of His people, as they intercede for Him to come to help them. It is a divine mystery that we do not seek to explain: God's eternal plan includes intercession, which brings Him in to give victory to His people. That is the truth that Moses and Jehoshaphat were relying on.

It is not for us to understand 'the secret things which belong to the Lord', but to carry through 'things that are revealed, that we and our children may do them', as Moses himself said (Deut. 29:29). One of those revealed things is for us to pray for God to come in and handle the situations we face.

There is nothing too hard for God to handle; that is part of the first commandment: God is always first. We must say: Lord, come in and handle this thing and forgive me for not thinking of you in it. The power of God is the basis for our prayers.

The Necessity of Intercession (9:7-28)

Why is intercession so necessary, since God said 'I'm going to give you the land? It's my promise to you.' Why has Moses got to intercede—in three different periods of forty days and nights—fasting, and praying, and agonizing, if God said He was going to give it to them? Why not just claim it, without any intercession?

Here's why intercession was so necessary then and is now. It's because of the unbelief, hardness of heart, inconsistency, and sometimes utter rebellion, of the people of God against the Lord, who is a consuming fire in His resplendent holiness. It's because of our unholiness and our unlikeness to the holy, beautifully burning fire of God's being that requires us to exercise tremendous prayer and, sometimes, fasting. It's not that God isn't willing to keep His promises, and isn't generous—He is! But it's our unholiness and our unworthiness to receive them without somebody interceding, that is the background to God giving over these promises to us—who are so frequently, cold followers of Him. Intercession for us sinners is the ground for God blessing us, without denying His own character.

Verses 7–8 talk about it, but verse 6 had set the tone here in chapter 9. Moses says: understand that the Lord God is giving you this good land, not because you're so good but, indeed, in spite of your being stiff-necked. He says, it's going to take a lot of praying, if you are to get anything that is good. Then he tells the story of the golden idol that Aaron had molten and fashioned while Moses was on Mt. Sinai, forty days and nights, receiving the Ten Commandments. When he came down, he saw what they had done! They had gone into a sinful orgy in the worship of an idol, a disastrous breaking of the very first commandment.

In properly angry response, Moses broke the tables of the law, stamped the golden calf, and made the rebels drink it. Then he goes back up and fasts another forty days and nights, interceding. God says 'Don't worry Moses; I'll blot them off the earth and out of your loins, we'll raise up another nation'. But Moses prays, O Lord, don't do that; have mercy upon them.

Some 1,400 years later, Paul, in praying for the unbelieving Jewish people, takes up the same words: 'I could wish myself accursed to God for my own beloved people, the Jews, to be saved' (Rom. 9:3). God heard Moses, and He will hear Paul in due time, according to 2 Corinthians 3. The point for us is that God answered the intercession.

Moses goes on to list other incidents: Taberah, Massah, Kibrothhattaavah, and Kadesbarnea. They wouldn't enter the Promised Land at the beginning, when they had just left Egypt, because of unbelief, but Moses intercedes forty days and forty nights and God spares them.

What hope is there for our increasingly apostate Western nations? It all depends on whether or not people of God start interceding in a way we have not seen in years. I remember before the American national elections in 1980, speaking to a gathering of Christians of all denominations and races, on the Courthouse Square in Dillon, South Carolina. The meeting had been organized by Dr. Bill Monroe of Florence Baptist Temple. We were there to intercede together for our nation; it was non-partisan.

I, among others, was asked to speak a little. I chose one verse, Ezekiel 22:30: 'And I sought for a man among them, that should make up the hedge, and stand in the gap before Me for the land, that I should not destroy, but I found none.' That's what I urged on God's people in Dillon that day, calling the people of both black and white churches to stand in the gap; to come kneel down in the gap. I thought then and I think now exactly the same thing—this is the only hope to save any country.

It's an unchanging principle from Deuteronomy 9, that judgment upon the people of God can be averted and divine blessings made over to them, only if there is active intercession on their behalf. You might say, let's organize a Christian political party; it's too late for that. But intercession is not too late, and we could go back to what is said of Moses in Psalm 106:23, 'Therefore God said that He would destroy them, had not Moses His chosen stood before them in the breach, to turn away His wrath, lest He should destroy them'.

We now have a far greater than Moses, who ever lives to make intercession for us (Heb. 7:25). But Christ our great intercessor, Moses, Jehoshaphat, Paul and others, all call us to stand in the gap for the needy people and nations of our time. They call us to intercede that at this late hour, God will turn away His wrath and give us another opportunity. Instead of seeking to start some large political movement, why not start going to Wednesday night prayer meeting at your church? If it does not have one, humbly ask the leadership to start one, and promise your support. Start having family worship, where you intercede, together with our children, for people and issues that all will know about. Our God generally starts great changes, not in an impressive way, with much media coverage, but with small groups of humble believers in insignificant 'fly-over' zones, who pray in their homes, day-by-day, and in their churches (small or large), faithfully every week. At least do that, and if you need to do more, the providence of God will lead you. Always be happy to start small!

26

God's Grace in Action

Deuteronomy 10:1–11

These eleven verses of chapter 10 are a wonderful exhibition of God putting to work His wondrous, matchless, fathomless grace towards unworthy sinners. St. Augustine defined grace as 'unmerited favor.' That is to say, God dealing with us infinitely better than we deserve. He deals with us in grace because of who He is, not because of who we are. That is Israel's and the church's greatest and only hope: the grace of God as He deals with us unworthy persons.

There are three points in these eleven verses: first, an answer to prayer (Deut. 10:1, and 10,11); second, a renewal of a broken covenant (10:1–5), and third, a restored priesthood (10:6–9).

An Answer to Prayer (10:1, and 10,11).

Verse 1 says that Moses was to make a second copy of the two tables of stone, and in verses 10 and 11, God says to get ready to march into the land that He was still giving them, in spite of the fact that by their disobedience, they have justly deserved being denied entrance.

There's an interesting phrase here in the first three words (in English) in 10:1: 'at that time'. Moses is pointing to the last verses of chapter 9, when he prayed for Divine forgiveness for the sinful people of Israel, who had committed adultery, fornication, and idolatry. He urgently asked God not to blot them out, but in His grace to give them another chance.

God answered his prayer, apparently right after he prayed it, by saying something like: 'Moses, I am instructing you to build an Ark to house the second tables of stone, because I'm giving you another chance to live your life on the basis of who I am by My grace, and by My holiness.' Hence, God is communicating forgiveness: 'Yes, I do forgive the people everything they did wrong. And not only that, I am going to lead them into the land that I promised to Abraham, to Isaac, and to Jacob. I'm going to renew the covenant with them and I am calling them back to their first love,' as He says to one of the churches in Revelation.

Isn't it wonderful how God answers specific prayers specifically? So, to know the grace of God and have it conveyed into our lives, it is clear that we've got to pray and ask for it, and to be specific about it.

Let me contrast two verses in the Bible about whether you pray for grace, or whether you don't pray for grace. The first one is Jeremiah 33:3. 'Call unto Me and I will answer thee and show thee great and mighty things that thou knowest not'. God says, I will show you some tremendous things, but—you have got to call on Me and ask Me for them.

That's one thing: calling unto God saying, Lord, do everything you've got planned for us, and use these prayers to convey that grace. In James 4:3 we find the opposite attitude—characteristic of many churches and many of us sometimes—namely: 'You have not because you ask not'.

Have you ever wondered why we do not receive some of the things we long for? It may be because we are not asking, interceding, praying.

Now Moses, a great, noble man of God, wasn't perfect, but he was one of the great saints of Scripture, and is our example in so much. He sets the example, when he asked for God's grace to those people and to himself and—wonderful thing—got it. Psalm 86:7 promises: 'In the day of my trouble, I will call upon thee, for thou wilt answer me'. In the day of trouble, call upon God and God says, 'I will answer you'. Moses was in terrible trouble: the sin of those people required that justice should blot them out from the earth. But God used Moses to call upon Him and extended wondrous grace to an unworthy people.

Any time we go to a prayer meeting we don't go and say, now we are very worthy people; we certainly have done well, and on the basis of how well we've done, we would like you to do this and this. Nobody with any Christian sense would pray like that. When you go to a prayer meeting, you're gathering to ask for more grace. That's what Moses asked for: grace to the unworthy, grace to be bestowed on a sinful people. And wonder of wonders, God gave it!

So in these opportunities let us gather and ask for more grace in the sense of Romans 5:20: 'But where sin abounded, there did grace much more abound'. You might say, 'Well I feel that I am not doing well; I'm sinful, so I ought not to go to a prayer meeting.' To the contrary! 'Where sin abounded', where it's getting at you, go to the place of prayer; and where sin abounded, you will find that by the mercy of the Lord, grace much more abounded. The devil has a vested interest in keeping you out of any prayer meeting, because he knows something that at times the church doesn't know, that if God's people ask in the name of Jesus for more grace, God will give it and overwhelm the sinfulness that seems about to pull us down into a dark hole.

Yet, for all God's willingness to extend grace, we seem hesitant to receive it. But let us remember how St. Augustine describes grace it is 'unmerited favor' not because of who we are, but because who God is. He extends this grace in the merits of Christ.

Probably the best definition of grace in the Bible is 2 Corinthians 8:9: 'For ye know the grace of our Lord Jesus Christ who though He was rich, yet for your sakes became poor that you through His poverty might be rich'. God is making available all the grace we could ever need in every particular situation, even in the dark, hidden things in our lives. God knows all about it; and is making grace available through Jesus who has paid for our sins and has made available the power to do better. But still we have got to ask for that grace; to want it enough to articulate the precise areas in which we wish God to convey to us that grace.

As we start a prayer meeting, think of Ezekiel 36:37: 'Thus saith the Lord God; I will yet for this be inquired of by the house of Israel to do it for them; I will increase them with men like a flock'. God says, I'm available; I'm going to be inquired of; insofar as you ask Me, you're going to get a tremendous increase for the asking. But you've got to ask in order to receive.

God is willing and indeed, eager to be inquired of: 'I will yet be inquired of by the house of Israel' for this. These verses are clear: to get the blessing, to get that grace translated into the flesh and blood responses of our lives and those of other people for whom we are praying, we must actually go to the place of prayer and do the asking.

A wonderful verse, Isaiah 30:18, says: 'God is waiting to be gracious unto you'. Isn't that encouraging? Think of the needs of my life, of my sins, my failures, and the times I trip up; I thought I'd do well and didn't; what does God, who knows everything, think of me? As Isaiah says, God is attending upon me, waiting to give me more grace, if I will only ask it.

Hebrews 4:14–16, gives us great encouragement to come to the place of prayer, there to seek grace where sin has abounded:

> Seeing then that we have a great high priest, that is passed into the heavens, Jesus the Son of God, let us hold fast our profession. For we have not an high priest which cannot be touched with the feeling of our infirmities; but was in all points tempted like as we are, yet without sin. Let us therefore come boldly unto the throne of grace, that we may obtain mercy, and find grace to help in time of need.

God used Moses' intercession to save a sinful nation from destruction, and to give them a second chance to enter this beautiful land of promise. That's the first point: prayer answered.

The Renewal of a Broken Covenant (10:1–5)

In thinking about the meaning of covenant in modern English, we might use the word 'relationship'. In Scripture, God establishes the terms of that relationship. One fine scholar spoke of it as 'a bond in blood'. Covenant is central to the entire book of Deuteronomy. God requires perfect obedience to His terms, and then, in matchless grace, He provides, in our place, the required responses. What He does to restore the broken covenant shows us that a holy God, who is a consuming fire, is at the same time full of the most tender mercy and grace.

So, covenant is important in Deuteronomy, and in the New Testament Jesus comes precisely to make over this covenant to us. He shows us the results of this in John 15:9, 10 and 14: 'As the Father hath loved Me, so have I loved you; continue ye in My love. If ye keep My commandments ye shall abide in My love, even as I have kept My Father's commandments and abide in His love … Ye are My friends if ye do whatsoever I command you'.

We have seen that the second giving of the law in Deuteronomy is to remind the people, of precisely who God is. He is the one to whom their primary relation is established. Since God is our primary relationship, we are to live in terms of His character: to walk in terms of God's holiness and love and grace. That is exactly the point of the Ten Commandments: 'Be ye holy for I the Lord am holy' (Lev. 11:45), which is picked up in 1 Peter 1:16: 'Be ye holy for I the Lord am holy'.

To honor God, to respect and help our neighbor, and to be charitable to the poor, is to live our earthly existence in terms of who God is. In other words, love God first and secondly, love your neighbor as yourself. That is how Jesus summarizes the two tables of the law, that were in the holy Ark. LOVE is the basic relationship that is to give the quality and the shape to our life on earth.

In answer to Moses' intercession, God gives the rebels another chance, giving them two benefits: first He spares them from the destruction they deserved, and secondly, something even more, He gives them the undeserved reward of a beautiful homeland. That is surely grace upon grace: 'where sin abounded', as when they worshiped the golden calf, 'grace did much more abound' (Rom. 5:20). It's double grace: sparing from destruction and providing every possible material benefit His people could need in this earthly life.

So the Ten Commandments are to be lived out in the lives of His people, out of sheer gratitude for God's grace upon them. They don't live it out to get the grace; they have already been given it, and it requires them to give everything they are back to the Lord, who so graciously forgives their sin and provides all they need.

Now concerning the depositing of the divinely given law, there seems to be a contradiction in Deuteronomy 10 with what we're told in Exodus 31. In Deuteronomy 10 Moses says, 'God told me to build a box', that is, the Ark; but in Exodus 31 it says that the Ark was built by Bezalel. But careful study will show how there is no contradiction.

First, God told Moses to build a box (the Ark), and He gave him, as it says in Hebrews 8:5, 'the pattern of the tabernacle', including the Ark of the Covenant up there on the mount. When Moses got down to the foot the mountain, God had endowed this very talented craftsman named Bezalel with the Holy Spirit, so that he could do wonderful woodwork and other kinds of marvelous craftsmanship. Then Moses told him how to make the box with its mercy seat, and Bezalel did so, according to the pattern revealed to Moses by God. The Ark was housed in the Holy of Holies in the Tabernacle, and later in the Holy of Holies of the Temple built by Solomon.

Through the long history of the Old Testament, the Ark, containing the two tables of law, was there as a standing reminder to God's people, both of the requirements of God, and of the covenant of grace that had been renewed. God's grace is visibly shown in what was on top of that box: namely, the mercy seat.

Nobody has ever been able completely to carry out the Ten Commandments—to love God above everything else in their life, and to love everybody else as much as you love yourself. But the mercy seat makes provision for our breaking those commandments, so that we will not be put out of the covenant and destroyed. Upon this mercy seat the High Priest of Israel would come once each year, bringing the blood of a sacrificial animal. He sprinkled the blood between the two cherubim, first making atonement for his own sins and then for the sins of the people, coming out of the holy place with the Aaronic benediction to all the people: 'The Lord bless thee and keep thee; the Lord cause His face to shine upon thee; the Lord lift up His countenance upon thee and be gracious unto thee and give thee peace'.

In sum, the mercy seat over the Ten Commandments shows us always to keep these two together: our sins, and the blood of the Lamb. In the Old Testament it was the blood of sacrificial lambs: 'Without the shedding of blood there is no remission of sin' (Heb. 9:22). Ultimately, however, the lambs pointed towards a supreme substitute provided by God—what Revelation 13:8 calls 'The Lamb slain before the foundation of the world'.

The whole world was waiting for this. When Jesus was baptized by John the Baptist at the River Jordan, John said to the people, 'Behold the Lamb of God that taketh away the sins of the world' (John 1:29). The broken covenant was renewed with the covenant of grace, which Hebrews 8:6 says is based upon better promises; that is to say, it is a better covenant than the original one, because the Lord Himself keeps it for us and makes over His covenant-keeping into our lives.

It is not a covenant that is temporary—as in a sense the original Mosaic one was—but everlasting (Heb. 13:20–21). It is an everlasting covenant as it cannot be broken by any of the elect, because Jesus has stood in for us. It is made better by two things.

First, the blood of Christ secures us from all sin, because it is the supreme sacrifice of the infinitely worthy and holy Lamb of God that meets every need and failure of my life perfectly, in a way that the blood of lambs, rams, bulls, and goats could only typify, but not fulfill in and of themselves.

Second, the Holy Spirit, on the basis of the sacrifice of Christ, brings the Ten Commandments from off the table of stone and puts them in our hearts. That's what happens within a Christian.

Some people think that to be a Christian means that you have no relationship to any law (including God's law), but that is not right. Grace does not destroy the law. Jesus says He is not come to destroy the law, but to fulfill it (Matt. 5:17). Grace takes the law out of the box, out of the Book, and by the miraculous renewing power of the Holy Spirit in the new birth and in keeping us Christian, works it inside of us, so that we actually want to do the Ten Commandments. We are divinely motivated towards holy obedience.

A saved person, a born-again person, is not perfect; but he is motivated in a way that an unsaved person could not be, because those not yet saved do not have the Holy Spirit. Jeremiah 31:31–34 speaks of the new covenant, the covenant of grace, the everlasting covenant:

> Behold, the days come, saith the LORD, that I will make a new covenant with the house of Israel, and with the house of Judah: Not according to the covenant that I made with their fathers in the day that I took them by the hand to bring them out of the land of Egypt; which my covenant they brake, although I was an husband unto them, saith the LORD: But this shall be the covenant that I will make with the house of Israel; After those days, saith the LORD, [here's how He gets it out of the box and into me] I will put my law in their inward parts, and write it in their hearts; and will be their God, and they shall be my people. And they shall teach no more every man his neighbour, and every man his brother, saying, Know the LORD: for they shall all know me, from the least of them unto the greatest of them, saith the LORD: for I will forgive their iniquity, and I will remember their sin no more.

On the basis of the merits of Christ, we're forgiven, kept in the holy presence of the Lord, and motivated to do His will by the indwelling Holy Spirit. We do so by virtue of what Colossians 1:27 tells us: 'Christ in you, the hope of glory'. Christ comes inside you, with the motivation to love the Lord and to love people. Galatians 5:22–23 tells of the fruit of the Spirit: a supernatural thing that grows deep inside of you, and is expressed in the way you treat other people and the way you relate to God: namely love, joy, peace and meekness, with patience, self-control and faith: that is how the Ten Commandments are lived out in a constant relationship to God.

A Restored Priesthood (10:6–9)

Deuteronomy 10:6 mentions the death of Aaron, the first High Priest, Moses' brother, and then the continuation of the holy priesthood in his son, Eleazar, and in the Levitical tribe of which Moses and Aaron were a part. This is remarkable—for a good reason; Aaron seemed to have put himself out of the priesthood by his severe disobedience (Deut. 9:20). While Moses was on the mount, Aaron led the people into making an idol, a golden calf, and going into a terrible orgy. But by Moses' intercession God forgave Aaron.

What rich grace of God! God forgives a failed minister, a failed priest. He restores him, and restores the priesthood to his family (Deut. 10:8). It is like Jesus did after Simon Peter denied Him three times: Jesus appears in His resurrection body by the sea, and restores Peter, saying, 'Simon, son of Jonah, lovest thou Me? Feed My sheep; feed My lambs'.

Extending this principle beyond Aaron and Simon Peter, Scripture tells us that every Christian, along with other believers, shares in true priesthood, so that together we are a kingdom of priests. We're able to get through immediately to God and bring others into the presence of God, by praying for them and talking to them and living with them. We would all be put out of the priesthood were it not for the intercession of our great High Priest, Jesus, who is a priest forever after the order of Melchizedek (Heb. 5:6). The Aaronic priests died; somebody had always to replace them, but Jesus lives forever, so that He maintains our priesthood, thereby keeping our influence with God and for others, always valid.

Let us close with this: God is waiting to be gracious unto us through the priesthood of His Son, which He Himself provided. He waits to show us great and mighty things that we know not. He waits to cause grace to abound even more, where sin abounded. But He says, come and ask for it: 'come to the waters', Isaiah 55:1, 'and drink freely and without price'; come and claim My grace, and I will be there to give it to you.

27

A Circumcised Heart

Deuteronomy 10:12–22

The heart of this passage is found in verse 16, about a religious ritual which is central to biblical religion and one of the major aspects of Old Testament godliness—namely, circumcision which was crucial to being a part of Israel, to belonging to God.

What this passage (along with many others) tells us, is the true meaning of circumcision. It shows why it was so important to mark you out as a child of God, as inheriting the grace, the salvation, that is in His divine covenant. And therefore, also shows us that physical circumcision pictured something absolutely essential to true salvation, namely a circumcised heart. That is the essence of what it is to be a believer, to be a child of God.

Let us notice two points in this passage: first what the grace of God requires of us; and the second is what the grace of God provides for us.

What the Grace of God Requires of Us (10:12-13)

We have seen how, in the first half of chapter 10, Moses was rehearsing the glorious grace of God to the children of Israel, in getting them out of Egypt and forgiving them time and again, instead of destroying them. Now they're by the River Jordan, soon to march into a Promised Land that they had forfeited many times by their misbehavior; yet God was gracious to them. Hence, Moses has spent a good bit of time in this chapter (and in the first ten chapters) saying, 'This is how God led you. This is how gracious He has been to you. The fact that you're His people is a gift of His undeserved, unmerited favor or grace.'

Then, in verse 12, there is a very important phrase, 'and now'. It is a transition from history, the story of the grace of God upon Israel, to the giving of a commandment. This is how God dealt with you, saved you by His grace, forgave you by His grace, and now will give you this wonderful country by His grace and therefore, this is how you must behave. Chapters 5–10, and on into chapter 11, are an exposition of the first commandment. Now, we are nearing the end of Moses explaining what the first commandment means in the lives of the people of Israel. In the rest of Deuteronomy he will go through the other Ten Commandments.

These chapters, and particularly this section, says for us to look at how wonderfully God dealt with you in the past, and thereby you will see why you should keep the first commandment. That is the basis of everything God wants out of your life.

The first commandment is put in the negative: 'Thou shalt have no other gods before me'. But here in 10:12-13, Moses puts it into the positive, by way of several verbal forms.

What does the first commandment mean positively, in terms of your daily life? To show us, we are given five infinitives in verses 12-13: to fear, to walk, to love, to serve, to keep. It's very close to Micah 6:8: 'He hath showed thee, O man, what is good; and what doth the Lord require of thee, but to do justly, and to love mercy, and to walk humbly with thy God?' These words, special to me, are written on the outside of Gerard Hall, one of the oldest buildings at the University of North Carolina, Chapel Hill—the University's worship center for a long time. They are, in many ways, a summation of biblical religion, both in its Old and New Testament phases.

The Apostle Paul says this in a slightly different way in Romans 12:1-2. After explaining how we are elected by grace, and saved through the blood of Christ, he adds:

> I beseech you therefore, brethren, by the mercies of God that ye present your bodies a living sacrifice, holy, acceptable unto God, which is your reasonable service. And be not conformed to this world; but be ye transformed by the renewing of your mind, that ye may prove what is that good, and acceptable, and perfect, will of God.

In short, keeping the commandments. Jesus summarized the whole law, when asked what is the first and greatest commandment: 'Thou shalt love the Lord thy God with all thy heart, mind, soul, and strength ... and thy neighbor as thyself'. God put us in the world to love God above all, and our neighbor, next to that. God's grace, or the mercies of God, as Paul says, calls for a consecrated life.

What Grace Provides (10:16-22)

The realization that God requires our heart can disturb us self-centered people; that He requires our deepest motives to be offered up to Him every day, which means to walk, to serve, to love, to keep, walk humbly with God, and therefore, do right to others. It is a very demanding requirement. How could any son or daughter of Adam and Eve offer back to God what His grace requires?

How could you live a consecrated life, even one day or part of a day? Here's how: with a circumcised heart (see verse 16).

It is instructive to realize that the Hebrew, *karath b'rith* (to make a covenant) literally means to 'cut a covenant'. This 'cutting'—particularly after Adam falls, and the Lord's intervention with the promise of the gospel, when He calls Abraham by grace—shows us that God's covenant with us involves our mortal frame. The sign of entrance into that covenant in which God saves us, keeps us, multiplies us, is always, in the Old Testament, circumcision.

Circumcision, at eight days old, was a picture of the new birth, for when the male member was cut round, it shows us that where physical life comes forth in each generation, by means of procreation, the life of another generation is passed down in an orderly fashion by the plan of God, demonstrating a profound spiritual truth. Circumcision, the rite of blood, is saying that where human life is passed down, there has to be a death, for 'the soul that sinneth, it shall die' (Ezek. 18:20). There must be the shedding of blood, for 'without the shedding of blood is no remission of sin' (Heb. 9:22).

In other words, to inherit the faith and to be right with God, it is not enough to be merely physically procreated by our parents; but it takes a certain kind of death and shedding of blood.

The ritual of physical circumcision is done on the male child by someone else. That is a picture of a change in the heart that's done to you by God. God's covenant plan provides a picture of a miraculous action, based on the shedding of blood, done by God Himself on our behalf. It is done by the infinitely powerful Holy Spirit, who comes to change the heart based on what the Son of God in the flesh did in our room and stead. We can regard from that point of view, the final and supreme 'circumcision of Christ,' as His having been slain, when He was pierced for our sins on the cross of Calvary, and then raised to newness of life in the empty tomb.

To be right with God, to be saved, to appropriate His grace, to live in His grace, to have His presence in this world, and to go into His heavenly home that He has prepared for you, you need a new, circumcised heart. Physical circumcision pictures spiritual circumcision, or regeneration by the Holy Spirit.

Jeremiah 31:33 says: 'But this shall be the covenant that I will make with the house of Israel: After those days, saith the Lord, I will put my law in their inward parts, and write it in their hearts; and will be their God, and they shall be my people'. God will send His Holy Spirit to change the heart, so that literally, the law in which Moses says 'walk in it, keep it, love God and love others', can actually take place by the miraculous action in the new birth, by the mysterious power of the Holy Spirit, putting in you a profound desire making you want to be like the Lord who saved you.

I don't think it could realistically be claimed by any honest Christian that they had perfectly walked in the love of God every day, in every way. I most certainly couldn't. In the new birth, while you don't become sinlessly perfect in your own responses while you are on earth, nevertheless, a miracle happens, an otherwise unexplainable re-orientation of motivation. It is a change of heart, following which you really want to please God, to love God—you do love Him—and to love Him more; you want to do good to other people, to do right; and when you don't, you hate it, and want to confess your sin and seek to be more consistent with who you really are in Christ in the new birth Ezekiel speaks of this:

> Then will I sprinkle clean water upon you, and ye shall be clean; from all your filthiness, and from all your idols, will I cleanse you. A new heart also will I give you, and a new spirit will I put within you; and I will take away the stony heart out of your flesh, and I will give you an heart of flesh. And I will put my spirit within you, and cause you to walk in my statutes. And ye shall keep my judgments, and do them (Ezek. 36:25–27).

As Moses requires us 'to walk and to keep the commandments', Ezekiel shows that this is a possibility only when God takes away the heart of stone that we have by inheritance from Adam. That is, we are born selfish, and much prefer to put our own ego first, and others a distant second, and God only, insofar as we think He might be able to help us, maybe a distant third.

But the glorious news is that hardness of spirit, that self-centeredness, is profoundly broken and removed, when the Holy Spirit puts a heart of flesh within us that is tender, that really does love God and wants to love others and be good to them! It is a wonderful miracle, pictured in physical circumcision.

In line with Moses, Jeremiah, and Ezekiel, Jesus speaks of this 'Except a man be born again, he cannot see the kingdom of God … except a man be born again he cannot enter the kingdom of God' (John 3:3, 5). The new birth, by action of the

Holy Spirit of God is stated in a slightly different way: 'if any man be in Christ, he is a new creation. Behold, all things are passed away; all things are become new' (2 Cor. 5:16-17).

I want us to note in the rest of this chapter, particularly from verse 16 onwards, that there are three accompaniments of the new heart: first, godly kindness; second, beauty of character, and third, increase in numbers and influence.

First, godly kindness, particularly described in Deuteronomy 10:18-19. We are told there to love the stranger, to give him food and raiment, (remembering that you were strangers in Egypt). In verse 17, the person of the circumcised heart is told not to regard persons, not to take bribes, but rather to do right. We are never to use somebody's lack of power to run over them: instead, we feed them, help them, and seek to be good to them.

When we are helping the needy, particularly the powerless, we are carrying out what Jesus said in one of His parables, that when we put on a feast and invite others who can invite us back, we really haven't put into practice what Deuteronomy 10 calls 'walking, keeping, and loving'. It's when you invite somebody who can't invite you back, who hasn't got anything by which you could benefit, that you are fulfilling Deuteronomy and the parable of Jesus.

When you love and help the poor and powerless, you're showing what God is like in human life. Jesus speaks of this:

> But I say unto you, Love your enemies, bless them that curse you, do good to them that hate you, and pray for them which despitefully use you, and persecute you; [and here's the bottom line] that ye may be the children of your Father which is in heaven; for he maketh his sun to rise on the evil and on the good, and sendeth rain on the just and on the unjust (Matt. 5:44-45:).

This kind of human kindness demonstrates what a true child of the heavenly Father acts like. And in that way, you show, at least a little bit in your own actions, what God above is really like.

This is a matter of no small importance, as shown when Jesus talks about the last Day, and the great assize: the final assessment of how men and women have lived.

> Then shall the King say unto them on his right hand, Come, ye blessed of my Father, inherit the kingdom prepared for you from the foundation of the world; for I was an hungered, and ye gave me meat; I was thirsty, and ye gave me drink; I was a stranger, and ye took me in; naked, and ye clothed me; I was sick, and ye visited me; I was in prison, and ye came unto me. Then shall the righteous answer him, saying, Lord, when saw we thee an hungered, and fed thee? or thirsty, and gave thee drink? When saw we thee a stranger, and took thee in? or naked, and clothed thee? Or when saw we thee sick, or in prison, and came unto thee? And the King [mighty God on the majestic throne] shall answer and say unto them, Verily I say unto you, inasmuch as ye have done it unto one of the least of these my brethren, ye have done it unto me (Matt. 25:34-40).

You and I cannot do much to change the world, but it is given us to be kind to the needy. It is really a supernatural witness to the world as to who God is, when we show human kindness. I do believe Scripture teaches and the history of the church proves, that basic human kindness and goodness and the mercy shown by Christians to others prepares the way for the preaching of the gospel. That certainly happened in the first century Rome.

We have records to show that in the first and second centuries in Rome, when Christians were being persecuted and in face of all kinds of lies told on them, they continued being kind. They would rescue abandoned babies left under the bridges of the Tiber to be eaten by dogs. Christians would rescue old people put out in the elements so they would die more quickly, and care for them in Christian homes. Many of them were converted. The church was not rich, and yet did a tremendous amount to feed the pagan poor in Rome. People began to realize that the things that were said about the Christians were lies, and they said, 'We have never seen such human goodness; we believe they have something we don't have; maybe this gospel they preach actually has something to it'. It changed public attitudes.

Is it a far stretch to suggest that in the United States, Britain, and Western Europe, the church has lost a great deal of ground as far as people taking seriously its preaching? And that the only way the churches in America and the West are going to begin to regain lost ground and attract attention to the church's message, is to start again profoundly ministering to the needy around us?

If so, history shows that it will not go unnoticed even by secular humanists. Maybe there are already some small signs of this taking place, in a very unobtrusive manner: crisis pregnancy centers doing wonderful work; Christian schools, with scholarships for poor children; soup kitchens; and many free medical clinics. A growing number of Christian people in this country and Britain are doing acts of kindness that are never recorded in the papers. But we still have a long way to go.

Most of us couldn't do anything dramatic, like giving two or three million for the causes of the needy. But we can do a little, and this is a way of keeping the first commandment positively. Often in the good timing of the Lord, such humble acts of kindness really do open the door for the proclamation of the gospel, and fulfilling Jesus'
summary of the law, love God first and your neighbor as yourself. Godly kindness, in small ways as well as large ways, results from a new heart, from circumcision of the heart, from new birth by the Holy Spirit.

Secondly, beauty of character is another accompaniment of the new birth, or of a circumcised heart. The person's character becomes much more beautiful. The last clause of Deuteronomy 10:13, 'which I command thee this day for thy good', means you could do far more good for yourself and do more to become a beautiful person, by putting God first and others ahead of self, than any other thing.

Putting God first, and thinking of others, has a way of displacing our natural self-centeredness and inborn selfishness. But with a circumcised heart, we walk and serve in love. It blesses others around us and gives us true nobility of spirit. Not many of you will remember William Bennett, who wrote *The Book of Virtues*. He had been on President Reagan's cabinet, and said about the generality of prosperous folk in America, that 'we live well', *i.e.* we live prosperously; but 'we no longer live nobly'.

The English word 'snob' comes from a shortening of a Latin term, *sine nobilitate* (without nobility). A 'snob' is a person who is thinking of self, and wishes to impress and get ahead at all costs, is not concerned for the welfare of those whom he or she wishes to displace or impress. So *sine nobilitate* means 'self, self, self', whereas nobility of spirit means 'God and others' and thinking of what you can do for them.

Cardinal John Henry Newman, talking in the nineteenth century about the basic characteristic of an English gentleman, said that a gentleman—and this is true of a lady—deeply wishes to keep from giving undue pain to any other person. Now that is nobility of spirit.

Deuteronomy 10:21 shows that living for God—Him first and then others' next, practically thinking of them—actually brings God's beautiful praises down upon us. What an amazing thing, in verse 21: 'He is thy praise'! While some commentators say that this expression means that 'you praise God,' I believe that rendering misses the meaning. Of course, we are told to *'praise ye the Lord'* (Psalm 150, and elsewhere), but this verse is saying, *'God is your praise'*, i.e., the praises of God, that which makes Him splendid, noble and beautiful, and pure, uplifted and wonderful, comes down into the character, and into the face and life of somebody who is living for God and others: God is your praise; and beauty. 'Let the beauty of the Lord our God be upon us, and the works of our hands establish thou them' (Ps. 90:17). The very beauty of God comes down upon His people. We see something of this in Proverbs 31, describing the virtuous wife, who is praised by all her family and by the whole community, because of her helpful life. Notice verses 25–31:

> Strength and honor are her clothing and she shall rejoice in time to come. She openeth her mouth with wisdom and in her tongue is the law of kindness. She looketh well to the ways of her household and eateth not the bread of idleness. Her children arise up and call her blessed; her husband also, and he praiseth her. Many daughters have done virtuously, but thou excellest them all. Favor is deceitful; beauty is vain; but a woman that feareth the Lord, she shall be praised.

God's praises and moral beauty have come down within her and upon her. 'Give her of the fruit of her hands and let her own works praise her in the gates'.

We find yet another illustration in Acts 16:25–30, when Paul and Silas were in the Philippian jail. An earthquake—a miracle—occurred; the chains fell from around their ankles. When the jailor realized that the prisoners could escape—knowing that it was his life for their life—he pulled out his sword to commit suicide, a better fate than the torture he would have undergone for letting prisoners escape.

But Paul and Silas say: 'Do thyself no harm', we're not leaving. The moment the jailor saw their nobility of spirit, that they were concerned about what happened to him and didn't want him to commit suicide, he was broken apart in his spirit, and cried out, 'Sirs, what must I do to be saved?' I want to be like you; what would it take? They answered, 'Believe on the Lord Jesus Christ and thou shalt be saved'.

The third fruit of a circumcised heart is increase in numbers and influence in the society where you live. A reference, according to many older Christian writers, is found in the Song of Solomon 5:16, where it says that 'He is altogether lovely'. Some Church Fathers and some seventeenth-century Puritans believed that 'the beloved' of the Song was speaking ahead of time of our Redeemer. (Not all interpreters agree on this!) Regardless of who 'the beloved' is, all are agreed that the daughters of Jerusalem say in 6:1: 'Tell us where he is! We want him too!' That indicates that there is something about being taken up with the beauty of the Lord, so that some of that beauty comes down upon you (probably when you are least aware of it). Others then say 'Take us where you got it!'

Even when the children of Israel came out of Egypt, we are told that 'a mixed multitude followed them'; that is, a host of Egyptians. Why? Because for all the slavery and oppression that God's people had been subjected to, they saw the blessing of God—the covenant working within them—and the miracles that the Lord was doing, and so they said, 'Let's join ourselves to the Israelites; we would like to have that blessing! Let's go with them and risk everything.'

Billy Graham used to say that you can argue against the doctrines of Christianity, and many do; but pagans simply cannot argue against a changed life. In 1949–1952, during the revival on the Isle of Lewis, an island off the Hebridean coast of Scotland, a woman of church background, but not yet a true believer, had been dragged to a prayer meeting. Though they had services in the church, they would go to the homes of people, and pray half the night or more. She says this:

> We emerged from the room and were ushered outside to Christians who shook our hands. They were so thrilled, so happy; they beamed with joy. The more they shook our hands the more miserable and convicted I felt. They assumed that I was part of the happy throng that had come to the Lord Jesus, but I was as miserable as sin. I did not belong here and felt like a fish out of water. The more they rejoiced, the sadder I became. They stood outside the house and sang; it was two in the morning and the singing was simply out of this world. I had never heard anything like it. Opposite me in the large circle of rejoicing Christians, a young girl sang with the rest. The light of God was on her face and I saw there something that I had never seen before. I knew she had something that I did not have, and I would never be at peace until I found it.

What really got her to go over the line was to see the light of God, the joy of God, the praises of God, upon His people; for her, it changed everything. As far as I know, none of us is up to this point living in scenes of real revival (though it may come, in the timing of God). But why don't we take the prayer of Moses in Psalm 90: 'Let the beauty of the Lord our God be upon us, and establish Thou the works of our hands upon us'; that others may be drawn in and know what it is to have a circumcised heart.

28

THE BLESSINGS AND CURSINGS OF GRACE
Deuteronomy 11

This substantial passage plainly sets before us the blessings and the cursings of the covenant of grace. Normally we think of 'grace' as blessing and kindness, goodness and sovereign mercy. Yet there is a dark side to it, on account of human sin that also involves cursing to those who finally reject the grace that is proffered to them.

In other words, this passage shows us something important. God's grace does not leave us without a choice to make. Grace provides us wonderful blessings that we do not deserve; but it also holds us accountable. There is blessing when we give our hearts to the God of grace; there is cursing when we only conform externally and keep our hearts for ourselves or for another god.

The accountability is demonstrated graphically in this scene that they would soon enact across the river Jordan, in 11:29-32; and also in Deuteronomy 27:14-26, where we hear the blessings on Mt. Gerizim and the cursings on Mt. Ebal.

The cursings and the blessings come from the same source, namely a holy God, who is ever gracious God. In Deuteronomy 27 we are told that six of the tribes of Israel were to stand on Mt. Gerizim, the mount of blessing, and the other six on Mt. Ebal, the mount of cursing. People who know the geography of that country tell us that it is like a natural amphitheater between Gerizim and Ebal. The deep hollow valley between them forms the most wonderful acoustics in an open-air auditorium—apparently like being in La Scala in Milan.

In this 'auditorium' the Levites would read the law of God, the Ten Commandments, including the blessings attached to obedience, and the people standing on the mountain of blessing, would say 'Amen, Amen!' Then they would read the warnings of the covenant, describing the curses if you turn your back on God. Then the people standing on the mountain of cursing would say 'Amen, Amen!'

It was a graphic lesson, heard by well over a million people. It is a ceremony that renews the covenant. God is saying, you're going into a new experience—leaving the wilderness, going into a permanent country—and your life is to be based on who I am, on My revealed law. It loudly states that there is tremendous grace as you live in terms of these holy words. But there's also frightful cursing for trampling underfoot this divine grace.

Let us notice four main points in this chapter: first, the splendor of God's grace; the second point brings out the generosity of God's promises;

the third, the seriousness of God's warnings; and fourth, the right response of God's people.

THE SPLENDOR OF GOD'S GRACE (11:1-2)

In the first two verses of chapter 11, the people are reminded yet again how of all God had done for them and now are about to enter the beautiful country He's giving them. And all of this they didn't earn by their good works or personal merits. Every bit of it was the gift of God's splendid grace, although that did not remove the necessity of their response to such grace.

How beautifully His grace was shining at the Red Sea, in the spreading of the blood and the sparing of the lives of the first born; and how beautifully that splendid grace was shining in the fiery, cloudy pillar over the tabernacle, and how wondrously God wanted His grace to shine as they would march into the Promised Land; and soon the walls of Jericho would come tumbling down!

Such munificent grace was a clarion call to live holy lives, as a proper response to the splendor of God's grace! It was founded in grace, because they did not deserve it. It was because of who God is that He did these things for them. That's what it meant to be an Israelite, by grace, not by merit:

> The Lord did not set His love upon you, nor choose you, because ye were more in number than any people; for ye were the fewest of all people. But because the Lord loved you, and because He would keep the oath which He had sworn unto your fathers, hath the Lord brought you out with a mighty hand, and redeemed you out of the house of bondmen, from the land of Pharaoh, king of Egypt (Deut. 7:7-8).

In other words, because of who God is, our lives are to be lived as a response to the divine grace. That grace-based life was to be true in Israel, and later in the Christian church. The New Testament constantly shows that we believers are not in the church because we're more wonderful than others outside, we are there only because of God's grace. Ephesians 2 has to be taken into account with Deuteronomy 11. When Paul says, 'You hath he quickened, you hath he made alive, who were dead in trespasses and sins', he is referring to us, the Gentiles. Ephesians 2 goes on to say: 'in the time past you lived according to the world', [under the devil; controlled by the lust of the flesh], but God who is rich in mercy, for his great love wherewith he loved us, even when we were dead in sins, hath quickened us together with Christ; by grace are ye saved—and raised us up together'.

Surely, we see here in Ephesians 2 (as well as in Deuteronomy 11), that we are included in the people of God now, not because we were any better or more worthy than anybody else; it's the sheer grace of God that He reached down and formed a church and began raising people from a dead relationship with Adam to a living relationship to the Lord. The splendor and beauty of God's grace is spoken of here in Ephesians 2 as raising us with the same power that raised up Christ's resurrection body; and one day, at the appointed time, the resurrection bodies will be absolutely surpassingly splendid.

THE GENEROSITY OF GOD'S PROMISES (11:13-15, AND 22-25)

Here, God's generous promises extend in three directions: to the people, to the land, and to the political, military situation.

First, to the people: in verse 9, they are told that they could prolong their days in a relatively happy and wholesome place. Verse 21 speaks of multigenerational blessing: fathers, mothers, children, grandchildren, and great-grandchildren, experiencing what the text calls 'the days of heaven upon earth'. It's never perfect in this world, of course, for we live in a fallen world, but you can have real joy and tremendous blessing—something like reflecting the days of heaven upon earth—in your families and in your homes and lives. As a general rule though, at times His mysterious providence dictates otherwise,

Then there's a promise to the land, in verses 10-12, in contrast to Egypt. For instance, in Egypt, one had to irrigate. I remember in school learning about the shaduf, an amazing contraption that would lift water into the fields when the Nile would overflow. It was generally successful, but took hard work, requiring lots of slaves and manpower.

But unlike that, Israel would be a green and pleasant land of hills, where the Lord gave rain without human labor. Thus it was a land flowing with milk and honey. Those of you who have visited the Holy Land may wonder about this description. But Israel has changed; it is a much dryer climate than it was 3500 years ago when it had a marvelous climate. God's eyes are upon this land all the year, like a mother with a new baby. You may remember the gospel song, 'His eye is on the sparrow, and I know He watches me.' And another one:

> He makes the rose an object of His care;
> He guides the eagle through the pathless air;
> and surely He
> will remember me,
> My heavenly Father watches over me.

In addition to promises to the people and to the land, God gives through Moses some general promises regarding international, political, and military situations. When I was a child in the American South (in the 1940s-1960s) I heard many church people say that we must not connect our religion to politics and military matters. Probably the desire to keep religion inside the doors of the church was because we did not want to see what God was requiring of us in racial matters. But God is the God of everything. Nothing is excluded from a relationship to God or God's control, including tribes, races, armies, navies, air forces; technological developments; motivations of generals, presidents, and dictators; 'The heart of the king is in the hand of the Lord; He turns it withersoever he wills like as the rivers of water' (Prov. 21:1).

While I do not believe that any modern state stands in the same relationship to God, as did Old Testament Israel, it is probably the case that where there is a large church population in a modern country, it will usually affect the standing of the country, possibly including military matters. There is reason to believe from history that in many cases, God handles the enemies of countries which have multitudes in them whose hearts are right with Him. But its outworking in the modern age is a complicated matter that one cannot trace out too far, and is never removed from the mysteries of providence.

But one still can think of instances of this protection of populations. I mean not just the infallible promise given to the church that 'the gates of hell shall not prevail against it', which has no exceptions, but of regions that have historically been, to some real degree, Christian. That is, the divine protection is given to the church, not to any one country since the New Testament. Yet we may, at times, perceive examples of that protection even outside the church, in countries or regions where the church is strong. One thinks of a remark made by Stalin in the late 1930s, when the Pope was highly critical of his atrocities, such as brutally murdering multitudes of Ukraine farmers. Stalin was, not surprisingly, very angry and responded: 'How many battalions does the Pope have?' What was he saying? 'The church is nothing; they don't have an army. Who do they think they are to criticize me?'

Some 50 years later, after Stalin, his empire and USSR Communism had collapsed. But the church he despised as having no battalions, whether Protestant, Catholic, or Eastern Orthodox, did not collapse. This, I suggest, is not far from the principle of Deuteronomy 11. Think of the hymn:

> O where are kings and empires now, of old that went and came?
> But Lord, Thy church is praying yet, a thousand years the same.

And so God says, I'm making promises for Israel concerning their surrounding enemies: 'If you will put Me first, I'll take care of all your enemies. If you don't, you're not going to enjoy what I will let come on you'. So this second point includes three generous promises in this gracious covenant, as we have just seen.

The Seriousness of God's Warnings (11:6-17, and 26-29)

As well as the blessings of grace, the same passage speaks of the curses of the covenant of grace. That is something we must face. In Deuteronomy 11:6, a terrible experience is mentioned about two men who rebelled against the express command of God, Dothan and Abiram (or Abihu). For their disobedience to the covenant words, Moses told the people to draw back from these men and their tents; then God literally caused the earth to open and swallow them up in their tents and everything they had—a painful illustration of not taking seriously God's warnings.

It may seem harsh to us, but it was to show us that the essence of sin is personal rejection of God. If one makes a decision, 'I will not have this man reign over me,' one is engaging in a knowing rejection of His authority over my life. 'I'm going to live for myself; I'm going to live on my own.' To reject God, which some do who have been massively privileged, is to lose everything.

Verse 17 says that idolatry—turning your back on God and following something less than God as an integrating point of your life—will cut off the rain and cause the fruits of the earth to dry up. I have been looking at this a little bit, and it seems to me that God's moral judgments against a country often start in the realm of agriculture. If He is sounding a trumpet warning for the need of repentance, he usually starts by cursing agriculture, the basis of the whole economy. After agriculture is cursed, the general economy goes into decline. Verse 28 implies that other kinds of curses will follow. While God's grace is marvelous and great, His warnings are very serious indeed.

IV. The Right Response of the People of God (11:18-21, and 32)

What should the people do? First, learn the law, that is, learn God's will; second, do God's will, and third, be sure you are in the remnant.

First, verse 18 says that we are to learn God's law by spending time learning Scripture, and giving it first place in our home. Verse 19, as translated in the Septuagint, essentially states: 'have your children memorize holy Scripture.'

Although no educationalist by formal training, I am aware that there are times in children's lives when they can maintain in their young minds massive amounts of sounds and pictures and words. During those years, it is relatively easy for them to memorize, and so they should be taking in a great deal of Scripture, (or in our Presbyterian setting the Westminster Shorter Catechism). In my office at the seminary in Charlotte, I've got more than one diploma from the old *Christian Observer*, showing that one of my great aunts, myself and some others memorized, and recited at one sitting, the questions of the Westminster Shorter Catechism. What a wonderful heritage to take with you all the rest of your life!

Secondly, do things God's way. 'Be ye doers of the word and not hearers only, deceiving your own selves' (James 1:22). There's no worse kind of deception, than to know and not do! We see it in highly educated ministers who have a moral failing, and lose their reputation and ministry. It is a dreadful matter to be a hearer of the Word, and not a doer. It is always easier to tell others to do it, than to do it ourselves—a potential danger for any true ministry. That problem did not stop with the Pharisees of Jesus' time!

Moses is saying to the children of Israel: 'If you are going to go in my will, so that grace proves to be a blessing in your life here below, then you've got to keep this law.' And the law is essentially the covenant, your relationship to God. As we have seen, Deuteronomy 11, (which concludes chapters 6-11) is all about the exposition of the first commandment, 'Thou shalt have no other gods before me'. For that to be true through the generations to come, for this grace to continue in your children, they need to see you putting God first; to be in a real heart relationship with God, for all this to take place in your life, and then in that of your children.

When you are in this heart relationship to God, you will be a doer of the Word, and not a hearer only. But just to go along with the externals, and never let them impact my life, will lead to the most horrendous curse. So, Moses warns that, if the Israelites do not instruct their children and set a good example; if they finally give in to the temptations of the world, the flesh, and the devil, and wind up turning away from God to follow idols, they would be thrown out of the land. But if they love the Lord their God with all their heart, mind, soul, and strength, as summarized in 11:32, if they put God first, then they would be secure in that land and tremendous blessings would follow them.

We must see what happened six or seven hundred years after Moses, after Joshua had led the people into this beautiful Promised Land. The vast majority gave themselves over to idolatry; they were perhaps hearers of the Word but not doers; their hearts were hardened; they did not have circumcised hearts. They lost nearly all the external blessings of the covenant of grace. Thus, in accordance with the warnings of Deuteronomy, they were taken away from this wonderful Promised Land.

God had given them many opportunities. God is very patient. It took Him about 700 years before the axe fell, constantly sending the prophets to call them to return to Him. And yet I want to conclude with this: even at the worst, when the vast majority of Israel turned out to be apostate, to have hardened hearts, and were deported to Babylon for 70 years, still God kept a remnant among them.

Ezekiel 11:16 says to the remnant, 'I will be unto you a little sanctuary in the countries where they shall come.' No matter how bad it gets, the Jerusalem temple is torn down and you lose your country—if the church gets rotten and apostate, so that God has to judge it—still those who put me first, will find that I will be a little sanctuary to them. When the great majority is under judgment, and loses the blessings of God's good providence, the remnant do not lose grace itself! God will preserve them to something better.

And others in the corrupt mass will be blessed through them.

Paul talks about that in Romans 9:27, 'Isaiah also cries concerning Israel, though the number of the children of Israel be as the sand of the sea, a remnant shall be saved.' Huge numbers would be judged as hard-hearted, not circumcised in heart, no new heart, no love of God, so that they had to be judged with the world. But a remnant would be saved, a certain number of elect that really did love God. Paul goes on to say (regarding God's grace upon Israel and His future plans for the Jews): 'Even so at this present time also there is a remnant according to the election of grace' (Rom. 11:5).

There is mystery here, beyond human explanation. But let us grasp that the most important thing in our life is for us to know that we are in the remnant of grace. That is to say, we humans can't look into the predestinated purposes of God. But we can look to the promises of grace. And God says, 'Whosoever believeth in Me shall not perish, but have everlasting life'. We can look to Christ on the cross, dying for sinners, and say, 'Lord, I am certainly a sinner, but from what your Word says, that qualifies me to come to the cross. So I wish Your blood to be applied to my sins and to my life. Change me, circumcise my heart by Your supernatural power. Or, in terms of Jeremiah 31:33, put a new Spirit within me, so You will be first; You will be my God in such a way that nothing would ever come ahead of You.'

To say that, and to mean it, indicates that we are in the remnant. I can't tell you secrets of God's election; that's not my business. But I will tell you this: the remnant is where you want to be, no matter what happens externally in any country. You can be there, by being face to face with Christ, heart to heart with God, saying, 'Lord, I will have You first. Remove anything in me that would keep You from being first.' That is to be in the remnant according to the election of grace. May God have us all there, all our life, and then what follows our life will be nothing but glory.

29

The Second Commandment

Deuteronomy 12:1–11

This chapter in Deuteronomy is an exposition of the second commandment, 'Thou shalt not make unto thee any graven image, or bow down to it'. To put it positively, this is a commandment about purity in our worship of God.

There have been times in church history, when worship (or liturgy) and church architecture and furnishings have constituted major points of discussion, and at times, controversy, or even wars (as in the 1630s in Scotland and then in England). When the sixteenth-century Protestant Reformers rediscovered the gospel of salvation by the grace of God through faith in Christ, millions of people began thinking of how such a God of grace could be rightly worshipped. The story of this would require several volumes, but here I only make the point that when people see more clearly who God is, they are possessed by a new and driving concern to worship Him as He would have them do. Equally good Christians come out with rather different readings of what the Lord requires, but all true believers do wish to get it right. A careful reading of Christian leadership across the ages will indicate that as they sought to formulate the worship of God properly, many of them turned to Deuteronomy chapter 12.

It is plain from history that as they sought to work out the proper worship God required in His written Word, there were considerable divisions among many Protestants, from the sixteenth century down to the twenty-first. Again, there is massive research, but I cannot explore that important issue. Instead, let us ask, why were the people who rediscovered the gospel so concerned to make changes in the church, at all costs, so that God could be rightly worshiped?

It is because God is the most important factor in the universe. If you ask somebody what's important, maybe it would be their health or their family life, or how their children are; whether they have a decent job or enough income to survive. Those things are indeed important, for God cares about those things and commands His people to help others materially (as we see in Matthew 25).

Yet it is hard for us to remember in a materialistic age, that the most important reality we ever face is who God is. Who God is determines everything else that will happen to us. And since God is God, and we are humans, the most crucial activity in which we ever participate is worship of God. Therefore, nothing matters so much as how we worship God. That is why the Reformers and the Puritans, among others, wanted to do the best they could to study Holy Scripture in order to see how God requires to be worshiped. Deuteronomy 12 was one of the central texts that they looked to, to see how we—even after a thousand years of the Medieval heritage—could get worship just right.

I think many scholars are correct in noting that the Calvinist reformers in particular went back to the Jewish synagogue, and saw how simple and pure was the worship, without any accretions, pictures, and statues: just basically, the word and prayer, singing and offerings. They wanted to do the best they could to come and meet the Lord, by worshiping Him in the way they thought He had prescribed in Holy Scripture, based on the first commandment, 'no other gods before me', and the second commandment, 'no graven image'.

There are two points in these eleven verses that I want to look at: first, Moses is preaching to the children of Israel just before Joshua leads them over the Jordan into the Promised Land; God, through Moses, is getting them ready to order their lives in a way that will be God-honoring, so they can enjoy the blessings of that land, and be preserved in it, by putting God first, and getting rid of any graven image that the pagans have.

To that end, they are told to do two basic things: first, clean out the false worship of the land of Canaan; and secondly, set up true worship of the great Jehovah God. The Reformers of the 16th and 17th centuries felt they were doing just that in their own generation. It is doubtful that they always got everything right, but at least you could say that their hearts were in the right place.

Clean out False Worship (12:1–3)
These first three verses show us what it means, practically, for Israel to carry out the second commandment of not allowing graven images and not bowing down to man-made idols. Deuteronomy explicates the Ten Commandments in Exodus 20 in very practical day-to-day terms that anybody can understand. But it's not only a question of whether we understand it, but also of whether we choose to obey it with all our hearts.

Hence, in these verses, the children of Israel—and all of God's people since that time—are told to clean out all polytheism and get rid of all false worship that is concocted from the human religious spirit. By the way, just because something is religious doesn't mean it's right. In this world, there is true religion and false religion, and it is clear that God wants us only to walk in true religion.

What does that mean? It means going by Holy Scripture. It never ceases to be a task for every generation to clean out idols and to destroy false worship. Why is it so hard? Why do you have to keep coming back to it? I think the reason is given to us by John Calvin. He often said that the mind of fallen man is a perpetual 'factory of idols.' In other words, part of the fall—in which we all descended from fallen Adam and Eve—is that we like to create our own gods. Contrary to that self-worshiping spirit, the Bible says that we are created in the image of God, and therefore, He is original; He has priority and primacy. But the devil perverted us when we fell, so that there is a tendency in the pagan spirit to want to create God in our image, so we can then control Him, and become more comfortable with our idol. That is the reason why fallen people, even very cultured and very educated ones, tend to come up with idols of their own imagination, with which to replace the true God of Holy Scripture.

That may be the greatest task the church has to face every generation: breaking down idols and setting up true worship. Hence God said through Moses to the children of Israel, when you get across the Jordan you're going to find the loathsome products of an idol factory made by pagan Canaanite religion. They will be everywhere you turn, on all the high hills, under many a green tree; you're going to find remnants of pagan worship, and with them, all kinds of false ideas about who these different gods are. They will be competing for your loyalty.

Therefore, the first thing I want you to do, says the Lord, is to take an axe and a torch; and chop down those false places of worship and burn them up. True religion, true salvation, can never co-exist with idolatry and with false imaginations about who God may be; we are required to clean them out and destroy them utterly. Verses 2 and 3 mention four different things to be done by true worshipers of the Lord: deal firmly with all places under green trees, on high hills; overthrow all altars of false gods and graven images, tear down groves—those were groves of trees, and sometimes involved wooden statues that had been carved out and were set up, sort of like totem poles.

Moreover, the Canaanite religion, like that in many other parts of the world, had corrupt sexual orgies in those groves; it was a fertility religion with no holds barred, resulting in fertility for animals, crops and people for another year. But God says that is absolutely false; sexual corruption in the name of worship is an abomination in My nostrils. Hence take your hatchets and axes and chop down those phallic symbols, those totem poles, and put the torch to them; purify the land.

In the story of Gideon, in the book of Judges, this chopping down was one of the things that Gideon needed to do, before the Holy Spirit would anoint him to conquer the Midianites in the name of God. The Midianites were able to oppress the children of Israel for so long, because Israel had corrupted the worship of God, and had taken idols into their own homes. Gideon's father was an important man, and he had one of those pagan groves outside his house. So, even before God the Holy Spirit called Gideon to come and be anointed, the first thing he had to do was chop down that grove by his father's house. He did it at night to avoid being killed for destroying a place of pagan worship. He was, in his own way, following Deuteronomy 12:1–3; he cleaned out the grove, and then God endowed him with the blessing.

Also, we are told in verse 3 to destroy the names of these false gods. The name represents the character of God and the presence of God. In a certain sense these false gods of idol worship have behind them a certain reality. There's only one real God of course, the Creator of heaven and earth. But there are evil spirits who would often enter those idols, and into those horrendous worship services. Thus, God says, do not take their names on your lips.

That would be why some people criticized the apostles in places where the Holy Spirit was working, and people were getting saved. It worried people because one of the first things that happens when you're saved and you meet the Lord, is that you realize you need to purify your life and stop doing some things you used to do, so that you may instead consecrate yourself, your family, your household, and your thinking to God, as we see in Romans 12:1–2.

That sort of thing happened at Ephesus, where they brought a tremendous number of books with magic formulae and blessings and curses in the names of false pagan gods. The new converts to Christ brought a whole library to the apostles, and what did they do with this library of phony, pagan, religious antiquity? They burned them up, because they did not want the names of these demons, these false gods, taken on their lips.

It is clear why it so important to get rid of pagan ways of worship, and to get rid of calling on idols, and the evil spirits that sometimes lurk behind idols. The reason being that false worship, idolatry, and occult practices give Satan an entrance to your body and to your soul, and can pervert and destroy you. Therefore, God says to flee this kind of thing like the plague.

Now let me apply this briefly: this is one of the reasons why a Christian should never set foot at a fortuneteller's place. You might say, 'well, aren't fortunetellers fakes?' Some of them no doubt are, maybe most of them are, but there is such a thing as what the Bible calls 'a familiar spirit', an evil spirit that can tell people who are demon possessed certain things that will happen in the future; I would not deny that this could be the case with some unhappy people. And so, if in determining what's going to happen to your life in the future, you say, 'Let's go to Madame So-and-so; she will tell us,' then what you're doing is giving the powers of evil an entrance into your life to bring corruption, and possibly disaster into your present, and into your future.

Therefore, all of that kind of occult practice is absolutely ruled out by the second commandment. We live our life in purity, as best we can, before the presence of our gracious God. Yet many people have said, 'Isn't this being narrow minded? Isn't this being very radical to say you should have nothing to with these kinds of false worship, because after, all these people are sincere and have some interesting ideas'.

I reply: Scripture teaches us that there's nothing wrong with being radical when it's a question of rooting out soul-destroying sin. To be gentle with falsehood, and to compromise with idolatry, is sin in the eyes of a holy God. The prophet Jeremiah says more than one time that this is what happens to people who follow false gods or demons, or their own silly ideas. Jeremiah said 'they followed vanities and became vain'; 'vanity' is an old English word that means 'empty' (the Hebrew word is 'breath'). They followed idols and false religion, which finally are empty of good spiritual reality and they became empty, like the empty things that they followed. To have traffic with false religion, with idolatry, and with impure worship is to pollute our own spirits, and to give the evil kingdom power over us and inside of us, to rule in our lives and make us vain or empty, and ultimately set apart for final separation from God.

History shows us that something powerful happens where Christianity starts going forward in strength. Recently, I was talking with David, a fine African Christian scholar from Kenya; he was the moderator of the Presbyterian church of Kenya. It has twice as many members as all the Presbyterians in the United States put together. Great growth to a very large size has also marked the Anglican church in Kenya. By the way, these African churches are made up of conservative Bible believers; they haven't gone liberal like so many in the Episcopal and the Presbyterian Churches in the USA; they fully accept the reality of the supernatural, unlike many churchgoers in Europe and America. David, noted that as Bible-believing Christianity spread in Kenya and Uganda and other parts of Africa, it was always accompanied by a tremendous decline of demonism. Witch doctors are denuded of their power; idols are chopped down as people don't participate in idol worship.

One thing that seems to happen is this: when these groves, high places, idols and places of evil pagan worship are destroyed, Satan loses a beachhead, and when they put witches and fortune tellers and such to flight, some of them actually get converted, for the devil doesn't have a contact point to control the population the way he once did.

Therefore, God wants Israel to cross the river and have a country that is based on pure worship, so that the presence of God in its beauty and goodness and peace may prevail, and the people not be oppressed by evil spirits that will separate them from the Lord, and send them into perdition. That's the first major point of Deuteronomy 12:1-3—to clean out the land of false, idolatrous worship.

SET UP TRUE WORSHIP (12:4-11)

Moses tells us here that God will eventually appoint only one place of true worship. He doesn't tell them where it is right now, but it will be one central sanctuary that they would come to for all the festivals—where the holy tabernacle with the mercy seat and the sacrificial system would be set up. It would be 400 or more years before God guided David to choose the central shrine of worship on the hill of Zion in Jerusalem. It is significant that the Lamb of God, slain from the foundation of the world, would be slain very near that central point of worship.

Where did they worship before the time of David? They set up the tabernacle, with the mercy seat, in a place called Shiloh. That would be the one place of true worship until the tabernacle was moved to Jerusalem.

Why only one place of worship for Israel is not hard to figure. Because there is only one true God, therefore, there is only one place of worship. God's Word specifies who He is and how He is to be worshiped, and so we do not have the authority to negotiate away His prescribed way of worship. There's only one way to worship the one God. In Jewish times, it was the sacrificial system with the mercy seat, which pointed to who Jesus Christ is. That was and is the true way to meet God.

Any other way, though you might get temporary peace and people speak well of you politically, you will lose your soul and the country will be destroyed. Mark my words: only one God, only one way of worship, only one way of eternal salvation. We have seen earlier that the tabernacle is pointing to the human nature of Christ and all that He accomplished in his incarnation, in His suffering on Calvary, and in His death and glorious resurrection. That is God's ordained way that we may approach Him.

This is made plain in Hebrews 10:14-20, speaking of the New Covenant:

> For by one offering He, that is Christ, hath perfected forever them that are sanctified. Whereof the Holy Ghost also is a witness to us, for after that he said before, 'This is the covenant that I will make with them [Jeremiah 31:33] after those days, saith the Lord, I will put my laws into their hearts, and in their minds will I write them; and their sins and iniquities will I remember no more. Now where remission of these is, there is no more offering for sin'. Having therefore, brethren, boldness to enter into the holiest by the blood of Jesus, by a new and living way, which He hath consecrated for us, through the veil—that is to say, His flesh.

The 'veil' is the tabernacle; that was His flesh; all of that is the way that Jesus gets us to God.

In John 4:19-26 we can see a change that will come in worship. The woman at the well says, 'We Samaritans worship God on Mount Gerizim, and the Jews worship God at Jerusalem. Which one is right?' Jesus clearly says that salvation is of the Jews; the Jews are right, as far as it goes. But with Jesus coming in the flesh, and soon to offer up His life as a sacrifice, to be raised and seated on the throne of glory, and to send down His Holy Spirit into the world, there would be a tremendous change in the place of worship—no longer centered at Jerusalem. It would be anywhere in the world, as Jesus explains to the Samaritan woman.

> But the hour cometh, and now is, when the true worshipers shall worship the Father in Spirit and in truth, for the Father seeketh such to worship Him. God is a Spirit; and they that worship Him must worship Him in spirit and in truth.

Worship God anywhere, in the name of Jesus, and you have immediate access to God Himself in heaven, and to all the intended blessings of God, if you are coming sincerely in the name and in the merits of our Lord Jesus Christ.

Regarding the fairly radical restructuring of worship that took place in the sixteenth-century Protestant Reformation, a great deal of ritual and ceremony was simplified, in hopes of making the gospel teaching clearer. When I was a student at Union Theological Seminary in Richmond, Virginia, we often had distinguished speakers. One of the ones I liked the best was a Russian Orthodox priest and theologian, Father Alexander Schmeman, who gave a series of lectures on Christian worship.

He remarked that years ago he had gone into Presbyterian churches and had been shocked at their barrenness, plainness and simplicity. They didn't have the beautiful pictures and the incense and the gorgeous ritual in their services that he was used to in the Eastern Orthodox churches. He thought: 'Why in the world would anybody worship God in that plain, barren way?' Later he raised this question to a friend, who was in the Reformed tradition, who replied: 'We don't have all these gorgeous rituals and pictures, for we don't feel that the second commandment allows it. But he added a second reason: namely, God is so beautiful, that we don't want to put any man-made thing, or any humanly concocted ritual, that would obscure the beauty of God. All these complicated images and rituals can take people's eyes and hearts away from the Lord, who is so very beautiful.'

Well, I hope that is why—at least at their best—the Reformed churches have sought to keep it plain, so that this beautiful God may come to us in His Word and in His Spirit and in the sacrament. Father Schmemann then said that after that, he came to appreciate the simplicity of the Protestants in their way of worshiping God as they believed God had told them to do, in Spirit and in truth.

God help us to hear it; God help us to get a fresh vision of His beauty and to be motivated by His Spirit to worship Him the way that He deserves; and everything in our lives will be moving in a right direction.

30

Practical Help in Old Testament Worship

Deuteronomy 12:12–32

In these twenty-one verses, we have practical helps in Old Testament worship, and it certainly has some application to New Testament worship in its own way. There's a hymn that we sometimes sing,

> There's a wideness in God's mercy like the wideness of the sea;
> there's a kindness in His justice which is more than liberty.

This chapter, you will see, is about the wideness of God's mercy in the rather strict requirements that He gives on pure worship. Even in that strictness, God considers our humanity, and is kind and tender to us. In light of the first two commandments (and this section in Deuteronomy is expounding the second commandments, 'no graven image', and what it will mean in the Promised Land) the divine purity required in true worship is very demanding on us. Yet these verses show that since God makes merciful allowance for our human weakness and needs, we really can do it with His help.

God gives clear requirements, and yet He helps us, so that they are not truly burdensome. 'His commandments are not grievous' (1 John 5:3); in the Greek the particular word is *barus*, like 'barometer'. His commandments, properly understood and practiced, do not weigh you down or crush you; actually they uplift you because God's kindness, mercy, and love always come to us when our hearts are set on keeping them. Let us notice three points; first, what is demanded in biblical worship; second, what is mercifully allowed to help us get through it; and third, the consideration required of us towards other people in this process.

What is Demanded in biblical Worship (12:13-14, 26)

Once Israel would cross into the Promised Land, they were required to conduct all official worship services—especially those involving ritual sacrifice and giving tithes and first fruits—at a central shrine that God would show them, initially Shiloh and then the Temple on Mount Zion, in Jerusalem (after the days of King Solomon), where all were required to come at certain times of the year.

It was demanding to come to a central shrine of worship—Shiloh or Jerusalem—because it required people to walk, or perhaps those who had animals to ride, a few days' journey. The more land they were given, then the further they had to go. When Jesus was twelve years old, he walked with Mary and Joseph and the pilgrims from Nazareth, all the way to Jerusalem; it was quite a walk and they camped along the way.

We saw in the previous chapter why there was one central shrine; it was to enforce legitimate worship through a scripturally-based priesthood, rather than allowing everybody to cook up their own ideas which would eventually wind up being pagan and humanistic, rather than reaching God.

Now this very principle—to worship where God said and the way God said—is in the Old Testament, but its main point is taken over into the New Testament. We see it in 1 Timothy 2:5: 'There is one God, and one Mediator between God and men, the Man Christ Jesus'. Only one! That's as exclusive as anything Moses gave Israel.

Now after Christ's incarnation, His Virgin Birth and His holy life, atoning death and resurrection, the requirement is no longer one central, physical place of worship but one holy Name. After Jesus has come, it's not the place that is the issue, but one Name, which stands for everything that the place meant in Old Testament times.

We see this in Acts 4:12: 'Neither is there salvation in any other; for there is none other name under heaven given among men whereby we must be saved'. Thus, one place in the Old Testament; one name in the New Testament. Not only in Old Testament times, but also today, the only true way to worship God is through the biblical sacrificial system and the one true priesthood. There was the priesthood of Aaron in the Old Testament, fulfilled in the priesthood of Melchizedek, namely that of the Lord Jesus Christ, in the New Testament. The Levitical priesthood was given to the Jews to prepare for the fulness of salvation, and it was fulfilled in the Lord Jesus Christ for all who will ever believe in the Redeemer throughout the entire world to the end of time.

Two other demanding requirements are added to the central place of worship. No consumption of animal blood and no sacrifice.

No consumption of animal blood by any of the people of God was allowed; you cannot eat meat and leave the blood in it (Deut. 12:23, 27). This same requirement is carried over into the New Testament, at the first Apostolic Council in Acts 15, (the general assembly of the Christian church in the days of the apostles): 'That ye abstain from meats offered to idols and from blood and from things strangled and from fornication from which, if ye keep yourselves, ye shall do well' (Acts 15:29).

Why do both Old and New Testaments say that we are not to eat animal blood ever? Why is that important to godly worship? I think it's well explained in an excellent book, *Davis Bible Dictionary*, which brings out the point that 'The life is in the blood' (Lev. 17:11, 14; Deut. 12:23). The blood represented life, and life is so sacred before God, that the blood of murdered Abel is described as crying out to God for vengeance from the ground (Genesis 4:10). Immediately after the flood, the eating of blood of the lower animals was forbidden, although their slaughter for food was authorized, in Genesis 9:3–4. So the law was laid down, 'Whoso sheddeth man's blood, by man shall his blood be shed' (Gen. 9:6), which is the basis for capital punishment for murder, because of the blood and what it means. Dr. Davis says:

> The loss of life is the penalty for sin, and its typical vicarious surrender was necessary for remission of sin: in Hebrews 9:22, 'Without the shedding of blood there is no remission.' In sum, under the Mosaic law, the blood of animals was used in all

offerings for sin, and the blood of animals killed on the hunt or slaughtered for food was poured out and covered with earth, because it was withheld from man's consumption and reserved for purposes of atonement, Leviticus 17:10–14 and Deuteronomy 12:15 and 16. The blood of Jesus, the blood of Christ, and the blood of the Lamb are figurative expressions for His atoning death.

That's the best explanation I have seen. A few times in my life, I have gone to a hospital where somebody was clearly dying. In some cases, I did not know where they stood with God, and wished to help them if possible. In the ICU, I have more than once said, 'Do you believe that you're covered by faith in the blood of Jesus for the remission of your sins, and thus prepared to die and meet the holy Judge?' I have felt it necessary to confront them directly, even at the possible cost of embarrassing them, so I could offer them the only hope—the only open door to forgiveness and heaven—the blood of the Lamb. All of this helps to explain why we don't eat animal blood: it is out of our reverence for the blood of the Lamb, shed at the immense cost of God Himself to put us in the right with God.

And secondly, no idolatrous sacrifices—especially child sacrifices (12:31) which were part of worship to Molech. People would sacrifice their babies, their little children, and pass them through the fire, with people beating drums to drown out the screaming. It was an idolatrous, pagan, satanic kind of sacrifice to which God says: Have absolutely nothing to do with it; root it out.

I remember reading about the Roman Empire and the Carthaginian general Hannibal, with his army of elephants, which, at first, Rome could not beat. But the war turned against Carthage, and when the Romans got to Carthage they found something that is still there; if you go to Carthage they can show you a huge hewn-out place in the earth that was the place where they burned babies alive, and sacrificed their own children. The Romans were shocked to find that place of child sacrifice, where they saw thousands and thousands of little skeletons of babies and small children that had been sacrificed, burned as it were to Satan. So the Romans said that people like this deserve to be wiped off the map, and they destroyed Carthage and sowed salt over it.

It would be easy to object and say that this was a different culture, ages ago. But let me ask you this question: how about abortion? Particularly in the United States of America, since 1973, the anniversary of Roe v. Wade, far more babies have been slaughtered than had been killed in all the wars we have ever had, from the French and Indian down to the Iraq and Afghanistan Wars. You might say yes, but that's different, for the Carthaginians were part of the pagan Canaanite religion, and we are not. So then, why do we take life?

Is it not because most of the Western world is ultimately worshiping an idol of selfish ease and personal comfort; keeping their money, and protecting their time so they will not need to bother with a baby? So it really is an idol that doesn't have a name, except SELF. And that's the hardest one to deal with—harder than Molech. It is just as demanding an idol; it demands your babies, to please the sinful self.

What is Mercifully Allowed in Old and New Testament Worship to Make it Bearable and Pleasant (12:12,15,20)

We need to discern what is allowed to help us cope with what could be rather difficult—merciful provisions made by God to make imperfect worship humanly possible and pleasant. God loves you enough that He likes things to be pleasant for you. Isn't that wonderful? He doesn't want you to be living depressed and feeling hard done by; God's not like that. He is loving, kind, and full of joy Himself, and He wants your worship and your life as centered in worship finally to be as pleasant as possible in an imperfect environment.

Four provisions or practical aids to true worship are given, especially in the Old Testament with a certain application for us. First, in consideration of the long distance of travel, the Lord made it easier in certain regards, as we see in verses 15, 20, and 21. Second, verse 15 talks about personal uncleanness, not being entirely right to participate, and says that the Lord will accept you anyway. Third, people at a distance can still take part in the blessings of worship, even if they're not able to go, as in verse 15, and fourth, an atmosphere of joy is what the Lord wants for your worship and for your general mental condition, as in verse 12 and another verse I will mention.

First, God says you do not have to go all the way to Shiloh or Jerusalem to sacrifice animals for regular household food; that's made clear in verse 20: 'when the Lord thy God shall enlarge thy borders as He has promised thee, and thou shalt say I will eat flesh because thy soul longeth to eat flesh, thou mayest eat flesh whatsoever thy soul lusteth after'. So, God is saying, in order to have good meals of animal meat, you don't have to go all the way to Jerusalem to do it; you can do it in decentralized fashion at your homes, to make it easier on you and pleasant for the family.

Second, personal uncleanness does not prevent one's being able to share in the slaughtered animals at home, that is, if you have not perfectly carried out all the ritual requirements that appear in Leviticus, and there are many, which would be hard for everybody every day to have done for absolute purity. So the Lord says, you don't have to have carried them all out to share in the meal with your family and with the people of God. You can still safely partake; I will have mercy upon you.

That principle is illustrated in 2 Chronicles 30:18–19. When King Hezekiah put on a big Passover, and people came even from the separate and largely apostate Northern Kingdom, he prays for them and says, 'The good Lord pardon every one that prepareth his heart to seek God, the Lord God of his fathers, though he be not cleansed according to the purification of the sanctuary'. What it means is that in our own New Testament times, we do not have to be sinlessly perfect, thank God, to enjoy the good gifts of the Lord. What God is looking for is the heart; He knows if your heart is right, if you really do believe—and He's aware that you are not exactly where you ought to be—God says, just come and partake and I will bless you anyway.

In that vein, 1 Timothy 4:4–5 shows that you don't have to be perfect to enjoy the good blessings of God in this life: 'For every creature of God is good, and nothing to be refused, if it be received with thanksgiving; for it is sanctified by the Word of God and prayer'. Thus, personal uncleanness will not keep us from all the blessings of God, if at least the heart is fixed sincerely on the Lord.

The third merciful provision for true worship is that people can still share in the blessings of worshiping, even if they can't get there physically (Deut. 12:15). What could that mean today? Let's say, for example, that we have old folk in rest homes; they can't get out to church now. Yet they can, in some sense, share in the blessings of Christian worship. Members of the congregation can go to them and pray for them; we can remind them of the great ministry they can still exercise in prayer. Who knows what their intercession for us can accomplish?

Paul in 2 Corinthians 10 says we conquer Satan, not with physical weapons, but with spiritual weapons which are mighty through God in pulling down of strongholds, and that includes those used by Christians laid up in rest homes.

And then fourth, an atmosphere of joy (Deut. 12:12 and one other place): 'And ye shall rejoice before the Lord your God, ye, and your sons.' God wants you to have real joy when you come into His presence. You know how it is in Psalm 122:1: 'I was glad when they said unto me, let us go into the house of the Lord'. Nehemiah 8:10: 'The joy of the Lord is your strength'; God wants you to enjoy Him, appreciate Him, love Him and rejoice and be happy before Him; that is what will make you strong. One of the best advertisements your life will have for Christianity is that you demonstrate, to some degree, a certain sweet, quiet joy. It will not fail to impress many. True Christian worship involves 'joy unspeakable and full of glory' (1 Pet. 1:7-8).

Consideration Towards Others

The Lord teaches that we are to keep in mind when we worship, that we are to act charitably towards others. In the Old Testament time, God's people were to remember to support the Levites. They didn't own land, and so they received part of the tithes for their support. Moses is saying that his people were to invite them to eat with them, and in general to be very considerate of them.

While the Levitical system is no longer part of the New Testament economy, the principle remains that part of worship is taking up offerings to help others. We see this in 1 Corinthians 16. Immediately after the greatest discussion of the nature of the resurrection body, Paul says: 'Now remember the collection!' It is similar in Acts, Galatians, and elsewhere in the New Testament. We are told to consider our servants. Today that means our employees. Deuteronomy 12:12 and 18 tell us to share with the workers. When God is doing you good, you do them good. Give them food.

James 2:15–16 talks about that, that real religion is not when you say to somebody be warmed, be filled, but you actually give them those things which are needful for their bodies. Some would argue, 'But, I'm interested in souls.' Fine, but you can't get to the soul, unless somebody knows you care about their situation, including their body.

Jesus speaks in Matthew 25:34 and 36 about the last assize, and says that one of the things God will be assessing is whether you went to prison, and visited those who were locked up; whether you gave food to the hungry, and drink to the thirsty, or clothing to the naked, That practical charity is one of the signs of true conversion and genuine Christianity.

Biblical worship, whether in the New Testament phase or the earlier Old Testament phase, is intended to shape the rest of our daily life. And when true worship is in our purview, it changes us; it shapes our lives from the inside out. It changes you into a mode of more personal purity, a more compassionate sharing with the needy, and more internal joy and gladness.

That is why Paul, after giving all the tremendous doctrine in the first eleven chapters of Romans, then applies it all by commanding in Romans 12:1–2: 'I beseech you therefore, brethren, by the mercies of God, that ye present your bodies a living sacrifice, holy, acceptable unto God, which is your reasonable service. And be not conformed to this world; but be ye transformed by the renewing of your mind'.

Transformed! That is very close to Deuteronomy 12. In both texts, we see worship as part of God's beautiful transforming process in your inner life that nobody sees but God, 'that ye may prove what is that good, and acceptable, and perfect will of God.'

31

God's Name and Exclusive Worship
Deuteronomy 13

The Bible has its hard sayings, but they always are well grounded, and when you look at them carefully, you can see very good reasons why God speaks in a rather severe tone against misuse of His name and taking the name of a false god upon our lips.

I would compare the use of the name of God to marriage which God has set up so that in many respects it images His relationship to His people. Israel was like His wife in the Old Testament (as in Hosea), and in the New Testament the church is the bride of Christ (see Ephesians 5). Marriage is intended by the Lord to be pure and exclusive of any other: and that reflects His relationship to His people. Exclusiveness and purity of a relationship to God is essential when we come to the issue of worship. Worship is what you really give your heart to.

I once heard somebody say that what parents really worship is what their children will value the most. Children may well get angry with their parents, and go in a different direction, but it does seem that they cannot fail to value in first place what their parents really valued in the first place. In this regard, I think of a friend from childhood, who, I fear, worships money. I knew his parents well when I was a little boy, and for years afterwards. Although they were church people, they appeared to come close to worshiping money. Their son reacted against them very strongly, for they did not handle him well. Perhaps to punish them, he rejected the Faith. Yet what did he keep? He kept their deepest motivation (as best I can tell)—the love of wealth. That is an illustration of what Deuteronomy 13 means; not about wealth and money, but about idols.

God made us in His image and sent His Son to die for our sins; therefore, God wants the central affections of our hearts. That means we only worship the living God: Father, Son and Holy Spirit, and no other God; we don't allow anything or anyone less than God to have first place in our bosom. Otherwise, God says, you are engaging in an act of spiritual adultery. Worship My Name and through My Name who I am; let that be first in your affection, and all will be well.

Chapters 13, and most of chapter 14, deal with the third commandment: 'Thou shalt not take the name of the Lord thy God in vain'. We know that before the people of Israel go across the River Jordan and enter the Promised Land, Moses is speaking to them of how they are to live. He is taking them through the Ten Commandments, and saying what it will mean practically to keep the first, second and now the third commandment.

A careful look at this commandment will indicate that not taking the name of the Lord our God in vain is not primarily a prohibition of foul language (though of course it does include that), but more to the point, is a prohibition of any other way of worship, except through the name and the character of God, and the way of salvation He has provided. To do otherwise is to pollute the name of the Lord. This commandment guards against the temptation to join in with the pagan worship as the Canaanites were observing it.

In certain quarters of our Western culture today, one could think that not a few are reverting to some kind of nature worship! It is necessary to respect the environment, but we are to be careful not to soak up the assumptions of pagan nature worship (for example, of 'Father Time' and 'Mother Nature'), or to get involved in pagan nature rituals and their assumptions. God has given us an exclusive and pure way to worship Him, excluding every other avenue of worship.

Old Testament history shows that 500 or 600 years after this time, Israel finally would give in to false worship, adopt false gods and would lose everything and be departed to Babylon for seventy years. With prophetic insight, Moses is saying, for your security, your well-being, your immortal soul, and for the welfare of your children, do not take any name into your hearts and on your lips, but the name of God.

In Deuteronomy 13, Moses gives three cases of violating the name of God by giving in to false worship, and thereby inviting destruction from the Lord. These examples come from what we call 'case law' ('if … then'); for example, *if* a false prophet has a lot of power and you follow false gods, *then* he should be put to death.

There are three cases here: first, temptation to apostasy when there is a charismatic leader, a powerful leader, who can do signs and wonders, or a dreamer who can foresee the future (1–5). Second, temptation to apostasy by a close friend or family member, who leads you into destruction, because you love them and lack in discernment (verses 6–11), and third, corruption of an entire city by apostasy, turning away from God to something other than God (verses 12–18).

Temptation to Apostasy by a Powerful False Prophet (13:1–5)

The Bible relates plenty of prophecies and dreams in both Old and New Testaments; for these are some of the ways that God revealed His will to His people. For example, the dreams of Pharaoh interpreted by Joseph, or the prophecy of the boy and then the grown Samuel. They showed the will of God.

But an important exception is given here: if some prophet can do wonders, or some dreamer or fortune teller can accurately predict a number of things that really do happen, one must immediately reject them and their message, if they say to follow after some other god. But how could it be that false prophets can have supernatural power? Yes, at times, it does mean precisely that, because the devil still has a certain amount of power that he can parcel out to some of his servants.

Paul in 2 Thessalonians 2:9 speaks of a massively powerful false prophet, 'whose coming is after the working of Satan with all power and signs and lying wonders'. Yes, their malign power is real—at least for a time. Revelation 9:19 speaks in images of evil, God-hating beings whose power is in their mouth and in their tails, for their tails are like serpents and with them they do hurt.

Satanism, voodoo, occult practices and Wicca worship is claimed by some to be going 'mainstream' (though I do not actually observe this even among most pagans). One illustration would be the occult, voodoo and Satanism that has had such a stranglehold on the city of New Orleans for so many generations. Why? It must be because the Evil One is able to communicate supernatural powers to some who are in league with them; he later destroys them, but for the time being he gives them power so that they can impress, deceive, and mislead foolish people. I tend to think that Satanism in its various manifestations is on the increase in the rich, materialistic countries of the West. As much of the population has turned its back on the gospel, it has left a vacuum, and the powers of evil have rushed in to fill it. That may be part of the explanation for the strange mass killings in our own days. Chuck Colson and Dr. James Dobson have interviewed people in prison that had been engaged in some of those unspeakable atrocities, and who said they had been involved in different sorts of Satanism. This shows that breaking the third commandment has severe consequences.

Moses therefore says, beware of seeking spiritual power from anywhere but God. It's out there, but don't go near it; don't take any name on your lips when you're seeking spiritual help or seeking to make sense of your life; don't seek it anywhere but with God. There is the blessed Holy Spirit who is the greatest of all, but there are also evil spirits that are still in the world; they are mere creatures, and thus infinitely less than God, but still have a certain amount of power.

That is why 1 John 4:1 says: 'Try the spirits to see whether they are of God'. How do we test to know whether a spirit is of God? Simply by the Word of God written. From time to time, people will come along who seem very impressive, and may have a certain kind of spiritual power. But it is not clean and pure spiritual power; it will pollute you, rather than build you up. These people will say to you, 'Follow me, because I have a new revelation of who God really is. You don't need to be loyal to the God of the Bible; He is too harsh, too strict, too demanding; you can't ever have any fun. I have shown you some power; come with me and I will give you an easier religion; you won't have to deny yourself; you won't have to take up your cross; you won't have to seek to be a pure man or woman; I can offer you fun, and power, and advancement.'

Hence, Deuteronomy 13:5 calls for execution of false prophets who speak rebellion against the Lord—a tough penalty, but it was the only way to protect the holy covenant community from being wholly corrupted and Satan taking over.

What about today? No modern nation that I know of executes Satanists and those who teach open rebellion against the Lord. Years ago, there used to be laws against public blasphemy in all the Christian countries, but that's long gone. To the contrary, some who openly blaspheme God and His Word are given high teaching posts in some of our universities. Far from being fired (or executed), they are rewarded.

But keep in mind that 'the triumph of the wicked is short'. I wouldn't like to be in their shoes when they pass through death, and when judgment day comes. What good will wealth and fame do then? The most severe penalty that Christ gave to His church is a spiritual penalty, not a physical penalty. The church has the power of the Word and the Holy Spirit; only the state has the power of the sword. We are living in a different economy to Old Testament times, when, more or less, church and state were together. But since New Testament times, church and state have been largely separate; the Christian church imposes only certain spiritual penalties—not civil or physical ones—on blasphemers.

But do not make the mistake of thinking that these spiritual penalties are nothing! Actually, they are at least as effective, and certainly longer lasting than physical penalties. Read 2 Corinthians 10 about this matter. The final and worst penalty the Christian church has ever had, and still has, is the penalty of excommunication of a person, who refuses to repent of rebellion against God, of blasphemy, of denial of the Trinity and the way of salvation and the Word.

I've been in ordained ministry forty years, but I've only been involved in one excommunication. The person was given every opportunity to repent, but proudly refused. The only way the honor of Christ could be upheld and the purity of the church preserved, was for him to be excommunicated, sad though it was.

Does this sound hard? Does it seem unloving? Well, Jesus, the man of love; the love of God incarnate, says in Matthew 18:17 to treat the impenitent as a heathen man or a publican. That means that such a person is then cut off of any possibility of going to heaven (Matt. 18:19); the church has the power of the keys; what you bind on earth is bound in heaven, what you loose on earth is loosed in heaven. They can't go to heaven unless they repent.

In some cases, excommunication may work to reclaim an idolater, blasphemer or massively immoral person. In 1 Timothy 1:20 they excommunicated a man so that he could learn not to blaspheme. Paul seems to be saying that if the church applies the most severe penalty on him, it <u>might</u> lead him to reconsider his position and repent and be saved at the last. At this stage of advanced secularism, we can't clean up the country. But at least we can work to keep the church pure, to honor the name of God. If we do that, by and by, I think, it will definitely begin to affect a corrupt country, in a more pure and godly direction.

Temptation to Apostasy by a Friend or Family Member (13:6–11)

Rather than by wonder workers or fortunetellers with supernatural power, here the temptation comes by a close personal relationship, somebody you value very highly. God's Word always teaches us to love our families, even to sacrifice ourselves, if necessary, for their welfare. Christ loved the church that way, and we are to love our family that way, that is clear. But the exception is if the devil uses a valued friend or family member to try to turn you against God, to go apostate, to make you quit believing the Bible, then cut them off; for the salvation of your own soul and the safety of the rest of the family depends upon it.

Years ago I knew of a family, and as I recall, the great grandfather had written a book that was unsound; it denied who Christ is, and seriously so. Because of their loyalty to this older member, several members of that family, although they were technically participants in the church, did not believe. A few got gloriously saved, and they broke loose from the influence of an unbelieving ancestor. But some felt that they could not confess Jesus Christ as the Son of God and the only way of salvation, because they were loyal to their ancestor. The kind of family loyalty, where you put your relatives before Christ, is not worth it (Matt. 10:34–39).

Apostasy could happen in any family, and if so, the devil gets in and tries to use them to lead others astray. Therefore, they would have to be dealt with severely, and their ideas never tolerated even for a moment. That's the only way they could be saved. Conniving with thinking which is clearly against God's Word, even with somebody you love, not to hurt their feelings, is the worst thing you could do against your eternal salvation. Moses is clear; Jesus is clear.

Corruption of an Entire City by Apostasy

God ordained the destruction of the Canaanites, and hundreds of years later, Jerusalem was to be wiped out. Jericho had already been put under the curse, as we see in Joshua 6. Joshua says that Jericho is to be destroyed with its inhabitants, buildings and possessions, and then burned, because of its idolatry and immorality that had increased, and reached up to heaven. Then (in Joshua 7) Achan thought he would beat the system; he stole gold and some Babylonish garments and hid them in his tent. Soon he was found out, and because he had taken the cursed thing, he was put to death.

Now since the time of the New Testament, God's people do not have the responsibility or the authority of doing anything like wiping out a sinful city. God doesn't ask us to do anything like that. But there is an application that we still have as true Christian people:

> Be ye not unequally yoked together with unbelievers; for what fellowship hath righteousness with unrighteousness? and what communion hath light with darkness? and what concord hath Christ with Belial? (2 Cor. 6:14–15).

So those three cases are probably the three main ways that the devil employs as he tries to mislead the church, and corrupt Christian families over the ages. Hence we always need to remember the purity of God's holy name, Father, Son, Holy Spirit, one true God in three persons; who He is requires us to avoid at all costs any kind of paganism, any kind of false religion, any denial of holy Scripture, and any participation in immoral, corrupt practices. To put it positively, we mention only God's name in worship, and no other. And to live like that, you must know who is first place in your heart. That is the right way to live: with a pure conscience, always applying to the cleansing blood for keeping in the right with the Lord. To give our hearts to the Lord who says, 'Thou shalt not take the name of the Lord thy God in vain', is the source of joy and pure spiritual power.

Charles Wesley wrote this hymn about God's name:

> Jesus, the name high over all,
> In hell, or earth, or sky:
> Angels and men before it fall,
> And devils fear and fly.
>
> Jesus, the name to sinners dear,
> The name to sinners giv'n;
> It scatters all their guilty fear,
> It brings them peace of heav'n.
>
> Jesus the prisoner's fetters breaks,
> And bruises Satan's head;
> Pow'r into strengthless souls He speaks,
> And life into the dead.
>
> Oh, that the world might taste and see,
> The riches of His grace!
> The arms of love that compass me,
> Would all mankind embrace.
>
> His only righteousness I show,
> His saving truth proclaim:
> 'Tis all my business here below,
> To cry, Behold the Lamb!
>
> Happy, if with my latest breath
> I may but gasp His name:

> Preach Him to all, and cry in death,
>   'Behold, behold the Lamb!'

What a wonderful poetic way of summarizing the meaning 'Thou shalt not take the name of the Lord thy God in vain'!

32

Clean and Unclean Animals

Deuteronomy 14:1–21

Although I am sixty-four and was brought up by my parents and grandparents to be in church, twice on Sunday and generally on Wednesday nights, and thus have heard thousands of sermons, I have never heard a sermon on clean and unclean animals. When I started getting this sermon ready, I knew why. It takes some digging. But anyway it's part of the Word of God, and all Scripture is inspired (2 Tim. 3:16) 'and is profitable'; and there is definitely profit here for the people in the Word of God. We must need Deuteronomy 14, or it would not be in Holy Scripture. So with that confidence I speak to you on a passage that is demanding to get into.

The passage is still part of the exposition of the third commandment, 'Thou shalt not take the name of the Lord thy God in vain'. We are given two major points: don't take the name of God the wrong way when you are hit by grief (verses 1–2); and don't take the name of God in the wrong way in what you eat (verses 3–21).

Do Not Take the Name of God in Vain in Time of Grief (14:1–2)

These first two verses of Deuteronomy 14 teach us that God's name is to be hallowed. Jesus says to pray every day (in the Lord's Prayer), 'Hallowed be Thy name'. On the day when we have lost a loved one, we have to pray as on any other day, 'Hallowed be Thy name'. We have to seek the grace to say with Job, when terrible things have happened, what Job said to his wife, who told him to curse God and die, 'The Lord hath given, the Lord hath taken, blessed be the name of the Lord'.

Deuteronomy 14:1 precludes our grieving like pagans when death enters our family or circle of close friends. The pagans in the ancient Middle East went to great lengths in dealing with death. The Canaanites would cut themselves with knives, shave their heads, or make gashes between their eyes, along with screaming and other kinds of emotional outbursts.

I remember when I was in the seminary in Richmond, that a hospital chaplain came and spoke to us one day. He said that he had seen in the hospital one time a woman whose husband had just dropped dead of a heart attack. Another chaplain went up to her to express condolence, and she spat in his face. Believers are never to act this way, primarily because of the third commandment. It dishonors the name of God, as though He did not have the right to take us when He wants to. We are never to engage in excessive grief, like pagans who have absolutely no hope for life after death. That kind of grief is an outburst against the goodness and wisdom of God, a violation of the third commandment.

St. Paul gives us the right balance in handling deep personal grief when we lose loved ones: 'That ye sorrow not even as others which have no hope' (1 Thess. 4:13). Of course, Christians do feel sorrow over death; that is perfectly valid and truly spiritual. It cannot be wrong to weep and grieve at the breaking of the family circle, for Jesus wept (John 11:35) and still feels our grief: 'We have a faithful and a merciful High Priest who is not unable to be touched with the feeling of our infirmities, but was tempted in every point like as we are, yet without sin' (Heb. 4:15). He is touched when we grieve.

I knew of someone who in a sort of super-spiritual way claimed that when there was a death in the family he would say, if you have faith you won't express any grief because they are gone to a better place, so don't in any sense be sorry. But that is not right! Paul says we 'weep with them that do weep, and rejoice with them that rejoice', (Rom. 12:15). If you tell somebody they can't feel any grief, you are short-circuiting the necessary outworking of the grief we feel at the death (which is an enemy); it is part of our function as Christians to share grief and help carry the load with other believers.

Notice that Paul does not say in 1 Thessalonians 4:13 that we have no sorrow over death, but rather that our sorrow is not like the horrid anguish of a materialistic pagan who has absolutely no hope. Our sorrow could not be like that, for death has lost its sting for the believer. Jesus on the cross took the penalty of our guilt, and thus removed the poison and darkness of death, so that for every believer, physical death becomes an open door into a place of light, the blessed realm of God's throne and the company of the saints and angels, the loved ones who have gone ahead of us, and beauties so wonderful as to be indescribable. And so Jesus says in John 14:19, 'because I live, ye shall live also'.

Thus the Holy Spirit brings the reality of the resurrection hope into every grieving Christian heart, and helps us get through our sense of profound loss. The fact that we don't act like pagans when we lose loved ones is a powerful witness to an unbelieving, hopeless world, of the sheer goodness of God and of our trust in the integrity of His holy name.

I know of a family in Jackson, Mississippi, who many years ago lost a baby well into a pregnancy. People lived across the street who were not Christian believers but were nice people and brought food to this family when they heard. A few months later, the lady who had brought the food came and said the whole family had been gloriously converted. It all started, she said, on seeing how they handled the loss of the child, in confidence and faith in the Lord, and they decided there must be something there that they didn't have.

Do Not Take the Name of God in Vain in What you Eat (14:3–21)
This Old Testament truth should not surprise us as Christians, for Paul says in 1 Corinthians 10:31: 'Whether therefore ye eat or drink, or whatsoever ye so, do all to the glory of God'. Now eating to the glory of God—to the honor of His name, and thus keeping the third commandment—is done in a very different way in the New Testament. But let us look first at what it involved in the Old Testament, and then see the changes that occurred after Jesus comes.

In Leviticus and Deuteronomy, God's people were told which animals were clean and which were unclean. They were allowed to eat and to sacrifice at the tabernacle, only clean animals. The details of clean and unclean foods are listed for us in Leviticus 21 and here in Deuteronomy 14.

Actually, the distinction between clean and unclean animals goes way back before Moses; he codifies it under the inspiration of the Holy Spirit, but we are told in Genesis that Noah put into the ark one pair of each species of unclean animals, and seven pairs of clean animals, probably to provide enough for holy sacrifices as an offering when they got off the ark.

Let us look at the three categories of clean and unclean animals, and then consider the reason that lies behind the very concept of an animal being clean or unclean.

There are three categories of animals corresponding to earth, water, and air. The land animals are listed in verses 4–8; the water or aquatic animals in verses 9 and 10; and the air animals, namely the birds and certain flying insects, in verses 11–20. We are told which ones are pure or clean, and which ones are impure, so that in each of the three categories the distinction is made plain for the people to understand.

First, the land animals. The clean ones part the hoof—look at their feet—cleave the cleft into two claws, and chew the cud (v. 6). For instance, a cow has a split hoof divided into two claws, and chews the cud. And yet the pig has a split hoof, but does not chew the cud (v. 8). A camel chews the cud, but does not split the hoof (v. 7). So the pig and the camel, the swine and several other animals, are unclean.

Second, the water animals: clean ones have fins and scales; they may be eaten. But shell fish and eels do not have fins and scales, and so are impure and excluded from the Old Testament diet.

Third, the air animals: most birds seem to be allowed as clean, but verses 12–19 exclude as unclean birds of prey such as eagles, vultures, owls, bats, and creeping things that can do a little bit of flying. So these are the details as to which are clean and which are unclean.

But what could have been the reason that God pronounced some animals clean and others unclean? Jewish and Christian commentators, and scholars across the ages, have found it difficult to discern exactly why some animals are clean and some are unclean. The medieval Jewish theologian, Moses Maimonides, said that the human mind could not know exactly what the reason was, although he thought it might have something to do with the health of the body, and also protection against certain ancient pagan practices such as boiling a kid in its mother's milk. Some of the church fathers followed some of the Jewish Hellenistic scholars such as Philo, and allegorized everything; they pretended that certain animals represented virtues, while other animals represented vices. Thus a hawk was said to represent violent stealing and killing, and a snake was said to represent dangerous trickery.

But the trouble with allegory is that you have no objective control over the real meaning; it's left up to the imagination. The Bible itself never, anywhere, allegorizes these animals. It simply presents certain types as pure and others as impure, without any reference to supposed human moral characteristics of virtue or vice.

Other scholars have argued that the dietary or kosher laws were really about good health, especially in a hot climate. That is, pigs can give you trichinosis, and shellfish are scavengers, and maybe would pass on some type of illness. I once read a book by a Baptist minister, claiming that if you followed the Old Testament dietary laws you were far less likely to get cancer. That may or may not be true; I'm not a medical expert and simply don't know. All I can say is that in Deuteronomy 14 and Leviticus 11, and other passages that deal with the Holiness Code for food, health is never mentioned as the real reason. There may be something to this, but it's not the reason given us in the Scripture.

Some of the modernist liberal scholars have said that clean and unclean have no reason whatsoever. It is either a primitive idea or a merely arbitrary decision of God without meaning. But surely that cannot be right, for God is a God of order. Everything He does has the most wonderful meaning in terms of who He is and what the creation is like.

But what would be the reason? I remember years ago talking to a friend in Lausanne, Switzerland; he had read an article by the American anthropologist, Mary Douglas. He thought that she may have given the reason. She wrote an article that makes more sense than anything I have seen so far. According to Dr. Douglas, impurity in an animal seems to go back to the effects of the fall of Adam. When he fell, something terrible happened across the whole created order, because he was the crown and the representative of creation. When sin and the fall and death came on him, it came on the whole created order.

Now before the fall, all animals must have been clean, for God pronounced at the end of creation week that everything was very good, and to say that it was very good, precluded anything unclean. But by the time of Noah's flood, as we have seen, and no doubt long before that, some animal orders were considered ritually unclean. What had happened to make them unclean? At the fall, for instance, the ground was cursed and thorns began to infect the ground. They weren't there before.

Thus all creation was affected by the fall. Romans 8:20-23, looking forward to the great blessings that will come at the end, speaks of this:

For the creature was made subject to vanity, not willingly, but by reason of him who hath subjected the same in hope, because the creature itself also shall be delivered from the bondage of corruption into the glorious liberty of the children of God.

The fall of Adam sent a shock wave all through the created order, so that some types of animals must have degenerated from the perfect and beautiful forms that they previously had. For instance: Satan came and inhabited the body of a serpent, a snake, and evidently at that time snakes walked upright, and were very beautiful creatures. But because of God's curse on Satan and the animal he inhabited at that moment, God cursed serpents so that they went down and slink and move around on their belly ever since. The beautiful structure of the serpent was devastatingly changed. Evidently that was not necessarily the case with every species of animal, but with many of them, degenerating from the structure they previously had; that is the issue presented for us in Leviticus 11 and Deuteronomy 14.

As the ground was cursed, there came a structural disorder apparently in camels, pigs, eels, hawks, and so forth. Camels no longer chew the cud; eels no longer have fins and scales; snakes walk on their bellies; penguins no longer fly; their original perfect structure degenerated from its original form due to the fall.

It's not evolution, it's devolution or degeneration from the original beauty that they had because of the fall of Adam and its effect on the creation. In others words, animals that are pronounced by God as unclean have been profoundly disordered by the fall, more than the other animals; I don't know why certain ones were and certain ones were not. These unclean animals are a continuing sign of God's judgment upon sin, and that is why they were forbidden to Israel.

There had to be perfection of structure. For instance, we are told that a priest, a descendant of Aaron or of the Levites, could not serve in the tabernacle, if he in any way had a physical deformity. A malformed or diseased lamb could not be brought for a sacrifice; it had to have a health and a beauty and perfection of structure to be offered. Therefore, if Mary Douglas is right, the unclean animals are considered to be lacking in perfection of structure, and hence are excluded from sacrifice at the Temple, or food on the table.

Now I want to move on and look at how profoundly things changed concerning what you eat with the coming of Christ in the New Testament. Here is the key to it all; John the Baptist cries out at the baptism of the Lord at the River Jordan, 'Behold, the Lamb of God that taketh away the sin of the world' (John 1:29). The word for 'world' is *cosmos;* it means not just the sins of the people—of course, all who would ever believe, sins are taken away in principle—but it also means the curse on the ground (and on animals); in principle, it's paid for, and eventually will be totally taken away.

As we see in Romans 8:20-22, even this physical realm shall eventually be redeemed, restored, and renewed; sometimes called 'the regeneration' by virtue of the victorious work of Christ in his death and resurrection. As one hymn proclaims,

> Stars and skies and seas and all,
> by blood are cleansed from the fall.

What God did in the death and resurrection of Jesus was so massive and powerful that it affected everything, including the physical realm. Yes, our soul, yes, our diseased body, but also everything else in the environment was, in principle, cleansed and is being prepared for complete restoration in God's due time. In that way, order and beauty will be brought back finally in perfection, in place of disorder and ugliness.

That is why in Acts 10, God, in principle, purifies all animals and says that they are fit to be eaten by His people. We see how this works in Acts 10:9-21. Peter was called to go to a Gentile, Cornelius, a Roman centurion, with the gospel; Peter was naturally very hesitant to take the gospel to a non-Jew, an impure Gentile. However, while on the roof praying and in a trance, he sees a sheet being let down from heaven by four corners, full of all kinds of clean and unclean animals.

Then God said to him, 'Simon, arise, kill and eat' these unclean animals. Peter answered, 'Lord, I can't do that; I've been brought up on and have honored the Jewish dietary laws; I can't eat unclean animals'. The Lord responded to Peter, 'Do not call unclean what I have cleansed.'

There are two main points in this passage: one is that the church, almost totally Jewish at that stage, is being prepared for its missionary outreach to the rest of the world, including to Gentiles. The second point is that the death and resurrection of Jesus has done something to the animal realm to render, in principle, all animals clean for God's people to be able to eat.

Is there any evidence of this massive change anywhere else in Scripture? It helps explain the words of Jesus in Mark 7:15: 'There is nothing from without a man, that entering into him can defile him: but the things which come out of him, those are they that defile the man.' Hence, it is not unclean meat but what is in your heart that matters; and the distinction between clean and unclean foods no longer applies.

At the first Apostolic Council, or General Assembly of the church (Acts 15), because so many Gentile pagans were getting saved, there was some debate among the leaders of the church, as to whether these Gentiles must first become Jewish, i.e., be circumcised, and adhere to the dietary laws. The council decided it was not relevant to make them go by the various Judaic laws as far as circumcision and pork were concerned, because Jesus' blood had taken care of all that and rendered it no longer an issue: Acts 15:19–21:

> Wherefore my sentence is, that we trouble not them, which from among the Gentiles are turned to God: But that we write unto them, that they abstain from pollutions of idols, and from fornication, and from things strangled, and from blood. For Moses of old time hath in every city them that preach him, being read in the synagogues every Sabbath day.

We may then, with clear conscience, eat the various sorts of animals (including ritually unclean ones) because everything is made clean to us in and through Jesus Christ. Yet we're always to think of Christ, and give thanks for His bounty for us every time we eat or drink. 'For every creature of God is good and nothing to be refused if it be received with thanksgiving, for it is sanctified by the word of God and prayer' (1 Tim. 4:4-5). Christ has restored, in principle, the created order, and if we believe in Him and pray, everything is just right. So Titus 1:15 says, 'Everything is pure to those who are pure'. All foods, for instance, are now pure, if your heart is pure through the saving work of Christ that you personally receive.

So we learn from this passage that what we eat or drink is to be consecrated through faith in Christ and prayer in His name. That is the significance of the table blessing in Christian homes; even the food we eat is a time to remember that everything is consecrated to Christ, so that we may better enjoy Him and serve Him. Let every meal you eat remind you of the wondrous cleansing effect of the blood of Christ in rendering all things pure to those who have born again hearts.

At the same time let us remember that we are on the way to what Jesus calls 'The Regeneration'. That means the total renovation of all things in the whole created order; all of it will be wonderfully put right. There will be a beautiful restoration that Romans 8 speaks of: seas and skies, animals, fish, birds, plants, our own physical bodies—all will be brought back to beauty, to perfect structure, and lasting glory, on the basis of who Jesus is, and what He did for His creation. Everything is to be delivered from bondage to sin and in purity to share the glorious liberty of the sons of God. What a Savior and what a hope is ours! We thus honor God's name in times of loss and at every meal.

33

The Tithe

Deuteronomy 14:22–29

As far as I know, there's no simple recipe to be happy, but whatever stage we are in life, if we wish our experience and our influence to be as productive and as happy as possible, we can do certain things: love God and love our neighbor as ourselves, and forgive everybody who has ever offended us. Those things certainly are part of a truly happy and fruitful life (though none of them precludes us from trials and loss).

This text brings forth two additional things I want us to talk about, which are very important for anybody to have a good and a happy life: namely, the Sabbath and the tithe.

Deuteronomy 14:22–16:22 is a large section dealing with the fourth commandment: 'Remember the Sabbath day, to keep it holy'. And we are seeing how, after a prologue, Deuteronomy is structured in terms of practical advice on how to carry out the Ten Commandments. We have looked at the first three commandments; now we are going to look at the fourth commandment, and what it would mean in our lives.

Moses, in this long text, is showing the people of Israel, just before they cross over Jordan, how deep and broad is the Sabbath principle for our healthy, happy, and useful earthly lives. The purpose of the Sabbath is not merely to abstain from work one day out of seven, though it certainly requires that, but it also gives us a weekly time of rest and praise, when we once again appropriate the transcendence and the presence of this glorious God. This is something we very much need in a busy life. We are to give God heart-felt praise for everything He's done for us, if we are going to be able to experience that profound rest of body and soul and spirit that is so essential to happy and holy lives.

I've sometimes talked to people who were emotionally having a bad time; I have asked them, 'Are you keeping the Sabbath day, one day out of seven?' They answer, 'No.' And then they stay frazzled and worried, and torn up on the inside, to such a degree that they can't get their emotions calmed down in any given week. In view of that kind of disturbance of spirit, God is giving us a very great blessing in this commandment. His commandments really are, as 1 John says, not grievous, not burdensome.

These verses give the first practical outworking of the Sabbath. The Sabbath principle is extended by Moses to practical life, by means of the tithe. Verses 22–23 say the people of God are to give the tithe (ten per cent) of the seed of the field, of grain, wine, and oil, thus including all agricultural produce from fields and vineyards and so forth; and also the tithe of animal increase such as cattle, sheep, and goats. Giving the tithe would be a practical way of showing gratitude to God from whom all blessings flow. We rightly sing 'Praise God from whom all blessings flow', and every time we give the tithe we are, in a sense, turning that beautiful doxology into money; that is, in the practical outpouring of our lives, we are saying, 'O God we praise You because we know every blessing flows down from You, and we are privileged to give this small amount back to You.'

Let us note three things in this section: first, how the tithe and its connection with the Sabbath worked out in the Old Testament agricultural economy; second, how it works out after Christ has come for all nations, whether agricultural or urban; and third, blessings promised in the Old Testament and the New Testament to those who praise God and rest in Him by tithing.

The Tithe in Old Testament Israel (14:23)

We note three differences between what was happening in Old Testament Israel before Jesus came, and the situation with believers today. First, since the Old Testament was an agricultural economy, where the harvest was once a year and thus people got their income once a year at harvest time, the tithe was to be gathered in once a year. Most of us today are not in that situation, for generally we are paid some kind of weekly or at least monthly wage.

Then there's a second difference: when it was possible, once Israel crossed into the Promised Land, they were to take the farm increase to wherever God would locate the temple, wherever the tabernacle would be set up, as we see 14:23. But the Bible is realistic; Moses is very merciful and understanding, and tries to make these things work out in the complexities of the real world. He knew that the Promised Land would be a fairly capacious area, and in some cases it would be hard to get sheep and goats and cattle and olive oil and grain to the central place of worship, first at Shiloh and later Jerusalem. Hence you might not be able to get all your tithe to the central worship shrine, with little or no means of transport or maybe a cart for wealthier people to ride on. For that reason, the Lord says through Moses, if it's a long way to the central shrine, then sell your agricultural produce at a market price, put the money in a bag and, bringing your family, come with it to the tabernacle or temple. And when you get there, spend part of that money to provide a wonderful banquet for your family: good food, good wine, and whatever you would like, and join in the celebration with the saints of God at the central place of worship, eating and drinking together (verses 24 to 26). The rest of the money would go to the Lord's work at the tabernacle or temple, part of it to support the Levites (the tribe of Moses and Aaron) whom God had not allowed to have any grant of land, so that they would be scattered through Israel as the moral instructors and as the teachers of the children.

The third difference is that in Old Testament times before the incarnation of Christ, the years worked on a Sabbath principle—the Jubilee—a cycle of seven years. That is, certain things were done in some years as regards the tithe, and other things were done in other years in a cycle of seven, which God said He would bless. We'll look at that in more detail in our next chapter.

Specifically, at the close of every third year—the third year and sixth year of the Sabbath cycle—the tithe was to be used differently from years one, two, four, five, and seven. Each third year, the families of the believers were not to go to the central temple, but rather take the produce to the nearest town and deposit it for the use of local needy people, who owned no land: the Levites, the strangers (what we would say today were immigrants), widows, and orphans. In this way, true biblical religion reminds us always to make physical provision for the needs of the poor around us.

Jesus said you will always have the poor with you; to help the needy in physical ways is to show praise and honor to God because He is creator of rich and poor; all are alike before Him in equal value as far as human worth and immortal destiny are concerned. And this giving would give the families of Israel a rest and a joy in their spirit which cannot be experienced unless His people are generous. God has seen to it in the way He has set up the Sabbath cycle, and we must notice here that giving to the needy not only helps them, but also blesses those who give. If we are unwilling to help the needy, there will be a lack in our inner attitude, in our motivation, in our very spirit—a certain lack of rest and joy that can only be known when we give as God requires.

Then, interestingly, in the seventh year there would be no tithe. Why? Because the seventh year was a sabbatical year when one was told not to plant the crops, not to trim the orchards and the vineyards, for God had promised that He would provide. And so, since they didn't plant crops, they would not have a regular increase; they would have enough to eat, but, for that reason, God did not ask for the tithe in the seventh year.

What Does the Tithe Mean Today?

How binding is the biblical tithe after the appearance of Christ? The epistle to the Hebrews in particular, shows that Jesus fulfilled the rituals of the temple in His own holy life, His suffering, His death, His resurrection, what we call in the Westminster Confession of Faith the 'ceremonial law'. He fulfilled the seven year sabbatical cycles in His wondrous finished work, and yet Hebrews quotes Psalm 95, where it says 'strive to enter into His rest' (which we shall discuss in later chapters).

So, how does the tithe work today? First, Sabbath and tithing still hold as valid life principles for the people of God after Jesus came, till the very end of time. Jesus says in Matthew 5:17–20:

> Think not that I am come to destroy the law, or the prophets: I am not come to destroy, but to fulfill. For verily I say unto you, Till heaven and earth pass, one jot or one tittle shall in no wise pass from the law, till all be fulfilled.

We have previously considered how the ceremonial law, and also many parts of the judicial law were truly fulfilled, and thus surpassed in Christ, so that they are not relevant in the same way, since He took care of them in his finished work. But the moral law, the basic Ten Commandments including Sabbath and tithing continues in force, even after the work of Christ. I think one of the best expositions of this continuance of the Sabbath principle was given by the Southern Presbyterian theologian, Robert L. Dabney, in his beautiful essay on the Christian Sabbath.

Concerning the Christian Sabbath, after our Lord appeared in the flesh, the actual day of the week was changed from the last day of the week to the first. After Jesus' resurrection and sending down of the Holy Spirit, we find that the Christians meet on the first day of the week, which we call Sunday, or sometimes the Lord's Day or Christian Sabbath.

The Roman Emperor Constantine rightly regularized Sabbath observance in the fourth century to be on Sunday; Saturday was the last day of the old creation, whereas Sunday, or Lord's Day, is resurrection day—the first day of the new creation. Hence, every Sunday is resurrection day. We remember that in Jesus' resurrection, we too are raised in principle into the new life: abundant, eternal, beautiful life here on earth, and then in heaven hereafter, for the kingdom of God is made possible by the death and the resurrection of Jesus.

This change of Sabbath day is also seen in John's gospel. After Christ's resurrection, Jesus breathed on His disciples the Holy Spirit, and then we find them gathering in *octaves*, groups of eight. That means that on the first day of each week, they were together worshiping the Lord. And that's usually when the risen Christ appears in the latter part of John's Gospel: on the first day of the week.

And then we find in 1 Corinthians 16:1 that they are taking the offerings on the first day of the week, the day of worship. The principle of the first day of the week for worship and meeting with the risen Lord is seen in Revelation 1:10, when the beloved apostle John says: 'I was in the Spirit on the Lord's Day'; that is when he received all these visions of the book of the Revelation. The Lord's Day, the first day of the week, was the beginning of the new creation. While the day had changed from Saturday to Sunday, the principle of Sabbath remained exactly the same, as a necessary part of a happy and a healthy Christian life.

All of this shows that the principle of the tithe was definitely kept in the New Testament era. After the resurrection of Christ, the necessity of giving, at least a tenth, was certainly nowhere removed. It's often said and rightly so that the tithe is not, as such, specifically mentioned in the New Testament; but you find, if you look carefully, that the principle is very clearly there.

For example, 2 Corinthians 8:12–15: 'For if there be first a willing mind, it is accepted according to that a man hath, and not according to that he hath not'. In other words, it is saying that whatever your income is, you give a portion of that, and don't say 'I'm going to get rich some day, and then I'll be generous.' No. God expects you to give out of what you have available now; to give your portion back to Him, not to what you fondly imagine you might have in the future.

Paul continues: 'For I mean not that other men be eased, and ye burdened. But by an equality'. Now what would equality be? Equality means that all the people of God, depending on their circumstances in any age, whether rich or with little, are to give an equal percentage (which will vary a great deal as to amount). There is no doubt that in the New Testament era, the ten percent is required, as it was all through the Old Testament. Hence Paul says: 'that now at this time your abundance may be a supply for their want, that their abundance also may be a supply for your want: that there may be equality: As it is written, He that had gathered much had nothing over; and he that had gathered little had no lack'.

Now not everybody agrees; some have argued that since Christ fulfilled the law, we should not have to tithe. But that is surely a wrong conclusion, for with the fuller reign of grace, we should be at least as generous as the people of God in the Old Testament, who had not seen Jesus clearly yet, if not more.

Certainly, Christ fulfilled and rendered unnecessary the continuance of ceremonial law, because you don't need the shedding of the blood of animals, since the precious blood of Christ fulfills it all. But He affirmed and even deepened the moral law, such as personal purity, weekly rest, worship, and tithing. Read the Sermon on the Mount to see how Jesus, far from throwing out the law, is saying yes, I fulfilled major parts of it that you are not obligated to fulfill because

I've done it; but the moral principles still remain, so that your life can be healthy and beautiful in the power of the Holy Spirit, as you live by those principles. In sum, while the tithe is not specifically stated in the New Testament, I think the teaching in 2 Corinthians 8, about 'equality', conveys it.

Indeed, right after the resurrection chapter in 1 Corinthians 15 (the fullest discussion of life in our resurrection bodies), we are immediately instructed about giving in the next chapter: 'Now concerning the offering…' What is Paul saying in 1 Corinthians 16? Because of the certainty of the resurrection, your physical future is guaranteed; your body is going to be raised in beauty and glory and power like the Lord Jesus Christ's. Now, since that's true, I want you to show that you are thankful by giving to the work of God in these offerings every week.

The fact that the church is always to have in mind the poor and the needy is shown us in James 2:15 16:

> If a brother or sister be naked and destitute of daily food and one of you should say unto them, Depart in peace; be ye warmed and filled; notwithstanding ye give them not those things which are needful to the body, what doth it profit?

Now the church's ability to help those in need usually comes from the tithe, which enables us as the people of God to fulfill our responsibility to help the needy.

Let us answer one further argument that is sometimes raised against the tithe and the sabbath. A secular society resents the Sabbath because it testifies that God exists and is first; it is deeply marked by profound selfishness, and seeks respectable reasons to avoid both. Here is probably their main argument: Sabbath and tithing were part of the Mosaic Law, but as Christians we are out from under the Law of Moses and we dwell wholly in the grace of Christ, so therefore no Sabbath and no tithe.

But if you take the Bible seriously, you will understand that Sabbath and the tithe go back long before the time of Moses. Long before Sinai, Sabbath was instituted in the Garden of Eden, and God says to keep it. Some of the English Puritans used to say that there were two sweet relics left from the Garden of Eden. One is Sabbath, and the other is marriage. It was God's plan for the entire human race, even before Moses, back to our first parents as part of God's moral law for all His image bearers. Therefore Sabbath observance is necessary if we are to have a healthy and happy structure for our earthly lives. You couldn't do many things much better than regularly to keep the Sabbath day holy.

This pre-Mosaic status is also true of the tithe. We see, for instance, Abraham giving tithes to the mysterious priest-king of Salem, Melchizedek, in Genesis 14:20. In Genesis 28:22, Jacob, roughly 500 years before Moses, promised God the tithe when he left home to go to his mother's people. He said, 'Lord, if you be with me, I promise to tithe everything I get hold of'. And though he went through tribulations, God did richly blessed him. Hence, Sabbath and tithing were valid before Moses, during Moses' time, and after Moses in what we call the New Covenant.

It is an open secret that many people who are in financial straits have decided to start giving the tithe. If they do, I believe that in most cases, God supernaturally sends in more. Many people are never going to get out of financial straits until they do what God said. It is as the Apostle Paul says, 'the equality'. Give that, and you will find that God is waiting to be gracious.

God Promises Blessings for Tithing

Bring Me all the tithes into the storehouse that there may be meat in Mine house and prove Me now herewith, saith the Lord of Hosts, if I will not open you the windows of heaven and pour you out a blessing that there shall not be room enough to receive it (Mal. 3:10).

God's honor, if I may respectfully say so, is on the line! He says to try Me, trust Me, prove Me. You can rightly do so by giving the tithe! Then see how God will directly intervene in your lives for great blessing.

Second Corinthians 8:15 refers to Exodus 16:18, about God providing the manna. Well, God provides other kinds of manna, just what you need; maybe to do with health, or a relationship, or money or something else. He knows what you need, is very generous and will provide: 'As it is written, he that had gathered much had nothing over and he that gathered little had no lack', and thanks be to God, that promise puts the motivation in you to be helpful. In the next chapter of 2 Corinthians we see a great principle of tithing and giving in the New Testament: 'But I say, he which soweth sparingly shall reap also sparingly. And he which soweth bountifully shall reap also bountifully. Every man according as he purposeth in his heart, so let him give; not grudgingly, or of necessity, for God loveth a cheerful giver' (2 Cor. 9:6).

Isaiah says that the Lord is 'waiting to be gracious' to you. I believe that very often God has some real blessings in our lives, and He's waiting to see if we trust Him enough to keep His Sabbath holy and to give Him the tithe. Then He'll release the blessings.

In conclusion, to keep the Sabbath requires you to have a certain amount of faith that God is going to take care of you the other six days of the week. Most of us have many things to do in our profession, and we may feel that it is hard to keep the Sabbath, with so many demands on the other days. Yes, but you've got to trust God by not doing anything other than resting and praising and giving on that one day, because you are saying, 'Lord, if You don't bless the other six days of the week, they won't be worth anything anyway'. So why should I take the pressures of the whole world on my shoulders seven days a week and wear out and be frazzled and uneasy and unhappy; I am resting one day out of seven and trusting You for the other six'. It's true faith, overcoming doubt; we all have to fight this.

Paul says, 'God is able to make all grace abound unto you'. God supernaturally works in our circumstances and stretches money. Indeed, He does! There is not a human explanation for it. But if we hold it back and won't give it, what we are really saying is 'Lord, I'm not sure I really do trust You in the material, money realm'; and if you won't keep Sabbath you are saying, 'Lord, I do not really trust You in the temporal realm in this thing of time, because doesn't everything really depend on me?' What a loss! And what a gain that we remove blockages to further blessing of God where He can make all grace abound towards us when we keep His day holy and give Him His tithe, and anything more that the Lord might lead us to give.

34

The Sabbath and Poverty
Deuteronomy 15:1–11

This section of Deuteronomy expounds the fourth commandment, and particularly what the commandment means when Israel, His people, enter the Promised Land, and how they are to live out the Sabbath principle. It may surprise us that the Sabbath principle is a major way of dealing with poverty in a very practical manner. The principle was one of the major ways that the people of God in the Old Testament would be able to help the poor, and maintain a healthy, structured economical society at the same time, thereby honoring God. This text then shows us the connection between Sabbath and serious reduction of poverty.

Every nation on earth in all times has had to deal with poverty. Some nations are far poorer than others, but even among rich nations—the United States, Canada, Great Britain, France, Germany, and others—there are still plenty of poor. Jesus said: 'The poor you always have with you' (Matt. 26:11). Deuteronomy 15:11 says: 'The poor shall never cease out of the land'. What do we do, as a believing people, concerning the poor?

In the United States, you have certainly heard your parents talk about the New Deal in the 1930s, as an attempt to try to handle the depression; and many of us well remember the so-called Great Society under President Johnson in the 1960s. Economists don't agree whether those programs worked or not; I'm unable to say, but as a believing people, what would we say about helping the poor, in accordance with the Word of God?

God's Word does deal with it. Deuteronomy 15 and Exodus 23 speak of handling poverty in terms of the Sabbath principle of Sabbatical cycle of years, with the seventh year to be observed as one of rest. During that seventh year, not only were they to rest for their labors for a year and let the land lie fallow, but they were to forgive the debts of all the poor people that had borrowed anything from them.

In Deuteronomy 15:1–11, we study how the Sabbath principle takes care of an unpayable debt. In the next section, we will deal with something most of us have never heard a sermon on—the Sabbath and slavery. But for now we will deal only with the Sabbath principle and crushing loads of debt.

As we have said, Old Testament agricultural society—structured in terms of the theocracy—worked on a cycle of seven years, the seventh year a year of rest (later we will talk about the larger cycle of seven times seven years, that is, the Jubilee, which fell in the forty-ninth year). In addition to this year of rest, there was a profound rest of soul, in knowing that you were not under debt. One of the greatest rests of soul is not to owe anybody anything. It is very hard to live, owing heavy debts that are difficult to pay, a burden that one carries in their spirit all the time. But to feel that all your obligations have been honorably met, so that you don't owe anybody anything gives a wonderful freedom of spirit.

God's Law provided a way to come out; God instructed His people to forgive the debts, and God says He would make it up to them. This is made clear here in Deuteronomy 15; when you help the poor in the name of the Lord, and forgive a debt, God will bless you: 'For this thing the Lord thy God shall bless thee in all thy works, and in all that thou puttest thy hand unto' (Deut. 15:10).

In the last text, we spoke about the tithe, and how God blesses those who give. But God also blesses us for being compassionate, involved, and generous to the poor, and does all kinds of things to help us that we probably don't even know that He is working for us.

Even in a rich country like America, people carry a tremendous load of debt: business and personal. Apparently the United States has the lowest rate of savings of any industrialized nation. I am not an economist, but I think it is the case that we have been a people who have lived far beyond our means. If you think back to your grandparents' generation, how restrained they were, how conservative they were, how simply they lived, how generally none of them were in debt. But then they didn't have anything like the kinds of comforts we have. Somewhere along the line, our people felt that they were willing to go into debt to obtain the comforts they desired. I don't know when it happened, but it was most likely after World War II, when so much of our country decided to live beyond its means. An aspect of that, especially since the 1960s, has been the credit card, people spending what they want, to have things they desire, and thereby continually postponing payday, thus getting more and more in the hole.

Two things are said in Deuteronomy 15:7–8 to those of us who are in a better financial position than those who are massively indebted and ready to go under. First, soften your heart towards the needy. And secondly, open wide your hand (Deut. 15:10). In plain language, put your hand into your pocketbook, and give.

Deuteronomy 15:9 warns us, (and even as Christian people who have the Holy Ghost, and are on the way to heaven, we have to be reminded not to be hard-hearted towards the needy around us), and tells us that how helpful we are to the poor depends directly upon the state of our heart. Basically, the state of our heart is determined by our relationship to God in Jesus Christ, and thus, Romans 5:5 says 'the love of God is shed abroad in our hearts by the Holy Spirit who is given unto us'. Walking in the love of God, appropriating the love of Christ for us in the gospel, has a practical ramification of softening our heart, giving us a tender and compassionate heart to the needy. It is not possible really to accept and experience the love of Jesus to my soul, and then to be hard-hearted and mean towards the needy.

We see this in many places in the New Testament; for instance Ephesians 4:28: 'Let him that stole steal no more, but rather let him labor, working with his hands the thing which is good, that he may have to give to him that needeth'. Here Paul teaches that Christian ethics not merely requires us not to steal, not to cheat anybody, but also to work hard. Hard work enable us to have some extra to give to those who are needy.

I saw this in the lives of my mother and father, who were believers. They were not perfect, but spent much time going to the homes of the poor with food and money, to help them in their time of need. I often rode in the back seat of the car, as they took these trips of mercy, and it has stuck in my mind all these years. They were carrying out Ephesians 4:28, 'Give to him that needeth'. If our children or grandchildren could see us doing that, it would have a lasting influence in their lives. Romans 12:13, after all the wonderful doctrine of justification through grace by faith, says: 'distributing to the necessity of the saints, giving hospitality', meaning our heart is to remain tender towards our neighbor.

Now what is the driving force to keep us giving and helping? Deuteronomy 15:15 gets to the point: 'Remember that thou wast a bondsman, a slave in the land of Egypt, and the Lord thy God redeemed thee; therefore I command thee this day'. All of us were enslaved to sin, lost and undone without God and on the way to hell, although we might not have known it. We had little hope concerning eternal life, but Jesus came and the Holy Spirit drew us to faith in Christ. God has given us everything. When we die, what we'll take with us is a saved soul, and what we gave away will be waiting for us on the other side; that's all by grace.

So look at how generously God has dealt with us. He says, as I was to you, now you be that way to needy people around you. It's not that they deserve it; once we say that we will only help those who are very deserving. Stop and think: when was I ever deserving? He came when we were in great need, and so we go to people in great need. In other words, what is being said in Deuteronomy 15:15 is what Jesus says: 'Freely have ye received; freely give'. As I have been generous and merciful and open handed to you, now you treat other people that way.

Now what is the relevance of the Sabbatical cycle in the New Testament after Christ has come? It is clear, as we saw previously, that the weekly Sabbath day of rest carries over into the New Testament, and therefore we are obligated and privileged to observe weekly Sabbath until the end of time. But it is different with the seven year cycle; there is no indication anywhere in the New Testament that the seven year cycle was incumbent upon the church to observe. The cycle was tied to the theocracy of Israel in the Promised Land, and indeed doesn't seem to have been observed after the Babylonian captivity, as far as we know.

But now that the gospel goes to all nations across the world, with all kinds of economies—rural, urban, industrial, agricultural—there is no indication that the Sabbatical cycle carried over. It would be part of what our old theologians called 'the ceremonial law'. The temple stood for the blood sacrifices, the Levitical Aaronic priesthood, the various feasts, and so forth were fulfilled in Christ's death and resurrection, and in that sense surpassed. The Sabbatical cycle seems to have been in that category.

The Westminster Confession of Faith clearly teaches that the basic moral law (enshrined in the Ten Commandments) carries over directly to us, because it is a lasting expression of the character of God. But some aspects of the Law do not carry over with the same authority. Paragraphs 3 and 4 of the Chapter on the Law reads:

> Beside this law, commonly called moral, God was pleased to give to the people of Israel, as a church under age, ceremonial laws, containing several typical ordinances, partly of worship, prefiguring Christ, his graces, actions, sufferings, and benefits;

and partly, holding forth divers instructions of moral duties. All which ceremonial laws are now abrogated, under the New Testament.

To them also, as a body politic [that means a theocracy, tied to one land], he gave sundry judicial laws, which expired together with the State of that people; not obliging any other now further than the general equity thereof may require.

The obligation that may be in something like the Sabbatical cycle of years would be the general equity (the principle of fairness). While, since the New Testament, we are not under the law of Jubilee and release of debts, the principle of fairness—of consideration for the image of God in poor people—carries over. We have to think, what would it mean for us now.

The Epistle to the Hebrews, particularly chapters 9, 10, and 12, explain how the ceremonial law really was fulfilled in Jesus (Heb. 9:6-10).

Now when these things were ordained, the priests went always into the first tabernacle, accomplishing the service of God. But into the second went the high priest alone once every year, not without blood, which he offered for himself, and for the errors of the people; the Holy Ghost this signifying, that the way into the holiest of all was not yet made manifest, while as the first tabernacle was yet standing; which was a figure for the time then present, in which were offered both gifts and sacrifices, that could not make him that did the service perfect, as pertaining to the conscience; which stood only in meats and drinks, and divers washings, and carnal ordinances, imposed on them until the time of reformation.

Hebrews 9:11f. says that Christ, being come, has fulfilled it, so that the old tabernacle and ceremonial laws, many of the rituals, and even the yearly cycle are not relevant in the same way, other than the continuing obligation of general fairness or equity. Hebrews 10:11 speaks of 'the law having a shadow of good things to come'. The laws—ceremonial, judicial, Jubilee—were good, but they were a foreshadowing, of all that Christ would do; they were not the full reality of the things, for Jesus Himself was the full reality to which they pointed. He fulfilled them all: 'Lo, I come to do Thy will, O God. He taketh away the first, that He may establish the second' (Heb. 10:9). He removes all the regulations and gives us something in their place.

Later, Hebrews 12:25-29 speaks of things that can be shaken, that is, certain aspects of the Old Testament economy which were honorable and wonderful for their time, but at length they were shaken down so that the kingdom of Christ could stand forever in their place.

Now that we have the new reality in Christ, we are to remember the poor, to help and be merciful to them in a way that might actually cost us some money—maybe a lot! Hebrews 13:16 says: 'But to do good and to communicate, forget not; for with such sacrifices God is well pleased'. 'Communicate' means, in this context, to give away.

Let us add another principle to the Westminster Confession of Faith's teaching: under the fullness of the gospel we are to be at least as generous as the people of God in the Old Testament, when they were under the shadow of the gospel. They could foresee a Messiah coming. Abraham, Isaac, Jacob and the rest were saved, as Hebrews 11 clearly demonstrates, but they didn't have the fullness of the knowledge of the Lord Jesus Christ in the way we do in the Scriptures, and in the Holy Spirit who makes the presence of Jesus real to us. Surely, when you know him directly, you will wish to be at least as generous as the folk were under the Old Testament, as they were waiting. The principle is: we gladly do more, not less, for those in need.

Jesus says: 'As the Father hath sent Me, even so send I you' (John 20:21). And that's been the story: when the church has been at its brightest in loving the Lord and being holy, it has done the most for the poor people to change their situation.

In the Reformation in Scotland, the Medieval Roman Catholic Church owned a third of the land, but it had become corrupt and sinful. It needed reform, so John Knox and other men of God had to decide what to do with the Church's wealth, including fabulous estates, castles, and accounts in banks. Hence the General Assembly of the Church of Scotland met and decided to take the wealth of the expropriated Catholic Church and use it in three ways: for the support of the ministry and upkeep of the buildings of the churches in Scotland; for universal education and establishment of a free school, for every child in Scotland in every parish; and for poor people, administered through local parishes.

I think they were reflecting Deuteronomy 15 and Exodus 23 in those concerns. It didn't work out because the aristocrats and the nobility expropriated a lot of the money that should have gone to the church and the school and poor people. But in principle, the concern of the Reformed Church in Scotland for the poor was a valid part of the general equity of the Sabbatical cycle of years.

The Word of God teaches us, at the very least, the general principle of 'freely have you received, freely give'; always to be on the lookout for any way that we can help to do whatever we can for those in need. This will be the more important if the economy grows weaker, and large numbers cannot eat or find housing. When things are very difficult, we have the grand opportunity to make the sacrifice of giving in His name. If so, the reality of the grace of God in Jesus is going to shine out in this land like it maybe never has. May God equip us for this, and give us two things: tender hearts and open hands, by His Holy Spirit's grace.

35

The Sabbath and Freedom from Slavery

Deuteronomy 15:12–18

This passage deals with the Sabbath principle, especially as it concerns release from various kinds of slavery. You might think: even here in South Carolina—the center of slavery at one time—this sermon is 140 years out of date. Well, stay with me, and you might find out that it is very up-to-date in several respects, so we want to give this part of the Word of God our attention.

Earlier, we noted that several chapters in this section of Deuteronomy (parts of chapters 14, 15, and 16) are all an exposition of the commandment, 'Remember the Sabbath Day to keep it holy', and that, after the historical prologue, Moses expounds, one after another, the Ten Commandments in very practical ways, to show us what they mean for our daily lives

The passage shows us how the Sabbath principle has relevance for different sorts of slavery and particularly, how to come out of different kinds of slavery. To grasp this we must consider two kinds of slavery. The kind we always think of is physical slavery, or continued indentured servitude. But there is also another kind, for which this passage (and other ones) are relevant, and that is economic slavery or debt slavery. Hence, we are to look at what God's Sabbath principle says about these two sorts of slavery: reprehensible, physical slavery is happily finished in most of the world, but the other is very much with us.

Physical Slavery

For reasons of war, or other economic and cultural reversals, many people over the centuries have been placed in bondage, and enslaved to work for other people. That has been the case since sometime after the fall of Adam down to the nineteenth century. One of my sons lived in a particular country in Africa and served with the United States Peace Corps, and he told me that that country still has physical slavery. So in some societies, sad to say, you still have it. But we in the Western world got rid of it a good while ago.

Some of you may have seen the film, *Amazing Grace*, about the life of William Wilberforce, a great Christian evangelical aristocrat in England in the early 1800s, who worked for years and years to get slavery outlawed in the British Empire. He fought at times almost single-handedly against it. About the time he died in the 1830s, they did finally get rid of slavery across the British Empire. But it took us in the United States about another thirty years, until 1865, before slavery was outlawed in our country. No doubt we are glad it is finished, and wish it hadn't happened. We are still paying a very high price for the shameful slavery that was the case here not so long ago.

Now what does the Bible say about this? Certain forms of slavery were temporarily tolerated in the Old Testament, just as polygamy was. Neither polygamy nor slavery was required by Scripture, nor was either one set up by God's law. They were a second-best but were tolerated until something better would come. Polygamy and slavery were carefully fenced in with many regulations by the Bible to keep them from being any worse than otherwise they would have been, and eventually the coming of Christ and the power of the gospel would purge them out. But it took many years, because to get rid of these bad practices was going against the self-serving tendencies of fallen human nature in nearly every culture.

Jesus spoke about divorce and re-marriage more than once. In Matthew 19:8, Jesus said concerning divorce that, 'from the beginning it was not so'. Neither polygamy nor slavery was part of God's beautiful plan for creation in the beginning; rather, they are results of the fall and of the degeneration of society.

The basic New Testament principle that would overturn all slavery is found in Galatians 3:27-28,

> For as many of you as have been baptized into Christ have put on Christ; there is neither Jew nor Greek; there is neither bond [slave] nor free; there is neither male nor female. For ye are all one in Christ Jesus. And if ye be Christ's, then are ye Abraham's seed and heirs according to the promise.

The liberating principle is: we are one in Christ, and therefore, we have full and equal access to the heart of God and the same personal value before God. Every one who is in Christ, therefore becomes part of the spiritual seed of Father Abraham, the father of the faithful. It is that principle that would eventually get rid of the onerous practice of slavery.

In 1 Corinthians 7:21, Paul is speaking to the various problems in the church at Corinth. In the Greek and Roman classical culture, of course, slavery was a major institution. So what advice would he give to a slave who got saved and joined the church? 'Art thou called being a servant?' In other words, did you get saved while you were still somebody's slave? What should you do? 'Care not for it'. In other words, don't let it worry you; rather think about who you are in Christ. And then he says: 'But if thou mayest be made free, use it rather'. In other words, if there is any way you can get out of slavery, perhaps by earning extra to pay your way out, you ought to do it; it is good for all in Christ, men and women, to be free citizens, where possible. But even where the economic situation is such that you can't get out of it, you still are given this absolute dignity and honor of being in Christ.

Then Paul's little letter of Philemon deals with delivery from the institution of slavery. Onesimus was a slave who ran away; he 'hot-footed it out of town'. Later he was converted under Paul's ministry, and then waited on Paul and was a great help. The man from whom he ran away was actually a Christian—Philemon—and he was a friend of Paul who had stayed in his house. So Paul sent the runaway slave, Onesimus, back to his master Philemon. Then Paul wrote this letter, admitting that it had been illegal for Onesimus to run away, but saying that he had been very helpful to him; and that he has become your brother in Christ. He wasn't a believer when he left, but now he is a Christian, and if he owes you any money, if he took anything when he left, I'll pay it back out of my pocket. Paul adds, remember one thing, you got converted by me and you owe me a good bit. But if you want me to pay you back, I'll do it.

Receive him forever [actually, open your heart as to a son]; not now as a servant, but above a servant, a brother beloved, specially to me, but how much more unto thee, both in the flesh and in the Lord? If thou count me therefore a partner, receive him as myself. If he hath wronged thee, or oweth thee ought, put that on mine account; I Paul have written it with mine own hand, I will repay it; albeit I do not say to thee how thou owest unto me even thine own self besides (Philem. 15-19).

Obviously there is no doubt here that Paul is very strongly hinting, set this brother in the Lord free; don't hold him in slavery; but I am leaving it in your hands.

In sum, the New Testament teaches that in the beginning, there was neither polygamy nor slavery; all were equally created in the image of God; all are equally precious and dear to God. Everyone is fallen; all the descendants of Adam are fallen into sin; Jesus died for all in terms of every tribe, tongue, race, island, nation. His blood was shed for all sorts and conditions of people—for the bond, for the free. And we are to treat them that way. The only principle that really matters in our relating to other sons and daughters of Adam, is this: are they in Adam or are they in Christ? As far as race, this is the only thing that matters in the Bible. We are all born into the fallen race of Adam. And then the race of the last Adam, by regeneration, by faith, by the miracle of God's mercy, is taken out of the first Adam and placed into the last Adam, whereby we have been made Christians.

That is the only distinction that really matters to God; not what country you're from, not what you look like, not what tribe, not what economic standing. Those things have some relevance in human affairs, but they do not matter to God. What matters to God is whether you are in Adam, condemned and lost; or whether you are in Christ, so that you will be with God forever.

Wherefore, as by one man sin entered into the world, and death by sin; and so death passed upon all men, for that all have sinned:
(For until the law sin was in the world: but sin is not imputed when there is no law.
Nevertheless death reigned from Adam to Moses, even over them that had not sinned after the similitude of Adam's transgression, who is the figure of him that was to come.
But not as the offence, so also is the free gift. For if through the offence of one many be dead, much more the grace of God, and the gift by grace, which is by one man, Jesus Christ, hath abounded unto many.
And not as it was by one that sinned, so is the gift: for the judgment was by one to condemnation, but the free gift is of many offences unto justification.
For if by one man's offence death reigned by one; much more they which receive abundance of grace and of the gift of righteousness shall reign in life by one, Jesus Christ.)
Therefore as by the offence of one judgment came upon all men to condemnation; even so by the righteousness of one the free gift came upon all men unto justification of life.
For as by one man's disobedience many were made sinners, so by the obedience of one shall many be made righteous.
Moreover the law entered, that the offence might abound. But where sin abounded, grace did much more abound:
That as sin hath reigned unto death, even so might grace reign through righteousness unto eternal life by Jesus Christ our Lord. (Rom. 5:12-21)

Now there is something here in Deuteronomy 15, particularly verses 12 and 18, that one wishes our Southern forefathers had taken seriously. large numbers of whom were Bible believers, and yet slave holders. If they had only gone by this passage, how different American history could have been! Here is what I mean: Deuteronomy 15:12 and 18, say: 'But if thy brother, an Hebrew man or a Hebrew woman, if he be sold unto thee and serve thee six years, then in the seventh year thou shalt let him go free from thee.' According to Galatians 3, the equivalent of 'Hebrew man or woman' would be 'in Christ'; you put on Christ and you become a brother in the Lord.

Earlier, we considered the principle of equity, spoken of in the Westminster Confession of Faith. Let us think about slavery under this principle. Since Christ fulfilled the Old Testament ceremonial law, one could argue that it is the same with letting indentured servants or slaves go free after six years of service. Is that really required under the gospel?

Well, general equity is the principle of fairness, according to which Christian people would be at least as fair, just, and generous in their dealings with others, as were the Hebrew people of God under the code of Moses. We wouldn't do less under grace than we would under the stricter requirements of the law; rather, far more! If our forefathers who held slaves had followed the principle, then they would have gladly released their servants after six years, if not sooner, for most of the African-Americans became Christian believers, and thus, would have been in the category of 'true Hebrews' and could have been integrated peacefully into the American economy, without severe dislocation, bitterness, hatred, or war. Had our Southern ancestors been obedient to God's Word, I wonder what it would be like now?

If you don't do things God's way, following the general equity as your guide, it is always a lot cheaper than if you do not. If you violate the summary of the law (love to God and to your neighbor) you will pay a very high price; whereas if you seek to honor it as best you can, seemingly costly at the time, it will be far less costly than if you don't go by it.

A Second Kind of Slavery

There's a second kind of slavery, not immediately in view in this passage, which has already been dealt. Still, I want to talk about it, because it is in view in verses 1–11 of this chapter. It is the principle of debt—too much debt—enslaving the people of God. Physical slavery is finished in this country since 1865, and we're glad it's gone. But while economic slavery is generally not so bad as physical slavery, it does bring people into desperate circumstances, where life for some of them does not seem worth living.

Now the Sabbath principle has something powerful to say about dealing with debt, which can become a dreadful master. Many years ago some wonderful Christian friends went into rather heavy debt in order to get hold of extra land. Soon they got under tremendous pressure as interest rates went up drastically in the late 1970s. One day, this wonderful Christian mother said, 'I believe I have learned my lesson. I won't get into debt the next time to get hold of any more land, because ...' and then quoted Proverbs 22:7: 'The debtor is slave to the lender.' I can see her face as she said it, and it has stuck in my mind almost like an arrow in the flesh.

Too much debt can become a massive burden to the spirit, destructive of the personality and indeed of marital relationships. Look at this statement from the *Wall Street Journal*: 'American household debt has more than doubled in a decade to 13.8 trillion at the end of 2007, from 6.4 trillion in 1999, the vast majority of it in mortgages and home equity lines, according to federal data. But the value of United States householders, the biggest asset, their homes, is now falling.'

I remember in the 1970s, a conservative Bible scholar said that the way he took the Old Testament passages like Deuteronomy 15, was that nobody should go into debt for a house mortgage for longer than six years; if people would limit their indebtedness to six years, it would be a way to liberate the population in a certain period of time. I don't think you can really prove that after the end of the Old Testament theocracy. On the other hand, we could at least go by the general equity (as in the Westminster Confession of Faith) of the Sabbatical cycle, and be very careful not to commit to more than what we can reasonably pay back.

Another principle is, never take out debt on the basis of how you hope your income will increase. I know a huge church in Charlotte that almost went under twenty some years ago. They convinced the bank to lend them money based on the rate the congregation was growing. (They were in a growing area of Charlotte and in the last three years had grown such-and-such a percent.) So they said, how about lending us some money for the way we will have grown five years from now? The bank did so. Then they started having problems in the church, including a membership that instead of growing, was now declining. It seems that they had not thought through the general equity of not getting indebted like that. In sum let us remember two things, 'The debtor is slave to the lender' (Prov. 22:7), and 'Owe no man anything but to love one another' (Rom. 13:8).

One of the ways we experience Sabbath rest, even beyond our ceasing from work and unnecessary travel, is to learn not to get heavily indebted. People who are indebted beyond what they can reasonably pay back, have little or no rest in their spirits and cannot rest. Maybe they are under huge credit card debt, or a house mortgage far beyond their means; maybe they still owe large educational loans. If so, it is important to get competent advice on how to get out of it, and to make all necessary adjustments in one's living expenses in order to do so. Practicing personal and familial modesty is a great spiritual principle here, and without it, one cannot generally get out of debt.

Another commandment that will help us avoid debt is: 'Thou shalt not covet'. If we can take the cross to our self on coveting, so that we no longer insist that we should have as much as everybody else, and are willing to go into debt to keep up, then we could soon enough be in a position to experience a sabbath rest in our spirits. The point here is not to wish to show off in comparison with others, and instead say to ourselves, 'I will live simply, on what the Lord gives me now. I want to look everybody that I pass on the street in the face, to owe no man anything, but to love one another'.

This requires modesty of spirit, a fruit of the blessed Holy Spirit. When you experience even some measure of it, you will find a quiet rest of spirit; something that will mean more than you could ever calculate, on the Sabbath Day when you seek to rest. Rest from debt is one of the beautiful principles of the holy Sabbath day. God help us to heed and to live in that sort of Sabbatarianism, so that we can become ever more free and happy!

36

Consecration

Deuteronomy 15:19–23

This little section is about the all-encompassing principle of consecration, that is most important to our lives, and to the advancement of the Christian church in every age. One of the highest honors that can ever be paid to a fellow Christian is when somebody in the church or community says, this person really is consecrated.

In 1966, when I worked for a summer as a seminary student in some small churches. In one of those little towns in rural Mississippi there was a minister whom everybody said was truly consecrated, which I found to be absolutely right. As an illustration, one of the townspeople pointed out to me that, in general, the custom was that people would bring food to the minister's house, but this good man and his wife were constantly delivering food which they had cooked for poor, elderly, and sick people. They had never had a minister who was that generous, and I would add that in fifty years I have seen very few in his category. He was a very humble person and full of prayer and exuded the presence of the Lord. Though I may be partial, I would deem him and a Lumbee Indian preacher whom I knew from Pembroke, North Carolina, who also constantly visited the sick and dying, and gave away everything he could get his hands on, for the sake of Christ, as two of the most consecrated people that have ever touched my life. They encouraged me to seek the route of consecration.

Now the term 'consecration'—often used in the Christian church—is rooted in the Old Testament, not least here in Deuteronomy 15:19–23, and in Exodus 13 and Numbers 18. So what does 'consecration', mean, as we look in these texts and in some New Testament passages?

Let us note three points. First, consecration is part of the Sabbath principle; second, the necessity of being set apart or being made different, is part of consecration, and third, consecration is seen as sacrifice in the New Testament.

Consecration is Part of the Sabbath Principle

We have seen previously that this section of Deuteronomy is divided into ten major parts, each expounding one of the Ten Commandments. The part we are in today is 'Remember the Sabbath Day, to keep it holy'; so consecration is seen in the context of the Sabbath principle and will help us understand what consecration really means.

The Sabbath principle itself is a sort of a consecration, a setting apart, in the temporal area—one day set apart to God out of every seven: 'Six days shalt thou labor and do all thy work, and so forth, but the seventh is the Sabbath of the Lord thy God'. It's the consecration of our time. You don't work; you worship, you praise, and you have to engage in acts of necessity or mercy—get the ox out of the ditch, take care of the sick, and so on.

Some seek to avoid Sabbath observance by asking, but doesn't all our time belong to God? Yes, but don't use that as a way to get yourself off the hook. Even if all your time, and indeed, every breath you take belongs to God, you are still under obligation to give the entirety of one day out of seven to him. You cannot do that if you go shopping or attend professional sports events! So Sabbath keeping is a consecration of time to God.

What is the most valuable thing you have? You might say, money to pay my bills. That is true; you want to honor the Lord by paying your bills on time, and you want to be able to help people. But you can lose money and get it back. Something you can't get back is time. The most valuable thing you have got is time.

I recently read about a banquet held at Princeton University for Albert Einstein in his later years. Someone asked him, 'Dr. Einstein, if you could be given by us a gift that you would really like, what would it be?' He said, 'It would be a jar filled with more time.' In Sabbath keeping, you're showing God that you're giving something very, very precious—the most precious thing you have—which is your time. Sabbath is consecration in the temporal area of our lives.

Similarly, the devotion, offering or setting apart of the firstborn of men and animals to the Lord, is consecration in the area of personal familial life and economic growth. Now the money comes in—that's important. So temporally, we consecrate one seventh of our time to the Lord every week. But then, in terms of human increase and economic increase, Old Testament believers consecrated to God the firstborn of all the cattle and sheep. And then later when we get to Deuteronomy 21, we will see the meaning of the consecration of the firstborn son to the Lord.

The Necessity of Being Set Apart or Made Special Is Essential to Consecration

This latter part of Deuteronomy 15 deals with growth in the economic area, and also with matters involving human growth: both are to be consecrated in different ways to the Lord. Now the major form of wealth in Old Testament times was flocks of sheep and herds of cattle and goats; animal husbandry was the principal form of wealth in the ancient world, and still is in much of the world.

Some of our Gideons were recently in Africa to give out Bibles, and they met a consecrated young man of that area, who was also a Gideon. He said he was looking forward to getting married, but he still had to make enough money for three more cows to give to his potential father-in-law, in order to get the hand of this man's daughter. Some of the Gideons said, 'We'll give you money to get these extra cows to drive down to your would-be father-in-law's house.' And he said, 'No, no, the Lord will send it in; I don't want you to give me the money.' So in many parts of the world, the number of animals is your wealth. Job had a lot, but the main things listed are camels, sheep, goats, cattle, and so forth; he was the richest man in that part of the world.

One thing I found out about our own ancestry as I started to write *Carolina Scots,* dealing with why our ancestors left the Isle of Skye and other places in the early eighteenth century and came to North and then South Carolina, was related to the dropping price of cattle, the main form of wealth. While the Puritans in England came because of religious persecution, our own Highland people came because of the price of cattle. The form of wealth that most people in the world have lived by since the dawn of time is animal husbandry.

The firstborn of every cow, sheep, goat, or camel, is to be set apart to the Lord; a considerable transfer of wealth to God. It's a way of saying, I recognize the goodness of our Creator God, our Savior, our Provider, and I consecrate to Him, as He has commanded, the firstborn that opens the womb of this cow, this sheep, or whatever you have. While Sabbath keeping is *temporal* consecration, *material* consecration involves setting apart some of the increase in reproduction within animal husbandry to the Lord, and was expressed negatively and positively.

Negatively, firstborn livestock such as oxen were not to be used to work in the field. Firstborn sheep were never to be sheared—to get the wool for weaving or selling. Consecration of the firstborn reminded everybody that these animals are special; they are devoted to God.

Positively, firstborn animals could be sacrificed at the central shrine of worship—the tabernacle, and later, at the temple in Jerusalem. It was fine to sacrifice consecrated firstborn animals because they belonged to God. And the setting apart of the firstborn of animals and mankind is a reminder of the Passover—recalling how the tenth plague required the death of the firstborn son of every family, from Pharaoh's palace down to the slave hovel; all were slain by the destroying Angel of Death. The firstborn of every animal, the cattle, the sheep, the camels, and all the rest was slain—a tremendous loss in the chief form of wealth, animal husbandry.

But the children of Israel were in the Land of Goshen, a separated part of Egypt, and had smeared the blood of the sacrificial lamb by divine provision, on the doorpost of every house. This also protected the barns, the sheep stalls and cattle stalls, so that the destroying Angel passed over them, and did not visit devastation on the sons of the Israelites, nor on their cattle, their sheep, or any of their animals. They were literally under the blood.

Whereas the Egyptians had been taken in their own sin during the tenth plague, without the protection of the substitutionary atonement, the Israelites remembered that their firstborn had been spared by divine grace. Therefore, it was proper for them to consecrate all their firstborn to the Lord, because they would remember, after all, that these were a gift from the Lord. (We will deal with the firstborn of the human family at a later time).

Finally, there should be no defect in the animal to be sacrificed. According to verse 21, you cannot use the animal to work in the fields; you cannot shear the sheep for the wool; but it is appropriate, if you want to take it to the central shrine for a sacrifice, because it belongs to the Lord anyway.

However, you should not take a defective animal that is malformed or has some kind of problem that makes it unhealthy or not the very best. You only give God your best.

At a much later time, this is commented on in Malachi 1:6–9,

A son honoreth his father, and a servant his master; if then I be a father, where is mine honor? And if I be a master, where is my fear? saith the Lord of hosts unto you, O priests, that despise my name. And ye say, Wherein have we despised thy name? Ye offer polluted bread upon mine altar; and ye say, Wherein have we polluted thee? In that ye say, The table of the Lord is contemptible. And if ye offer the blind for sacrifice, is it not evil? And if ye offer the lame and sick, is it not evil? Offer it now unto thy governor; will he be pleased with thee, or accept thy person? saith the Lord of hosts. And now, I pray you, beseech God that he will be gracious unto us; this hath been by your means; will he regard your persons? saith the Lord of hosts.

which says that one of the problems at the end of the Old Testament economy is that people were bringing junk to the Lord and keeping the best to themselves. To do that is to invite judgment, but far worse is the disrespect it shows to God Himself. The principle is found in the old hymn which begins:

> Give of your best to the Master;
> Give of the strength of your youth.
> Throw your soul's fresh glowing ardor
> Into the battle for truth.

Consecration as Sacrifice in the New Testament

The law of offering the firstborn of animals to the Lord was not necessary after the incarnation of Christ: God's firstborn is Jesus Christ, whom God gave for us; He left the glories of heaven; He fulfills all of the typical Old Testament requirements—they are honorable, they are right, they are good, they are true, but they are fulfilled in Jesus. When the Father offers His own Son on the cross, that fulfills the economy of the firstborn. So, offering the firstborn of animals is no longer required.

On the other hand, there is still what we may call 'the general equity' of the principle of sacrifice and consecration of what you have, or at least part of what you have, that still carries over to our times, after the New Testament revelation. The nearest we have to consecration of the firstborn would be the tithe. Therefore, we take basic truths from Deuteronomy 15 and other passages I have referred to (Num. 18, Exodus 13 and so forth), and see how they apply today.

Listen to the teaching of the Apostle Paul in Romans 12:1–2:

> I beseech you therefore, brethren, by the mercies of God, that ye present your bodies a living sacrifice, holy, acceptable unto God, which is your reasonable service. And be not conformed to this world; but be ye transformed by the renewing of your mind, that ye may prove what is that good, and acceptable, and perfect, will of God.

The idea here is that the best you will ever have, in principle anyway, is that you will be willing to say 'Lord, I am willing for you to have first refusal.' If the Lord will say, 'no my son, or dear daughter, I don't really need that right now, you can have it back,' then fine.

One consecrated Christian woman in the last 300 years was Susanna Wesley, the mother of the great evangelists, John Wesley and his brother Charles Wesley, the hymn writer. What a mother she was! She was the mother of 19 children, and her husband was a very poor vicar of the Church of England; they were always poor, struggling, with never enough money. But what a fabulous job she did, raising those children for the Lord!

One time when John and Charles had finished Oxford University, they felt called to mission to Savannah, Georgia, which was pretty wild at that time, with a wild ocean to cross, and diseases and possibly hostile natives when they got there, Somebody spoke to Susanna Wesley and said 'Ah, sister Wesley, we feel so sorry for you; for your two most brilliant sons, who have done so well at Oxford, and had such a bright future before them, have gone to the dangerous colony of Georgia.' Susanna, looking them right in the eye, said, 'Look here, I couldn't be more pleased that my sons are consecrating themselves to the Lord in Georgia.' She added that she wished she had 15 more sons so she could send every last one of them to the mission field, because Jesus Christ deserves the best that she had, and she would gladly offer them up to the Lord.

That sort of consecration of Susanna Wesley played a part, through her sons, in changing much of the English speaking world in the next century, through the revival that accompanied the Methodist movement. I believe that when God wants to work powerful changes in society, He raises us consecrated people. It could also be said of the consecrated Calvinists in the mid eighteenth-century revival, such as George Whitfield, Jonathan Edwards, and Samuel Davies. One verse of the hymn, O Zion Haste, says:

> Give of thy sons to bear the message glorious;
> Give of thy wealth to speed them on their way.
> Pour out thy soul for them in prayer victorious,
>   And all thou spendest, Jesus will repay.
>   Publish glad tidings, tidings of peace,
>   Tidings of Jesus' redemption and release.

We will conclude with a contrast between two verses about attitude. The most important thing about a person is their attitude, which pretty well determines how you are able to deal with them in business, in the home, or in a social setting.

There are two different attitudes: one is found in world, before it is touched by the grace of God, a worldly attitude. I think that a worldly attitude is not really whether somebody smokes, drinks, or dances, or wears makeup, or such fairly superficial external things; that's not what it is to be worldly, although even so, careful moderation and consideration of others is always called for in all matters.

You will find a worldly attitude in what Satan says to God in Job 2:4, where the evil one accuses the Lord of protecting Job too much; that God has put a hedge about him. Satan argues, the only reason Job honors God and praises Him is that He doesn't let anything bad happen to Job. Job doesn't really love God, he just loves what God gives him. Then Satan summarizes the attitude of the world and the people under his control—which Job was not, though Satan hoped he would be: 'Yea, skin for skin, all that a man hath will he give for his life.'

Here is worldliness: here is the attitude of the world, and of those who don't even know that they are under Satan's dominion—'skin for skin, everything that a man hath will he give for his life'. In other words, put yourself first, break any and every moral principle, if it takes it for you to stay on top. Take care of number one and let moral considerations go, if it is necessary to protect your interest. That is natural to a fallen world. It is the essence of what is rightly called worldliness.

In contrast, Revelation 12:11 expresses the attitude of God's people; this is consecration: 'And they overcame him (the devil) by the blood of the Lamb and by the word of their testimony and they loved not their lives unto the death...' and then it goes on to say, 'Rejoice, hallelujah, hallelujah!' Many in the world are going to praise God and rejoice, if they see some people who are consecrated enough not 'to love their life to the death'. Nobody with good sense wants to get killed, wants to put themselves unnecessarily in the way of danger. But when God says, 'Dear son, dear daughter, serve me here, and don't ask any questions; do what I say', they reply, 'Lord, I love you; Jesus gave everything for me; you've got the right to ask of me my best; I'll go'.

That is how the mission of the church has worked for 2,000 years; we're still larger and expanding more rapidly than Islam, because you have had men and women over the ages who loved not their lives unto the death.

It is entirely fine to enjoy living, to appreciate the good creative gifts of God in your family, good food and drink, and friendship; good music, good books, and, when possible, pleasant houses. But don't love it to the death! Don't love living so much that you violate moral principle and forget who God is. You are to love Christ better than your life. When a selfish world sees that Christians are consecrated, that they put the honor of Christ and the interest of others before self, it shocks the world. They can't believe that somebody is not finally, totally self-centered and selfishly motivated. Instead, even worldly eyes see that the consecrated ones actually care for God, honor God, and care for other people. That has broken many a worldly mind open to receive the love and light of the grace of God in Jesus Christ.

How will we reach a secular world, now in late stages of moral declension? While prayer, preaching and the sacraments, as well as soul winning, are always called for, every day, the most important, foundational thing we can ever do is be consecrated Christians. You might be disappointed by this answer, and object, 'I asked you a political question; I asked you a cultural question, and you have given me an answer of piety!'

Don't discount consecration as a powerful factor in changing the real world. I was reading recently about Gorbachev, who is now a member of the Russian Orthodox Church. He was the biggest politician at the time of Ronald Reagan and Margaret Thatcher, and head of an atheistic, communist nation, with massive power. Why did Gorbachev join the church?

The article said that he had very consecrated grandparents and especially, a consecrated mother. Apparently, he never forgot that, even when he was heading up the Soviet Union, and that memory of consecration may have had something to do with the fact that he later worked for the atheistic Soviet Union to unravel. I remember when he came to North Carolina ten or twelve years ago, one of the things he requested was to be taken to visit Billy and Ruth Graham. So there you see consecration: humble grandparents, humble mother, and one of the biggest politicians of the twentieth century, being changed by it.

Take my life and let it be, consecrated, Lord, to Thee.
Take my moments and my days; let them flow in endless praise.
Take myself and I will be, ever, only, all to Thee.

37

THE PASSOVER

Deuteronomy 16:1–8

This text brings before us the foundational festival of biblical religion, the Passover. In the larger section (verses 1–17) you find three pilgrim festivals of Israel: Passover (or unleavened bread); the Feast of Weeks, and the Feast of Tabernacles (the great harvest festival of Israel). They are called pilgrim feasts, because all Israel was required to come as pilgrims to the central shrine (Shiloh and later Jerusalem) three times a year.

We read in the Gospel of Luke that when Jesus was 12 years old, He came with His parents and the pilgrim crowd from Nazareth, up to Jerusalem to observe the festival of Passover. All three festivals for the pilgrims were based on the weekly Sabbath. That is to say, the calendar of three pilgrim festivals was based on periods of seven, computed each year in accordance with how many Sabbaths had passed. This festal calendar is part of Moses' explication of what the fourth commandment, 'Remember the Sabbath Day to keep it holy', means in the life of God's people in the Promised Land.

In this message, we will look at the first eight verses, and the first of the three pilgrim festivals—Unleavened Bread or Passover. We shall note three points: first, the reason for the Passover; second, the reason for unleavened bread; and third, the place of the Passover in the Christian church.

THE REASON FOR THE PASSOVER (16:1–2)

Passover is first in the festivals of Israel, because it is the foundational celebration of all biblical redemption. It is the way God chose to deliver His people from bondage in slavery, to the freedom of new life in communion with Himself. It is based on the shedding of the blood of the animal substitute; the shedding of the blood of the unblemished lambs' blood in the place of God's people.

In Exodus 12:2, which speaks of the setting up of the Passover, it says that the Passover is 'the beginning of months, the first month of the year to you'. Once they left Egypt, the calendar was rearranged whereby the first month—in the earlier part of the Old Testament called *Abib*—was called *Nisan*, from the time of the Babylonian captivity, when they adopted Babylonian names for the months.

What we see here is something very important about the rolling around of the years. In biblical religion, the year is based on the shedding of blood for our sins. That's very important!

Whenever we face a new year, it is most important to remember that as we face the unrolling of time, whose outcome is always uncertain for us, we face it as those who have been forgiven, and will be forgiven of all their sins through this animal substitute. This shows that redemption is the basis of how we live out our years.

I think that is why Christian people, who realize their privileges, ought to have an easier time facing life than non-Christians who, as unbelievers, can never do enough to make themselves right, and therefore tend to be uneasy in spirit. The world is fallen, it will never be perfect; and some people live under tremendous stress trying to control everything, trying to make it right, or even perfect. Naturally, they know they haven't gotten there, and it makes some people's lives, particularly the more conscientious ones, very difficult indeed. But biblical religion teaches us to face every year, every week, every Sabbath, with the knowledge that 'I am forgiven; I am ransomed by the blood of the Lamb; I don't have to make everything perfect; I can't. But God accepts me because of the One who shed His blood in my room and stead.' And then strangely enough, it sets you free to do something positive, and not to be bound by worry.

In Exodus 12, we see the setting up of Passover, when they were still in Egypt in slavery. God told Moses that He was going to do something tremendous, and that He wanted him always to remember it. We still remember it to this day, particularly in the Lord's Supper. God says, I want My people, Old Testament and New Testament, till the end of time, to remember what I am doing in what will become the basic festival of all biblical worship. 'Speak ye unto all the congregation of Israel, saying, In the tenth day of this month they shall take to them every man a lamb, according to the house of their fathers, a lamb for an house.'

The principle here of substitution is the basis of true religion, the way home to God, the way to have peace in your heart. The only way God has appointed for us to be saved and to live in joy is through substitution of an innocent victim in our place. Therefore, we focus on the lamb.

Verse 6 says that you shall keep it until the fourteenth day of the month—the Sabbath principle, still observed in Judaism; in fact the date of Easter in Christianity is still based on it. Notice verses 6–7: 'the whole assembly of the congregation of Israel shall kill it in the evening. And they shall take of the blood, and strike it on the two side posts and on the upper door post of the houses, wherein they shall eat it'. So we're talking about blood atonement; that's the only way that you can know God, that you can be accepted by God. The liberalism, the modernism, which in the early 1900s wanted to be so sophisticated, taught that we commend ourselves to God by education, by culture, and by good works, which is absolute folly. It is true that good works are called for, but only after you have received the blood atonement, that is the basis of our approach to God.

Verse 8 then speaks about eating the roasted lamb; the lamb was slain and its blood smeared on the doorposts, and then the family was to eat of the lamb. It is a picture of communion with God, who provided the sacrifice at His own expense.

Earlier, Deuteronomy 16:1, tells us: 'God brought thee forth out of Egypt by night', it is a clear reference to the destruction of the firstborn in Egypt, the tenth plague, when God sent the Angel of Death over all Egypt, over the cow stalls, the folds of the sheep and of the goats, and over every house, from Pharaoh's palace to the slave hovel, taking the life of the firstborn of mankind and of animal, except in the land of Goshen, where the Israelites lived, where they had sacrificed the lamb, and smeared its blood on the doorposts, and on the lintel over the door. When the Angel saw the blood he passed by, and the lives of their firstborn were all spared.

You might ask this question: Wouldn't it be true that the Israelites were sinners as well as the Egyptians? The answer is, yes. Moses himself had murdered a man; the Israelites were far from perfect. So why did the Angel of Death not destroy them when he saw the blood? St. Paul tells us in Romans 8:32: 'He that spared not His own Son, but delivered Him up for us all, how shall He not with Him freely give us all things?' God spared the firstborn of Israel because in due time, 1450 or so years later, God would give His own Firstborn on Calvary's cross to pay for their sins. The blood of the lamb was pointing toward the blood of the Lamb of God; that's why it was effective.

Note that they were to eat this feast together, as Deuteronomy 16:6–7 makes clear—a change from the original Passover, when they didn't have time to come together; it was crisis time. So they slaughtered a lamb in every house, and ate it by families. But Moses said, Once you get into the Promised Land it's going to be different; then this will be a pilgrim festival. I want everybody in the land to come together, the blood to be shed at the tabernacle (or temple), and all to eat together. It's a picture of sharing the new life that God gives to all His people at the place of worship, sacrifice, and resurrection.

The Reason for Unleavened Bread

Deuteronomy 16:3-4 requires there to be unleavened bread at this feast, the reason being, 'Thou shalt keep the feast of unleavened bread; (thou shalt eat unleavened bread seven days, as I commanded thee, in the time appointed of the month Abib; for in it thou camest out from Egypt. And none shall appear before me empty' (Exod. 23:15). In Exodus 3:7 we read: And the Lord said, I have surely seen the affliction of My people which are in Egypt, and have heard their cry by reason of their taskmasters, for I know their sorrows'. So the unleavened bread is also called in Deuteronomy 16, 'the bread of affliction'.

What does it mean? They didn't have time to put leaven in the bread; leaven is yeast, and it needs to have several hours to make the bread rise, as all of you who bake would well know. To get out of the country before Pharaoh's army could reach them, they took the flour and water in the kneading trays, and bound it in their clothes on their back, so that they could bake it very quickly on the way.

Hence, having no leaven in the bread meant that it wasn't as tasty a bread, thus it is called 'the bread of affliction,' reminding them of their long affliction, of hundred of years of slavery. But less tasty bread was a small enough price to enable them to remember what they had been through, and to give God thanks. 'You will remember your affliction, and your uppermost thought will be that affliction has become glorious freedom.'

So, the absence of leaven speaks of haste—they had to get out fast—and they were supposed to remember their affliction. Leaven also may mean something else, as I would gather from 1 Corinthians 5:6–8. There, Paul draws an analogy between leaven and insincerity in religion, or leaven and impurity of life:

> Your glorying, your boasting is not good. Know ye not that a little leaven leaveneth the whole lump? Purge out therefore the old leaven, that ye may be a new lump, as ye are unleavened. For even Christ our Passover is sacrificed for us. Therefore let us keep the feast, not with old leaven, neither with the leaven of malice and wickedness; but with the unleavened bread of sincerity and truth.

Paul is saying that absence of leaven speaks of simplicity of life, of turning from wickedness and lies and falsehood, and seeking to be absolutely right and true and honest and open with God. Paul picks up Deuteronomy 16, Exodus 12 and Exodus 23, taking it on into the New Testament, and thereby reminding us of this: while the eating of leaven or unleavened bread is no longer an issue for us as such, it does remind us at the beginning of every worship service that we must confess our sins. We come before God, in private prayers, in family prayers and particularly in the church, having lived another week or another day, where there is 'leaven', impurity, lack of sincerity or straightforwardness in some of the things we have said or done. And true biblical religion always calls for sincere, open confession of our sin for God to purge us out, and make us clean and fit once more to stand in His presence.

Something very important about worship, needs to be emphasized today. Deuteronomy 16:8 says: 'and on the seventh day shall be a solemn assembly to the Lord thy God'. What is meant by 'a solemn assembly'. Whatever else you say about Christian worship, there is to be a solemnity about it, a seriousness, an earnestness about worship, simply because worship is, first of all, about God. Peter makes this point when he was getting ready to go to the house of Cornelius, in Acts 10:33: 'We are all here in the presence of God.'

If Christian worship be true worship, the most important thing is that we have assembled in the presence of God; and that definitely says something about the demeanor of the minister and the people who are engaging in worship. For hundreds of years that has been assumed to be the case, though I fear, less so now. Throughout the churches, Protestant and even Roman Catholic, there is a tremendous difference in how people are now approaching God in worship. Some services—I have been to them—start with a joke, end with a joke, are light and frivolous all the way through, almost more like an entertainment session or a cocktail party, as though it is merely a work of the flesh, and as though God's holy presence is irrelevant. You might ask, 'What denomination are you talking about?' I'm talking about Presbyterian, Baptist, Methodist, Episcopal, Lutheran, Roman Catholic, and some others. You may also say, 'You must be talking about liberals'. No, I'm not. They may be into it, but conservatives, it seems to me, are just as bad as the liberals in the kind of worship that is running through many of the churches at present.

I wish to refer you to *Reformed Worship*, a fine resource on this point by Dr. Terry L. Johnson, pastor of the grand old Independent Presbyterian Church of Savannah, Georgia. He says, 'The influences of the baby boom generation, mass culture, and the charismatic movement, have converged to bring rapid, controversial, and popular change. The forms of traditional worship: historic orders of service, organs, hymns, metrical psalms, creeds, pastoral prayers, and biblical sermons have been jettisoned in favor of the forms of contemporary culture: soft rock, talk show format, a friendly and informal atmosphere, overhead projector and topical sermons addressing felt needs.'

I was recently told of an advertisement by some people who are starting a church; they said it will be contemporary, won't make you feel uncomfortable, and you can walk around during the service eating hot dogs, drinking coke or coffee; there are soft chairs; you will feel perfectly at home. Well, how does that fit with what Deuteronomy 16:8 says is a 'solemn assembly'? Wouldn't we want to worship God the way He has told us to do in His Word? How can you take upon yourself to say that people like so-and-so, and they don't like so-and-so; we're going to give them what they like. But if you follow the Bible, if you are a servant of the Bible, you don't have the right to do that and still call it Christian worship.

The Westminster Confession of Faith (chapter 21, paragraph 1) states: 'But the acceptable way of worshiping the true God is instituted by Himself and so limited by His own revealed will, that He may not be worshiped according to the imaginations and devices of men, or the suggestions of Satan, under any visible representation, or any other way not prescribed in the Holy Scripture.' Then in paragraphs 3 and 5: 'Prayer, with thanksgiving …the reading of the Scriptures with godly fear, the sound preaching and conscionable hearing of the Word. … singing of psalms with grace in the heart … the due administration and worthy receiving of the sacraments instituted by Christ, are all parts of the ordinary religious worship of God.'

When the woman at the well in Samaria asked Jesus how we were to worship, God would it be in Samaria or Jerusalem, He replied: 'God is Spirit and they that worship Him must worship Him in Spirit and in truth'. True Christian worship is a solemn assembly. That doesn't mean you can't be joyful; it's not a funeral service! It can be full of life and gladness, of course, where appropriate. But we know that God is here; God is holy; we are unholy; we are taking something on ourselves to believe that we are coming into His presence.

Hebrews 4:15–16 speaks of our drawing near to God in worship. James 4:8–10 in like fashion says that we are coming into God's presence. Isaiah 55:6 says that we are seeking, and calling upon God. The Psalmist says:

> One thing I have asked from the Lord; that I shall seek that I may dwell in the House of the Lord all the days of my life to behold the beauty of the Lord and to inquire in His temple'. And then verse 8: 'When thou saidst seek ye my face; my heart said to thee, thy face, O Lord, will I seek (Ps. 27:4).

Such texts show us that Christian worship is a solemn assembly that requires profound reverence. Jesus told us when we pray, to pray this way: 'Our Father which art in heaven, hallowed be thy name'. Reverence! Solemnity! 'Worship the Lord with reverence and rejoice with trembling' (Ps. 2:11); 'At thy holy temple I will bow in reverence to thee' (Ps. 5:7); 'O come and let us worship and bow down; let us kneel before the Lord our Maker' (Ps. 95:6). So this Passover is to be a solemn and reverential assembly. Why? Because God is there.

THE PLACE OF PASSOVER IN THE CHRISTIAN CHURCH

Paul in 1 Corinthians 5:7 gives us the clue as to how Passover fits into Christianity: 'For even Christ our Passover is sacrificed for us'. Christ is our Passover! Yes, we believe in Passover, but now it is fulfilled, caught up and renewed in Christ. All four Gospels put the Lord's Supper (or Last Supper) into the context of the Jewish Passover and its fulfillment. For instance, Mark 14:1, 'After two days was the feast of the Passover and of unleavened bread', and the chief priests and the scribes sought how they could kill Christ. Mark goes on to say that Christ instituted the Lord's Supper. Mark, and the other Gospels put the Last Supper in the context of the Jewish Passover.

Therefore, what we must say is this: all of the Old Testament Pascal lambs point forward to the Lamb of God that taketh away the sins of the world. That's what John the Baptist said at Jesus' baptism in the Jordan: 'Behold the Lamb of God that taketh away the sins of the world' (John 1:29). All of the morning and evening sacrifices and the Day of Atonement, every blood shedding of every lamb in Israel, was pointing towards THE Lamb of God that taketh away the sins of the world. And Revelation 13:8 shows that all of history, even the creation of the frame of the earth and the sun and the moon and stars, their rotation, and the movement of every day, every hour, every moment of history, is in terms of the Lamb of God, slain before the foundation of the world. The cross was in God's mind before He made the world, which He well knew would fall into sin, and the remedy for sin would be in the slain lamb, all of which is in the all-encompassing plan of God.

Now look at Acts 8:27 and following. It's about the man from Ethiopia, a eunuch of high authority, under Candace, queen of the Ethiopians. He had come to Jerusalem to worship; he wasn't a Jew, but he was seeking the God that he knew the Jews properly represented. Afterwards, 'he was returning home and sitting in his chariot' and reading Isaiah the prophet—probably out loud as was the custom in the ancient world and no doubt, having a slave to drive his chariot. He was reading from Isaiah 53, the suffering Lamb.

Sent by the Holy Spirit of God, the evangelist Philip was on that very road, where he heard this man reading Isaiah 53: 'The man of sorrows and acquainted with grief' section. Philip went up and said, 'Do you understand what you are reading?' The Ethiopian said, 'No, not really; I'd like some help, so come up into the chariot.' So Philip goes up there. The eunuch asked, who does this mean? Who is this talking about, this suffering one, this Man of Sorrows and acquainted with grief that gave up His life? 'Then Philip opened his mouth and began at the same Scripture, and preached unto him Jesus'.

All of this shows us that Christ fulfills the Old Testament Passover, and replaces it with the Lord's Supper, which sets forth His fully sufficient, one-for-all atoning death for sinners. The Old Testament Passover was wonderful, but it had to be repeated every year. On the contrary, Jesus' sacrifice is what the Greek in the New Testament calls '*ephapax*': 'once for all'; it was so fully sufficient, that when the infinite One rendered up His soul on our behalf, it availed for all time: past, present, and future. And so it's 'once for all'.

Because of this eternally availing nature of His finished work, we can say that the Holy Spirit brings the presence of the risen Christ into the Christian Passover, the Lord's Supper; the bread and the wine speaking of His pierced body, and His outpoured blood for all who will receive it in faith. The Holy Spirit makes this now risen Christ present to the faith of all those who believe the Gospel, who eat the bread and drink the wine; it's a way of saying 'God is here in his infinite grace.'

We were speaking of a solemn assembly, but some people these days argue that solemn or serious worship might turn people off. Not for a moment! Not if you've got the real thing; the real thing is God. What worries me about certain types of worship is that they exclude God! I have to ask, why go through a human exercise of often tacky entertainment? What have you got then? Nothing! What I say is, get all that out of the way; go by Scripture, so that God—the living God; the holy Trinity: Father, Son and Holy Spirit; the fountain of living water that cleanses, renews, gives joy and peace and gladness inexpressible—so that God can be there, to share the benefits of His Son's death and resurrection, in fresh power and grace.

In addition to desiring to please God, when we sincerely wish the best for God's people, it means meeting the Living God in the grace of the gospel, with the real continuing presence of the risen Christ coming down, and penetrating into your life. That is probably one of the greatest forms of evangelism you'll ever know: Christian worship services, where the Holy Ghost comes down and makes Jesus' present in the preaching of the Word, and in the administration of the sacraments. Vital worship services constitute a tremendous outreach to the lost. Even unbelievers can tell when God is there!

The best thing you can give anybody, whether the most secular, degenerate person, or the most highly sophisticated unbeliever, is that God would come down and be there in the worship of His people. So, 1 Corinthians 14:24–25 says that this is what will happen in true Christian worship. When the Holy Spirit is making the risen Jesus real, and the unbeliever stumbles into the service, something's going to happen. The context is talking about prophesying in a known tongue, a known language, so that people make sense of it:

> But if all prophesy, and there come in one that believeth not, or one unlearned, he is convinced of all; he is judged of all. And thus are the secrets of his heart made manifest; and so falling down on his face he will worship God, and report that God is in you of a truth.

So the Sabbath, one day out of seven, reminds us that God is here. Then the Passover, the Lord's Supper, reminds us of the price that had to be paid by God, for God to be here in His grace and mercy and love: the shedding of the blood of His beloved Son, and His resurrection, and the Holy Spirit coming down to apply it. And that's what Christian worship is all about. May God help us to experience it every Sabbath day, and especially every communion day.

38

The Feasts of Firstfruits and Tabernacles
Deuteronomy 16:9–15

Three Great Hebrew Festivals

It is truly amazing how full the Old Testament is of Jesus Christ, His person and His work; and our part in Him. These Jewish festivals were set up in the time of Moses, approximately 1400 years before Christ was born in Bethlehem, yet the order of these feasts speaks to us most remarkably of the exact things that were accomplished in the death and resurrection of Christ, and then the outpouring of the Holy Spirit at Pentecost. From the order of the feasts and their content, we are given a most amazing portrait of Jesus Christ, the saving work and the eternal hope we have through union with Him, and what He has done in our place. He is the one whom the feasts foreshadowed; He is the reality, and He fulfills to the letter what these Jewish festivals meant. If that were the only reason, you would have a pretty good line of evidence for believing that the Holy Bible is inspired; 1400 years before Christ, the Old Testament was precisely setting forth what the Messiah of Israel, the Savior of the world, would do.

The three great festivals of Old Testament Israel in Deuteronomy 16 all mean something for the New Testament church. The ones we will look at now are the festival for the Firstfruits or Weeks (verses 9-12), and the festival of Tabernacles or harvest (verses 13-15).

These ancient pilgrim festivals of Israel show us that the relationship of God to His people proceeds from a certain foundation in a particular direction. The foundational festival of Israel, already mentioned at length, is the Passover, the basic festival, followed by the festival of Firstfruits, which speaks of the resurrection and of the outpouring of the Holy Spirit, which took place when Jesus' blood sacrifice was fully accepted by the Father and which fulfills all that we owe the law and pays in full the dire penalty for breaking it. We see this in how He raises His Son up and then pours out the Holy Spirit to make the Son ever present with every believer.

The final great Jewish festival of the year is the harvest festival, or the feast of Tabernacles or ingathering. It looks forward to the last thing that will occur, when the curtain of earthly history rings down—the return of the Lord Jesus Christ, together with all His people, Old Testament and New Testament, through all times, ages, races, and climes.

The Festival of Firstfruits

This festival was held at the beginning of the barley harvest. You know that the first thing we harvest is wheat and barley. I can remember while at the University of North Carolina, coming to the family farms as soon as the university let out for the summer and helping in the wheat harvest. That's the first of the crops harvested both in ancient Israel and in North and South Carolina.

At the beginning of the barley harvest, people from all over Israel would gather at a central shrine to celebrate (Shiloh and later, Jerusalem). Verses 11–15 specifies that the people of God were to count seven Sabbaths after the ritual of the sheaf offering. That is to say, when they had the first of the harvest—the barley harvest—they were to reap the first of the barley crop and make a loaf of barley bread. Then the High Priest would go before the tabernacle, lift it up and wave it before the Lord, from which time they were to count exactly 50 days, which, in the Greek translation of the Hebrew, is rendered 'Pentecost'. So 50 days after Passover—after the blood had been shed and they had eaten of the roasted lamb and rejoiced in redemption—the feast of the firstfruits of the barley harvest or festival of Weeks was held.

The festival of Firstfruits looked forward to the time that the Holy Spirit would be poured out on the waiting church, when the Holy Spirit, who comes from the risen Christ and the Father, was given in large measure. Jesus was killed during the Passover, three days later, He was raised in the same body in which He was crucified. We are told in more than one place in the New Testament that He was raised by the Father; that he was raised by his own power, and that he was raised by the Holy Spirit. Fifty days later, the Holy Spirit would come on an assembled church in an upper room in Jerusalem, and baptize them with the spirit of resurrection and glory, the same glorious resurrection power that raised Jesus. He was raised by the glory of the Father, and that same glory would descend on the church (Romans 1).

Now in the great resurrection is the counterpart of this festival of firstfruits, and it gives us a clue as to what it means: 'Christ is become the firstfruits of them that slept; and afterward they that are Christ's at His coming' (1 Cor. 15:23). At the end of Passover week, on the first day of the new week (the Christian Sabbath or Lord's Day) Christ was raised up in His formerly crucified body, and a stunning thing happened. We are only told about this occurrence in the Gospel of Matthew and it shows us what the festival of Firstfruits really means. Jesus is the firstfruits of them that slept, and Matthew 27:53 reports there went out a power from His resurrection body that caused a number of graves to split open in the graveyards of Jerusalem; and many bodies of the saints were raised by the power of Jesus; then they walked around and were seen by the believers!

What took place is an exemplification of the principle given us by Jesus in John 12:24: 'Except a corn [or grain] of wheat fall into the ground and die, it abideth alone. But if it die it brings forth much fruit.' Jesus died as one—firstfruits of them that slept—sleep here means to die. But when He was raised by the glory of the Father in the power of the Spirit, that power went out and literally lifted up many deceased saints, lifted their bodies out of the grave. He died as one; He was raised as 'many', including, of course, Himself. That shows, in a preliminary way, what it was for Him to be 'the firstfruits of them that slept'.

This sharing of resurrection was also seen in the ritual of the wave offering. The High Priest would walk around holding the barley loaf up, a picture of one grain that dies and becomes fruitful and turns into an entire loaf; and a picture of the union with Christ of all believers, becoming one body with Him, one loaf in the bread of life.

The Apostle Paul explains the significance of this feast of firstfruits in Ephesians 1:23, where he is speaking of the church, His body, 'the fullness of Him that filleth all in all'. Then chapter 2:1, prepares us for a reference to the true meaning of Firstfruits: 'You hath He quickened; you hath he made alive who were dead in trespasses and sin'. In Jesus' death and resurrection, He did something to all of us who were spiritually dead towards God which Paul goes on to speak about in verses 5–7: 'Even when we were dead in sins [cut off from the Lord, on the way to perdition] God has quickened us [made us alive] together with Christ, by grace ye are saved, and hath raised us up together and made us sit together in heavenly places in Christ Jesus'. Although it does not use the words, it would be hard not to see the true significance of the feast of the Firstfruits in these verses. They point to the resurrection of Christ, and then how that resurrection unites believers together with Him, by the power of the Holy Spirit, exactly what Firstfruits appointed by Moses showed forth prophetically.

The Old Testament feast of Firstfruits speaks of the fruitfulness of that which dies. When you entrust a seed to the ground, you believe that it will be fruitful and reproduce more than one seed: indeed, many. This feast was looking to Jesus, the Seed, the seed of Eve, the seed of Abraham, who would be put into the ground and because of His holy life and perfect sacrifice, God the Father would raise Him, and not just raise Him, but raise the whole church. Across the long years of the expansion of the gospel in the world, the Holy Spirit comes and imparts the resurrection of Christ, to all who believe, in perfect accordance with the Father's plan. Hence the feast of Firstfruits is speaking of Pentecost, the down-coming of the Holy Spirit.

Pentecost, at its basis, means that the same Spirit, who by the glory of the Father raised the Son from the dead and the deceased saints in Jerusalem, that same Spirit comes down on the church to give it resurrection power, and then sends out the empowered church to the whole world, with heavenly authority, to raise the spiritually dead, and make them one with Christ, united by grace through faith with the risen Lord. The Son from glory sends down the Holy Spirit, with the power of resurrection, to join all who will become believers to Him: 'He hath raised us together with Him' (Ephesians 2).

Now in the Old Testament festival of Firstfruits the believers were told they were to celebrate the festival two ways: first, with joy; second, with generosity. Joy is easy to understand: what a wonderful thing it is to know that this physical life does not end in the extinction of our personality, that beyond death there is the newness of life; and indeed, more than that; even during this brief earthly life—when we have to face sin and struggle and temptation, sickness and breakdown of the body and death—even now we are in touch with the resurrection power that comes from the Father and the Son from the glorious throne, and so it gives us great joy.

That is precisely the story of the Christian church. It is God, as it were, sending His Son to drop as a seed in the graveyard—fearfully abused—but raised in beauty and power, and at the same time, also raising many with Him, and ever after touching people with the Holy Spirit, making them alive forevermore with Jesus Christ. This is how the church expands: God gives us everything. But then He, at least in principle, has the right to ask of us everything. The ultimate would be God saying, 'You're mine; I've given you everything. Now I wish you to be available to be dropped as a seed of wheat into the ground and die to yourself, die to your own plans. My power will be put forth from the throne—the same power that raised My beloved Son from the dead—from your death to self, death to your own plans. And I will do miracles. And you go down as one, and then out of your life will come much fruit.'

That is essentially what is said to us in John 15: 'Every branch in Me that beareth fruit He pruneth that it may bear more fruit'. The joy is simply this: to celebrate the feast of firstfruits is to know that God has made this crop fruitful; out of death He has brought forth life. Even now, as my life is yielded to Him in faith, even though it seems like I am losing and giving everything up, God will make my little life fruitful, so that somehow it will touch others with resurrection power. That has empowered the Christian church over the years, knowing they could afford, if God asked them, to give up everything, because they already had been given in Christ, absolutely everything. Any sacrifice He calls on us to make will be fruitful in resurrection power to touch others. We hear the joy of this in the hymn:

> Jesus lives, and so shall I.
> Death! Thy sting is gone forever.
> He who deigned for me to die
> Lives, the bands of death to sever.
> He shall raise me from the dust;
> Jesus is my hope and trust.

'Because I live, ye shall live also' (John 14:19). Now that settles all questions as to how much of myself I will let the Lord have. Jesus lives! So shall I! I'm alive in Him; if He wants it, He can have it, and He will then make it fruitful. So they celebrated the feast of firstfruits with joy, joy that resurrection always comes after every crucifixion.

Secondly, they celebrated the feast with generosity. God said, now be generous and give; bring all you can to the Lord's work; help the widow, orphan, and foreigner, who have no power; reach out, touch them, bless them, because of who I am to you. Why should we help others? Because of who God is to me. I really believe this: full assurance of eternal life makes people open their pocket books and be very generous. The people who are most sure of heaven, from my own experience, will be the ones who will do the most for you and give you the most.

I once had a South African black student, from the Bantu tribe who knew the resurrection touch of the Holy Spirit in his daily life, and was filled with joy and faith. He often spoke of the generosity of the Lord in his life (although he chose to live mostly on corn-bread gruel, so he would be ready to go back to Africa). I found out some of the incredibly generous things he did to help people, rather than saving up for his return to a difficult area. It would not be proper to list these things here, but only to note with joy how his sense of co-resurrection with Christ made him a fountain of love and practical assistance to many.

His life was a reflection of what happens at the end of the great resurrection in 1 Corinthians 15. Having talked about how sure and wonderful the resurrection is, Paul says 'Therefore my beloved brethren, be ye steadfast, unmovable, always abounding in the work of the Lord, for as much as you know that your labor in the Lord is not in vain.' So, resurrection says 'abound' and being fruitful in the Lord; and then the very next verse, 1 Corinthians 16:1: 'Now concerning the offering'. These two chapters of 1 Corinthians reflect the meaning of the festival of the firstfruits: glorious resurrection, life after death, the seed dying and being raised up, after which Paul says: 'Now concerning the offering' which I want you to take up to help the needy saints in Jerusalem. In this movement from chapter 15 to 16, we see generosity in those who have been raised with Christ.

There is something else of equal importance, that goes along with giving, namely, telling people about what God has done for you. Sometimes we call it evangelism, or soul winning, but it simply means sharing very good news with somebody. At its most basic level, you can humbly tell them what it meant to you for Jesus to come into your life. You don't have to follow a fancy program or a complicated theological explanation—good if you have the background—but anybody, any man or woman, no matter what their level of education, if they know Jesus, can simply tell somebody else and share the good thing God has done for you. That is still one of the main ways the church advances.

We have recently seen with admiration what is happening in the Anglican Church in Nigeria, under the remarkable primate of Nigeria, Archbishop Akinola. Twenty-five or thirty years ago, with some of the other leaders of the Anglican Church in Nigeria, (now grown to over 25 million), he started a program called '1 plus 1 plus 3.' That is to say, one Christian—including bishops and archbishop—makes friends with somebody, and tells them about Jesus and invites them to believe in Him, and to be empowered with His resurrection. So that's '1 plus 1'.

Then you spend three years discipling this one person you brought to the Lord to become a disciple of Jesus. I can't remember the exact numbers, but when they started there were nine or ten million Anglican Christians, and now after twenty or twenty-five years, there are 25 million Christians. That sort of thing is a modern illustration of the meaning of the feast of firstfruits: life after death: Jesus has risen, the saints in Jerusalem are the firstfruits, and then in due time, we ourselves become alive with Christ, and united to the loaf; hence, we celebrate this ever-expanding resurrection with joy and invite others.

THE FEAST OF TABERNACLES

Then the second festival is that of tabernacles or the final in-gathering, the grand harvest festival of Judaism, as we see in verses 13–15. Leviticus 23:24 tells us that this seven day feast was to begin after the grain was stored and the grapes made into wine, and stored for the next year; so this feast was to last from the fifteenth to the twenty-first of this particular month. During that time, the people gathered at the central shrine and dwelt in booths or tabernacles; hence the words 'feast of tabernacles.'

I remember reading in 1975 a fascinating article in the *National Geographic* about the Hasidic Jews, particularly in Brooklyn. They are among the most pious in current Judaism and try to live as literally as they can by the Old Testament. To celebrate the festival of Tabernacles, because many of them live in high apartment complexes, they get palm branches and other kinds of tree limbs and spread them over fire escapes. Then they go out on the fire escapes and sleep for seven days, to observe the festival.

Dwelling in booths in the Old Testament (and with the Hasidic Jews today) reminded the people of God of two things: first, that they camped for forty years in the wilderness, in tabernacles, a tent you could fold up and move when the fiery cloud or pillar moved. It also reminded people of the final ingathering when the Lord of harvest would come back and, as the hymn says, 'Gather all His people in; free from sorrow, free from sin.' And it reminded them that in our earthly life, we are only in the tabernacle, not a permanent dwelling place here below; we do have a dwelling place of surpassing beauty, but it's not here.

Paul in 2 Corinthians 5:1–4 is reflecting the significance of the feast of Tabernacles as he calls our body 'this tabernacle', which one day is going to be dissolved, and then we shall have a building 'eternal in the heavens'.

> For we know that if our earthly house of this tabernacle were dissolved, we have a building of God, an house not made with hands, eternal in the heavens. For in this we groan, earnestly desiring to be clothed upon with our house which is in heaven; if so be that being clothed we shall not be found naked. For we that are in this tabernacle do groan, being burdened; not for that we would be unclothed, but clothed upon, that mortality might be swallowed up of life.

Today, Christian people are not called upon to celebrate every year the festival of tabernacles, nor to dwell in booths to do so. But it does mean something. It reminds us that during our whole earthly life, we are in a tabernacle of clay that has many flaws, and one day the jar is going to be broken (read Ecclesiastes 12). But there is something wonderful on the other side of it!

And so all our life as believers on earth is, in a sense, a pilgrim festival of tabernacles; we're just in temporary tents. We don't want to get too possessive of anything we've got down here, because it's not our home, only a tent that can quickly be folded up. We have something far surpassing it in worth and value and in glory.

I remember in the 1940s and 1950s as a child, we used to hear on the radio gospel groups like the Chuck Wagon Gang, who were often singing very lively and memorable lyrics about soon going home to heaven. (Even then as a child, I knew it was not great music, but I loved it!) One of their 'foot-moving' tunes, with memorable words was:

> Every day I'm camping in the land of Canaan and with rapture I survey its wondrous beauties grand.
> Glory, hallelujah, I've found the land of promise, and I'm camping, camping, in Canaan's happy land.

That's what we're doing—we're campers. We don't take life ultra seriously, because our citizenship is not here. This body is just temporary; it will be raised in the resurrection; it will be beautiful and wonderful. We remember our past redemption in blood—that's Passover. And then we think of Pentecost, the Father united me to the Son, and so I celebrate being in Him with joy and generosity, giving to others; and then tabernacles—I've got something better beyond this body and beyond this earthly life.

I conclude by reading you a little passage from *Of the Imitation of Christ* by a wonderful fourteenth century devotional writer, Thomas à Kempis:

> My son, when you feel the desire of eternal bliss to be given you from above and long to depart out of the tabernacle [see, that's the word] of this body that you may contemplate My brightness without shadow of turning, open your heart wide and receive with your whole desire this holy inspiration. Give greatest thanks [and that was reflecting the festival of the tabernacle—thanksgiving] to the heavenly Goodness which treats you with such condescension, visiting you mercifully, stirring you up fervently, powerfully sustaining you; lest through your own weight, you sink down to earthly things. For you do not obtain this by your own thought or endeavor, but by the mere condescension of heavenly grace and Divine favor. To the end that you may make progress in all virtue and obtain greater humility, preparing yourself for future conflicts; and endeavor to cleave unto Me with the whole affection of your heart and to serve Me with fervent willingness. . . Do not ask God to give you

what is delightful and profitable to you, but ask Him for that which is acceptable to Him and tends to His honor. For if you judge aright, you ought to prefer and follow My appointment rather than your own desire, or anything whatsoever that is to be desired. I know your desire, and I have heard your groaning. You long now to enjoy the glorious liberty of the sons of God. Now you delight in the everlasting habitation, your heavenly home full of joy, but that hour is not yet come. [tabernacles is looking forward to something we've got a foretaste, but we don't have it yet] There still remains another time, and that a time of war, a time of labor and of trial. You desire to be filled with chiefest good, but you cannot yet attain it. I am He. Wait on Me, says the Lord, until the kingdom of God shall come.

(Calvin, in *Institutes of the Christian Religion,* has a beautiful section on the Christian life, where he is very clearly reflecting Thomas à Kempis).

I close with this line from the hymn, 'I've Found a Friend':

The eternal glories gleam afar, to nerve my faint endeavor;
So now to watch, to work, to war, and then to rest forever.

39

GOD'S AUTHORITY IN THE COURTS

Deuteronomy 16:16–20

In Psalm 119:96, we read: 'Thy commandment is exceeding broad.' That is to say that the commandment of God, the Word of God, is so broad and far-reaching that it touches every aspect of the lives we live on earth. Here we see that the fifth commandment—'parental' honor—teaches the principle of respect for every authority that is legitimately placed in our lives, resulting in a generally happy and well-functioning country. So the commandment of God even speaks to the justice system: how you run the courts, the police, and the rest of it.

This text brings before us three matters: first, the conclusion of the fourth commandment—the Sabbath principle (verses 16–17). Secondly, the beginning of the next major part of Deuteronomy (a commentary on the fifth commandment), which leads us to consider courts of justice throughout the land (verse 18). Third, the main point is how God's authority as our heavenly Father, requires fairness in the courts, and in all justice systems (verses 19–20).

THE CONCLUSION OF THE FOURTH COMMANDMENT (16:16–17)

Here we note that the conclusion of the fourth commandment is applied to the feasts which are based on sevens: in other words, the Sabbath principle, which is lumped together at the very beginning of the system of justice with the police, the courts, and various commissions that could be set up in any country. So immediately before the new section, we are reminded that the people are to keep the three pilgrim feasts at a central location each year.

When Moses says that the males shall appear before God, most commentators think that doesn't mean that the females and children couldn't go; it simply means that the whole household does not have to pack up and move three times a year. In that case, who would feed the cattle, and so forth? It means that the males have to go, if they are physically able; but if their wives and children are in a position to go with them, they would do so.

It is significant to note that the Bible here in Deuteronomy, before discussing why the police, the judges and the courts should be perfectly fair and honorable, talks about regular worship of all the people, showing us something very important. It is highly unlikely that you will be fair in a government, whether at very local level or national level, unless people have some sense of the reality of God and His holiness and

His grace; that is, unless the people regularly worship God as a central part of their lives. So we might conclude that the three pilgrim festivals (Passover, Firstfruits, Tabernacles) spread throughout the year, are the spiritual context for doing right in every legal transaction, and for judging honorably.

Why is regular worship by a country's population so important for doing things honestly and properly? The reason is that it takes constant immersion in the fear of God, in which God seems real to us, to develop the point of view where we care about who He is and what He thinks. That godly attitude means that we give officials, and even individual men and women, who have even the smallest sort of authority—parents, teachers and others—proper respect.

A true servant of God in any kind of official post, is to keep God before his or her eyes, and not show favoritism to any power bloc, nor any currently favored or unfavored group. You can never run a fair system of justice unless the officials fear God in their hearts more than they fear man. That is basically a supernatural virtue, and why regular worship of the population is so important for there to be honesty, integrity, and fair dealing in any state or country.

Hence, the three yearly religious festivals were a way of carrying out what David said in Psalm 16:8: 'I have set the Lord always before me; because He is at my right hand I shall not be moved'—meaning, I shall not be moved from righteousness. How can you not be moved from righteousness? Remember the old African-American spiritual, 'Anchored in Jehovah, I shall not be moved'? The only way you cannot be removed from doing right, particularly when it might hurt you in the short run, is to set the Lord always before you and to think: God requires of me righteousness in this situation, no matter what it may cost.

Therefore, I shall seek to do it. That's the only thing that can prevent government officials from doing what Exodus 23:2 warns against: 'Follow not a multitude to do evil'; the widespread idea (apart from grace) that everybody else is doing it; I don't want to be thought odd. But that is where our Christian integrity shines out most, when, for the love of God and fear of Him, and desire to do good to others, we are willing to stick out like a sore thumb and be called, perhaps, unpleasant names; that determination of integrity makes any country a very good place to live.

So we can summarize the first point by saying, regular worship keeps the machinery of a good government oiled, so that people tend to seek what is right, rather than their own self interest.

Fair Courts of Justice (16:18)

Now we are making a shift from the fourth commandment, the exceeding broadness of the Sabbath principle, and the various feasts into a new section, Deuteronomy 16:18–18:22. It is a practical commentary on what it means to say, 'Honor thy father and thy mother that thy days may be long upon the land which the Lord thy God giveth thee'. I suggest that when you go home, you look in the Westminster Shorter Catechism on this commandment, where the Catechism unfolds what it means, not only to honor father and mother, but all legitimate officials over us—from the king or leader of state, on down.

Now the Holy Spirit is leading Moses to say to the people, before entering the new land, that when they do enter it, the fifth commandment must be carried out in several different levels. The level that is particularly put before us here is the level of the law courts, of doing justice in society. The officials are to seek to do right in the courts, based on who God is: that He is our Heavenly Father, that He is to be remembered and He is to be honored in every judgment or every decision that we render. Peter speaks about this very clearly: 'Submit yourselves to every ordinance of man for the Lord's sake, whether it be to the king as supreme or unto governors as unto them that are sent by him for the punishment of evil doers and for the praise of them that do well. For so is the will of God that with well-doing ye may put to silence the ignorance of foolish men'. And then going on down to verse 17: 'Honor all men; love the brotherhood; fear God; honor the king' (1 Pet. 2: 13–15).

This means that justice should be readily available, no matter what part of Israel you lived in. In the days of walking or going by animal, it would take a long time to get from south to north, from east to west. So God orders that every good sized town would have a court system set up. The court was to be held—notice the words—'in the gates' of every town large enough to have walls and gates. The gates were where everybody passed through to do their business, get in and out of town, and which would be shut at night.

Some archeologists who have dug up ancient walled towns in parts of Israel—particularly in the southern part of Israel—have found gates of stone, inside which were benches of stone, where you went to make land transactions, and to deal with inheritance, murder, and other things. So two things are being taught: justice, a just law court, ought to be available so that everybody can walk to it within a part of a day. And the courts are to be visible, not in a 'smoky back room', where we don't know what is decided or why. It was to be out in the open, so the public could stand and hear the arguments on both sides of a case. Thus justice was visible, and it probably put a certain pressure on the elders and the judges of that town, to be honest and not to pull a trick for their own self interest.

So the point is, justice should be available to ordinary people where they can get to without much trouble; and it's to be visible, so that they can see, and that those who have power cannot be underhanded. Thus the accessibility and visibility of the courts helped lend respect to the officials, who were over the people in a town or larger district.

My parents always told me when I was a little boy, 'If you get a whipping at school, you'll get another one at home;' so of course, I didn't tell them when I did get one. The ones I got were well deserved, so it didn't bother me; but I was very careful not to tell my parents. What were my parents doing? They were not mean; they were inculcating respect for legitimate authority. It seems to me that it's rather different today in many quarters. Many parents back up their disobedient children against proper authority. I am told they sometimes even threaten to sue the school, if their child was even mildly disciplined.

Why? It is loss of fear of God. They go by emotion, instead of thinking through, in accordance with God's Word what is right and what is best for their children. Not to teach a child to respect authority does something very bad to a child's attitude for many years to come: maybe for their whole life. One of the best things Christian parents can do is to try to teach their children respect for authority, and it is not always a simple matter.

You might ask, how are we going to do it? Well, you aren't going to do it if you just want to keep the child happy with you! You've got to hold the line and where necessary—moderately, of course, never abusively—sometimes you've got to use the rod. If children are not brought up to show due respect to the authorities they are under on earth, how in the world could we expect that they would ever show respect and honor to the God in whose image they are made, before whom they must stand, whom they do not see; if you don't respect those you can see, it is far less likely you will respect the One you cannot see.

This text also adds words to the judges and other officials. God lays three charges or requirements on everybody that has official governmental power over the public. This is especially centered in judges, but it would also avail for everybody else with even minor authority. Three basic rules are laid down: first, not to turn aside justice; second, not to show favoritism; third, never to take a bribe. Let's look at each one.

First, not to turn aside justice; in the old Authorized Version it says, 'thou shalt not wrest judgment', meaning not twist it. What does it mean, to turn aside justice or twist the situation? It seems to mean failing to do what you know is right in a given case. Even though you clearly see it, your personal sympathies and interests lie in keeping justice from being done. It involves a twisting of the principles of the law in order to let a guilty person off, or to convict an innocent person whom you don't like or whose group you wish to punish, for whatever reasons. Now clever lawyers and judges can do this. But if they do it, they wrest judgment. It hurts people, and that's bad enough, but it's more serious than that; it is a direct attack on God's holy character.

That's the kind of wresting of judgment that was done in the time of Elijah upon a humble citizen Naboth, who lived in Samaria, and had a vineyard near the palace of wicked Queen Jezebel and King Ahab. Ahab decided that he wanted the vineyard so he could pull up the vines and plant a herb garden for his own use. So he offered to buy it from Naboth. But Naboth was a good Israelite, and he knew the law that you are not allowed to alienate ancestral land from the family. He was not being obstinate; he was under the Word of God not to alienate land from the family. That was poured into me as a child: 'Don't do it! Never get rid of family land!'

The king got depressed, and his wicked, but creative wife, Jezebel, set up a court and hired false witnesses to say that Naboth had blasphemed God and the king. The witnesses were believed by a thoroughly dishonest court, and Naboth was condemned to death and was stoned. Ahab took his vineyard and turned it into a little garden.

Well, that isn't the end of the story. Elijah sent word to Ahab and Jezebel that they would pay, and pay dearly with their lives; the very vengeance of God would come upon them and destroy their house. And in due season it happened.

I remember reading many years ago an amazing article in the *Legal Journal*—sent me by one of my law professor friends—written by a Jewish lady, a member of the bar of New York and later a professor in a law school in the Philippines, Helen Silving. She shows how Anglo Saxon jurisprudence, the way we run our government on the basis of fairness and righteousness, comes out of the Old Testament. She particularly shows that the issue of Naboth's vineyard, summarizes the major point of the Magna Carta of 1215, —'due process of law'. Due process of law requires that things are to be done fairly and visibly in terms of the righteousness of God. That is what has made our (at least formerly Christian) countries great; that is why immigrants are always pouring in here. Yes, it is because of our economies, but you couldn't have that prosperity, liberty, and hopefulness, unless it was based on a just law system and due process of law. Helen Silving shows how much the development of law in the countries of the West has been based on precisely avoiding the turning aside of justice that occurred in Naboth's vineyard.

In our own Carolinas, one can often see sad illustrations of the turning aside of justice.

For instance, in Hilton Head, South Carolina, government officials apparently were offered money and advantage, if they would slap unbelievably high taxes on humble people, who (like Naboth) had ancestral land that they had lived on for generations. The officials raised the taxes because they knew that ordinary people could not pay. Then greedy real estate developers who seemed to have been in cahoots with the officials, were able to buy the land at bargain prices. Ancestral homes had to be sold for practically nothing to greedy real estate people who then started building expensive houses, which raised a lot more taxes, than the simple abodes of—in most cases—African-Americans.

Now, in a sense, you can say that all of this was perfectly legal. But it was a denial of justice, a wresting of the judgment of God and a dishonoring of the character of God to treat people like that for personal and corporate gain. You may say, they got by with it. But don't forget that the officials who had the power and misused it for personal gain will one day stand naked and humbled before the bright shining judgment seat of the eternal God, to whom they will give an answer for wresting judgment during their earthly life. Then they will experience through endless eternity something that will massively outweigh the paltry, unjust gain they got on earth by abusing their power. We have to remember this: the more authority we have, the more we will have to answer for.

Then a second requirement for those in official positions: 'Thou shalt not respect persons', that is not to show favoritism to anybody or any group, whether rich or poor; whether educated or illiterate; whether black, white, Chinese, Hispanic, or whatever. All persons, because they are created in the image of God, are to be equal under the law.

That is what our American forefathers meant when they used to say, 'We believe in a government of laws, not of men.' I fear that in not a little of modern politicking, what they are doing is trying to pivot one group of the population over against another group. They believe in a government of men, or competing interests. But no! That will tear a country apart. The only right way is that we believe in a government of laws, not of men.

Then a third thing is required of judges and all police and all officials: not to take a bribe. I don't want to be getting into nasty stories, but in a neighboring county I believe six or eight members of the Sheriff's department who were the drug squad, and therefore, were supposed to keep drug sales from happening, are now in federal prison, because they made considerable money by stealing drugs they confiscated, and selling them themselves. When money is available, it takes integrity of character, primarily is based upon fear of God, to say no, I will not sell justice; I will not corrupt my name, and the name of the Lord by hurting these people for temporary financial gain.

This takes us back to the importance of worship, of belief in God, as the first line of defense against corruption in government. I suspect that if we don't have some kind of religious revival in the United States and return to faith in God, and repentance towards Jesus, we are in for even more corruption and grief. Of course, it will make some people angry, but we need to keep in mind how brief our tenure on life is. All officials should be able to say, 'If I die within an hour and stand before God to give an account for my life, do I want this corruption on my record? No I don't!' And that's the way to live. 'I have set the Lord always before me; because He is at my right hand, I shall not be moved' (Ps. 16:8).

One of the biographies of John Wesley records

that he was asked in his old age: 'Mr. Wesley, if you knew you were going to die during the night, what would you do today?' John Wesley gave him a direct answer: 'Well, at 11:00 am I would preach the regular service that we have on this day. And then I'm supposed to go see elderly Mrs. So-and-so who is homebound and sick, and I would do that at 1:00 pm. And then at 3:00 there is a meeting of the officers of the church; I would go to that. And in between 6:00 and 8:00 I have six more visits, and I would make every one of those visits. I would come home, read my Bible, pray, go to bed and die.' You see, John Wesley had it right. Let's live every day as though it were our last day: 'I have set the Lord always before me; because He is at my right hand, I shall not be moved'. That is the word for ordinary Christians, and particularly, the word for all who have any kind of authority. When we take that seriously, what a blessing it is going to be in our land; what rich dividends it will pay for years to come.

40

Integrity in Worship and Judgment

Deuteronomy 16:21–17:7

This section is about having no other authority but God speaking in His Word; or you could say that the requirement of integrity in worship extends to the justice system of a land that acknowledges God as the Lord.

When Harry Truman was President, I am told he had a sign on his desk in the Oval office: 'The Buck Stops Here'. In other words, he was, at least in executive terms, the highest authority during his years as President. And so it is a fair question for us all, who have to frame our lives in terms of some system of values, to ask, 'Where do those values come from? Where does the buck really stop?'

This passage answers that question: first, no substitute authority, no authority but God; second, therefore no hypocrisy, no turning away from God to derive how you worship, and how you set up the laws and apply them.

No substitute authority (16:21–22)

These verses start out with a picture of what it was like in ancient Canaan where the children of Israel were, after Joshua led them across the River Jordan. The land was pagan, and you would find dotted throughout the land of Canaan would be poles, called in Hebrew *Asherah*, standing for pagan gods and near places of worship. Besides these poles—maybe trees or carved poles like totem poles, the pagans would have court and deal with various controversies in terms of the pagan gods whom those poles represented. They didn't get their justice system or their form of worship from the revelation of God (the five books of Moses) but from various pagan concepts.

Moses tells the people that when they cross Jordan and begin conquering the land, the first thing they are to do is go throughout the land and chop down and burn those poles, because that was an alternative place where 'the buck stopped' for the pagans, where they worshiped and particularly where they exercised justice in terms of what we would call 'lying spirits', or unholy gods. In the story of Gideon in the book of Judges, the first thing the holy angel who showed up to Gideon and terrified him, said to him, 'Go chop down those poles on your father's property; chop them down and burn them, because that is a false system of authority and values; destroy them. And then I am going to do something big.'

I have wondered what might be, in our modern culture, the practical equivalent of the *Asherah* or the pagan poles, where people came up with their own ideas of how to worship God and with what would be right or wrong with the law system? Could it not be the twisting of perfectly clear laws to allow what traditional Christianity has considered immoral forms of sexuality? Are we not moving from biblical morality to a humanistic point of view where evil is good and good is evil?

What can we do? I believe that bad leadership, with false and destructive judicial decisions, and liquid laws are the chastisement of God on a formerly Christian people, who are not doing right. Going back to Gideon, the Midianites had long since been turned loose on the children of Israel, who were involved in idolatry. God let them come in, as He brought chastisement on His well-loved people, in order to bring them to repentance. The angel tells Gideon to chop down the Asherah, to show that God is the God of Israel, and that He alone is the one in whose character the laws should function. Are we, formerly Christian people, in the Western countries above that kind of terrible providential rebuke?

Even before we come to think of providential reversals on our civil societies, we must first deal seriously with a primary question, a spiritual question. It says often in the Holy Scriptures that judgment begins inside, at the house of God. That's why Jesus cleaned out the temple. If there is going to come a change for good in a country that has been formerly Bible-based, the judgment, the cleansing, has got to start among believers within the church—where it always starts. Then, when you have a church that becomes taken up again with zeal for the holiness of God, with love for His character, with devotion to His Son, Jesus, with a renewed determination to follow Him, no matter what the cost, God can begin doing all kinds of unexpected things, great and mighty things we could not even imagine, as He did with Gideon.

But first, God's honor has got to be preached; God's holy love must be preached; sin has got to be denounced, as to what it is; and the gospel tenderly held forth to people, who may have become unconcerned, materialistic and self-satisfied. When the church starts moving back towards God, when hard hearts begin melting, and get real with the Lord, and right with one another, it is amazing the changes that can come almost overnight in public polity. God will do it. A lot of things we can't do, but one thing we can do is seek to put ourselves in the right with the Lord, and with anybody we need to be right with; and God will do the rest. God really exists! He is really in charge! He has never vacated His throne. It is time for us to sing: 'All to Jesus I surrender; all to Him I freely give. I will ever love and trust Him, in His presence daily live'.

If we really mean it, I don't think you even have to get the majority in a church to get things right. All you have to have is a newly consecrated minority, and it will be amazing what God can do about the wicked, corrupt political system. Above all else, as we see these things, we should not become discouraged, but pray!

The same is required in the New Testament, as in 1 Timothy 2:1–2: 'I exhort, therefore, that, first of all, supplications, prayers, intercessions, and giving of thanks, be made for all men; for kings, and for all that are in authority; that we may lead a quiet and peaceable life in all godliness and honesty'. That's one reason I'm saying that we are going to keep this prayer meeting going; having just two or three doesn't make any difference—two or three can have the power, if God is in it. He has chosen the weak and foolish things of this world to confound the mighty; if we wait for that which is impressive and showy, we'll get nowhere. Take the broken, and lowly, and humble, and say, Lord, it's not much, but it is yours, and we're available; we're going to pray. And thousands of thousands of points of light will begin shining, coming down and shining into this pagan world. So first of all, no substitute authority for God.

No apostasy (17:2-7)

Apostasy is a violation of the first two commandments: 'Thou shalt have no other gods before me', and 'thou shalt not make any graven image', and a violation of the fifth commandment, 'Honor thy father and thy mother', of which this whole section of Deuteronomy is an exposition. The most basic parentage we have is our heavenly Father. I know some people have had an abusive father, and that's bad. But in the gospel, one can, to a large degree, recover from that, because as believers, we have the perfect, wondrous heavenly Father, and therefore, He is to be honored, and nobody is ever to take His place in our affections.

To worship anyone or anything but God is the most serious violation of the covenant of grace: 'I will be your God and you will be My people'. That's the essence of the covenant, beginning with the promise of the gospel to Adam, all the way through to the new covenant, in and through Christ.

In the Old Testament prophets, it is often called spiritual adultery, or whoring after other gods. I suppose it is the most basic temptation of Satan intended to destroy the welfare of the people of God, and to sully the honor of God. Apostasy finally led Israel into Babylonian captivity. Turning from God ultimately destroys the structure of human life; that's what we're seeing now in this country—it's the beginning and could get far worse—unless God intervenes—and if not repented of, will finally land us in outer darkness, and total eternal perdition; it needs to be told and warned. That's where apostasy gets you.

In other words, apostasy in the Bible is considered highest treason. Several of us in here are old enough to remember in the 1950s, when a man and his wife committed high treason against the United States, turning over to the Soviet Union the secret of the atom bomb, and were executed. Their actions are what made the cold war last as long as it did. But to turn your back on God and follow a phony god, material things, or personal pleasures, is an even higher treason than that against any nation, because God—who made the nations—is the most important of all. That is why, in the Old Testament, apostasy was met by capital punishment (stoning).

Now it's different in the New Testament economy, in the church, which does not have the power of capital punishment. In John 8, when the woman taken in adultery was dealt with by Jesus, He said to the crowd: 'Let him who is without sin among you cast the first stone' (referring to Deuteronomy 17; the person who bore witness against the sinner had to lay hands on the person who was to be stoned, first, to say that if their testimony was false, God would get them with something worse than stoning). The crowd all went away, Jesus forgave her, and told her to go and sin no more.

The most serious thing the church can do is to excommunicate an absolutely unrepentant sinner. We don't excommunicate absolutely every sinner, because everyone's a sinner, elders and ministers included. But repentance is called for, and we gladly forgive and try to put things right as best we can. A person would be excommunicated only for what is called in the old Book of Church Order, 'contumacy'—absolute refusal to tell the truth about what was done and to repent of it.

The closest we would ever come to the equivalent of capital punishment, is if somebody absolutely dishonors God, and will not say it was wrong, and is not sorry for it. They would have to be put out of the church, to honor God. If they later repented, well and good; we'll take them back in.

Matthew 18:17 says that if somebody has done wrong, you send a small committee to see if you can get it right, without making it public unless you have to. But if they won't listen, 'in the mouth of two or three witnesses that every word may be established'. Jesus is following the law in Deuteronomy that one witness is never enough to condemn a person, because it could be a personal issue that people would be willing to tell a lie about, and thereby accuse somebody of something they had not done, to get back at them. Thus, both Moses and Jesus say it takes two or three witnesses who will bear public testimony, face to face with the accused. And Jesus said, 'If ye shall neglect to hear them [the church authorities] tell it unto the church. But if he neglect to hear the church, let him be unto thee as a heathen man and a publican. Verily I say unto you, whatsoever ye shall bind on earth shall be bound in heaven; and whatsoever ye shall loose on earth shall be loosed in heaven.'

Let us note in passing, Deuteronomy 17—and what Jesus says in Matthew 18—is reason enough that Christians must assiduously avoid engaging in gossip. One of the evils of gossip is that just one person who gossips is not accountable; they can spread poison, and they don't have to face the person they are accusing, so are not held accountable. But Moses and Jesus say that it takes two or three, and it has to be public: facing your accuser, so they can answer you.

What would apostasy look like in the church? It would be this: church leadership—people high up, ministers, theology professors, Bible professors—beginning to deny the holy Trinity, the divinity of Jesus, that there is only one way of salvation, through the blood of Christ. It involves denying the final truth of the Holy Scriptures. Many have, in those ways, gone apostate, 'having a form of godliness but denying the power thereof', the top leadership in many a church.

In my earlier years, one of the things that tired me in the denomination we were raised in, was fighting apostasy in the upper echelons. If the Christian churches of the Western world—in Europe, Britain and later in the United States—had dealt with apostasy the way Jesus and Moses said, when we had cause to rebuke or, if necessary, put out unrepentant apostate leadership from the Protestant churches, none of our countries would be in the rotting, moribund condition they are in.

You may object, if you dealt with apostasy, wouldn't that bring conflict to the church and cut down on the number of people in the church? It would, at least at first. But a small church that is trying to do right on the basis of the Word of God, and the holiness and love of God, that church would be a massively potent instrument for good in any society; whereas a larger, compromised church—where the general public know they don't believe—and which tolerates unbelief and immorality in their leadership, loses almost all influence, and is disdained by the very pagans themselves.

I conclude with this: I believe, if we are to face all that is happening so fast, the only hope is a Holy Ghost, heaven-sent, heart-melting, character-changing revival from Jesus on His throne. God is in charge of revival—what can we do? I know He is in charge; I know the Holy Spirit is sovereign; we don't tell Him what to do. But our Lord said in Luke 11, that the Holy Spirit is given in answer to prayer. We can't dictate to God, but we can ask Him. Jesus gave us such authority, when He said that if an earthly father will not give his son a stone if he asks him for bread, he will not give him a scorpion if he asks him for a fish, how much more will your heavenly Father give the Holy Spirit to him that ask Him?

If we had thousands of prayer meetings, with five, six, ten, a thousand people—it doesn't make any difference—a few thousand prayer meetings across the country from the Atlantic to the Pacific, from the borders of Canada to Mexico, and we had them in England, we had them in Scotland, we had them in Ireland and France and Germany, and so forth, Australia and the rest, as they have them in China, and in Africa, what changes we would see!

41

The Foundation of Justice

Deuteronomy 17:8–13

Sometimes in Charlotte, one sees a bumper sticker that says 'If you want peace, work for justice.' Well, I don't know what the person who put on the bumper sticker exactly means by that, but if you mean the right thing by it, it is a biblical truth, that if you want peace, work for justice. To put it another way: what is the foundation of justice? What should we work for? How should we base our life as citizens and as church people?

The answer to that of course is the righteousness of God. The basis of true justice between human beings is always the character of God. That character is revealed in two complementary ways.

To the nations it is revealed through the human conscience. Everybody is born with a basic sense of right and wrong; read Romans 1–2. People have conscience inbuilt, because they are in the image of God, even though we are sinful and twisted in many ways, there is still an inbuilt sense of right and wrong, of fairness, truth and of a certain justice. So we could say that all the nations with their different ideas, groups, and cultures, are still having to work within a certain sense of the justice of the God who created them, a sense of right and wrong, which is the basis of all human law. Ultimately behind it stands the character of God in whose image we are created.

God reveals His pattern of justice in an even more clear way to Old Testament Israel and to the New Testament church; and Holy Scripture announces it to the entire world. He gave you this word: do it according to the *torah,* to the law, to the Ten Commandments, and to the whole revelation of what God says is right and wrong.

So these two things are the basis of true justice, and the closer churches and nations approximate the character of God in the structure of how they organize their lives, the more peace, and indeed, the more human happiness and fruitfulness you are going to have.

Let us look at four points in this text, which is a roundabout way of seeing what Deuteronomy makes plain—the foundation of justice is the character of God, as revealed to conscience and Scripture, where, before Israel passes over into the new land, God is saying, 'When you get there I want you to set up a system of justice that will be fair, and be based on who I am, and things will go well.' A higher court will be there (there will be local courts); the court's legal basis; the court's finality; how the system of courts applies in the world today.

A Higher Court (17:8-9)

Through Moses, God set up a good system of justice for the land that Israel was to enter, with two kinds of courts. First, there were local courts in every village, and then the highest court in what would become the central place of worship (Shiloh, then Jerusalem). Local courts, which dealt with most problems arising locally, in the village square or the city gates, where responsible men, who knew the truths of God's Word and its legal principles, rendered judgment. This was a decentralized system of courts that were easy to get to. So these were the local courts which took care of most problems and seem to reflect what Moses' father-in-law, Jethro, suggested, when he told him to choose seventy elders, so they could adjudicate lesser controversies. Then if the controversy was very difficult and the elders couldn't handle it, they would appeal to Moses, the higher court. This system of appeals is reflected in what they would do in the Promised Land, even though Moses would not be with them, with one centralized higher court that would be located at the place of worship, tabernacle or temple.

It is hard to know what constituted a case too difficult for the local elders and Levites to deal with, but from what is said here, particularly in verse 8, it would seem that it was something like certain kinds of physical assault—maybe felonious assault as we would say in our system—kinds of manslaughter, maybe involuntary or voluntary manslaughter, and rather complex lawsuits, perhaps regarding division of estates, or other kinds of problems. Anyway, it would be a comfort for the people of God to know that even after Moses and those seventy elders had gone, there would be a system of local courts based on God's Word and character, with a central court for more difficult cases, where they could get a fair hearing. Justice would bring peace in the society, and would be a great comfort and a tremendous blessing.

The Court's Legal Basis (17:10-11)

The court's decision was to be based on the law of God revealed to Moses: 'which they shall teach thee' (verse 11), that is, the revealed will of God in His Word, at this stage the five books of Moses, in process of being written. In other words, the Ten Commandments and the general principles of teaching surrounding those commandments would be the grid through which godly scholars would decide your case. To make such decisions, these judges had to be well instructed in the revealed will of God, and we see that in verse 11, which speaks of *torah*.

That is the reason why to this day, as far as I know, the Jewish people are the most highly literate people in all the world, and always have been; no other nation has had so large a percentage of educated persons, in the Middle Ages or even today. Why? Primarily, because you taught your children to read and write, so they could meditate in the law of God and live in the light of that law in all their choices and decisions. So, the higher court would be based on the law of God that all the people were learning, and many of them knew well. They knew they would get a proper decision, even though it might be sometimes uncomfortable for them; they could rest in the fact that it really would be right.

The Court's Finality (17:12-13)

That is why these courts are included in this section of Deuteronomy, which expounds the fifth commandment, 'honor thy father and thy mother'. We give honor to our earthly parents because they reflect something of who God is as our heavenly Father. All legitimate authorities—judges, teachers, police—are owed respect, and reflect something of the proper authority that the heavenly Father has bestowed upon them, and which is necessary to run a nation, and to keep the peace.

So God's holy honor is involved in the decisions rendered by the highest court in Old Testament times, for it made its decisions on the basis of the revealed will of God in His Word. There was no appeal beyond the highest court. Today in American parlance, we would say it was the Supreme Court. To reject this decision was counted direct rebellion against the Lord and would be visited with the death penalty. That was appropriate in a theocracy, which Israel was at that time, in a way inappropriate in a modern constitutional republic, monarchy, or democracy; none of these can claim that same kind of supreme authority that the highest court bore in the Israelite theocracy.

The Meaning of the Highest Court for Us Today (17:12–13)

That brings us to the fourth point: what does this system of foundational justice that works out through these courts, based on the Bible, mean for us today? I have had to ask that question so often as I am preaching through Deuteronomy, envisioning a historical setting which is now long past. Yet, as God's eternal Word, what does it mean for us now? Let me look at it in two ways: first, how the justice in this system of courts does not apply today; and secondly, how it still applies today.

First of all, how it does not apply. The Westminster Confession of Faith, chapter 19, paragraph 4, says that the Old Testament people of God constituted a theocracy, with particular ceremonies, with blood atonement through animals, with worship rituals, with certain kinds of courts, and many sorts of regulations, which have now been fulfilled in Christ, and therefore have passed away in detail as to their function. But we still have, says the Westminster Confession, the 'general equity of the law', that is, the principles of justice and fairness in all five books of Moses and the rest of the Old Testament, which still illumine our way, if we don't want to walk in the darkness.

Israel was a theocracy limited to one land and valid for that time. But when Jesus comes, those requirements are fulfilled in every detail. In Matthew 5, which we will come to later, Jesus tells us that he is not come to destroy the law, but to fulfill it. In fulfilling it, many of its specific requirements no longer apply, for several reasons. For one thing, you don't have the morning and the evening sacrifice of lambs, because Jesus Christ shed His blood on the cross of Calvary, and that is the final, once-for-all sacrifice that fulfills everything that was meant in the sacrifices of rams, lambs, goats, and bulls; no more blood needs to be shed.

By the same token, the ceremonies related to the sacrificial system, like the Day of Atonement, and other important ceremonial matters have been taken care of in the sacrifice of Christ. When He dies, it's like the Hand of God splitting the veil of the temple in two from top to bottom, as a way of showing that people now have access to the holiest place of all, because Jesus has died an all sufficient death in their place, always giving them direct access to God. Therefore, much of Leviticus, Deuteronomy, and Exodus is taken care of, and it is no longer appropriate for them to be carried on.

Another difference is that Israel was one nation, one land. Jesus fulfills all that and honors it to the full, but then He sends His disciples to all the nations: 'Go ye into all the world and preach the gospel' (Matt. 28:19); disciple the nations, all tribes, all *ethnoi*, all groups, 'teaching them to observe all things whatsoever I have commanded you; and lo, I am with you always, even to the end of the world.' Now the theocracy of Israel passes into the Kingdom of Christ. It was a local, national system and had an important place; but it is fulfilled and now transmuted into something broader, deeper, wider, higher, that is available for every nation, every tribe, every race, every tongue, every group in the entire world.

We are under a different economy, the Christian economy, which is international in its scope and far-reaching. The system of courts, with local courts and a central court, is obsolete, because we don't worship God at Jerusalem anymore. As To the woman of Samaria who asked, 'Should we worship God at Mt. Gerizim or at Jerusalem?' Jesus said, 'The hour is coming and now is when they that worship the Father shall worship Him' not in either of those places, (although salvation is of the Jews), but they shall worship God 'in Spirit and in truth', meaning everywhere. So, a court tied to the temple, which was destroyed in 70 AD, and since then to any one country, by definition, could no longer apply in the same way.

But secondly, how do these principles of a system of justice based on who God is, apply today to the problems of our complex society? There's got to be a way to handle controversies; there is never going to be a generation until the end of time without legal, moral, financial, business, land and all other kinds of controversies—including felonious assault, manslaughter, murder, breaking of contracts and so forth. How would it be handled?

Let me try to simplify this a little. The Westminster Confession of Faith, chapter 19, paragraph 5, talks about how the basic principles of morality based on who God is, as expressed in the Ten Commandments, still apply in the world today:

The moral law doth forever bind all, as well justified persons as others, to the obedience thereof; and that, not only in regard of the matter contained in it, but also in respect of the authority of God the Creator, who gave it. Neither doth Christ, in the gospel, any way dissolve, but much strengthen this obligation.

God's character exercises pressure upon us in two ways: on the nations, including the unconverted, and all mankind, and thereby providing for them a somewhat peaceable life. And upon the elect, upon believers, upon the church, in a different, a clearer, a more precise way.

But first, how does the character of God bring pressure upon the pagan nations, since many of them either don't know about the Bible, or wouldn't accept its authority if they did?

We have previously noted that every man and woman, every baby, is born with an innate sense of right and wrong. We still don't know exactly how the psychological sensibilities of a baby develop, in growing to age two, and to age four, and so on. How are they able to get a sense of right and wrong? At least we can say that every baby is created directly in the image of God, which means that they have an inborn sense that will develop as they get older, in the environment around them, as they learn many new things; they learn a particular human language and thereby begin to understand many other things. It is amazing what a baby knows by age two, and how that is increased by age four! They say teaching the mother tongue is a supreme educational achievement, and that therefore, a mother is probably the supreme educator, because the greatest task of all is to teach a baby the mother language, whether it is Chinese, English, Latin of old, or whatever. And we don't know how it all comes together.

Noam Chomsky of Harvard, of Jewish background, has suggested some ideas as to how it works, but I will not try to repeat him. All I know is this: babies and young ones have got a sense of right and wrong, and particularly when you read about the conscience in Romans 2, that your own conscience either accuses you when you've done wrong or encourages you when you do right, you can see this as the light of God that is in every person who has ever been created in God's image.

You might object as follows: since all are sinners, does this not skew our perception? Yes! 'There is a way that seemeth right unto a man, but the end thereof are the ways of death' (Prov. 14:12). So yes, you need more than that, but if you didn't have that, no society could ever have functioned, because it would be total anarchy. So conscience brings something of the character of God and makes the functioning of justice, whatever kind of system of courts in different tribes and cultures, possible for all places on the earth. The sinfulness of humankind is not powerful enough to keep this from happening.

For instance, while we can't say that in a pagan country we can directly impose the Bible on the courts, still to some real degree, more or less, even pagan courts are bound by the natural way. That is to say, by the conscience of the population, which inexorably dictates that some things are right and some things are wrong, and that the courts have got to go by that.

Then secondly, regarding the church. Israel in the Old Testament (the church under the old economy) and now the Kingdom of Christ, the church in the New Testament, are far more privileged. They have been given the written Scriptures, the Word of God, the Old Testament, and then after the time of Christ and His apostles, we have the New Testament. Up until the early twentieth century, various Christian denominations held up the moral law of God, which deeply impacted the attitudes of Western culture.

We can think of how this has worked with the officers of the Christian church: God clearly revealed His will that the elders, including teaching and ruling elders and deacons, would be males; the husband of one wife, if they are married. The Bible never indicates that there is any difference in worth or intelligence or value between a male and a female; women are equally intelligent to men, equally valuable to God, equally in the image of God; they have the same eternal destiny that any male has; they have the same access through the blood to God. The Bible puts the highest value on both the male and the female; that's not at issue if you take this biblically.

But without entering into questions of personal worth, which the Bible doesn't, there are certain rules for the good ordering of society in the church that the Lord has placed in the male, because Paul says Adam was created first; that doesn't mean he was any better than Eve, he wasn't; but he came first, and for things to work properly, the male has a certain limited primacy.

And so to know who should be officers of the church, the churches went to the Bible. That was understood until the 1960s and 1970s. Then many of the mainline churches changed their procedure. Why? It was because of the pressure of modern thought and the pressure of feminism. Apparently, they decided that they could not withstand the pressure from a changing society, so began to disregard what God's Word said in this matter.

Let us conclude: we are given in the Old Testament the foundation of justice, a certain court system that doesn't apply the same way any longer, internationally. Our Christian system is adaptable to every kind of culture, but the principles of equity, of fairness, still apply. The Ten Commandments, the basic moral character of God as explained by Moses, provides the structure for how we ought to live, how the church ought to be run, how the nations ought to be run, and how our homes ought to be run. That gives us the structure; there is no doubt about that.

But the law, the holy structure, as we sincerely believe, does not, cannot give us the power to do it. If you went home only with an emphasis on the law, you would be depressed. I would! The law doesn't give you the power to keep it. If anything, as it shows us the holiness of God and what we ought to be in the different relationships to life, and thereby, it condemns us. What's the use of it then? What gives us the power to walk in terms of God's light? The Holy Spirit is the one who does it; the Holy Spirit gives us the power.

Jeremiah 31:31 tells us God will write His law in our hearts; He will give us a new spirit. The Holy Spirit comes and implants in us a firm desire to please God. A newborn person, a saved man or woman, in the new birth, has been given the Holy Spirit, who makes us have a longing to please God, and to do right in the highest sense. Many times we violate what we know is right. But then, 'If we confess our sins He is faithful and just to forgive us our sins, and cleanse us from all unrighteousness' (1 John 1:9). Therefore, we pick up and keep going. The law was never given to provide the power to be holy and to do right. But it does helpfully give us the structure of it.

Jesus shows this in Matthew 5, the Sermon on the Mount, where he takes the law, and then expounds it and expands it in many directions, thereby showing what it means. And Paul does that in Ephesians 4:28; he takes the law 'Thou shalt not steal' further. 'Let him that stole steal no more; but rather let him labor…that he may have to give to him that needeth'. Jesus takes the law and expands it to what it really means for living; Paul takes the law and expands it to what it really means to be like Jesus Christ. But these principles of godly living, in and of themselves, do not give us the power to carry them out. What does then? Obviously the Holy Spirit, and the new birth.

Now let us look in Ephesians 4:21–24, and this is the key to where the power lies:

> If so be that ye have heard Him, and have been taught by Him, as the truth is in Jesus, that ye put off concerning the former conduct the old man, which is corrupt according to the deceitful lusts; and be renewed in the spirit of your mind'; [like Romans 12:2—your attitude shifts when the Holy Spirit comes in] 'and that ye put on the new man, which after God is created in righteousness and true holiness.

So a profound inner shift of attitude is given in the new birth, and continually maintained by the Holy Spirit. In the Sermon on the Mount, (Matthew 6:3–4), where Jesus is expounding mercy and almsgiving, Jesus says, 'When thou doest alms [when you show mercy to somebody] let not thy left hand know what thy right hand doeth, that thine alms may be in secret and thy Father which sees in secret, Himself shall reward thee openly'. This shows you where you go to get the power to walk in the structures of biblical justice. It indicates that holy living comes primarily from 'dwelling in the secret place of the Most High' in the depths of our soul, or as Psalm 16:8 puts it: 'I have set the Lord always before me'. In the secret place of my life, where God is the most important factor, I dwell before Him; I confess my sins to Him; I believe in His Son, and make myself available to His Holy Spirit to send me out. All obedient lives are empowered from the secret place.

42

THE KING OF ISRAEL

Deuteronomy 17:14–20

I sometimes think, as I teach young people, that in much of the world we have less and less concept of what it is to be a king. We see political power flowing from the people, and we elect presidents and representatives. I like our system, I approve of it; but because we see the top winners as politicians who are elected, and who can be kicked out, we may not be able to identify so well with what the Bible is teaching about kings. While that is understandable, we may be losing something by it.

C.S. Lewis said somewhere that the whole office of king, along many other things in the organization of people, was primarily given to teach people something about what God is like. Kings had, and in some countries still do have, an important governmental function with its own justification, as does our president and prime ministers and others. But Lewis has a point that kings were given for a higher function even than being head of a human government, which would eventually pass away: it was to represent one of the characteristics of the God who made the universe out of nothing, and will control it to the end, and judge it in the end. From this ancient office, we learn something about what God is like.

Many of you, no doubt, were at one time catechism children, and one of the easier questions to memorize was the one on the offices of Christ: Prophet, Priest, and King. In the Old Testament, these are given primarily to show us what God is doing for us in the Lord Jesus Christ as our Savior and our Lord. He is our Prophet; He is our Priest; He is our King. I am thinking today of what Deuteronomy 17 says about kingship, and will refer to other texts dealing with kingship. We know that kingship in Israel functioned for a long time, but eventually passed away. Yet what it represented never passed away: a supreme kingship over all things.

Significantly this chapter of Deuteronomy is in a larger section, as I have told you, where Moses is expounding the practical ramifications of the fifth commandment: 'Honor thy father and thy mother', which, as St. Paul says, is 'the first commandment that has a promise'; 'that thy days may be long upon the land which the Lord thy God giveth thee'. Indeed, verse 20 speaks about prolonging one's days, and blessing upon the children. It's a way of saying that human government, at least at its best, is a reflection, in a limited way, of the fatherhood of God and His fatherly care, and so we are to render it due respect insofar as it deserves it, because of God himself.

When you come to medieval, and even modern kings, at their best, they are given to show something of the kingship, fatherhood and authority of the Lord God Almighty over the universe. More particularly, kings were meant to instill in people's attitude the concept of the Lord Jesus Christ as the final and eternal King of Israel and King of the church.

An interesting passage in John 1:46–51 introduces the disciple whom we otherwise do not hear much about, Nathanael. One of the things he is honored for is that very early in the public ministry of Jesus, after His baptism, Nathanael got the point of who Jesus really was. At first, he did not seem to start off well, when he exclaimed, 'Can any good thing come out of Nazareth?' (verse 46). He came from the more orthodox side of the Jewish section of the south, and he knew that Jesus had been raised in Nazareth. But then Jesus says something to him that Nathanael knew had to come from supernatural knowledge, and he immediately recognized who Jesus was, not just a human prophet out of Nazareth; He was far more than that. So Nathanael was apparently the first one to get it, even before the leader of the disciples and apostles, Simon Peter.

Notice verse 47: 'Jesus saw Nathanael coming to Him, and saith of him, "Behold an Israelite in whom is no guile!"' Now 'Israel' was the name of Jacob, and 'Jacob' means supplanter, or trickster; so Jesus is playing on Jacob's name-change, from supplanter or trickster, a person acting with guile to get the best of you, to Israel, or prince with God. And he says: 'I see Nathanael' as having the characteristic of his ancestor, Jacob *after* his character (and his name) was changed to 'prince with God'. Nathanael had said to Him: 'Whence knowest Thou me?' How do you know me? I hadn't been introduced to you. Jesus answered and said unto him: 'Before Philip called thee, when thou wast under the fig tree, I saw thee.'

I can't say for sure; the text doesn't give us a lot of information, but it must have been something involving supernatural knowledge on the part of Jesus, that He saw Nathanael under a fig tree. That impressed Nathanael, but what was far more significant was that Jesus saw into his very character, that he represented the best in Israel. Nathanael is bowled over that Jesus, whom he has never met, knows exactly who he is. And then he answers in verse 49: 'Rabbi, Thou art the Son of God; Thou art the King of Israel.'

He was the first one to see that Jesus, with His supernatural knowledge and divine ability to see through to the very core of our being, has to be the King of Israel. Then Jesus says, if you think that is something, just wait a while; you are going to see far more! Jesus never denies that Nathanael is right, that He really is the King of Israel. At the time Nathanael is speaking, in the early ministry of Jesus, Israel had not had a king for some 600 years. But Nathanael says, I have found a King! Jesus is the one that all the others were standing for; they were mere shadows of Him.

Three points emerge from this text: first, appointment of kings (verses 14–15); secondly, limitation of powers—an early king's power is always limited (verses 16–20); and third, some application to what this means to us in a constitutional republic or so-called democratic society (verse 20).

Appointment of Kings (17:14–15)

A careful reading of these verses shows that God did not command Israel to have kings. Indeed, through Samuel, He solemnly warns them of the bad things that will happen if they insist on having a king, in 1 Samuel 8. John Calvin has a famous sermon on that passage, which I translated many years ago. God definitely did not say, 'It is My commandment that you have kings;' He warns them that in wanting to be like other nations, some very deleterious consequences will follow. However, Deuteronomy 17 shows that He does allow kings. You might ask, why does God allow some things He does not command? The answer to that is hidden in His secret providence. But at least one reason could be that God allows it because it will be a foreshadowing of His own authority and of the Kingship of His Son over a renewed universe.

The form of government commanded up to this point in Scripture, is for Israel to have elders and judges in the time of Moses, with the addition of priests after Aaron. These offices were commanded. But in this section, Moses says that when you get into the Promised Land, you are going to want to have a king, because you will want to be like others, and I will allow that subject to certain moral and legal restraints upon any king of a godly people.

Moses gives two requirements for the appointment of kings: the first was unique to the time before Scripture was completed, because it required direct revelation from God; God Himself must make the choice of who would be the king, which He did through the prophet Samuel.

The first king that God told Samuel to choose, was a handsome, tall young man, who looked like he would be wonderful—Saul. He turned out to be a disaster. Why would God let somebody be chosen who would turn out to be a disaster? Literally Saul had a mental breakdown, after severe disobedience to God, and got into the occult and witchcraft! We don't know exactly why God chose someone, who went astray very rapidly.

This shows us that God and His holy character stand behind every throne and every government. No king is ever given absolute power; no king, president, prime minister, congress or parliament is absolutely pure or right or true. The holy shadow of God stands behind and above every throne and every chair of government; and it shows that the only place we can trust for the future is the throne of God. Lesser earthly thrones have their place, and we have to cooperate unless they clearly go against the revealed will of God; then we have to resist and demote them, sometimes at great cost to a people.

The first chosen king went astray. It's not that God didn't know what he would do—He knows all things so He knew what he would do. The tragedy of Saul at least shows us that God can use His people to bring down governments, when they are severely out of line with His will.

Samuel Rutherford, the great Scottish Reformed theologian of the seventeenth century, who helped write the Westminster Confession of Faith, also wrote a powerful book, *Lex, Rex* (the law and the king), giving the historical and biblical rules in which a tyrannical government could rightly be overthrown. Rutherford taught that kings are to be respected, insofar as they maintain something of proper morality. But when they seriously deviate—like Saul—they can be, and should be, brought to heel for it.

After Saul, God chose a very fine king, David, who nevertheless had some moral failings from time to time. His line continued until the deportation of the Jews to Babylon over 550 years after David. He was a man after God's own heart; he had some sins and he paid dearly for some of them, but nonetheless, he was on God's side. Much about David is a direct reflection of who Jesus is; some things are not, because Jesus is not a sinner, but David does reflect many things about the office of Christ as king; otherwise we would not know just how rich is the administration of Christ to His church.

The Limitation of the Power of Kings (17:16-20)

The power of kings is divinely limited, as is that of all civil governments. Does any government have all power over you, body and soul? No. That is brought out in the American Declaration of Independence and the Bill of Rights to the Constitution; even the American government, set up after they had overturned the authority of King George III of England in these colonies, was still strongly limited in its power. The teaching of the founders was not unrelated to the 'Glorious Revolution' in 1688 in England, which itself owed much to English Common Law, Catholic Canon Law, and finally, the Bible. In company with these ancient authorities, they brought out the important fact that the people have inalienable rights that God has given them, which did not come from the civil government but from God. Hence, civil governments have to be held accountable by the people, for they are directly created in God's image.

That is the point of limitation of the power of kings. No government has absolute power. Only God has, because He is totally holy, pure, and does everything right. Human agents and institutions are finite and sinful, and will misuse their power, if not kept in check. A pastor and elders have legitimate authority within a church, but they don't have absolute authority over it; they are under the Scriptures, and, if necessary, can be removed if necessary. A husband has a certain delegated authority over his wife and children, but he doesn't have absolute authority; she is to obey him only in the Lord, and he can be dealt with if he seriously abuses his position.

It's the same with kings, presidents, and prime ministers; they are to be respected and followed, unless to do so implicates you in direct sin against the character of God, and then you've got to pay whatever price it costs to bring them down, but only after a long time of abuse, and under most serious provocation.

Lord Acton of England wrote extensively on the source of liberty and the history of government. He was a British aristocrat and as brilliant a thinker as I have ever seen. He brings out that a major problem of human government is that it tends to seek more and more power, and to decrease the liberty of the population in order to be more powerful—a continuing problem to this day. Sometimes governments go so far as to seek to put themselves in the place of God, as we saw under communism, now largely failed since 1989 and 1991. They wanted to be God—a basic temptation of Satan: 'Ye shall be as gods, knowing good and evil.' It took a long time and a lot of suffering, and a great deal of praying and tears to bring them down. Human civil government is definitely subject to that temptation.

In Moses' economy, God laid on restraints—negative and positive—that would limit the power of future kings of Israel. Let's look at those briefly in these verses 16-20.

Negatively, God gives three restraints—one of them would seem very strange to us, the other two make sense. One was not to amass horses, not to go down to Egypt to get a bunch of horses. Egypt was a place at that time that bred and raised the most wonderful horses in the ancient world. If they went down to Egypt to get horses, they would be impressed with Egyptian culture, and look to them for guidance, and maybe lose their liberty, for they had once been slaves down there.

Many scholars say that maintaining a large number of horses meant a large standing army, because the way you moved an army around was with cavalry, involving horses and sometimes chariots. It was not the Lord's will that the kings of Israel would have such an army. It didn't say that he couldn't have any army, and it certainly didn't say he couldn't raise an army to fight when attacked. Why this restraint? There's a number of reasons: to maintain a huge standing army would require too much taxation on the people, and would force large numbers of them into conscripted military service, thereby weakening families. Also, the central government, with a huge standing army that it is paying a lot to maintain, will be eager to get into wars with its neighbors; whereas if they don't have all that military force, they are less likely to fight. Hence, the king is not to increase horses.

The second thing he is not to do is to increase wives. Obviously, that's not the perfect will of God, which is for a man to have one wife and a wife to have one husband. But we need to remember that the kings getting many wives was not merely lust driven—I'm sure that is part of it—but a wife is the way you would conclude a political alliance with another country. For instance, King Solomon took one of Pharaoh's daughters, and that concluded a treaty. In addition to her, he had many other wives, and got trade agreements with different countries, thus breaking God's law. One of the problems with all these wives is that he let them set up their own chapels, and bring in their own priests, serving idols, no less. And it stole away his heart.

King Solomon, the smartest man who ever lived, the wisest man in the world, wound up losing everything, destroying everything—he, who had so much wisdom to impart—because of his lust for foreign women, and his lust for power violated those very principles he was trying to teach in the books of Proverbs and Ecclesiastes. Despite everything, he left a situation in which his son lost most of the kingdom.

The third negative of restraining the power of the king is that he is not to amass great wealth. It doesn't say he couldn't have wealth, but he is forbidden to amass great wealth. The silver, gold, ivory, and the amount of successful trade they had in one year is almost hard to believe! We are given lists of it, and it all but boggles the mind! There's nothing wrong with having some wealth, but the trouble with <u>great</u> wealth is that it usually takes your heart away. When you have tremendous resources, often something bad happens. Once you get a great deal of money and other kinds of resources, you start thinking about it nearly all the time, and a slow process begins in your attitudes: God starts becoming unreal, and then you begin to think that you are smart; even if you got it by inheritance, you will still think that you are somehow outstanding. In that case, your heart begins to grow cold on God, in favor of all the material things that you are going to have to leave very soon anyway.

All this wealth can even cause us to make moral compromises in order to maintain and increase it, in which case we can lose our soul. 'What shall it profit a man if he gain the whole world and lose his own soul? Or what shall a man give in exchange for his soul?' asks our Saviour (Matt. 16:26). A king amassing great wealth would be tempted to do two things: fleece his people to get more out of them, squeeze the powerless to get more of their possessions; take advantage of the widow and the orphan and the weak. His gathering horses to maintain his army, gives him a tendency to pick a fight with people around him, and to use them for cannon fodder. So he is not to do those things. That's the negative limitations.

Then the positive limitation (verses 18–20): the king must learn Holy Scripture and carry it out.

Good human government is to be based on the principles of the Holy Bible. The interesting thing said here is unique to Israel. Not all monarchs knew how to read and write, but among the Israelites, the kings were to be literate. And it was required that the young king, maybe starting when a boy, was supposed to write out a good bit of the law—maybe the Ten Commandments, maybe more than that—take a quill, ink, and parchment and write out what God says to do. Then he was to meditate on it. Psalm 1 would fit in here, written by David, the first good king of Israel:

> Blessed is the man that walketh not in the counsel of the ungodly nor standeth in the way of sinners; but his delight is in the law of the Lord, and on that law he doth meditate both day and night. He shall be like a tree planted by the rivers of water.

David was inspired to write many of the Psalms; but in addition to that, he no doubt meditated day and night on what God said a king ought to be like. The major resource of a good government is said by David in Psalm 16:8 to be this: 'I have set the Lord always before me; because He is at my right hand I shall not be moved.' Now what do we do with our mind, if we have any power, position, money, good looks, sports ability, or any connections? Whatever we've got, we are to set the Lord always before us, and thereby to think of what God would have us do with whatever he has given us. That is the key to happiness and to joy.

I don't know if any of you would have remembered the ceremony in Westminster Abbey in 1953, when Queen Elizabeth II was crowned. The Archbishop of Canterbury, when crowning the king or the queen of England and the British Isles, presents them a copy of the Bible and asks him or her to take an oath on that Bible. The Archbishop says: 'Here are the lively oracles of God,' and calls on him or her to meditate in it day and night, and seek to govern by its authority. The coronation oath in Great Britain is very biblical.

What Kingship Means in a Modern Republic (17:20)

Look at these words in verse 20: 'to the end that he may prolong his days in his kingdom, he and his children'. 'Prolong his days' is reminiscent of the promise in the fifth commandment, 'Honor thy father and thy mother that thy days may be long upon the land which the Lord thy God giveth thee'. So to meditate on the written law from God, day and night, has a way of blessing one, and prolonging one's days in the land, and prolonging your children's days with *shalom,* peace, meaning well-being—with things working right, and the absence of unnecessary grief, defeat, disaster, blight, and horrible wars.

So I conclude with 1 Timothy 2:1-4. We in America, have not had a king since 1776. The Israelite theocracy has ages ago passed away. But we do have a King, *the* King, Jesus Christ over His church. We also have lesser governments that in some measure are meant to reflect something of the kingship of God. We give them due honor, insofar as they do that, and we are supposed to pray for them. Scripture commands us: 'I exhort therefore, that, first of all, supplications, prayers, intercessions, and giving of thanks, be made for all men; for kings, and for all that are in authority; that we may lead a quiet and peaceable life in all godliness and honesty' (1 Tim. 2:1-2). We pray for them, and as God blesses them in their function, even if they are not personally saved, He can still use them in His own way, so that His people can have a quiet and peaceable life.

Why? Just so they can be happy? No; it is in order that the function of Christian evangelism, the saving of the lost and the changing of character into Christ-likeness, and the building up of the church can occur, as we see in verses 3-4: 'For this is good and acceptable in the sight of God our Savior; who will have all men to be saved and to come unto the knowledge of the truth'. Decent government that is prayed for makes it much more likely that we can save lost men and women and gather them into the kingdom, as well as leading a reasonably calm and peaceful life; that is what government is for, to provide a structure for the advancement of the church. God help us to pray in that direction!

43

How to Guide Your Life: The Word of God

Deuteronomy 18:1–22

We are now looking at Deuteronomy chapter 18. Previously, I finished chapter 17, which is exactly half way through this major book. Now we are beginning the last half of Deuteronomy.

Deuteronomy 18 is fairly close to the comforts found in Psalm 23: 'The Lord is my shepherd', and sets before us a strange contrast between two ways of guidance: one by the Shepherd, and one by the devil—a bad kind of guidance-seeking and a holy and happy kind of guidance-seeking, that all the people of God are commanded to follow.

I start with the forbidden pagan ways of coping with the unknown future—verses 9–14, the negative, and still very relevant. Secondly, the rest of the chapter, verses 1–8 and 15–22, the positive: how God really does guide His people to the end of their life, and to the very end of earthly history.

Forbidden Ways to Know the Future (18:9–14)

The Canaanites for generations had followed pagan ways to try to handle the future and face the unknown, and that is one of the major reasons the Lord gives for being morally right to run them out of the land, and to give the land to the children of Israel. Verses 10 and 11 give us one of the strongest prohibitions in the entire Word of God against all dark forms of spiritism.

One is putting children to death by fire in order to appease the Satanic thirst of some evil spirit, who might then turn around and help the parents prosper one way or another. We have archeological evidence of a great deal of that, even outside the Bible. When the Romans had finally conquered Carthage, and were breaking it up, they found burning fields—still there today. The Romans themselves, pagan as they were, were shocked that the Carthaginians had burned their own babies to false gods; they found thousands and thousands of charred bones of babies and little folk in that burning field. The Romans said that if Carthaginians were that terrible, it was only right to wipe them out, to burn the city, and sow salt on the fields, so nothing would grow.

Along with other forbidden ways to seek the help of the dark unknown, let me summarize certain related forms of Satanic practice, under more modern names. It is sufficient merely to list some of the forbidden practices: fortune-tellers; witches; spiritists; mediums; horoscopists and necromancers.

I remember about 30 years ago in Dillon County, a terrible instance of necromancy. There was a particular house in the county, where a morally degenerate lived with his cronies, who were trying to make contact with the dead spirits. Some bad things happened and some of them came to see me, to see if I could undo some of the damage that had occurred. They were not members of my church, but they knew who I was. I think it best not to say any more about it, other than to say that the outcome, both to the people involved and to the grand old house, was horrendous. One would not expect things like that in a conservative, fairly Christian state like South Carolina.

I have often asked myself: why does there seem to be more of this kind of thing than when I was first ordained forty years ago? The reason, I think, is that the more humanistic our culture becomes, the more the gospel is lost and people turn from the Bible, then the more a vast spiritual vacuum is left. As the saying goes, nature abhors a vacuum—something will fill it. Who fills the spiritual vacuum when people aren't relying on the Holy Spirit as explained in the Word of God? Evil spirits from the dark realm! It's a silly theory of some of the modernists a hundred or more years ago, that there were no evil spirits and no devil; in fact, they did not realize how much they themselves were under his control.

Again, it's not edifying for me to go into it very much. I could give instances that I have read in the mainline press—such as the Wall Street Journal—which suggest the possibility that evil spiritism lies behind at least some of the bizarre murders that have occurred over the last twenty or thirty years. All I'm saying here is this: don't discount the reality of the evil realm; beware of it; keep yourself free from it; it is all too real.

Verse 12 says that these Satanic practices are 'an abomination to the Lord'. 'Abomination' means literally impure, disgusting to a holy God; something He particularly abhors. Why are false ways of seeking guidance from the spiritual world an abomination, an insult in the face of God? Because to consult a dark, unseen power is to turn to someone other than God. Psalm 27 says: 'Seek ye My face'; and true piety says, 'Yea, Lord, thy face do we seek.' Messing with any form of Satanism says, 'I do not seek the face of God; I want some easier way to get in contact with the other world that doesn't make moral demands on my life.' That's the issue. We will not have God reign over us; we will get help from some other place, and that's why it is an abomination.

This chapter concludes Moses' exposition of the fifth commandment, 'Honor thy father and thy mother'. Our supreme Father is our Father in heaven, the Lord God Almighty. We are to honor Him above everything else. That's clear. To consult evil spirits, whatever form they would take, is to dishonor our heavenly Father in the extreme. To seek to know the future apart from the revealed will of God in Holy Scripture means that I chart the course of my life not from God, but from some unseen world of lesser and dark spiritual powers—stars, palm readings, horoscopes, evil spirits—and basing my life on an immoral basis. To say 'I can get help, I can get guidance for the future, but I don't want God to do it because then I'd have to obey Him' is why this kind of thing is so wrong. Hence, to try to get in touch with dark powers is to reject the most basic call of God in Holy Scripture, which is 'Trust in Me.' Jesus says 'Follow me; If you love me, keep my commandments'. Jesus says in John 10: 'I am the Good Shepherd; my sheep know my voice and they follow me; a stranger they will not follow'. To go to the Satanists, fortune tellers, palm readers, witchcraft people, and any of that, is to turn one's back on the Good Shepherd, to reject Him for an evil power, which will wind up destroying the person who follows it.

This is stated bluntly in Isaiah, which followed Deuteronomy many years later:

> Behold I and the children whom the Lord hath given me are for signs and for wonders in Israel from the Lord of hosts, which dwelleth in Mount Zion. [In other words, follow the Lord]. And when they shall say unto you, Seek unto them that have familiar spirits, and unto wizards that peep, and that mutter; should not a people seek unto their God? For the living to the dead? To the law and to the testimony; if they speak not according to this word, it is because there is no light in them. (Isaiah 8:18-19)

Leaving the negative ways behind, where do we get good, healthy, wholesome guidance for the difficulties, the challenges, and the uncertainties of our lives? Everybody has difficulty in living and in facing the future; 'You know not what a day may bring forth'; it can change so fast. Your health may go; the stock market can go bust; the country may get into a war; members of your family get killed; a business may come under tremendous pressure: nobody is able to chart the future very far; a day at a time, even an hour at a time, that's the best we can do. So naturally, any normal person wonders what comes next; what can I do; how can I cope with the things that lie ahead? That is a longing in every human heart, saved or unsaved. God has graciously said, here's the way to cope with what you don't know, with what you can't control, with a future that's too big for you; it's this: follow my revealed Word that I have given to you, in a way that you can understand enough of it to be pure and relatively happy while down here, and at last go to a heavenly home.

God's Guidance and Provision for the Future (18:1-8, and 15-22)

Verses 1-8 deal with the priests and Levites; and then verses 15-22 deal with the institution of prophecy out of which the Old Testament was written. In these two ways, priest and Levites and the institution of prophecy—and the final Prophet who was to come—the people of God were given the pure and true way to find what God wants them to do for the rest of their lives. Isn't it wonderful that you can raise your children, and honestly tell them that God has guided you, and that He will guide them exactly the same way, even though you don't know their future anymore than you knew your own future, but you know God? And if they will go His way they are going to make it! As the line in the hymn says, 'With salvation's walls surrounded, thou mayest smile at all thy foes.'

The first section, verses 1-8, is the appointment of priests and Levites. They were a divinely chosen tribe—of which Moses and Aaron were part— and had two major responsibilities.

Some of them, the descendants of Aaron, were to serve as priests, to offer sacrifices, make pardon available for sin, and grant holy benediction to all the people: 'The Lord bless thee and keep thee; the Lord be gracious unto thee; the Lord lift up His countenance upon thee and give thee peace'. They were to stand between a holy God and a sinful people, performing and assisting in worship ritual at the tabernacle or in the Temple.

Others were teachers, preachers, and moral examples, scattered throughout the other eleven tribes of Israel, going to where the people were, and teaching the children to read and write. The Jews were and are the most literate of people, because of their respect for the Word of God, and the Levites were the teachers, teaching literacy and teaching the basic truths of Scripture.

The Lord makes it clear that He doesn't let them have farmland, agriculture being the basis of the economy of all the other tribes. As it takes a lot of work to run a farm, having to be there each day, giving it your full attention, the Levites were not given land. Moses said that the Lord is their inheritance, and therefore, free from the duties of farming. Hence the people were responsible for maintaining them and their houses, so that they could fulfill their functions of priesthood, representing the people to God and God to the people, and teaching the next generation the will of God.

Obviously, the people are encouraged to give them the support they needed and to do so generously, because God is no man's debtor. Everything the people gave to support the Levites would be given back to them in personal and national blessing, ten thousand fold and more. This is one of the principles of the tithe which we read about in Malachi 3:10–11: how richly God would repay their support of the Levites.

Malachi is saying that the Lord will bless the farms; He will bless agriculture, if they will bless the priestly tribe.

The second way instituted by the Lord to give specific guidance to His people throughout all the ages is the institution of the office of prophecy, as we see in verses 15–22. Out of the divine office of prophecy comes the Old Testament. Why am I preaching on Deuteronomy? I couldn't do it, if it were not written down. The writing down of the Bible came out of the institution of the office of prophet. Moses, endowed by the Holy Spirit, wrote the first five books of the Bible, including Deuteronomy, and then the Holy Spirit would work in the other prophets. So you could say that the entire Old Testament, and later the New Testament, come out of the institution of prophecy.

Verses 15–18 explain that as Moses must die (at the age of 120) God will replace him as both mediator—the one who stood between a holy God and sinful people and made intercession for them—and teacher with his brother Aaron, who offered the sacrifices. God would put the spirit of prophecy that had been in Moses into other chosen men, who would follow him in the generations ahead, choosing who would be prophets, as He did who would be king, and who would be priests. And who would be able to intercede for the people and explain to them how to live and cope with difficulty, and how to follow God when it seemed hard to do.

Verse 16 relates how scared the people were on Mount Sinai, a huge mountain, which was literally shaking all over with the presence of God—like an earthquake—and beaming out stupendous rays more awesome than the noonday sun with the pure holiness of God; and so they begged Moses that he would be the one to speak to them the will of God, and not God Himself; they couldn't stand God being that close with His purity and power. Hence the Lord and Moses agreed to their request, and the Lord put His holy words in the mouth of Moses, and in the mouth of other men whom He would choose, all the way down through the Old Testament and indeed into the New Testament. This is explained in principle in 2 Peter 1:20–21: 'Knowing this first, that no prophecy of the Scripture is of any private interpretation [in other words it is not a matter of human opinion]'.

Relativists say that since there are different religions, it is impossible to know if any one of them is right. Thus, they conclude: you look at it your way, I'll look at it my way, and we'll all get there at the same place. No! Prophecy is not a matter of the opinions of one human cultural group. It is a divine revelation from heaven, from

God Himself, so that it is firmly true; 'For the prophecy came not in old time by the will of man; but holy men of God spake as they were moved by the Holy Ghost' [and the word *moved* in Greek is *fero*, to be carried along like the ocean carries a ship or the air carries an airplane or a mother carries a baby, to bear along, as the Holy Spirit was bearing along the penmen of Scripture in the Old and New Testament, so that it was literally a divine product.

Deuteronomy 18:19-21 warns against false prophecy. Anytime you have a valuable currency, you will have counterfeits. People are always trying to counterfeit dollars, pounds, or euros, and now they are trying to make it harder for counterfeiters, by putting red strips in dollar bills, so they are more difficult to reproduce. It is similar in the spiritual realm: where you have the true spirit of prophecy, the devil is going to raise up people to give you a cheap, phony alternative that would destroy those who follow it. Verses 19-21 say that if somebody engages in false prophecy, he is to be put to death. How would you know that it is false prophecy? It is simple: if what they say is not in accordance with written Scripture, particularly if somebody is predicting the future and it does not come to pass, he is a false prophet. In Old Testament times, such people would be executed. We don't execute them now, but we excommunicate them, and do not listen to them.

I know of one man—whose soul I cannot judge—who sold a lot of books on the end of time, and at least, four or five times, he specifically predicted the exact year that Jesus Christ would return (in the 1970s and 1980s). That shows him to have been a false prophet. You have that kind of thing in 1 Kings 22:11-28, where there was a false prophet named Zedekiah, and the true prophet of God was Micaiah ben Imlah. Micaiah, was called before King Ahab who asked: 'Will this battle that I'm going to fight prosper?' And Micaiah told the truth and said 'No, don't go up and fight this battle; you'll come back dead if you do; it will not prosper'. The king was infuriated, and had him put in prison and said to torture him. But Zedekiah knew he would get a promotion at court, and told the king to go up and he would prosper. But Micaiah said to Ahab, If you come back alive, I'm no prophet. And so Ahab followed false prophecy.

People who follow false prophecy do not enjoy the consequences. So when Ahab came back, he had been shot with an arrow that went through an open place in the joints of his armor, and he was bleeding to death. Thus, as Elijah had prophesied, the dogs licked up Ahab's blood from the chariot, as they washed it out when they got back to Samaria. That's what God thinks of false prophecy.

The institution of prophecy for Israel looks forward, not only to people like Moses and many others who are great and wonderful and give us the Bible; but here in chapter 18:15 it looks forward to a final Prophet, whom we could truly call the sealing Prophet. It is the Lord Jesus Christ; He is the ultimate, the supreme Prophet who fulfills all other prophecies in Himself. Other prophets spoke the Word of God; Jesus in His flesh is the Word of God, fulfilling it all. And this verse is quoted three places in the New Testament which apply it directly to Jesus Christ: John 6:14, John 7:40, and also Acts 3:19–23, which takes this word and applies it to Jesus directly in this preaching of Peter:

> Repent ye therefore, and be converted; that your sins may be blotted out, when the times of refreshing shall come from the presence of the Lord. And he shall send Jesus Christ, which before was preached unto you; whom the heaven must receive until the

times of restitution of all things, which God hath spoken by the mouth of all his holy prophets since the world began. For Moses truly said unto the fathers, A prophet shall the Lord your God raise up unto you of your brethren, like unto me; him shall ye hear in all things whatsoever he shall say unto you. And it shall come to pass that every soul which will not hear that prophet, shall be destroyed from among the people.

Then, in Hebrews 3:1–6, there is a comparison and contrast between Moses as a true prophet, and Christ as the final Prophet. It demonstrates how much more Christ is able to do for us as our final High Priest, than even Moses, as great a man as he was. In Hebrews 3:1–6, our eyes are all focused on Jesus, as it gives this promise: 'We are His house'—that is to say, we are His dwelling place, His temple, lively stones of His temple, 'If we hold fast the confidence and rejoicing of the hope firm to the end'. Hold on to that hope, and it will be your life, for He is your life. Follow Him! Jesus said to the disciples: 'Follow me', and He still says it to us.

44

The Law of Retaliation
Deuteronomy 19:1–21

We have dealt with the Cities of Refuge previously. With that in mind, we begin with verse 14 of Deuteronomy 19. The very last verse of that chapter gives us the major subject we will now look at: the law of retaliation. Here's the question every person in every public body faces at sometime or another: is it good or bad to retaliate? Or would it sometimes be good to do it and sometimes be bad?

The Bible gives us very clear answers on this issue in a fallen world. When Adam sinned, all his descendants became sinners, and therefore we all do wrong things. From the time Adam and Eve fell, until Jesus returns, you're going to have the issue of retaliation: how you handle evil that's done against you. This chapter, and some others I'll make reference to, give us guidance in a matter that is very important for living in a fallen world.

Deuteronomy 19 starts a new section in the book, leading us into Moses' exposition of the 6th commandment, 'Thou shalt not kill'. For several Sundays, we have been in the 5th commandment, 'Honor thy father and thy mother'. But now, Moses is taking the 6th commandment and is explaining the practicalities of how it's going to work out in the land that the Lord will lead Israel into, through Joshua. Although they are the Lord's people, they will commit sins; they will do wrong things, and their sins are to be dealt with in a fair and judicious way.

This section on not killing runs from the beginning of chapter 19 until about the middle of chapter 22. As I said, I will not comment on the first several verses of this chapter, because I dealt with the Cities of Refuge previously, except to say that this idea of Cities of Refuge, mercifully giving locations where a person who has committed involuntary manslaughter can flee to, is obviously a part of this exposition of Moses, regarding not killing; that is, we should not kill, without it being absolutely requisite, on the basis of what God teaches us.

We are going to look at verses 14–21, which cover three subjects, all of them one way or another related to killing—at first sight not obvious, but we will find out as we go along. First: boundary markers or landmarks, verse 14; second, malicious false witness in court, verses 15–19; third, the law of retaliation, verses 20–21.

Land Markers (19:14–21)
Landmarkers are important. In some countries, especially desert countries or countries with a lot of rocks, the landmarks are in stone. But

normally in the east coast of the United States, we follow the old English way of measuring by metes and by bounds. I remember as a child going with my father and great uncle, re-running the lines of the plantation, and I learned something about blazes on trees while running a line that had been set 200 years before by our ancestors, and it was very challenging; some of the trees were gone, and many other things had changed.

Moses is telling the people how they should act when they enter the Promised Land. They would be a nation to whom God directly granted a large area of land, which would be divided between the tribes excepting Levi, and apportioned to them by Joshua and the high priest. Many study editions of the Bible have maps that tell you where the lands of Judah (in the south), Dan (in the north), Reuben (on the other side of the Jordan), Asher (next to the sea), and so forth were situated.

In the providence of God, through Joshua, the captain of the hosts, and through Aaron and his successors, the land was portioned out to the eleven tribes, and it would be theirs right on. Then within the tribes, the different families were given specific metes and bounds of land. Thus it was through legitimate leadership that God had appointed—the high priest, the captain of the hosts, and the judges—that everybody held their land; so it was as if God gave you the land—an important point to keep in mind.

In Deuteronomy 19:14, the authorities establish the security of boundary markers or landmarks. These were meant to safeguard each family's property from being stolen by someone else. Some dishonest people still attempt to steal land by moving a landmark; I once knew of that happening in Colleton County, in the Low Country of South Carolina, when a man willfully moved an old landmark to try to increase his field. To move a landmark in Israel would be a direct attack on the Lord who granted that land to a tribe or family; that is the background of verse 14.

Why does Moses put stealing land in the category of killing? You would think it would have been put in the less serious category of 'Thou shalt not steal'. In fact, the two categories are closely related as I will show you.

I think there are two reasons why Moses considered moving landmarks to be in the general category of murder. Firstly, in a rural society, which Israel was for a long time, the people grew their food on the land: gardens, vineyards, olive yards and grazing of animals. To take the land of, let us say a powerless person, perhaps a widow or orphan, would deprive them of groceries and reduce them to poverty or possible starvation that would wind up leading to their death. Secondly, moving a landmark and stealing land is, through the code of Moses, not very far from killing. What do I mean?

It is often said that if someone breaks into your house, they will also kill you, if they think it necessary, if you surprise them. That happened in about 2008, in Moore County, North Carolina, where a high school girl, sick with a fever, was at home, rather than school. Her parents were at work and left her by herself, which they later, every hour of the life, regretted. A wicked man broke into the house to steal televisions and whatever else he could get, and saw the teenage girl sick in the bedroom, and brutally murdered her, so she couldn't report him. Later I visited the family cemetery, where the girl is buried. Her heart-broken parents tend the grave like a shrine, with pictures of her, constantly changing flowers. My heart goes out to them.

There is a major case in 1 Kings 21, which we have already discussed in some detail, where wicked Queen Jezebel stole ancestral land from

Naboth. The prophet Elijah heard about it, and sent direct word to Jezebel that God would bring her down, and dogs would lick her blood from the ground, which happened in due season, showing that God takes very seriously trying to steal someone's land or property.

Let us conclude these thoughts on the importance of the integrity of land boundaries, and other kinds of property, from Proverbs 23:10-11: 'Remove not the old landmark; and enter not into the fields of the fatherless; for their Redeemer is mighty; he shall plead their cause with thee'. And Deuteronomy 27:17: 'Cursed be he [by God!] that removeth his neighbor's landmark. And all the people shall say, Amen.' (That is one of the reasons Jezebel came down). They are saying we will live, O God, by Your way, by honoring the integrity of property, and hence we will not steal that which may actually remove somebody's life. So that is the first point, integrity of the landmark.

MALICIOUS WITNESSES IN COURT (19:15-19)

A criminal case is in view in these verses. In some cases, criminal matters could involve the death penalty, and that is why Moses is discussing malicious false witness, not under the later probation 'Thou shalt not bear false witness against thy neighbor', but under murder. Why? Because, in a criminal case, if false witness is given, then an innocent person whom the false witness hates or envies could be wrongly put to death. That is why Deuteronomy 19:15 requires there to be more than one witness, otherwise a malicious or jealous person could have someone imprisoned or put to death, just because they hate them or want their property.

The biblical law is fair at this point. Verse 16 and 19 state that if the judges find out someone has lied against another person in court—has borne false witness—or has accused them of something they never did, then the court is to do to them the same thing they were to do to the person they defamed, whether beating, imprisonment, or execution. This had a wonderful way of cutting down people's eagerness to bear false witness in court in order to hurt or even kill others.

Competent lawyer friends tell me that many frivolous and unfair lawsuits in the United States today that are clogging the courts could be cut out, if we restored the principle here in Deuteronomy 19:15, that somebody that brings an unfair lawsuit, the same thing will be done to them that they wanted done to the person whom they severely inconvenienced and falsely accused. I am told that such a provision would cut down the backlog of cases by probably eighty per cent, thereby making the work of the courts massively easier.

THE LAW OF RETALIATION (19:20-21)

I know that some of you will have a negative feeling about the concept of retaliation. In some cases, of course, you're right; but not in every case. We must think of this practice as the Bible defines it, and not as the modern humanist does. The old term for retaliation in judicial procedure is known by the Latin words, *lex talionis*, the law of retaliation. I wish to say three things on the law of retaliation: first, what retaliation—as taught in the Bible—does not mean; secondly, what it does mean and why it's important to the true biblical understanding of it; and thirdly, what Jesus says about it.

Lex talionis certainly does not ever mean to take personal vengeance against someone who has hurt you. Some months ago I was told about a thing that happened not far away, in Robeson County, North Carolina. One young male was driving his car and went past another, apparently whom he didn't like; each one rolled down the window, and the one who was passing cursed the one he was passing. Then the one who was cursed became infuriated. He went home, got a gun, chased down the young man who had cursed him, and shot him dead. That is the precise opposite of what the law of retaliation in Deuteronomy means. It never gives us the right to take personal vengeance, when we have been unfairly or viciously offended. Romans 12:19 tells us what God would have us do: 'Dearly beloved, avenge not yourselves, but rather give place unto wrath'. Precisely when we feel infuriated, the inspired Apostle instructs us 'give place to wrath', meaning, don't let wrath get hold of you; step away from it. Don't let wrath get the best of you: 'For it is written, Vengeance is mine; I will repay, saith the Lord'. God will see that proper vengeance, at the right time, in the right way, will be given to those who have hurt you unfairly. Leave it to Him; do not take it into your own hands.

So then, what does the law of retaliation actually mean? It is, in fact, the very foundational principle of all criminal justice; every valid justice system in the world is ultimately based on *lex talionis*, and here is what it comes down to: the punishment must fit the crime.

Doesn't that make sense? The punishment must fit the crime; it must never exceed the seriousness of the crime. The angry young man in Robeson County, who cursed somebody he didn't like, was acting sinfully. However, what he did do, did not merit death, so the action of the boy who killed him was worse. The punishment has got to fit the crime.

Or take what verse 21 says, (and many people have used this to criticize the Bible, much as they are out of line in doing so): 'An eye for an eye, a tooth for a tooth.' What is that saying? You only take one eye or one tooth; you don't take both eyes or all the teeth. The gravity of the crime determines the gravity of the punishment; there is a direct relationship established here between the evil act and its punishment. One is to go by impartial principles of justice, based on the righteousness of God, not by overheated emotion.

Take for instance, where parents have to be careful not to over-punish a child. Most of us poor parents have probably transgressed by over-punishing at times. But we must be zealous to remember that in the family, as well as in the courts, the punishment must always fit the crime. That provides the basis of a fair justice system, of a peaceful, honorable society, and of a godly home.

Now the third question about retaliation is more widespread than you would think, even extending to some denominations; it is this objection: since Jesus teaches love and forgiveness, we truly follow Him, it precludes any retaliation whatsoever. A question like this can be properly answered only by comparing Scripture with Scripture. Indeed, one passage in the New Testament seems to disallow any kind of retaliation. Jesus, in the Sermon on the Mount, says; 'Ye have heard that it hath been said, An eye for an eye and a tooth for a tooth. But I say unto you, That ye resist not evil; but whosoever shall smite thee on thy right cheek, turn to him the other also' (Matt. 5: 38–39).

The Lord is making a distinction here between personal attitude about how people treat us in our ordinary relationships and formal court cases. He was not here, the best I could tell, talking about a court case; He is talking about personal attitude towards one when we are offended; in general, those are two different things.

Let me give you an illustration of this from the life of John Wesley. Once he was preaching in the north of England, out in the fields, because the Church of England wouldn't let him preach in cathedrals anymore and thousands upon thousands were flocking to his ministry. It had been raining and the fields were muddy, but the Holy Spirit had been working, with people getting saved. There was one hostile unbeliever, who hated Wesley, and made his way to the front of the crowd. He took into his hand a big ball of mud, and when he got to Mr. Wesley, he smashed the mud into his face and said, 'There! That's what you deserve!' John Wesley certainly had the Holy Spirit in this matter! He replied, 'God bless you, sir.' And that wicked man was broken down and began weeping, and on the spot repented of his sins. Hundreds and hundreds saw it. I believe that is the kind of thing that Jesus was speaking of.

Or take a godly wife with a difficult husband, as in 1 Peter 3:1–2, 4.

> Likewise, ye wives, be in subjection to your own husbands; that, if any obey not the word' [if a husband obeys not the word, he is not going by the Bible], 'they also may without the word [without your saying anything] be won by the conversation of the wives'; [that means the conduct of the wife: her attitude, her life] 'while they behold your chaste conversation coupled with fear [the fear of God]. But let it [the beauty of the wife] be the hidden man of the heart, in that which is not corruptible, even the ornament of a meek and quiet spirit, which is in the sight of God of great price.

Peter gives hope to women who were converted, but still had husbands who were not. He says that their husbands may be changed, not by their preaching at the husband every day, but by their godly life and Christ-like attitudes. Hard-hearted males, proud males, can be broken down and won by their wife not taking personal vengeance on them (even through fussing).

Or again, how about an unpleasant church member, who says he is a Christian, but in the community, he is unpleasant and mean? What do you do with that? The first thought is to pay them back. But no; what Peter says is in accordance with Jesus and Paul, teaching us not to render personal vengeance (1 Pet. 3:8–11).

So there is to be no personal vengeance. It takes the Holy Ghost to overcome the desire to do so and the presence of the crucified, risen Christ in us, at a deep level. It is wise, I think, for us to pray for this spiritual assistance ahead of time, before the offense comes. If we wait until we are offended, it may be too late, and we will react with emotion that short-circuits our good sense. I think that might be part of what Jesus means in the Lord's Prayer, 'Lead us not into temptation, but deliver us from evil'. 'Lord, don't let me get into a situation today in which I would over react to someone's offense, and by it dishonor you, even before a wicked person. Since that wicked person needs to see a good witness for Christ, in order to be changed, let me faithfully represent you in this hard situation.'

This, I think is the personal level, on which we do not retaliate. But at the same time, Jesus and His apostles do not undercut the necessary work of civil courts, which are always based on the law of retaliation, by which the punishment must fit the crime.

Think of it this way: if Jesus had meant you can no longer have civil courts, and nobody can be punished, even when the punishment does fit the crime, then society would have descended into anarchy, and it would have been hell on earth with everything destroyed 2,000 years ago. That cannot be what He meant.

Can one prove that distinction between personal vengeance, and legitimate authority of courts to punish wrong doing? Yes! Elsewhere in the Sermon on the Mount, Jesus affirms the legitimacy of civil courts, and of the punishment they mete out based on the law of retaliation. In the same chapter, Matthew 5:25–26, (and this is as much a part of the Sermon on the Mount as the verses not to take personal vengeance):

> Agree with thine adversary quickly whilst thou art in the way with him [that means on the way to the court house]; lest at any time the adversary deliver thee to the judge, and the judge deliver thee to the officer and thou be cast into prison. Verily I say unto thee, thou shalt by no means come out thence, till thou hast paid the uttermost farthing.

Here, Jesus is speaking to somebody who has done wrong. He tells them to settle it out of court. This means that the court has a legitimate right to exercise punishment in accordance with the nature of the crime. So why not settle out of court? Hence, He is assuming here, and clearly teaching, the legitimacy of courts and the law of retaliation, which is their basis.

The Apostle Paul, who had met the risen Lord and studied the Old Testament, and who knew the mind of the Lord, if anybody ever did, he affirmed the legitimacy of the court system and the principle of proper retaliation (not personal vengeance, but proper, legal retaliation within the system).

> Let every soul be subject unto the higher powers. For there is no power but of God; the powers that be are ordained of God [that's the government]. Whosoever therefore resisteth the power, resisteth the ordinance of God [government is an ordinance of God]; and they that resist shall receive unto themselves damnation [that means judgment, not necessarily where a soul winds up]. For rulers are not a terror to good works, but to the evil. Wilt thou then not be afraid of the power? Do that which is good, and thou shalt have praise of the same. For he [the civil official] is the minister of God to thee for good. But if thou do that which is evil, be afraid; for he beareth not the sword in vain. (Rom. 13:1–4).

Hereby, Paul says that the state has the power to apply punishment in accordance with the nature of the crime, and in some cases by use of the sword or capital punishment [for certain, carefully defined cases]; 'For he is the minister of God, a revenger to execute wrath upon him that doeth evil. Wherefore ye must needs be subject, not only for wrath, but also for conscience sake'. So there we have it: a justice system that is, to some degree, based on the principle of retaliation when carefully defined, meaning that the punishment never goes beyond the seriousness of the crime. And when our personal lives are lived in union with Christ our risen Lord, our ever-present Redeemer will help us to respond with immense grace, beyond anything we have in the flesh, if we look to Him and say to Him day by day, 'Lord, lead us not into temptation but deliver us from evil.' And He can do it.

45

Holy War

Deuteronomy 20:1–20

One of the advantages and disciplines of being a minister who preaches through books of the Bible, chapter by chapter, is this: it makes you preach on subjects you never would have dealt with in all your life. If I live another sixty-four years, I doubt I would preach on the subject of holy war. But I come, in this chapter of Deuteronomy, to that very subject. I remember what Paul says in 2 Timothy 3 that 'all Scripture is given by inspiration of God and is profitable'; so even this chapter, which may ring strangely in our ears, is profitable for doctrine, for reproof, for godly living. So, I approach this subject because it's in the *rota* of Deuteronomy. But it could be the proverbial 'elephant in the room.'

The subject has come to the fore during the last twenty or so years, with the rise of radical Islam, notably 'ISIS', which claims that cutting heads of 'unbelievers', and running the film of it on social media, is a valid part of holy war. Or, the attack on the Twin Towers in 2001, was a proper action in holy war, as were the blowing up of the train in Madrid, the bombings in Brussels, etc. Few people across the world, as far as I know, would believe in that kind of a holy war. In fact, it is anything but holy; it is demonic—of the devil—and we do well to be against it.

However, the holy war spoken of in Deuteronomy 20 is very different. It, in fact, is holy in the sense that it is in accordance with the moral character of the God who made the universe, and created the human race in His image. The kind of war envisioned in Deuteronomy 20 is very limited and restrained; it operates under particular rules and laws which keep it from being a widespread, scorched earth, anti-humanitarian conflagration.

Because of the fall of Adam, all of us are born with a sinful nature. The book of James asks: 'Where do wars come from?' (James 4:1). They come from within, from our fallen nature. Until the end of time, till Jesus returns, we're going to have trouble, including wars. The question is not whether or not we face a reality of war, but how do you deal with it?

Deuteronomy tells us some matters about how God would have His people conduct a war, so that it would be in line with what St. Augustine called in the fifth century 'a just war'. It is that which I want us to look, under three points: the first, when is killing ever legitimate? (this section is part of Moses' exposition of the sixth commandment, 'Thou shalt not kill'). Moses seems to be saying, there are a few (not many) times when killing is necessary.

When is Killing Legitimate? (20:1)

The first verse says that there are times when the men of God have to go out to battle; when citizens are called to leave their homes and go to the battle field to serve as soldiers. In doing so, if it is necessary for them to kill an enemy combatant, it is not a violation of the sixth commandment in any way. So, in a legitimate war, killing is by definition called for, although it has to be carefully hemmed in by other rules of war, such as not killing the innocent, and indeed, not going to war if there is another way to handle it.

Also it is legitimate to kill a thief, who is breaking into your home, and is attempting to steal or attack the family. That is explained in Exodus 22:2, which says: 'If a thief be found breaking up and be smitten that he die, there shall no blood be shed for him'. Defense of the home is a right that is backed up by Holy Scripture.

Legitimate Exemptions from War (20:2-9)

Although war may be required, verses 2–9 give four exemptions from what we call in modern countries, the draft. These people are not draft-dodgers; their not taking part is legitimate. God says there are four categories that can be let out of joining the army: someone who has just built a new house and not lived in it (verse 5); someone who has planted a vineyard and not yet harvested it (verse 6); one who is engaged to be married, (verse 7); and—a little different from these—someone who is of a terribly fearful spirit is to be sent home from the battle (verse 8).

What's the reason for these exemptions? The first three are illustrations of the loving kindness of God our heavenly Father, who desires His chosen people to enjoy life in the Promised Land. God is full of joy, and wishes to spread that joy to all His people, including as far as He deems proper, the time they spend on the earth. God is never harsh. Many people who won't go to church, or who have a negative view of Christianity, feel that God is mean. They know that He is powerful, but they think that He does not have a kindly face and loving heart; they wrongly see Him as a dark, terrible power, out to get them.

However, the God of the Bible is a loving Father of the Son, bound to the Son with the bond of the Holy Spirit, and has made us to share in His life and love. 'God so loved the world …' (John 3:16). In 1 John 'God is love' (4:8) and 'God is light' (1:5). A gracious side-effect of God's love and light, and kindness and fatherly nature, is that He has put us in a world where He desires for us, in our own way, to enjoy living.

On Puritanism people have different ideas. I would say there is a good kind of Puritanism and there is a bad kind. The good kind of Puritanism holds that we want to live our whole life as in the presence of God—as the English poet John Milton says in his sonnet #7, 'As ever in my great taskmaster's eye'. The good Puritanism says that the main thing about being here is about God and we want to refer everything in our experience to God; thus we want to avoid what is impure and unclean and to live clean lives of purity and joy by His grace. That is the valid kind of Puritanism, which is profoundly God-centered.

A bad kind of Puritanism is really a misunderstanding of what these good men in the seventeenth century were saying. Some of them may well have had a negative tendency, but most were happy, well-balanced people.

The bad kind of Puritanism is where God does not want me to enjoy anything in this world; if anything is beautiful, attractive, lovely, tasty, desirable, it must be bad. So therefore, I am to deny myself every legitimate pleasure, so that I can dwell in a vale of tears and a land of shadows, until I am set free from it all by physical death. This is also found in other religious traditions. But it is not biblical. Jesus, speaking about our abiding in the vine and being in Him, says: 'These things have I spoken unto you that My joy might remain in you and that your joy might be full' (John 15:11). His beloved apostle says: 'These write we unto you that your joy may be full' (1 John 1:4).

Then 1 Timothy 6:17 says what God is really like, as you think about the good things of life: 'The living God who giveth us richly all things to enjoy'. But some will argue that this refers only to spiritual joy. Well, of course, we read: 'Rejoice in the Lord, and again I say, rejoice!' Our primary joy is living in the presence of God, and knowing where we are going after we leave this world. But Scripture also teaches that God gives us other things 'richly to enjoy': good food, good drink, marriage, happy relationships, beauty of nature, and so forth.

The Psalms are full of this: 'Let everything that hath breath praise the Lord' (Ps. 150). When the Psalmist speaks of angels, birds, and creatures in the sea, he describes the trees of the fields clapping their hands together. In another psalm, God says, 'I would have fed thee from the finest of the wheat and the honey from the comb' (Ps. 81:6). This shows us that God is the one who has set it up that we may have considerable joy; not only spiritual joy, which is primary; but also physical joys, which are perfectly legitimate: 'For He hath strengthened the bars of thy gates; he hath blessed thy children within thee. He maketh peace in thy borders, and filleth thee with the finest of the wheat' (Ps. 147:13–14). Those are some of the physical pleasures that God takes much joy in sharing with us.

This sharing of divine joy with His image-bearers is the reason for the first three exemptions: God wants these young men to share some of these joys, before perhaps having to give their lives on a field of battle. That's the kind of generous Father He is. Most of us have had good fathers; none of them was perfect, but they were probably good fathers, and wished to give us good things, the best they could. Our heavenly Father is even more generous and caring than any earthly father; keep that in mind.

The fourth exemption is different. It allows the captain in the various divisions to dismiss a soldier who is absolutely horrified of battle. The captain has common sense to know that once the battle is joined, it is likely that this man will turn and run. I was told by some of the veterans of the first Gulf War that when the battle was joined, huge numbers of the Iraqi soldiers started running, led by their officers. Their officers, when they saw the Western allies coming, turned and fled and the ordinary troops followed them.

Deuteronomy is very wise; it's better to let a few fearful troops go home, than to infect the whole brigade with fearfulness, and to get them cowering and running in the other direction. That is why Gideon in Judges 7 dismissed so many soldiers, saying everyone who is fearful, should go home.

One final word: Deuteronomy 20:1 commands: 'Be not afraid of them' when you see it's a bigger force than yours and better equipped. Israel, at this time, did not have horses and chariots; they acquired them only later, under Solomon. But at this stage they were merely foot soldiers and the Canaanites were much better equipped. But God tells them not to be fearful and to trust in Him.

God also encouraged them to remember what He did for them in Egypt, which had horses and chariots aplenty, and they were a pack of slaves, whom nonetheless God favored. So, they were able to flee across the Red Sea, which then overcame this massively well-equipped Egyptian army. God says, remember that is what I am like; don't be terrified; don't let your hands become frozen as you consider what your enemy is like. Consider them, but think the most of Me. That is a legitimate kind of 'Puritanism' at its best: think of God in everything that happens; think of Him first always.

Let me apply this to modern life. In Deuteronomy 20:2, the priest goes out to the army before the battle and encourages them in the Lord. In other passages, they would bring the Ark of the Covenant, and put it in the middle of the army to encourage the people. But it's necessarily different today; our High Priest is not on earth. He is in heaven on the right hand of the Father. Yes, He's interceding for us, watching over us, and even closer to us than the High Priest could be to those Israelite soldiers, but we don't see Him. So while He does not come literally down to army, navy or air force, He is at work by His powerful providence, taking care for His people in situations of great danger, including us in our own little battles.

Thinking about this further, how does our High Priest come to us to help us when we need it? Ephesians 6:12 and following says: 'We wrestle not against flesh and blood but against powers and principalities, high places, against the wiles of the devil; therefore take unto you the whole armor of God'. This means that Christians, all the Church, from the time Christ baptized it in the Holy Spirit at Pentecost, until He returns at the end of time, the Church has battles; and every believer has struggles against dark powers, sometimes stronger than we can handle. How does our High Priest, who loves us more than anybody has ever begun to love us, how does He come to us, as we face these struggles? Two ways are mentioned in these verses in Ephesians 6.

The first way is the sword of the Spirit, which is the Word of God—the Bible, the promises of the Bible, what God says He will do, and how you stand with Him, what He is going to accomplish in letting you get into this trouble (which according to Romans 8:28 will work together for good). The sword of the Spirit, the Word of God, enables you to overcome many an enemy. The second way is prayer in the Spirit. Paul speaks in Ephesians 6 of the weapon of 'praying always with all prayer and supplication in the Spirit'. These two are ways our High Priest leaves heaven every time His people have need, far more effective than the Israelite High Priest to encourage us in our battles: the Word and the Holy Spirit that brings the risen Christ into the midst of the situation to do exactly what He wants done.

Instead of being paralyzed by fear, we can face difficulty. Every time you get into trouble, maybe not of your own making, you have a painful decision to make; will I be paralyzed by worry, anxiety, fear, bitterness, grief, hopelessness? Or will I do what David says in Psalm 16:8 and 'set the Lord before me; because He is at my right hand, I shall not be moved'. I shall not be knocked down, knocked flat, or run over.

Rules for just war (20:10-20)

A distinction is made between cities inside the Canaan, and those outside it. God told Moses, Joshua, and the people of Israel to wipe out the cities inside Canaan. Archeology shows that this culture had reached a rare peak of rottenness, moral corruption, degradation, and filth that was offensive to God, far worse than the more restrained pagan lands around them.

Long before, God had spoken to Abraham, saying that one day the iniquity of the Amorites would be full and they would be wiped out. God gave the Canaanites a long time to repent! They wouldn't repent, and even got worse. Finally, the iniquity of the Amorites was full and God said it was time to clean house.

Some might ask, does God have a right to do that? Psalm 24:1 says: 'The earth is the Lord's, and the fullness thereof'. Acts 17 says that He has appointed the various tribes, different boundaries in the world, by His providential direction. God has the right of judgment; He and He alone knows when a culture has been given so many opportunities, that in its unrepentant arrogance, it sends up such a stench to heaven, that the Lord needs to wipe it out.

That is what He does in the movement of the children of Israel. After forty years of wilderness wandering, it was time for divine judgment to fall on the tribes of Canaan. However, that was unique to the Old Testament period and was legitimate because God told them to do it. But the physical wiping out of a nation is never the task of the church.

The church's task is one of warfare, but it is spiritual warfare. 'Onward Christian Soldiers' is very different from a physical sword, or a neutron bomb, or whatever else. Christian soldiers go forward on their knees. Our kind of warfare is to win the lost to Christ; the call to battle is given by Jesus in Matthew 28:

> Go ye therefore into all the world and teach all nations, baptizing them in the name of the Father, and of the Son, and of the Holy Ghost; teaching them to observe all things whatsoever I have commanded you; and, lo, I am with you always, even unto the end of the world.

The church at no time is called to wipe out a particular tribe or country. In His providence, God sometimes does that, He is the one who will make that decision. Our warfare is spiritual.

We tend to feel that spiritual weapons are not so good as physical ones. We fear that the spiritual approach is weak; maybe it is halfway unreal to us, so that it will not make any difference. I beg you to believe the Bible which says spiritual weapons make far more lasting weapons than any physical weapons. They can accomplish things that physical weapons never could accomplish, and are given to the people of God as a church. 'For though we walk in the flesh, we do not war after the flesh; (for the weapons of our warfare are not carnal, but mighty through God to the pulling down of strongholds)' (2 Cor. 10:3-4).

When the blessing of God is upon them, spiritual weapons of Scripture and prayer, will take you much further, far deeper, far higher than swords and hand-grenades. They will be, instead of killing, resurrection-bringing. The spiritual weapons—the Word, the gospel, prayer, the Holy Spirit, will transform nations—carnal weapons can only wreak havoc.

In the Roman Empire, the early church, up to the time of Constantine the Great in the fourth century, had no weapons. They were persecuted, hated, lied about; but they were constantly increasing through the spiritual weapons of preaching the gospel, living holy lives, and suffering for Jesus with integrity, hope, and love. Eventually, Constantine declared that Christianity was the religion of the Roman Empire—which by and by collapsed. Then Christianity spread all over the world. Spiritual weapons, more powerful than the sword, overcame the world.

Now that doesn't mean that a modern state doesn't have the right of warfare; I believe they do. There are times when a civil government has to engage in battle to defend its borders, and the people of God are obliged to help them.

Finally, a remark on protecting trees in warfare (verses 19-20). It tells us something about what God is like (incidentally, a positive effect of preaching expositorily is learning things about what God is like). God created nature and loves it. Read the nature Psalms, like Psalm 65 and many others, to see how much God loves the nature He created.

Hence, in warfare, God said I want the fruit trees protected, and not to cut down more trees than absolutely necessary to build a battering ram or a ramp. God made the natural environment; He loves it. In the New World He's going to restore it perfectly and beautifully, and wants us to respect it in the meantime. Psalm 148:9: 'Mountains, and all hills; fruitful trees, and all cedars' are called upon to praise the Lord. Just the existence of the trees, the growing of various fruit, the wonderful smell of a cedar or a juniper or a pine in the summer evening, in the breeze, is praise to God, and He wants us to care for and protect them.

So this rather unusual chapter is in the part of 'Thou shalt not kill', where Moses is explaining what it means, and shows that sometimes war and self defense is necessary, and is not murder. It also explains that even in case of a just war, some citizens are properly exempted, and also that when you are engaged in war, the world around you is not to be scorched, not to be destroyed; but is to be protected as much as you can. All of this shows God's love for us; God's love for the world, and His glorious plans for the future. I conclude with 2 Peter 3:13: 'Nevertheless, we, according to His promise, look for new heavens and a new earth, wherein righteousness dwelleth'. This passage is already pointing toward what God is going to do for all that are His.

46

The Sacredness of Life

Deuteronomy 21:1–23

This substantial passage demonstrates in many directions the sacredness of human life. Chapter 21 is a continuation of Moses' exposition of the sixth commandment, *'Thou shalt not kill'*; and he is explaining at large the principles in the real world of what it means to obey this commandment.

The sixth commandment is rooted in the sacredness of human life which is a donation from God, because every person is created immediately in the image of God. That directly affects how we treat other people every day, every hour, universally. That is to say, we are never to hate people, disrespect them, curse them, or murder them, because, even though we may consider them very nasty and unworthy—which may be true in many instances—they are still in the image of the holy, glorious God. I'll say this: a country where human life is still considered to be sacred, is a wonderful place to live. Four main points in chapter 21: first, atonement for unknown murder, verses 1–9; second, protection for a captive bride, verses 10–14; third, a rebellious son, verses 15–21; and fourth, execution by hanging, verses 22–23.

Atonement for an Unknown Murder (21:1–9)

I remember maybe 30 years ago seeing in the *Dillon Herald* a very strange picture on the front page. My wife saw it, and immediately threw it away before the children could see it. It was a picture of a murdered young white man somewhere in his twenties. His body had been discovered along highway 95 between Latta and Dillon, South Carolina. The reason the police had his picture published in death was to find out if anybody knew anything about him. He had no identifying papers; they didn't know who he was, couldn't get any information; they buried him in a pauper's grave, and I never heard if anything was ever found out about this man.

Now that sort of thing is envisioned in verses 1–9, of Deuteronomy chapter 21. Let's say a murdered body is found in a field somewhere, and it's not known who killed him, or maybe her. Human life is so sacred that the territory around a murdered body, at least in the Old Testament times, was considered polluted until proper atonement could be made for the murdered person. Now Genesis chapter 9, at the end of the flood event, teaches capital punishment for murder, and it gives a reason people why are not to be murdered. If somebody commits murder you must put them to death. But here's the issue: what do you do when you don't know who killed somebody, like this man in his twenties that was found between Latta and Dillon all those years ago?

In the Old Testament times, the elders of the nearest village would measure where the body was found, and find out where was the closest city or village was. Then they would notify the elders of the nearest village or city to begin taking action. They were to take an unworked heifer into an unworked valley, and break its neck, cut its head off, as a form of atonement for murder. Here we have the basic principle by which we are saved: it is the principle of substitution—someone dying in another's place. That is the only way any sinner can ever, under any condition, be offered forgiveness and pardon, the principle of substitution.

So after they had made atonement by slaying this heifer, the elders who represented all the people of this now polluted territory, were to wash their hands in a bowl of water and plead their innocence before the Lord. I suppose that is rooted deeply in human nature, because we read in the New Testament that that precisely is what Pontius Pilate did. After falsely condemning Jesus to be crucified, he asked that they should bring a bowl of water—he's a Roman, not a Jew, but it is deep in human psyche that you need cleansing for murder—so he washes his hands and says, I am innocent. Of course it didn't work for Pontius Pilate (for he knew that he was guilty of being an accessory to the murder of Jesus), whereas it would have worked in the Old Testament village. But the washing of his hands would have been all in vain. It was like that with Lady Macbeth. Many of us remember a little of Shakespeare's *Macbeth*, where Lady Macbeth supposedly tried to wash the blood off her hands from the innocent King Duncan, whom she had killed.

But on the contrary, Deuteronomy presents the idea of a holy community, which is something that we don't think much about. Serious sin affects the whole lot so that when something, particularly willful murder, occurs, the whole community needs cleansing to remove the pollution and the wrath of God upon it. That goes exactly contrary to what modern people think, even church people.

What we are in the modern West is sometimes called 'individualists.' Particularly that has been the case since the liberal, European enlightenment of the eighteenth century. Everybody thinks: 'I am a disconnected, free, autonomous individual. What I do is my business; what you do is your business, and if others have done something bad, it has no effect on me whatsoever, so why should I care that somebody was murdered, even next door? It has nothing to do with me.' But that's not biblical.

Let me read you from what the apostle Paul says in 1 Corinthians 12:26–27. He's certainly not dealing with murder, but dealing with the principle of corporate connection, community connection, that God sees us together and that one does affects the others in the eyes of God: 'And whether one member suffer, all the members suffer with it; or one member be honored, all the members rejoice with it. Now ye are the body of Christ, and members in particular'.

Without exploring the issue, I do think, as far as I know, that the most horrendous sin in our country today is the ever-increasing mountain of guilt that is piling up because of legalized abortion every day. We do nothing to stop this the killing of the unborn. There can't be sufficient atonement for this until the sin is repented of. What would it look like to repent? Let's be specific. It means stop doing it; stop allowing it; and then over it you will have deep, broken-heartedness that it ever happened. What then is our responsibility? Look at Proverbs 31:8–9: 'Open thy mouth for all the dumb [the unborn can't talk] in the cause of all such as are appointed to destruction. Open thy mouth, judge righteously, and plead the cause of the poor and needy'. The most dangerous place to be in the United States of America is in a mother's womb, and God has said we are to plead their cause, because they can't speak for themselves; so for us to speak out is required.

Protection of a Captive Bride (21:10–14)

In ancient warfare, women at times were taken captive, later to serve as wives of the victors. Now God had told His people to wipe out all of the Canaanites, because of the vile degradation of the Canaanite culture, which meant they would all have to be wiped out. Hence, the Israelite soldiers could not form a marital union with any Canaanite woman. But there were many countries round about Israel, or what would become Israel, that weren't nearly so degenerate as the Canaanite folk. Sometimes, if Israel had to engage in war with particular cities of those other nations which weren't so degenerate as Canaan, it might be that an Israelite soldier would see a beautiful young woman and then say to his captain, I would like to have this young woman to be my wife. And so what we have here is something the Lord allowed in such cases. But the Lord set up particular protections for the captive woman, so she would not be abused and mistreated. The idea here is that the captive woman would be taken to the home of the Israelite, and cleansed, and given proper Israelite clothing, and allowed a full month to mourn for her parents, whether they were dead or whether she had to leave them; and then she would become one of the people of God by becoming married to this man.

John Calvin in his commentary thinks that that month would have been a time, not only to give her different clothing, and let her hair grow back, but that it would have been a time when she would be instructed in the Israelite religion, the true religion. That might be right; although the text is not necessarily specific on the matter, it would make sense—according to verse 13. And then in verse 14 she is still given holy protection. Let's say the young Israelite soldier thought she was beautiful, took her, and then she doesn't please him, they don't get on very well, and he feels like he doesn't want to stay married to her. At the very least, God says through Moses, she remains a free person; she cannot be sold into slavery; she cannot be made merchandise of. If you are not willing to live with her in marriage, she still has got to be protected and to that degree, honored.

So here's the principle: even formerly enemy people are still to be treated with dignity and respect, because they too are in the image of God and their life is sacred.

A Rebellious Son (21:15–21)

Here Moses seems to move from the sacredness of an individual life to the sacredness of the family unit. Thus he discusses the relationship of parents to their sons. First, it comes up in the question of inheritance: Jewish biblical law teaches what is called in Latin *primogeniture,* and it was carried on in English common law, and in several of these American colonies. *Primogeniture* means 'firstborn'; the right of the firstborn. The firstborn son gets preference in the will of God because he came first, and also he bears most of the responsibility for the care of the parents when they are aged. The issue here is about the firstborn, and that is established in other biblical passages; but something is brought up here, where polygamy was tolerated for a time in Israel (although Jesus says in the New Testament that God's original plan was marriage between one man and one woman).

But even when in the Old Testament economy, a certain form of polygamy was temporarily tolerated, it was still hemmed in with careful regulations to keep any of the wives or their children from being abused. Let us say that if a man has two wives, maybe he doesn't like the original wife as much as he likes the younger wife, the second wife; and so he decides to give a larger share of the inheritance to the younger son of the second wife, and he thereby would break the law of *primogeniture*. But Moses said you cannot do that; God will not bless that. Even if you don't like the older wife and you prefer the younger wife, you must honor the son of the older wife, if he indeed is firstborn, and thus give him the larger inheritance. So this shows that the law of *primogeniture* is to be adhered to, regardless of personal preference. Personal preference cannot overrule the clear teaching of the Word of God.

Now this shows great respect for the sacredness of the family. That's something that is pretty well broken down in America. Many people will say that you should have a certain respect for the individual, and probably most people would, one way or another: except for the unborn. But not too many think that a very high honor and respect is to be laid on the family unit; but God puts it there.

Then the second matter that is brought up here is a painful one to think about: it is the case of an incorrigibly rebellious son. He is a rebel; he is a drunkard; he may be violent; he wastes the family money, as far as he can get hold of it; he is irresponsible; and he disdains family honor, breaks the heart of his parents and grandparents, and breaks the unity of the sacred family unit. Now in such a case, the parents could bring him before the city elders; (the parents themselves did not have the right to put this young man to death), but what they could do was bring him to the judicial authorities that God had set up, to the village elders, who operated according to the principles of the Old Testament, and say: Here's the situation with our son; now you decide. And if the city elders said this young man is incorrigible, he has violated every principle of family trust, then he must be judicially executed. So that is a rule that is laid down in the Old Testament.

However I will say this: it must not have happened very often. Scholars have combed through every verse of the Old Testament, and nobody has ever found even one case of the actual execution of a rebellious son mentioned anywhere in the Old Testament. So it looks like, as far as we can tell, this regulation that was laid down as a possibility, does not appear ever to have been carried out in Israel, at least so far as we know. Probably what really happened was this: most parents of a terrible adult child would probably act more like the father that Jesus talks about in the parable of the prodigal son in Luke chapter 15, who awaited and prayed for a drunken, wastrel, rebellious son. When the son, finally down in the hog pen, lost everything, wasted everything, at last came to himself and repented—remembering who his father was.

I don't believe anybody is going to repent in this modern world, unless they remember who God the Father is. And so he goes home and the father runs out from the front porch, I suppose, when he sees the boy coming, and embraces him with joy and total, 100% forgiveness. Interestingly, this father- who represents God Almighty—says 'This my son who was dead and is now alive'.

Forgiveness of wayward children is a sort of foretaste of the resurrection.

Execution by Hanging (21:22–23)

Those who committed murder were to be executed, as we saw, because of Genesis chapter 9. And then their body was to be hung the rest of that day upon a tree. They were probably executed most likely by stoning, and then the body taken and tied to a tree. It was a sign of the curse of God against the breaking of the sixth commandment, *'Thou shalt not kill'*. Tying their body up to the tree so that the public could behold it, served as a deterrent to further murder in society at large. But even here, the body of the executed criminal is to be disposed of by the end of the day with a certain respect, because even the serious wrong-doer is still in the image of God. He may be lost, but he is still a lost soul in the image of God; that has to be remembered. Their body was to be taken down before nightfall and decently buried. John Calvin says in this passage that it was a way of banishing inhumanity and barbarism from the chosen people. If you show disrespect for deceased bodies, it has a way of engendering barbarism in a population. That's why decent, respectful burial is always called for.

Deuteronomy 21:23 is directly quoted by the apostle Paul in the New Testament in Galatians 3:13, and it's very significant that we should conclude this passage, which is about the sacredness of life and murder, with the grace of God. Man's worst, humanity's worst offense against God is striking out at the image of God by killing others; yet it all winds up with the potential of the grace of God being extended to those who have violated the commandment. And so Apostle Paul in Galatians 3:13 quotes Deuteronomy 21:23 and says *'Cursed is everyone who hangeth on a tree'*.

Paul applies it to the body of our Lord Jesus Christ on the cross of Calvary, which was made from a tree with a beam across it. What he is saying is this: in face of all these awful things, how could atonement ever be possible, so that we are all not literally burned up with the fire of a holy God, and sent down to hell? What hope is there?

There is hope through the tree—through Him who hangs on a tree—through the Lord Jesus Christ, bearing our sins in Himself. Let me read you 1 Peter 2:24: 'Who his own self bare our sins in his own body on the tree, that we, being dead to sins, should live unto righteousness; by whose stripes ye were healed'. It is the perfect fulfillment of the illustration of the principle of substitution, and then striking off the head of the heifer. I want to read you two little passages in closing, from two of my favorite theologians. One is St. Hilary of Poitiers who wrote a book on the Trinity around the year 350:

> The one, only begotten God, ineffably born of God, entered the virgin's womb and grew and took the frame of poor humanity. He who upholds the universe, within whom and through whom are all things, was brought forth by common childbirth. He at whose voice archangels and angels tremble and heaven and earth and all the elements of this world are melted, was heard in childish wailing. He by whom man was made had nothing to gain by becoming man; it was our gain that God was incarnate and dwelt among us, making all flesh His home by taking upon Him the flesh of one. We were raised because He was lowered. Shame to Him was glory to us. He being God made flesh His residence, and we, in return, are lifted anew from the flesh to God.

And a little further in this book he says:

The Son of God is seen as man; but God is present in His human actions. The Son of God is nailed to the cross; but on the cross God conquers human death. Christ the Son of God dies; but all flesh is made alive in Christ. The Son of God is in hell; but man is carried back to heaven.

It's the principle of glorious substitution and covenant, corporate identification.

And then finally from John Calvin in his *Institutes of the Christian Religion*, Book 4:

> This is the wondrous exchange, which out of His measureless benevolence, he has made with us, that becoming Son of man with us, He has made us sons of God with him; that by his descent to earth he has prepared an ascent to heaven for us; that by taking on our mortality, he has conferred his immortality upon us. Accepting our weakness, he has strengthened us by his power that, receiving our poverty unto himself, he has transferred his wealth to us; that taking weight of the iniquity upon himself which oppressed us, he has clothed us with His righteousness.

I say to you, Christian people: go home like the captive bride was taught in Israelite religion, cleaned up and clothed with the garments of the people of God—go home by faith clothed in the righteous garments given to us by faith in the Lord Jesus Christ.

47

The Broadness and Beauty of God's Law

Deuteronomy 22:1–12

This part of Deuteronomy may strike us as strange; how does it all fit together? What binds all these rather strange commandments together is this: God's law is broad and has the benefit of engendering beauty in life and society. 'Thy commandment is exceeding broad' (Psalm 119:96). These first 12 verses are a vivid illustration of the commandment of God being 'exceeding broad', stretching in every kind of direction. Who would have thought of all these things lumped together? Probably because of various cases having arisen within Israel, God has made them into a pattern which somehow reflects His beauty.

Deuteronomy 22:1-12, seems to be a transition between Moses' exposition of the sixth commandment, 'Thou shalt not kill', and the seventh commandment, 'Thou shalt not commit adultery', with some things relating to killing and others related to sexual purity, and a few other matters added in. While difficult to outline, we can say that the exceeding broadness of God's commandment covers six different areas which do not always seem closely related one to another.

In that light, let us look at what God's holy requirements leading to beauty mean in these six areas: first, taking care of your neighbor's livestock, verses 1–4; second, prohibition of cross-dressing between male and female, verse 5; third, respect for nesting birds, verses 6–7; fourth, a parapet or guard rail around the roofs of flat houses, verse 8; fifth, no intermixture of species, verses 9–11; and sixth, decorations of the hems of one's garments, verse 12.

Take Care of Your Neighbor's Livestock (22:1–4)

First, we are told in this 'exceeding broad' commandment that we are to take care of our neighbor's livestock, who have wandered away from the fold. I remember when I was nine or ten years old on the Old Blue plantation up in North Carolina, with my great aunt and uncle, getting a phone call during a big thunderstorm from some of our neighbors, (our cousins), saying that a bunch of our hogs had broken loose; probably the lightning scared them, and 30 or 40 had broke out of the hog pen and got into the woods on our cousins' properties. I remember my great aunt and uncle putting on rain gear and big hats, taking sticks, and—while the storm was still going on—going out to drive the pigs back to our place, lest they got into the field and caused damage.

In another situation about twenty years later, when I was a student at Edinburgh, one of our professors kept bees, and told us that one day he got a phone call from a neighbor, saying that there was a big swarm of bees that had swarmed in the park near his house, which they believed were his swarm, and indeed they were. So the professor went over and recaptured the swarm, and brought them back to the hive.

Both of those situations are illustrations of how God is showing us who God is: that is, you help somebody if their animals have run away. From verse 4, I think you could apply it to modern-day cars or trucks. If on the road your car or truck breaks down, then someone should help you get to a filling station; that would be part of the exceeding broad commandment of God.

My vehicles haven't broken down many times in the last 30 or 40 years, but some have a few times. One time in Mississippi I was taking our son Angus to catch a ride somewhere in an old white truck and it broke down on the highway as we were passing through deep woods. I don't think it was more than two minutes, when somebody pulled over, and said he would take us to Meridian. What few times I have ever broken down, within five minutes, some 'good Samaritan' has always stopped and rendered aid. That's the way it ought to be; living as a godly person, caring for the neighbor's livestock, or the thing that would be the equivalent of a horse today. (I will add here that the states where I have lived have been heavily Christian, which may explain why so many have been willing to help).

But in general today, even in Christian areas, the temptation is not to get involved in somebody else's need—whether lost animal, broken down car or truck. We feel very busy. But God's way for us is to seek to help those in need, even when it is inconvenient. How much happier it makes people's lives! And it is a godly kind of happiness, based on His character!

No Cross-Dressing Between Male and Female (22:5)

The technical word for this is transvestism. Why should clothing be an issue? Let's go back to the basics. From the book of Genesis, and the rest of the Bible, we get the basic distinction between the sexes, male and female, which is a very good gift of God. It is rooted in the formation of Eve from the side of Adam. God saw that it was not good for the male to be alone, and so He gave him this wonderful, appropriate helper, Eve—and indeed, all of her daughters, till the end of time. So the gender differences are divinely ordered. This reality comes from Him. Out of this gender difference comes fruitful marriage, propagation of the human race, and perhaps most important of all, the increase of the Christian church. That's behind the prohibition of a male trying to act like a female, or a female trying to act like a male. So let's keep that in mind, and then we will make some sense out of this.

Now as far as the clothing you put on is concerned, I don't feel it's possible to be overly precise, because styles change in different countries and over the centuries. Some things are acceptable in one culture that are not in another, and some things are acceptable today that would not have been acceptable at Reedy Creek 100 or even fifty years ago. So you have to leave some flexibility in trying to think about this. For instance, in Scotland for a very long time, men have worn kilts. That is perfectly acceptable and manly. Anybody who might laugh at it, would not be laughing at the kilted army, with their swords charging towards the enemy, with bagpipes skirling; you would run in the other direction. So it depends on the culture or the country.

Or for instance, since the 1970s in most Western countries, women have worn dress pants or pantsuits, and that has become acceptable. Although I remember the first time I saw it, when I came back from Edinburgh, was when my mother's sister had on pants. I gave her such a hard time about it that she had to go home and put on a dress. But since then the custom has changed, and there's nothing wrong with it.

What is the basic principle? That's the issue. Cultural matters such as acceptable clothing change and you can't be dogmatic about varying tastes over the generations. Still, I think the principle is modesty and appropriateness to the culture around us in how we dress, how we comport ourselves, and even bodily language.

John Calvin in his *Commentary on Deuteronomy* said it well:

> This decree also commends modesty in general and in it, God anticipates the danger lest women should harden themselves into forgetfulness of modesty, or men should degenerate into effeminacy unworthy of their nature. Garments are not in themselves of so much importance, but as it is disgraceful for men to become effeminate, and also for women to effect manliness in their dress and gestures, propriety and modesty are prescribed not only for decency's sake, but lest one kind of liberty should at length lead to something worse. Decency in fashion of the clothes is an excellent preservative of modesty.

One of the contributions the Christian church can make to the culture around it—where you have the unisex movement, metro-sexuality, and that sort of thing—rather than being critical or saying very much, is to set a wholesome example, by seeking to preserve modesty and appropriateness, not only in what we wear, but in gestures that we make and the way we speak. That helps the church be salt and light and preserve from further corruption a society that is casting off divine restraints, including the basic differences between male and female. In the matter of how we dress as the Lord's people, God is saying, show them a better way. And it will make a difference.

Respect for Nesting Birds (22:6–7)

I am 64, have almost never missed church on a Sunday all those years, but I have never heard anybody preach on nesting birds; well, I'm hearing it today! In Deuteronomy 20, we saw that the fruit trees are to be protected in war time. Here in chapter 22 one is to set free a female bird that is either sitting on eggs, or has actually hatched the young fowls, the biddies.

This text says that if really needed by a hungry person who finds the nest, which has blown onto the ground, that person has the right, if needed, to take the young or the eggs. But they must set free the hen, the mother bird. What can be the reason for this prohibition? It might be that something of the special relationship that God honors between parents and children, something of that is so important, so basic, and so honorable, that it is reflected even in the animal kingdom. Family relationships among humans reflect the Trinity. Now animals are not created in the image of God, and yet maybe the animal rearing of their young in some sense is a dim spark of light from the familial communion of God within the Holy Trinity. Certainly, not killing the mother bird enables the species to continue to reproduce, so that particular species will not be wiped out in any territory. Thus the people of God are to respect, as we would say today, the ecology in their own way: the trees and birds. That is a sign of what God wants us to be like.

A Parapet Around a Flat Roof (22:8)

Even today, in parts of the Middle East, people build houses made of bricks, baked clay, or stone; and in the evenings, sit on the flat roof of the house, getting the evening breezes, eating and drinking with the family or neighbors, particularly in the hot months. So the Lord says, when you have a flat roof, be sure you build a guard rail all the way around it, so nobody will fall off and get hurt. That's a common sense application of the sixth commandment 'Thou shalt not kill'.

Not to kill, implies doing the best you can, even in the construction of your house, or your property around your house, to protect human life—not unlike the signs you see in construction sites, 'This is a hard hat area.' A hard hat area is the same kind of idea: let's do what we can to protect human life.

An illustration of what occurs when you do not take protective measures was recounted to me by the friend of many of us, Jean-Marc Berthoud of Lausanne, Switzerland. He was speaking at a conference, where he and other speakers were seated on a very high stage. They put the chairs for the speakers near the very back of the six foot high stage; but they hadn't put a guard rail or a parapet on the back. His chair fell off the back. It didn't do serious damage, but was not a pleasant experience. He said to me afterwards, that it was an illustration that if they had gone by what Deuteronomy 22 says, he wouldn't have fallen six feet and possibly been badly hurt!

No Mixture of Species (22:9-11)

This prohibition is not easy to interpret. We need to go back to God's original creation in the first two chapters of Genesis, where God made the different species. The word *min* in Hebrew means 'kind' generally a broader term than species, for when Genesis says that God made the different kinds, it is clear that they included variations within the basic kinds, by which you can have a cat or a lion or a tiger coming from the same original kind. Thus, God created the basic kinds with potential variations within them—animals, fowl, fish, and vegetative life. They are to some degree, fixed at the original creation. So this assumes a non-evolutionary view, for God's Word says that He made these different kinds (including many possible species); He made them to reproduce 'after their kind'. They would have reproductive seed, whether they be a fruit tree or an animal, male and female; within them is the male seed and the female egg, so that they reproduce after their kind, but with no possibility of development from one kind to another. Scientific evidence has never indicated such a thing.

Hence, the Genesis teaching on creation, and validity of the reproductive cycle of the different kinds, seems to lie behind what Moses is saying here, as he teaches God's people to do what they can to preserve the purity of the species, and not to mix them up. With my limited biological knowledge, as best I can understand, this does not prohibit genetic research on seeds, within a basic kind, so as to make the plant more disease-resistant or more fruitful. I can't see that that is anyway ruled out by this, because it wouldn't violate the principle. But it does prohibit the horrendous idea of trying to mix the human species with animal species in certain types of fertilization programs. That's absolutely prohibited by this section of the Word of God, and by other sections. That much is clear, even if much else is dark.

In Deuteronomy 22:11, we find another complex matter not easy to discern: the prohibition of mixing together certain types of fabric. When Deuteronomy was written it meant that you wouldn't make a garment of wool and linen worked together in the same fabric. The best I can understand it, this prohibition does not seem in any way to have been taken over into the New Testament economy; there is not the slightest indication anywhere, even in the later strands of the Old Testament and certainly in the New Testament, that in the life of salvation we would need to worry that linen and wool were combined in a particular bolt of cloth.

Tassels on the Hems of One's Garments (22:12)

Why such an odd commandment, that in a long garment you are told to put tassels that would swing back and forth, as the person wearing the garment walked? There is a parallel passage in Numbers 15:37-41, which casts light and makes sense of all this: the wearing of tassels on long garments is a way of reminding the ancient Hebrew people of God that they are different from the pagans; they've got something extra and different, something reflective of another world. Tassels moving around as a person walks are to remind them that they are to keep the law of God. This extra decoration on garments is not in any sense to show off, but to remind you that you are to live in terms of the holiness of God.

Thinking of this, my mind went back to Psalm 90 said to have been written by 'Moses the man of God', who also wrote Deuteronomy. While he never remotely mentions tassels in this psalm, he does speak about reflecting the moral beauty of God in human character. Verse 17 says: 'And let the beauty of the Lord our God be upon us; and establish thou the work of our hands upon us; yea, the work of our hands establish thou it'. The beauty of God is what Moses is praying to be upon His people—moral beauty—and that seems to be the heart of what was being conveyed in another context, in another generation, by the tassels in the garment.

One final reference is found near the end of the Old Testament in Zechariah: 14:20-21. I think the idea of various instruments and the beauty of God were brought together in this, one of the last books of the Old Testament prophets, which speaks prophetically of Christ, including His entrance into Jerusalem on Palm Sunday.

> In that day shall there be upon the bells of the horses, HOLINESS UNTO THE LORD; and the pots in the Lord's house shall be like the bowls before the altar. Yea, every pot in Jerusalem and in Judah shall be holiness unto the Lord of hosts; and all they that sacrifice shall come and take of them, and seethe therein; and in that day there shall be no more the Canaanite in the house of the Lord of hosts.

Holiness to the Lord, on the pots and the pans and the tassels of the horses that have bells!

So what we find in true Judaism and Christianity, in which Judaism is fulfilled, is that God the Holy Spirit (who makes present the beauty of God, and is the very fragrance of the person and loveliness of God), comes down into human flesh and blood—life—and brings the beauty of Christ, as it were, the fragrance of Jesus, into the lives of those who seek to honor God every way they turn. This is prayed for in a hymn:

> Let the beauty of Jesus be seen in me,
> All His wonderful passion and purity.
> Oh, Thou Spirit divine, all my nature refine
> Till the beauty of Jesus be seen in me

One could object that this interpretation is nothing but spiritualizing. But I do not think so, for Deuteronomy 22 makes it very practical what the beauty of Jesus, the moral beauty of God, looks like; you help your neighbor like the good Samaritan; his animals go astray, his car breaks down, and you help him. Something of the moral beauty of God shines every time you do it. Or you are going through the woods and you don't take advantage of the mother bird, you help her get free, or you spare the young ones. That's something of the moral beauty of God shining in a little way in a man or woman who does this. Or you build your house, and if there is an empty well on your property, you fill it up, so that nobody falls in and loses their life. A small action like that shows something of the moral beauty of God, as you keep in mind your property, making arrangements that it would not lead to anyone being hurt, as far as possible. And modesty in dressing is a way to reflect, in a humble and quiet manner, the beauty of the Lord our God upon us.

So I think all of these rather strange ideas to us are brought together in the broadness of God's law: 'Thy commandment is exceeding broad'; and it is part of what is given to put us in a position where the beauty of the Lord our God can be seen even in little things that we do, in the little ways we live; God's beauty can shine and God will accomplish what He wishes out of that.

48

Holiness of God in Engagement and Marriage

Deuteronomy 22:13–29

This rather grim passage is about the holiness of God in engagement and marriage. One of the characteristics of the Bible is that it is very realistic, and takes an honest look at things that happen in human relationships, including the things that are very nasty. It gives a way to deal with the various relationships within fallen human nature, with a view to holiness and, in some cases, to redemption.

We should note here a verse from the prime penitential psalm by David (Psalm 51), composed after he had committed adultery with Bathsheba and then had her husband, Uriah, killed. He went on without repentance for a long time, and finally was confronted by a holy prophet, after which God gave him brokenness of heart and true repentance. One of the things he said in composing this psalm was this: 'Thou requirest truth in the inward parts'.

Holy Scripture says that the eyes of God are always upon us; the eyes of Him with whom we have to do, constantly survey every aspect of our being, mental, physical, and spiritual. God's eyes penetrate the deep places of our life, where God requires truth. God requires integrity in the inmost part. There is nowhere that the integrity of the innermost being any more clearly works itself out than in the male/female relationship.

In this passage, Moses is explaining what the seventh commandment, 'Thou shalt not commit adultery', really means, in a number of the ways involved in the relationship between the man and the woman. Moses' point of view is very realistic; he says several things could happen and wants you to be honest enough to look at it. He gives us six different kinds of cases that show how the holiness of God's pure character is to shine into the male/female relationship, three involving married women, verses 13 to 22; then three involve unmarried girls, verses 23–29.

Purity with Married Women (22:13–19)

Think of the case where a man marries a young woman, and for whatever reason, turns against her. In order to get rid of her, since he hates her and is sorry he married her, he tells a lie and claims that she was not a virgin when they married. Now, if that were true, in Old Testament Israelite law, it would mean that his wife would be subject to the death penalty, and he could get rid of her that way. It was a serious charge if your wife was not a virgin when you married.

Then the girl's parents demand a public trial before the elders of the city. The father of the accused young woman presents evidence of his daughter's chastity—presumably the bed sheet he had saved from the night of the marriage. If the girl is indeed innocent, the elders discipline the man, probably with public whipping, though we are not told; what is listed is that the man is fined 100 shekels of silver, which was a lot of money, double the usual price of a bride, because the law of restitution we looked at earlier teaches that when honor is offended in that way, then the man had to pay double the amount, 100 shekels of silver instead of 50, which would have required several months' hard work. And the man cannot get rid of his wife. Moses allowed divorce in certain cases, but divorce would not ever be allowed in this case; he would have to continue to live with her in marriage and to treat her right.

The second and different case is in verses 20–21. If the girl indeed was guilty of having been impure, she was to be executed in front of her father's house. Why there? It was a way of rebuking the parents for not having restrained their unmarried daughter from immoral practices.

I was once asked advice about a younger minister, whom I very highly regarded and still do. He was a fine man, but his oldest daughter was allowed by her ministerial parents to live in an immoral way: to stay in their house, to abuse alcohol, and run with men. Well, she got herself into trouble, which was a great embarrassment to her family, and to the church of which this man was the pastor. But he wouldn't do anything; he let her keep living at home, and I don't know how long it was, but she got into trouble again. Yet the parents wanted to keep her living in the Presbyterian manse with all the privileges of a daughter, and no discipline, and let her continue drinking heavily and running.

I was asked to give him some advice, which I did. I think I did it kindly, but very firmly and honestly; and he refused to accept the advice I gave him as to what he ought to do. Well, it was terrible for that church, and he had to leave. And then a while later he had to leave his ministry of the PCA; it could have been prevented if he had done what I and some others advised him, and then later he had much grief because of it. I will say no more. So we are talking about something not just in Old Testament Israel, but today.

The third case is adultery of a married woman, and the basis of this is Moses explaining what the seventh commandment, 'Thou shalt not commit adultery', means in this fallen world. Some people would like to live in an ideal world, and their religion only deals with an unreal, ideal world, but that's not the Bible. The Bible deals with the real world which is sometimes nasty. But God helps you deal with that nasty world. So a married woman commits adultery with a man, and they are both to be put to death, as also stated in Deuteronomy 5:18 and Leviticus 20:20.

In our modern culture, that comes across to us as extremely harsh. But I remember hearing many years ago R.J. Rushdoony saying something like this: in modern nations, everybody understands capital punishment for treason against the state; for example, in the 1950s when a man and his wife gave secrets of the atom bombs to the Russians, and were put to death. This biblical scholar said that in the Old Testament, the issue was not treason against the state—no such crime existed—but treason against the family which incurred the death penalty. I will come back to that issue a little later.

Purity with Unmarried
Women (22:23–29)
Moses also deals with how unmarried women are to be treated with purity, as in the case of a

betrothed girl (verses 23–24). Let me say that in Old Testament and, indeed, in New Testament culture, betrothal in Israel was more serious than engagement in our Western countries today. It involved the high moral standards of actual marriage, even before the wedding.

The situation here involves a betrothed girl seduced by some man in a city—the element of being in the city is important because she could get help by screaming out. As she didn't cry out when this man seduced her, the elders of the place where she came from assumed it was a consensual act, and that she went along with it. Old Testament law put that in the same category as adultery. Hence both transgressors, the female and the male, were to be put to death.

In the fifth case, verses 25–27, the girl is taken advantage of by a man in the field of the countryside. There was nobody she could cry out to for help, and the elders assumed she did not consent to it and put it into the category of rape. Thus, the girl was set free and considered totally innocent; only the man was executed. That is why in many Western countries that were at one time Christian, rape was considered to be a capital crime, as well as murder. To say the least, where rape was dealt with in that way, you had far less of it; it made the streets much safer and cut down on raw violence.

A sixth case is brought before us in verses 28 and 29 here (also Exod. 22:16–17). An unmarried girl, who is not betrothed, is taken advantage of by a man. In that case, the man is judged, not the girl. There's a twofold penalty, so you can see how sophisticated biblical law is, and how fair it is in the various circumstances; they did not deal the same punishment out to everybody, but carefully considered the circumstances, like any good court of law would do. The twofold penalty to the man who violated an unbetrothed woman involved paying the bridal price to the girl's father and never being able to divorce her. Moses' law allows divorce in certain circumstances, but that was not available in this case. But, according to Exodus 22:17, the girl's father does not have to accept the marriage, if he deems the man unworthy. In this case, he would have to pay the father, but the father would not have to accept a person who would lower the moral or cultural standing of the family as a whole.

Putting all of this together, while some of you might feel shell shocked to come to church and hear such things, we have to keep in mind that we are dealing with the real world, where everything is not ideal. God's Word gives us the approach in this case. So what happens to all of these laws of these six different cases when you come to the New Testament, when you take us to our Lord Jesus Christ, the New Testament, and the Church? How would we respond to these various cases?

Here's what I would say: the principle of God's holy character requiring sexual purity in male/female relationships is exactly the same; the principle of holiness between men and women is the same in the New Testament. Let's look at that positively, and then negatively, in terms of the principle of God's holiness in physical relationships after Christ has come.

Positively, consider Ephesians 5:21-33—you know it well—speaks of how husbands should love their wives, as Christ loved the church, a sacrificial love, a very high standard indeed! And then it speaks of wives submitting to their husbands as they would to the Lord Himself. Ephesians 5:27 shows that a true Christian marriage—they are all imperfect of course—can be sincere and pretty good; they can be models of the very holiness of God, and the love of God in human life, that others can see as a testimony that God is holy, God is good, and God is love.

A good marriage is a more powerful testimony, day in and day out, than any sermon—and I believe in sermons. Look at this from Romans 13:12–14 in the NIV version, which may be more understandable:

> The night is nearly over; the day is almost here. So let us put aside the deeds of darkness and put on the armor of light. Let us behave decently as in the daytime, not in orgies and drunkenness; not in sexual immorality and debauchery; not in dissension and jealousy. Rather clothe yourselves with the Lord Jesus Christ and do not think about how to gratify the desires of the sinful nature.

That's our privilege, and the Holy Spirit helps us. What a testimony to a lecherous society!

Now let's look negatively at the principle of the Old Testament law taken into the New Testament Church. Consider when very serious sexual sins are committed of an egregious nature. For instance, 1 Corinthians 6:9–11: 'Know ye not that the unrighteous shall not inherit the kingdom of God? Be not deceived: neither fornicators, nor idolaters, nor adulterers, nor effeminate, nor abusers of themselves with mankind, nor thieves, nor covetous, nor drunkards, nor revilers, nor extortioners, shall inherit the kingdom of God'. But then get the next verse: 'And such were some of you'; Paul is talking to real people in the church, saved people on their way to heaven, who had lived in these terrible sexual practices that were condemned in Deuteronomy 22, Romans 13, and 1 Corinthians 6. 'But'—and here's the hope; here's the joy of the gospel—'ye are washed, but ye are sanctified, but ye are justified in the name of the Lord Jesus, and by the Spirit of our God'.

What an open door God has set before us! These people had done all kinds of things, some of them had broken every sexual more that God said not to do. Although they could have died in their sins, God says to the sinner, 'Come in, repent and believe in the Lord Jesus and you will be washed whiter than snow, as though you had never committed a sin in your whole life! You can be cleaned up, because Jesus paid for it, and the Holy Spirit will apply if you will repent and come in through that open door'.

The story in John 8:1–11, is about a woman taken in the very act of adultery. She had committed adultery; they got her, and there was no question about her guilt. And so, Jesus coming near in the providence of God (planned from eternity) showed grace in this woman's life. They asked, 'Rabbi, should we stone this woman, because that is what is taught by Moses?' Jesus says, 'Let him that is without sin among you cast the first stone'. Everyone went away with their heads down, Pharisees, Sadducees, and others, from the oldest to the youngest. Why did the oldest go first? Because they had more sense; the older ones knew how sinful they were; maybe not in that way, but in other ways. Did Jesus approve of adultery? Of course not! But He said to the woman, 'Neither do I condemn thee; go and sin no more'. He sets before this woman an open door of forgiveness and eternal life, and that is what God's church is here to do.

Sexual relationships, dealt with in the Old Testament, are summarized in two passages in the New Testament, showing a new, wonderful, cleansing, pure, true attitude, made available by the Holy Spirit in our lives, after Christ has come in the flesh. First, Colossians 3:1–14 (NIV):

> Since, then, you have been raised with Christ, set your hearts on things above, where Christ is seated at the right hand of God. Set your minds on things above, not on earthly things. For you died, and your life is now hidden with Christ in God. When Christ,

who is your life, appears, then you also will appear with him in glory. Put to death [the Authorized says mortify], therefore, whatever belongs to your earthly nature: sexual immorality, impurity, lust, evil desires and greed, which is idolatry. Because of these, the wrath of God is coming. You used to walk in these ways, in the life you once lived. But now you must rid yourselves of all such things as these: anger, rage, malice, slander, and filthy language from your lips. Do not lie to each other, since you have taken off your old self with its practices and have put on the new self, which is being renewed in knowledge in the image of its Creator. Therefore as God's chosen people, holy and dearly loved, clothe yourselves with compassion, kindness, humility, gentleness, and patience. Bear with each other and forgive whatever grievances you may have against one another. Forgive as the Lord forgave you. And over all these virtues put on love, which binds them all together in perfect unity.

And then, from 1 Thessalonians 4:3-8:

It is God's will that you should be sanctified: that you should avoid sexual immorality; that each of you should learn to control his own body in a way that is holy and honorable, not in passionate lust like the heathen, who do not know God; and that in this matter no one should wrong his brother or take advantage of him. The Lord will punish men for all such sins, as we have already told you and warned you. For God did not call us to be impure, but to live a holy life. Therefore, he who rejects this instruction does not reject man but God, who gives you his Holy Spirit.

What I am preaching would be a counsel of despair, except for these grand texts. God gives you His Holy Spirit! It was the same, wasn't it, in 1 Corinthians 6 where you are washed, sanctified, justified, and it is the Holy Spirit, who makes it real, the personal presence of God in Christ, the third Person of the Trinity. When Jesus is away from us, since His body is up in glory, He sends the One who binds Him and the Father together in love and purity: the Holy Spirit, who comes in to enable us to live the Christ life, including in the area of relationships and sexual purity. There is a power from above that, if we will ask for it; God will send, as the Psalmist says, 'straight from the sanctuary' to enable us to rise above all that the Devil stirs up within you, in the attempt to pull you down. The Holy Spirit is far greater than the devil, for 'greater is He that is in you than he that is in the world' (1 John 4:4). Possessed by that Spirit, ever looking to the Holy Spirit, we say, 'Lord, make it <u>real</u> for me, to walk in the Spirit; it will be God's good pleasure to give good gifts to His children who ask Him.'

49

Holiness in Unexpected Places

Deuteronomy 22:30–23:14

This is a rather unusual passage, to say the least. It is speaking about the holiness of God in unexpected places of life. In the Hebrew text, Deuteronomy 22:30 is actually the first verse of chapter 23, so I am following that division. Moses is expounding here the broader meaning of the seventh commandment, 'Thou shalt not commit adultery'; and he takes it in many rather unexpected directions. But there is a basic context that holds all together—the holiness of God, His purity is to be reflected in our bodies, even in small personal functions. This same holiness is to be reflected in who is allowed to take part in the worship of the congregation of Israel as a constituent member.

In this text we find God's holiness shining in some unexpected, unusual places. At first sight, some of these are issues that seem very strange to us; but it all makes sense, once you remember Psalm 24: 'The earth is the Lord's, and the fullness thereof'. In other words, God wants to shine His beautiful purity through absolutely every aspect of our being, including the body. This unusual text ties together some peculiar things, such as incest, physical mutilation, personal sanitation, and varying degrees of fellowship with pagans.

I want to look at four main areas of life in this fallen world. Throughout the passage, we see that the world is fallen and humanity is impacted by sin. But even though humanity is fallen and corrupted, nonetheless, God's beautiful holiness is able to shine through it, in an uplifting and redemptive way. God's holiness is speaking to us through Moses of how we are to live when things are complex, confused, and impure.

Here are the four things I want us to note: first, prohibition of marrying one's stepmother, 22:30; second, prohibition of physical mutilation, 23:1; third, varying degrees of prohibition of incestuous and pagan groups coming into the holy congregation of Israel, verses 2–8; fourth, personal cleanness in the camp, or in the life of service, verses 9–14. Through them all, God says, 'Let My holiness shine and it will make a difference; and the world will know, so it can be brought from impurity to a higher level of purification, and indeed of beauty.'

God's Holiness Prohibits a Believer from Marrying his Stepmother (22:30)

We see an illustration of this in Genesis 35, where the oldest son of the patriarch Jacob, Reuben, had relations with his father's concubine Bilhah. In Jacob's blessings as he was dying, in Genesis 49, we see that he remembered this offense and Reuben missed out on tremendous blessing, because he had violated this principle. In my lifetime, I've never heard of anybody doing this, but I did have a distant cousin, who shamefully married his adopted daughter after his wife died, much to the distress of the family and the community. Time showed that the blessing of God was definitely not on this forbidden union, and in principle, I would say, that it was the same kind of thing as Deuteronomy 22:30. Not surprisingly, the lives of this couple were ever after marked by much grief.

Human happiness always calls for a basic integrity and purity in personal life, especially in the relationships we choose. It is always best to do things God's way, and thereby to avoid what He says to avoid. I've read various books over the years on happiness: some pretty good and some very superficial, but I don't remember any of them telling people that the most important foundation of true happiness is to honor the holiness of God in your personal life, and in your marital relationships. That's not the only thing that matters, but it is one of the foundational planks to a happy existence in this difficult world.

God's Holiness Prohibits Personal Mutilation (23:1)

Ancient commentators, such as some of the Rabbis, have said that this refers to pagan worship rituals, where in the pagan cult, frenzied people would submit to gender mutilation. Scholarship shows that that did occur many times, and in some parts of the world, I am told it still occurs. I would deem that in the United States of America, and the Western world in general, as far as I can tell, the modern day equivalent would be sex change operations; such a horrendous procedure is clearly forbidden by this verse, not to mention some other places.

On the other hand, to get the balance, it is clear that accidental genital damage, or that which is caused by illness, is not in view here. When it's not someone's fault that they are not able to reproduce, it is not unholy; indeed, God makes a very gracious promise to such people when it is definitely not their fault (e.g., Isaiah 56:3–5).

We know that God always looks on the heart of the individual, whatever the state of their physical body may be; it is the heart, the spirit, what we are on the inside, that really matters to God. If we love God and wish to honor His holy standard, physical problems that we cannot help do not in any way interfere with God's beautiful light shining through us in every way.

God's Holiness Excludes Some Categories of People from Full Fellowship in the Covenant Community (23:2–8)

These are: those of incestuous, i.e., illegitimate incestuous birth, and those of certain incestuous nations. But a more open door is given to two other nations for reasons to be explained, so let's look at this carefully.

First, those of incestuous, illegitimate birth (verse 2). It is important to look at the original Hebrew. The normal Hebrew word for an illegitimate child is not used here. From other places in Holy Scripture, it is clear that people born out of wedlock were definitely accepted into the worshiping people of God, assuming they were believers, and tried to follow the Lord. The Hebrew word here is unusual; it is used in only one other place in the Old Testament, Zechariah 9:6; it seems to mean the product of incestuous relationships, probably connected to ancient cult prostitution. This prohibition was meant to discourage that kind of pagan religious wildness and confusion among the people of God.

Then we are told that there were to be no Moabites or Ammonites to enter the Lord's congregation to the tenth generation—roughly 200 or 250 years of genealogy. There seemed to be two reasons for this exclusion of Moabites and Ammonites: one reason is given in this text; for another reason we have to look in Genesis 19, in the story of Lot and his two daughters.

The first reason, given in verse 4, is that the Moabites and Ammonites absolutely refused to sell water and bread, which the Israelites offered to buy peacefully; they would not help them on their way to the Promised Land. The Moabites hired the prophet Balaam to put a curse on Israel, which God turned into a blessing. In so doing, they opposed the holy purposes of God for His people, and they would have to bear the consequences of that. The second reason for excluding ten generations from Moab and Ammon was that they were the products of incest between Lot and his two daughters, recounted in Genesis 19. From one daughter came the Moabites; from the other daughter came the Ammonites.

Yet this general rule that the holy people of God were not to welcome incestuous persons or their offspring into their fellowship as worshipers, does not seem to have excluded the possibility of many gracious exceptions. For instance, one of the most morally beautiful women in all of the Old Testament is surely Ruth. She was a Moabitess; she was welcomed into Israel as the wife of one of their leading men, Boaz. In the first generation—not the tenth—a Moabitess was welcomed in and became a part of Israel; indeed, in the providence of God, she became the great grandmother of the greatest king Israel ever had. She was the grandmother of Jesse and the great grandmother of David (some generations are missing so that she is a more remote ancestress than that). By becoming the great ... grandmother of David, she was the direct ancestress of the Messiah of Israel, the Savior of the world, the Lord Jesus Christ.

Ruth the Moabitess is listed in the genealogies in the New Testament. So, evidently this general rule against fellowship with incestuous peoples still did not close the door to individual conversions, if their heart was turning toward the Lord. Also Isaiah 56 talks about the stranger—probably the forgiven stranger; if they keep the Sabbath, if they want to follow the Lord, they are welcome. Indeed, if the heart of an individual Moabite or Ammonite person was like that of Ruth (Ruth 2:12), then absolutely every door was open for him or her. This is what the fine man Boaz said to the noble young woman, who loved her mother-in-law and came out of Moab to Bethlehem: 'The Lord recompense thy work and a full reward be given thee of the Lord God of Israel under whose wings thou art come to trust'.

Then in verse 7 we are told of another exclusion that is not nearly so strict as the Ammonites and Moabites: the Edomites and the Egyptians could enter the holy congregation after only three generations—about 70 or 75 years. Why the difference?

There seem to be two reasons: first, the Edomites, and then the Egyptians were not of incestuous background. Also the Edomites, through Esau their father, were close kin to the Israelites. In addition, we are told that for many years before the Egyptians finally enslaved the Hebrews, they had been pretty good to the children of Israel, in giving them a protected place to live. In light of that, God says, remember that for the most part you were in a good place, in the land of Goshen, part of Egypt, and so He opened the door to them after three generations.

Yet even here, if you look in other places in Scripture, individual exceptions of grace were certainly made, even in the first generation, for

Edomites and particularly for Egyptians. We read in Exodus that when the children of Israel came out, many Egyptians had been spiritually awakened, and accompanied them through the Red Sea and into the wilderness; they are spoken of as 'a mixed multitude'—a mixture of Israel and Egyptian—and they were in some sense believers, so they were allowed to come, even in their first generation. These exceptions show us that even in the strict rules of the Old Testament, such as in Deuteronomy 23, individual repentance and faith always opens doors to God and to His people's fellowship that would otherwise be closed. How much more is that true in the New Testament economy, after Christ has come, and the church goes out to all people! We read in Matthew 28, the great commission to carry the gospel into all nations, all tribes, all groups, whether they are incestuous or not; everybody is now, regardless of background, cordially invited to come to Christ.

How could you have that much change between the strictness of the Old Testament, where you can not have incestuous pagans as part of the community of faith, and the New Testament, where everybody, in principle, can come?

In Old Testament times, there were various ways to get sin covered; one of them was the ritual of the scapegoat. The High Priest of Israel would lay his hands on the head of a scapegoat they had tied up, and would confess the sins of Israel over him. Then the scapegoat was untied and was allowed to flee out into the wilderness. Sin causes death, puts you in hell, makes you become God-forsaken, if persisted in. This ritual is a picture of the principle of substitution: the scapegoat runs off into a God-forsaken place as our substitute. He becomes God-forsaken in the dark, terrible wilderness, in order that the repentant people of God may come back into the holy, loving presence of the Lord. The scapegoat makes the difference, and opens the door to everybody.

The scapegoat, of course, is a picture of the Lord Jesus Christ. In His suffering on Calvary for all our sins, for the sins of the world, He cries out at the height of His suffering: 'My God, My God, why hast Thou forsaken Me?'(Ps. 22:1). In that mysterious suffering—we don't know how it happened—the sins of all who would ever believe are transferred to the head of the sacrificial Lamb of Calvary, the scapegoat of the world. He takes their God-forsakenness—that of the Ammonites, the Moabites, the Egyptians, the Americans, the Africans and the Chinese: He takes their God-forsakenness on Himself and bears it away into outer darkness. That marvelous transaction opens the way for anybody who calls on His name, and believes, to be brought into the tenderest love of our holy God. That's the difference!

I want to read you two New Testament passages about this. Ephesians 2:12–16, speaking of us pagan Gentiles:

> That at that time ye were without Christ, being aliens from the commonwealth of Israel, and strangers from the covenants of promise, having no hope, and without God in the world. But now in Christ Jesus, ye who sometimes were far off are made nigh by the blood of Christ. For He is our peace, who hath made both one, [true Israel and pagan Gentile who now believe] and hath broken down the middle wall of partition between us; having abolished in His flesh the enmity, even the law of commandments contained in ordinances [Like Deuteronomy 23—He takes care of it!]; for to make in Himself of twain one new man, so making peace; and that He might reconcile both unto God in one body by the cross, having slain the enmity thereby.

And 1 Peter 3:18: 'For Christ also hath once suffered for sins, the just for the unjust, that He might bring us to God, being put to death in the flesh, but quickened by the Spirit'. So here's the glory of the gospel—it's really true—it's why we have missions; it's why we preach every Sunday; no matter what your physical, spiritual, mental, or cultural background, no matter how polluted, how sinful, how rotten, how shameful, if you will look to the Lamb of Calvary, to God's final scapegoat, the door to glorious purification and immediate access to the heart of God will swing wide open for you, and for anybody else who sincerely that wants it. One hymn says:

> Near, so very near to God,
> more near I cannot be;
> for in the Person of His Son,
> I am as near as He.

Another hymn sings:

> There is a place of quiet rest,
> near to the heart of God.

That place was purchased at the expense of Christ who takes our God-forsakenness, and gives us His nearness to the Father.

Therefore, this means that we sinners, through this glorious gospel, can live the rest of our lives in immediate nearness to the heart of the holy God. Our life can be the outflow of God's life. That's what it is to live; nothing compares to that! You really don't have to worry about anything else, if you have that. That's all that is truly worth having—nothing like it!

Personal Physical Purity in the Camp (23:9–14)

The picture here is of maintaining purity, as one joins other believers in seeking to win the battles of the Lord for truth. It may be in a literal army camp or a navy ship or a missionary outreach, or teaching as a Christian in a school or in a church, or soul-winning or trying to raise children right: we can live this way, whatever our call to defeat Satan, so as to liberate people for the truth. I remember a hymn we used to sing when I was a child: 'Give of your best to the Master.' There is a line in it: 'Join in the battle for truth'. I said to God as a child that I would like to be in that army to do battle for truth.

Let me deal with two matters brought up in this text. I want to deal with them in propriety and respect, but also in such a way that it will make the point clear, with things we don't normally speak about, but God talks about it, so it's clear that we have to deal with it if we are going to be His servants.

Now God's holiness calls us to deal, in a respectful way, with two issues that are mentioned here by God: one is nocturnal emissions and the other is personal sanitary functions that are necessary for us to keep living. Now neither one of these things, the nocturnal emission, or the personal sanitary function; neither one is in any way sinful or a reflection on the integrity of the person. But there is a proper way to deal with these things that are part of our bodily existence. In the first case, those affected are to wash off, and then it's fine. And then in the second case, one is to go about these necessary physical functions in privacy and decency outside the camp, and thereby to maintain personal hygiene and public sanitation. Someone might say this is odd; well, I reckon so. But it's probably the case that the general good health, hygiene and sanitation of modern nations, is rooted in the Old Testament, in biblical laws such as these.

Let me conclude with a question of what you might be feeling, because I felt it, as I was trying to prepare all of this. Here's the question: isn't all of this very strange and, to say the least, unexpected in the context of true spirituality and godly holiness? Isn't it odd that this kind of thing is here? Well, I think we have to submit ourselves to this point, that the Bible gives us a different way to look at life from what you get on the streets. The Bible calls us to adjust our thinking. In fact, personal sanitation really is not strange or separate from spiritual holiness, if we have a biblical viewpoint. What the Bible, Old Testament and New Testament, shows us is this: God's holiness and His call to live our earthly lives in closest fellowship with Him, includes both mind and physical bodies.

Some Christians talk only about the mind. That's the starting place and hence, very important, but the physical body is also involved. You hear less about that, but Jesus, God's Son in the flesh, died to save our souls and our bodies. His bodily resurrection shows that His holy purity is meant to permeate our entire physical being, as well as our spiritual being.

Let's go back to the New Testament briefly, and see how this works. 'For Christ also hath once suffered for sins, the just for the unjust, that he might bring us to God, being put to death in the flesh but quickened in the Spirit' (1 Peter 3:18). That is, He died for us, took our God-forsakenness and gives us His nearness to the Father. Look how that is to work out in the verses following. In 1 Peter 4:1–3, we see that Jesus brought you near to God, so that this is what it means for your body, as well as for your mind:

> Forasmuch then as Christ hath suffered for us in the flesh, arm yourselves likewise with the same mind [the mind of Christ]; for he that hath suffered in the flesh hath ceased from sins; that he no longer should live the rest of his time in the flesh to the lusts of men, but to the will of God. [It's a miracle; it's an available miracle through Christ]. For the time past of our life may suffice us to have wrought the will of the Gentiles, when we walked in lasciviousness, lusts, excess of wine, revellings, banquetings, and abominable idolatries.

That used to be your story, but it's not anymore! To show you this is an issue that is not dealt with enough from the pulpit, an organization called 'Harvest', ministers to people with homosexual, lesbian, and other kinds of problems, and they do a wonderful job. Their latest journal states: 'The Barna Research Group has determined that there is virtually no statistical difference between the sexual behaviors of Christians and non-Christians; in fact, they have determined that among born-again Christians, 28% believe that looking at pornography is morally acceptable, and that 20% believe that homosexual behavior is morally acceptable. Among born-again young adults, i.e., 23–41 years old, 18% have had sex outside of marriage and 36% have viewed pornography in the last thirty days.' Then it raises the question: how many church leaders address these issues compassionately from the pulpit?

How we handle very personal physical functions is a way of demonstrating God's holiness in three areas: first, remembering God's purity which we do by showing respect for ourselves, in terms of proper privacy and clean lives. It is wonderful to have respect for yourselves; there is a certain dignity that God wants you to have because you are His, and it entails privacy and cleanliness.

Secondly, we are to remember the holiness and purity of God by showing respect for others—usually known as modesty. And third, we show respect for God, thereby remembering His purity, because we were created in His image originally. The image was twisted by sin, but we are being restored to that beautiful image, through the work of regeneration and sanctification in union with Christ.

Let me conclude this way: we are all human and not one of us, I would think, could justly say, 'I am a totally righteous person, and I point the finger at you, because you have sinned.' The answer to that is 'all have sinned and come short of the glory of God' (Rom. 3:23) and 'there is none righteous, no not one' (Rom. 3:10), as well as the words of Isaiah 53:6: 'all we like sheep have gone astray'.

Well, what then? What if we have violated some of these precious principles of purity in body, mind, and in personal relationships; what if we have done some of these things in the past, and even maybe the recent past? The gospel says that we do not have to be controlled by the failures of the past, even the very recent past. The devil says you won't ever get out of it; you can't change; you're too bad; your flesh is too strong; the Spirit's too weak; you're not to get anywhere, just carry on and stay down.

But no! God's Word says otherwise! The Creator of heavens and earth, the One who has all power, the One who lives and functions in holiness and in grace, says, 'You do not have to have your future controlled by your past. It can be different when I put forth my power in your life; but you've got to ask me! And I'll do it.'

I conclude with a thought taken from Psalm 130:3-4, on which the great Puritan theologian, John Owen, did one of his most beautiful writings. He discusses the issue that is in the heart of all honest people: 'If thou, Lord, shouldst mark iniquities, O Lord, who shall stand? But there is forgiveness with Thee, that Thou mayest be feared'.

John Owen says that you can translate from Hebrew 'that Thou mayest be feared', as that 'Thou mayest be worshiped'; that is to say, you can directly experience true fear of God, as involving you in direct worship and love of God, because of His forgiveness, no matter how you would be condemned for what you've done in the past. You can come to God, and find cleansing and hope and supernatural assurance that it will be different. And thus you can live a godly life; your future can be controlled, not by the confusion of a corrupt world and the down-pull of the flesh, but by the presence of God in Christ, made immediately present in the Holy Spirit. God make it to be so for all of us.

50

God Turns Curses into Blessings

Deuteronomy 23:3–6

Proverbs 29:27 gives us an amazing insight into the psychology of the fallen human person, who does not love God. The first part of the verse is something we may find hard to understand at first glance: 'An unjust man is an abomination to the just'. Now we can easily understand the opposite of it: somebody who is sold out to do wickedness will naturally be resented by honorable people. That's no surprise. But the second part of the verse is the surprise psychologically, though it shouldn't be. Here it is: 'He that is upright in the way is abomination to the wicked'.

When we see someone who is living a criminal life and full of viciousness, hatred, and dishonesty, we find naturally them to be an abomination. But what may be odd to us is the opposite: the worldly spirit finds a man or woman, in whom the light of God to some measure is shining, to be a personal abomination. In other words, a godly life is offensive to a world that is going in the other direction. Paul says in 2 Corinthians 2:15–16: 'We are a savor of life unto life to those who are being saved … we are a savor of death unto death', a veritable stench, to those that are lost. And in 2 Timothy 3:12 he says: 'Yes, all those who live godly in Christ Jesus shall suffer persecution'. Keep that in mind, and it will help you understand the strange psychology of fallen humanity.

Another thing to keep in mind is the command in Philippians 4:4: 'Rejoice always in the Lord; and again, I say, rejoice'. Well, how are we going to keep these two things together? On the one hand, the Bible forewarns us that all those who live godly in Christ Jesus shall suffer persecution; and a sincere, Christ-like testimony will be very, very offensive to some people around you, and you have to expect it. So how, as you contemplate another week, are you able always to rejoice? Here is how: no matter what amount of external persecution or resentment a Christian testimony may raise in the culture where we live, then is the time to bring to mind the principle of Deuteronomy 23:5, 'But the Lord thy God turned the curse into a blessing unto thee'. Remembering that the gates of joy every morning, every evening, are open, when you get up in the morning and when you go to bed at night; 'Nevertheless, the Lord thy God turns the curse into a blessing unto thee'; and suddenly, you find yourself right at these wonderful open gates of joy, with a fragrance of heaven wafting out from them.

Let us note three points from this short text: first, curses are sure to come to the Christian (verse 4); second, our God turns curses into blessings for His people (the first part of verse 5); third, why God is in the business of transmuting curses into blessings (the last part of verse 5).

Curses Are Sure to Come to the Believer (23:4)

We should never be surprised if some would place curses upon us, when we think of the blessed Lord Jesus Christ, who was full of holiness and love in the flesh; He was absolutely nothing but kindness, goodness, and truth in human nature. And how the light of God was concentrated in all of His being, so that the beauty of what makes heaven, heaven—the shining light of the throne—was down in the flesh and blood responses of the Lord Jesus Christ, and everywhere He went the light of heaven was going!

But then what did they do to Him? 'These things I command you that you love one another; if the world hate you, you know that it hated Me before it hated you' (John 15:17-18). Jesus goes on to say that the servant is never above His Master. If the blessed, holy, true, loving Son of God in the flesh was hated by a fallen world, motivated by Satan, how in the world do we think that we can be universally popular, when the likeness of Jesus is becoming manifest in us? So the Lord says in the next few verses: 'If ye were of the world, the world would love his own' (John 15:19-21).

That's the problem! You're an alien; you make them uncomfortable, without even recognizing it.

> Remember the word that I said unto you, the servant is not greater than his lord. If they have persecuted Me, they will also persecute you; if they have kept My saying, they will also keep yours, but all these things will they do unto you for My name's sake (John 15:20-21).

Whatever trials you may be going through, however painful, you can handle them, if you remember that it is all for His name's sake; it is for Jesus' sake.

A minister who is preaching the truth is at times hated by some in the congregation for preaching Jesus. But a minister who is called of God is able to bear up under it and do well, because he remembers: it's for Him; it's for Jesus; Jesus is worth it, and some of the very ones who hate the preacher of uncomfortable truth, I am happy to say, will get gloriously converted. So, if Jesus was cursed, and you know He was, then the Bible says—remembering Deuteronomy 23 and 1 John—we must expect at least a little bit of the same type of treatment, from time to time. Indeed, if you are never criticized, then what are you preaching?

I personally know a fine minister elsewhere in the Carolina, who was literally kicked out of his church by a congregation controlled by modernists, who told him: we hate your preaching of Jesus! He went on to another congregation, one who loved Jesus, and it rejoiced in his preaching.

Have you ever noticed in your own life that there are times when you get a new resolve in which you feel that the Lord is moving to make heavenly changes in your own life? So you seek a new consecration and you make a new surrender to the Lord. The Rev. William Still of Aberdeen used to speak of 'the sweetness of a new surrender'. Well, when you make it, very often about the same time, there will suddenly come an unexplained attack of the devil, perhaps by someone you would have thought better of. Out they come! Perhaps some odd thing happens that is unpleasant or hurtful. And it's at the very time that you know the Lord has led you to a deeper commitment to His Son.

One of the authors of the Westminster Confession of Faith explains it as well as it could be explained: the saintly Scottish minister and professor, Samuel Rutherford, who spent some time in jail and under house arrest, and used his jail time to write some wonderful spiritual letters. In one of them, he said: 'He that stands closest to his captain is the surest target for the archers.' Doesn't that make sense?

Yet, if we keep in mind Deuteronomy 23:5, howbeit our God turned the curse into a blessing, we will happily take our stand with this glorious Captain and fear not the future, because we remember the larger purposes of God. The theme of the message at present that you and I as Christians will constantly be calling to mind is this: the larger purposes of God. That thought will keep you from being pulled down into a dark hole just by thinking of something bad that happened. Well, all right, it was bad; but you won't go down in a sink hole, when you remember the larger purposes of God.

GOD TURNS CURSES INTO BLESSINGS FOR HIS PEOPLE (23:5A)

In the Middle Ages there was a very popular myth about the philosopher's stone; everything it touched turned into gold. As far as we know, such a stone has never existed. But there is something far better than that! We serve a God who is able to take everything that is meant as evil against us, every curse allowed to come our way, and transmute it into something better than gold, something that will endure the fires at the end of time, something that will build us up in Christ-likeness and reach out in holy influence to others and make positive changes in the very ones that may be against us. It is this: our God turns curses into blessings, because He's a most gracious God and is well able to do it.

The background here is Deuteronomy 23, where it talks about Balaam, who was a prophet of Mesopotamia. Although we lack details, this indicates that there were people outside Israel who knew God to some degree, and had spiritual power. Hence, the king of Moab, Balak, was very uneasy at seeing the Israelites out of slavery in Egypt, on their way to take possession of Canaan. They would be a rival people, and naturally, he wanted them to fail, so he hired the most powerful spiritual man in that part of the world in his day, Balaam, and said, 'I'll pay you, and pay you richly, if you will come and put a curse on these Israelites.'

Balaam replied: 'I can't do it'; but the king promised him more money and sent more distinguished people from his court, so that finally Balaam reluctantly agreed to go, and do something he sensed was not right. And God finally allowed it, after giving him certain warnings. While Balaam was on the way, he noticed that his donkey was acting strangely, and quit moving, after which the exasperated prophet started beating and cursing the donkey. Suddenly his donkey is allowed to speak: 'Why are you beating me?' In shock, Balaam looked and saw a holy angel with a drawn sword, who said, 'I would have killed you, if it hadn't been for your donkey.'

Not surprisingly, Balaam said something like: 'Lord, I'm sorry that I was doing this prophecy for money; I'll go back home.' But the Lord said 'No, you go ahead'. What God doesn't tell him is what we soon find out: God's going to tell him to take the curses and turn them into blessings.

So he goes, and joins the pagan king on a hill; the sight must have been very impressive. We don't know how many children of Israel there were—probably over a million—in their camps, and in the middle of that camp, was the holy Tabernacle, presumably shining with the light of

God. Balaam must have been deeply shaken by perceiving that God was among them.

Twice in Numbers 23 and once in Numbers 24, Balaam attempts to put a curse on Israel. In 23:7 the king of Moab told Balaam to curse this great people who so frightened him (Num. 23:7). But when Balaam saw the mighty camp with the light of God in it, the Holy Spirit took charge of his eyesight, his mind, his affections, and his tongue:

> How shall I curse whom God hath not cursed? Or how shall I defy whom the Lord hath not defied? … Who could count the dust of Jacob and number the fourth part of Israel? Let me die the death of the righteous and let my last end be like his (Num. 23:8).

Balaam is saying something like, 'Oh, it is so wonderful; the blessing of God is so much upon them; I wish I could be with them when they die, so that I also could die that way, because I know I would be saved and go to a better place!' The king is absolutely furious: 'I hired you to curse them and you have put a blessing upon them!' Balaam said, 'Didn't I tell you that I could not go beyond what God says?'

The other times he attempts to lay a curse on them, God takes over, and it becomes a tremendous blessing. We see some of the results of the blessing announced by Balaam in the Scriptures as we read on through Deuteronomy, and the rest of the books of Moses. The blessings of Balaam turned into flesh and blood action, and really worked! Maybe Israel got special blessings from Balaam that would never have come to them if he hadn't tried to curse them! Think about that!

This same principle is seen in the experience of Joseph. In Genesis 50, his frightened brothers who had sold him into slavery, said to him, after their father Jacob had died: 'We hope you will be kindly to us.' Godly Joseph gladly replied: 'Of course I will, don't you worry': 'You meant this for evil but God meant it for good to save much people alive as it is this day'. And so this curse, this hatred of his brothers that led Joseph being sold into slavery, was the prelude to tremendous blessing, which later involved the salvation of the entire nation of Israel. God freed him, saved the nation, and preserved the seed of whom Messiah would be born, who is our Lord and Savior. Even we Christians have a part in the blessing of Joseph; God turned this curse of jealousy and hatred into a blessing to Israel, and then to the world, including us!

Think of how this principle works in the undeserved sufferings of Jesus. He suffered more than any other man. It is proper to apply (as does Handel in his *Messiah*) Lamentations 1:12 to Jesus: 'Is it nothing to you all ye that pass by? Behold and see if there be any sorrow like unto my sorrow, which is done unto me, wherewith the Lord hath afflicted me in the day of his fierce anger.'

God worked through the greatest crime that ever occurred in human or cosmic history, when sinful men, motivated by Satan, sought to kill God Himself, God in the flesh; in fact they did kill Him, according to His human nature. Of course, God cannot die, but He willingly submits to the worst that they can do in the human nature that is personally united to the Deity, when He submits to the worst thing ever done: the slaying of the innocent, holy, righteous Son of God in the flesh.

Out of the greatest curse the devil could ever bring about, came the greatest blessing God Almighty could give us: the forgiveness of all who will ever believe; the ransoming of the church, every tribe, nation, tongue, every island of the sea, every continent—millions upon untold millions, through all the ages. The salvation of all the elect come directly through that curse laid on

Him on the tree—as it says in Deuteronomy and in Galatians—where He became a curse for us.

The very universe itself will be renewed, restored, purged, beautified, sanctified, glorified and, as part of that, our bodies will be raised out of the graves just like His. The world's greatest blessing came out of the world's worst most horrendous curse. That is the case with our Savior. If God could take the worst curse that ever occurred—what they did to His well-loved Son, which was in His eternal plan, as we see in Revelation 13:8—and turn it into absolutely boundless blessing, then He is always taking lesser curses that come against the followers of Jesus Christ, and bringing good out of them.

Sometimes a disappointment in a romance feels like a curse, but later you will know a divine blessing was in it. Maybe you didn't get a job for which you applied; it felt like a curse, but later you may know that a divine blessing was in it. Or somebody you counted on, whom you thought was a friend, suddenly—almost irrationally—turns against you, and no longer has any use for you; it feels like a curse. Yet, tremendous blessing is down the road, if we can keep in mind Deuteronomy 23:5: 'Howbeit our God turned the curse into a blessing'. And in Psalm 121: 'He that keepeth Israel shall neither slumber nor sleep'. When some curse comes toward you, it is not that you were out of the eye of God. He doesn't slumber; He doesn't sleep; He doesn't forget you; He's as busy as He was when Jesus was crucified and then resurrected and enthroned in glory, when through the merits of His Son every curse was transmuted into great blessing. Only now, He is transmuting every hurt and pain and curse that comes to His people, into some kind of larger blessing! That is why in Romans chapter 12, we are commanded not to repay evil for evil, but to return good for evil; not to take personal vengeance, because God says 'Vengeance is mine saith the Lord; I will repay'.

It is wonderful to be a Christian, and to be, as it were, freed of responsibility of hating people, of being embittered against them, of thinking of how to get them back, as soon as you have an opportunity. Instead, we rest in the knowledge that God is going to do it, and He'll do it just right! I can't afford to take vengeance, because I would do it in the flesh, and I won't get it right. So I can leave it to a loving God, who slumbers not nor sleeps, and always keeps Israel. Therefore, you turn these things over to the Lord, and sometimes the world is amazed that you don't hate anybody; that you can be kind to those who have notably disappointed you, because God is always in the business of transmuting curses into blessings, and in those blessings, good things happen beyond you. Some people will get a certain sense of this, by which some fragrance of this quiet kindness becomes fruit to eat. They will be changed in a way they would not have, if God had not entrusted you with the stewardship of undergoing that difficulty.

As a Christian people, if we keep in the front of our minds the invisible hand of God always at work in our lives to transmute curses into blessings, we will be camping at the gates of joy, the gates of Him who turns curses into blessings; and we will be truly a happy people, saying and meaning, 'We know that all things work together for good to them that love God, to them that are the called according to His purpose' (Rom. 8:28).

Why God Is Always Transmuting the Devil's Curses into Blessings for His People (23:5b)

Deuteronomy 23:5 tells us plainly, 'because the Lord thy God loved thee'. How can I have the faith to believe that the invisible hand, which I cannot see, is being used by God to turn a curse into a blessing? This is the time when we have to walk by faith, not by sight. But how, when He is letting these terrible things happen to us? You may be tempted to say 'Why me?' Just remember that God is transmuting every difficulty, or curse, against you, into a blessing, because God loves you. That's the final word: 'God is love', according to 1 John 4:8, and then in John 3:16–17:

For God so loved the world that He gave His only-begotten Son that whosoever believeth in Him should not perish but have everlasting life.

And then in 17,

For God sent not His Son into the world to condemn the world, but that the world through Him might be saved.

Think of the plan of salvation. God in heaven moved, heaven and earth to get you saved. Look at what it took, what it cost Him! God is moving all things to get us to our heavenly home at the end. Look at what that takes on His part and that of the holy angels! God did not stop moving heaven and earth in your interest in the first century A.D., or in the hour of your conversion. He is doing it all the time; He will continue to do it until the last moment. 'He that spared not His own Son but delivered Him up for us all, how shall He not with Him freely give us all things?' (Rom. 8:32).

Notice the future tense of the verb, '*shall* freely give'. Yes, God so loved the world that He sent His Son—in the first century A.D.—and it was wonderful for all ages! It is the basis of my salvation, that God raised Him from the dead. But God *will* freely give us all things, because of this same Son, and His same love. God loves me and could not quit loving me and you, His people. He did it when Jesus went through oceans of grief to get you saved, and has guaranteed to get you home. Surely you don't think He's going to give up on you now! He will freely give you absolutely everything you need for life and godliness, so that His holiness can shine through you, and you can know His joy, by which you can avoid being a vengeful person, and be a solid, loving, fruitful person.

Some of us need different things, depending on family background, on education, on the pressures we are under. God will give it all. So we remember His beneficent hand—invisible to us, nearly all the time. But by faith remember that His hand is transmuting every curse into a blessing; thereby, you are camped at the gates of joy.

Isn't it a good time to confess to God our lack of faith in seeing His beneficent hand over our lives? Isn't it a good time, after confessing, to seek the grace and anointing of the Holy Spirit that we may give God constant thanks for what He's doing: 'In everything give thanks, for this is the will of God for you in Christ Jesus' (1 Thess. 5:18). May it be so.

51

INSTEAD OF STEALING, GIVE

Deuteronomy 23:15–25

In this section of Deuteronomy 23, we move from the seventh commandment, 'Thou shalt not commit adultery', to the eighth commandment, 'Thou shalt not steal'. The Holy Spirit, through Moses, describes how we treat the possessions of other people, as well as our own possessions, so that we do not steal, but instead are generous.

It is wonderful how this section in the Old Testament, and then a passage or two in the New Testament, do this, saying, avoid certain sins (most of the Ten Commandments are negative). But then God is not through; He adds something positive, as here in Deuteronomy, and much later in Paul's Epistle to the Ephesians.

That full godliness in Old and New Testaments not only says 'do not steal', but goes on to tell us to give something! When a person lives like that, you are seeing the beauty of the character of the Lord expressed in human life. Such a life can have much influence, and should always accompany preaching. That probably has far more influence, really and truly, than preaching.

Some commentators have said that such verses as Deuteronomy 23:15–25 are just a rag bag, filled with different kinds of laws—nobody knows where they came from—and are thrown together without any theme. In actual fact, it makes wonderful sense: the many different kinds of laws make wonderful sense when you see that all of Deuteronomy is based upon the exposition of the Ten Commandments, as we have often noted.

But in this section, we are in the eighth commandment, and it goes on many more verses. So when you ask, why would you have something like a vow, and then move on to deal with eating somebody's grapes, and after that are told not to bring dirty money to God's house; what is the possible connection?

Here's the connection; in this physical world, a world of relationships influenced in some ways by the devil, God wants us to live a life of beauty and integrity, particularly as regards God's property and the property of other people, and never to take from another person, but instead to help them. That is one of strongest ways of expressing what true godliness is all about.

We see here five different regulations that seem in odd juxtaposition, but it all makes sense, when you remember that 'the earth is the Lord's and the fullness thereof, the world and they that dwell therein' (Psalm 24). This means that every way we turn, in a sense, is meant to become holy ground. Therefore, God says: you do things that are spiritual, that are physical, that are financial, that are agricultural, and so forth; I want you to show in all of these ways who I am, thereby, fulfilling, negatively and positively, the eighth commandment.

Five areas of integrity are called for as God's people deal with the possessions of others. First, verses 15–16 protect a runaway slave; second, verses 17–18 instruct us not to bring dirty money to the Lord's house as a way of paying a vow; third, verses 19–20 give rules concerning interest or usury for believers; fourth, verses 21–23 instruct us to pay what we vow and to be careful what we vow; and fifth, verses 24–25 deal with free grapes and free grain. All are held together within the theme 'Thou shalt not steal', and being a generous person with whatever you've got.

Protect a Runaway Slave (23:15–16)

In ancient Middle Eastern law codes, such as the Code of Hammurabi, we are told that if a runaway slave comes to your place, you must return him to the man from whom he escaped; not to do that would be considered man-stealing. That was the general rule in the ancient Middle East. But God says something entirely different: if a slave runs away (perhaps due to abuse) and shows up at your door, you have a decision either to return him to his owner, or to let him go free and help him get established.

God says, 'I want you to be merciful to them, and let them go free; freedom, liberty is of me.' So, while it's true that the Old Testament law code, and the New Testament one, do temporarily tolerate a certain kind of slavery, (because that was the way it was then), the basis is there for overturning slavery, and finally, gloriously, getting rid of it. The commandment in this passage is one of the ways that would help get rid of slavery.

We haven't had slavery in our country since 1865 (except perhaps sexual slavery), but it still exists in some other countries. Yet the principle always pertains—even where we no longer have the wretched system of slavery—people are more important than money.

No unclean money is to be brought into the Lord's house (23:17–18)

Here we see a second rule connected to 'Thou shalt not steal': no unclean money, no dirty money is to be brought to the Lord's house in order to pay a vow. One of the reasons God ordered the Israelites to wipe the Canaanites out totally, was because they held the particularly immoral and degenerate form of religion, known as fertility cult (see 1 Kings 22 and Hosea 4).

Ancient art has been found in caves and in other places depicting this kind of activity, e.g., Pompeii. The fertility cult involved temples with male and female cult prostitutes, and people would misbehave with either or both, and then pay the temple priests money for the privilege. The money supported the degenerate temple. There is plenty of archeological evidence for it.

Not surprisingly, when a holy God looked down on that kind of lewd activity in the name of religion, He commanded Joshua to clean them out. God had given them many opportunities to change and repent for a long time, and He waited 'until the iniquity of the Amorites was full' before saying, 'Wipe them out!' because they used religion as a form to cover up the most lurid, degenerate kind of physical lust.

We still see that sort of immoral activity near the end of the Old Testament, involving God's own people:

> ... and all the graven images thereof shall be beaten to pieces, and all the hires thereof should be

burned with the fire, and all the idols thereof will I lay desolate; for she gathered it of the hire of an harlot, and they shall return to the hire of an harlot. (Micah 1:7)

God goes on to say how thoroughly He must devastate the culture that uses religion to cover up and to give an excuse for personal, massive immorality. If the kind of worship people are engaging in goes against the holiness of God, it is an abomination to the Lord; it must be broken down and the people that engage in it will be broken down and separated from a holy God, unless they sincerely repent.

I remember a number of years ago at RTS Charlotte, a student who had been converted in his early twenties and then went to university in North Carolina, where he took a religion class, had an assignment to go to some kind of 'off-the-wall' religion to see how they worshiped. This young man, a good fellow, made contact with somebody who was into Satanism or the Wicca cult. Without wishing to give a description of what he saw, it was every bit as vicious, lewd, and awful as what is described here in Deuteronomy.

Not many of us are tempted to be involved in something like that. But I will say this: worship, to be acceptable, has to be offered in spirit and in truth, and has to be based on the written Word of God. The one right way to approach God, where we honor Him as holy and gracious, is through the shed blood of His Sacrificial Lamb, which we accept by faith, having repented of our sins and then offer Him our praises in ways He has prescribed. In no other kind of worship but that will we meet the living and true God. Worship must be cleaned up wherever necessary.

Charging Interest to Believers (23:19–20)

What possible kind of connection is there between charging interest to other believers and cult prostitution? Well, cult prostitution involves paying God dirty money, as we just saw. The focus of the subject seems to change with charging interest to other believers. This is prohibited for good reasons. Let us say that some fellow believers are in need, and you lend them some money. In that case, you are not to charge them interest; because if they are in dire straits, it might be hard for them to pay it back. The text does say that on a business basis, usury or interest is legitimate to a foreigner (no doubt that means foreign tradesman or businessman). But within the Lord's people, within the family of faith, or the body of Christ, we are to let them have money within reason as they need it, and as they pay us back, we are not to charge them any interest.

The principle is that it is better to lose interest to help a needy brother or sister in the faith, than not to help them. God will always repay you your lost interest, and more. When we are generous to the point of self-sacrifice, we find hidden springs of joy bursting up beneath the surface into our lives. We never lose anything by being generous to the needy, especially within the family of faith.

Pay Your Vows (23:21–23).

It is easy to see how this is connected to 'Thou shalt not steal.' It is made clear here that a vow is always voluntary, or it wouldn't be a vow. You can't take a vow for somebody else; for instance, when somebody joins the church, it's a voluntary vow. Other than that, the most important vow that we take in our earthly life is marriage. Nobody is going to make you join the church and nobody generally would make you get married.

There are other kinds of vows. Somebody might say, 'Lord, if you will do so-and-so, I vow that I will do so-and-so.' That may be acceptable, depending on the situation, but be very careful; don't vow something that would be too hard to pay. If you make a vow, be sure that you are willing to carry it through, no matter how much trouble it is to you.

I used to pastor a church where, whenever I took in young folk as communicant members, I would always stand before the church and read this passage to them: 'When thou vowest a vow unto God, defer not to pay it; for He hath no pleasure in fools; pay that which thou hast vowed. Better it is that thou shouldest not vow, then that thou shouldest vow and not pay' (Eccles. 5:4–5:) Also I often ask people whom I am counseling before marriage, 'Are you sure you want to do this? Do you realize what you are getting into? Nobody is making you do this; if you decide you want to do it, I'll go along with it; and I'll pronounce you man and wife, of course. But are you sure you want to be this bound?' To make a vow and not to pay, is to steal from God. At one time, that was probably generally accepted in our culture, but not now. Here, we believers have the opportunity to be different, and to shed light in a self-serving, often faithless society.

Free Grapes and Free Bits of Grain (23:24–25)

It may surprise us that this matter is related to 'Thou shalt not steal', but careful thought will show how. In Matthew 12:1–8 Jesus and the disciples one Sabbath day were walking near a grain field and were hungry, and took a few heads of wheat, which they rubbed together and ate. The Pharisees criticized them, not for doing that (they knew that it was based on Deuteronomy 23) but because they did it on the Sabbath. But Jesus said it was not a violation of Sabbath. Without exploring the good reason for that, let us go back to the general principle of this text: farmers were to be generous and were to allow passers-by to wander into the fields, and pick a handful of grapes or to get some ears of wheat.

But there were limits to that. Nobody was to get enough grapes so that you could fill a vessel and nobody was to take a scythe or sickle and start reaping the wheat; both would be stealing. So God protects the farmer's property rights and everybody's property rights. Without violating those, there is a certain generosity that God encourages us to exhibit, by being generous to those who are passing by.

What we have to remember is that God is always watching, watching everything we do. It is hard for us to imagine that the mighty Sovereign God is intensely interested in everything we do, in every step we take. God is very pleased when you and I are very generous so that we let somebody take some of our grapes, or some of our wheat, or whatever. We are not to feel upset because some needy person took some small amount of something that we owned, for God will give you more! 'Give, and it shall be given unto you; good measure, pressed down, and shaken together, and running over, shall men give into your bosom. For with the same measure that ye mete withal it shall be measured to you again' (Luke 6:38).

In sum, the five varied rules are not a random collection of strange laws thrown into a rag bag. On the contrary, they are details in a deep and wide exposition of 'Thou shalt not steal'. What is wonderful is that it deals not only with not stealing, but it takes us beyond that to the point of generosity, so that in this short earthly life, we have the privilege of expressing something of the generosity of our heavenly Father.

Ephesians 4:28 brings all of this together. Paul is talking about the behavior of a person who is born again, and how they have 'put off the old man and put on the new man'. Paul shows how we change in not only avoiding particular sins, but in going beyond that to do something positive. 'Let him that stole steal no more'. That's the eighth commandment. But then he adds: go beyond it, (like Deuteronomy 23:24–25): 'but rather let him labor, working with his hands the thing which is good that he may have to give to him that needeth'.

One reason to have a job, when physically able, is not only to keep us from having to steal to feed our family, but also so that we will have enough left over to help others. We should work hard enough, so we have some surplus we can share with those in need. In doing so, you and I have the privilege of showing what God in heaven really is like, and of confirming in this little way the gospel: 'For God so loved the world that He gave His only begotten Son'.

52

The Far Reach of the Eighth Commandment

Deuteronomy 24:1–7

If we are desirous of being holy, you can know that it is one of the things you are given in the new birth. One thinks of the words of Robert Murray McCheyne of nineteenth-century Scotland: 'Lord, make me as holy as it is possible for a pardoned sinner to be made.'

Well, in Deuteronomy, we are given a very far ranging, deep and precise picture of what the holiness of God's people looks like, as they live in a fallen, sinful society. These seven verses of Deuteronomy 24 show us the far reach of the eighth commandment. In the fifties, when Westerns were popular, you used to hear the expression, 'the long arm of the law'. This is the far reach of the eighth commandment, 'Thou shalt not steal.'

Psalm 119:96 says 'Thy commandment is exceeding broad'; the particular application of it here is that it is our privilege to reflect the holiness of God in the way we deal with our possessions and other people's possessions: never to steal from them, but to be generous to them—a tremendous Christian testimony. Nothing could be a worse slap in the face of the gospel—I've seen it—than a noted Christian who is dishonest, who steals. In another part of South Carolina, I have been told of an outspoken man in an evangelical church who goes on missions and talks in an evangelistic manner, yet is known in his law practice to be dishonest and to steal: not illegally, but to take immoral advantage of the situation. That has hurt the testimony of the church which he attends.

On the contrary, one of the ways we can show the beauty of the holiness of God, is not merely by talking (though that has its place), but by respect and by integrity in dealing with the possessions of others and our own. The basis of this, and of the eighth commandment, is simply the character of God—who God is. God is holy. His character is one of pure integrity, not only integrity that would never take what is someone else's but massive generosity that would give out of His own bounty to help them.

God, our heavenly Father, instead of stealing from us, instead of being hard with us, on the contrary gives to us, with incredible generosity. That's the basis of the gospel, isn't it? 'For God so loved the world that He gave ...' (John 3:16). To take unfairly somebody's belongings is the opposite of God, because God gives. Hence, that lawyer who says he is a big Christian, and is using the legalisms of the system to take what belongs to others, is denying who God is, because our

God is One and has the most perfect, sterling, pure integrity; instead of taking, He gives.

To live a life of integrity, never trying to trick somebody out of something but rather thinking of where it is possible to encourage them, is a tremendous opportunity to show what God is like, that God is good. Certainly, to be honest and generous is not the same thing as the gospel; it doesn't mean that you have necessarily explained the gospel. But it often is a first step, so that the outsider will hear your testimony to the Lord. It prepares the way for people to believe that there is a God, that He is good, and that He saves, when they see loving integrity in the lives of His saints.

In the first verses of chapter 24, we have four cases of the far-reaching holiness of God in some unexpected areas—exactly how it was in the text we looked at in our last message. Again, we may wonder why all these commands are thrown together, since they deal with so many different kinds of things. But when you consider that it's the eighth commandment being expounded in different areas where you have to go in a given week or over a period of time, everything makes sense; all are tied together by the spirit of the commandment, 'Thou shalt not steal'.

The four cases are: stealing within the context of marriage and the family, verses 1-4; not going to war the first year you are married, verse 5; not taking a millstone as a pledge on a debt, verse 6; the fourth, stealing people to sell into slavery, verse 7.

Stealing Within the Context of Marriage (24:1-4)

This text deals with an unusual case of divorce, in which the estranged wife is prohibited–if the opportunity should arise–from remarrying the first husband, who put her out; we don't know exactly why, although it says that he found some uncleanness in her; we know it is not adultery because the penalty for adultery was death by stoning. It simply says that her husband finds in her some uncleanness. You can look in all the commentaries and in the studies of the rabbis, and nobody knows exactly what it means.

The two schools of the rabbis, the conservative *Shammai* and the liberal *Hillel*, are said to have disagreed on it, and weren't exactly sure what it meant. But whatever it was, it was something profoundly offensive to the husband. When Jesus speaks of divorce, he does not seem to allow anything as a cause for divorce other than adultery. Paul in 1 Corinthians 7 allows desertion as a grounds for divorce, but when Jesus speaks of divorce in Matthew 19 and Mark 10, He gives one cause and that is adultery.

So I assume that this particular regulation does not carry over into the New Testament code of ethics. But it had to have meant something important when the Lord gave it through Moses. What? Why would prohibiting a man who kicked out a wife, and maybe years later wanted to take her back, be put in the commandment about stealing?

Generally the idea is this: if a man goes through a divorce procedure to put away his wife, God through Moses, says you cannot go back and remarry the first husband. Why? Possibly that would be to protect the interests of the rejected woman, and the idea seems to be that she probably received some money, maybe a divorce settlement of a possible second husband, who died and left her a good bit of money, which the unworthy first husband sees as an opportunity, and so he decides to try to talk her into remarrying him.

Whether that is true or not, I cannot say, but we know that marrying for money has a long history. It usually does not have the blessing of God upon it. So, if the first husband is allowed to take her back, it would be like he was stealing her money, because legally in Israel, as in the Carolinas until the early twentieth century, the male had control of the money and property, according to ancient English Common Law.

So—assuming this is envisioned by the text—if he marries her in order to get hold of her money, it would be a violation of the eighth commandment; and it is also a false basis for marriage.

I haven't known of many people who married for money, but I have known or been told of a few, and all were unhappy and in general, turned out badly. It is possible that some I do not know of worked out well. But marriage is too precious to base it on financial considerations alone. I grant you, a father would have the right if somebody wants to marry his daughter, to make sure he has a job or would be able to get one; that is a legitimate concern. But you can't have the blessing of God, if you base this relationship on nothing but money.

Other than your relationship to Christ, the relationship of marriage is the most important you will ever have in this life. It should not be based on desire for monetary advancement, because marriage, as you see in Ephesians 5, is a reflection of who God is as the Trinity: Father, Son, and Holy Ghost, in a fellowship of holy love. Also, marriage sets forth Christ's love for His bride, the Church. Every good Christian marriage, although they are all imperfect, still show to the world something of who God is, that 'God is love' (1 John 4:8).

A godly marriage is primarily giving. It's not that you don't get anything out of it, for that is legitimate; but its proper focus is thinking of building up the other person. Trying to base marriage on money, social prestige or political advancement, without profoundly caring for the other person, is grasping instead of giving. In marriage, as elsewhere, true love gives.

Not to Go to War the First Year You are Married (24:5)

A man who is newly married may not be drafted into military service for one year, to give him time to encourage his wife so they can get to know each other, and also to give them time to reproduce, so the family name will be carried on, in case when he does go to war, the worst happens. If the Old Testament government had required the young husband to be drafted, and then if he were killed in a battle, it would constitute stealing from his young wife. God says that would be a violation of the eighth commandment. That's how far reaching the holiness code of God really is.

Let me make one other point here: notice the phrase in verse 5, 'cheer up his wife'. Our God is a God who is full of joy. When God saves us, He wishes us to have a great deal of joy in our own heart, as we see in 1 Peter 1:8, 'joy unspeakable and full of glory'. In our relationship with people to whom we are close, such as a wife, husband, parents, and children, they can tell if you have good cheer or joy. Because God is the God of joy, there is something about that relationship with him that makes good cheer a predominant note in our life. Hence the Lord wishes the young man to 'cheer up his wife'.

Good cheer in a marriage is one of the great creational blessings of God, who provides good things for our physical life, as well as for our spiritual life. We see this in Jesus. His first miracle was at the wedding of Cana in Galilee, where He turned the water into wine. That is a way of showing not only that He is God in the flesh, but that He wished to provide good cheer for the wedding guests. God wishes marriage to have much good cheer in it. What a privilege it is, and a happy testimony, when you have a good marriage. And when we're least aware of it, people are watching, so we've got opportunity to reach out for Jesus Christ; to accomplish that, often the way is made ready for the gospel to be explained and believed, just by the way we live, for example, by not taking financial advantage of any person or having good cheer in marriage and family. People watch. It does make a difference.

Do Not Take Part of a Millstone as Collateral for a Loan (24:6)

Some of you have been in more primitive cultures, where they grind the grain every day using millstones, turning it by hand, which provides the flour to make the bread. In view of that, God says, don't take part of their millstone apparatus as a pledge for money owed.

While the Old Testament did not allow the Jews to charge one another interest, they could charge interest to a business man or trader from outside, a non-believer. If you made a loan, you could take something of value from the person to ensure they would pay you back. That's sensible, and God approved of it. But there was a limit: He said not to take either the upper or lower millstone as a pledge because they would not be able to grind the wheat and make bread that day; you could be taking their life from them. That is the connection with the eighth commandment 'Thou shalt not steal'; don't oppress them by taking something that they need to maintain the family life.

So, what if they have a millstone but not much beyond it? If you don't take that, how will you get your money back? The text doesn't openly tell us, but it is better to suffer loss than to oppress somebody who owes you money. God is able to make it up to you. If you lent some money and to get it back you would literally have to go into what they use to make a living or eat their bread, God says don't do it. I can see your sacrifice and can repay you most generously.

Moreover, if the last thing they had was the millstone, at least they can't borrow any more money from you until they pay you back! I do think it's legitimate, if somebody has borrowed money, and gave you nothing as collateral, for you not to lend again, until such time as they pay you back. You might want to lend to them again (or perhaps make an outright donation). That's something that the Holy Spirit will guide you in, as you deal with people. We don't want to do anything that would 'steal their life', but on the other hand, I don't think the Bible anywhere encourages irresponsible borrowing.

It is tempting to discuss the serious debts of western countries (in trillions of dollars, pounds, or euros). But I am not an economist, and will simply say that nations, like families, can live far beyond their means. Then the price must be paid, often with severe disturbances in society.

No Man-Stealing (24:7)

Here the Lord, on the basis of the eighth commandment, prohibits the kidnapping of people in order to sell them into slavery. We know that Joseph, son of Jacob, was kidnapped by his brothers and sold as a slave to merchants who were going to Egypt. That happened in our own country until 1865. God definitely disapproves of man-stealing, because the Lord requires that all persons be treated with dignity, respect, and freedom.

The strong must not take advantage of the weak, because God who is omnipotent doesn't take advantage of us. This prohibition goes back to the eighth commandment. God hasn't stolen anything from you; He's given you everything: your creational life, your body, your hearing, your sight, your sense of taste, and all these relationships. He has given you most of all His precious Son in the gospel, and heaven through

Jesus Christ who paid for it. Therefore, if He is living in us, we do not take what is not ours; least of all we would not take advantage of weaker people. It is disappointing that the Christians of the Southern United States obstinately refused to see this, and a high price is still being paid for it in American society, as we face the twenty-first century.

As Christians, we should want everybody to be free: 'Stand fast therefore in the liberty wherewith Christ hath made us free, and be not entangled again with the yoke of bondage' (Gal. 5:1). That is spiritual liberty, which, before God, gives you a certain dignity and security that is at the basis of every physical and political liberty.

Drawing all of this together: we can work for the freedom and the dignity, and the uplifting, spiritual and physical, of everybody else, as far as we have anything to do with it. Whatever opportunity we can take, let us take it. Thus, the eighth commandment, as expounded here, shines holy, beauteous light on many areas of life, thereby giving us practical opportunities, day by day, in different directions, to show how very good God is. An English hymn by Joseph Hart says:

> How good is the God we adore,
> Our faithful unchangeable Friend!
> His love is as great as His power,
> And knows neither measure nor end!

Thus our life is meant to reflect how very good God is, as we are walking in the Spirit. You can't keep the law in your own strength—your law-keeping is not what saves you, it's Jesus' blood—but nonetheless He inhabits you, and wants you to go in a direction that is pleasing to the heavenly Father. Enabled by the Holy Spirit, we have the opportunity to show to an unbelieving and hard-hearted world, 'how good is the God we adore, our faithful, unchangeable Friend'.

May the Holy Spirit give us the grace to walk in His way.

53

No False Witness

Deuteronomy 24:8-16

This brief section is subsumed under the ninth commandment, 'Thou shalt not bear false witness against thy neighbor'. Honest talk and truthful witness are two of the brightest marks of being a Christian. Jesus said 'Let your yes be yes and your no be no; anything beyond this cometh of evil' (Matt. 5:36). In the political systems of most countries today, differing parties, in order to win elections, often twist news to their advantage, in what is known as 'spin'. It is, at its worst, a violation of the ninth commandment.

Moses explains this commandment and what it means: namely, speak the truth and only the truth, in four different cases: first, Miriam's punishment, verses 8-9; second, mercy in lending, verses 10-13; third, timely payment of poor workers, verses 14-15; fourth, murderous false witness, verse 16. They may seem to be very different, but all four are bound together by the idea of speaking and acting with truth and mercy. That's one of the ways we show the world what our God is like, the God of all truth.

Miriam's Punishment (24:8-9)

Moses didn't have but one sister, Miriam, and she slandered him in Numbers 12:

And Miriam and Aaron, spake against Moses because of the Ethiopian woman whom he had married ... And they said, Hath the Lord indeed spoken only by Moses? Hath He not also spoken by us? And the Lord heard it (Num. 12:1-2).

In verse 9 it says: 'And the anger of the Lord was kindled against them; and He departed. And the cloud departed from off the tabernacle; and behold, Miriam became leprous, white as snow; and Aaron looked upon Miriam, and, behold, she was leprous'.

Miriam violated the ninth commandment by saying something like: 'You don't need to listen to our brother Moses, as though he is the only one bringing you the Word. That Word could come also through what I, Miriam, and my brother, Aaron, tell you; it is time to listen to us. Anyway, who can be sure that God really is speaking primarily through him?'

For that direct attack on the revelation of God, the Lord smites her with the terrible condition of leprosy. Moses was a great intercessor, a true leader of God's people, and one who was merciful to opponents. Numbers 12:13 says he was the meekest man on the earth, displayed as he prayed for his erring sister, who had sought to defame him out of selfish jealousy and pride!

The Lord graciously heard His servant, and directed that Miriam be chastised by having to go outside the camp for seven days, and then go through the ritual cleansing. This episode was given as a warning to God's people never to slander others, and particularly never to slander those who are speaking God's truth to them.

Miriam stands as a warning to many. There's a better way, found in using your mouth to praise and bless God, instead of criticizing and cursing the Lord's servants (related to and expressed differently in James 3:8-10). Paul gives us this better way in Ephesians 4:29, well worth memorizing and then practicing all our days: 'Let no corrupt communication proceed out of your mouth, but that which is good to the use of edifying, that it may minister grace unto the hearers'. That's the better way for us; that's the way of safety in the use of our tongues.

Mercy in Lending (24:10-13)

The second case that flows from not bearing false witness calls for mercy and respect to be shown to a debtor, who has made you a verbal promise to pay you back what you lent him.

We saw previously that no interest or usury was to be charged among Israelites, within the family of faith. However, you could take a pledge of security from a person, something of value to encourage them to pay you back. Even so, the Lord tempers that with respect for the person who is in debt. He says if somebody owes you money, show him or her respect by not pushing into his house to grab the pledge. Instead, stay outside and ask him voluntarily to bring you the pledge.

The case moves on to a person with nothing of value but a sheepskin rug or blanket. I have some given to me when I was preaching in Australia. In Old Testament days, sheepskin rugs were used much as in Australia or New Zealand today, to sleep under at night. Possibly it was the only thing of value a poor man had, and so he gives you the sheepskin rug that he normally covers himself with at night, in order to serve as his pledge. You can keep his rug during the daytime as a pledge, to remind him to pay you back, but at night, when it is getting cold, you should take it back so he can sleep under it; if you do so, he will bless the Lord that you have had mercy on him. Then you can come back the next day and get it.

Why bother every day to get it? Because if during the daytime you keep the only really valuable thing he's got, it will keep him from borrowing more and contracting more debt. Think about it: it is no favor to poor people to encourage them to go into debt that they cannot repay. That's the biblical teaching.

That attitude played a big part of the sub-prime lending crisis that almost brought the American economy down. People with no pledge, no down payment, and no steady income were rushed into houses that they could not afford. The United States Congress passed a bill encouraging this kind of irresponsible lending in 1999; and in 2008 the proverbial chickens came home to roost. Disobeying clear biblical principles always extracts a high price, in our personal lives and in society, though usually it takes several years to see the consequences come to your door.

Thousands or millions of people were encouraged by an unethical lending system to promise something they knew they could never perform. It is a serious violation of the ninth commandment, 'Thou shalt not bear false witness'; you do not make a promise that you know you cannot carry out. Other than the saving gospel of the Lord Jesus Christ, I would say there is nothing in this world so precious to any individual man or woman as our honor, which is inextricably bound to our word.

Timely Payment of Poor Workers (24:14-15)

We deal here with day laborers. Workers who live on a subsistence level may need payment day by day, at the end of each day, in order to buy some bread to feed their children. There are some people who are that poor, that near the line, and we've got to respect them. Not to pay them what they are owed in a timely fashion is a failure to keep your word to them, and thus a violation of the ninth commandment, 'Thou shalt not bear false witness'.

I remember reading, maybe twenty five years ago, that some huge companies in our country have a policy (called stonewalling) of not paying small suppliers what they are owed for months after they were supposed to have paid it, in order to make interest on the money. Such injustice in delayed payment can cause small businesses to go under; unable to meet their payroll or pay their light bill. It is a double violation of God's commandments: a violation of the ninth commandment, not to bear false witness, not keeping one's word to the supplier, the little man; and also a violation of the eighth commandment, 'Thou shalt not steal'.

As Christians in our own corner, let us always be enthusiastic to pay everything on time, to honor every business promise made, in order to honor the God of all truth. Then sometime, somebody might say, I believe God is real and good because I have seen your honorable integrity.

Murderous False Witnesses (24:16)

The concept here is that the innocent, whether father or son, is not to be punished for a relative's sin. Personal responsibility and accountability are at the basis of all biblical justice. Thus you could not have a father put to death because he has a bad, licentious, immoral son. Nor could you have a son put to death because he has a terrible father. This verse is talking about the way evidence is given in court: honest evidence must be given only against the person who has committed the sin or done the crime. It is never right to speak in a way that will make the relative guilty by association. That would be to violate the ninth commandment, subvert justice, and, in some cases, might even lead to taking the life of an innocent person, just because they are kin to somebody who is terrible.

This kind of integrity in a court that does not punish a son for his father or a father for his son, is very different from the situation given us in Deuteronomy 5:9; there is no contradiction. Deuteronomy 5:9 is speaking of the sin of idolatry, and how, if fathers and mothers get involved in idolatry and bring up their children in it, it will bring a curse to the third and fourth generation: 'Thou shalt not bow down thyself unto them [false idols] nor serve them, for I the Lord thy God am a jealous God, visiting the iniquity of the fathers upon the children unto the third and fourth generation of them that hate me.' What exactly is this saying? How is this different?

What it is saying is that the holy, wise, and patient providence of God does indeed let later generations of those who sell themselves out to idolatry, inherit the consequences of their fathers' sin, if they continue in the sin of worshiping something or someone instead of the true God. It will bring a curse for generations to come.

Let me try to apply this to what is now happening in the United States of America. The New England Puritan father, Cotton Mather, ministering in Boston in the late 1600s and early

1700s, noticed that something had happened in New England by the early 1700s that was very discouraging. The Calvinists in New England, had been successful; they were very thrifty, hardworking, and praying—and had, as a general rule, done right. Thus, they were getting rich by trade and in other ways. Yet Cotton Mather warned those early colonists that they were losing their zeal for God, and instead of having their heart placed on God, like their grandparents, their hearts were placed on money, and what money could buy, and were cutting corners morally.

The colonists, were, Cotton Mather feared, already beginning to make an idol out of wealth. We usually don't see physical idols in America, so far as I know. But we have a different kind of idol, something that is in the place of God, an idol of the heart, an idol of the mind. Cotton Mather warned the people that they were making an idol out of money, and loving money more than they loved God. Any kind of idol will take you away from God.

Now both kinds of idolatry—physical idolatry, or emotional and heart and mental idolatry, where you put money or sex or power in front of God, and begin to give yourself to that instead of to the Lord—both kinds always bring devastating curses, let's say after three or four generations, on the population of a nation that was once privileged and refused to repent of its idolatry.

God has a way of doing something to idols. In the Exodus event, God smashed the chief idols of Egypt, including the economic idols, with the ten plagues, devastating the economy of Egypt. Let me ask you this: what do you think God is going to do if the Europeans, the Americans, the British, and the rest, continue worshiping an economic idol, and not turning away from it? Why would any of us think that privileged western countries should always be immune from judgment, when the Egyptians weren't? And the Israelites weren't; when they were taken into captivity, it was for their idolatry.

God always gives time for repentance; He sends His prophets, and He gives His Word. But if His tender calls to repent are consistently refused and people keep bowing down to an idol, including money, God will smash that idol. That may be the only way to save the souls of deluded multitudes, to gain their attention to become placed once again on the only thing that really matters: forgiveness of sin, holiness, and eternal life in Jesus Christ.

Always keep in mind that idols cannot help you in the hour of death; they will fail you in that hour. More than that, Deuteronomy 5:9 warns that if you give yourself to idolatry and raise your children in it, it will destroy them to the third and the fourth generation, unless somehow they are able to break out of the cycle of worshiping things instead of God.

The ninth commandment does not merely require us to speak the truth, not to bear false witness, not to put things above God, but also requires us to *think* the truth. The Bible says that 'as a man thinketh, so is he'. The most important thing is, what do you think about God; who is your God? What is He like?

We have to be aware that because He is invisible, we may be tempted to put our affections on something less than God that we can see. We live in a materialistic generation. Most of us find it difficult to live in terms of the spiritual. In order to keep anything from taking the place of this glorious, holy God, we must keep at the front of our mind who God is. And that will automatically smash idols in our affections. If you never think about God, if all you watch is foolish television, or the internet, you start soaking up a deluded idolatrous culture.

Thus, in order to keep the ninth commandment, not to bear false witness, but instead, honorably to keep every promise and to speak according to the way things are, you've got to keep thinking of what God is like. That is your greatest protection and the only hope for the country; that a serious minority of Christians will think about what God is like, and act on that basis!

Have you ever wondered, how could the holy Son of God in the flesh have chosen to remain on the horrendous cross of Calvary, when—as the gospel hymn affirms, 'He could have called 10,000 angels'? Of course He could have; He's God in the flesh! Yet He said: 'The cup which my Father hath given me to drink, shall I not drink it?' The sinless One drank that cup of the wrath of God, for my sins and yours; He voluntarily stayed on the cross to drink it to its dregs. From what we can tell, as He was doing this for us, God His Father was in His mind above all else, God's holiness, and the salvation of the church were in His mind, when He had said earlier in Gethsemane: 'Not My will, but Thine be done'. He experienced hell, so I would never have to go to hell; He paid its price. Now that is the God whom we worship! That is the God, a self-sacrificing, holy, loving God who said, 'Don't you put an idol in front of Me; don't you let any good gift that I have given you come before me in your affections. I am the one who made you; I love you; I have given absolutely everything to save your soul, and get you to heaven.' How could we possibly turn our back on such love and follow some paltry false, failing idol? This we must keep in mind, and we will be safe, no matter what else may happen.

In closing I want to quote a prayer from two Psalms, and to recommend that we make it our personal prayer.

In Psalm 51, the penitential Psalm, verses 6–7, we find David praying. He had committed very serious sins. But after many months, he confessed them with a broken heart. God heard him, and He will hear you; He will hear me.

> Behold, Thou desirest truth in the inward parts,
> and in the hidden part.
> Thou shalt make me to know wisdom.
> Purge me with hyssop and I shall be clean;
> wash me and I shall be whiter than snow.

And then Psalm 139:23–24, the conclusion of this wondrous Psalm: 'Search me, O God, and know my heart; and try me and know my thoughts. And see if there be any wicked way in me, and lead me in the way everlasting'.

I want to make this promise: if large numbers of God's true people pray those two Psalms and mean it, we may still see God exercising His mercy upon us in our corrupt societies across the contemporary world.

54

How to Treat the Disadvantaged (Part I)

Deuteronomy 24:17–22

This is a passage on how God wants us to treat the disadvantaged and powerless people in our midst. In this text and following, we move to Moses' exposition of the tenth commandment: 'Thou shalt not covet'. At first sight, this does seem to be directly about not coveting, but there is more here than meets the eye.

In modern Britain and America, we don't use the word 'covet' too often, but we know its basic meaning: to covet is to strongly desire for yourself something that belongs to someone else. It has been widely noted that usually one of the underlying causes of an economic and social crisis is untrammeled greed. Greed is an aspect of covetousness. And when the leadership of a society, and much of the body politic as well, is eaten up by greed, eventually the country experiences major problems, sometimes ending in social disaster.

But the kind of coveting we are warned against in Deuteronomy 24 is not the kind of coveting we normally think of. It's stinginess, a holding of one's blessings so closely to one's bosom that one is unwilling to share their abundance with the needy and the poor, when you could easily do so without losing your substance.

Moses teaches God's people not to be stingy towards the disadvantaged. He mentions three cases where we can see how it works. First, equal protection under the law, 24:17a (the first part of the verse); second, mercy in lending, verse 17b; third, gleaning, verses 19–21; and fourth, the reason God gives through Moses why we should be compassionate to the disadvantaged, verses 18 and 22.

Equal Protection Under the Law (24:17a)

Scripture everywhere teaches that God is no respecter of persons, as for example in Acts 10:34 and many verses in the book of Proverbs. Yet respect of the high and mighty is something that is hard for us not to be involved in. We have to fight it as much as anybody, because one of the effects of the fall of Adam, is that we have the problem of twisting things away from how God wants it, so that we cater to the rich and powerful and look down on and possibly take advantage of the poor and the powerless. But God says, 'As my people you must strive never to do that; instead, give equal protection to all.'

Moses presents three classes in society at that time who were particularly disadvantaged: the 'stranger' (in the King James Version or 'sojourner' in other translations); like an immigrant worker. Then the orphan and the widow are mentioned. In any legal process in the court, if you are serving on a jury or as a judge, these politically and economically powerless persons are never to be treated unfairly, but the same as the established aristocracy of a town or a state; this is what God says.

The book of James takes this principle of fairness from Deuteronomy 24, and expands it in the life of the church:

> My brethren, have not the faith of the Lord Jesus Christ, the Lord of glory, with respect of persons. For if there come unto your assembly a man with a gold ring, in goodly apparel, and there come in also a poor man in vile raiment; and ye have respect to him that weareth the gay clothing, and say to him, Sit thou here in a good place; and say to the poor, stand thou there, or sit here under my footstool; are ye not then partial in yourselves, and are become judges of evil thoughts? (James 2:1–4)

James is saying to give a cordial welcome to every person. If well dressed with an obviously prosperous background, greet them cordially. Some may be poor and broken down; greet them cordially. Treat them equally, one as well as the other. That is how it is to be in the church. In the state, in the political and judicial area, economic status, race, or family connection must never cause us to pervert justice. 'Thou shalt not wrest [twist or take from] the judgment of thy poor' (Exod. 23:6).

One way we can show an unbelieving world who God is, is by impartial fairness in our dealings with persons of every sort and condition. Somebody who is evenhanded, personally courteous to everybody, as far as they humanly can be in daily life, and then—if voting on a jury—trying to make a fair decision, without respect of person or whatever, is a wonderful witness to a secular public that 'maybe God really is good, because this person is treating me fairly.' The human mind works that way.

Mercy in Lending (24:17b)

We have already seen that the Israelites were allowed to take a pledge of some valuable thing from a person who had borrowed from them, to help ensure they would pay it back. But in the case of a widow, who, in general, was seriously disadvantaged economically, the person who lent her some money was not to take a pledge from her, particularly a garment that she wore or a blanket that she needed to keep warm at night. Moses forbids it because it would make her suffer. It's better not to get your money back than to make a poor person unnecessarily suffer; take her word that she will pay it back. It is a merciful way that the Lord provides to deal with lending to poor widows and a specific way of showing them and the public, what kind of God we serve: He is considerate and kind, helpful and generous to us, and expects us to be that way to other people.

To live this way certainly removes some of the bitterness of a hard life, and gives a quiet inner peace to the person who is acting considerately. Treating disadvantaged widows or others well, is a way to win every time, and not to lose in God's eternal values. Generosity always wins, over the long haul.

But it is not always easy, for because of sin we tend to be partial and stingy, pass by on the other side and ignore the need. So how can we imperfectly sanctified Christians avoid greed and stinginess? God tells us how, particularly through the testimony of Paul:

Not that I speak in respect of want [of need]; for I have learned, in whatsoever state I am, therewith to be content. I know both how to be abased [when you are really poor and hurting and people have turned their backs on you and disappointed you, and you feel really terrible], and I know how to abound [you have those days or weeks when things are going wonderfully; children are healthy and giving you a good report; income is better, and we all have felt that and been grateful when it happened]. Everywhere and in all things I am instructed both to be full and to be hungry, both to abound and to suffer need. [Now here is how he learned it; Paul had to learn it! Paul was a holy apostle, and he had to learn it, and if he had to work hard, I will certainly have to work hard at it] I can do all things through Christ which strengtheneth me (Phil. 4:11–13).

Presumably even Paul did not have it in him to be content when abased, or to keep equity and not get proud, when abounding; through Christ, who was in him, he learned how to do it, and that is held out for us all. He also says: 'But godliness with contentment is great gain' (1 Tim. 6:6–8). Godliness can be had whether you are abased, your stocks went bust, company closed, one or two of your children lost their jobs, or if you are on retirement income, and inflation has got you where you can't keep buying gas or whatever. Godliness is not dependent on the economic situation. Or if you are doing well when your ship came in and everything seemed rosy, godliness with contentment is still the great gain. Be content, whether down or up or in the middle.

Most of us are probably somewhere in the middle. But whether currently up or down, you can be a happy and productive person in the Lord: 'For we brought nothing into this world, and it is certain we can carry nothing out'. When you die, you don't take any material things with you. But there is something you can take: godliness and contentment, to go with you on the other side of physical death, up into the light.

Whether you have little or much in your house, godliness with contentment is great gain. If you've got some food and clothes, you are extremely well off, particularly if your soul is saved, without which there is no contentment. And if you have the Holy Spirit and assurance of forgiveness of Christ, then truly the economy and the political situation will not affect very much the godliness with contentment, the great gain, which being in Christ gives to you. You could lose ten worlds and still have it. 'For what will it profit a man if he gain the world and lose his own soul?' (Matt. 16:26).

Colossians 3:1–5 helps us work out this godliness with contentment, so that we do all things through Christ who strengthens us; then we won't be discontent, and won't be greedy, and, when we have something, we won't be stingy. We will be well balanced, helpful, kind, loving persons—tremendous testimonies for the gospel.

Mean people are a terrible testimony for the gospel. But how can you avoid being that way? It's hard not to be stingy or greedy; it's hard to think well of everybody and to treat them right. Yet as the Apostle tells us: 'I can do all things through Christ'. Here is where we come into contact with the power: 'If ye then be risen with Christ ... ', that is, every believer has experienced spiritual resurrection in his soul. Now your body won't be resurrected until the end of time, but your soul is resurrected the moment you are given the grace to believe in Jesus. You're risen with Him; which is why we won't be devastated either way various elections go, for our citizenship is somewhere higher than America, or we would be in very worrying shape indeed, wouldn't we?

If ye then be risen with Christ, seek those things which are above, where Christ sitteth on the right hand of God. Set your affection on things above, not on things on the earth. For ye are dead, and your life is hid with Christ in God. When Christ, who is our life, shall appear, then shall ye also appear with Him in glory.

One day in this world, everything is going to be just right, when He comes back and the cosmos and all things in it are renewed and, as part of that, we will be shining as His saints: what a day! But until then 'Mortify', that is, put to death; say 'no' to the lower parts of yourself (Col. 3:5).

In and through our union with Christ, although He is up there and I am down here, yet in one real sense, I am already seated with Him in heavenly places (Eph. 2:6). He knows how to help me deal with my covetousness; Jesus will help me mortify it. We can mortify covetousness (as mentioned in Colossians 3:5) as required by the tenth commandment. We can mortify it by continual actions of day by day, thinking of Christ; that's the only way. If you haven't got time to do this, then you haven't got time to be a Christian. Who isn't busy? Set your affections—deep motivations—if you could have something you really want, it must be Christ. Look to Him and think about Him through the day, and when you are tempted to be hard with somebody or to be unduly worried, or to be feeling unhappy that you haven't got something somebody else has, then think of Christ, seated up there in wonderful love to you, with nail prints in hands and think of all that He did for you. That way, you and I will become more and more free from greed or stinginess, because we will then inwardly realize that if we have Christ, we have absolutely everything that we can ever need.

55

How to Treat the Disadvantaged (Part II)

Deuteronomy 24:17–22

We saw previously that this section of Deuteronomy is an exposition by Moses of the meaning of the tenth commandment, 'Thou shalt not covet'. It is particularly applied this way: if we hold onto our blessings too tightly, what money or possessions we may have, it is a form of coveting. So Moses says: 'Thou shalt not covet', and, specifically, it means that we are to be merciful to the poor and disadvantaged in the society in which we live. To that end, we are going to look at verses 19–22, the biblical law for gleaning.

Anybody around my age would probably remember that sometimes in Sunday school they would hand out a little bulletin which sometimes had on its front a classical picture of Ruth gleaning in the barley fields of Bethlehem. She and her mother-in-law, Naomi, were poor widows, with practically nothing, but the biblical law of gleaning enabled them to survive, and indeed, to beget an important line in Holy Scripture.

Gleaning is one of the ways God gives His people across the ages to help the poor, and those who are, one way or another, financially or politically disadvantaged. Jesus said in the Gospel of John, 'You always have the poor with you' (12:8). It was true when Moses was speaking; it was true in the lifetime of Jesus; it is true today. It was even true in a society that claimed they would get rid of poverty—Communism—and it is true among Capitalists (though not nearly so bad under Free Enterprise). Under any system, even under fairly good ones, you will have people for various reasons—sometimes it is their fault and sometimes not—who are poor, and who therefore need help. Because of Christ's compassion, which is engendered for us in the new birth, the Holy Spirit brings forth compassion in the believer towards those who are in bad shape.

We are going to limit it today to talking about gleaning. Now most of you know what gleaning is, and even though we live in an agricultural area, as far as I know, we don't do any gleaning.

The law of gleaning said they were not to strictly take everything they could from the harvest but they were to leave some, so the poor people would be allowed to go into the olive groves, the vineyards, and the wheat or barley fields at the edges, and let them gather the remains to meet their needs.

Grain, wheat, barley, olives, and grapes were the main crops of ancient Israel; today in Dillon County I reckon it's cotton, tobacco, soybeans, wheat and corn. So we remember, as I told you, the beautiful story of Ruth, a Moabitess with an Israelite mother-in-law Naomi; and when Naomi heard that things were better in Israel, that they had some crops now, she migrated back. And Ruth said, 'I will not leave you; I am going with you, come what may.' And so Naomi and Ruth got to Bethlehem where Naomi and her family had come from. Naomi had a distant kinsman named Boaz, a property holder and farmer, and a godly character, and she told Ruth to go into his fields and glean.

Ruth did so and Boaz was very impressed. He had heard about her and her excellent character, and her love for her mother-in-law, and so he commanded his workers to leave some handfuls on purpose. Charles H. Spurgeon once wrote a lovely little book, *Handfuls on Purpose,* showing how God does that for us all. Then Boaz said, I want you to advantage Ruth in this gleaning. They did so, and she took home bushels and bushels of grain, much to the joy of her bereaved mother-in-law.

Then Boaz set his eyes upon her, and they went through the legal procedures of the levirate law of marriage, so that he married this fine young woman. What is significant about it is this: it is always well to obey the principles of God. Moses said, I want to help you to help the poor by allowing gleaning on your property. Boaz did so, and guess what came of it, affecting you and me? If it hadn't been for that, we wouldn't be in this church; there wouldn't be a church, humanly speaking. Because Boaz takes Ruth as his wife, and their direct descendant was King David, whose direct descendant was our Lord Jesus Christ, God the Son, who came into our race by miraculous action into the womb of the blessed virgin Mary, who was descended from Ruth. So the humanity of our Lord Jesus Christ was inherited from Ruth and Boaz.

Now think of it! What if they had disobeyed? What if they had said 'I am not going to help the poor; I don't want them on my property; I don't want to see them!'? Ruth and Boaz would not have married and become the direct ancestors of David, son of Jesse, and the ancestor of Jesus. So we're direct beneficiaries, of the law of gleaning.

There is a great deal of detail about gleaning in Leviticus 19 and 23. I would like to bring up three points, three advantages of gleaning. I believe you will say that this makes as much common sense as you have ever seen in your life about any social policy.

The Spiritual Privilege of Relieving Poor People

If you ask how is giving, in any sense, an advantage? It is a great blessing when God says, 'I am granting you something to give to those who have less than you.' This means a person who gives is being blessed. In the Book of Acts, Paul quotes Jesus (this is the only place we find him doing so in the New Testament): 'It is more blessed to give than to receive' (Acts 20:35).

There is an illustration of it in 2 Corinthians 8:7: 'Therefore, as ye abound in everything, in faith, and utterance, and knowledge, and in all diligence, and in your love to us, see that ye abound in this grace also'. What's the grace? Giving! Our being able to give is a grace, something better than we deserve, that God has bestowed upon us; giving is a grace from God to His child.

Most of us would wish for more grace in our lives. One of the answers to prayer, when I am saying Lord, show me more grace, is when He directs you to share some of your leftover increase with the disadvantaged. When you give to others in the name of God, it is as much grace beginning to operate in your life, as when God heals your body, or increases your inward joy, or sends you a check in the mail. It's just that big a grace!

Gleaning Increases Social Harmony

You are not going to have a classless society—the Communists didn't; the Socialists don't, and we who live under Free Enterprise do not—it's impossible. But you can have one that is more just and gives people opportunity to move up. Gleaning helps increase harmony between different kinds of people in a society. It does it by making provision for the landless to survive honorably without stealing. And they can keep their dignity without obsequious begging, because they are allowed to glean from those who have been blessed in their increase.

I would say that gleaning was a way to fulfill the prayer that would later be written by Solomon, who was descended from the wonderful gleaner, Ruth. Proverbs 30:7–9 is a good prayer to pray. Have your children, when they first start their job, as a life goal in their job and in their marriage, to write out this as a prayer; see if you think it's helpful. You can get terribly rich and forget God, and think you got it by yourself, but the opposite is equally bad, and so we ask God to keep us from both:

> Two things have I required of Thee; deny me them not before I die: remove far from me vanity and lies; give me neither poverty nor riches; feed me with food convenient for me; lest I be full and deny Thee, and say, Who is the Lord? Or lest I be poor, and steal, and take the name of my God in vain.

This is a wise prayer, and gleaning helped the prayer to be fulfilled, in the sense that the wealthier person shared, and the very poor person didn't have to steal and dishonor whom He knew the Lord to be.

Gleaning Required Work on the Part of the Poor

The farmer did not hand him out the picked grapes or cut the wheat himself; the poor people had to do that for themselves. Then they had to take it home and grind the wheat or mash out the grapes, or prepare the olives, grapes and grain to be stored and eaten. It took a lot of work in the field and the home. It is always best for poor and disadvantaged people who are physically able, to work, even in little jobs. It is also always best even for rich people with tremendous income and their children, and far more godly, that they work and bring their children up to work hard, whether in an impressive big job or in a little job.

The fourth commandment, 'Remember the Sabbath Day to keep it holy', requires six days of labor, but the seventh to be kept as the Sabbath of the Lord. So we have every right to enjoy the seventh or Sabbath day of rest. I think that the modern idea of a four day work week really is contrary to the principles of Scripture. I also think the modern ideal—going back to Bismarck of Germany in the nineteenth century—of retiring at sixty-five and then doing nothing productive until you die, also runs contrary to the will of God as revealed in Scripture.

It has been shown in many psychological studies that not to work makes genuine happiness impossible. Laziness and inactivity can even break down a person's emotional stability, and sometimes their mental health. Forty years ago, as I remember, a sociologist did a study of the Amish up in Pennsylvania. He discovered that the Amish community had little jobs for everybody in the community; from ninety-five years old, and able to do something, down to the age of twelve,—everybody had a little job, making them feel an important part of that community, and doing something that mattered and helped others. The sociologist found a very high degree of good mental health among those Amish, partly related to the fact that everyone had a place and was encouraged to do some kind of a job—a little one or a big one.

I am told that in a number of mental institutions and rehab centers, those who generally made the most improvement seemed to have become involved in some kind of work, using their hands, using their minds, making something useful, doing something productive; and it is widely believed that doing even a little work that amounts to something, actually increases people's recovery from mental or alcohol or drug problems. So when God says to work six days, He means what He says; it's best for us and best for many whom we could help by what we have earned.

What is the Bible's solution to poverty? A big question. Let us take a look at the big picture as I understand it.

The Bible's approach to poverty is profoundly different from that of socialism. Socialism, while held by many good people, forcibly takes from the productive and bestows it upon the non-productive, who by their improvidence often waste it, and come back for more. Thus one could make a good case to say that income redistribution, through the modern socialist tax codes of most countries, flies in the face of the Deuteronomic principle, of gleaning.

Gleaning certainly required something from the haves—let them get into your fields, after the main harvesting. It certainly required something from the have-nots: get out there and work; do the best you can to gather it up, process it, and store it. It made the haves and have-nots better people; both could keep their dignity and not bow their heads in shame to anybody else.

But here's the question. To get to Reedy Creek Church, you come through miles of beautiful land in order to get here to this agricultural district. But people who live in Charlotte, Raleigh, Columbia, New York, Atlanta, Los Angeles, and so on—most people—don't live in an agricultural district such as we live in.

What then would be the modern equivalent of gleaning? I have thought about it, and I'm not exactly certain, but I have some idea of what it may be. Is it not the case that the modern equivalent of gleaning, where you have gardens—most of us have vegetable gardens—would be to share with the needy after you have enough to eat and after you can or freeze for the winter? Or if, after cooking enough, you spread the food you don't need to those whom you know would be glad to have it; many of you already do that.

Also I wonder if gleaning could mean something like sharing free computer time when the computer would otherwise be down, and somebody who hasn't got much money and won't tear it up, could be allowed to use it? Or when getting a different computer, give your old one to somebody who couldn't buy one. In our own family, since we have been given so much, we made a decision several years ago never to sell an old car, but to give it to a worthy poor family to help them get to their job.

There are other things we could consider—ways we can help—without breaking ourselves down and robbing our children. Some of you could come up with creative ways to do so. If we wish to be generous and to bring God's mercy to the many needy persons He puts around us, the Holy Spirit will lead us as to precisely how to do it. He motivates us to be good to those in need, and will give us the practical wisdom to see ways that would be a modern day equivalent of something like the principle of gleaning.

Why Be Compassionate?

Moses in verse 18 makes perfectly clear the reason why we should be zealous to help people; and why Israel was told to be compassionate to disadvantaged immigrants, widows, and orphans. It was because Israel itself had been severely oppressed in Egypt and got to the stage where they had nothing but God in heaven. But in wondrous grace, God operated in supernatural, miraculous mercy and power, to bring them out, and deliver them from slavery. So God says, 'When you had nothing, I had mercy on you, intervened, helped you, and delivered you; that is the attitude I want you to have to everybody around you, who is in need.' Jesus said:

'As the Father hath sent Me, even so send I you' (John 20:21). That is the way that many people will practically see who Jesus is, and be prepared to receive the gospel of grace.

Now you could say it is true that Israel was in Egypt in slavery, but what about us? Well, we were not literally in Egypt, nonetheless, we were in bondage to sin, to Satan—the worst Pharaoh of them all—before God mercifully stepped in and saved our souls. We were under evil powers, and thus were spiritually dead, and on the way to hell.

The New Testament teaches that God had compassion on us and redeemed us at His own precious cost when we had nothing to demonstrate our merit, when we were spiritually bankrupt: 'Forasmuch as ye know that ye were not redeemed with corruptible things, as silver and gold, from your vain conversation [that is your empty way of life] received by tradition from your fathers; but with the precious blood of Christ, as of a lamb without blemish and without spot' (1 Peter 1:18-19).

God redeemed us, when we had nothing, by taking the beloved Son of His heart and sending Him down here to take on our nature and yet remain God; keeping the law and suffering the penalty of sin, thus paying all the price of sin for anyone who will confess His name. The generosity of the divine compassion is seen in what the love of God gave: 'For God so loved the world that He gave His only begotten Son, that whosoever believeth in Him should not perish but have everlasting life.' This is the basis of all Christian compassion to the needy. According to John 3:16, it is the love of the Father in sending the Son that motivates us to give. I don't see how anybody could have received the love of God in Christ, and not be a compassionate giver.

Let us close by looking at John 20:21-22, when the risen Christ showed up after His resurrection, and spoke to His disciples: 'Then said Jesus to them again, Peace be unto you; as My Father hath sent me, even so send I you'. He is saying, 'I came out from heaven to do this for you, and I am sending you out to do something on the analogy of what I did when I left the Father in heaven, and came down to earth for you.'

And our answer is, 'O Lord, we are not worthy! We are not as motivated as we should be, and there are things that hold us back, and we sometimes don't want to do it; how in the world can we do it?' Verse 22 shows how; it turns this from a counsel of despair to an encouraging promise that we can truly receive: 'And when He had said this, He breathed on them, and saith unto them, Receive ye the Holy Ghost'. It is the power of the Holy Spirit that keeps us in union with Christ, and keeps us motivated, and doing good works. This will enable us to demonstrate, in our own little way, something of who Jesus, whom the Father sent, truly is, and who says to us, 'So send I you.'

56

Fair Punishment

Deuteronomy 25:1–3

This text is about declaring the innocent, innocent; and declaring the guilty, guilty; and meting out the appropriate punishment in terms of God's law for those who have done wrong. One of the great strengths of the Holy Bible is that it is a realistic book, written for people who live in a fallen, sinful world. It is different from some spiritual biographies of the saints, because, not infrequently, the authors withheld information about the saints' failings. Some spiritual biography is unrealistic, in that it presents in roseate tones, a life that was no doubt Christian, but wasn't angelically perfect. However, the Bible tells you and Bible equips men and women to live in a world that is not ideal, that is fallen and selfish, and where there is much wrong. Hence, God's Word gives us the information, gives us the approach to handle every kind of difficulty— including societal wrongdoing. These first three verses of Deuteronomy 25 are primarily dealing with fair punishment of wrongdoing.

It may seem odd that a text about fair punishment is placed here, where Moses is expounding the tenth commandment, 'Thou shalt not covet'. What he is saying is, do not covet the justice that is owed to any person; do not desire to withhold justice from them for any reason, whether because of sentimentality or partiality.

After having judged fairly, where the party is guilty, the court has to administer punishment. It is wrong to withhold a fair sentence and the consequences that flow from wrongdoing. Now this may well fly in the face of sentimentality. Many fondly say that if you are a nice person, you should not be punished. But that is not from God. God says that not to give fair justice, including punishment when called for, is breaking the tenth commandment, and withholding from them something of value.

The basic idea is that God's law requires judges to administer a fair and impartial sentence on everybody, regardless of their background. After a properly administered legal case, the judge declares the innocent party righteous, and the guilty party to be sentenced. That is the basic point of justice: render to everyone their deserts. In God's long-term scheme of things, this is what I want you to think about, because, in many respects, it goes against our normal thinking. But in God's long-term scheme, it really is always best for the righteous to be recognized as righteous, and for the guilty to receive fair and reasonable punishment for their wrongdoing.

When in the wrong, it is best for them to be punished for wrongdoing; that's what the Bible is saying. How could that be right then? In answer, let me give you some passages of Scripture: 'Because sentence against an evil work is not executed speedily, therefore the heart of the sons of men is fully set in them to do evil' (Eccles. 8:11). It is treating a person wrong, coveting their justice, not to punish them speedily, because it confirms a wicked heart where they are hatching more evil, as many sitting in prisons are doing. Yet their life might have been changed, if they had been given fair justice, which includes punishment. So punishment for the guilty is actually a benefit <u>for</u> the guilty, as well as for the nation.

Hebrews 12:5–11 speaks of this in very personal terms: family terms.

> And ye have forgotten the exhortation which speaketh unto you as unto children, My son, despise not thou the chastening of the Lord, nor faint when thou art rebuked of him. For whom the Lord loveth, he chasteneth, and scourgeth every son whom he receiveth. If ye endure chastening, God dealeth with you as with sons; for what son is he whom the father chasteneth not? But if ye be without chastisement, then are ye bastards, and not sons. Furthermore we have had fathers of our flesh which corrected us, and we gave them reverence; shall we not much rather be in subjection unto the Father of spirits and live? For they verily for a few days chastised us after their own pleasure; but he for our profit, that we might be partakers of his holiness. Now no chastening for the present seemeth to be joyous, but grievous; nevertheless afterward it yieldeth the peaceable fruit of righteousness unto them which are exercised thereby.

God's Word says that you cannot have a society where there is peace in people's hearts, unless they are dealt with fairly for their wrongdoing.

The sentimentality that refuses to punish either criminals, or let us say in a much lesser fashion, a child, is lacking in truest love for the person who needs to be punished. That may seem strange to you, but that is what the Bible says: 'He that spareth his rod hateth his son; but he that loveth him chasteneth him betimes' (Prov. 13:24). Children require legitimate, careful, and non-excessive chastisement. 'Chasten thy son while there is hope and let not thy souls spare for his crying' (Prov. 19:18). I can testify here that I made many mistakes in raising our children. But I honestly do not regret the fact that when I thought it necessary, I applied the rod; I don't regret it; I'm glad I did it. I wish I had done some other things much better, and I wish I hadn't said some things—the Lord knows about that; but I do not regret in my older age that I have at times, punished those children; I'm glad I followed God, at least in that way.

Proverbs 29:15, 'The rod and reproof give wisdom', so not to punish is to steal wisdom—one of the most precious gifts a human being can have—that the guilty could have gained. If you are brought up without chastisement, or if criminals don't get chastisement, they fail to develop wisdom which means they live as fools—and fools lose their souls! 'But a child left to himself bringeth his mother to shame'.

I remember an excellent black police officer in Jackson, Mississippi, an expert on the gangs in Jackson, speaking one time at the Reformed Seminary. He said that the gang was a substitute family. Maybe they didn't get love at home, and if they didn't get love, they probably didn't get proper chastisement. But the gang will chastise them, if they don't act in accord with the gang's nefarious purposes, until they are loyal to the gang. In other words, they have been deprived of having learned the wisdom of self restraint—a wisdom we all have to learn. Personal relationships will be fairly well ruined for life—you can count on it—if you don't learn at an early age, a certain amount of self restraint; that is one of the worst things that can happen to a human being.

A lack of wisdom in a child can be the result of the lack of proper chastisement and of proper love. When you have unusually surly children in school, and the school needs to call in the parents, sometimes the parents are worse than the children; They are spoiled, unrestrained, emotionally abusive; they are adolescents in an adult body. Society is getting in a serious condition when you have at least two generations—and some cases three—that were not punished at home. It's too late when you put them in jail, for then they have failed to develop the wisdom and the beauty of self control. What a high cost society pays, extra police having to be hired, heavy court dockets as the courts are jammed, crowded emergency rooms, and property destroyed! But it could have been different, if we had gone by God's Word.

Before getting to more severe crimes, as in Deuteronomy 25:3, let us look at crimes not so severe; sins that are minor, but, if not dealt with, will get worse. One of the best gifts a parent can give a child is to teach them responsibility for their actions—a beautiful gift. Not to do so when they are young, may be to render them emotionally and morally unfit for the rest of their lives.

So how do we, as men and women who are in Jesus Christ by the Holy Spirit, deal with things like sass, dishonesty, and disrespect to others? On most occasions, I believe that non-corporal punishment is best, such as things like withholding of pleasures or restriction of activities, or a firm verbal rebuke, and requiring an apology and restitution. In general, these things are far better and sufficient.

However, sometimes—I think it pretty rare—you may need to apply the rod. When you do so, never be excessive or do it harshly; do not do it in anger; it's better not to do it at all, if you are full of wrath. Occasional corporal discipline is far superior to a household where there is constant fussing and an atmosphere of unpleasantness, and resentment between parents and child. It is far better to get it over with, and clear the atmosphere. But above all else, whether corporal or not, the punishment must never exceed the seriousness of the offense. It is always better to under-do than to overdo. Looking back, I would say that sometimes I overdid it.

Deuteronomy 25:2–3 deals with an adult who knew better, and did something seriously wrong—we are not told what. He is taken to court and the just judge says he is to be beaten with forty stripes. Let me just say a few words about that, because if I don't I will lose people. I am well aware that in the last 250 years, more or less, in the Western world of Europe and America, there has been a strong revolt against public whippings for wrongdoers. Courts have generally substituted monetary fines or time in jail, instead of corporal punishment. Maybe sometimes that is best; I don't know. But this refusal to administer public whipping, let's say, seems to have come about as a result of the humanistic European enlightenment which, at its worst, tends to replace God with man as a sort of deity himself. From that point of view, man is God, and therefore, you can't whip God. I seriously doubt that most people who oppose public punishment would go that far; I am merely suggesting what may underlie this revulsion in its origins.

Certainly, one can raise reasonable objections against public whipping, putting in the stocks, or other kinds of punishment. But do you believe that our refusal for the last 250 years to allow any kind of public whipping for serious wrongdoers has caused society to progress, for people to feel better and the streets to be safer? What do you think? Was it progress not to do it God's way? I'll leave it to you to answer.

Going back to Deuteronomy 25, the Deuteronomic law had the advantage of meting out fair and swift justice. If we refer to Ecclesiastes again, delaying justice is asking for further, and maybe worse, trouble. Think of the people sitting in the jails and prisons, who can't get a hearing in court; that may not be their fault; the courts are jammed. But the biblical way of doing it has the advantage of meting out fair and swift justice to malefactors, while at the same time preserving their essential human dignity. Hence they were allowed to whip with only forty strokes of the cane.

The rabbis during time between the two Testaments had reduced that to forty strokes minus one, lest somebody made a mistake in the counting; they didn't want them to go over forty, because it would tend to dehumanize the person who is in the wrong, a thing you'd want to avoid; the Bible always protects their humanity. The Apostle Paul knew about this, and says in 2 Corinthians 11:24: 'Five times received I forty stripes minus one', one of which we read about in Acts 16; there are other times of which we are not told. So the police authorities, according to Old Testament law, could never exceed forty stripes.

The reason for this is given in verse 3: '... lest thy brother seem vile unto thee'. The dignity of every man and woman, created in the image of God, is never to be forgotten—even when they are being punished for wickedness. Hence a fair, restricted punishment does not really dishonor the criminal. The restriction recognizes their God-given human dignity.

I think the best discussion I have ever seen of this is by C. S. Lewis in a remarkable article he wrote years ago entitled *The Humanitarian Theory of Punishment*. He deals with this very passage in Deuteronomy 25, and points out that the biblical terms 'worthy to be beaten' and 'according to his fault' emphasize the essential issue, and that is desert. He says that it is desert, what one deserves, that links punishment with justice, according to the proper sentence. To be punished, even if strictly, because we have deserved it, is to be treated as a human person made in God's image. A few times in my childhood career I got whippings in school; in every case I richly deserved them. It did not damage my psychology; it did not make me hate the teacher; I knew I deserved it, and I was fine about it; and I very carefully didn't tell my parents, because I knew that I would have received another whipping at home. In fact in one case I lied to them about it.

But this concept of 'deserts'—somebody actually deserving something—is not acceptable to the modern humanism that controls our culture; they reject it. What do they put in its place? It is the liberal theory of therapy or psychotherapy; that's why courts employ so many psychiatrists. There is no objective standard of right and wrong to which we are to be held accountable, because humanism denies the existence of God and His holy character, which gives us the standard of right and wrong, and by which, if you follow it, you are blessed. So what you are left with is psychotherapy. As C. S. Lewis says, it is dehumanizing. Instead of getting your deserts, you are subjected to psychotherapy and made less than a responsible human in God's image. The idea of psychotherapy is that they are criminally sick, not sinful. Maybe it's their parents; maybe it's their environment; maybe they were too poor; maybe they were too rich. They are sick and need to be cured, not punished.

It is very clever, but devious and detrimental. Just look at our society; look at the schools; look at the jails. Instead of a straightforward punishment in terms of a holy and fair law of God, the wrongdoer is subjected to a battery of psychiatric tests, and perhaps then drugs and other forms of treatment. C. S. Lewis mentioned how this kind of psychological therapy actually dehumanized people and kept them from facing their sins and growing up, and maybe even having the chance of getting right with God, because they through a proper dealing out of justice to them, they could come to realize that He is the one to whom they are finally subjected .

An extreme example of this was in the Soviet Union, where the horrible Lubyanka prison in Moscow was a psychiatric prison. Often people who opposed the communist regime, and many others, were convicted, put into this psychiatric prison for healing, and often drugged into being zombies or given electric shock treatment, and other terrible things, supposedly to heal them, so they would go out and support the regime.

Some European countries have already declared it illegal to whip a child. If it gets bad enough, the child might be subjected to the whole therapeutic bureaucracy, rather than appropriately and moderately dealing with his or her faults. That takes away from the parents what God gave them: the responsibility to chastise, to love, to train, and, where needed, to give children the kind of discipline that will help them learn the wisdom of self-control. That's the state coveting what is the parents', and is profoundly sinful and destructive of our culture. If I am not mistaken, we have been reaping the results of that since the 1960s—and maybe longer.

To be a responsible person, somewhere along the line, you have to realize that your actions have consequences; that wrong must be righted. And it can be righted! The good news here is that something can be put right. It says in Proverbs 20:11 and in other places that 'even a child is known by his doings, whether his work be pure, and whether it be right'. A child is responsible. It's a different responsibility for a fifty-year-old man; and a fair justice system will take that into account. But even a child is in the image of God, and is thereby responsible, so the parents have to be sensitive to see about that.

Let me conclude this way: the basis of true justice is for each one to get what he or she deserves. I could give you the old Latin tag for that: *suum cuique*, 'to each his own'. That, by the way, is the very point of why Christ left the glories of heaven and came into a shadowy, hatred-filled world to take our place on the cross of shame, to pay the price of our infinite guilt and sin, and to put us in the right with God, at His own immense expense. Jesus Christ, God's Son in the flesh, rendered His pure and holy soul an offering for sin; He paid what we owed! We couldn't pay that! Jesus paid it on our behalf.

When thinking about what it cost Him, you can't think about it too much: Jesus paying the penalty, taking our punishment, re-establishing true justice between God and man, making it possible for us to be counted righteous, if we believe. Notice two passages about this: Isaiah 53:4–6:

> Surely he hath borne our griefs and carried out sorrows; yet we did esteem him stricken, smitten of God, and afflicted. But he was wounded for our transgressions, he was bruised for our iniquities; the chastisement of our peace was upon him; and with his stripes we are healed. All we like sheep have gone astray; we have turned every one to his own way; and the Lord hath laid on him the iniquity of us all.

Then, in verse 12, this wonderful good news available to every sinner, myself included:

Therefore will I divide him a portion with the great; and he shall divide the spoil with the strong because he hath poured out his soul unto death; and he was numbered with the transgressors [there where I was standing, he came and stood, not only with me but in my place]; and he bare the sin of many [anybody asking for Him to bear his sin—anybody], and made intercession for the transgressors.

And, in a slightly different way, we find the same message in 1 Peter 2:21–24:

> For even hereunto were ye called: because Christ also suffered for us, leaving us an example, that ye should follow his steps; who did not sin, neither was guile found in his mouth; who, when he was reviled, reviled not again; when he suffered, he threatened not; but committed himself to him that judgeth righteously; who his own self bare our sins in his own body on the tree, that we, being dead to sins, should live unto righteousness; by whose stripes ye were healed.

This is the gospel. It's amazing!

So to conclude: Christ honored the principle of fair punishment, *suum cuique:* the punishment of what we deserved as the only way of establishing true justice in the universe. We sinners are saved through faith in Jesus, who came below to render fullest justice to God. In our earthly lives, we seek to honor God's principle of upholding human dignity, by declaring the righteous to be in the right, and declaring the wrong to be guilty, and seeing to it that they are granted a fair and a modest punishment. It is always in the larger context of the unmerited, forgiving, transforming grace of God for whosoever will.

57

Never Covet

Deuteronomy 25:4–19

This section from chapter 25 has the theme 'never covet'. Looking at our country, coveting or envy of others and what they have, is eating up the social fabric of the United States, like car battery acid poured on a fine linen tablecloth. No doubt, some poor people want to get the possessions of the rich, without having to do any work; and some very rich people are never satisfied with what they have, so are willing to seek to manipulate companies, and even influence money supply so as to get more, at the expense of the general public. I don't think there has ever been a time when the Tenth Commandment and what it really means has been any more relevant or needed than in the Western countries today.

These verses are a part of Moses' exposition of what the Tenth Commandment means; it is a profoundly attitudinal commandment. We sometimes say somebody has an 'attitude problem', and this is an attitude question that only the written Word of God, and the blessed Holy Spirit, can change in a person. Now it takes a little bit of thought to connect it all, when you look at the different scenes that Moses describes in these verses. It takes thought to figure out how these different subjects fit into the commandment not to covet, not to strongly desire something God hasn't given you.

These different scenes, five of them that we are going to look at briefly, show us how deep and far reaching into our attitudes, and into our outward actions that flow from our attitudes, is the commandment from God Almighty not to covet, not to eat ourselves up with desire to have what is not ours: first, consideration for working animals, verse 4; second, levirate marriage, verses 5–10; third, unfair, vicious fighting, verses 11–12; fourth, unjust wages and measures—and I would add dishonest bookkeeping verses 13–16; fifth, blotting out the godless tribe, the Amalekites, verses 17–19. These five things all make sense in light of 'Thou shalt not covet'.

Consideration for Working Animals (25:4)

It may surprise us that verse 4 deals with caring for animals, but it should be no surprise, for God's Word covers everything in principle, in order to help us to cope with the real world, including animals. It is because 'This is my Father's world'; even the animals belong to my Father.

I was coming two weeks ago from Monroe, North Carolina, to Pageland, South Carolina, on the way from Charlotte to Dillon, and I saw something I had never seen before. It was a small black bear, maybe 50 pounds, that had been hit by a car; he had obviously run into the road and been killed, and was lying there beside the road. I didn't know bears had gotten that far up towards Charlotte. I thought, this is God's animal. God's sparrow falls to the ground, not without the will of God. The oxen that were used in ancient Israel, and still are in India and various parts of Africa are used to do a great deal of heavy work, and are in the Father's purview.

In Israel, the oxen would be hitched up to a sledge, and when the grain, the wheat, barley or spelt, was reaped, they would put the grain on a stone threshing floor, and cause the oxen to walk over the grain with the sledge—back and forth—so that the sledge would mash the grain and separate it from the stalks. In that context, the Lord says 'do not muzzle the mouth of the ox', a sign of God's consideration for animal life so that, from time to time, the hardworking ox could benefit a little from the blessings of the harvest.

That's the kind of God we serve; He cares about the animals, in the spirit of Psalm 145:15–16: 'The eyes of all wait upon thee; and thou givest them their meat in due season. Thou openest Thine hand, and satisfiest the desire of every living thing'. An ox, a bird, and a fish are living things, and it's to God's glory that their appetite, one way or another, be satisfied. The general principle is in Psalm 145:9; this is the kind of God we serve; now remember what He is like: 'The Lord is good to all and his tender mercies are over all his works'. We could say this: God is like that and wants us to become like that, with tender mercy, insofar as you are able, to everything you come in contact with. In other words, true godliness, true sainthood, engenders a kindness, even towards animals, where appropriate. Proverbs 12:10 says 'A righteous man regardeth the life of his beast'.

Paul takes this same verse 4 of Deuteronomy 25, into human life. In 1 Corinthians 9:9 he says that Christian people are to provide financial aid for those who spend their lives laboring in the Word, since they generally do not have time to hold a secular job in order to earn much of an income. God always richly repays generosity, whether towards animals or towards the servants of Christ. Not to give them their fair due is covetous, and when we are covetous, instead of making us happy it makes us unhappy and dissatisfied, and we lose tremendous blessing.

Levirate Marriage (25:5–10)

The word 'levirate' comes from Latin *levir*, the Latin word for brother-in-law. The idea is that one of God's chief mercies in created human life would be that you have descendants. God does not give every good believer a descendant, but the general rule is that it is a blessing of God for a man and a woman to have children to carry on the spiritual heritage, keep the land, and carry on the family name. Sometimes though, a godly man and woman marry, and suddenly the husband dies. Therefore, his young wife is a widow before she is able to have any children. So the Lord makes merciful provision for young widows to enable them to be remarried in the faith, and to raise up children in honor of the deceased husband. The law provided that she would be able to marry her brother-in-law, her deceased husband's unmarried brother, if he had one. It was generally thought to be his duty to marry the bereaved sister-in-law.

This still takes place among Christians in Kenya. Many of you remember Rev. Samuel Maina, a wonderful African pastor, who plans to be a seminary professor in Africa. Samuel visited us and preached here at Reedy Creek and at First Presbyterian, in Dillon. When I was teaching in Jackson, Mississippi, Samuel was one of my students. His wife came from Kenya, a beautiful Christian woman of much faith and character. She had needed open heart surgery but died during surgery. I was with them during that trying time. They took her body home to be buried in Kenya.

In two or three years, it was the custom with the people he came from that he would marry his deceased wife's unmarried sister, and so he did. I have met her, and she is also a lovely Christian woman. The custom of marrying a brother-in-law extends in Kenya also to a sister-in-law. That way you can keep the land in the family. and the first child that would be born, would be named for the deceased, so the name would not die out in history.

This shows us that God is considerate of our desires and feelings; and, in case a brother-in-law does not want to marry his bereaved sister-in-law, He has provided a way he could get out of it, by going through a legal ceremony, before the elders, in which the rejected sister-in-law spat in his face as a sign of humiliating the man for not being willing to take this responsibility. Then she was to pull off one of his sandals, because one of the ways to show ownership of land in Israel was to walk with your two feet and plant your feet on the land. Although legal documents were put into a clay jar showing your having bought the land, you also had to walk on the land to make it yours. Taking his shoe off, means he cannot have the land that he would have had, if he had married his brother's widow.

We see the levirate law in the book of Ruth. When Boaz, who wasn't as much kin, said I will gladly marry Ruth, he was fulfilling the law of levirate marriage. Now, we have a Lord and Savior Jesus Christ, who is our 'kinsman redeemer.' God is His Father, but He enters into the womb of the virgin Mary, to be made a true human, and thus in a position to represent us, His kinsmen, according to the flesh. This 'kinsman redeemer' takes us on in our poverty, and as our 'next-of-kin', ushers us into His untold wealth. We recall that His physical descent, through the virgin Mary, goes back to Boaz and Ruth through David and Jesse. So Boaz and Ruth, obeying this law for Old Testament Israel, is what the Lord used to provide the entire world this glorious Savior Jesus Christ. It shows us that God's way of doing things is always the front door to fuller blessing.

Unfair, Vicious Fighting (25:11-12)
It bears repeating: the Bible is very realistic. It never hides from us the fact that life in this fallen world can be nasty and dangerous. Because of that, God gives us a right way to cope with some of the worst things that can happen, to keep ourselves from doing evil. In this case, there is a fight between two men, and the wife of one of them decides to intervene in the fight, to give an advantage to her husband. It is never said that a wife cannot help her husband in a fight, but God's law prohibits the wife taking the adversary by 'the secrets' because that might disable him later from being able to carry on the family name by reproducing.

Now if a wife did a thing like that, which is so strictly forbidden, then she was to be severely punished. Fighting must not be vicious, and especially, it must not be done in a way that would cut off lines of possible descent in the future, because childbearing is one of the chief blessings of God to His people. Apparently, Moses considered that such vicious action would be coveting someone's future family line, by taking such action against him, when at a disadvantage, that would disable him from having a family.

Unjust Weights and Measures (25:13–16)

It does not take much contemplation to see why weights and measures are to be even-handed - the same for everybody. We can read from other extra-biblical texts about business practices in the ancient Middle East. There are accounts of merchants with two different sets of weights; one for buying, and another for selling, manipulating the uneven weights to make more money at the expense of the customer. Amos 8:5 indicates that this dishonest practice had come into Israel and would bring down divine judgment: 'When will the new moon be gone, that we may sell corn? And the Sabbath, that we may set forth wheat, making the ephah small, and the shekel great, and falsifying the balances by deceit?' That is a prime instance of coveting. How many law suits are jamming the court dockets, because of various forms of coveting through people using dishonest weights and measures?

We were all taught, by parents or in school, that honesty is the best policy. That's not just an old saying; it summarizes the truth of God Himself:

> A false balance is an abomination to the Lord; but a just weight is his delight. When pride cometh, then cometh shame; but with the lowly is wisdom. The integrity of the upright shall guide them, but the perverseness of transgressors shall destroy them. [That might be why some economies break down.] Riches profit not in the day of wrath; but righteousness delivereth from death. The righteousness of the perfect shall direct his way; but the wicked shall fall by his own wickedness. The righteousness of the upright shall deliver them; but transgressors shall be taken in their own naughtiness (Prov. 11:1–6).

I try to read the *Wall Street Journal,* and from what I can tell, the juggling of financial reports in big companies, in order to make quarterly stock reports look better, and sell more shares—along with other dishonest practices—has been one of the major factors in the breakdown in what was once the world's greatest economy. Covetousness, leading to lying and dishonest practices to advantage one's business, advance one's career and get larger end-of-year bonuses and promotions costs our economy and society a great deal. When God said: 'Thou shalt not covet,' it required honest balances, fair measures, and honest accounting; no cheating and lying in business.

Cutting Off the Amalekites (25:17–19)

The Amalekites were a war-like desert tribe, who were especially hostile to Israel and the one true God, hating God and also the Israelites because they represented God. That hereditary hatred continued for hundreds and hundreds of years. So, God is saying, blot them out, and a major problem will be taken care of.

We meet the Amalekites, in Exodus 17, soon after Israel had come through the Red Sea into the wilderness. Israel was organized with the elderly, sick and weak at the back end of the camp; and perhaps not unlike a hospital brigade, were carried slowly along as best they could. The Amalekites had spies, and so knew about 'the hospital brigade'; so they took vicious advantage of Israel, and attacked the elderly, sick, and weak, with no soldiers to protect them.

The Amalekites apparently were better equipped and may have outnumbered Israel in trained fighting men. And Joshua leads the Israelite troops against the hostile God-hating Amalekites. But Israel had a weapon that the

Amalekites didn't know about; it was a secret weapon, one we should take hold of today.

Moses, with his hands held up in intercessory prayer, is up on a mountain looking down and interceding all day long, until the battle is won against this greater enemy. Victory against overwhelming odds was given in answer to prayer. Yet they did not disappear.

Later, King Saul lost his throne for refusing to obey the command to blot out the Amalekites. In 1 Samuel 14-15 he spared them, because he coveted their goods—cattle, sheep and other forms of wealth—and thought he didn't have to go strictly by what God said. Saul overrode God's command, and lost his throne for it.

Then generations later, in the book of Esther, is the great enemy of the Jews at that time, Haman, a man in high position in the empire. We read that he was an Agagite, which was a latter day, direct descendent of the Amalekites. He was jealous for the wealth they had gathered by honest labor, and he especially hated them because they represented the one true God. Being very close to the emperor, Ahasuerus, he arranged a pogrom to wipe out all the Jews, hoping to kill every one.

But a godly Jewish man, Mordecai, who had a niece named Esther, got word that Haman had gathered the political power to wipe out the people of God. Mordecai then sent word to his niece, wife of the mighty emperor: 'Go to your husband, Ahasuerus, and intercede for the Jews'.

She would be taking her life in her hands, but she said, 'I will intercede, if you will get the people of God to fast and pray on my behalf'. To go into the king's presence uncalled for, could end in losing your life, unless he extended the golden scepter. So all Israel fasted and prayed that God would make him do so. And through the intercession of the saints God overcame one of the most wicked plots in all history.

We can't always get rid of Amalekites; they keep emerging in new forms. But here is the encouraging teaching of the Word of God: satanically-inspired enemies of God and Christ and His people can be handled through intercessory prayer. Fussing or despairing is uncalled for, because Christ is risen!

So what can we do? Get in touch with the risen Christ on His throne in intercession, which can defeat the covetous designs of immoral, selfish multitudes. Intercession can make supernatural changes; we don't know how God will do it, but he can do it for the benefit of his people. Any time he deems they have prayed enough, he will intervene and interpose his power to turn things in a better direction. What you can say is this: believing prayer accomplishes the impossible. Jesus says: 'The things which are impossible with men are possible with God' (Luke 18:27). Once you live your life counting numbers in order to assess what might happen in terms of human possibilities, and hopelessly trying to be with the popular crowd, you are living on a naturalistic, humanistic basis.

That's not how God instructs His servants to work. Instead, we are to come with very little, bow down, and call out in Jesus' name as we intercede. The intercession of God's people in the name of Jesus, who has all power in heaven and on earth, becomes a bridge between heaven and earth, so that the power of God comes down and accomplishes the impossible. That is what we are called to do.

Listen to this hymn:

> Christian! seek not yet repose,
> hear thy guardian angel say;
> thou art in the midst of foes;
> watch and pray.

Deuteronomy

Principalities and powers,
mustering their unseen array,
wait for thy unguarded hours;
watch and pray.

Gird thy heavenly armor on,
wear it ever night and day;
ambushed lies the evil one;
watch and pray.

Hear the victors who o'ercame;
still they mark each warrior's way;
all with one clear voice exclaim,
watch and pray.

Hear, above all, hear thy Lord,
him thou lovest to obey;
hide within thy heart his word,
watch and pray.

Watch, as if on that alone
hung the issue of the day;
pray that help may be sent down;
watch and pray.

~ Charlotte Elliott

58

Tithing of First Fruits

Deuteronomy 26:1–15

This section is about the tithing of our first fruits, and part of a larger section where Moses is explaining what the tenth commandment means in practical life—'Thou shalt not covet'. Coveting makes a person dissatisfied and unhappy, on the inside, and frequently hard to get on with—perhaps bitter and sharp, on the outside as they deal with people. It is to be avoided like the plague, especially by true Christians; it's the last thing we want to give way to.

Moses is giving us a positive way to overcome a very negative force in the lives of many, helping us overcome any tendency to covet what others have, by means of faithful tithing. How?

Coveting means you're focusing on what you want, and perhaps what somebody else has that you don't have, whereas tithing means you are thinking about what you can do for somebody else, and how you can be a blessing in the kingdom of God. Tithing means giving; coveting is based on wanting. So the healthiest, happiest people psychologically and spiritually, are those who focus not on getting, but on giving. This kind of giving instead of bringing you loss, gains you far more than you gave away.

We note four points in this text: first, we tithe our increase to God's kingdom, verses 1–4; second, we confess the faith anew, verses 5–10; third, we remember the purposes of the special third year tithe for poor people, verses 12–13; and fourth, we pray for a divine blessing upon those who tithe, verses 14–15.

We Tithe Our Increase to God's Kingdom (26:1–4)

In an agricultural economy, one brought the tithes of the first fruits to the sanctuary—wheat, grapes, olives, etc. In Dillon County, you might bring one bale of cotton out of ten. One tenth of the increase was dedicated to the purposes of the kingdom of God, and administered by the priests and the Levites. In our post-industrial society, even if you're a farmer, the store of value and medium of exchange is cash. So we tithe our regular cash income, and bring it to the modern equivalent of the storehouse, namely God's church.

There are hard passages in Scripture; this passage is not one of them; it is among the clearest in the Bible, simple and straightforward. The problem is not lack of clarity, but the will to obey a simple command from God. Jesus said: 'If ye love me, keep my commandments' (John 14:15). And tithing is one of the crucial commandments coming out of the principle of not coveting, setting our spirit free not to be niggardly, but to be loving. If we love Jesus, it is not at all hard to figure out what we are going to do with the 10% of what the Lord allows us to gain.

We Confess the Faith Anew (26:5–10)

It is possible that these verses constitute the first of the biblically based creeds in all of history, not unlike reciting the Apostles' or Nicene Creed, hundreds of years later. In Deuteronomy 26, the faithful people brought the tithe into the Lord's presence, and recite these sacred words to recall how good God had been to them and to their ancestors, and had redeemed them.

This shows us that tithing is a response to the love of God. I can't imagine that somebody whose heart is hard, or somebody controlled by bitterness, would be very much of a tither. Yet it is possible; the Pharisees, I suppose show that, but in general, tithing comes from a heart that is grateful to God for His goodness.

This confession states the basics of what God has done for His people, the farmers of Israel, everything going back in sacred memory to their father Jacob, also called Israel. He wandered about in tents, from place to place, seeking 'a city which hath foundations, whose builder and maker is God' (Heb. 11:10). He is called in the Authorized Version a 'wandering Syrian'—in the Hebrew it would be closer to say 'wandering Aramean'.

Aramea is roughly what is today called Iraq, in the Fertile Crescent. Jacob got into trouble from having cheated his brother Esau, so that he had to flee. Yet God met him, and got him through the difficulties of living with his Uncle Laban, who gave him his two wives, but also cheated Jacob many times. After several years, Jacob decided to come back to his elderly father Isaac, and to face the probable wrath of his brother Esau, whom he had painfully offended. Yet God answered his desperate prayers for protection from Esau and his small army. He came back 'with two bands'—that is, with two wives, and a number of children. So, this far-from-perfect patriarch, Jacob, was greatly blessed.

In later years, a terrible famine occurred; everything was drying up. But Jacob was still not forsaken by God, for through His strange providence of using evil to bring about good, He let Joseph to be sold into slavery, who prepared the way for his elderly father, Jacob, and the other eleven patriarchs, to go down into Egypt for refuge, so they could survive and do well. These things are recalled in this creed or confession.

Egypt was a place of blessing, but was soon to become a place of testing, for the descendants of Jacob. The whole of earthly life often combines those two things. I have never known of anybody who lived an earthly life and got nothing but blessing. It is not possible in God's providential plan for us. You will get much blessing, and I believe, as a Christian, you will get more blessing than testing, but you are also going to get testing.

Why? Because God is shaping your character for eternity; we'd be mushy jellyfish if we got nothing but blessing; I reckon most of us are sinful enough to wish we got nothing but blessing, but it's not possible. Blessing predominates, I believe, for the Lord's people; but there is also testing, trials, and hurts. So, there was a blessing: the people of Israel increased from less than 200, within 430 years, to well over a million people—a massive increase, a massive blessing. But in the later years, they were enslaved and beaten, and cruelly mistreated. But then God intervened.

God heard their crying, their tears, their groans, and, remembering the covenant He had made with Abraham, Isaac, and Jacob, he intervened and did many a miracle to get them out of Egypt, through the Red Sea, through the wilderness, into a beautiful land that flowed with milk and honey.

This ancient confession reminds us of something important for every believer—the mystery of election. Have you ever wondered, why should I be a Christian, when other people I know, who are smarter than I am, better looking than I am, richer than I am, are not believers, and are not going to heaven, unless they change? Why would somebody like you and me in the providence of God have been chosen? Why did we hear the gospel and believe it, and come over the line in faith and repentance? Why? It is the mystery of election; there's no explanation of it.

We must never think, however, that our being Christian means that we are somehow superior or finer than others; that can't be right. Israel wasn't, and we're not. The relation is based on God and His choice and His love, not on us. 'The Lord did not set His love upon you, nor choose you, because ye were more in number than any people, for ye were the fewest of all people; but because the Lord loved you' (Deut. 7:7-8). That's it! Election goes back to the love of God, and you stop with that—the love of God. Why am I a Christian? It's the love of God. Didn't your mom and dad believe? Yes, but why did they believe? It's the love of God. Were they perfect? No. So how are you a Christian? It is the mystery of election in which the last word behind it all is the sheer love of God to the unworthy, the few, the nothing.

St. Paul says much the same:

> 'For ye see your calling, brethren, how that not many wise men after the flesh, not many mighty, not many noble, are called; but God hath chosen the foolish things of the world to confound the wise; and God hath chosen the weak things of the world to confound the things which are mighty; and base things of the world, and things which are despised, hath God chosen, yea, and things which are not, to bring to nought things that are.' (1 Cor. 1:26-29)

We base nothing—and I can believe I'm in the group—nothing on ourselves; and on such, God mysteriously and wondrously laid His matchless love, 'that no flesh should glory in his presence'.

Similarly in Romans 9:9-11: 'For the children' [Rebekah, Isaac, Jacob, and Esau] 'being not yet born, neither having done any good or evil, that the purpose of God might stand, not of works but of Him that calleth'. So even after I get saved, it is not in consideration of my works that God would have saved me. He set me apart, He chose me, before I was in any position to do any works; it depends on Him who calls; it depends on God, which is, to our human minds, a mystery.

We are nothing! Yet He lifted us up, chose us, called us to Himself in Christ, and saved us, and will get us home to heaven. How do we express our gratitude for that? One of the major things you can do is to give to God's work, the tithe, and do all you can to help the poor and the needy. Matthew 25 tells us that on the last great day when the whole universe is assembled, Jesus will say, 'I was in jail and you came and visited me; I was poor and naked and you brought money and clothes and you helped me.' And His people reply, 'Lord, when did we do that?' Jesus answers, 'Inasmuch as ye have done it to one of these, the least of my brethren, ye have done it unto me.'

That is how we pay back Jesus, by helping those who are needy.

REMEMBER THE PURPOSE OF THE SPECIAL THIRD YEAR TITHE (26:12-13)

Israel was required to tithe every year, but a special tithe was appointed every three years to help the sojourner—what we would call today the landless immigrant—the orphan, the widow, or those in society who are disadvantaged economically. The church is to reach out to them with special care, if we are going to show who Jesus is.

We could call this God's effective welfare program. In every society, whether a democracy, monarchy, dictatorship, or tribal, you are always going to have poor, needy and disadvantaged people. Every third year, a special tithe was taken up, to be administered to those in some kind of need.

Jesus said that the essence of the law is: 'Thou shalt love the Lord thy God with all thy heart, thy soul, thy mind, and strength, and thy neighbor as thyself.' It is impossible to love God sincerely and truly, and not reach out a helping hand to the neighbor in need, whether at home or abroad.

According to 1 John 3–4 it is impossible to love God, whom you have not seen, if you do not care for the brother in need, whom you have indeed seen. When I was about twenty, I lived a year in France, and went every Sunday to the French Reformed Church. I noticed that after every communion service, it was a law of the French Reformed Church to take up another collection after the service, for the poor and the disadvantaged people in the parish, whether church members or not.

Today, in the United States, many churches have a food bank to help anyone in crisis. My mother used to pull a shift at a soup kitchen run by the Episcopalian and the Presbyterian women of Lumberton for poor people. She went every so many days with the other good church women. Most boards of deacons in any church keep a fund to assist those in crisis. In today's declining economy, with people losing jobs, houses, cars and so forth, I would say we are going to need more of this kind of practical mercy than ever.

I heard my mother and father and grandparents talk about the depression, when I was younger, so I know something about it from family talk. I'm not saying what lies ahead will be a depression; I have no way to know that; I hope not. I was told that during the depression, many churches and individual believers found ways to help the poor. These were a valid, modern application of the third year special tithe, and will demonstrate to a secular society, which has written off God and the Bible, who God really is, what his love and mercy are. We need to remember that the opportunities that lie ahead really are just that: opportunities, not burdens; an effective way to touch many a life that would never listen to the confession made by Israelite farmers: 'A wandering Aramean was my father …', and God did this and God did that for us. The only way some people will listen to that confession is when they are being helped by the believers.

A Prayer for Divine Blessing Upon All Who Are Tithing (26:14–15)

This is a prayer for those who are going in the opposite direction from coveting; that is, those who are tithing to the Lord, and giving to the needy. In both yearly and third-year tithing, it showed that God had already blessed them, to have given them enough money both to live on, and to have something left over to assist others.

This special tithe for the poor is like saying: Lord, do it again; you have blessed us in the past; Lord, do it again! Keep doing it; keep doing it! In a sense, every act of tithing, every act of relieving the needs of the disadvantaged, is a prayer for more of the blessing of God in our lives so that we can continue being a blessing.

God said to Abraham, 'I will bless thee and make thee a blessing!' And so, God blesses us, not to stop with us, but that the waters of mercy and living waters of faith and purity and truth break forth through us, as we are available to help the work of God's church, and to help the needy whether at home or far away.

> Bring ye all the tithes into the storehouse, that there may be meat in mine house, and prove me now herewith, saith the Lord of hosts, if I will not open you the windows of heaven, and pour you out a blessing, that there shall not be room enough to receive it (Malachi 3:10).

God does give us the legitimate right to test Him in this way. He says, 'I will be glad for you to test me, and see if I am true to my Word; see if I carry out my promise in your life; and here's how: bring the tithe to the church, and continue special giving to the needy; bring it, and then watch very carefully what I'm going to do in your life and in your circumstances. See if I am who I said I will be; I give you the right to test me at this point.'

I will say this in closing: if any of us are worried about the future—we may be in for all kinds of changes—what could we do to make the future better? Here's one thing: we can tithe faithfully to the Lord, and give more generously than ever to the needs around us or far away. You can't change elections and things like that, but we can give as generously as possible, as faithfully as possible. God says, 'Now watch! Be on the lookout and see if I do not open the windows of heaven and pour you out such blessing that you cannot receive it; it will be more than you can take in, and it doesn't matter who is in office; that has nothing to do with it. You be faithful to me, and I am going to do something that you will know about.'

59

The Covenant Confirmed

Deuteronomy 26:16–19

These verses show us the covenant confirmed: a covenant is made and then here confirmed. Most of us are married, or at least, we have all been to weddings, and we remember the high point when the sacred vows were taken. Marriage is a kind of covenant. One confirms the marriage covenant in words like these: 'I John, take thee Mary; I Mary, take thee John.' Those words constitute the confirmation of the most sacred covenant we can make in this life, other than when we profess faith in Jesus Christ before the church, which is the most sacred.

This kind of covenant confirmation is presented in this text. It sweeps back to the fifth chapter of Deuteronomy, and it includes all of Moses' exposition in between. Moses has been explaining what it means to be a holy people, a godly people, dare I say a beautiful people, in the Promised Land, essentially saying, you must reflect God's character. This brings us to the confirmation of the covenant, in these verses, where God promises something to us and we promise something to Him—like a marriage—with mutual promises of the most sacred and binding nature.

This text prefigures what we find in the New Testament, as it describes how individual believers profess Jesus Christ as their Lord and Saviour. First, these verses in Deuteronomy 26 show us what Israel promises to God, verses 16–17; secondly, what God promises to Israel, verses 18–19. The whole of a godly and happy life on earth, and stretching into eternity, is included in confirming this personal and corporate covenant with the gracious Lord God Almighty.

What Israel Promises to the Lord (26:16–17)

Note that God is the one who specifies what Israel is to promise Him. In fact, God sets up marriage, and, though we are not given exact words, we are told the point of what we are to promise to our spouse. God also sets up what happens when we join the church; again, not the exact words, as in the Book of Church Order, but the basic thing we are to do, the terms of the covenant. God, sets up what He wants Israel to promise to be and to do, if they are going to live as His people, and be taken into eternal life and blessing. Israel is told to promise God with all of its heart to keep God's commandments and to love God with all the heart and soul.

First, keep My commandments, verse 16. Moses has minutely explained exactly how to walk in the Lord's light, by unfolding the outworking of each one of the Ten Commandments. Jesus summarizes the Ten Commandments this way: love the Lord your God, with all your heart, mind, soul, and strength; and your neighbor as yourself. We could not possibly be loving God and our neighbor, if we steal from them, bear false witness against them, or even kill them. Those things are precluded, because the God of love and holiness calls us to walk in love and holiness, which means treating people in a right way.

Of course we know that no human being since the fall of Adam and Eve could possibly do everything right. But Jesus came, not only to die for our sins, but to keep the law as our substitute, as our Head, as our Representative; Jesus keeps the covenant in our place, that Adam should have kept and Israel should have kept and didn't. Jesus perfectly fulfills the law; He loved God above everything. You see that in the Gospel of Luke, where He gets up well before day to pray to His Father, taking all His desires, and focusing them on God; and in the Gospel of Matthew, in Gethsemane, saying: 'Not my will but thine be done'. Jesus renders to the Father heart-felt, perfect, total keeping of the law in my and your place, if we are believers. He fully keeps the law of God in our place, and pays the penalty of my sin, when He dies on Calvary. These two realities are both good news: together they constitute the gospel. When I die and go before the Lord, the Lord will, in a very real sense, consider my life, which has been so imperfect and so weak at its best, to have been perfectly righteous, to have kept every aspect of the law, in motive and in outworking towards God and towards man, because of Jesus' life in my place.

Yes! Jesus did it in my place. God sees me when I pray, and hears me when I pray, as if He were hearing the voice of Jesus. When I leave this body and go into His presence, He sees the likeness of His Son who loved Him from the heart and kept all His commandments, as our representative. Jesus did it, and we were in union with Him through the Holy Spirit in His doing of it.

However, the fact that Jesus kept the law for us does not mean that we have no relationship to law-keeping. We're saved by Christ, not by the law; that's clear. But Jesus never revoked the Ten Commandments for His people. Read the Sermon on the Mount in Matthew 5, and see if Jesus ever said: 'Christians don't need to keep the law.' Of course not! He explains what the law means; He offers cleansing in His blood when we don't do it, and He offers the filling of the Holy Spirit to help us do it better. To know Jesus is to be face to face with the heavenly Father and to seek to walk in His will, and to carry out His good law. 'If ye love me, keep my commandments' (John 14:15). We cannot sincerely profess that we love Jesus, if we willfully live a life of breaking His commandments. 'So first, keep My commandments.'

The second thing Israel promises in these holy vows is to God, who says, 'Love Me with all your heart and soul.' The prophecy of Jeremiah 31 perhaps more clearly than any other chapter in the Old Testament ties together Old and New Testaments. Particularly verse 31, Jeremiah promises that in the new phase of the covenant of grace, God the Holy Spirit will come into somebody who is a sinner, but is beginning to believe, and will write on the fleshly tables of their heart, the law, the Ten Commandments, in living letters. That's a graphic way of saying that when you become a Christian, when you come to the Lord, the Holy Spirit gets inside your spirit and radically changes your deepest desires.

How? Nobody can say, other than to say that we are embodied, created spirits, while the Holy Spirit is an uncreated Spirit, who therefore, as infinite God, is able to come inside the deepest wellsprings of my created spirit, and change my most basic motivations, so that now, I really do want to please God our heavenly Father, to walk in His will, to do His law. That's part of regeneration, new birth, and God Himself makes this supernatural change in us.

Yet even though in the new birth, we really do wish to please God, we often don't live up to it. We still have to fight with the flesh, with the remnants of indwelling sin. We see in Romans 7:21: 'When I do right, evil is with me'. Yet even in this struggle, the desire to be and do right, so as to please your heavenly Father never goes away. Therefore when you sin, within you there is going to be a drawing back to God; you will be sorry about it and repent.

Let me ask you this: is the difference between a Christian and a non-believer the fact that the Christian never sins and the non-believer does sin? That can't be right. Christians do commit sin: 'If we say we have no sin, we deceive ourselves, and the truth is not in us' (1 John 1:8). So what is the difference between the Christian who has committed some kind of sin, and the non-believer who lives in sin?

Christians, at least, no longer live in sin as their native atmosphere. The difference is that, unlike the non-believer, the Christian will be repentant and grieved that they let the Lord down. The non-believer's only worry is that they might be inconvenienced if caught.

Without wanting to be judgmental or go into details, I remember when a famous televangelist had a serious moral fall (in the 1980s). I thought the saddest thing about it was that he seemed only to be concerned with losing the finances that supported his ministry. From what he was reported to have said, he did not appear to be sorry to have dishonored God, and hurt the church. If you are God's child, who has the law of the Lord written on your heart to please the Father, you may seriously fall and do something very wrong. But if so, you will be broken, grieved, and willingly withdraw, at least for a while, to show humble repentance at having let down the Lord.

I have sometimes wondered what the key to Proverbs could be. Of course, the key to the book of Proverbs is probably: 'The fear of the Lord is the beginning of wisdom and the knowledge of the holy is understanding.' But maybe deeper than that, the Lord says, 'My son, give me thy heart.' A Christmas carol—In the Bleak Midwinter—by an English lady, Christina Rossetti, says in its last verse:

> What can I give Him,
> Poor as I am?
> If I were a shepherd
> I would bring a lamb,
> If I were a wise man,
> I would do my part,
> Yet what I can I give Him?
> Give Him my heart.

That's what God wants. You can't bring perfection to the Lord; you have to look to Jesus for that. Your heart, the real you, is what God is interested in; give Him that by the help of His Spirit, and all these other things will certainly work out.

Verse 17 says, 'Thou hast avouched the Lord this day to be thy God'. Much like the wedding vows, what you are saying is 'Lord, I am all Yours.' Don't get married until you can say to that other person, 'I am all yours.' We say that much more profoundly, of course, to our Savior. Many of you will know other gospel hymns about giving the heart.

While our relationship to God is not primarily legal but one of most tender love, we do seek to walk in the law to please the Lord and to be helpful to others, because God loves us and we love Him. Jesus said: 'If ye love me, keep my commandments'. The law is given in a tender, passionate love-relationship between God and His people.

Evangelism works when the sinful, unbelieving world sees an obedient Christian people, a loving kind of people, and through them perceives that God is real and God is love. Then you can do your evangelism, and your witness to the gospel has some credibility. But when the church is unholy, disobedient, and unloving, it causes the watching, skeptical world to think that atheism is perfectly justified. I don't believe that the European enlightenment, with its terrible unbelief in the eighteenth century, could have occurred, if the church had stayed holy and loving. God wants us to be obedient, and to that end, He wants our heart.

What the Lord Promises to Israel (26:18–19)

The Authorized Version of verse 18 says, '*The Lord hath avouched thee to be his peculiar people*'; '*peculiar*' in modern translations is properly rendered 'treasured' people. The Lord of Lords and King of Kings, the sovereign, majestic potentate of the universe, from the splendid throne of glory, looks down on us believing mortals (still imperfect, but believing in Jesus) and considers us to be His treasure! Think of that!

The One before whom stretch the streets of gold in the celestial city, and the gates of pearl and all the splendid beauty of the heavenly world, considers the likes of us to be His special treasure. Before Thanksgiving, I went to the bank safety deposit box to take out some of the old family sterling silver to be used at the banquet; I then returned the 'treasure' to the deposit box for another time. Any reasonable person wishes to take good care of an irreplaceable family treasure. Now God thinks far more of us than we think of the most wonderful centuries-old family silver—no comparison!

God treasures all His children, His blood-bought, ransomed children, far more than any earthly thing you and I may have inherited. I wish we could believe it: how much God thinks of us and treasures us? Go to the cross and you will find out—to the last drop of the cleansing blood.

I remember, as a teenager, hearing one of the older members of our extended family say about someone else, their parents were 'pitifully fond of them', that they absolutely loved this child. I hope it is respectful to say that God is 'pitifully fond of us' as children. I can still hear my great-aunt saying those words, and they struck my fancy.

We find out at the cross that God's greatest treasure was His well-loved, only-begotten Son, His eternal Son in closest union with Him, and He gave Him to go through all He went through, so that through His person and work, we could become God's own treasure. That's how much He thinks of us! Don't ever have light thoughts of how much God thinks of you, or how profound and deep, far reaching, sweet and kind and self-sacrificing is the love of God to sinners! Say to yourself at the beginning of every year, 'This year I'm going to think more about the love of God to me and to His people.' Some of you will know the hymn:

> His love has no limit, His grace has no measure;
> His power has no boundary known unto men.
> For out of His infinite riches in Jesus,
> He giveth, and giveth, and giveth again.

God considers us His treasure—that's the first thing.

As part of his 'wedding promise' to His people, God promises 'to make thee high above all nations which he hath made' (verse 19). God is pledged in sacred wedding vows to exalt His people. I want to add some thoughts from other parts of Scripture, and not least from Deuteronomy.

God exalts His people, even though they are not yet sinlessly perfect. Still, if they are really His, they realize their weakness and their need and unworthiness, and find their holiness in the grace of God, not in themselves. God exalts such people, particularly insofar as they are little in their own eyes. Isn't that a paradox?

How could anybody get elected politically if they are little in their own eyes? Much of the press tries to kill you anyway! Proper humility goes totally against human society; how does a humble person get elected to anything? That shows how far off our thinking is from the will of God. But it is precisely as we are little in our own eyes, that God is in a position to lift us up.

Moses is described here as the meekest, the humblest man in all the earth. But remember that he is the very one, whose face, when he came down from the mountain, was shining out with the light of God so brightly, that the people were terrified with the holiness of God getting that close. So they asked him to put on a veil. The text specifically says that Moses did not know his face was shining. He didn't feel special and holy and bright and resplendent. He only knew that he had been in the presence of God, and knew how wonderful God was. He was little in his own eyes.

God can afford to lift up before the nations, only a humble people, who find their glory in the Lord, not in themselves. It may become more difficult in years ahead in our culture, for true Christian people, but if so, we will have a chance, by our humble circumstances, to reflect more brightly than ever, the beautiful light of God in the moral darkness that is descending on secularized nations. All you need is a humble people, taken up with the glory of God, whose light begins to shine through them. Then by and by, the country might change again in the right direction, if that should be in God's secret will.

In closing, I want us to turn to the New Testament, to Ephesians 1 and 2, and see how God's promise to lift up His humble, believing people, works out after Christ has come. Especially in Ephesians 1:20-23, it speaks of the resurrection power of Christ that comes in and makes us Christians,

> Which he wrought in Christ, when he raised him from the dead, and set him at His own right hand in the heavenly places, far above all principality, and power, and might, and dominion, and every name that is named, not only in this world, but also in that which is to come; and hath put all things under his feet, and gave him to be the head over all things to the church, which is his body, the fullness of Him that filleth all in all.

Our exaltation is because our Head is exalted, Christ our Representative, our Master, the Person who fulfills the covenant for us; He is on the throne and is lifting us up, as we are taken up with Him. The devil can't stop it. Then in Ephesians 2, notice verses 4-6:

> But God, who is rich in mercy, for his great love wherewith he loved us, even when we were dead in sins, hath quickened us together with Christ (by grace you are saved)'; and then get this in verse 6— every Christian, the humblest one of the lot, the little child, the old man or woman broken down in the rest home: 'and hath raised us up together [that means together with Christ], and made us sit together in heavenly places in Christ Jesus.

Thinking of final things, what is the goal of your life? Surely the highest goal you could have for your life would be Christ-likeness, being more taken up with Him and lifted up with Him, and have Him shining through you in the particular circumstances that His providence determines for you. That is the background of all true evangelism, of getting men and women saved, of reaching an unbelieving culture. It's not cleverly arguing philosophy—I'm willing to try to do that—but, in most cases, that's not likely to make a lot of difference. It's simply this: Christ-likeness, shining out of humble men and women in their daily life, takes unbelieving hearts captive, and breaks them open, to be translated from the darkness into God's marvelous light, when they see it in somebody else. Surely that's the highest goal you could have for the rest of your life. It's fine to have fifty goals, or a 'bucket list' as the popular saying goes. Well and good! But this is the highest, and all the other 49 should fit into this one.

I will close with this question: what do you think God is going to be doing during the rest of our lives on earth? Well, according to Deuteronomy 26:16–19, and according to the verses in Ephesians 1–2, God is involved in the business of exalting His people, and the exaltation occurs the more rapidly, the lower they are in their own eyes, and the higher He is in their eyes. Supernatural wonders occur in people who are watching, often when we are least aware of it. God will be exalting His people as they go down the road, and we ask Him that we could be among them.

60

Curses of the Covenant

Deuteronomy 27: 1–26

This chapter deals with the curses of the covenant, and later, we will look at the 28th chapter, which relates the blessings of the covenant. The pronouncing, in responsorial fashion, of the consequences of the violation of the basic law of God—a series of cursing—took place at an outdoor ceremony. We must consider this ceremony which confirms the law, and what is required by it. The ceremony itself was unusual in the history of Israel, but the nature of it may not be entirely strange to us today.

Some of you go to college football bowl games, and in a sense, the gathering of thousands of people, sitting in large stadiums, may be somewhat like this tremendous gathering of Israel (at least as concerns huge crowds, though not the content of what is seen and heard). There was a large and deep valley with high hills or mountains on each side of the valley, Mount Ebal, and across the valley, Mount Gerizim. Moses instructs the people to gather on those two mountains, for the better hearing of the human voice; six of the twelve tribes of Israel on the mount of cursing, Ebal, and six tribes on the mount of blessing, Gerizim. It probably added up to over half a million on each mountain, with a hollow valley between them. Apparently this provided wonderful acoustics; according to the structures of nature, hundreds of thousands of people could hear the echoing of the human voice from mountain to mountain across that deep and hollow valley.

The ceremony was like it was later in the temple in Jerusalem, where psalms that we call responsorial were chanted or sung by Levitical choirs, or by the people, half standing on one side of the temple, and half on the other side. They would go through a psalm which had a refrain, such as Psalm 136: 'For His mercies aye endure; ever faithful, ever sure' (as paraphrased by John Milton). It was as if the two mountains, with the deep valley in between had become a sanctuary.

As the congregation pronounced first, God's curses on lawbreaking and then God's blessings on obedience of the law, the whole atmosphere echoed with the sounds of the Holy Word of God. Then the people would say *AMEN!*—meaning 'so be it,' or 'let it be established'. For the assembled people it meant: 'we set our seal; we covenant with this; we accept this; we put ourselves under this curse; we put ourselves under this blessing.'

Even today, when you say 'Amen', we are confirming the covenant. I have sometimes wondered imaginatively what it must have meant to the little children and teenagers who were alive at this time, to be a part of this amazing covenant ceremony, far more exciting than any football game, and how thrilled must have been the elderly, leaning on their canes and staffs. I wonder if maybe the birds, the hawks and the sparrows, settled down on their perches in the trees or on high rocks, to listen; maybe even the foxes stuck their heads out of their dens, to hear these amazing liquid sounds of the Word of God coming from the people of Israel.

As a background or preparation for this ceremony confirming the law of God, containing the moral requirements of His character, the Lord has the people erect two stone monuments on Mount Ebal, huge stones dug down into the earth so they remain upright over the ages against wind and storm. Perhaps like the monoliths at Stonehenge in England or the ancient stones from apparently the same time as Stonehenge, in the Isle of Lewis, in a place called Callanish?

By divine instruction, they were to set up these monoliths, and put white lime plaster on them so they could write in large letters the Ten Commandments, so they could be clearly read and understood by the ordinary person. Now that's an argument for plain preaching! For that reason alone, many of us would conclude that services should be relatively simple, and preaching should be plain (as the Puritans termed it) to convey who God is, and what He is requiring and offering.

In the twentieth century, some archeological digs found what maybe was this series of stone monoliths—ten huge standing stones over ten feet high and weighing tons—where Israel was likely to have gathered on that day. The plaster is clearly long gone with the rain, wind, and snow. Some archaeologists believe that these may be the stones that would have been erected on Mount Ebal as the first monument, reminding the people of the covenant that God was making with them, as they took possession of the land.

There is a second monument also very important, an unhewn rock altar, made of field stone. They were to gather the stones from the field and build an altar for blood sacrifice and whole burnt peace offerings. Moses said not to take chisel and hammer to shape the stones so the people would not be tempted to make an idol; the altar was to be made of stones that God provided in nature, to be used for the shedding of blood, not an idol for the self-expression of the artistic, religious thoughts of mankind.

For us today, the two monuments obviously mean what they say: first, keep the law if you are to be this nation that God has constituted; secondly, it provides sacrifice if one breaks it. In so doing, they prophetically portray the two aspects of the work of the Messiah of Israel, Savior of the world, the Lord Jesus Christ.

The ten standing stones with the Ten Commandments written on them in plaster, speak of what theologians have classically called 'the active obedience of Christ', meaning Jesus saves us, not only by His death but by His life as well. For any person to please God and get into heaven, he or she must keep the law of God, within the heart, and with the outward actions. 'This do and thou shalt live', says Joshua.

Elsewhere, we are told that 'naught that defileth shall enter heaven'. The life of the believer is to express God's holy law. But that's the problem for us all: we are fallen; we are descended from fallen Adam and Eve; at our best, we really don't make it. So God sends His Son in the likeness of sinful flesh to be a human, and at the same time to remain the Son of God. He keeps the law of God for us, in our room and stead, so that it is accredited to our account. You cannot get into heaven without keeping the law, unless somebody else kept it for you; that's the only way.

Let me explain: in God's covenant with Adam, the Lord said: 'Do not eat of this particular fruit', for 'in the day that thou eatest thereof thou shalt surely die' (Gen. 2:17). Disobedience brings death: 'The wages of sin is death' (Rom. 6:23). By necessary implication, if you obey, you live: 'this do and thou shalt live'. Therefore, Joshua says, 'choose life', choose obedience. Somebody has to keep the law for us. 'This do and thou shalt live' means receiving eternal life, which comes by giving the heart to God, who sent His Son to love and obey Him in our place, whereby He makes up for our disobedience by His life and by His death.

Does not our conscience testify that we have never kept the Law as we should have? But Jesus is actively obedient in my place, and in the place of everyone who trusts in Him. For instance, Jesus says to the Father in the Garden of Gethsemane, 'Not my will, but thine be done.' Jesus turns the human will of everyone who believes, back through His own holy obedience to the Father. Once we were looking the other way, but now, because of our Mediator, we are brought face to face with God; Jesus turns humanity around by His own obedience.

Consider how John the Baptist protested when the Savior comes to be baptized at his hand in the River Jordan. John said: Why would you be baptized? This is for sinners! You ought to baptize me. And Jesus says, 'Suffer it to be so; for thus it becomes us to fulfill all righteousness' (Matt. 3:15). Jesus is fulfilling righteousness in the place of sinners. Though not a sinner, He undergoes the baptism of sinners; He obeys for sinners; He repents for sinners. He says on the cross, 'It is finished!'—the work of obedience.

Galatians 4:4 says that God sent His son, Jesus, made of a woman, under the law, which expresses His character and that of His Father; He is made under the law, so He can fulfill its terms on my behalf. That's the only way any man or woman will ever get into heaven.

Romans 5:19, contrasts the disobedience of Adam and the obedience of the last Adam: 'For as by one man's disobedience many were made sinners, so by the obedience of One [Christ Jesus] many shall be made righteous'. Jesus is fulfilling the law in His holy life, so that in Him, really and truly, I am sincerely able to say in response to the curses of law breaking and to the blessings of law keeping, Amen! We are told in 2 Corinthians 1:20 that Christ is our 'Amen'; He speaks the Amen for us: 'For all the promises of God in him are yea, and in him, Amen'. That's the first monument: the law, standing for Jesus' active obedience. Keep it!

The second monument is a rough, unhewn altar made of field stones, for the shedding of blood, to represent the payment of the price of sin and cleansing from guilt. It is a picture of Mount Calvary a number of miles away and of Jesus dying on the cross some 1400 years after this outdoor ceremony, when Jesus dies outdoors on Golgotha. We have seen already Romans 6:23, 'The wages of sin is death'. Ezekiel 18:4: 'The soul that sinneth, it shall die'; Hebrews 9:22: 'Without the shedding of blood there is no remission of sin'.

So this altar represents the blood propitiation that our Lord Jesus Christ would perfectly render, paying for all the penalty of the offended law of God in our room and stead. The first monument represents Christ's law keeping in our place; the second monument represents His death, paying for all of our sins in our place. This is salvation beautifully pictured on Mt. Ebal.

The ceremony also involved the reading out of the covenant, led by the Levites; as the people heard them read out, they were to echo with 'Amen, Amen!'

We are told which six tribes were on Mount Ebal, the hill or curses, and which six tribes were on Mount Gerizim, the hill of blessing. There has been some difference among rabbinical scholars as to why certain tribes were on the hill of blessing, and others were on the hill of cursing.

It may be that on the hill of blessing are the tribes that are the direct descendants of the true wives, Rachel and Leah; while on the hill of cursing are the tribes descended from the handmaidens or concubines of Jacob, and not his full-fledged wives, with the exception of Reuben, although he is the descendant of Leah. That may be because of the offense he committed against one of his father's concubines that caused him to lose the rights of the firstborn.

Other scholars have said that the placement of the tribes on Mt. Ebal, the mount of cursing, because they had tribal lands on the north side of that hill; whereas the tribes put on Mt. Gerizim, were given tribal lands on the south side. We do not know for sure, but what really matters is that all were called to obedience and to sacrifice.

A very important feature is that, in verses 15–26, the curses start with secret sin: things you can do in private, and get by with, as far as the community is concerned. Verse 15 deals with a secret idol; probably a small molten image made and kept in the house. In our modern culture we in America are not likely to use idols, as they would in some parts of China or India and elsewhere, but we do have idols of the mind, 'idols of the imagination', as Professor Herb Schlossberg wrote in his book *Idols for Destruction*. He shows that an idol is something that replaces God, thus keeping God from being first in your thinking, your affections, and in your motivations. Our kinds of idols in the Western world are in the mind; they may be materialistic, or some intense personal goal outside the will of God, but, whether material or mental, they are always some aspect of the created order instead of the Creator Himself, and that is what idolatry is. What's denounced here is secret idolatry that people might not know you are involved in.

Later verses deal with disrespect of parents, as in verse 16. Verse 17 deals with people surreptitiously moving land markers so as to steal land. Verse 18 prohibits misleading blind people—and prohibited by 'Thou shalt not kill'. Verse 19 deals with lies told in court to advance your own interest and to defraud the powerless: as in 'Thou shalt not bear false witness'. Or it may not be in open court but done more secretly, like gossip, to make yourself look better, and hurt somebody you resent. Verse 21 speaks of bestiality. Verses 22–23 deal with various types of incest.

I have been told by two different people who teach in community colleges in the South (not in Dillon County), and know the lives of the students reasonably well, that counselors in talking to students hear that they come from families where there has been incest. It seems to be that with the decline of belief in the gospel in America, incest is increasing. One of the serious problems with incest is that it is generally secret, and you can get by with it for a while.

Verse 24 prohibits secretly striking one's neighbor, hoping that nobody sees it—a violation of 'Thou shalt not kill'. Verse 25 prohibits killing on contract (something we popularly think of as done by the Mafia).

For our purposes here, I am not going to expound most of these sins, for I reckon they are unfortunately all too clear to us. But I am going to ask this important question: why would the first pronunciation of covenant curses pertain to secret sins? Why did Moses not start with public sins, open sins? The reason may be given in the Penitential Psalms, such as Psalm 51, a penitential Psalm of David after he had violated Bathsheba and had her husband killed. After months of hardness, David was confronted by the prophet, and was broken in repentance. 'Behold, Thou desirest truth in the inward parts and in the hidden part Thou shalt make me to know wisdom' (Ps. 51:6).

Another of his Psalms, Psalm 139, verses 1–4, 7, and 23–24, deals with what we really are in our heart; the secret life is where he starts:

> O Lord, thou hast searched me and known me. thou knowest my downsitting and my uprising; thou understandest my thought afar off. thou compassest my path and my lying down, and art acquainted with all my ways. For there is not a word in my tongue, but, lo, O Lord, thou knowest it altogether. Whither shall I go from thy Spirit? Or whither shall I flee from thy presence? Search me, O God, and know my heart; try me and know my thoughts; and see if there be any wicked way in me, and lead me in the way everlasting.

Therefore, before anything else in the Christian life, we have to be real with the God who sees all. As God said to Samuel when he was going to choose a king: 'Man looketh on the outward appearance; but the Lord looketh on the heart', (1 Samuel 16:7). The first spiritual issue you and I have got to deal with all our lives, is not so much what we do outwardly and publicly—that will come later. The first thing is who we really are on the inside. Hence in a covenant relationship to God, essential integrity in the heart and mind is always called for as the first issue; not sinless perfection, for none of us could offer that, but an essential integrity inside, where God has come and is doing His cleansing, uplifting work in the Holy Spirit inside us, where God always starts with every individual, with what we are within.

I have noticed in studying the history of revivals, although I could not lay it down as a universal rule, that many revivals have started with the Christians coming under conviction of secret sin. So far as I know, when the Holy Spirit is poured out from on high, the first thing He does is make people feel the filth and the shame of secret sin and their own uncleanness.

In the wonderful biography of Jonathan Edwards by Iain Murray, Jonathan Edwards preached a sermon May 14, 1741, and an eyewitness said that, 'Many had their countenances changed; great numbers cried out aloud in the anguish of their souls;' they felt their inward sins. You can get by with it and it not bother you, but when the Holy Spirit comes in new power, He literally breaks you down, so that you feel with agony your insincerity and your duplicity. The eyewitness to this sermon then used this interesting phrase: 'Several stout men fell as though a cannon had been discharged and a ball had made its way through their hearts.'

Joshua 8 tells us something very important that we are not told in Deuteronomy 27 and 28, namely, that while half of the people of Israel were on one mountain and half were on the other, the Ark of the Covenant was in the valley between the two mountains, that amazing wooden box covered with gold—with representatives of the angelic orders at each end—containing the tables of the Law. Upon it was the mercy seat that received the blood. This holy Ark that was where all Israel could look down on it and see it.

What did the Ark of the Covenant stand for? In Hebrews 4–8, you will see that the Ark prophetically depicts the human nature of our Lord Jesus Christ, His incarnation, becoming our flesh, without committing sin. It depicts His atoning death; the mercy seat received the blood. The law was on the inside, as the law of God was in the heart of Christ. And it depicted, in its own unique way with angel wings sweeping up, His glorious resurrection on our behalf. All that is to say that this ceremony, with the two stone monuments, and then the Ark of the Covenant in the valley, says: look to the Ark; look to Him whom the Ark so fully represents; look to Jesus Christ. Look to Him in all your imperfection, your weakness, your sins, your brokenness, your failure, and your grief. Particularly if and when the Holy Spirit comes to our churches in new power, a lot of us are going to repent in ways we never have, because we will see and feel the uncleanness of our secret sins, as well as our open ones. Like the tribes of Israel did on that day, looking to the Ark; we shall look to Christ whom the Ark pictures. Then life begins to move in a beautiful direction.

We can see how this happens in Psalm 132 (a song of degrees) in verses 8–9 and 15–16; how looking to the Ark, looking to Christ, cleanses, purges, and transforms in beauty, the life that looks in that direction.

> Arise, O Lord, into thy rest; thou and the ark of thy strength. Let thy priests be clothed with righteousness; and let thy saints shout for joy. I will abundantly bless her provision; I will satisfy her poor with bread. I will also clothe her priests with salvation; and her saints shall shout aloud for joy.

As they look to the Ark, to Christ, these wondrous things will occur: transformations that at first are invisible and then keep on working more visibly, as we flee from secret and open sins.

I want to close by reading a hymn written by a Southern Baptist missionary, Dr. James Edwin Orr, who knew something about revival.

> Search me, O God,
> And know my heart today;
> Try me, O Savior,
> Know my thoughts, I pray.
> See if there be
> Some wicked way in me;
> Cleanse me from every sin
> And set me free.
>
> I praise Thee, Lord,
> For cleansing me from sin;
> Fulfill Thy Word,
> And make me pure within.
> Fill me with fire
> Where once I burned with shame;
> Grant my desire
> To magnify Thy Name.
>
> Lord, take my life,
> And make it wholly Thine;
> Fill my poor heart
> With Thy great love divine.
> Take all my will,
> My passion, self, and pride;
> I now surrender, Lord,
> In me abide.
>
> O Holy Ghost,
> Revival comes from Thee;
> Send a revival,
> Start the work in me.
> Thy Word declares
> Thou wilt supply our need;
> For blessings now,
> O Lord, I humbly plead.

May God hear the cry of our hearts.

61

BLESSINGS OF COVENANT OBEDIENCE

Deuteronomy 28:1–14

In this text, we come to the blessings of covenant obedience. We sing when we open the Sunday service, *Praise God from Whom all Blessings Flow,* and thus we start thinking about God and how every blessing comes from God. In a sense it is always a joy to speak about the blessings that God sends down. As far as I know in the Old Testament in its entirety, there is no passage that goes any more particularly or fully, into the blessings that flow down from God, as does Deuteronomy 28:1–14; it is a kind of a doxology.

Some commentators have suggested that this text is the Old Testament form of the Beatitudes of Christ in Matthew 5—'Blessed are the poor in spirit; blessed are the merciful', and so forth. 'Blessed' basically means 'happy'—but more than that, truly happy, truly joyful. The word 'blessed' is, today, almost completely a religious word, and therefore seems remote from daily usage. In modern parlance it is something like true and lasting happiness. One aspect of our being created after God's image, in His likeness, is that we long for blessing or true happiness and this passage is about true happiness in the biblical sense.

Let us note three points from this text: first, the order of the blessing—I shall be comparing chapter 27 with chapter 28; second, how the blessing comes—specially addressed in verses 4, 8, and 13; third, the ground of blessing—where you go to get it, especially verses 1 and 7-8.

THE ORDER OF BLESSING BETWEEN DEUTERONOMY CHAPTERS 27-28

The covenant ceremony on the mountains of Gerizim and Ebal started by calling out the secret sins that God's people tend to commit, and then saying that those secret sins are to be confessed, and the Lord's help sought to forsake these secret sins. Not forsaking them leads to serious consequences, that is, cursing.

In the first 14 verses of chapter 28, we are given a list of the blessings that follow on honest dealing before God with our secret sins, and what a catalogue it is! In other words, to be real with God, we must deal honestly with our personal and secret sins. And then the blessing comes! You don't get true happiness from God without dealing with your own sins honestly before Him; that's the point of Deuteronomy 27 and 28.

The order of these two chapters can be thought of in terms of the spiritual principle found in Proverbs 28:13-14: 'He that covereth his sins shall not prosper; but who so confesseth and forsaketh them shall have mercy. Happy is the man that feareth always; but he that hardeneth his heart shall fall into mischief.' Deuteronomy 27 is like verse 13, and Deuteronomy 28 like verse 14. So, happiness or blessing follows true and sincere confession of sin and dealing before God with what you are really like.

I have mentioned the history of some of the trans-Atlantic revivals previously, and wish to share a passage from a recent book, *Scotland Saw His Glory: a History of Revivals in Scotland*, pertaining directly to the order of cursing and blessing found in the two chapters of Deuteronomy under discussion. The year 1638 saw tremendous revival in Scotland that was marked by the signing of the National Covenant, after the Holy Spirit had been poured out in the preaching of the Word and administration of the sacrament. (Eventually, this movement would lead to civil war in the United Kingdom, but that is not our story for today).

One of the first things to happen before they signed the Covenant, which ultimately led to civil war and eventually the introduction of what we know as modern liberties, is that as the Word was preached and the glory of God was coming down in the pulpits of Scotland, vast numbers assembled outside the churches to sign the Covenant that they would be God's people. They first promised that they would forsake their sins, feeling they had to begin there because when the Spirit of Christ came in such a powerful way through the gospel, people were smitten for their sins: church people, magistrates, ministers, and academic professors. This shows that when Christ comes close, people first feel unclean, sinful and broken open, because of their sins.

Alexander Henderson, one of the commissioners from Scotland who helped write the Westminster Confession of Faith, says that he was present in Greyfriars Church in Edinburgh, where thousands were standing in the cemetery to sign the Covenant. Henderson noticed that some of them opened their own veins, so they could sign in their blood. But something powerful had happened before they signed: they experienced a tremendous sense of their sinfulness and their uncleanness, and they were broken open and confessed it all to God. Partly as the result of that, much of the Scottish nation changed.

Here is what Alexander Henderson said: 'This is a note of the power of God that He has touched the hearts of the people and there never was such a howling and a weeping heard amongst them this long time as there is now. And yet it is not a weeping only for sorrow, but a weeping for joy.' In other words, yes they were broken for their sins, but the love of Christ and the atonement of God had fully cleansed them and gladly received them; they were restored. So part of the weeping was because of the love of God to sinners. 'How oft there has been preaching to the most part of the congregations of this land, this long time past, and yet people have never found the power of it working upon their hearts; but all was now changed.' Another minister, John Livingston, said, 'I have seen above one thousand persons all at once, lifting up their hands, and the tears dropping down their eyes.' There was a tremendous outpouring of the Holy Spirit, and the confession of sins, many of them secret; then the blessings of God followed upon these individual Christians and upon the whole land.

This principle runs through the whole of Scripture. We see it in Nehemiah 8:9, where, after Ezra had read the law to the worshiping people, they began to weep. Romans 3:20b explains why: '…for by the law is the knowledge of sin.'

I have said before that there is no recipe for revival (contrary to several books I have read).

Holy Spirit revival comes from the Holy Spirit; and the Father and the Son decide when to send Him. Revival is always a sovereign work. That was the case in 1638, 1740, and in 1858. Certainly, people were praying in 1858 that He would come in power, but nobody knew ahead of time that He would do so in the way He did. But it is to be noticed that a characteristic of true revival is that that when times of renewal and restoration come, large numbers of the people of God have come under the conviction of sin, and seek to split with their secret sins. They realize that God is displeased, and will do anything to please the Lord. Sometimes it seems that this leads to even further blessing. So, what very often happens in times of revival illustrates well the first point we wish to make today: the order of blessing, as one moves from chapter 27 on to chapter 28 of Deuteronomy.

How the Blessing Comes (28:4,8,12).

Look carefully at Deuteronomy 28:2: 'And all these blessings shall come on thee and <u>overtake</u> thee'. They overtake you! It's like you are walking down the road and somebody comes by in a car and quickly overtakes you. Maybe they stop and offer you a lift—at least they used to—but the blessing is not that you went out and got it; it overtakes you. It comes from behind, catches you, and overtakes you. Often God sends it when you are least expecting it. By blessing, I mean true happiness.

Years ago, the founder of a well-known Christian college often said: 'You do not find happiness; you stumble over it in the pathway of duty.' So if in a high school, or more likely a primary school, the teacher asks the children 'What do you want to accomplish with your life when you grow up?', you get some interesting answers. Often it is to be a fireman or policeman. Later in life, other professions become more popular. Whatever it is, if your goal is to make yourself happy, you won't find it. Many years ago, Rev. James Philip of Holyrood Abbey Church of Scotland wrote:

'In verse 2 of Deuteronomy 28, it is said that these blessings will 'overtake' God's people, and this in itself is highly important in view of the contemporary search for, and preoccupation with happiness, that bedevils so much of our society. Happiness is not to be found by seeking it. It comes to those whose minds and hearts have been gripped by something bigger than personal happiness, and steals on them unawares; it overtakes them when something greater than themselves has commanded their souls. So it is here; the blessing of God overtakes those whose hearts are gripped by a passion to obey God's Word.'

The Ground of Blessing, or the Place Where You Find Happiness (28:1,7–8)

The ground of blessing is brought before us in this passage: Deuteronomy 28:1–14 and the Beatitudes in Matthew 5, teach, in somewhat different ways, that covenant obedience is the ground of further covenant blessing (although the obedience itself is grounded in the coming of the Holy Spirit, as a major aspect of the Covenant of Grace).

Deuteronomy 28:1, 'And it shall come to pass if thou shalt hearken diligently to observe and to do his commandments', I am going to set you on high and all these blessings will overtake you. Deuteronomy 28:13: 'and the Lord shall make thee the head and not the tail if that thou hearken unto the commandments, to observe and to do them'; and Matthew 5:5 and 7: 'Blessed are the meek for they shall inherit the earth; blessed are the merciful, for they shall obtain mercy'—that's the place where these kind of blessings are to be found.

Isaiah speaks of judgment as 'God's strange work': 'that he may do his work, his strange work; and bring to pass his strange act' (Isa. 28:21)—judgment! If judgment is God's strange work, then this expression means that it is not the thing He most desires to do. His normal work is blessing! So obedience in the covenant to which God has called us and enabled us to be there, is the ground of blessing; when your face is turned towards God and you are seeking sincerely to obey Him, is where you get blessing. Your being there is based on God's grace, not any works you have done or will do by yourself in the flesh.

You might ask, Do you have to be perfectly obedient? Of course not; no one but Christ was ever perfectly obedient. You don't have to be angelically perfect; there is no such person. But covenantly obedient means that the Lord has your heart: 'the Lord knoweth them that are His', as the prophet says. If you are in the covenant, then if you sin, at least you will repent and say Lord, restore me. You will deal with secret sins as in Deuteronomy 27, and then there will be further blessing. But the Lord does have your heart; you do want to please Him; and He knows that very well indeed. His Holy Spirit has operated in your heart so you are in this position.

Let's look at Psalm 147:11, which makes it clear that the grounds of blessing are for those who are standing in the place where they would like to please their heavenly Father: 'The Lord taketh pleasure in them that fear him and those that hope in his mercy'. Can you believe that as great as God is—running the sun, the moon and the stars; keeping the planets rotating; directing the laws of thermodynamics, keeping everything working; ten thousand times ten thousand angels bowing before Him—could be interested in my attitude? He most certainly is. That's who God is. And Deuteronomy says that God literally, actually, takes pleasure in those who fear Him, those who reverentially trust Him, those who say Lord, I want to obey you; help me. God, the great, mighty, majestic, sovereign God in heaven, is actually delighted by such a response! That is who God is. And to those who are seeking to please God, He comes down and puts further blessings upon them. That's the teaching of Scripture. Obedience in the covenant, desire to please the heavenly Father, is the ground of further blessing.

But now it is time to make an important distinction, or else we won't get the biblical balance. Obedience is the ground of blessing, but it is never the cause of blessing. Covenant obedience, seeking to please Jesus in our life, and repenting when we don't, is the place where you find the happiness and the blessing; but it's not what causes it. The cause that we get any kind of blessing is told us in Deuteronomy 7, the same book, verses 7-8:

> The Lord did not set his love upon you, nor choose you, because ye were more in number than any people; for ye were the fewest of all people; but because the Lord loved you, and because he would keep the oath which he had sworn unto your fathers, hath the Lord brought you out with a mighty hand, and redeemed you out of the house of bondmen, from the hand of Pharaoh, king of Egypt.

The cause of every kind of blessing, even of our believing and repenting, is the electing love of God, not from anything in us, but because of who He is. The same thing is told us by the apostle Paul in Ephesians 1:3-6 in the New Testament, and it is exactly in line with Deuteronomy 7:

> Blessed be the God and Father of our Lord Jesus

Christ, who hath blessed us with all spiritual blessings in heavenly places in Christ; according as he hath chosen us in him before the foundation of the world, that we should be holy and without blame before him in love; having predestinated us unto the adoption of children by Jesus Christ to himself, according to the good pleasure of his will, to the praise of the glory of his grace, wherein he hath made us accepted in the beloved.

So, the source of all spiritual blessing, as it says in Ephesians 1:3, is because of what happens in Ephesians 1:5—He predestinates us unto adoption as His children; it's by grace. We don't deserve it. Hence the cause of all blessing, whether it is being chosen, and as a result of that, the Holy Spirit removes the chains from your personality, so that now you are free to reach your hands out in faith, and believe in Jesus and receive the gospel, and repent when you are out of line, and then be more sanctified as the Spirit is working to deny self and follow the Lord; all of these things are what we mean by obedience. But keep in mind that the cause of it all is the electing love of God in Christ, and the sheer grace of God; that is the cause.

But the grounds of further blessing, not the cause, but the grounds, the place where you get the happiness—as much as God wants you to have on this earthly pilgrimage—is covenantal obedience to the Lord.

I will close with this verse from the hymn by Robert Murray McCheyne:

> Chosen not for good in me;
> wakened up from wrath to flee;
> hidden in the Savior's side;
> by the Spirit sanctified.
> Teach me, Lord, on earth to show,
> by my love, how much I owe.

May what was said of Abraham be said of us: 'I will bless you and make you a blessing'.

62

Covenant Curses

Deuteronomy 28: 15–29:1

As far as I know, this is the longest passage in all of the Bible dealing with divine curses on covenant-breaking—54 verses. What is really happening in this text? I want us to note three points: first, and this is a question many of us will have when we read such solemn, grim, terrible passages: why would a loving God pronounce curses? Second, what are the curses God pronounces; and third, how to get out from under the curse.

Why Would a Loving God Pronounce Such Curses?

We saw in the last two messages on Deuteronomy 28:1-14 the pronouncing of blessings. But then the next 54 verses are given to divine curses; four times more space is given to the curses than to the blessings in this 28th chapter. Why is that? It is certainly not the case anywhere in the Bible that God is harsh, or that God is ever eager to curse or to punish. Lamentations 3:33 says that 'He afflicts not willingly the sons of men.' Isaiah often speaks of judgment as God's 'strange work;' that means that it is unusual. The implication of that is that God's normal work, God's regular work, is blessing.

The prophet Micah says God 'delighteth in mercy', Micah 7:18. Psalm 81 shows the constant desire of God to bless His people; read verses ten through 16: 'Oh, that My people had a heart to obey Me … I would have given them the finest of the wheat, the honey from the comb'—a loving Father, longing to bless us. That's the picture in Psalm 81 and many other places. 1 John 4:8 says that 'God is love'. Our God is a wonderful heavenly Father, gracious, pure, kind, merciful. So, why then is all this space in Deuteronomy 28 given to threatening curses upon serious disobedience of His people? Why four times as much space as is allotted to the blessing?

One of the old commentators said that the reason is clear, although maybe we hesitate to accept it; it is because in the fall of our first father Adam into sin we inherited a corrupted human nature that inclines us easily to be disobedient. Even within the Christian experience of salvation we have to struggle against the temptation to disobey the Lord in order to please our fallen flesh.

The Apostle Paul talks about it in Romans 7. It is easy enough for a person who is not a Christian to be like this, but even Christians can be struggling to be obedient. Romans 7:15: 'For that which I do I allow not; for what I would, that do I not, but what I hate, that do I'. He is speaking as a Christian. Then verses 17–21: 'Now then it is no more I that do it, but sin that dwelleth in me'. Even in the Christian, after we are regenerate, after we are born again, there are remnants of sin:

> For I know that in me (that is, in my flesh) dwelleth no good thing; for to will is present with me, but how to perform that which is good I find not. For the good that I would, I do not; but the evil which I would not, that I do. Now if I do that I would not, it is no more I that do it, but sin that dwelleth in me. I find then a law [that means a principle], that, when I would do good, evil is present with me.

Now isn't that, honestly speaking, where we all are, at least much of the time? Therefore, you have got to have passages like Deuteronomy 28:15–68 to show us that even though God primarily desires to bless us, He has to give a great deal of time and attention and space in His Word to warning us to flee self-destructive behavior to which we are all too inclined. These severe warnings are out of tender love—remember that—not out of harshness. They are God's way of saying 'Do not commit suicide. To commit apostasy against me will destroy you.' I'm told that some states have a law that for those who are caught for drunk driving, before they can get their license back, have to watch movies of terrible wrecks with human carnage, as a warning not to do it again.

Here is really the nub of the question: why would a loving God punish apostasy in His people? Why would He send curses to those who willfully forsake His covenant of grace? It is because God's love is holy. The prophets and the Psalms often speak of the Lord as 'The Holy One of Israel'. It is interesting that in the Gospel of Mark, when the demons saw Christ doing His miracles they cried out 'This is the Holy One of God; flee from us!' In our generation people will be sitting in churches this very Sunday morning, and will accept some aspects of the love of God, but will not accept His holiness.

Well then, they are not in touch with the true God. The modernist theology takes some bits of God's Word that it likes, and rejects those parts in Scripture that it doesn't like. By so doing, what they have produced is an idol, a figment of their own imagination, which will fail them in their hour of death. The one and only true God has the attributes of holiness and love, of mercy and judgment; they are always together in the real God, the God of the Bible. God's holy character, is the stability of this universe. To deny that God is holy would mean you had an idol, and it would be a cancer that would eat up everything, including the concept of right and wrong, and everything would collapse into nothing.

This is not complicated. If God is not holy, everything collapses. For instance, let us say you opened a school, and said that in this school there is going to be nothing but love—no punishment, no unpleasant discipline, nobody fails. But what would you do about the big bully who terrorizes the smaller children? He couldn't be punished, so you would say to the victim, 'You must put up with this. Don't ask for protection because this is a loving school; we don't punish bullies.' But that would not be love; it would be the total denial of justice and the triumph of cruelty. In truth, discipline and justice make true love possible.

Let me give you another illustration. Take a marriage: you could foolishly say that because of love, each partner can do exactly what he or she wants to, without any sort of accountability or discipline. Let us suppose that the husband constantly runs to other women; that every day he is abusing alcohol and drugs, and regularly beats his wife. But because of this crazy definition of love, she is to say nothing unpleasant to him, and not seek any relief or help, because that wouldn't be loving and would make him feel badly. We all know that is not love. It is the triumph of brutal, corrupt self-centeredness, making true love impossible. You surely see the point; real love, God's love, always has a holy structure to it, which includes accountability, discipline, and painful consequences for disobedience to the Lord's way. Otherwise society could not work. God is like that; yes He is love, but He is holy love. And you and I are made to need love and holiness. Holiness entails discipline and proper curses for violation of God's wondrous love. Otherwise it would be no love.

What Curses God Pronounces on Covenant Disobedience

One German Old Testament commentator, Delitzsch, divides this long series of curses into five major sections and we will follow his outline.

First, the curse and all its forms, verses 20–26. Note verse 20: 'The Lord shall send upon thee cursing, vexation, and rebuke.' Several passages from the prophets teach that God sent idolatrous Israel into captivity: God sent the Assyrians and the Babylonians upon them. I won't discuss all those passages, just one, Amos 3:6: 'Shall a trumpet be blown in the city and the people not be afraid? Shall there be evil in a city and the Lord hath not done it?' That does not mean that God commits evil; that is impossible. In this case, evil means the consequences of being attacked because you are sinful, and God let them come in on you to destroy you. No military reversal is accidental; no crop failure is accidental. Deuteronomy 28:22 lists seven curses and the number seven in the Hebrew world of thought stands for totality or finality (seven churches of Asia, seven spirits of God, and so forth). It is saying that every possible experience in human life can serve as the hands and the feet of God, either to bless us or to curse us.

Turn your back on God, says Amos, and go home and lean against the wall, and when you do, a serpent bites you (Amos 5:19). Trust in money, as many do, instead of God, and the money either evaporates or it becomes a cauldron of torment to destroy your soul. There is no way to escape the judgments of God against apostasy, for every way we turn, His holy wrath is waiting for us. That is clear in Psalm 139:7–12:

> Whither shall I go from thy Spirit? Or whither shall I flee from thy presence? If I ascend up into heaven, thou art there; if I make my bed in hell, behold, thou art there. If I take the wings of the morning, and dwell in the uttermost parts of the sea; even there shall thy hand lead me, and thy right hand shall hold me. If I say, Surely the darkness shall cover me; even the night shall be light about me. Yea, the darkness hideth not from thee; but the night shineth as the day; the darkness and the light are both alike to thee.

Every way you go, it's going to work out wrong, if you turn your back on the One who matters the most, your Lord and God. That's true of an individual, of a people, and of a church.

Verse 23 speaks of drought that destroys crops and ruins the economy. It means that timely rains depend on God, and drought and flood are used by Him to bless or curse his people. John Calvin says in his *Institutes*, Book , 'Not a drop of rain falls, but at the express command of God' (1.16.5). He adds, 'although the future is uncertain to us, there will be no event which God hath not ordained' (1.16.9).

Second, in this list of terrible curses, you have diseases of body and soul, including oppression by enemies, especially in verses 27–34; diseases such as the boils of Egypt, scab, itch, madness, and blindness (verses 27-29). These seemingly refer to the sixth plague on Egypt. But now it comes upon the descendants of those who had escaped in the land of Goshen, where they were sheltered under the blood; they are not under the blood, because they have abandoned the covenant.

Some of these diseases we don't know. Medical science tells us that syphilis eventually drives people crazy; it's called general paresis; I wonder could AIDS be a divine curse on the arrogant disobedience of our countries? (some innocent people get it, but in general, it goes with certain types of sexual disobedience).

Third, rejection of the people from covenant fellowship (verses 35-56). Verses 38 and 40 speak of the destruction of the economy, the basis of which is nearly always agriculture. Recently, somebody showed me from the paper that in one day, 40,000 people in America lost their job, when Caterpillar closed down many of its plants. And in the *Wall Street Journal*, the fire department in Miami had 35 jobs open, and there was a picture on the front page of 1,000 men and women standing in line for those 35 jobs!

Verses 41-44 speak of people's loss of their homes, and eventual exile. Verse 43 speaks of the immigrant taking over and dispossessing the original citizens. Verse 44 speaks of once prosperous people, who used to rent to the rest of the world, becoming impoverished debtors, dependent on hostile foreign countries financially. We don't know how much of American obligation, bonds and the rest, is owned by the Middle East and by China. That is our fault; not theirs!

Verses 45-46 explain why everything we once counted on for personal and national security is beginning to collapse around us. Here, it is because you would not listen to the voice of God. You say, I don't understand how this could happen in America, in Iceland, in the U.K. or Ireland, which have been so blessed in the past. These curses can come on us, as well as on any other disobedient people, because we will not listen to the voice of God. Continued refusal to listen, eventually means rejection of many areas from the blessings of covenant fellowship.

The fourth kind of curse is enumerated in verses 47-57: the horrors that will occur when the heathen take over, when pagans get the reins of power. Let me summarize briefly: what happens is that the population experiences a loss of mercy in those who govern them, as in verse 50. Familiar institutions that protected them, compared to high and towering walls of security, now fail and are powerless against non-Christians (verse 52). In some cases, and this I reckon is the worst part of it all, a once decent population can descend to the horrors of cannibalism. It happened in the siege on Jerusalem; Josephus relates it in A.D. 70, and it happened long before that in the siege on Samaria about 721 B.C., and it has happened in modern times.

One of the greatest novels of the twentieth century, equal to Dostoevsky and Tolstoy, was written by an Italian Christian, Eugenio Corti, entitled *The Red Horse*. Corti lived through the horrors of World War II as a young man; he was a university student and was sent to Siberia with the Italian army into which he had been conscripted. As you read it, you almost feel the cold. He relates what happens in the concentration camps, where they put captured soldiers. They got so desperately hungry that you had to watch out at night, because people would come to where you were sleeping and, if you were weak, would finish you off and take parts of your body to eat. This was happening in the 1940s.

The fifth kind of curse that comes on covenant disobedience is hardening of the heart to disregard the glorious name of God (verses

58-68). Verses 65 and 66 refer to fear, sorrow of heart, and a quaking or shaking, and horrid insecurity; a stress that leaves you trembling like a leaf replaces a once healthy fear of the Name of God. That's the direction people will go when they consistently break the covenant and forget who God is.

How to Get Out From the Covenant Curse

How to escape this curse is an intelligent question. Chapter 29:1 summarizes the whole of history, going back to our response to the covenant that the Lord made with our fathers. To walk in this covenant brings blessing, as we saw before. But to disregard and to trample underfoot this holy covenant assures cursing upon our society. So what if we are now living in days that may be increasingly characterized by divine curses on our once Christian society? Is there any hope for us whatsoever?

The clue is given us in Joshua 8. It relates the same thing that we saw earlier in Deuteronomy, about the mountain of cursing and the mountain of blessing. Joshua 8:30 tells us that the altar of sacrifice was built on Mount Ebal, the place of cursing. Isn't that interesting? Where the covenant curses were pronounced, God had Joshua erect the altar where the blood of the sacrificial animals was shed.

That is the ground of all our hopes. We are never without hope, no matter what the political or moral situation is around us, because the altar is available on the mountain of cursing to those who seek it. If by our unbelief and disobedience we get into the place of cursing, an altar is provided whereby the curse can be removed. That Old Testament altar in the place of cursing points forward to the Lord Jesus Christ, who bears away our curse insofar as we identify with him through faith and repentance. As in that song by Getty, 'O to see the dawn of the darkest day', of Christ becoming a curse for us, and by that means, taking the curse away. That goes back to Galatians 3:13: 'Christ hath redeemed us from the curse of the law.' Deuteronomy 28 is the curse of the law, the broken law; and although we are seeing it abroad in our culture just now, let us remember the Lord, of whom it is rightly said: 'being made a curse for us, for it is written,"cursed is everyone that hangeth on a tree"'.

What is our hope, as we face a possibly darkening future economically, and before that, morally and politically? It is for us to come back to God's altar, to come face to face with Christ on the cross of Calvary, there to humble ourselves through brokenness and confession, honest confession, of all our sins. Then He will shelter us in His grace, and as Ezekiel 11:16 says, even if we should be in some kind of captivity, He will be to us 'a little sanctuary' until the storms of judgment be past. And if enough people really do it, if they come to the altar in increasing numbers, you will see very major changes for the good in all the lands where it happens.

I close with two verses in Psalm 142, written by David when he was in the cave. Saul had gone crazy, and was involved with witches and was trying to kill David. The country was being oppressed by the Philistines; Israel was feeling the curses of the covenant. But here David prays in verses 6-7: 'Attend unto my cry, for I am brought very low. Deliver me from my persecutors, for they are stronger than I'. And aren't they! 'Bring my soul out of prison that I may praise thy name. The righteous shall compass me about, for thou shalt deal bountifully with me'.

A book was written maybe forty years ago by Merlin Carothers, *From Prison to Praise*. I do not remember its details, nor can I say that I would necessarily agree with all of it. But he does rightly bring out the point that by returning to God, we can move from loss and grief, to praise of God. And if enough true believers will come to the altar that God has provided on the mount of cursing, God will work. No matter what else is going on outside, God will work and we can move from prison to praise and we will be where God wants us to be. Things may be tight and short and difficult in the future; they may well be, but we will find a God who deals bountifully with us.

63

Take the Covenant Oath
Deuteronomy 29:2–15

This fairly brief passage is a command and an invitation to take the oath of the covenant to be the Lord's and nobody else's. It must have been a very impressive sight, something over one million people: men, women, and children gathered near Shechem, on the sides of hills and a huge valley, who were called by God to take this oath of the covenant before the Lord would lead them into the Promised Land through Joshua, who would replace Moses. This tremendous gathering, the oath to worship God in a pure fashion, and what came after it, shaped the history of the world.

That covenant oath that Israel took, more than anything else, other than God's grace behind it, is the reason that the Jews are still an important part of the world today. The other kingdoms have passed away long ago, but the Jews are still here, as are Christians, their spiritual descendants. Taking this covenant oath, not only made possible the survival, first of Judaism and then of the renewed Judaism—true Christianity—but also provided to the whole world a healthy law structure, a fair law code, the possibility of a sound economy, safety, health, and large-scale happiness for millions, all going back to this swearing of the divine covenant, about 3,400 years ago between the plains of Moab and Shechem.

We are not completely unaware today of swearing a covenant oath, to live by it, and hence to devote everything we are and have to it. There have been swearings of renewed forms to the divine covenant, and these covenant oaths, taken by our ancestors, have made possible good laws, holy lives, healthy societies, and generally happy people. For instance, in 1620 the Pilgrim fathers, who migrated to Plymouth, Massachusetts from Plymouth, England, while still on board the Mayflower, made a covenant. They were going into a wild territory, far north of Virginia, that, as far as they knew, did not have any law code, other than the customs of some Indian tribes. Those evangelical Calvinist people, made a biblically-based covenant on board the ship, forty-one of them adding their names to it. It is still known as 'the Mayflower Compact', and is often considered, in one sense, the basis of all American law.

We read this about the Mayflower Compact of 1620:

Forty one of the band when at Cape Code signed the well known covenant by which they mutually and solemnly combined themselves into a civil body politic for the better ordering and preservation of the object, and by virtue thereof to frame, enact, and obey such just and equal laws as from time to time should be thought most meet and convenient for the general good of the colony. They declared that their enterprise was undertaken for the glory of God, for the advancement of the Christian faith in this new world and for the honor of their king and country.

A similar event happened about 18 years later in Scotland, in Edinburgh and all over the mother country of most of us. A covenant, known as the National Covenant, was sworn in 1638. While a student in Edinburgh, I lived in a New College residence, and not very far behind it was the medieval Greyfriars Church—long since the Church of Scotland—with a huge graveyard going back to the Middle Ages. Thousands of people gathered there in 1638; the Holy Spirit had been poured out in such measure that the Puritans in Scotland—and then in spreading into England—felt they needed to repent for not having really carried through the Reformation as thoroughly as the Bible said. They pledged themselves and their children and everything they had, to live by the Word of God, on the basis of grace.

Many people were weeping, and some literally took knives and opened their veins and signed their name in blood. Many of those 1638 covenants are still extant in some of the churches of Scotland and in the Royal Scottish Museum. It is generally recognized that what happened at that covenant signing in 1638, and in the next 50 years of struggle and wars, led to the Glorious Revolution in 1688, which established religious and civil liberty for Great Britain, and then for many other parts of the world. The liberty, that about a hundred years later occurred in the American colonies, would not have been possible if it had not happened first in the mother country, in that covenantal way. Nearly all the countries that have constitutional liberty, and fairness and equity, individual dignity and sound structure, can trace these blessings back to what those grand old Scottish Christians were doing in 1638 and to some degree to what the Pilgrim Christians were doing on these shores in 1620.

In both of those covenant oath-takings, in Plymouth, Massachusetts and in Edinburgh, the people who were prepared to sign and swear the oath had in their minds various places in Scripture, including Deuteronomy 29. So it is one of the most relevant passages of the Word of God for everything you could ever wish for, while you are living in earth.

I want to look at three major points from these verses: first, a solemn assembly, verse 2 and 9–12; second, a failure of discernment, verses 2–8; third, a call to decision, verses 9 and 12.

A Solemn Assembly (29:2, and 9–12)

First, we note in verse 2 that all of God's people are called to stand together as one body, where they were reminded of what the Lord had done for them in bringing them out of Egypt, and through forty years of wilderness wandering. This provided the background to exhort them to give themselves, body and soul, and their children, to live for God, by taking the covenant, by swearing the holy oath, to be His people forever. In verses 9–12, we note that every class of people, people of every age, from high to low, from young to old alike, were required to give themselves afresh to God in taking the covenant oath. Whether prince or workman: drawer of water, hewer of wood, male and female, all were in on it; their future would depend upon it.

A Failure of Discernment (29:2–8)

In verse 4, we see a failure to discern who God was, and what His work in their lives meant, up to this point. There are two aspects to this failure of discernment.

First, God lists His blessings to these people in verses 2 and 3 and 5–8. We have talked about them previously: the Exodus event, military victories, supernatural protection of shoes and clothing, to keep them from wearing out, heavenly manna to feed them, water from the rock, and now, this beautiful land of which they already had (which we call trans-Jordan), which God had already given them, after destroying the kingdom of Og and Bashan. Hence, God, through Moses, is listing how wonderfully he has treated them, how generous he has been to them, as a heavenly Father, Captain, and Friend.

The second aspect of this failure—and this is the sobering part—up to this point the generality of the people have not discerned the meaning of what God has done for them. Notice verse 4: 'Yet the Lord hath not given you an heart to perceive and eyes to see and ears to hear unto this day'. All these good things have been done to you from birth, and yet you don't know what it means! You haven't appreciated who did it and what it requires of you! With all of the supernatural blessings that have surrounded you for forty years, Moses is saying, you still do not see what it means. You take the divine interventions of God into space/time history for granted, as though you deserved them, or as though you did them yourself. This same attitude is mentioned at length in Psalm 78:5–8:

> For he established a testimony in Jacob,
> and appointed a law in Israel,
> which he commanded our fathers,
> that they should make them known to their children:
> That they might set their hope in God,
> and not forget the works of God,
> but keep his commandments,
> And might not be as their fathers,
> a stubborn and rebellious generation:
> a generation that set not their heart aright
> and whose spirit was not stedfast with God.

Psalm 78:22 and 31 show the bitter outcome of forgetting who had done all this for them:

> Because they believed not in God,
> and trusted not in his salvation…
> The wrath of God came upon them,
> and slew the fairest of them,
> and smote down the chosen men of Israel.

This same verse 4 of Deuteronomy 29 is quoted by Paul, in Romans 11:7–8. Romans 11 is about the mystery of the Jewish people largely rejecting Jesus as Messiah, a great grief to Paul and hard to understand. In Romans 11:7–8, he takes some of the words directly from Deuteronomy 29:4:

> What then? Israel hath not obtained that which he seeketh for; but the election hath obtained it, and the rest were blinded [the election is the chosen remnant]. (According as it is written [and this is referring to Deuteronomy 29], God hath given them the spirit of slumber, eyes that they should not see, and ears that they should not hear;) unto this day.

In other words, Paul has to go back to Deuteronomy to get any kind of approach to the hardness of Israel's heart, when they largely rejected Jesus Christ as their Messiah and Lord, some 1400 years after Moses spoke these words.

What does God say through Moses that should make Israel discern the meaning of all their divine blessings? What would it take for them to realize that the most important thing about life is God? Verse 4 says, to put it positively: God has to give you a heart to perceive, eyes to see, and ears to hear. Isaiah 6 talks about the same thing.

Jesus brings forward this principle, in the chapter on the new birth in John 3, where he says: 'Except a man be born again, he cannot see the kingdom of heaven.' You don't see it! You sit in a church 50 years, and you literally don't see what it means, or get the point, until something happens inside you that is called the new birth or the new creation. Similarly in John 6:57–58 and 65, we hear the words of Jesus, where He is talking about the Jewish leadership who were rejecting Him. Jesus says that to receive Him, is 'to eat his flesh and to drink his blood':

> As the living Father hath sent me, and I live by the Father; so he that eateth me, even he shall live by me. This is that bread which came down from heaven; not as your fathers did eat manna, and are dead; he that eateth of this bread shall live forever.

It is saving, personal faith in Jesus, that is eating the bread. And then in verse 65: 'And Jesus said, Therefore said I unto you, that no man can come unto me, except it were given unto him of my Father'.

Similarly, the church of Laodicea, in Revelation 3:18, is told what they need: 'I counsel thee to buy of me gold tried in the fire, that thou mayest be rich; and white raiment, that thou mayest be clothed, and that the shame of thy nakedness do not appear; and anoint thine eyes with eye-salve, that thou mayest see.'

It all goes back to the supernatural eye-salve—that is to say, the Holy Spirit repairing the moral blindness of the fall of Adam with which we are born, changing us from the inside out, so that now we see God, and what He has done, and have a heart to follow Him. The most valuable thing that a human being could ever have is the eye-salve, the Holy Spirit's unction, so that we can see—as Jesus says in John 3:3—the kingdom of God. How could you buy something that valuable? You haven't got that kind of money.

Well, Isaiah says: 'Come and buy food and drink without money and without price'. This means, ask, humbly and simply. In 2 Corinthians 3, Paul again discusses the situation of the synagogue rejecting Jesus; but he ends with the great hope and great joy of the future. He says that a day is coming, when the vast majority of the Jews will have their eyes opened by God, and they will see their Messiah, and willingly come to Him:

> And not as Moses, which put a veil over his face, that the children of Israel could not steadfastly look to the end of that which is abolished; but their minds were blinded [and then the same expression as in Deuteronomy 29:24]; for until this day remaineth the same veil untaken away in the reading of the Old Testament; which veil is done away in Christ (2 Cor. 3:13–18).

They hear the Torah every Sabbath and their eyes are blinded from seeing the One who is the completion and the fullness of the Torah, which is Christ. That will change one day. It will be a miracle of miracles, and God alone will be able to do it.

> But even unto this day, when Moses is read, the veil is upon their heart. Nevertheless when it shall turn to the Lord [that is, the nation Israel, the Jews], the veil shall be taken away [the blindness of understanding where their own law points them to is going to be removed]. Now the Lord is that Spirit; and where the Spirit of the Lord is, there is liberty. But we all, with open face beholding as in a glass the glory of the Lord, are changed into the same image from glory to glory, even as by the Spirit of the Lord.

Now what Moses is saying, is true, not just of the Jews in Moses' day, but of all persons who have experienced anything of the blessing of God in their lives; all need an opening of the eyes to discern what the goodness that has surrounded them really means. Their eyes need to be opened, in order to discern that God has been good to me, and is calling me to live in His covenant. This is the goal of human life, above everything else.

Many otherwise intelligent, cultured, and well-off people, are like dumb, fat, well-watered, well-fed, sleek farm animals or perhaps a big animal in the woods; they live as though they had no soul, and as though there were no God. They just live on the level of the physical, and lurch every day closer to the grave, towards final disaster. How much do you lose when you lose perception of who God is, and what He has done for you, and the direction He calls you to go? Everything!

One can think here of what old King Nebuchadnezzar said, before he went crazy for a few years. He said in Daniel 4:28–32:

> All this came upon the king Nebuchadnezzar. At the end of twelve months he walked in the palace of the kingdom of Babylon. The king spake, and said, Is not this great Babylon that I have built for the house of the kingdom by the might of my power, and for the honor of my majesty? While the word was in the king's mouth, there fell a voice from heaven, saying, O king Nebuchadnezzar, to thee it is spoken: The kingdom is departed from thee. And they shall drive thee from men, and thy dwelling shall be with the beasts of the field; they shall make thee to eat grass as oxen, and seven times [that's seven years] shall pass over thee, until thou know that the Most High ruleth in the kingdom of men and giveth it to whomsoever He will.

Here is an important historical question: verse 4 says that most of Israel up to that day had not discerned who God was, and what His blessings meant; they still did not get the point of how good He was, and how they owed Him everything. If that is the case, then how was it that Israel has endured unto this day?

The answer is found in the mystery of election: God elects a remnant, as for instance in Isaiah 1:9, 'Except the Lord of Hosts had left unto us a very small remnant, we should have been as Sodom and we should have been like unto Gomorrah'. Isaiah 10:20–22 adds:

> And it shall come to pass in that day, that the remnant of Israel [that's a small percentage, a corner of the cloth], and such as are escaped of the house of Jacob, shall no more again stay upon him that smote them; but shall stay upon the Lord, the Holy One of Israel, in truth. The remnant shall return, even the remnant of Jacob, unto the mighty God. For though thy people Israel be as the sand of the sea, yet a remnant of them shall return; the consumption decreed shall overflow with righteousness.

In other words, mysterious, divine election guarantees the endurance of a remnant of the chosen people. Our covenant God has always seen to it that there is a remnant, a certain percentage known only to Him, whose hearts are opened to discern the Lord in their lives, and to cast themselves upon the grace of God, saying, 'Lord, here I am'.

We hear this truth in Jesus' words in Luke 12:32: 'Fear not, little flock [remnant]; for it is your Father's good pleasure to give you the kingdom'. That is why Israel endured, and that is why the church has endured against every possible odd. There is a lot about election in Deuteronomy 29, and in Romans 8, 11, Ephesians 1 and other places.

As I teach it every year at the seminary, I always have to conclude that it is mysterious, and I never have once attempted to explain election. I'd have to be as big as God to do that, and I'm just a little human. But I will say that there are two sides to it, and if we hold these two sides together, we will be all right. Here are the two sides of the one truth of election:

First, universal human responsibility. All humans, all in the image of Adam, are obligated to discern what God has done for them. They are created in His image; He has given them life; He has spared them so far from judgment; He has given them gracious calls; they are obligated to discern that God is the One they must deal with. Everyone is obligated. Read Romans 1 and 2; Psalm 19; Psalm 8, and so forth.

But the other side of the truth is divine election. It is a fact that the sons and daughters of Adam and Eve will not discern or perceive, without the Holy Spirit renewing our personality and our hearts, and opening our spiritual eyes and ears. Now the pressing issue for us human beings is not God's election; for God is big enough and wise enough to take care of that just right. Rather the issue for us is to be keen to answer God's call, to swear the oath, to live in this covenant, to live in the covenant of faith that God provides in the Old and New Testaments, especially as they lead us to Jesus, through the ministry of the Holy Spirit.

A Call to Decision (29:9–11)

Moses issued a call for decision to this vast assemblage in verses 9 and 12. Verse 9 shows that God wishes to prosper you. Do you know that? Micah says about God that 'He delighteth in mercy'. And Lamentations says 'He afflicts not willingly the sons of men'. God's heart is wonderfully loving. The hymn writer Faber says,

> For the love of God is broader
> than the measure of man's mind;
> and the heart of the eternal
> is most wonderfully kind.

Yes, it's true. God wants to prosper you; God does not want to hurt you. But the only place where God is properly able to prosper us is in the covenant of grace, the plan of salvation that He arranged. We see this point in Romans 10:1: 'Brethren, my heart's desire and prayer to God for Israel is that they might be saved.' They have a zeal, but according to verse 3, they are ignorant of what it really means. They haven't perceived. Then, like Deuteronomy 29:9 and 12, which call us to swear the oath in faith and claim the covenant for ourselves, Romans 10:6–9 states:

> The righteousness which is of faith speaketh on this wise [and this is from later on in Deuteronomy 29]; say not in thine heart, Who shall ascend into heaven? (that is, to bring Christ down from above;) or, Who shall descend into the deep (that is, to bring up Christ again from the dead.) But what saith it? The word is nigh thee, even in thy mouth and in thy heart; that is, the word of faith, which we preach; that if thou shalt confess with thy mouth [that's swearing the covenant, in the New Testament form] the Lord Jesus, [or that Jesus is Lord—He's my Lord] and shalt believe in thine heart that God hath raised Him from the dead, thou shalt be saved.

In closing, some of us might feel hopeless, knowing that unless God touches our hearts, we will not want to swear the covenant; we will not desire to confess Jesus, even when He is offered, unless something happens to us spiritually. Well, from God's point of view that is true enough. But there's this to be said always: divine election is true, but human responsibility is equally true; hold them together, for the Bible holds them together, without explaining how it all fits together.

If the Holy Spirit does not anoint you with the eye-salve, you are not going to believe; you are not going to swear the covenant. That's true, but at the same time, Jesus says in Luke 11:13, that if a good earthly father will not give his son a scorpion when he asks him for a fish, and will not give him a stone when he asks him for a piece of bread: 'how much more will your heavenly Father give the Holy Spirit to them that ask him?' Jesus says, ask the Father for the Holy Spirit and He will take care of it! But in order to do so, you've got to want it!

Jesus said: 'If any man will do His will, he shall know of the doctrine, whether it be of God, or whether I speak of myself' (John 7:17). If you want to know if Jesus is God, if Jesus is Savior and Messiah, if He is truly your hope in life and death, then Jesus said that if you are prepared to do the Father's will, He will gladly show you who Jesus is. Jeremiah 29:13 says, 'Ye shall seek me, and find me, when ye shall search for me with all your heart'. You can find God and know Him with your heart, soul, and spirit, if you 'give it all' to seek Him. If you really want this thing above everything else, God will show you Himself. It's a promise from God; He doesn't lie; He's not hesitant to show Himself.

Proverbs 1:23: 'Turn you at my reproof; behold, I will pour out my Spirit unto you; I will make known my Words unto you.' Say this: 'Oh God, help me turn around; help me turn around now! You have rebuked me; help me accept the rebuke for not having perceived you, and not caring. Help me turn around.' Our gracious God replies, 'I will pour out my Spirit' and He will get you exactly where you need to be! God doesn't lie.

One more encouragement for us to take the covenant oath from the depths of our heart is this: God says through Moses that He will include our children in the blessings, if indeed we will take the covenant. Deuteronomy 29:14–15 tells us, 'I am making this covenant for those who are not here.' That means they are not yet born; but God, by His grace, is including them. Deuteronomy 7:9 says: 'I will be gracious to a thousand generations'. We don't know exactly how it works, but 1 Corinthians 7:14 says that if a believer is living with an unbelieving spouse, and the unbeliever will let the believing spouse stay with them, he or she is not to walk out; stay with them, if only one is a believer. The reason is this: if you stay with them, your seed will be holy; your children, even of only one believer, will have a special relationship to God that worldly children don't have, at least, not as of yet. That's the truth of the covenant being made, not only with those standing there, but also with their long-term descendants.

We have discerned this kind of pre-ordained blessing for generations to come in one of the ancestors of our family, who came from the Isle of Skye to North Carolina long ago. Most of his children emigrated with him, but he left some descendants on Skye. It is wonderful to see that now, about eight generations later, his descendants both on the Isle of Skye, Scotland, and in North Carolina, are still in the covenant. Micah says that God 'delights in mercy', and He does so over long generations. He wants to bless you and your seed. But you need to answer His call to make certain that you are in the covenant of grace.

64

IDOLS DESTROY, BUT GOD SAVES

Deuteronomy 29: 16-29

This passage brings before us in a vivid way that idols will destroy a people, but God will save and bless you if you put Him first. This text brings out that the most significant thing about your life is that you never put anything in front of God in your mind or in your affections; then your actions will be right actions that God can bless.

To put something in front of God is to engage in a certain kind of idolatry, which finally winds up wreaking havoc on the life given over to it. Remember that in the Ten Commandments, the first few start with God: 'Thou shalt have no other gods before Me'; in the Lord's prayer that Jesus gives us, the first few petitions of the Lord's prayer address our relationship to God: 'Our Father which art in heaven, hallowed be Thy name...' This passage, in a very concrete way, shows us that our only hope is to follow the same order, seeking for God to be in first place. This will require the Holy Spirit working within us. And if so, we and our children will dwell safely all through the future.

There are two points in this passage: first, the certainty of Divine curses upon idolatry, verses 16-21; second, the verdict of history against nations that God had to bring down in His wrath, verses 22-29.

THE CERTAINTY OF DIVINE CURSES UPON IDOLATRY (29:16-21)

The certainty of Divine curses upon idolatry is something we do not like to think about. Our reluctance makes one recall the famous line of Scarlett O'Hara's, 'I'll think about that tomorrow', in Gone with the Wind. Or it makes you think about cartoons in which an ostrich sticks his head in the sand, on a beach, where they are getting ready to test an atomic bomb. Do that if you want to, but you will pay a high price, as did the ostrich.

In verses 16-21, we find three truths: first, how easy it is to see idols (verses 16-17); second, how hard it is to see one's own heart as it really is (verse 19); and third, how certain is the execution of the wrath of a holy God (verses 20-21).

First, how easy it is to see the idols in our culture: idols are the things that God hates the most, because they come between Him and the affections of His people. Idols are the very sins that are the most destructive to the human soul. People are worried about catching AIDS, and rightly so, but very few are worried about what idolatry will do to them, which is far worse. In verses 16 and 17, we see that Egyptian culture had been chock full of idols. In Egypt, the river Nile, crocodiles, snakes, jackals, dogs, and particularly the Pharaohs, were all considered some kind of god, and people worshiped them as gods.

Egyptian culture did what Paul denounces in Romans 1. What they, and all idolatrous cultures do, though in different forms, is to take an aspect of the created order, something less than God, and put it in the place of God: 'and changed the glory of the incorruptible God into an image made like unto corruptible man and to birds and four footed beasts and creeping things … and who changed the truth of God into a lie and worshiped and served the creature more than the Creator who is blessed forever. Amen' (Rom. 1:23-25).

To give oneself over to any kind of idol was in Egypt a statue or animal, or rulers; in India it is various kinds of animals: cows and statues; in our Western world it is something in the mind—idols of nature (making nature a god), or history, evolution, politics, or maybe money or sex or power. They become idols, just as destructive as the ancient crocodile or the Buddha.

Something bad happens to people who follow idols; their moral character becomes profoundly degraded. Romans 1:24 speaks of it: 'wherefore God also gave them up to uncleanness through the lusts of their own hearts to dishonor their own bodies between themselves.' Now every culture—whether ancient Egypt, Rome, or modern America and Europe—has its own form of highly visible idols. You can't live in a culture or in a country without being aware that there are idols that might be attracting your mind or your affections. Hosea 8:4 speaks about the people of northern Israel: 'They chose them idols to their own destruction.' Once a people gives its heart to idols in the place of God, unless they repent, they are going to be destroyed.

What do you think makes idols, taking different forms in different cultures, so attractive to people? I believe it's that they do not demand moral holiness; they do not demand splitting with your sins in order to follow the character of God. They let you go on the way you are, and maybe give you some kind of little thrill or help, but don't ask you under any condition to change your life. History shows that this attracts a big following.

The second point, in verse 19, shows that it is very hard to see one's own heart. By that I mean intellectually and spiritually; it is hard to figure out, sometimes, what we're really like. Verse 19 shows the self deception of people, particularly those brought up in the faith, which is most people in America and Britain. In verse 18, Moses says that some of them had turned away in their affections from God, putting something in God's place. Then in verse 19 he says, (and here's where it is so hard to figure ourselves out), 'they bless themselves in their own hearts'.

They have replaced God with something else; God is no longer first; they are no longer willing to split with their favorite sins; but still they want God to prop them up in self-centered ways. They bless themselves, though, because of their fine religious background—generations of Israelites. In our case we may be from generations of Presbyterians, Baptists, or whatever. But if they could have honestly looked into their own hearts, they would have seen that they were replacing God with the idols of their culture—maybe those of Egypt, maybe those of Canaan. In our case, maybe it's the things that appeal to American and European culture.

When you replace God with an idol, you no longer accept His Word for what it says. You change it so you don't have to change your life. The surest sign that a church has turned its back on God and replaced Him with some aspect of the created order, culture, politics or whatever, is that it will say that the Bible cannot mean what it says, when it alleges that God is going to judge people for sin. Our God is not like that! They fondly claim that the wrath of God will not fall on sinners—at least, not on them.

One could do a whole psychological study on verse 19. People who have turned their back on the real God, and replaced Him with something less, literally feel good about themselves but don't know how close they are to eternal destruction. Proverbs 4:23 says (literally from the Hebrew): 'Before all keepings, keep thy heart; for out of it are the issues of life.' The Authorized Version says: 'Keep thy heart with all diligence; for out of it are the issues of life.' What's going on in the heart determines whether you are going to have eternal life, or be separated from God. Deuteronomy 29:19 says that it is hard to discern one's self, once one has gotten into idolatry. The first person we deceive is our self, when it comes to feeling good spiritually, and even denying the written Word in order to do so.

Third, how certain is the execution of the wrath of a holy God against the sin of idolatry that is unrepented of (verses 20–21)? I believe that if people engage in idolatry, and have not gone past the point of no return, so that they repent, God will forgive them. But if they don't repent, eternal disaster is sure to follow. People don't like to accept that certainty.

I have a friend, a Christian business man, whom I have known for a long time; he lives in California. He said to me a number of years ago (speaking of southern California, but it could be true in South Carolina), that whenever you go to a funeral, everybody becomes a Universalist. No minister ever hints that a soul could be lost and in hell for not receiving Jesus. He said that whenever he attended a funeral, in every case the minister, whether evangelical, moderate or liberal, was functionally a Universalist.

Why? Because they foolishly think God will not judge anybody. So we deceive ourselves and go on. What a price to be paid! In actual fact, Deuteronomy 29:20 says that if somebody keeps on in idolatry and refuses to repent, the Lord 'will not spare him'. How different from what many of the preachers and theologians are saying! But we must go by what God says through Moses, that the Lord will not spare him. If there ever is a split between what God says and what the preachers say, I'm going with God, as best I can understand the issue.

Along these lines, Romans 1 and 2 are, in one sense, an exposition of Deuteronomy 29 and 30. In Romans 2:6–9, Paul is saying that the real God, not the idol god that keeps some people from having to face their sins and be honest about their sinful hearts, but the real God:

> who will render to every man according to his deeds: to them who by patient continuance in well doing seek for glory, and honor, and immortality, eternal life. But unto them that are contentious, and do not obey the truth, but obey unrighteousness - indignation and wrath, tribulation and anguish, upon every soul of man that doeth evil, of the Jew first, and also of the Gentile.

That's the real God, the one you and I are going to face at the last, not the god conveniently concocted by self-serving humans. The frightening expression 'God gave them up' is used three times in Romans 1:24, 26, 28.

> Wherefore God also gave them up to uncleanness through the lust of their own hearts, for this cause God gave them up unto vile affections, even as they did not like to retain God in their knowledge, God gave them over to a reprobate mind.

The worse thing that can happen to you in this earthly life is for God to give you up. It's the worse thing that can happen to a denomination too. Does He ever do it? Obviously He does. Both Deuteronomy and Romans talk about it, along with others. Just think of how many mainline denominations have severely weakened their moral standards to accommodate the declining culture.

It is very serious when people have been in idolatry for such a long time, and refuse to repent, that God gives them up, or God gives them over. The modernist idea, which is held by more evangelicals than you would think, is that God never punishes anybody for sin; but this is to fly in the face of the clear teaching of the Word of God.

The Verdict of History Against Nations That God Had to Bring Down (29:22-29)

Note two truths under this point: first, what history teaches us; second, what God hides from us.

What history teaches anybody who is willing to learn is that the centuries are strewn with the wreckage of nations and churches that turned away from God and His written Word, to addict themselves to popular idols. Sodom and Gomorrah (verse 23), Assyria, Babylon, Persia, Rome, and the northern and southern kingdoms of Israel are all on the rubbish heap of history, except for the remnant of the southern kingdom, which God brought back.

We in the western world are subject to exactly the same holy, moral forces that eventually brought down all these others. God brought them down after having given them many opportunities to hear His prophets and to repent. But they stubbornly refused to do it. We today may not be too far from what happened in the northern kingdom of Israel, in the eighth century B.C. Hosea 7:2-3; and then 6-10 unveil what was happening then, and what seems to be happening now: 'And they consider not in their hearts [they deceive their hearts] that I remember all their wickedness; now their own doings have beset them about; they are before my face. They make the king glad with their wickedness'—the political process praises sinful activities as though they are wonderful; the media loves it, and then verses 6-9:

> … for they have made ready their heart like an oven while they lie in wait; the baker sleepeth all the night; in the morning it burneth as a flaming fire. They are all hot as an oven, and have devoured their judges; all their kings are fallen; there is none among them that calleth unto me. Ephraim, he hath mixed himself among the people; Ephraim is a cake not turned. Strangers have devoured his strength.

– immigrants, foreigners, outsiders are going to get your best possessions—'and he knoweth it not; yea, gray hairs are here and there upon him, yet he knoweth it not.'

This illustration seems to set before us a distinguished man, taken up with his own strength and abilities, but he doesn't realize how he is aging. He doesn't look in the mirror, where he would notice that gray hairs are coming, which he would have seen if he had been in touch with his heart before God. It is a sign of what he must soon face, as his physical life draws to its inevitable end. It can be like that with a prosperous culture. The verdict of history is clear: countries that replace the triune God with idols, whatever kind of idol, if they don't repent, will be crushed by the judgments of God.

The second part of this point is what God hides from us. I suppose Deuteronomy 29:29 is one of the most famous passages in Scripture, 'The secret things belong unto the Lord our God, but those things which are revealed belong to us and to our children forever that we may do all the words of this law'. God hides important things from all mankind, the precise details of His future plans, including from His elect people. We call it 'His secret counsel'. Jesus said that no one knows the day of the hour of the return of the Son of Man; it is hidden in God's secret counsel.

Therefore, there is absolutely no point whatsoever in trying to guess exactly what the next ten years will hold, what the next century will be like, how long I will live, even what next week will be like. Scripture says you know not what a day may bring forth; it's in the secret counsel of God—leave it there! Listen to James 4:13–15:

> Go to now, ye that say, Today or tomorrow we will go into such a city, and continue there a year, and buy, and sell, and get gain; whereas ye know not what shall be on the morrow. For what is your life? It is even a vapor, that appeareth for a little time, and then vanisheth away. For that ye ought to say, If the Lord will, we shall live, and do this, or that.

I was brought up in a home where my parents said, if they would promise to do something in a day or two, 'If I live and do well'. As I remember, I'm told my great grandparents said from the Latin translation of this verse in James 4, *Deo volente*, or 'if God is willing'. I was brought up, as many of you were, not to make a certain promise as to what you were going to do in a week or a year, but to say 'if I live and do well' or 'if God wills', you will be there and do such and such. Your life is a vapor. A lot about you and me is hidden in the secret counsel of God, and really truly we should be happy about that, and feel at peace, because He will do everything right.

I went to see a very close friend of mine, a classmate from first grade through high school, up in Raleigh, who is facing death from cancer, and is now in a hospice. We were talking about that, and as he is a Christian, I knew I could be frank with him. I said something like this: God made the choice when you and I were born, and so I'm happy for God to make the choice when He wants us to die; it will be the right time. My classmate gladly replied: 'Yes, Douglas, that's exactly the way I feel.' He chose 1943 to be the year of my birth and I wish Him to choose the year of my death; it will be right. He gave us the best in our birth, and He is going to give us the best in our death. It is in His hands. You've never got to worry about that. God says to put your emphasis on, 'the things that are revealed belong to us and our children that we may do all the words of this law'; do what God said; get it in your mind:

> Blessed is the man that walketh not in the counsel of the ungodly, nor standeth in the way of sinners, nor sitteth in the seat of the scornful. But his delight is in the law of the Lord; and in His law doth he meditate day and night. And he shall be like a tree planted by the rivers of water (Ps. 1:1–2).

Psalm 119:9 asks: 'How shall a young man cleanse his way? By taking heed according unto Thy Word'. Get in close touch with God's Word; yield yourself to the patterns of its truth, and all will be well: 'Thy Word have I hid in my heart, that I might not sin against Thee' (119:11). Micah 6:8 is inscribed over the door of the first chapel that was built at the University of North Carolina: 'He hath shown thee, O man, what is good; for what doth God require of thee but to love mercy, to do justly, and to walk humbly with thy God?'

What is our appointed way for a safe future? What is our hope for our children in a rapidly declining culture? They are not, as far as we know, likely to have it as good as we who were born in the '40s and '50s. What about their future? Well, here's the appointed way for us and for them. God loves our children and grandchildren at least as much as we do, and indeed, more so. The appointed way is God's written Word. Trust God and His Word. Remove every idol from your heart and home, and seek God's Word and give yourself to it. As they follow you, your children will make it safely through an unknown future.

There are two ways to look at the future of the Christian church in America, and in the other countries. One is hopelessness, and lacking in biblical faith. The other is hopeful, that is to say, it is based on the resurrection of Jesus, and His total control over everything that ever happens. To live without hope means literally to give up, and wait for the worst: devastated stock markets, government oppression, maybe loss of freedom, all kinds of negative things.

But there's a better way: since Jesus is now on His victorious throne, He is guiding us into the future, which is surely His, just as much as the past. He has promised that the gates of hell shall not prevail against His church; nothing can happen but what He allows. The future may hold severe judgments for a sleeping church and a materialistic, immoral culture all around it. Yet, since the precious, loving, wondrous God is in control of everything, when He exercises judgment, mercy is always mixed in with it.

Let us close with a poem that was used by King George VI, on December 25, 1939, when Britain was at war, and the Germans seemed to be doing very well indeed, so that things looked terrible for the United Kingdom. In his Christmas Day speech to the nation, he quoted a poem by a Christian woman named Minnie Louise Haskins, and it is still the best way to face the future:

> And I said to the man who stood at the gate of the year,
> 'Give me a light that I may tread safely into the unknown.'
> And he replied, 'Go into the darkness and put your hand into the hand of God.
> That shall be to you better than light and safer than a known way.'

65

SUCCESS CAN FOLLOW FAILURE

Deuteronomy 30:1–10

This passage contains good news: it offers the possibility of having success after we have failed. God's Word teaches, particularly here, that failure does not have to be the last word for those who believe in God; it can be followed by an even greater success. We find two points in this passage: first, failure; and then second, success.

FAILURE (30:1)

Verse 1 of chapter 30 refers to 'The curse which I have set before thee', the meaning of which goes back to 29:28: 'and the Lord rooted them out of their land in anger and in wrath and in great indignation and cast them into another land, as it is this day'. Moral failure, based on long-lasting disobedience to God, would lead the people of God into captivity in a foreign country. At this juncture in their history, Moses—and this is one of the many places where the holy Bible shows its inspiration—is talking about the captivity, and predicting it about 900 years before it happened! The words in verse 28 are 'the Lord rooted them out', like pulling you up by the roots.

They had broken God's covenant over and over. God does not lightly judge: 'He afflicts not willingly the sons of men', says Lamentations. It takes a long time before God roots out His people, and a great number of years of disobedience. But finally, the last hour and judgment come. Scripture shows us how this finally occurred, especially in Jeremiah, Ezekiel and Daniel. Psalm 137:1–4 is a description of how they felt when they were led out of their ancestral home to have to live under foreigners.

By the rivers of Babylon, there we sat down, yea, there we wept, when we remembered Zion. We hanged our harps upon the willows in the midst thereof. For there they that carried us away required of us a song; and they that wasted us required of us mirth, saying, Sing us one of the songs of Zion. How shall we sing the Lord's song in a strange land?

SUCCESS AFTER FAILURE (30:1–10)

Some of the Psalms reveal how God's people felt, both during failure (as in Psalm 137), and then as they were restored as in Psalm 126, which describes how they felt when God had mercy on them after their repentance from severe moral failure. How glad they are that they will get back to Zion, out from under the heel of the foreigners: 'When the Lord turned again the captivity of Zion, we were like them that dream'. It was a dream—a beautiful dream come true; they had dreamed it for 70 years. 'Then was our mouth filled with laughter, and our tongue with singing.' Psalm 137 had said, we can't sing; we can't play the harp; we're too grieved; now the first thing they do is probably play the harps, beat the cymbals and tambourines, and sing; 'Then said they among the heathen, the Lord hath done great things for them. The Lord hath done great things for us; whereof we are glad. Turn again our captivity, O Lord, as the streams in the south. They that sow in tears shall reap in joy.' That's how it feels when you are coming out of failure and back into the success God wants you to have. 'He that goeth forth and weepeth, bearing precious seed, shall doubtless come again with rejoicing, bringing his sheaves with him.'

Behind God's wondrous grace to the children of Israel, and to all who have fallen into failure and ask for help to come out of it, and do come out of it, four things transpire: First, those who have failed are honest and call to mind why they failed. Second, repent of it before the face of God. Third, God does for them what they could never do for themselves. Fourth, the Lord will send massive blessings on those who really repent of their moral and spiritual failure. The last word in their experience will not be curses, but covenant blessings. That's God's intention and we see it happen to Israel.

First, then, we are instructed in verse 1 that when we, like Israel, have failed and start experiencing the curses of the covenant, we are to call to mind why we failed; that's the first step: 'Thou shalt call them to mind among all the nations whither the Lord thy God hath driven thee' (30:1). Call what to mind? The covenant you violated, the covenant with its promises of blessing and its threats of cursing. Remember that and connect it to the state you are in now, whether moral, physical, economic or familial.

Remember that if you hadn't violated it, you wouldn't be in this state, says Moses. Deuteronomy 29:25–27 makes it clear: 'Then men [foreigners, non-Christians, pagans make mention of it] shall say because they have forsaken the covenant of the Lord God of their fathers which he made with them when he brought them forth out of the land of Egypt'—in other words, you were redeemed; people know that you were redeemed by blood, but then you violated the terms of what God had called you to be through the redemption, 'For they went and served other gods and worshiped them, gods whom they knew not, whom He had not given them.' It may be a different religion, or it could be that you outwardly keep the same religion, but worship money or whatever; and 'the anger of the Lord was kindled against this land to bring upon it all the curses that are written in this book'. Call that to mind! Think of that!

To get beyond a failed life, or a bad stage of one's personal experience, it is always necessary to do something that is very uncomfortable or humbling—namely, go back to the roots of our failure and face the real problem. I think one of the strengths of the Alcoholics Anonymous Twelve step program is that they meet in groups, and go through twelve steps that help people who have been overcome by alcohol abuse, face what it was about them that made them place their life and hope in alcohol, rather than in God or other relationships. It encourages people to say, here's where it started; here's the downward spiral; here's where it still keeps me dependent on this alien substance.

It's like that in marriage counseling: people have to face behavior patterns where they violated God's will for them, but it is not easy to do. In most cases, none of you will reach the following extreme: a young couple with church connections had serious problems that the husband had not noticed in the least, even after about three or four years of marriage. But one day, the young wife went out to the tool shed, picked up a hatchet and started heading for her husband's head. He managed to stop her and get the hatchet away. He at last decided that they did need to go for counseling. She had suggested it before, and he had said no. So they went and the first thing he said was, 'I didn't know we had a problem!' That might be an illustration that the male is not as quick as the female to see that there is some kind of problem, seemingly hard for males to admit.

It is a human tendency in all of us, male and female, to do anything in the world to keep from facing who we really are, what got us into this thing that caused us serious trouble. But Proverbs 28:13 warns: 'He that covereth his sins shall not prosper; but whoso confesseth and forsaketh them shall have mercy'. That's all God asks! Confess it; forsake it. 'Confess' in Greek, is an interesting word; it is *homologeo;* comprising *homo* meaning 'same' and *logeo* 'to say'. When I'm confessing, I say the same thing about my own sins and failures that God says; 'That thou might be justified when Thou judgest' (Ps. 51:4). David says about his sins what God said. You're getting honest with God, and getting on grounds where you can be pardoned and come out of it to something massively better.

I believe we all have had enough experience to say this: the devil will work day and night to keep you and me from doing this, from confessing where we fail. The devil does not want you to face reality and so tries to block it. It's more pleasing to the flesh and more comfortable not to face the unpleasant truth, to remain the way we are. How can we overcome Satan in our own fallen flesh as we seek to avoid the truth? Make a prayer of the last two verses (23–24) of Psalm 139: 'Search me, O God, and know my heart; try me, and know my thoughts; and see if there be any wicked way in me, and lead me in the way everlasting'. When we are in serous failure, we may be like the prodigal son: we wake up and see we are in the pigsty.

The first step to help you get out is to recall who your Father is and how you've let Him down. Call to mind why you fail; every man and woman has to do that for failure to be followed by success; there is no other way.

Second, repent of your failure before God. Deuteronomy 30:2, 8, and 10 can guide us in this process: 'and thou shalt return unto the Lord thy God, and thou shalt return, if thou shalt hearken, if thou shalt turn to the Lord'.

The Hebrew word used for repentance is the word 'shuv'. It means going in one direction, turning around and going the other direction. It says to quit going in a sinful direction pleasing your flesh and thereby grieving the Lord, and to turn around from it. Your face has been turned away from God; you have not been going by his Word; turn around and confess it and come back to Him. This idea involves restoring face to face personal relationship to God.

In essence, the Bible gives us a personal view of sin; it's not merely that there is an external list of rules that I have violated. Rather, I failed God my heavenly Father, who loved me, and said, 'this is the way, walk ye in it'. Indeed, He made it possible for me to do it; and I willfully went in another direction, disappointing the Lord, as my face was turned away from Him. Repentance means turning back to Him, face to face.

Often, true repentance involves sorrow, but the Bible doesn't give any particular agenda or recipe that there has to be a certain amount of tears or sorrow. But I doubt that anybody who has seriously failed God would come back to the loving, holy Lord, without feeling sorry that they had grieved God.

Paul in 2 Corinthians 7:10 speaks of two different kinds of sorrow for sins; one is good: 'For godly sorrow worketh repentance to salvation, not to be repented of ...' means that although you are very sorry you grieved the Lord, you will remain glad that you repented and pleased Him; the other is not good: 'but the sorrow of the world worketh death.'

Here then are two kinds of sorrow: One is: 'I'm sorry that I am hurting; why did this have to happen to me; it's bad down here; it used to be better.' Some will even say, 'What kind of world is this, that somebody as fine as I am has to suffer like this?' This is worldly sorrow; it's like Esau who was shedding tears for what he lost, but it didn't do him any good: 'For ye know that afterward when he [Esau] would have inherited the blessing, he was rejected; for he found no place of repentance, though he sought it carefully with tears' (Heb. 12:17). He was very sorry he had disdained the blessing and sold it to Jacob: 'Oh look what I have lost! It hurts me; it's terrible, very terrible.' He never faced who he was, and never said, 'I was a profane, sinful person; I disdained the holy blessing that came from my father; Lord forgive me.' It was not godly sorrow.

Then think of the apostle Peter; he certainly failed Jesus Christ in a most shameful way, by denying the Lord three times. Matthew 26:75 says 'he went out and wept bitterly'. Esau wept, but this weeping of Peter was different. He is weeping because of the Lord he hurt, but Esau doesn't seem to be concerned about God and God's program. Later we see our Lord Jesus Christ restoring Peter by the seaside, by the fire at breakfast: 'Simon, son of Jonas, lovest thou Me ...' Yes, Jesus restores him to his ministry, one of the greatest ministries that ever was, after tremendous failure. Why? Because Simon Peter had godly sorrow, towards God. Worldly sorrow is only towards self.

Let me address a concern that more than one good person has felt. The devil will say that you have failed, and that any repentance on your part was entirely superficial. He may ask you, 'How do you know you will ever have godly sorrow? Maybe yours was only worldly sorrow.' But do not be overwhelmed. Instead of listening to Satan speaking inside you, look up to God, for He is able to give you godly sorrow, if you ask for it. Failure certainly makes us hurt, but is it only for self or primarily for God, whom we offended? Simon Peter ought to know, having failed his Master terribly. He did experience godly sorrow. In later years, Peter, when preaching about how Jesus was crucified and raised, says: 'Him hath God exalted with his right hand to be a Prince and a Savior for to give repentance to Israel and forgiveness of sins' (Acts 5:31).

Do not miss what a wonderful thing Peter is saying! Part of Christ's exaltation in His resurrection and ascension, and His power to dispense the Holy Spirit to all who ask, is that He has the authority to give the gift of repentance. You may object, but isn't that something we need to do? Yes, indeed, but how can I be certain that I have done it sincerely? On the basis of what the risen Lord now gives, if I didn't know whether I had godly sorrow or not, I would start crying out 'Lord Jesus Christ, from your throne, send the Spirit of repentance, who brings godly sorrow, so that I can get it right with you, and come out of the pig pen, and be sincerely grieved that I provoked you'. God will hear that prayer. Peter says that Jesus was exalted 'a Prince and a Savior to give repentance' to His people.

Third, what God will do, and what you cannot do, when you have failed. If it is a severe, moral, spiritual failure, God will do what you can't do. Deuteronomy 30:6 says: 'and the Lord will circumcise thine heart'.

Circumcision of heart can mean generally the new birth as in Jeremiah 31:33, where God says He will send the Holy Spirit to write the law on your heart; Ezekiel 36:26: 'I will take away the heart of stone' and put in a heart of flesh; and John 3, new birth. Such verses show us that circumcision of heart can be for those who have severely failed, and never been Christians, and by which God brings them to glorious salvation.

But it can also mean what the old Puritans used to speak of as 'melting the heart'. That's the way I would take it here, not to exclude that some would need the new birth, while they are in the pig pen. Yet I think this passage addresses real Christians, saved people, who through disobedience and taking on the qualities of the sinful culture in which they live, can get their faces turned away from God, and their hearts get hard towards God. But as the old Puritans used to say, the Lord melts the heart; the Holy Spirit melts the heart, so that there is once again, a tenderness of spirit towards the Lord, thereby renewing one's motivation and one's moral energies, to go in an entirely different, and now godly, direction.

Let us think of Psalm 110:3, (a Messianic Psalm) that says: 'Thy people shall be willing in the day of Thy power.' It is the power of God coming down, that both gives new birth and circumcises the heart of the lost, melting the heart of those who have been disobedient towards their Savior and Lord. God's power comes down into the moral pig pen, into the jail, or wherever, and make you willing.

Now here's a mystery of how two things fit together: God calls on us to repent and return, and to hearken to His Word; it's our responsibility; it's the only way out. But when we are doing that, something else is happening in the heavenly realms that touches us, that we don't see at first, and don't consciously even feel: God is working in us to enable us to repent and return. So which one is true? Does God do it, or do we do it?

Both are true at the same time, and it's not given us to figure it out any more than to recognize that both truths are in Holy Scripture. A good passage that may give some light on how this works is Philippians 2:12–13: 'Wherefore, my beloved, as ye have always obeyed, not as in my presence only, but now much more in my absence, work out your own salvation with fear and trembling.' You've got to do it! You've got to work out your salvation with fear and trembling. Listen to the covenant. Remember it. But then at the very same time, look at verse 13: 'For it is God which worketh in you, both to will and to do of His good pleasure.' God is doing it, enabling you. Even in the midst of a sermon like this, God is calling, and already working. Yes, you can do it now! Do what I have given you the strength to do, and I will give you more strength; I'm in it! It will work.

Fourth, God promises to send massive blessings on those who failed, but now are repenting, as they seek His face sincerely. The last word in their experience on earth will not be cursing; yes, they have experienced cursing, but it is going to be succeeded with tremendous times of blessing, such as they may never have seen before.

It was true of Israel, as we see in the books of Nehemiah and Ezra, when they got back home after 70 years of captivity. They got ready for tremendous blessings, one of which was the supreme honour that from them would come Messiah, who is our Savior and Lord!

Deuteronomy 30:9 says that God will make your body plenteous; He will give you children, and make your economy to abound with crops, cattle, fruit, and so forth. If that is not enough, later verse 9 says that God will joy over you; God will enjoy your return; God will be glad you are back, and you will feel something of the joy of God in your daily family and economic life. I suspect that there is little other than actually being in the glories of heaven, that can compare to that shared joy with God while we are still on earth!

Let us conclude this way: Israel violated the terms of the covenant and was led into foreign captivity for seventy years, because God had to put His covenant curses on them to wake them up, so they would repent and He could bless them again. Isaiah 26:9 explains it well: 'For when Thy judgments are in the earth the inhabitants of the world will learn righteousness.' May God grant us that the risen Christ, who is exalted to be a Prince and a Savior, will give us this kind of repentance, and all will be well!

66

The Truth is Not Hard to Find

Deuteronomy 30:11–20

This text is the precise opposite of modern relativism, which holds that you cannot know the absolute truth, for it does not exist. But what does the Word of God say? Jesus says in John 17:17, the high priestly prayer, 'Thy Word is truth.' This passage from Moses, near the very end of his life, presses home this point, and in so doing, shows that the truth is not hard to find.

Moses is getting ready to leave the people; it is time for him to die. He is saying, 'I have to leave you; God is calling me. You can't keep me, I've got to go. But you can keep the truth.' So he is about to conclude his long messages on the plains of Moab to the people, ere they went into the land of promise. To get them ready, he has been expounding what the Ten Commandments mean, how they teach us to walk with God in truth.

This is like the conclusion of a covenant ceremony we talked about earlier. Scholars who study ancient Middle Eastern forms of covenants have found that, for example among the Hittites, when the covenant is expounded, it concludes with a call to action. So Moses has no time to waste; within a few days God is going to take him. With that in view, he is saying, 'I'm leaving; now it's up to you to receive this truth and to act on it. That's the only way you can be saved. Otherwise you will lose absolutely everything, if you pretend that the truth is too complicated.'

We find in this passage two points. First, Moses tells us that the ultimate truth is not hard to find; and secondly, he gives a call to act on this truth by choosing life with God.

The Truth is Not Hard to Find (30:11–14)

In verse 11, Moses speaks of this ultimate truth by which we are supposed to live, in terms of God's commandment; in verse 14, he speaks of it as 'Word'. We can summarize by saying that it is the absolute truth about who God is, and what He requires of us as believers; it's the truth about what life really means, what lies beyond physical life, and how we can walk with God on earth and get to heaven. That's the ultimate truth; nothing is more important for a man or woman to know and act on,

One of the major points Moses makes in verses 11–14 is that these ultimate truths, the things that matter the most for each one of us, are not at all hard to find. Moses says that it is not hidden or far off; you don't have to go up to heaven, where you have some kind of vision and bring it down, or go into the deep places and bring it up. It is immediately at hand for anybody who wants it.

I remember when I was studying in Scotland, going to Dr. Francis Schaeffer's place, L'Abri, in Switzerland, in the late 60s or early 70s. I saw there a number of young people who had been experimenting with drugs and Eastern religions; but God got hold of them, transformed their lives, and they found Jesus Christ. Some of them said that they found that they already had the truth at home, in their Bibles, in the very houses in which they were raised. But they went shuffling off to other countries, supposedly in search of truth.

By grace, they found that Moses was right after all. One did not need to go way off. The truth of God is very close—if you want it.

That scene, so widespread in the 1960s, is long passed, but there are always other ways to avoid facing ultimate truth. Many use various theories of science to avoid God. While many scientists are atheistic, I read recently that forty per cent of scientists in America and Europe believe in God, and believe in some form of biblical truth.

The world famous scientist, Dr. Francis S. Collins, who completed the tracking of the human genome, working through three billion 'letters' in the DNA code is an illustration of a believing man of science. He finished this monumental task of mapping the genome, around 1999 and wrote, *The Language of God, A Scientist Presents Evidence for Belief*. I think he is a true Christian, though I cannot agree with his theistic evolution. But nonetheless, his testimony for the existence of God, the deity of Christ, and salvation through the blood is very strong indeed. He had been raised in a basically atheistic family; he was not necessarily opposed to Christianity, his parents didn't believe anything, and he had never been taken to church. Without much religious background, this bright young man was having a remarkable career in medical research, and was working in a hospital in Chapel Hill, North Carolina. But how did he meet God? It was not directly through his very able scientific studies but in a hospital room in the University of North Carolina hospital at Chapel Hill, when he was doing his residency. He went in to visit a simple country woman from rural North Carolina, who was a Christian. He tells us what happened:

> My most awkward moment came when an older woman, suffering daily from severe, untreatable angina, asked me what I believed. It was a fair question. We had discussed many other important issues of life and death, and she had shared her own strong Christian beliefs with me. I felt my face flush as I stammered out the words, 'I'm not really sure.' Her obvious surprise brought into sharp relief the predicament that I had been running away from for all of my nearly 26 years. I had never really seriously considered the evidence for or against belief.

The young doctor realized that he had met God at the hospital bed of a country woman, who loved the Lord, and confronted him with his need to know God. Moses had it right; you don't have to go far off; it's not terribly complicated, although the depth and range of God's truth always outruns our ability to comprehend it. Sometime after that, Dr. Collins read some of the works of C. S. Lewis, and things came together for him. But the simple truth is right at hand.

It's significant that these very verses, 30:11–14, are taken up and quoted directly by the apostle Paul in Romans 10:6–8. Paul is arguing against some of the Pharisees and others, who said that salvation through grace, justification by faith through Jesus Christ, is a new doctrine, not in the Old Testament, but something that people like

Paul invented. If it is not in the Old Testament, we don't have to accept it.

Paul replies by saying: you haven't read your Old Testament, for the Old Testament is full of salvation by the grace of God. Certainly that grace calls you to walk in God's law, but the basis of that salvation is God's grace. So Paul concluded that righteousness by faith in Christ is found in the law of Moses very clearly. To reinforce this, he quotes from Deuteronomy 30:

> the righteousness which is of faith speaks on this wise, Say not in thine heart, Who shall ascend into heaven? (that is, to bring Christ down from above;) or, Who shall descend into the deep? (that is, to bring up Christ again from the dead.) But what saith it? The word is nigh thee, even in thy mouth, and in thy heart; that is, the word of faith which we preach (Rom. 10:6–8).

Ultimate truth and salvation are just as close as the Word of God. Paul shows that the heart of the truth is the Father's testimony to what Jesus has done for sinners, that they could never do for themselves. And yes, salvation is that close! Nobody can say at the last day, 'Well I wasn't saved, Lord; it was too complicated philosophically and scientifically or it was in some other country from where I lived; we weren't sophisticated enough to know all of that.' God says, it was right in your house, in your Bible. Jesus was being preached. That's how close it was. He goes on to say in Romans 10:9: 'If thou shalt confess with thy mouth the Lord Jesus, and shalt believe in thine heart that God hath raised Him from the dead, thou shalt be saved.'

The truth is that somebody really did go into the heights above, where the ultimate truth is at the throne of God. Somebody really did go down into the depths beneath, where the spirits of the dead are existing in a different form. We are not called to do this, but the Lord Jesus Christ—who descended from the Father's throne into the womb of the virgin Mary, and was born of her in human nature such as we have, apart from sin, and suffered for our sins upon the tree—He went down into the deep places, and won the victory over Satan and his hosts. Then He came back to our realm, and made it possible for us to go to the Father. That's the ultimate truth that everybody needs to know.

The Call to Act Upon This Truth Deuteronomy 30:15–20

Moses, and the apostle Paul, centuries later, both call us to personal decision. It's something we must decide for ourselves. God sets before us either eternal life and all its bliss in His Son, or most awful separation from God and eternal lostness, if the Son be rejected by us. So we are called on by Moses, we're called on by Paul, to respond in faith and say, 'Lord, I wish to meet you in Christ in the Holy Spirit; whatever you have to offer to sinners, I want it. I wish to be forgiven, to have my life meaningful, and to live with you eternally. I don't know too much, but what little I know, I want to act on to the fullest extent of my capacity'.

Moses and Paul show us how near the truth is to us, a bright illustration of which is seen in the experience of the general Naaman from Syria, in the time of the prophet Elisha. The king of Syria told Naaman to go to Israel, for he thought the king of Israel could recover this man of his leprosy. The king of Israel was horrified, thinking it was a pretext of war. But somebody said to send him to the prophet Elisha, who would be able to heal him. So this great general, with all of his military retinue, drove up in their chariots to the abode of the prophet Elisha.

Elisha illustrated exactly what Moses means, in his words to this mighty general, who was eaten up by leprosy. He said for him to go and dip himself seven times in the Jordan River and he would recover from his leprosy. At first, the general was absolutely infuriated. He said to his assistants: 'we have much finer rivers in Syria: Abana and Pharpar—broader, deeper, cleaner, more sparkling, than this muddy Jordan, he is asking me to step into! Why didn't he come out and lay his hands on me, and say some words?' But one of his servants showed the wisdom of God when he said: 'Sir, if he had asked you to do something complicated, you would have done it; why don't you do what he says? something simple, something very near, as the Jordan River?' And the general thought better of it and went down into the Jordan River, where he was gloriously healed.

Most people who have problems accepting the Word of God, feel that they have an intellectual problem that justifies their not coming. Well, there are compelling intellectual answers, and as a professor and conference speaker, I have spent many years trying to give them. Of course, I only know some of the answers, but enough of them to rest satisfied in the truth of God's Word. Through it all, however, my observation is that it usually comes down to a moral problem, basically this: 'We will not have this man to reign over us.' I want to keep the lordship of my life, rather than turn it over to God.

But that does not make sense if you are lost! You're going down into eternal darkness, so how are you in any position to be your own guide? Yet part of our fallen condition is that we are afraid to give over control of our little life to another Lord! That's the real issue, though it is usually hidden deep inside the conscience of those who resist facing the truth about themselves.

Well, the great general did not want to step into the muddy Jordan; it was too simple, to the point of feeling humiliating to an important personage. But Moses says, 'The Word is very nigh thee'; and Paul says it's 'even in thy mouth that Jesus Christ is Lord'. God sets before us this decision; it makes people very uncomfortable, but what if it is worth it? An old hymn makes this point with power:

> Let not conscience make you linger,
> nor of fitness fondly dream;
> all the fitness He requireth
> is to feel your need of Him.
> This He gives you, this He gives you,
> 'tis the Spirit's rising beam.

As we move on into the latter part of Deuteronomy 30, we proceed on the foundation of what we did when we first came, as we trusted God's Word, and prayed for forgiveness. Then we hear three verbs in verses 15-20, which will characterize your life, after you are under God's Word: to love, to walk, to keep (i.e. the commandments). In verse 20 we find three more verbs (participles): loving, listening, clinging or cleaving (holding on to God). That is what the Christian life, the experience of salvation, is really all about: loving, listening, clinging; to love, to walk, to keep.

The message of these verbs is summarized in the words of Jesus in John 15:9-10, which express in personal, relational terms the meaning of cleaving, holding on to Him, loving, keeping; it all starts with love: the love of God. In Jesus, we accept that love and abide in that love.

> As the Father hath loved Me, so have I loved you; continue ye in My love. If ye keep My commandments—see the loving and the keeping—ye shall abide in My love—that's the clinging—even as I have kept My Father's commandments and

abide in His love'. Then verse 14 of John 15: 'Ye are My friends if ye do whatsoever I command you.

This love relation is the profoundest friendship of all. Within this friendship of all friendships, we are looking face to face with God.

Because of that, we wish to please Him, and so, Jesus says, 'If ye love Me, keep My commandments'. As we are always abiding in His love, 1st John says that we are 'walking in the truth', and 'walking in the light', because we are abiding in Jesus. He does it; He keeps us alive; He holds us to Himself. Millions of us often heard Billy Graham say: 'you cannot argue against a changed life.' Let us live in the light, and see what God will do around us!

67

The Future is Secure

Deuteronomy 31:1–13

This text brings before us essential truth about the future, in light of the soon-to-come death of Moses. It has often been said, as well-known Christian leaders die, 'The Lord buries His workmen, but the work goes on.' It's a way of saying that the future is going to be just as secure, without the great leaders, whom God in His providence has removed, as it was when they were here. When God takes home major leadership, naturally we grieve. But the real leader is always God, and He never leaves us nor forsakes us; therefore the future will be secure.

In these verses we note three points: first we look at Moses, the soon-to-die leader; second we look at the Lord, the ever-living leader; and third, at the proper response of faith to changes in leadership.

Moses, the Soon-To-Die Leader (31:2)

We are told here that Moses is now 120 years old. Let me say, that's not a miracle; that's not impossible. Even today there are people in the Caucasus Mountains, and in a certain area of Peru, who have indeed attained the age of 120.

Moses has reached 120 years old, and he feels the effects of that age, when he says: 'I can no longer go in and come out', a term in Hebrew for fighting wars, leading them in wars. He is saying: I have gone as far as I can go in earthly leadership; I have got to leave you. God is calling me home. But here is the important thing for the Israelites at that time, and for us today: he is saying: God really was your true leader all the time, and He will be just as present after I am gone and replaced by Joshua, as He was when I was in fullness of health and activity. So your future is secure, as you exercise faith in the One you do not see.

The Lord Was Always the True Leader (31:3–5)

Verse 3 states clearly: 'The Lord thy God, He will go over before thee', and He will do great things. In this new land, they would be facing fierce enemies, the Canaanites, who had fortified cities were militarily very able, and hostile to the Lord and to His people. The great one who led them, Moses, is being taken home. Here is the encouragement: it was not really Moses, but God all along, who recently gave them victory over Sihon and Og, in Transjordan. It was God who made it possible for them to be destroyed. And forty years before that, it was God who got them out of Egypt; it was God who got them victory over the Amalekites. Yes, He used Moses, the prayers of Moses, and the captainship of Joshua, but God was behind all their past victories.

In every generation, the real question is this: who are you looking to, no matter what happens? We are not to worry about the changes in leadership, for God has said that each generation cannot live but so many years, at the longest maybe 120. In most cases, you do well to make it to 85 or 90, and then the leadership has to change. But the real issue is to keep the eyes of faith on the Lord, who is always there and always directing affairs of His kingdom. Since the ever living One is always in charge of everything that happens, He will make the future exactly the way He wants it. Hence, every generation is to follow Hebrews 12:2, 'looking unto Jesus, the Author and Finisher of our faith'; and verse 3, 'consider Him that endured', by looking to Jesus.

THE PROPER RESPONSE OF FAITH (31:6–13)
Three responses of faith are called for in verses 6–13: first, be courageous (a command); second, keep the law (the Word) before your eyes; and third, live in the fear of God.

First, be courageous as you face a future that is likely to be full of uncomfortable changes, as verses 6 and 8 command. Fear of the unknown, not least, fear of the uncertainties in every future, is normal to human beings, for we have to live in a world that is always changing around us. But, insecure as the world around may make us, we must attune our ears to what Paul's words in 2 Corinthians 5:7: 'Walk by faith and not by sight.'

To act on something that you cannot see takes supernatural grace from God. That's where the men split from the boys; that's where the Christians shine above the dark attitude of the world, when they indeed walk by faith and not by sight. That is exactly what we are called to do; that's what Moses calls Israel to do.

It is well for us to remember that problems are also opportunities. What an opportunity Christian believers now have to demonstrate to the world, by their attitude of walking by faith, especially when the future, even that of Christians, humanly speaking, is very uncertain! What makes it possible to walk by faith and not by sight is the presence of the Lord, with whom faith keeps us in close contact. This God of the covenant has pledged Himself to provide for all our legitimate needs, including the handling of our enemies.

Circumstances can be daunting; but we have to remember that God is always greater than any set of circumstances, because He is the Creator of heaven and earth and everything in them. Circumstances are—from God's perspective—little, because all of them are finite, and God, the infinite Creator, can handle them; by definition, they are infinitely smaller than He. In this regard, notice verse 6 (it has been special in my life, as I will reveal): 'Be strong and of a good courage; fear not, nor be afraid of them. For the Lord thy God, He it is that doth go with thee; He will not fail thee nor forsake thee'. This verse was first spoken to ancient Israel, as they were on the verge of moving over the Jordan into the Promised Land, without Moses, but there is an sense in which it applies to believers in all ages. 'Fear not', for I will be with you.

As I was near graduation in Edinburgh about 1972, and not knowing where God would lead me, nor what He would provide, I was wondering and praying a great deal. At that time, an elderly Scottish saint, who went to the same church as I in Edinburgh, wrote out this verse and brought it to me. Believe me, it was a great encouragement, as I faced an unknown future. I daily turned it into prayer: 'Be strong and of a good courage; fear not, nor be afraid of them. For the Lord thy God, He it is that doth go with thee; He will not fail thee nor forsake thee.' It has been the Lord's plan at times to put me into testings and uncomfortable situations, but He has never once let me down; He has never failed to fulfill this promise.

I reckon that is why the 23rd Psalm is the most beloved passage in the Old Testament. I think the reason we love it may be because it is not so much about what we need to do for God, as it is about what God will do for us. Is that not why it comforts us; to be reminded that the Good Shepherd is with us, even in the valley of the shadow of death, where His rod and His staff will comfort us, and at the chosen time, will bring us into His house forevermore?

We can think of Amy Carmichael, a northern Irish missionary in India, who went through so much suffering, as she rescued young girls from prostitution in Hindu temples. Yet through it all (including many years of physical suffering with disease), she led a triumphant life. Here is a little poem she wrote:

> And a light shined in the cell
> And there was not any wall
> And there was no dark at all,
> Only Thou, Immanuel.
> Light of love shined in the cell,
> Turned to gold the iron bars,
> Opened the windows to the stars,
> Peace stood there as sentinel.
> Dearest Lord, how can it be
> That Thou art so kind to me.
> Love is shining in my cell,
> Jesus, my Immanuel.

Whatever the future holds, Jesus is going to be with us, and that is enough to remove the cancer of awful anxiety and carping fear.

Secondly, Moses commands us to 'keep the law before your eyes' (verses 9–11). The Torah probably means the covenant book that Moses expounded from chapter 5–26, the Ten Commandments, but maybe also, the whole Bible up to that time. It is to be kept fresh before the eyes of God's people, and thus, it is commanded that the whole law be re-read every seven years at a special assembly, at the Feast of the Tabernacles.

That seems to have been carried on for a long time, because hundreds of years later, after the return from captivity, Nehemiah 8 and 9 shows that they were doing exactly that. Nehemiah and Ezra had all the people assemble at the Water Gate, where the spiritual leadership were reading and explaining the entire law of God, and it turned into a time of powerful spiritual impressions.

Rev. James Phillip wrote on these verses: 'It was a means of quickening the soul, refreshing the heart, enlightening the eyes. It was a means of lifting up heart, soul, and mind to God.' That is what the reading of the law, and meditating on it, can accomplish, when accompanied by the working of the Holy Spirit.

Then the third thing we are commanded is in verses 12–13: live in the fear of God; conduct your life as though you are before the very face of God. To that end, note the four verbs in these verses: assemble, or gather; hear; learn; and fear.

First, assemble; that's for the seven year reading of the law of God, but also it certainly came to include the various yearly feasts where they had to assemble at the central shrine for Old Testament festivals. Then in later years, the same reading and hearing was done in the weekly gathering in the synagogue, where the law was read and preached on, and prayer was made.

We find Jesus and His apostles doing that, assembling every Sabbath day in the synagogue. They were carrying out what is said in Nehemiah 10:39: 'We will not forsake the house of our God', as well as Hebrews 10:25, where it says 'not forsaking the assembling of ourselves together' in worship.

To bring it down to the modern day: let us be faithful in attending weekly worship in God's house, for it is in the ordinary means of grace: the Word, prayer, and the sacraments, that God comes down, and enables us to live in reverential fear of Him; God makes Himself real to us in the Word and in the sacraments, so that our thinking is transformed; we literally become transformed thinkers in our attitude. 'And be not conformed to this world, but be ye transformed by the renewing of your mind, that ye may prove what is that good, and acceptable, and perfect, will of God' (Rom. 12:2). To be transformed in your mind, you have seriously to contemplate the doctrine: who God is, what He has done, and what He makes available and commands. To reach that goal, you have to assemble with God's people, so that together you may live in the fear of God.

Let us take the next two verbs together: 'hear' and 'learn' in Deuteronomy 31:12–13. It is saying, open your ears to what is important, and pay close attention. You know how you can be talking to somebody, and he is looking this way and that, and you quickly perceive they are not interested; it's not very respectful to you, so you just stop trying to say anything to them. God wants us to be at least respectful, and to pay very close attention to the Word, because of the One from whom it comes, our loving heavenly Father, who gave the Son of His heart to die for us and rise for us; He's done everything for us. You've got to have respect for somebody who did that much for you! Hence, we must 'hear' and 'learn'.

Finally, 'fear' the Lord your God. Fear in this context means 'reverential trust'; under no condition would you wish to offend Him, to let Him down. You fear the Lord your God and live in His presence because He is there and makes everything all right, in principle. We see this in the great John Wesley. He had been down with his brother Charles in Savannah, Georgia, on a mission for some time, and then took ship to go back to England. On that voyage, the ship got into a terrible storm and looked like it would be wrecked and everyone on board would meet a watery death.

While gathered together down in the hold, John Wesley noticed a group of Moravians, who were not in the slightest afraid, although it looked for certain that they would all be drowned. Yet they were singing with faces shining radiant. What were those Moravians doing? They were living in the presence of God. John Wesley realized that he himself wasn't, for he was terrified. Well, they survived the storm, but it raised some hard questions in his heart that he had never faced. Not long after that, he was converted; later in a meeting he said that 'his heart was strangely warmed'. It had been seeing those Moravians, living in the fear of God in a storm that could easily have led to their death; and seeing the practical difference it made to them to be walking by faith and not by sight soon changed everything for him. That is what opened John Wesley's heart, and he became one of the great evangelists of all history.

You could state it this way: the fear of the Lord removes lesser fears. That was true with the Moravians, and later with Wesley. Psalm 34:9 shows us how it works: 'O fear the Lord, ye his saints, for there is no want, or no lack, to them that fear him'. With all the uncertainties we face in a complex world, this assures us that since God is true and loves us, there will no lack to them that fear Him. That really and truly is sufficient for us to know, now and for all the future. Hence, Moses said to the people that if they wanted a secure future, they were regularly to meditate on the Word of God.

It is no different in the New Testament. In Luke 24, on what we call Easter Sunday afternoon, the risen Jesus—making Himself unrecognizable—unexpectedly joined some of the disciples, who were walking on the road to Emmaus. He asked them why they were so dismayed? They answered that the hope of their lives, the Messiah, had been killed, and that some claimed they had now seen him alive. Their major problem was this: if Jesus had truly been God's Messiah, how could He ever have been killed?

The risen Jesus (still unknown) got right to the point of their problem. He talked to them about the Law of Moses and the Prophets: 'And beginning at Moses and all the prophets, he', the risen Christ, although they didn't recognize Him yet, 'expounded unto them in all the Scriptures the things concerning himself' (Luke 24:27). And especially in the previous verse, 26, He tells them that if they had read Moses, they would see that the real Messiah, the Saviour, the Lord, was going to have to suffer first, and then get the glory.

The Old Testament had presented the coming Messiah (or Saviour) under the images of a lion and a lamb. But it seemed that Israel in New Testament times, only saw Him as a lion, not a lamb. So Jesus showed that, before He rose up as the conquering Lion, He first had to come as the Lamb. Jesus took them through the Law of Moses and the Prophets and lifted them from despair, by showing them who He was as lamb and lion, according to the written Word of God. That opening of the Word to hearts of faith is always God's answer to us in all our troubles and confusions.

68

Don't Make It Happen
Deuteronomy 31:14–30

These verses 14–30 are a solemn passage, and give a very important warning to the people of God, something like this: 'Don't make it happen!' God says through Moses, near the end of Moses' life, that if Israel makes the wrong choice, their future will be dark and tragic. He had already said as much in Deuteronomy 30:19, 'I call heaven and earth to record this day against you, that I have set before you life and death, blessing and cursing; therefore choose life, that both thou and thy seed may live.'

When people, greatly blessed by God, experience a dark future and go into very bad times, there's a reason for it; they made a wrong choice, they went against what God wanted them to do. These verses are saying: 'Don't make it happen.' If and when we choose a bad future, and many people do, it is always against the warnings that God gives us.

Think of how the Lord warned Adam and Eve: 'Don't eat of the forbidden fruit, for in the day that thou eatest it, thou shalt surely die.' Adam made the wrong choice and made the judgment of God happen. Now whatever else it means, it means this: God allows us humans to do things of which He does not approve.

I've heard people foolishly say that if God doesn't want me to do something, He will block it. That is silly. God gives us a choice. I'll grant you the fall into sin affects our choices. Nevertheless it's our choice, and it means He lets us make bad decisions if we insist on doing so, and then carries through with what He said He would do against sin. (And none of this is to deny God's all-encompassing eternal plan that includes all things, both good and evil). But God's knowing what we will do, never means that He makes us do evil. God didn't make Adam and Eve sin. God has never made me sin one time. If I did, and I have done so, I went against Him; and He warns us not to go against His will for our lives.

I want us to note in this respect three things: first, what God foresees the children of Israel will do; second, when he says they will do it and the price they must pay; and third, he sets a safe path by which they could move into a bright future, if they are willing to make the right choice.

What God Foresees They Will Do (31:16–18)

God foresaw that they would be spiritually unfaithful to the covenant. We have already noted many times that the covenant relationship is like a marriage, which is broken if one of the partners to it commits adultery: that's the image by which

God compares spiritual unfaithfulness to Him, and our relationship with Him—someone who commits adultery: 'This people will rise up and go a whoring after the gods of the strangers of the land' (Deut. 31:16).

In general, most modern people, even secular ones (as shown in various Barna reports) dislike adultery. Marriage, other than belonging to the Lord, is understood by a large majority of people to be the most precious vow we ever take in all our lives. Not surprisingly, the devil knows that belonging to the Lord is like a marriage and therefore the evil one wants to corrupt the most valuable relationship of our life, the one which determines where we will spend eternity.

Proverbs 7:9 paints a picture of a sinful woman trying to allure a somewhat naïve young man to do what he knows is not right, when it is dark: 'In the twilight, in the evening, in the black and dark night, behold there met him a woman with the attire of an harlot and subtle of heart and she said unto him come ahead and let us have a good time.' Verse 21 adds, 'and with her much fair speech'—the devil, and people who tempt you, will pour out much fair speech, putting the nicest spin on it. Part of their sophisticated remit is to make you feel better for not believing all the Bible, all the time. They tell you that a discrete moral looseness will keep you up-to-date; others will think highly of your intelligence, and you will be with the majority. So don't go, they advise, by a strict traditionalist interpretation of the Bible; instead, come on and let us be modern. 'Much fair speech'—you can enunciate it in religion, or in the physical relationship of sacred marriage, by issuing such excuses as 'it's our business; it doesn't hurt anybody and they won't know it' and such foolish things.

In verse 21, she allures him, and in the next verse, he goes after her 'straightway as an ox goes to the slaughter, or as a fool to the correction of the stocks.' A more literal translation of Deuteronomy 31:29 may be: 'Evil will summon you'. Evil puts on an attractive face for a while, and issues a call, for you to be unfaithful to your covenant vows, whether in marriage or whether to the Lord, especially when He requires you to be different from society. In all these issues, evil knows how to put on a very reasonable, attractive face: 'Come on, come on.' But God, our heavenly Father, audibly warns us to beware of moving in an unfaithful direction.

Now, if you are tempted, it does not mean that you are a bad person, for the devil will most of all tempt the servants of God. Temptation is not a sin; we can't help being tempted. Jesus was tempted—that's how we know it is not a sin—but He didn't yield. The devil will tempt you to go with the modern crowd, or to stretch a point in your marriage; the answer is to turn your face to the Lord.

Joseph did exactly that, when Potiphar's wife tempted him. She might have been a very attractive woman. She could have promoted him. But Joseph says, 'How can I do this great sin against the Lord?' It was Joseph's relationship to God, and the freshness of it and his sense of the holiness of the love of God, that kept him from giving in to that lustful wife of his owner.

In Deuteronomy 31:17, there is a very graphic phrase: 'I will hide my face from them.' Have you ever noticed that when you fall out with somebody, you won't look each other in the face; it's too painful and embarrassing? I remember a big wedding in our family, where I noticed that two of my second cousins, who were brother and sister, passed each other at the punch bowl and did not speak, but looked the other way. Later in the evening, I asked a relative, who knew them better than I, what was wrong? He said that they were fighting over their mother's estate in court. Bitterness will certainly make you turn your face the other way from someone against whom you are embittered.

God says that the worst thing that can happen is that 'I will turn My face away from you, if you openly, consistently disobey my will for your life.' What an unspeakable loss that is, for the greatest comfort of life is to have the face of God smiling upon us. There is nothing like living under the smile of a reconciled heavenly Father; that is the only real happiness. But if God turns His face away, because we are seriously breaking His covenant, disobeying His will for our life, it is very painful for us.

When He says, I will hide my face, isn't it the opposite of the Aaronic benediction in the book of Numbers? 'The Lord bless thee and keep thee; the Lord make his face shine upon thee; the Lord lift up his countenance upon thee, and give thee peace'? The priest would come out of the place of sacrifice, having made atonement over the mercy seat, the holy place, and said, 'The Lord bless thee and keep thee and cause his face to shine upon thee'. Such a benediction is a mighty source of blessing.

But if we willfully go against the Lord, a holy God is honor-bound to turn His face in the other direction. Verse 17 says that when God turns His face in the other direction, we will feel it terribly. When it gets bad enough, eventually somebody will finally ask, 'are not these evils come upon us because our God is not among us?' Not to look upon you, but instead, having His smiling, beautiful, loving, bright face turned the other way, leaves a vacuum where the dark powers are able to get at you. Verse 17 states the true answer: 'and they shall be devoured and many evils and troubles shall befall them'. In other places in Deuteronomy, we see that continued disobedience would involve loss of land, deportation, military defeat, drought, and famine, and all the evils and hurts that those things involve.

So God warns, 'Don't make it happen!' This could happen, but it doesn't have to. That's the good news; you don't have to make it happen. Deuteronomy 30:19, as we have seen, commands us to choose life and not death. But if we choose the wrong way, God says you will be subject to the law of the harvest: 'Whatsoever a man soweth, that shall he also reap'.

God Says When They Will Do This (31:19–23)

Without having set a precise date, Moses foresaw that masses of the people of Israel were going to commit spiritual adultery, and God would turn His face away from them. History shows that it did not occur until after the death of Joshua and the faithful elders who ruled with him, as we are told in the book of Judges.

This parlous process is not unknown in the lives of believers long after the collapse of Israel. The Rev. James Philip of Edinburgh wrote in 1984: 'The time when this happens to Israel [when they are going to give in after Joshua's death] is related to a spirit of complacency, because by affluence, Israel became too comfortable as the favored people of God. This is a supreme danger point in spiritual life, whether the affluence be material or spiritual.'

I have known of a few ministers, who had written some good books while relatively young, but during their 50s they fell into some shameful sins. They were at the height, it seems, of their spiritual powers; and that can be a danger point, just like when you get wealthy, and you feel satisfied with yourself. Jim Philip continues:

> The early years of Christian life have all the warmth and verve of enthusiasm, of great and dedicated

endeavor; as indeed frequently have our last days, But the danger point is the middle period. That significant middle period, when we may be at the height of our natural powers, has been the danger point for so many, when spiritual carelessness and complacency set in, and the never-had-it-so-good syndrome betrays us gradually and imperceptibly into a backslidden torporous spirit which can bring us to the point of becoming castaways.

Cotton Mather in Massachusetts, a famous Puritan minister, writing in the late 1600s and early 1700s, said in his book, written in Latin, *Magnalia Christi Americana* [*The Great Works of God in America*] famously observed that formerly Puritan New England, which had at one time such a powerful spiritual testimony, had by his lifetime begun losing its spiritual power and very identity as the people of God in America. Mather said: 'Godliness brought prosperity, and the daughter then turned around and ate up the mother.'

God Sets a Safe Way Before All Who Will Listen (31:24–30)

Even in the worst announcement of coming judgment on apostasy, God still sets before anybody who will repent, trust and obey, a safe and a happy way into the future. That is very encouraging! Maybe this passage has made a few of you feel depressed, or made you feel down, but even so, we have to be realistic. Even so, no matter how dark it gets, God sets before us an aisle flooded with light, and says, 'Come on into this aisle, walk with Me, walk in the light as Christ is in the light; His blood will keep you clean from sin, and I will take care of your future; it doesn't matter how dark things around you, how society seems to be crumbling, and coming down around your ears; trust in Me; choose life!'

By God's grace, you can do it! We must never use as the excuse 'everybody else is doing it' (i.e. these popular sins). That's the worst possible pretext to commit yet more sin. It is never an excuse that now the majority of people live together without being married, for instance. It is never an excuse that some of the biggest, most respectable churches no longer proclaim the cleansing blood of Christ as the only way of salvation. That's not an excuse for a preacher to say, 'I would like to get a bigger church, and maybe I have got to backpedal on all this.' No! It doesn't matter what they do; God will take care of them. We don't use their disobedience, their sin, and their apostasy to be the excuse for us to join them in being unfaithful. On the contrary, God says, 'This is the way; walk ye in it; you follow Me.'

In verse 23, Moses promises Joshua that if he stays in the Lord's will, God will supernaturally enable Joshua to lead the people into the Promised Land and the people will be blessed for a good period of time. It is amazing how one man's ministry, one soul that will be faithful to God above everything else, can influence tens of thousands; it has often been so. It has never been a legitimate excuse that the others are enjoying their sins—no, don't seek to partake of their enjoyment, but determine to follow the Lord, and He will not only bless you personally, but beyond that, will influence through you whom He wishes to influence, and all will be well with you and with them.

Moses said: 'Now take the Book of the Law.' I assume that is Deuteronomy, including chapters 5–26 where Moses is explaining what the Ten Commandments mean. There is an interesting picture here; can you almost see Moses talking to Joshua, and of course, the High Priest too, because nobody but the High Priest could go into the Holy of Holies in the tabernacle and later the temple—the innermost sanctum, in which was nothing but the Ark of the Covenant with the two tables of stone, the Ten Commandments, written with the finger of God. On top of the Ark, there was an unusual structure: a mercy seat. The two cherubim, with their faces veiled by their wings, to keep from looking directly upon the burning holiness of God, sat at each end of this mercy seat.

Onto this mercy seat, the High Priest would bring blood once a year, on the Day of Atonement (Yom Kippur) when he would sprinkle the blood on it, so the sins of the people could be covered for another year. Then he would go out with the Aaronic benediction, including the words, 'the Lord cause His face to shine upon you'.

This mercy seat speaks, finally (in epistle to the Hebrews), of Jesus dying on the cross of Calvary, shedding His blood, to forgive our breaking of the law, our apostasy, our sin, and our failure to do right and be right.

> Jesus paid it all;
> all to Him I owe.
> Sin had left a crimson stain;
> He washed it white as snow.

Or the hymn,

> What can wash away my sin?
> Nothing but the blood of Jesus!
> What can make me whole again?
> Nothing but the blood of Jesus.

In sum, the mercy seat speaks of what we call the passive obedience of Christ, the passion of Jesus Christ in our room and stead. He pays the infinite penalty of our breaking the holy law.

But then Moses said another thing. To see it, visualize the Ark of the Covenant in the darkness of the holiest of all, and notice that there is something right beside this holy Ark; there on a sort of ledge, you may see Deuteronomy, where Moses explained in practical terms what daily obedience to the Ten Commandments would look like in society. Hence, the Book of the Law is placed right next to the Ark of the Covenant, and this speaks of the active obedience of Christ; that is, Christ standing in my place, keeping the law; 'It is my delight to do the will of Him that sent me; I must work the works of him that sent me while it is day'. It is a way of showing Jesus loving the Father, and thus loving His moral character, which is His law, and keeping it, not only for Himself but for us. That book of the Law shows us the way forward.

God is saying: 'This is the way; walk ye in it'. Give you heart and soul and mind to My Son, and your future will truly be safe and secure; it will be a future upon which My face will continue to shine.

To whom does the law point us? Surely, to the Lord Jesus Christ, who fulfilled it, who paid its penalty, and then sent His Spirit to enable us to desire to keep it. Focus on Jesus; that's the way for the future; focus on Jesus, the Son of God, giver and keeper of the law in our place. Let us close with a hymn that is ascribed, by some, to Bernard of Clairvaux in the twelfth century:

> Jesus, Thou Joy of loving hearts,
> Thou Fount of life, Thou Light of men,
> From the best bliss that earth imparts,
> We turn unfilled to Thee again.
>
> Thy truth unchanged hath ever stood;
> Thou savest those that on Thee call;
> To them that seek Thee Thou art good,
> To them that find Thee all in all.
> O Jesus, ever with us stay,
> Make all our moments calm and bright;

> Chase the dark night of sin away,
> Shed over the world Thy holy light.

And let us say, Lord, shed it on us, and our land.

69

THE SONG OF MOSES

Deuteronomy 31:30–32:4

This text introduces the wonderful song of Moses, referred to in Revelation 15 which speaks of 'the song of Moses and of the Lamb'. It's a song we are all going to join together in singing!

In the Southern states, especially in country churches, we still sing, 'When we all get to heaven, what a day of rejoicing that will be!' One thing we will be doing in heaven is singing. We do not yet know the exact repertory of hymns in that beautiful place, but at least one of them, according to Revelation 15, will be the song of Moses and the Lamb. The Holy Spirit inspired Moses to write it, not just for the lifetime of Moses; it was composed for singing in the glorious realm around the rainbow-circled Throne!

Before getting into the Song, we consider four matters from Deuteronomy 31:30—32:4: first, the song's composer; second, the witnesses the song calls on; third, the song's effects; fourth, the authority exercised by the song.

THE COMPOSER OF THIS SONG (31:30)

According to Deuteronomy 31:30, its composer is clearly Moses. We know that Moses wrote another great song, Psalm 90. So among his many talents as a leader, a linguist, a prose historian, he was also a beautiful poet. He had led the people of God, as we know, out of slavery in Egypt through the Red Sea and through the wilderness. But now his time with his people is drawing to an end. God has told him: 'Moses, I am going to take you home, so get the people ready for transition of governmental power and of spiritual authority.'

One of the ways Moses did that was by preaching (and writing) Deuteronomy. Having gone through every one of the Ten Commandments, with much application to life in this world, he concludes with this beautiful song, or hymn, or psalm. Why did he conclude a book of historical nature with poetry?

The majority of Deuteronomy is straightforward prose, yet Moses concludes it in poetry. We know, from our own experience in school and in our adult life that it is much easier to memorize poetry than prose—especially if the poetry rhymes (which is not the case in Hebrew), or set to music (which is done frequently in Hebrew, as in the Psalms). Often we remember it all our life. It seems like Moses is trying to conclude the basic point of the covenant-teaching by saying that at the heart of every covenant is the promise: 'I will be your God and you will be my people.' In the Bible, the foundation and the goal of every covenant is that He will be our God and we shall be His people.

Moses phrases this in Hebrew poetry, which doesn't rhyme as in English, French, or German; it works another way, such as through parallelism, with contrast and comparison, and other literary devices. Hence, to the Hebrew mind, it would have been highly memorable and likely to stick in the mind. By this means, Moses gives them something to remind them that they are to be God's people, and He is to be their own God, and what that entails in walking, thinking, and acting. Evidently Moses expected the song to be sung over many generations. And that is exactly what happened, because Christ renews the song, revises it from the basis of His finished work, and we shall be singing this very same song when we get to heaven.

The Witnesses That the Song Calls Forward (32:1)

This verse is very poetic: the celestial bodies, the heavens and the earth, are called to witness to this covenant song. Since God created the heavens and the earth, the sun, moon, stars, planets, nebulae and galaxies, by being either the platform of human life and action or the illumination of it—the place where lives are lived and words are spoken—are somehow a mute witness to the relationship between the Creator God and His image-bearers, His people.

When aggressive pagan neighbors were working against Israel, and God raised up a deliverer, amazing things happened in the weather, to make the hard task of the deliverer much easier and to lay low those who were seeking to destroy God's people. In Judges 5:20 'the stars in their courses fought against Sisera'. So, all parts of God's universe, in ways we do not understand, including sun, moon, and stars, are used to reflect God's faithfulness to His people. We hear some echoes of that in the hymn,

> Great is Thy faithfulness, Lord unto me:
> Sun, moon and stars in their courses above,
> Join with all nature in manifold witness,
> To thy great faithfulness, mercy and love!

In reading the accounts of the Scottish Covenanter martyrs during the 'Killing Times' of the 1680s, we see that many of them, with confident heart in face of death, called on sun, moon, and stars as their witnesses! In doing so, they were in the company of Moses.

All creation is always, in ways that we do not yet understand, cooperating with God, and bearing witness to Him, and in a mute sort of way, reminding us that we should be faithful to our Creator. A remarkable Christian poem came to mind here by a nineteenth-century English writer, Francis Thompson, 'The Hound of Heaven'. The poem expresses creatively and imaginatively something of the witness of heaven and earth against those who try to flee the Lord. In part, this poem says:

> I fled Him down the nights and down the days
> I fled Him down the arches of the years
> I fled Him down the labyrinthine ways
> Of my own mind, and in the midst of tears
>
> I hid from him, and under running laughter.
> From those strong feet that followed, followed after
> But with unhurrying chase and unperturbed pace,
> Deliberate speed, majestic instancy,
> They beat, and a Voice beat,
> More instant than the feet:
> All things betray thee who betrayest me.

Across the margent of the world I fled,
And troubled the gold gateways of the stars,
Smiting for shelter on their clanged bars,
Fretted to dulcet jars and silvern chatter
The pale ports of the moon.

I said to Dawn --- be sudden, to Eve --- be soon,
With thy young skiey blossoms heap me over
From this tremendous Lover.
Float thy vague veil about me lest He see.
I tempted all His servitors but to find
My own betrayal in their constancy,
In faith to Him, their fickleness to me,
Their traitorous trueness and their loyal deceit.

Still with unhurrying chase and unperturbed pace
Deliberate speed, majestic instancy,
Came on the following feet, and a Voice above their beat:
Nought shelters thee who wilt not shelter Me.

So it was done.
I in their delicate fellowship was one.
Drew the bolt of Nature's secrecies,
I knew all the swift importings on the wilful face of skies,
I knew how the clouds arise,
Spumed of the wild sea-snortings.
All that's born or dies,
Rose and drooped with,
Made them shapers of mine own moods, or wailful, or Divine.
With them joyed and was bereaven.
I was heavy with the Even,
when she lit her glimmering tapers round the day's dead sanctities.
I laughed in the morning's eyes.

THE EFFECTS OF THE SONG OF MOSES (32:2)

In the Authorised Version of Deuteronomy 32:2, Moses says 'My doctrine shall drop as the rain.' In the Revised Standard Version, it is translated as a prayer, 'May my teaching drop like the rain.' You could argue it either way from the Hebrew. But either way, Moses is asking or predicting that this holy doctrine will saturate the souls of God's people like heavy rain pours its showers on the earth.

Isaiah 44:1–3 picks up this Mosaic prayer and turns it into a Messianic promise and prophecy:

> Yet now hear, O Jacob my servant; and Israel, whom I have chosen: Thus saith the Lord that made thee, and formed thee from the womb, which will help thee: Fear not, O Jacob my servant; and thou, Jeshurun, whom I have chosen. For I will pour water upon him that is thirsty, and floods upon the dry ground; I will pour my spirit upon thy seed, and my blessing upon thine offspring.

Isaiah, following Moses, is painting a picture of the beauty of holiness, of Christ's likeness, shining its splendors amongst a redeemed multitude of believers. Isaiah 44:6 shows us that it will be the Redeemer, the First and the Last, the Ancient of Days incarnate, crucified, risen, who will transform the formerly sinful millions into trophies of Christ's own beauty and character: 'Thus saith the Lord the King of Israel, and his Redeemer, the Lord of Hosts: I am the first, and I am the last [applied to Christ in the Book of Revelation] and beside me there is no God.'

In this way, the doctrine enunciated by Moses will be lived out in and through Jesus Christ the Redeemer. He does it for us, and, by His grace, He offers it to the entire world through faith and supernatural work of the Holy Spirit, to those who ask God to apply to them the redemption purchased by Christ. They can have the doctrine and the Holy Spirit pour it into them like the dew, like the rain, like the floods—and wash them, and cleanse them, and purify them, lifting them up, renewing them, and flowinng out of them, as the waters of life from their innermost being, as Jesus promised the woman at the well of Samaria.

The Authority Exercised By this Song of Moses (32:3–4)

The songs we write (if we have poetic talents) may be melodious and edifying, but they would not have supernatural authority. This one, penned by Moses at the inspiration of the Holy Spirit, has supernatural authority. In a certain, predictive sense, this song calls to mind the music of the last trump that shall sound and raise the bodies of the dead. Or we could think of the music of the trumpets of the Levites, as they were marching around the walls of Jericho, as God said, bringing down supernaturally the stone walls, as the music of the trumps shall raise the bodies of the dead.

The music of Moses' song, when heard in faith and appropriated in humility and trust, is an instrument God uses to change profoundly our attitude, like Romans 12:1-2, where we are instructed to be 'transformed by the renewing of our minds'. Rehearsing frequently such a song as this one, begins to transform us from self-centeredness to God-centeredness, from ugliness to beauty, from soon-coming death to everlasting life. The miraculous transformation, spoken of in this song, takes place because it is God who gives the song, through Moses, and then renews the same song through the Lamb.

Thus, in verses 3-4 Moses proclaims the glorious nature of God. What he sings comes to pass and shines with God's own glory. So let us look briefly at the greatness of God under two headings: first, Moses tells us that God is the Rock, and second, that God's works are full of pure integrity.

First, God is the Rock. This word *Rock* appears in the Song of Moses six times. *Rock* is a symbol of God's power and dependability. The great German commentator Delitszch says 'He is an unchangeable refuge who grants a firm defense and secure resort to His people by virtue of His unchangeableness or impregnable firmness,' expressed poetically in the hymn: 'How firm a foundation, ye saints of the Lord'.

The inspired Psalmist David takes up this picture of God as the Rock, in the Psalms! Let us consider just two of them. First, psalm 18:2–3,

> The Lord is my rock and my fortress and my deliverer; my God, my strength, in whom I will trust; my buckler, and the horn of my salvation, and my high tower. I will call upon the Lord, who is worthy to be praised; so shall I be saved from mine enemies.

… and Psalm 31:2–3:

> Bow down thine ear to me;
> deliver me speedily;
> be thou my strong rock, for an house of defense to save me.
> For thou art my rock and my fortress;
> therefore for thy name's sake lead me, and guide me.

God is a rock. These Psalms teach that we have somewhere to take refuge; we are not left to our own devices, no matter what happens around us, the Rock will never grow smaller or weaker, or less willing to take us in; the shelter will be there, for those who seek Him.

Secondly, Moses lists some of the holy ways God deals with His people. God has always been just, upright, and faithful to them, never doing anything but right. I remember years ago when first in the ministry up in Raeford, I was asked to preach a funeral for someone I didn't know. The widow, an older lady, said to me something that has stuck in my mind all these years about her deceased husband. She said, 'He always did me right.' What a great testimony! God has always 'done us right'.

Jesus could ask in the Gospel, 'Who convinceth Me of sin?' Nobody could. And Moses was able to say of God in Deuteronomy 32:4: 'He has been without iniquity.' Whatever else you say about God, He has no iniquity. 'God is light and in Him is no darkness at all' (1 John 1:5). Many things are unclear, mysterious and complex about God, and about our life on earth; but one thing is clear: God is pure, God is true, God is nothing but good, right, holy, and light. That's who He is. 'He is without iniquity.'

Now think of that! God, in all our lives and in all the lives of all His people, has never once done us anything wrong; not once. Most of us who are married, would admit that sometime we have done the other one wrong. If you have raised children, you have sometimes done them wrong. In every human relationship, unless you are extremely sanctified, you will have done somebody wrong. But God has never once done us wrong.

It is not easy to understand the book of Job, and it is important here, for it shows us from one particular point of view, that God is without iniquity. Job, assessed by God to be a righteous man, was allowed by God to be put through immense suffering at the hands of the envious devil. Job's ten children killed; he lost everything he had, and experienced horrid disease and suffering. His friends criticized him unfairly. In his terrible situation, he raises many hard questions.

But at the end of his immense suffering, instead of giving him an exact reason why God let his children be killed, and why he got this disease and why he lost all his money and his estate, God gave him something other than an intellectual explanation. In answer to his painful questions, God showed Job His glory! As He was doing so, He instructed Job to contemplate how amazing the created order is, and how little of it he could understand. Then the Lord said, 'Look at me', and He showed him His glory, at least as much of it as Job could bear to see.

Once Job saw the glory of the character of God, he was perfectly all right about the immense sufferings he had been through. And so he says: 'I have heard of thee by the hearing of the ear; but now mine eye seeth thee. Wherefore I abhor myself, and repent in dust and ashes' (Job 42:5–6. What he is saying is, 'O Lord, I was beginning to think you had done me wrong, letting me be hurt like this, All the rest of them are doing fine, but why me?'

God doesn't tell him why, but shows him the beauty of His love and His glory, His splendor and goodness; and Job says: 'That's my answer; I wish I hadn't even said all those things that implied criticism of you.' Job saw the glory and it was all right; he knew that God was without iniquity and that the center of the universe; the foundation of the world was solid; he could rely upon it.

I believe one day we will see Job; he is not a poetic figure, but was a real person living in the time of the patriarchs. Job will one day join all of us in a choir, all of us who have repented of our sins and trusted in Jesus. On that great glad day, Job will be there, and when we are singing together the song of Moses and the Lamb, enriched and reworked in light of what Jesus Christ, who is seated before them, has done. From that holy place, as revealed in Revelation 15:3–4.

We look forward to the coming of that grand day of all days!

I was recently on the phone with a good lady, to thank her for her wonderful job in typing all my sermons on Revelation. She told me that she and her husband have already paid for their funerals. Then she added, 'I got so excited thinking about getting to heaven, I could hardly wait!' We Christians can identify with what she means: Home! Home at last! We will reach that beautiful place of seeing and singing, because of Jesus' prayer for us and all His people:

> Father, I will that they also, whom thou hast given me, may be with me where I am; that they may behold my glory, which thou hast given me: for thou lovedst me before the foundation of the world (John 17:24).

And then will happen what the apostle Paul promises in 2 Corinthians 3:18,

> But we all, with unveiled faith, beholding the glory of the Lord as in a glass, are changed or transformed from glory to glory, even as by the Spirit of the Lord.

That's the effect of the song of Moses, and more particularly of the song of Moses and of the Lamb.

70

Remember the One Who Blesses

Deuteronomy 32:5–14

This passage teaches us to remember the One who has blessed us so greatly. All of you know the old gospel hymn,

> Count your blessings;
> name them one by one;
> count your many blessings;
> see what God hath done.

That's the idea. The first part of the song of Moses (verses 5–14) is essentially a command to remember what God has done for you, as in verse 7: 'remember the days of old'. To do so is the surest way for you to get back into the place of blessing. Let us note: first, the command to remember the blessings of God (verse 7); and second, the events that Moses told Israel always to remember (verses 8–14).

The Command to Remember the Blessings of the Lord (32:7)

Why would Moses in this song, lay so much emphasis on calling God's people to remember? He gives two reasons: first (verses 5–6), if you forget what God has done for you, you may become corrupt; your thinking will lead you down the wrong path, and you will change morally. Secondly, if you do call to mind what the Lord has done for you, you can get back to the place of high blessing (verse 13 and also 30).

If we forget what God has done for us we will soon enough become corrupted. It seems that human personality is made to focus on something outside itself, in order to stay in a healthy condition. But if you cease to stay focused on God, how you have everything from Him and how He has blessed you, you change. Your heart gets cold towards Him, your interests become increasingly self-centered, and eventually you will put something else in God's place. That's the message of verse 6: 'Is not He thy Father that bought thee?' and verse 17, 'they sacrificed unto devils, not unto God'. Quit remembering your blessings from God and you become a changed person.

This very process seems to lie behind the apostasy of the Western countries. Once they functionally forgot God as the center of their lives, they became modernistic, and thus, no longer held to the truth of the Scriptures and to their first love for the Lord Jesus Christ. In this downward decline, they neglected the importance of Bible and prayer. You don't have the same commonalities any more; you can't have the same fellowship you used to have. At first you wonder if it is your fault—but they have changed. That's one of the tragedies of the elite that gave leadership to American and European intellectual culture for the whole twentieth century. They have specifically worked to forget God, and that is the essence of what we call the politically correct rewriting of world history.

It is much the same in some areas of science, where evolutionary theory has replaced the Creator God. The year 2009 marked the 150th anniversary of the publication of Charles Darwin's *Origin of Species*. Why was Darwin's theory of biological evolution given such an amazingly quick reception, even though later research has demonstrated that it is highly questionable scientifically? It is because it seems to give a way that is intellectually respectable to forget that God is the Creator, and that the imprints of His special creation are everywhere to be seen, so that we are obligated to God.

In recent years, a great Jewish film maker, Ben Stein, made a film entitled, *Expelled*. In it, he interviewed the evolutionary scientists and creationist scientists. In Stein's interview with the atheistic evolutionary scientist, Richard Dawkins of Oxford, he paints him into an uncomfortable corner. The film documents how many outstanding scientists have lost their jobs, been refused tenure, or have had articles not published, because they raised problems with evolution.

Why is evolution so powerfully defended by our leadership, or those who tell us they are the leadership? Simply because they want to get rid of God, to prove that there is no need for God to have started this universe; it can simply be explained out of the material. This would mean that I can be my own God, and will not have to be told what to do by His Word.

Moses wants us to remember God and His blessings, because it can get us back to where we need to be. Let us look at the prophecy of Hosea 6:1 and 3:

Come, and let us return unto the Lord; for He hath torn, and He will heal us. He hath smitten and He will bind us up. Then shall we know, if we follow on to know the Lord; His going forth is prepared as the morning [the Septuagint has 'His coming is certain as the dawn']; and He shall come unto us as the rain [at times, rain can mean the Holy Ghost pouring out], as the latter and former rain upon the earth.

I take it they are referring to the crops, and while not impossible, it appears that a reference to the former rain as Pentecost, and the latter rain as various times of reviving is not clearly established in this text.

You know the hymn, 'Tell Me the Old, Old Story':

Tell me the story often, for I forget so soon
The early dew of morning has passed away at noon.
Tell me the same old story when you have cause to fear
That this world's empty glory is costing me too dear.'

Paul says: 'Having therefore these promises, dearly beloved, let us cleanse ourselves from all filthiness of the flesh and spirit' (2 Cor. 7:1). To overcome this sexually soaked culture that now accepts the most lurid sins as normal, we must remember the promises, and Him who promised, and from that follows, 'perfecting holiness in the fear of God'. Precisely what we remember is what our forefathers believed; in other words, the Word of God written. And you see it here in Deuteronomy 32:7: 'ask thy father and he will show thee; thy elders, and they will tell thee'.

The Events that Moses Told Israel to Remember (32:8–14)

Moses said, I command you to remember the Lord and His blessings, and it will keep you pure, and it will get you back where you need to be. Moses specifically said to call to mind three events and blessings God gave you: the calling of Abram (32:8–9); the Exodus (32:10–12); the settlement that is already beginning in the Promised Land (Deut. 32:13–14).

Moses is soon going to die and leave them, and is telling the people how to get into a successful future. By remembering what God has been to you in the past, what He has done for you in the past, you are going to make it fine in the future.

If you thought you were dying and still had your mind, what would you tell your children about their future? Here's the principle: the way into the future is to remember the past. That goes against the common sense thinking of most of Western culture today.

I have long felt that one of the strong points of the Southern culture in the USA, has been its deep remembrance of the past. Now we have had many sins as a Southern people, no honest person should deny it. But we do have strong points that I think are rooted in the revivals that worked the gospel deeply into the Southern character. One of the strong points is that, whatever your class or race, you generally have a deep remembrance and reverence for the past. That comes in with your mother's milk.

I remember about twenty years ago reading an article from *Chronicles of Culture* by an author from Michigan. He perceptively discussed, I thought, the difference between being a Northerner and a Southerner, and said he had lived in the South many years and was now back in Michigan. One of the things he most noticed was the deep historical consciousness of the Southern people, as contrasted with the frequent rootlessness of Northern and Western American culture. I remember the Mississippi writer William Faulkner having one of his characters make this now famous remark about living in Mississippi: 'The past is not dead; in fact, it's not even past.' Some things are painful for us to remember, such as long-time pervasive racism, and it needs to be repented of, and yet we may also take some honorable pleasure in recalling massive details of family ties and land, which is something most of us have been brought up to do naturally, day by day.

Whether Southern or not (and here I think of the Scottish Highlands): remembrance of what God has done for our fathers in the past is not backwardness. It's not a hindrance to future blessing; it is the only way to go forward. You read Hebrews 11, and it takes you through the history of the saints of God by faith: Abel by faith, Enoch by faith, Noah by faith, Abraham by faith, Sarah by faith, Moses—and on down to us. There has been the blessed continuance of the same saving faith in God and His covenant blessings, as recorded in Holy Scripture. That is what will take us forward into a future of light: that and nothing but that.

Bearing that in mind, let us look briefly at the three events recalled by Moses. First, the call of Abram (verses 8–9). It is simply this: election of unworthy people into God's covenant of grace, into his salvation, is always the foundation of present salvation and future hope, the ground of everything worth having. It means my salvation depends on God, not on me. In a way far beyond our grasp, verses 8 and 9 show that God, out of that huge world, chooses His own people to be His. We see this in Romans 11:4–7:

> But what saith the answer of God unto him? I have reserved to myself seven thousand men, who have

not bowed the knee to the image of Baal. Even so then at this present time also there is a remnant according to the election of grace. And if by grace, then it is no more of works; otherwise grace is no more grace. But if it be of works, then it is no more grace; otherwise work is no more work. What then? Israel hath not obtained that which he seeketh for; but the election hath obtained it, and the rest were blinded.

Much is mysterious, but we can safely conclude this: election depends on God, not on us, and our position is to praise Him for it, as seen in Romans 11:30–33. Praise Him for it! Don't explain it; praise Him for it. Don't be proud; you didn't deserve it. It's what He did. Remember Him! If you believe in Christ, it's because God elected an unworthy sinner to be where you are. Isn't He wonderful?

Secondly, remember the Exodus (32:10–12). Think about two illustrations given by Moses and the Exodus event: one from a human body, and one from bird life. Moses uses both to help us understand what was really lying behind the Exodus out of Egypt by God's power.

First, God will keep you as the 'apple of his eye'. We sometimes say that somebody's child is the apple of his or her eye, referring to the pupil of the eye. How much we protect the pupil by instinct, even before we have time to think about it! God has set up the body, so that the eyelid automatically closes if you are going to run into a limb, so as to protect the eye and particularly, the pupil, 'the apple of the eye'.

Psalm 17:8 makes reference to this, when it prays: 'Keep me as the apple of the eye; hide me under the shadow of thy wings.' Timothy Dwight a grandson of Jonathan Edwards and a president of Yale, saw revival during his administration there and wrote this hymn:

I love Thy church O God;
her walls before Thee stand.
Dear as the apple of Thine eye,
and graven on Thy hand.

Stop to think of it: Moses says God's people are as precious to Him as the apple of your eye, as your very pupil is to you; God thinks that much of us. What love! The fact that they were the apple of God's eye was why Pharaoh and all his troops, the Red Sea, the Amalekites or the Amorites couldn't get them. Why is there a church on earth, considerably larger than Islam? Because it is the apple of God's eye.

Then Moses uses another illustration to show what was happening in the Exodus, taken from bird life. Verse 11 says: 'As an eagle stirreth up her nest, fluttereth over her young, spreadeth abroad her wings, taketh them, beareth them on her wings.'

My father knew a good bit about birds, and I was told that the bird that has the greatest powers of flight and of sight, and the most amazing aviation abilities is the eagle. But, unlike some of the other lesser birds (such as sparrows), the eagle doesn't have the instinct automatically to fly. To train the little eaglet to fly, the parent bird stands on the nest way up in the mountains, or on a very high tree, and gets the little bird to stand up there with her. Then the parent flaps its wings, and the little eaglet naturally imitates the parent. In a later stage of training, mother eagle or father eagle starts tearing up the nest, making it a very uncomfortable home, so that little eaglet will be willing to leave that nest so as to take a chance on flapping the wings to leave the nest. But if the flapping of the wings of the little eaglet is not entirely successful, the parent eagle swoops under the little bird, catches it on the wings, and gives it another chance.

God was doing that to Israel in the Exodus event. You might ask, why does God let me go through these tests? Why doesn't God make it easier on me in my health, in difficult relationships, people disappoint me? Why this job is so bad or the country growing ever more immoral? God is teaching you to fly. God sometimes tears up our nest providentially, so we will be uncomfortable, and only then, are you willing to get out of the nest and go on to a larger place of service.

You would not do so, if He did not let discomforts come into your life. We're like that; we enjoy the familiar and the comfortable, even if these things keep us from growing. Even when we get out there, we don't know if we are going to make it or not. But isn't God wonderful? He is like the eagle, swooping down, just as we are about to go down, and catches us on His wings, so that we safely make it with Him!

St Patrick, who was used to convert pagan Ireland in the very early Middle Ages, preached all across the Island without any weapon. A hymn is attributed to him, called 'the Breastplate of St. Patrick'. This saintly missionary had no sword or knife, but he had his belief in the Trinity: that was his breastplate, his protection! Here is the chorus of this famous Breastplate of St. Patrick, and it is in the category of the protection that we believers have from God, who is even more solicitous of our welfare than mother or father eagle, whose wings come under us when we are falling:

> Christ be with me, Christ within me,
> Christ behind me, Christ before me
> Christ beside me, Christ to win me,
> Christ to comfort, And restore me
> Christ beneath me (eagles' wings!), Christ above me,
> Christ in quiet, Christ in danger,
> Christ in hearts, Of all that love me,
> Christ in mouth, Of friend and stranger.

The third thing Moses says is to remember settlement in the Promised Land—or immediately across the River from it, in verses 13–14. Note that when he is giving them this song to be learned and to be sung, they had only taken possession of that part of Israel that was on the east side of Jordan. Two and a half tribes were settling there with great blessing, although the men of these tribes would have to go to the front of the army to help the other tribes take the land of Canaan. It is clear that they were already experiencing some encouraging blessings in the first of the settlements: verse 13, 'He made him ride on the high places of the earth that he might eat the increase of the fields'.

Using an old expression, this first, trans-Jordanian settlement was 'a way token' for what God would do for all of Israel, and, I would add, for what He will do for the church. Always remember that God is generous, and wishes to deal generously with His people. Even if you come from a home that was not generous, always remember that God is different from stingy parents (or from a harsh orphan home). Do not go by your memories of bad people in your childhood; instead, determine to go by what His Word says, and it will show you His immense and kindly generosity; He loves to provide for you!

Moses mentions here honey and oil, curds or cheese, and so forth; good things of the created life while you are in this world. God gladly provides for His people in the lands where He has settled them. Psalm 81:6 expresses how much God wants to give you 'the finest of the wheat and the honey from the comb'. How generous He is!

The quickest way to lose such blessings is to forget the One who gave them to us, and foolishly to think that we got them by our own efforts, or perhaps that we deserve them. Moses calls us to focus on the blessings, and to remember that God gave them to us. But to forget the One who gave us the blessings is the quickest way to get a hard heart, and perhaps eventually lose it all.

If by grace, you have these blessings, (and most of us do), the way to keep them so you can share them with others is to remember the Lord; to remember that He is the source of every blessing. Be thinking much of Him, and that is one of the values of the observance of the Sabbath Day: to remember with gratitude remember the blessings of the Lord. And be specific about those blessings; 'Name them one by one!' That is always found in the attitude of a happy and a blessed people, in the day of Moses, or of ourselves.

71

THE HIGH COST OF FORGETTING GOD

Deuteronomy 32: 15-25

This passage brings before us the high cost of forgetting God. Previously we looked at verses 5–14, which exhorted God's people to remember all the blessings God had given them, and that remembering what God has done for us is the only safe and happy way into the future. That is followed by this passage which is a warning about the high price you will have to pay if you refuse to remember God and His blessings. Forgetting God means inevitably replacing Him with something else, with 'that which is not God' (verse 21). Great disasters always follow. In this text are two major points: first, Israel's sinful forgetting (verses 15–18); second, God's providential judgments that come down upon them (verses 19–25).

ISRAEL'S SINFUL FORGETTING (32:15-18)

In verses 15–18, Moses is predicting what the Holy Spirit has shown him is going to happen in the history of Israel, a prediction that will illumine what we see in the book of Judges, I and II Samuel, Kings, Chronicles, and the Prophets. It makes sense of the history of Israel, and is a constant warning to the church. This forgetting is sinful, particularly because those who forget God, who blessed them, are acting in an inconsistent way for those He has wonderfully taken care.

The inconsistency of turning your back on the Lord is shown in the name that He calls them in verse 15, Jeshurun, meaning 'my righteous people', that is, the people I have put into a saving and a right relationship with Me. I did all that for you so that you could be called Jeshurun, a righteous people, set apart and above the pagans. But when a people, who have been blessed with God's saving so many of them and giving them wonderful covenant opportunities, turn their back on the One who chose them and put them in a right relationship—or at least a potentially right relationship—with Him, they are doing two things at the same time. First, they are denying who God is. But they are also denying who they really are. To have been blessed, spiritually, and then to turn your back on the blessing, and act in a way that is contradictory to it by forgetting God, is to deny the real truth about yourself as one who has been put in the right with the Lord. To deny God means you deny yourself, which is like splitting apart your personality, so that you become a person badly divided.

We know what a terrible psychological condition that is, and it can also be a devastating problem in the spiritual realm. People who turn their back on the Bible and on the Lord, become split within themselves, between following a sinful culture and still knowing a great deal of what is right; it's what you call a confused self-identity that not only alienates you from God, but also guarantees inner disturbance and the inability to be satisfied with life. I reckon this inner division is what the Bible means when it says 'a double-minded man is unstable in all his ways'—psychological and political instability. In such a situation many internal griefs and external reversals are sure to come, as we will see in the second point today.

Two reasons are given us by Moses as to why it is so terrible to forget God, to turn your back on Him; why it is so inconsistent and massively ungrateful. First, because God has immensely blessed His people—you are then 'biting the hand that feeds you', and secondly, God begat you to be His own children, and so you are denying the family from which you come.

Hence let us remember how greatly God has blessed His people. Verse 15 says that they waxed fat and grew thick. People today don't like you to tell them that they have gained a lot of weight; in our culture, it is no longer considered a compliment, although it once was, especially among the poorer classes. We can understand why, because in subsistence economies, where it was hard to get enough to eat, to see that somebody was well-rounded and filled out was a sign that they had been blessed, and therefore it was a compliment to say to them 'you are shapely and it looks like you have prospered.' Thus, in this context, you have been well fed, well watered; you grew thick, meaning you have been in green pastures, beside still waters; God has prospered the well-being of His people. He has fed them 'with the finest of the wheat and the honey from the comb' (Ps. 81), giving them safe and quiet dwelling places, protecting them from enemies and pestilence, time after time.

And yet, in their prosperity, they have begun to take these blessings for granted, as though they got them without God's assistance. That may be the prime danger of prosperity.

How many prosperous Western people have become like King Nebuchadnezzar, who for some years, as a judgment for his pride, went crazy and lived out in the open fields, after which God gave him back his mind. Just before he went mad, Nebuchadnezzar was walking on the walls of Babylon, with its hanging gardens and a city of amazing wealth and prosperous culture. He looked around and congratulated himself: 'Is not this the great Babylon that I have built?' The judgment of God soon fell on him.

The second reason why this forgetting of God is so terrible is that He is our loving heavenly Father. In principle the seriousness of the sin is determined by the quality of the person against whom you sin. Of course, sin is sin, against anybody. But particularly when it is a noble, marvelous person, who has done you nothing but good, and you betray him, it is even more serious. Verse 18 makes this clear, when it speaks 'of the Rock that begat thee, thou art unmindful and hast forgotten God that formed thee.'

The Rev. James Philip, pastor at Holyrood Abbey in Edinburgh, referring to verse 18, writes:

> The word begat indicates that their defection was essentially a family matter, and was therefore fraught with all the seriousness and heartbreak that family tragedies bring and involve. It is a family sorrow and pain that God feels. It is the prodigal son story all over again, with a son's going into the far country and the father's heart being broken.

I saw a sad illustration of family grief, when a stranger from the North was involved in a terrible wreck on highway I-95, near Dillon, South Carolina, and was transported to the Dillon Hospital. Being a local pastor, the hospital asked me to visit him. The injured man was asked if he had any family whom he wanted to be notified. He answered that he had one son, but did not want him to be notified. When asked why not, he said: 'Don't you dare get in touch; we haven't spoken in years; we hate each other, and we will have no contact whatsoever.' This is an awful thing to happen in a family, and it can happen in those who claim to be in God's family.

God's Providential Judgments Upon Those who Forget (32:19–25)

We note three consequences of apostasy from God: first, the hiding of God's face; second, the provoking of the people who used to be so blessed, to jealousy of others; and third, the sure coming of providential disasters. Following the inspiration of the Holy Spirit through Moses, this part of Scripture has got to be preached, even though it is in a sense disturbing to preach and to hear, but if we hear it and take action, there can be hope on the other side.

The first consequence of apostasy is given in verse 20; God says, 'When you consistently, for a long time, forget me, deny me, suppress my blessings, I will hide my face from you.' That's ironic: you would think that the very thing that the forgetters want to happen is for God to hide His face, so they won't have to acknowledge His existence. But what they hadn't counted on was when God hides His smiling face from His people, then He also removes the blessings that they used to have in such measure, that they fondly thought were owing to their own cleverness. You cannot have the blessings of God for very long, without keeping God in your memory; that is, exercising faith. Verse 20 speaks of 'children in whom is no faith'. When blessed people forget God, there comes a point of no return, when He removes the blessings you used to have when you, your parents, and grandparents had faith.

In other words, if you cut off the roots of Christianity, you soon lose its fragrant, sweet-smelling, nourishing, beautiful fruits. You cannot have the fruits of godliness so long, if you cut the roots. That is something that the atheistic culture we are in, hadn't counted on; but they are going to go through the severe inconvenience of losing wonderful things that they had counted on and ascribed to themselves. When you lose God, you soon lose His blessings. We see that in Samson, in the book of Judges, apparently the strongest man who ever lived. Yet Hebrews 11 says that he died in the faith, so we'll see him in heaven, and this shows us that God saves all kinds of people.

Samson seriously compromised himself morally, and his concubine cut his hair off. His hair was important, because he had a Nazarite vow, which required having long hair to show that you are the Lord's servant. After losing his hair while asleep, Samson at first did not realize what had happened. Then his concubine called the Philistines in and when the formerly strong man got up from bed and tried to fight, 'he did not he did not know that the Lord was departed from him' (Jud. 16:20) and he became as weak as water. So they subdued him, tied him up, and put out his eyes. Without going into detail, later God gave him the grace to destroy the pagan temple, and thousands of idolaters in it. Yet Samson had lost a great deal, and as the pagan temple was destroyed, he also lost his life. The old Southern Baptist preacher of Memphis, Tennessee, Robert G. Lee, said: 'Payday someday.' If we continue to dishonor God, He will hide His smiling face, and the blessings we have known will be gone.

The second consequences of forgetting God is that God will provoke His ancient people to jealousy. That is what happened 1400 years after Moses. God took His time. He sent holy prophets to announce the coming of His Son. Then, in the fulness of the time, He sent His own Son in the flesh, to fulfill the prophetic requirements of what Messiah would be and do. But the Pharisaic leadership got their way, and rejected Christ, resulting in His cruel death on the cross. Since then, the covenant blessing of being the crucial people in the world has, at least for the time, been removed from unbelieving Judaism, though that is not the end of their story. For by inspiration of the Holy Spirit, Paul says that one day the Jews will become so jealous of the Christians that it will result in their conversion. Today, that seems impossible, but God says it will happen.

In Romans 10:19, Paul directly quotes these words of Moses from his Song in Deuteronomy 32: 'But I say, Did not Israel know? First Moses saith I will provoke you to jealousy by them that are no people, and by a foolish nation I will anger you.' Then in chapter 11:11: 'I say then, Have they stumbled that they should fall? God forbid! But rather that through their fall salvation is come to the Gentiles to provoke them to jealousy.' That's where we still are in world history, but he goes on to say later in this amazing chapter, in verses 25–26, that there is going to come a turning. The synagogue will have the Holy Spirit poured out; they will repent of denying the Messiah, and of their forgetfulness of who God is, and then the Lord will bring them back. It seems highly unlikely now, but with God all things are possible. Because God had spoken, it will indeed happen.

This shows that God sometimes provokes people who have been in the center of blessing to jealousy, by blessing other people who are humble enough to acknowledge Him. Something like that may happen again, if Professor Philip Jenkins' *The Coming of Global Christianity* (2001) is right. He divides the world into two parts, into the 'northern realm', wealthy Europe and America, Canada, Australia, and some other places, and the 'southern realm', Africa, China, and South America. Jenkins predicts that a strange change is going on in our lifetime.

The northern realm is becoming atheistic, denying God. They are refusing to reproduce themselves, and thus, do not have a birth rate high enough to replace the population, except for immigration. The Southern realm is seeing the biggest burgeoning of Christianity, probably since the Day of Pentecost. Huge numbers are coming to Christ in these places; some say around 10,000 a day in Africa and at least that many in China. At the same time, those places we tend to look down on in our prosperity, are having children and coming to the faith. If these trends continue, one day we, in once prosperous America and Europe, are going to be broken down, ashamed, and jealous at how God is blessing the massively growing churches in Africa and in China, unless, we stand up against atheism, which is a cancer eating away the vitals of faith in our countries.

The third consequence of forgetting God is listed in verses 23–25: the sending of providential chastisements, called 'mischiefs' or 'calamities'. Further down, Moses calls them 'arrows' that you get shot with, that stick in your flesh and soul. They convey God's severe providence, afflicting those who turn, willfully, their back on Him.

We are provided some details of how it works: verse 24 speaks about extreme weather and then poison from the dust—possibly meaning the increase of snake venom or maybe bacterial epidemics, new plagues and diseases that do not respond to normal medicine. Verse 25 is clear that military reversals of people, who used to be weaker than you, will follow; reversals that entail humiliation, defeat, death, and bondage for many.

It is a grim passage, indeed. But notice this: there's hope on the other side of it! In this connection, we are to remember the principle of Hebrews 12:6 and 9: 'For whom the Lord loveth he chasteneth, and scourgeth every son whom he receives. Furthermore, we have had fathers of our flesh which corrected us and we gave them reverence. Shall we not much rather be in subjection unto the Father of spirits and live?'

What is called for? We cannot change the culture. But in our own way, we can be sure that we are subject to the Father of spirits, and we will live. Whatever happens around us, God will secure us. If we're subject to Him, if we remember Him, and act on the basis of His existence and subscribe every blessing to Him, we'll make it. He promises us that.

Psalm 103 is the right one to remember at this juncture of new hope:

> Bless the Lord O my soul and all that is within me bless His holy name.
> Bless the Lord O my soul and forget not all His benefits.

Forget not the benefits! You and I can say: this week I am remembering the benefits; I will not forget them. Lord, forgive me when I have forgotten them. Help me to bring them to mind anew!

> Who forgiveth all thine iniquities,
> who healeth all thy diseases,
> Who redeemeth thy life from destruction;
> who crowneth thee with loving kindness and tender mercies.
> Who satisfieth thy mouth with good things so thy youth is renewed like the eagles.
> The Lord executeth righteousness and judgment for all that are oppressed.
> He made known His ways unto Moses,
> His acts unto the children of Israel.
> He will not always chide, neither will He keep His anger forever.

So, let us subject ourselves to the Father of Lights and live. Let us sit down at the table of His blessings, with thankfulness, repentance, remembrance, and a new consecration. That's what God says we can do by His grace.

72

HOPE FOR A SINFUL PEOPLE

Deuteronomy 32:26–52

In this short passage, we see hope for a sinful people. God has shown Moses that the future of a once blessed, once holy people, is going to be very grim, because of the sins they will commit and the chastisements that will come upon them. The nation is getting ready to go into a new land with great blessing upon it, but it is going to face severe judgments in the future. Yet Moses, foreseeing all of that, reveals the heart of God in these verses, when he says something like: 'Although it's going to get bad, there is hope for a sinful people, if they will hear God.' We notice three things in these verses: first, the opening of the thoughts of God (verse 26); second, God's zeal for own His glory, His character, or His honor, (verses 26–27); and third, God's sorrow at the blindness of His people (verses 28–29).

THE OPENING OF THE THOUGHTS OF GOD (32:26)

When you use an expression like 'the opening of the thoughts of God', you are saying a great deal, because He is God and not a man. It's hard enough to know what another human being is thinking, even in your family. But how could anyone know the thoughts of God, the infinite, majestic, sovereign One? Yet Verse 26 is clearly implying this. It starts off 'I said' I would do so and so; some have translated that, 'I thought'. The Tyndale commentary calls this little section a soliloquy in the heart of God.

Hamlet, in Shakespeare's play, has a soliloquy that probably a lot of us had to learn in high school; in a soliloquy, you are talking within yourself. So the Tyndale commentary says this is like God talking within Himself, a soliloquy in the heart of God. What an amazing revelation of the very heart of God!

That is no small matter. Think of Isaiah 55:8–9: 'For my thoughts are not your thoughts, neither are your ways my ways, saith the Lord. For as the heavens are higher than the earth, so are my ways higher than your ways and my thoughts than your thoughts.' And yet, great as the distance is between us, God has chosen to reveal the thoughts of His heart through Moses, to His people, and to us. The heart of God, the thoughts of God, are higher than ours, and therefore, we cannot go any further with it than what God reveals to us.

In Deuteronomy 29:29 we have already taken a look at it: 'The secret things belong to the Lord our God, but those that are revealed, to us and to our children that we may do them.' Yet God does reveal a certain amount about His heart, the primary revelation of which would have to wait until the New Testament, until the incarnation of the eternal Son of the Father. As H.R. MacIntosh of Edinburgh University used to say wonderfully, 'It is only in the face of Jesus Christ that we see most fully the heart of God the Father revealed.'

Hebrews 1:2-3 says that Christ is 'the express image of the Father'. In Greek, this word is *karakter*. This is only time this word is used in New Testament. It means that Christ is the character of the Father; He is exactly who the Father is, except that He is the Son, and not the Father. In every other way, they are exactly alike, as St. Athanasius used to say.

You remember in John 14:9, how Philip said to Jesus, 'Lord, show us the Father and we will be satisfied'. Jesus replied: 'Philip, hast thou been with me so long a time and dost thou not know that he that hath seen me hath seen the Father?' This indicates a fullness of the revelation of the heart of God in the New Testament. But already to a real degree, Moses shares part of God's heart, as it were a soliloquy, relating to the future of this nation, and the future of any large number of Christians, who get themselves into trouble, and what may lie on the other side.

God's Zeal For his Holy Character (32:26-27)

His zeal for His own character keeps God from destroying His own people. We see this when the Lord gives the reason why He would never totally wipe out the Jews. According to an old story, Frederick the Great of Prussia, asked his court chaplain, Zimmerman, 'Give me even a single proof for God's existence.' Zimmerman instantly answered, 'Your majesty, the Jews!' Why have the Jews endured and all the others gone? Nobody knows who is a descendant of an Amalekite, or a Midianite or a Philistine today, but they know who the Jews are!

God said to Israel, 'If you get out of my will, I am going to punish you severely, but I am not going to wipe you out totally.' God's reasons for not having wiped them out, I believe, are the same as when Christ made His promise to the church, that the gates of hell should not prevail against it. God through Moses gives two reasons why He's not going to wipe out the Jews, and then later, not going to wipe out His erring church.

The first reason relates to the haters of God and of His church. If they are able totally to defeat God's people and wipe them out, they will be able to say that God was not able or willing to protect His people, because we were great enough to destroy them, and we alone are great! So God said, 'I'm not going to let that happen.' That point is made by God in Deuteronomy 32:27: 'Were it not that I feared the wrath of the enemy lest their adversaries should say, our hand is high; we've done this'; it is similar to what Moses was praying in Deuteronomy 9:28, when he pleads with God not to wipe out His people: 'don't wipe them out', even though they are wicked, 'lest the land whence thou has brought us out say, because the Lord was not able to bring them into the land which He promised them, and because He hated them he hath brought them out to slay them in the wilderness.' God heard Moses; God was using Moses.

Even today, in a time of widespread secularism (atheism), I do not think that God is going to let the atheistic elite completely wipe out His people, especially when they say (or foolishly think) 'Our hand is high; we don't know if God even exists; if he does, he can't, or won't, do anything. He is not in charge of history; we are in charge.' Such voices of atheism will not be finally successful, because God is committed to the glory of His name. God says, 'I'm not going to let the pride of the enemy reach its goal, simply because it would be a reflection on my character.'

That is our hope for the future, and it's considerable. I'm never giving up, or feeling downcast or discouraged; and don't you! That is one of the great values of the Song of Moses.

The second reason why God will not let His people be wiped out is God's zeal for His own glory, as verse 17 says. The Lord has a zeal for His holy character to be shown. Why? Because He is the most beautiful reality in all the world. God is great. God is good. God is beautiful. God is light. God is lovely. God is wonderful. Therefore, He is zealous that His beauty of character, with its goodness, truth, mercy and grace should be known, and will work to do what is necessary in order that the only thing worth having, His glory and beauty and grace and goodness, shall without fail shine out, and will vanquish the darkness and corruption, and all the Satanic attacks against it.

Isaiah 48:9–11 refers to God's zeal for his glory:

> For my name's sake will I defer mine anger, and for my praise will I refrain for thee, that I cut thee not off. Behold, I have refined thee, but not with silver; I have chosen thee in the furnace of affliction'. [God does not say that He is going to keep us out of the furnace of affliction; He may put us there; we may be getting just to the edge of it now.] 'For mine own sake, even for mine own sake, will I do it; for how should My name be polluted? And I will not give My glory to another.

The cynical devil's crowd wants anything but God's glory; they want the glory to be theirs. But God says, 'You will not have it! I'll take whatever action is necessary, even when My people are weak as water, and inconsistent, and frail and failing; you shall not have My glory.' Ezekiel 20:8–9 says much the same:

> But they rebelled against me and would not hearken unto me; they did not every man cast away the abomination of their eyes, neither did they forsake the idols of Egypt. Then I said, 'I will pour out my fury upon them to accomplish my anger against them in the midst of the land of Egypt.' But I wrought for my name's sake, that it should not be polluted before the heathen, among whom they were, in whose sight I made myself known unto them, in bringing them forth out of the land of Egypt.

One commentator said that the pivot of the Song of Moses is zeal for God's holy character. That's it! That's the center, the pivot, that everything in the Song of Moses rotates around. Jesus has this same zeal for God's glory. Listen to His great high priestly prayer: 'And now, O Father, glorify Thou Me with Thine own self with the glory which I had with Thee before the world was' (John 17:5).

During Jesus' ministry on earth, He said, 'I have meat to eat that you know not of.' It was His zeal for the Father's glory, to be maintained in the salvation of the elect, that steeled Him to undergo His agonies on the cross. He knew what it would cost Him. That's the issue, I think, in the drawing back of Jesus in the Garden of Gethsemane, as He goes deeper into agony, for He is going to be made filthy, darkened with our sins. God hates sin, but He never hated His Son; He loved His Son, even when his Son was made sin, but Christ hated to become that which the Father disregards and He said: 'O my Father, if it be possible, let this cup pass from me' (Matt. 26:39). But beneath it all, He means, 'If it the only way God's glory can be maintained, and the lost sinners can be saved, is for me to go through this, then I will do it; hence, 'not what I will, but thy will be done.' It was zeal for the Father's glory that took Jesus through the unspeakable separation from the Father when 'God made Him to be sin, who knew no sin, that we might be made the righteousness of God in Him'.

The zeal that Jesus has for His Father's glory, carries on with great power in the church, and is one of the signs that the church is alive, and going to move forward. As it does so, it is animated by something of the zeal of the Son to the Father's honor and glory. This mighty zeal of Christ for His Father's glory was beautifully expressed in a sermon by James Henley Thornwell, Presbyterian minister and later, president of the University of South Carolina and then of Columbia Seminary. His sermon is entitled *The Sacrifice of Christ, the Type and Model of Missionary Effort* (1857):

> That supreme reverence for the glory of God which prompted Jesus to regard not his life dear unto him provided his Father's honor were maintained, must be the dominant principle of action in every Christian heart. The divine character must be sacred in our eyes. To be a Christian is to love God and to love God is to reverence his name. In proportion to the intensity of this principle will be our efforts to vindicate the divine honor from reproach. Darkness covers the earth and gross darkness the people. Without God [he means the pagan world and all the continents] they are yet seeking him; misled by their carnal minds, they can never find Him. They must lie down in sorrow. There is a light which can dispel this darkness, but it has never yet appeared in their hemisphere. There is a Name which can heal this sorrow, but it has never yet been pronounced in their dialect. Is there nothing in the spectacle of a world in ruins to stir the compassion of a Christian heart? Can we look upon our fellows, members of the same family, pregnant with the same instincts and destined to the same immortality, and feel no concern for the awful prospects before them? They are perishing and we have the bread of life. They are famished with thirst and we have the water of which if a man drink, he shall never thirst. They are dead and we have the Spirit of life. We have but to announce the Savior's name to spread the story of the cross, and we open the door of hope to the multitudes.

A zeal for the glory of God always carries with it a love for the multitudes in darkness, who, if they don't see His glory, lose it all. That has always motivated the church to give sacrificially to the cause of missions.

The Sorrow of God Over the Blindness of his People (32:28–30)

As Moses opens this divine soliloquy, he moves on to the future of the nation, in verses 28–29; and in that context expresses God's sorrow at the blindness of Israel. But let me ask you this: does God experience sorrow?

The Westminster Confession of Faith, chap. 2, says that 'God is without body parts or passions'. I assume that means God is without the passions of bodily parts, and that's true enough. But what God is referring to through Moses is not referring to bodily passion, but rather to the exercises of the Spirit of God, if I could use such an expression. I can't say very much about the sorrows of God, but I can take you to Jesus, who is the fullest expression of the character of the Father, as we have seen in Hebrews 1:3 and John 14:9. He is rightly called in Isaiah 53 'a man of sorrows and acquainted with grief.'

You could object, 'Yes, but that's in His manhood.' That is true, but His soul was intensely involved, for He says, 'My soul is exceedingly troubled, even unto death', (Matt. 26:28). Hence, there is something in His Spirit that must be in communion with the Spirit of the Father, over the sorrow over rebellion, sin, death, and hell that have devastated God's good creation. Yet we have to be careful here, for it is profoundly mysterious. We read throughout the Bible that the heavenly Father, God Almighty, has a most profound serenity always. His throne is maintained in a most holy serenity, so that God is never overcome by sorrow, although I believe in some sense that we cannot define, He experiences it, as He experiences joy and love. But sorrow never controls God; He controls it. That's about the most we can say on a holy and mysterious subject, upon which God Himself has not revealed much to us.

We're told in these few verses of the Song of Moses that God's sorrow was over two areas relating to His people whom He had blessed so much. Being omniscient, He knew that Israel would go off the rails. That was because first, they did not understand what got them into trouble; and second, did not realize what massive blessings they still could have after chastisement.

Yet the inspired text says that God is sorry, particularly that His people did not understand the source of their trouble. Verse 28 explains: 'They are a nation void of counsel, neither is there any understanding in them.' Put it this way: they looked only at the secondary issues, the human and the natural and the political economic factors. Certainly, there is a place for that, but what they haven't understood, and haven't wanted to be reminded of, is that the real problem is their disobedience to God. He is the prime cause; the other things are secondary causes. Whatever you may do with the secondary causes, you must get into line with Him who is the primary cause.

So, the end of verse 30 says 'except their Rock had sold them, and the LORD had shut them up', meaning, 'In times when you have done wrong, and I had to shut you up, I took away your strength; I weakened the knees of your young men that run in battle; I chased your horses away; I did this, I did that, I shut you up.' With only an eye upon secondary causes, we could reply: we weren't having a good day, and the Amalekites were stronger than we thought. But God says, 'That's not the issue; I shut you up; I was behind what happened when you lost those battles; I was speaking to you and you still don't understand, and so I'll have to do more next time.'

In Judges chapters 2–3, and 10, God is saying: 'I sold out My people because of their idolatry and abominable sexual behavior; I sold them out, and I let inferior groups come in and get the best of them, because I was speaking to them, and they still didn't understand why it happened; they only looked at the people who came in on them. Until you understand who's behind it, you're not going to get anywhere.'

Psalm 78:8 prays to be kept from this attitude: 'And might not be as their fathers, a stubborn and rebellious generation; a generation that set not their heart aright, and whose spirit was not steadfast with God.' Isaiah 42:24–25 speaks along the same lines:

> Who gave Jacob for a spoil, and Israel to the robbers? Did not the Lord, he against whom we have sinned? For they would not walk in his ways, neither were they obedient unto his law. Therefore he hath poured upon him the fury of His anger, and the strength of battle; and it hath set him on fire round about, yet he knew not; and it burned him, yet he laid it not to heart.

They had rather consider anything, any kind of cause, except God's doing it in order to deal with them. That is not supposed to be spoken of by nice people, but God's providence—if the Bible is true—is always directly behind the rise and fall of tribes, kingdoms, and nations, and in military victories and military disasters, Psalm 75:6-8 proclaims the same message, as does Isaiah 40:15 and 17.

God's dealing with the nations is always based on His true, changeless moral character. In a manner that is not revealed to the human mind, God uses historical events and realities of nature. As the years go by; He lowers some and He raises up others. Verse 30 summarizes this point, when it says that God is grieved over His people not understanding that God is behind what is happening, and, therefore, they need to get it right with Him. They still don't see, saying it's the economy, or a different political party; the weather or the spirit of the age. But God says, 'You don't understand! I'm behind these reversals.'

But Moses gives us positive hope in verse 30, that one should chase a thousand, and two put ten thousand to flight! That can happen when we're right with God, and thus in the center of His will, with zeal for His glory, to which we dedicate everything. In that case, God can take almost nothing and make it something tremendous. Think of how the Lord instructed Gideon to send back home the vast majority of the men who had come out to fight with him for Israel. That was to show that a very small number (only 300) could be used by God in a supernaturally mighty way, so that God alone would get the glory for the battle. A minority with God can always a win over an unbelieving majority. We see this principle is 1 Corinthians 1:25-29:

> Because the foolishness of God is wiser than men; and the weakness of God is stronger than men. For ye see your calling, brethren, how that not many wise men after the flesh, not many mighty, not many noble, are called. But God hath chosen the foolish things of the world to confound the wise; and God hath chosen the weak things of the world to confound the things which are mighty; and base things of the world, and things which are despised, hath God chosen, yea, and things which are not, to bring to naught things that are; that no flesh should glory in His presence.

God has chosen the weak and foolish things of the world to confound the mighty. It is true in the Western countries that the church does not have the impressive numbers it did up to the 1950s, but from this perspective, it doesn't matter. Indeed, great numbers might have been a holdback for us, for God will use the common, the lowly, the humble, for they are far less likely to be glorious in their own eyes!

But this humility is not always true of God's people. In Isaiah 9:9-11, Isaiah denounces the same sort of attitude earlier denounced by Moses. After serious reversals, the proud inhabitants of the Northern Kingdom did not get the point at all. Instead, they boasted that they could still take care of it, by rebuilding. 'And all the people shall know, even Ephraim and the inhabitant of Samaria, that say in pride and stoutness of heart, the bricks are fallen down but we will build with hewn stones; the sycamores are cut down but we will change them into cedars.' What they are saying is 'Yes, we've had a reversal, but we're going to come out stronger. We had brick houses, but now we're going to have stone mansions. We had a cheap pine wood, but we're going to have massive oak, and cedar and cypress; it's going to be better!' No brokenness in the hearts of these people! But God says through Isaiah, it's not going to be better until you repent: 'Therefore the Lord shall set up the adversaries of Rezin against him, and join his enemies together.'

In view of our recalcitrance, why is there hope

for the future? How can you realistically offer hope, when it's so bad? Turn to Joel 2, where hope for the sinful is especially concentrated, where it promises that if you will do this, you can get back to the place, where one shall chase a thousand and two shall chase ten thousand.

> And the Lord shall utter His voice before his army; for his camp is very great; for he is strong that executeth His Word; for the day of the Lord is great and very terrible and who can abide it? Therefore also now, saith the Lord, turn ye even to me with all your heart, and with fasting, and with weeping, and with mourning; and rend your heart, and not your garments, and turn unto the Lord your God; for he is gracious and merciful, slow to anger, and of great kindness, and repenteth him of the evil. Who knoweth if he will return and repent, and leave a blessing behind him, even a meat offering and a drink offering unto the Lord your God? (Joel 2:11–14).

Instead of being distraught over the pagan majority, bring your sins, your hardness of heart, and your lack of zeal for His honor and glory to the altar! Bring it to the cross of Christ and see what I will do! And then hear Joel 2: 21–27:

> Fear not, O land; be glad and rejoice. For the Lord will do great things. Be not afraid, ye beasts of the field, for the pastures of the wilderness do spring, for the tree beareth her fruit, the fig tree and the vine do yield their strength. Be glad, then , ye children of Zion, and rejoice in the Lord your God; for he hath given you the former rain moderately and he will cause to come down for you the rain, the former rain, and the latter rain, in the first month.

He's going to send down the rain, and, looking back from the perspective of the New Testament, I believe that would be the Holy Ghost. And then look at Joel 2:25:

> And I will restore to you the years that the locust hath eaten, the cankerworm , and the caterpillar, and the palmerworm, my great army which I sent among you. And ye shall know that I am in the midst of Israel, and that I am the Lord your God, and none else; and my people shall never be ashamed.

The gracious and faithful God has done that more than once with His erring people, once He leads them to repentance.

73

The Blessings of Moses

Deuteronomy 33:1–29

It is a great joy to contemplate the blessings of God, as they have come through His faithful servant Moses. While the Bible definitely teaches God's holiness, and therefore God's necessary judgments, it is a minor theme in the symphony of Divine revelation. The blessing of God upon His people and upon His world is the major theme of the entire Word of God. And that is the case with this wondrous book of Deuteronomy. We will look at the blessings of Moses and see, by the end of the message, that perhaps the major way that God wins people to the truth, in Judaism in the Old Testament, and in Christianity in the New Testament, is by blessing His people and making them a blessing in the earth, so that they attract others to themselves, who also desire the blessings of a happy and a satisfied life. Three points from this text: first, the majestic intervention of God for His people (verses 1–5); second, Moses' blessings upon the tribes (verses 6–25); and third, praise to God (verses 26–29).

The Majestic Intervention of God for his People (33:1–5)

Deuteronomy 33:1–5 deals with the interventions of God, when He comes down and makes a difference in the world of nature and of human personalities. God's arm—His right hand—intervenes; He is very present, and working out in the most practical and amazing way, his will.

There are other majestic interventions of God in Holy Scripture: the first one is creation out of nothing. God always was; there was nothing outside God, and at a certain point in eternity, God speaks worlds into existence, in the space of six days. Then God intervened when He called Abram, who was in a pagan, idolatrous land, to become the father of the faithful in all the ages. God intervened in the Exodus to get over a million slaves, who were nonetheless His people, out of Egypt, through the Red Sea in a wonderful way. God intervened on Mount Sinai, which was smoking and shaking with His divine presence, as He revealed His law; showing what His character is like, and how He has created us to live on the basis of His character, since we bear His image.

The main emphasis here is God's intervention at Mount Sinai. Something amazing was happening, and people were at first terrified, for the light of God was so bright that in a certain sense, it almost seemed darkness. That is one of the mysteries of who God is: He is so bright, He seems dark at times. Habakkuk 3:3–6 speaks of the same thing, of Mount Paran, near Sinai, and how God comes into this real world, and the world begins shaking, and is different on the basis of God intervening:

> God came from Teman, and the Holy One from mount Paran. Selah. his glory covered the heavens and the earth was full of His praise. And his brightness was as the light; he had horns coming out of His hand; and there was the hiding of his power. Before him went the pestilence, and burning coals went forth at his feet. He stood, and measured the earth; He beheld, and drove asunder the nations; and the everlasting mountains were scattered, the perpetual hills did bow; his ways are everlasting.

We note in these first five verses that when God came, He came with ten thousands of saints. That is to say, the holy angels accompany God when He intervenes to do something big in this world. In the book of Job, we are told that before the end of creation week, the angels were beholding the glories of creation, and praising the Creator for it, singing together for joy at seeing how wondrously God was working. So the angels were there at Mount Sinai; and at the call of Abraham; and at the Exodus, the angel of death was preparing the way for them to get out of Egypt. I guess the greatest intervention was at the birth of our Lord Jesus Christ, the virgin birth, which a holy archangel, Gabriel, announced to the Virgin Mary. Then when Christ was born in Bethlehem, a multitude of the heavenly host were praising God and singing: 'Glory to God in the highest, on earth peace, goodwill towards men'.

The angels seem to come when God comes down from eternity into time, and is working. At Jesus' resurrection too, the holy angel is there, sitting inside the empty tomb, clothed in shining white raiment. The angels are there when God is doing something of great significance on earth.

In all of our life, I believe that God is constantly sending angels to help all of His children. Psalm 34:7 says: 'The angel of the Lord encampeth round about them that fear Him and delivereth them.' Hebrews 1:14 speaks of the mysterious help of the holy angels to all believers: 'Are they not all ministering spirits, sent forth to minister for them who shall be heirs of salvation?'

Imagine these holy, beautiful creatures, humbling themselves to stoop down to be servants to us, to minister to us. That's the greatness of God; when He comes, the angels come; usually invisible, but at times some of the saints have seen them. Hence, these five verses demonstrate that God is a living and an active God, coming into this real world, getting done what He wants to get done, at the time He wants it done.

God is not a mere philosophical concept. He is the ever-living Triune God, who intervenes in this world, as He sees fit. He is never excluded from it.

That is what Moses is setting before the tribes of Israel. Later, David says in Psalm 16:8: 'I have set the Lord always before Me; because He is at my right hand, I shall not be moved.' So Moses is setting the Lord before these people. He mentions different kinds of blessings for the different tribes, but the binding concept, the foundational truth, is that God is the One before whom you live your life, and if you look to Him, and seek to follow Him in faith and obedience, great blessing is going to follow, and the world will be changed because you were there, in your own little way.

Moses' Blessings Upon the Tribes (33:6–25)

To work out Deuteronomy 33, it is necessary to go to Genesis 49, listing the blessings of Jacob—on his death bed—upon the twelve patriarchs, giving them blessings: sometimes warnings, sometimes rebukes, and predicting what the future will be for the twelve tribes. Moses, some 400 years later, takes some of the same themes, but with the revelation of the Holy Spirit, he reworks it and, in a certain sense, enriches the blessings.

Thus, following Genesis 49 and Deuteronomy 33, one could say that God's blessing runs in different ways upon the different tribes. As God blesses the different lines, it is finally to result in making them a blessing to others in the earth!

Looking at the twelve tribes in Deuteronomy 33, we find that just eleven are mentioned. As we trace biblical history, we notice that only a few of the tribes ever produced great epoch-making leaders in Israel's history, although all of the tribes were blessed in their own appropriate ways.

For example, Moses and Aaron came from the tribe of Levi; Joshua came from Ephraim; Gideon came from Manasseh; David came from Judah, and so David's descendant, the Lord Jesus Christ, came from the line of Judah; Paul the Apostle came from the tribe of Benjamin.

Even in later church history, it does seem that some family lines stay near God, and therefore blessings of widespread usefulness ensue through those generations. Many years ago, a very interesting book on the life of Jonathan Edwards was published, *Marriage to a Difficult Man*. It had an appendix in which the author traced out for some 250 years, what was known about the many descendants of Jonathan and Sarah Edwards. Then he compared them to a family of criminals in Virginia, evidently the products of incest, called the Jukes family, in which there was disobedience, unbelief, uncleanness, and curse upon curse, for generations. (Some of those descendants may have become saved, but that is not mentioned.) How different it was with the descendants of Jonathan Edwards: university presidents, brain surgeons, CEO's of great companies, presidents of banks, leading lawyers, governors, statesmen, ambassadors; altogether an amazing group of descendants! The line of blessing went down, and still is, apparently, in Jonathan Edwards' descendants. The same could be said of General Booth of the Salvation Army. Some have traced some of his descendants, and they tend to be top-flight, cultural, and still spiritual leaders. I remember the pastor of my wife's parents in Cambridge; I couldn't agree with his preaching, but he was a direct descendant of William Booth. I am told that it is the same with the remarkable descendants of Andrew Murray in South Africa, to this day.

Of the twelve tribes, one isn't mentioned, the tribe of Simeon. Jacob mentions him in Genesis 49, but puts a rebuke on him and his descendants because of bad things that Simeon had done (see Genesis 34). It would appear that by the time Moses is speaking, maybe the tribe of Simeon had more or less been assimilated into the larger and more important tribe of Judah. For whatever reason, Simeon did not have the significance of the other eleven tribes.

Looking briefly at the tribes that are mentioned: Reuben, the first born, would not have the prominence and joy of some of the others, because Reuben had committed fornication with one of his father's concubines, which caused him to lose the birthright and its considerable privilege. But even so, verse 6, says: 'Let Reuben live and not die [he is still given grace, he is saved] and let his men be few.' In other words, the Lord would not bless them with large numbers, because of what he did. It doesn't mean they couldn't be saved, but they won't have the prominence of others.

Then there's Judah: (from where we get the word *Jew*, or *Judea*). Judah was the progenitor of King David, the ancestor of our Lord Jesus Christ; the line of salvation to the world comes through

Judah as patriarch Jacob had predicted in Genesis 49. I will just take one point in Deuteronomy 33;7 which says that God will be his help over his enemies. That's important, because any time you are going to do something significant for God, any time special blessing is on the way, particularly when the blessing of larger service, is upon you, the devil is going to attack you in a strong way.

You have heard me quote many times a great Scottish saint and Puritan, Samuel Rutherford, who said, 'He that stands closest to his captain is the surest target for the archers.' Any time you are determined to do something for the Lord, anytime you have a new consecration, and are sold out to the Lord- as it were—as far as you can be, you are going to be attacked. But don't be discouraged. You might become fearful, and even feel that it is too dangerous to be consecrated, if you are going to be attacked. But it is not right to give in to such fears, for God will be your shield and your strength. It says that 'God is his help over his enemies.' How many times we see this in David! God was his help over his enemies. King Saul had the government, the army, the police, and was determined to kill this shepherd boy. But God was David's help.

Our Lord Jesus Christ, Judah's descendant through David and Mary, had to face the onslaughts of Satan, who wished to destroy Christ, or at the very least, lead Him aside from His mission of going to the cross. But Jesus said: 'Get thee behind Me, Satan.' Jesus refused to follow the satanic temptations, and God was His help. God never allows any opposition to come to any of His servants except He will overrule it for greater blessing. God will multiply your influence through these attacks.

Possibly, our feelings may be that we had rather not be attacked. But we have to keep in mind that God's in charge and will be your sufficiency, your shield, and your exceeding great reward. We are to remember Psalm 76:10: 'The wrath of man shall praise thee; the remainder of wrath shalt thou restrain'. God will never let any wrath of the devil, or of the people he motivates, come against you, except if in some way it builds up your character, increases your faith, multiplies your influence, and brings more glory to God than even if you hadn't been attacked.

Although I am not in any sense certain about a matter than has not been clearly revealed in Scripture, at times I have wondered if we shall have 'all the time in the world in heaven' to think about and to praise God for every attack we endured. I believe we may well think about things we went through on earth, and will see how frequently the angels were there, and how much God loved us when we didn't feel He was loving us. I think one of the things we will praise God the most for is the attacks of evil that He allowed to happen and press us hard. Then we'll see it was out of His love, because He said, 'I'm going to increase My glory; I'm going to entrust her, I'm going to entrust him, with the stewardship of difficulty and trial and suffering, because they're going to greatly increase, so that My beauty and splendor and radiance will shine out from them.' Hence, God will never leave us alone. He may not give us an easy path; He will not 'carry us to the skies on flowery beds of ease', but when we are safe home on the hilltops of heaven, by the shores of the crystal glassy sea, I imagine we shall be giving tremendous thanks to God for all He did for us. He did so for Judah, and He shall be with every believer. God is our help over every enemy. That is the spirit in which Moses would have us face the future.

The third Patriarch, Levi, verses 8–11, begat the priestly tribe of Moses and Aaron, and the generations of those who descended from them.

We are told that most of them stood against the unbelieving, complaining, unfaithful multitude in two different situations in the wilderness: Massah and Meribah. To do so and be faithful to God, they had to split from their relatives. We have all known people who had to divide from their families, at least for a time, and be thought very strange by their close relatives for fully obeying God. Maybe later the family would reconsider, but we are not told about that. What matters is that God said (as in 1 Samuel): 'Them that honour me, I will honour.' God did honour the priestly tribe of Levi over the ages, continued to use them as the teachers of the people, as well as their priests, until His own Son came as the final Prophet, Priest, and King.

Fourth, verse 12 speaks of Benjamin in lovely terms: 'the beloved of the Lord shall dwell in safety by him, and the Lord shall cover him all the day long and he shall dwell between his shoulders.' The Rev. James Phillip wrote in 1984, referring to Paul:

> The apostle Paul was of the tribe of Benjamin, and we may readily see how applicable this word would be to him in any number of circumstances. We could hardly doubt, could we, that there were times in his experience during his missionary journeying when he was under great pressure and in hazard and jeopardy of his life when he went to this ancient prophecy about his tribe and claimed its promise for himself, 'the beloved of the Lord shall dwell in safety by him?' It would be a Bible study of great enrichment simply to read through the apostle's missionary journeys and some of the autobiographical references to them in his epistles, like in 2 Corinthians 1 and 7, and lay this wonderful verse alongside them to see how full this divine provision was for His servant, and how richly this promise was fulfilled for him. Now that was some

1400 years later! God inhabits eternity, and His blessings are just as fresh as they were 3400 years ago. Why not? That's who God is; that is what God really is like.

The longest section, verses 13–17, is devoted to Joseph. It mentions 'precious things': valuable, beautiful, wonderful things in heaven, on earth, in the body and in the spirit, and relationships with people. It seems that the Lord was making it up to Joseph, because of his faithfulness to Him, when he was sold into slavery; hated of his brothers; lied about by Potiphar's wife, and cast into prison. Through it all, he remained faithful.

How generous God is! Not only did He reward Joseph personally, but He promised to bless His descendants down through the years. Interestingly, verse 17 speaks of ten thousands of Ephraim and thousands of Manasseh, in contrast to Reuben, where it says 'his men shall be few'. Joseph, through Ephraim and Manasseh, would become thousands upon thousands.

Having large number of descendants is a potential blessing of God; through them we can be a blessing to the future. If you bring up your offspring in the nurture and the admonition of the Lord, setting the Lord always before them, and they do the same with their children, there will be great blessing to the world.

The sixth and seventh of the patriarchs are Zebulon and Issachar, taken together in verses 18 and 19. Contrast Moses' statement here with what Jacob said in Genesis 49:15, that they would enjoy the pleasant things of life, but they would become servants to others. It is difficult for the interpreter to know exactly how this worked in the general economic weakness of these two tribes.

A mere guess might be that many of them become heavily indebted. Scripture says 'the borrower is servant [or slave] to the lender.'

But that may not be the only reason for their future loss of power and standing among the tribes. However, Moses gives encouragement in Deuteronomy 33:19, where he says: you are going to be given a new leadership; you'll get out of debt, if that was the problem, or out of poor behavior patterns. My grace will get you out, to where you'll really be a recognized, prominent, useful, fruitful leader.

This hope, held out to Zebulon and Issachar, teaches us something important. We can always go beyond our ancestors, if we need to. I suppose most people have some either very holy ancestors or some that were ungodly. Some may have been weak ones, but if they had at least enough faith, and obedience, through the grace of Christ, they made it, and we can too, even if we are not proud of them. With God's grace, you can go beyond anything that your ancestors ever did and ever were, if that is God's will for you.

The next tribe is Gad. Genesis 49:19 says 'a troop shall overcome him, but at the last he shall overcome.' Deuteronomy 33:21 says that Gad became a true leader, in the best sense of the word, because he was trusting in what God said. While many qualities are called for in good church leadership, the way they will be blessed the most by God, and used to make the most changes in the world, will when they are given over to the divine revelation, and to God who gave it.

In his Genesis 49 blessing, Jacob says that while Gad is going to be overcome, it is not the end. Moses is especially saying that by the power and grace of God intervening through your life, if you look to God and set the Lord before you, you can overcome whatever is against you. I sometimes say to people whom I visit in jails and prisons, something like, 'You have been overcome by a troop', whether by your own sins or hard circumstances, but you could overcome at the last. You can come out of this prison and be an overcomer, if you give yourself body, soul, and spirit to the Lord Jesus Christ. Many have done that through the prison ministry of Chuck Colson.

Then Naphtali, says Jacob, is 'a hind let loose', or 'a freed deer' (Gen. 49), but with Moses, in Deuteronomy 33:23, this tribe is said to be 'full of the favor of the Lord'. This seems to be saying that you go far beyond being set free (a wonderful blessing in itself) to having a prosperity and a stable influence for God. I do not believe that it is an over-spiritualization to think that God wants every believer to be, in his or her own appointed way, not, just a hind let loose, but 'full of the favor of the Lord'. When this kind of divine blessing is upon you, people can see that favor, and some of them will begin to want what you have, as must have been the case with Naphtali.

For Dan, in verse 22, a certain aggressiveness is predicted. That's not always bad. If we didn't have a certain amount of an aggressive spirit in the church of Christ, we couldn't be *onward* Christian soldiers, as it were. And we see Dan later capturing northern territory in a remarkable way. So there's a certain aggression predicted in one of these tribes and there is an element of it in all Christians. I have sometimes thought about my own ancestry: of my four grandparents three of their families were fairly relaxed and laid back. But one was fairly aggressive and high achievers. Whichever way our people have been inclined, the important thing is to seek the balance granted by the Holy Spirit in our own lives.

Finally, in verses 24–25, Asher is specially blessed: children, riches, friendship, and continued influence. One could look at a wonderful widow in Luke 2:36–38, who plays a part in the birth narratives of the Lord. She was either 84 years old, or had been a widow for 84 years—commentators aren't agreed. But, a descendant of Asher, she appears when Joseph and Mary present the Christ child at the temple in Jerusalem. She puts a wonderful blessing on Christ, similar to what Moses said about Asher: 'As thy days … so shall thy strength be', God gave this wonderful saint, Anna, the strength she needed at age 84, to speak to his parents of the redemption of Christ.

Praise to God (33:26–29)

Verses 26–29 lift up praise to God, particularly for His greatness. Moses says in verse 26 that God shows up when we need Him. He says the Lord rides upon heaven; that is, God is not only in the unseen, invisible realm of the crystal sea and the rainbow circled throne and the gates of pearl, but He also comes down into this natural, physical world when we need Him. In rain, and storm, and sunshine, He is controlling, directing, and intervening in the lives of His people. We are in no sense ever orphans.

Verse 27 says 'the eternal God is thy refuge, and underneath are the everlasting arms'. Over the long years of my ministry, whenever I go to a home where there has been a death, I nearly always pray, before the family leaves for the funeral, this verse: 'The eternal God is our refuge, and underneath are the everlasting arms.'

Verse 27 goes on to say that God will deal with our enemies. We have a part to play in this battle, for as James says: 'Resist the devil and he will flee from you.' Don't ask God to protect you from the assaults of Satan, unless you're willing to resist the devil, and then the devil has no choice. You resist him in the name of the Lord Jesus Christ, and the evil one has no choice but to flee the camp.

Moses adds in verse 28: 'Israel then shall dwell in safety alone: the fountain of Jacob shall be upon a land of corn and wine; also his heavens shall drop down dew.' Think of this as a concentrated 23rd Psalm—the psalm of the Shepherd—boiled down into one wonderful cup of strength and joy.

Finally, verse 29 concludes with these reasons to praise God: 'Happy art thou, O Israel, O people saved by the Lord.' These blessings of Moses conclude with the happiness of God's people who are saved by the grace of their Lord. True happiness. What is it? It is all in God, and He, out of free grace, makes it over to us as He deems best.

I said at the beginning that the most basic way of spreading the biblical religion, of introducing people to God and His salvation, is through the lives of happy people, who can thereby open the way for people to listen to the gospel of salvation. It is hard to win people to God if you're mean; but you are far more likely to win people to the Lord, if indeed you are happy.

Long after the time of Moses, Zechariah showed that the happiness of God's people draws in the pagans. 'Yea, many people and strong nations shall come to seek the Lord of hosts in Jerusalem, and to pray before the Lord' (Zech. 8:22–23). How are you going to get them to come to Jerusalem—now the church—to seek God's face and pray? How are you going to do it? It is not by fussing with them, not even with your own children:

> Thus saith the Lord of hosts: In those days it shall come to pass, that ten men shall take hold out of all languages of the nations, [the pagans, out of the whole world] even shall take hold of him that is a Jew [descendants of Judah and all of Israel, and 'the Israel of God', the Christians] saying, We will go with you; for we have heard that God is with you.

This is the fruitful background for evangelism and missions.

74

Death Has Lost Its Sting

Deuteronomy 34:1-12

The great resurrection chapter, 1 Corinthians 15:55, pronounces this transforming truth: 'death hath lost its sting'. I remember, maybe twenty five years ago, attending the funeral and burial of a dear old saint, who lived out in the country from my home town. She had apparently died very easily, and was found next day in a peaceful, dignified condition in one of the rooms of her old house. At her burial, her nephew said to me beside the grave, 'Death has lost its sting.'

When I look at these last words about Moses, I have to say, in all these arrangements for his funeral and his burial and what follows, death has lost its sting. In light of eternity, time in certain instances seems to flow backward, so that the future impacts things long before they appear. In that way, the resurrection of Christ seems to work backwards, as well as forward. The interaction between time and eternity is a mystery, but enough has been revealed to make us realize that what God did in Jesus Christ goes in both directions: not only future, but also past.

For instance, the blood of the cross goes backward (to cleanse the believers of the Old Testament) and forward (to cleanse all who confess their sins from now until the end of time). In a way like that, the power of the resurrection in some sense was already working backwards so that in his physical death, Christ was giving Moses a victory, not a defeat.

This is not a chapter that conveys defeat. I am glad to be able to finish Deuteronomy on such a victorious note. Let us notice five points: first, what God showed Moses before his death (verses 1-4); second, a divinely arranged funeral (verses 5-6); third, death at the right time (verse 7); fourth, the work goes on (verse 9); and fifth, the significance of Moses' life, or we could call it a kind of funeral sermon (verses 10-12).

What God Showed Moses Before his Death: (34:1-4)

Although it is never wise for us to be overly credulous about some spiritual claims, I do think that on some occasions, God has showed some of His people certain things, before their death, that lie in the future. I do not think that this is the norm, and I do not think we should ever ask for it, but sometimes, it has occurred, without anyone seeking it, so far as I know. He showed Moses exactly what was coming in Deuteronomy 34:1-4.

The Lord took Moses high up on Mount Pisgah, some 2,600 feet high, and I am told that if you went there today, on a clear day, you could see most of the Promised Land from the Dead Sea in the south, all the way to the Mediterranean Sea in the west, and northwards to Mount Hermon. Thus God told Moses, 'I'm going to let you look at nearly all this Promised Land from this vantage point on the mountain.'

You remember that Moses was not allowed to lead the people into the land, because of a sin he committed at the rock, when, instead of speaking to the rock to send out water, he smote it with his staff. God then told him that because of this transgression, he would not be allowed to go into the land. Even so, God still showed him grace and honored him very much. Although he could not lead the people into the land, God would let him see from afar the Land of Promise.

We noted earlier that scholars have found out in research over the last 100 to 150 years, that there is a certain formula in Deuteronomy and other places, concerning the legal conveyance of land. In order to give a valid title deed, a legal deed to property, one had to do certain things in the ancient Middle East, one of which was that if you were going to convey a title deed of land to someone, the person to whom the deed was to be made out had to see the land.

Hence, verse 4 is like God telling Moses, 'this is the beginning of the legal conveyance of this deed of the land to my people'. This same verse indicates that God is showing that this conveyance of land to His people is the fulfillment of a promise He had made to Abraham, Isaac, and Jacob. But He had also said: 'You will be pilgrims, strangers, and sojourners for a long time'. Indeed, it would be 600 years, with a little over 400 of those years spent in slavery in Egypt. Yet God had clearly promised that they were going to be a great and free people, with a wonderful homeland. Then in the fullness of the time (Gal. 4:4) God fulfilled His promise, although the fulness of God's time is not the same as ours! But, His word is as good as He is and is backed up to the hilt by the truth and the integrity of the eternal God, who cannot lie.

Therefore, He fulfilled the promise He made to Abraham: 'Look around you, Abraham; all this is going to belong to your seed' (Gen. 12:1). And yet, God operates on His own clock; it would be 600 years, from the time the promise was made to Abraham to the time that God showed Moses the land from Mount Pisgah. But it was the right time, and God did do it.

A Divinely Arranged Funeral (34:5–6)

During my lifetime as a relative of a large number of people, and also a pastor, I have helped to arrange many a funeral. But never one like this! Verse 5 says that the patriarch Moses died 'according to the word of the Lord'; that's important. In Deuteronomy 32:50, his death is spoken of as a command from God; a command, not a happenstance; not a mere byproduct of aging. Moses' birth had been at the right time, difficult as that time was for the people of the Hebrews in slavery in Egypt.

Pharaoh tried to kill the Hebrew baby boys, but it was the right time for His servant to be born. In the same way, your birth was at the right time, in the providence of God. And your death is going to be at exactly the right time for you to go home. I remember the first funeral I ever preached, of a handsome little boy about 11 years old, who was accidentally drowned along with another little boy. Some weeks later, the bereaved mother wrote me a letter, asking me some questions. Among them was this: since he died at only age eleven, was that the right time for him to go?

I knew that I was extremely limited in wisdom, but in the providence of God, I had just been reading Job 14:5. It seemed the best answer to the good mother. So, I quoted it: 'Seeing his days are determined, the number of his months are with Thee. Thou hast appointed the bounds that he cannot pass.' He was eleven years old; I don't know the mysteries of God, and I did not claim to go into them, but I believe, as a humble Christian, that God had appointed the number of that beautiful little boy's time on earth; there was a certain bound that he could not pass, and for him, it was 11 years old. For Moses it was a much greater age, which is generally easier for us to accept, as we think about the time of death.

Verse 6 says God buried him in a secret place. Only God knows where Moses is buried; therefore his grave site cannot be visited on a tour of the Holy Land. The fact that God buried him shows an intimacy and sweetness of fellowship between Almighty, Sovereign God on the throne of heaven, and the man of dust, Moses.

It must have been a strange, and certainly, an utterly unique funeral. Only God and the holy angels attended this funeral, and yet, according to Jude 9, the prince of demons also showed up. God had used Moses to defeat the power of Satan through Pharaoh in Egypt, and the devil was mad. The evil one showed up; and Jude says, 'He contended for the body of Moses.'

We don't know exactly what that means, and I am trying to be careful not to intrude on mysteries. The best I can tell is this: Revelation 12:10 says that Satan is 'the accuser of the brethren'; so Jude 9 may mean that the devil showed up in order to accuse Moses of his sins, as he had done before, when he asked God to be given free rein to destroy Job. The evil one protested that God had been too good to Job, who only loved the Lord for what God had given him. Along those lines, we could imagine Satan arguing that 'really and truly Moses was a sinner; he slew this Egyptian and buried him in the sand; He disobeyed you several times, and so he ought to belong to me.'

If I could guess what was happening, I would suggest that the devil wanted to stop Moses' divinely-honored burial, and all that it said about his relationship to God. But the devil could not prevent what must have been a majestic burial from taking place.

In terms of the New Testament, taking the experience of Moses some 1,400 years into the future, one of the mountains which Moses could have seen was not too far from Mount Pisgah, was Mount Hermon (or, as some think, Mount Tabor). Now listen to this amazing truth about God's later dealings with Moses. Yes, God had told Moses, 'You cannot in your natural lifetime go into the Promised Land, because you were disobedient, as you know, although I will let you see it.' But roughly 1400 years later, something wonderful happened, in which Moses' feet would go over into the Promised Land, and he would stand on Mount Hermon (or Tabor). Jesus was there, just before His passion, just before He paid the price for our sins in Gethsemane and on Calvary.

Before the passion of our Lord Jesus Christ, two persons from the Old Testament showed up to encourage this soon-to-be crucified Lamb of God, the soon-to-be resurrected Lamb of God: namely, Elijah and Moses, representative of the prophets and representative of the law.

Luke 9:30–31 says that they talked with the soon-to-be crucified Lamb of God about a matter of greatest importance to the whole world. What did Elijah and Moses talk about with Jesus, just before He goes into the agonies of the Passion? In the Authorized Version, it says that 'they spake with Him of the decease which He should accomplish at Jerusalem.' In Greek, it says 'they spake with Him of the exodus, which He should accomplish at Jerusalem.' What does that mean?

It means that what Jesus would do in Jerusalem,

outside the city walls and then in the tomb of Joseph of Arimathea, would constitute the great Exodus: the way out from slavery, the way out from sin, the way out from guilt, the way out from death, the opening into the Promised Land of eternal glory. From this perspective, Moses seems to be saying, 'Lord, the little Exodus that you used me to bring about through the Red Sea, where we smeared the blood of the Lambs on the various doorposts, so that the Angel of Death passed by, for that really to be valid and to reach its accomplishment, you need to go through this Exodus at Jerusalem and pay the full price that no lamb or bull or goat could ever pay because their blood is not infinite in its power and worth.' Elijah and Moses apparently encouraged our Savior to go through what He had to go through in Jerusalem, the truly great and final exodus.

Now how does that apply to the burial of Moses by God? It's just this: the devil might have shown up with accusation of Moses' sins. Yes, Moses was a sinner. Deuteronomy doesn't hide that; Exodus doesn't hide that; he was a sinner. He believed; he was saved; but he was still a sinner, and he failed God at several important junctures.

But still, God was going to take him directly to heaven, so that death had lost its sting. How does a sinner get into heaven? The devil wants to keep them all out, if he could; so we assume, without certainty, that that is what he was fussing about. Moses got into heaven the same way you and I shall get into heaven, through the blood of the Lamb. God had instituted the system of sacrifices through Moses and Aaron, but those daily morning and evening sacrifices and yearly Day of Atonement only pointed to the Lamb to whom Moses, 1400 years later, would be talking, not far from his grave on Pisgah, on another mountain, Mount Hermon. Moses got into heaven because his sins were covered by the blood of the Lamb in whom he had faith; that's the way you and I will get to our eternal home—there is no other way. The evil one must be infuriated, beyond all our conception, not to be able to stop it!

Moses' Death Happened at the Right Time (34:7)

Verse 7 makes it clear that it was not the natural process of aging that caused Moses' death. Although he was 120 years old, we are told his eye was not dim nor his natural force abated. God had kept his physical systems supernaturally strong, fresh, and young. Perhaps an illustration of this will be the promise to Asher that we looked at last week in chapter 33:25: 'Thy shoes shall be as iron and brass, and as thy days, so shall thy strength be'. Deuteronomy 8:4 applies this to the clothing of all the children of Israel for forty whole years: 'Thy raiment waxed not old upon thee; neither did thy foot swell these forty years.' What I draw from that is this: evidently during the exodus period in the wilderness there was a spirit of freshness and vitality and renewal that prevented their clothes and shoes from wearing out, their feet from swelling, and at least in Moses' case and maybe in others—maybe in Joshua, maybe in Caleb—it prevented their bodies from the normal process of aging. God can do that, if He wants to; He has all power, so why not? It was like a forerunner of the resurrection freshness and beauty of the body of our Lord Jesus Christ; it was working backwards.

Now all of this shows us that Moses did not necessarily need to die at this time, at least not physically; he was not worn out. But God ordained his death at this precise moment, and surely Moses would be happy to go home at that time, at the divine behest. Truly what Paul says in Philippians 1:21 is the case here with Moses: 'to die is gain'. Paul also says 'to depart and be with Christ is far better'.

You and I are in the midst of busy life; I hope your life is reasonably satisfying. As for me, I thank God for the different things He has allowed me to be and to do by His grace. I am grateful to be alive; however, to depart and be with Christ would be far better. For every child of God, to die at His time, is gain. It was so for Moses, and it will be so at our own preordained moment, if we are truly in the Lord by faith.

Remember this: if you are a believer in Christ, the day of your death will be the right day, and you will be very happy—more happy than you have ever been on this earth—on the other side of physical death. It will be the right day. Never, never worry about death. Never waste your time thinking of what year or what month or what day, or even for what cause you might die; don't waste your time on something like that. That is God's business; He will do it right. Therefore, it is in very good hands. What you need to be concerned about is the grace to be faithful unto the end, and to keep praying for that grace, to live to the fullness in the presence of Jesus. That's what you need to be concerned about—not when you are going to go. The time you and I go is predetermined before we were born, and it will be an appointed hour of release, to a much better place. What a happy way to look forward, to look to the rest of our life; what strength and gladness it gives us, if we look at it in that way. You know the hymn:

> But until then my heart will go on singing;
> Until then, with joy I'll carry on;
> Until the day mine eyes behold that city,
> Until the day God calls me home.
> ~ Ray Price

The Work of the Kingdom Goes On (34:9)

There is an old saying in the church, apparently going back to the Middle Ages: 'God buries the workmen, but the work goes on.' Moses had anointed Joshua to lead the people into the land, as later Elijah would anoint Elisha in his room, when the Lord took him up in the chariot of fire. Now that is one reason that the gates of hell should never prevail against the Christian church. There are many reasons, but one of them is that God keeps replacing His faithful workmen with the next generation. He gives them the Holy Spirit to enable them to carry out the spread of salvation in a way relevant to their generation and position. God will keep on doing that till the last Great Day through various workmen, but the work goes on.

The Significance of Moses' Life (34:10–12)

It might be stretching a point, but you could say that verses 10–12 are God's divine funeral sermon. It is at least possible, but not definite, that verses 10–12 might reflect what God said when He buried Moses. If so, it is the Divine assessment of the significance of one of the greatest men in the Old Testament, and one of the greatest men in all history. Verse 10 isolates the most important characteristic of Moses' entire life and ministry. How was it that this one man could change the world as he did, against such stupendous odds and indeed, considering some of the mistakes he made, and the sins he committed? How could one person be that incredibly useful and fruitful? We are told in verse 10 about Moses, 'whom the Lord knew face to face'. That's the key! Face to face! The concept of personality, what it is to be a person, as any scholar who knows anything about it will tell you, it comes from the Old Testament Hebrew word for 'countenance', particularly, 'face to face'—*panim*—that is what gives us the concept of personality.

It takes another, whom you face, before you really are a person, in the fullest sense. What about the unborn? Well, they are persons, because they are face to face with God their Creator, and they already have some kind of relationship with their mother. But particularly the most consequential thing about this man Moses was that he knew the Lord face to face; he went up into the presence of God when the whole nation was trembling down at the bottom of Mount Sinai, and was terrified, when everything was shaking. God instructed him to come up into the cloudy darkness, with frightening sounds of blaring trumpets. In that awesome place, Moses was face to face with God; the fountain of all personal blessing and fruitfulness.

It is the same in the New Testament, as we see in Philippians 3:7–8:

> For what things were gain to me, those I counted loss for Christ. Yea, and I count all things but loss for the excellency of the knowledge of Christ Jesus my Lord, for whom I have suffered the loss of all things and do count them but dung that I may win Christ—and verse 10, that I may know Him and the power of His resurrection and the fellowship of His sufferings, being made conformable unto His death.

I wonder if Moses, knowing God face to face, is not in the background of the basic Christian aspiration that Paul is praying for it in Philippians 3? St. Bernard of Clairvaux, in the Middle Ages may have written this hymn. Some lines from it express what Moses was already looking forward to in his face-to-face meeting with God:

> Jesus, thou joy of loving hearts,
> thou fount of life, thou light of men,
> From the best bliss that earth imparts
> we turn unfilled to thee again.
> Thy truth unchanged hath ever stood;
> thou savest those that on thee call;
> To them that seek thee thou art good;
> to them that find thee, all in all.
> Our restless spirits yearn for thee,
> where'er our changeful lot is cast;
> Glad when thy gracious smile we see;
> blest when our faith can hold thee fast.

Verses 11–12 summarize the miraculous work which God did through this man Moses, in overcoming Pharaoh and the biggest army in the world, and getting God's people successfully to the borders of the Promised Land. It speaks of 'mighty hand' in verse 12, and 'great terror'. Think of the terror of the destroying Angel of Death, and the terror when the waters of the Red Sea closed in on the Egyptian army. Mighty hand of God! Great terror of God! The holiness of God striking out against sin! And Moses was there when it happened.

In conclusion, it is very encouraging to me to remember that Moses' sins did not keep his life from changing the world. Nor did his imperfections keep his soul from going right into heaven, and later from seeing Jesus face-to-face. Moses knew that the blood of the Lamb was sufficient. Somehow David knew it; somehow Isaiah knew it; Jeremiah knew it; and one day, 1400 years after Moses' funeral, he would stand on the Mount of Transfiguration, once again face-to-face with this soon-to-be crucified, soon-to-be resurrected, holy, spotless Lamb of God. That was the true source of all his happiness and strength to labor each day; that gave him his strength to die happy, with eternal hope. That sovereign God: Father, Son, and Holy Spirit, is still using sinners, if they make themselves available, to expand his work of salvation on earth, and at the right time of His appointment, to get them home to heaven to be with Him forever more.

And so I conclude Deuteronomy, and this message of Moses' funeral, with a call from Jesus in Matthew 11:28–30 that we often read at the invitation to the Lord's Table:

Come unto me, all ye that labor and are heavy laden, and I will give you rest. Take my yoke upon you and learn of me, for I am meek and lowly of heart, and ye shall find rest unto your souls; for my yoke is easy and my burden is light.

Subject Index

A

Aaron, 96-97, 162, 169, 192
Abiram, 182
abortion, 120, 193, 294-95
Abraham, 20, 23, 38, 43-44, 60, 79, 104, 108, 130, 148-49, 222, 387, 459, 468
Achan, 201
Acton (Lord), 270
Adam, 151, 173, 206, 223, 281, 372, 378-79, 389, 427
Ahab, 252, 279
à Kempis, T., 246-47
Alexander, Archibald, 135
Amalekites, 148, 362-63, 421
Amish, 349-50
Ammonites, 50, 313
Amos, 84-85
Amram, 38
Anakim, 34, 37-38, 56, 159
angels, 460, 469
animals, 204-08, 359-60
Anna, 464-65
antinomianism, 101-2, 105
apostasy, 257-58, 390, 430, 439, 445-49
Ark (of Covenant), 168, 290, 381-82, 431
Asher, 464-65
Asherah, 255

Assyrians, 54, 85, 136, 391
atheism, 84, 160, 175, 213, 452
Aucas, 64
Augustine (St), 165, 287
authority, 249-53, 255-57, 262-63, 296

B

Babylonians, 54, 85, 183, 233, 257, 391
Bach, J.S., 122
Balaam, 65-66, 313, 321-22
Bancroft, J., 51
Bark, W.C., 52
Bathsheba, 305
beauty, 299-304, 325
Bennett, W., 175
Berlin Wall, 56-57
Bernard (of Clairvaux), 431, 472
Bethpeor, 65-68
betrothal, 307
Bezalel, 168
birds, 301-02, 442
blessing, 214, 319-24, 366, 368-69, 383-87, 389, 410, 446-47, 455, 459-65
Boaz, 313, 348, 361
Bolton, S., 112
Booth, W., 461
burial, 297

475

C

Caleb,   33, 56
Calvin, J.,   62-63, 83, 102-03, 122, 136, 186, 247, 268-69, 295, 297, 391
Campbell, D.,   111
Canaanites,   53-54, 203, 255, 275, 289, 290, 295, 326
capital punishment,   192, 198-99, 201, 257, 263, 279, 286, 293-94, 296-97, 306, 307
Carmichael, A.,   423
Carothers, M.,   393-94
Carthage,   193, 275
chastisement,   156-57, 256, 338, 354-55, 448-49, see also judgment
children,   129-31, 401, 408, 441
Christ, see Jesus and Messiah
church,   197, 243, 258, 265, 270, 291, 300, 308, 464
circumcision (spiritual),   9, 171-77, 413
clothing,   300-01
Cold War,   33
Collins, F. S.,   416
compassion,   86
confession,   236, 266, 384, 411
consecration,   10, 16, 45, 114, 122-23, 172, 227-28, 320
Constantine,   211, 291
contentment,   345-46
Corinth,   133
Cornelius,   207
Corti, E.,   92-93, 392
covenant,   9, 16, 107-09, 114-15, 133, 139, 153-58, 165, 167-69, 172-3, 371-401, 409-10, 413-14, 415, 427-29, 433-34, 441
Covenanters (Scottish),   434
coveting,   225, 343, 359-64, 365
Creator (God),   53, 68, 77-78, 109, 211, 302, 380, 422, 434, 440
Currid, J.,   19

curse,   153-58, 179, 182, 319-24, 377-83, 389-94, 403-06, 409-10, 461

D

Dabney, R.L.,   121, 211
Dan,   464
Darwin, C,   84, 440
David,   40, 79, 85, 269, 305, 313, 348, 393, 461-62
deacon,   368
death,   203-04, 379, 467-73
debt,   215-16, 224-25, 338-39, 392
Deism,   67, 84
Delitzsch, F.,   83-84, 391, 436
devil, see Satan
disobedience,   10, 37-42, 138-39, 142-43, 149-50, 165, 182, 338, 379, 384, 391-92, 409, 413, 429-30, 455
divorce,   222, 306-07
Dothan,   182
Douglas, M.,   206-07
Dwight, T.,   442

E

Eastern Orthodoxy,   190, 232
Ebal (mount),   179, 377, 380, 393
Eden (Garden of),   71-72, 83, 213
Edomites,   44, 313
education (Christian),   122-23, 129-31, 182-83, 219, 252-53
Edwards, J.,   117, 121-22, 127, 461
Egypt,   181, 234-35, 270, 351, 366-67, 403-04, 421
Egyptians,   135, 176, 313
Einstein, A.,   228
elder,   25-29, 262, 265, 296
Eleazar,   169
election,   10, 91-92, 112, 135-36, 142-43, 147, 184, 367, 386-87, 399-400, 407, 441-42
Elijah,   62, 252, 279, 283, 471
Elisha,   417, 471
Elliot, Elisabeth,   64

Elliott, Charlotte, 363-64
Ephesus, 187
equity, 10, 101, 224-25, 230, 266
Esau, 44, 50, 313, 366, 412
Esther, 363
evangelism, 245, 272-73, 374, 376, 465
evolution, 78-79, 84, 206, 440
excommunication, 200, 257-58, 279
exodus, 91, 131, 160-61, 442-43, 459, 469-70

F
Faber, F. W., 80, 400
faith, 31-36, 37-39, 41-42, 49, 52-53, 144-45, 161, 204, 214, 223, 298, 314, 398, 416-17, 422-25
faithfulness (of God), 22, 31, 44-47, 55, 126
family, 295-97, 306
fasting, 161-62
Faulkner, W., 441
fear, 57-58, 144-45, 289-90, 393, 423
fear (of God), 423-24
Firstfruits (festival), 241-44
foreknowledge, 148
forgiveness, 9, 86-87, 98, 105, 110, 135, 150, 165, 193, 234, 294, 308, 405, *see also grace*
future, 15-24, 55-58, 83-87, 188, 276-77, 321, 369, 391, 393-94, 396, 398, 407-08, 421-25, 427, 431, 441, 452, 463

G
Gad, 464
gender distinctives, 265, 300-01
genealogy, 154-55
generosity, 244, 289, 328, 331-32, 344, 369, 394, 397, 443, 463
George VI (King), 408
Gerizim (Mount), 179, 377, 380
Getty, K., 393
giants, *see Anakim*
Gideon, 187, 255-56, 456
Gilead, 52, 55

gleaning, 347-50
Glorious Revolution (1688), 396
glory, 134, 144, 184, 208, 242, 384, 437, 453-54, 462, 470
God (as consuming fire), 66, 77, 80-81, 110, 160-61, 163, 167, 410
God (nearness of), 68, 415-17
God (as spirit), 71-73, 77-78, 80
Golden Calf, 162, 169
Gorbachev, M., 232
gossip, 258
government (representative), 25-29
grace, 9-10, 42,103-04, 107-8, 114, 130, 134-35, 157, 165-70, 171-72, 179-84, 212, 217, 219, 229, 231, 238, 29, 348-49, 358, 375, 386, 395, 399, 401, 410, 416, 422, 430, 449, 464-65, 468, 471, *see also forgiveness*
Graham, B., 177, 231, 419
Great Awakening, 69, 135
grief, 203-04, 454-56

H
Haman, 363
Hannibal, 193
hardening (of heart), 392-93, 397-99, 439, 444
Hart, J., 126-27
Haskins, M. L., 408
Havergal, F.R., 114
health, 144
heart (new), 9, 108, 115, 157, 171-77, 373, 400, 413
Heaven, 81, 193, 200, 417
Hell, 81, 417-18
Henderson, A., 384
Herbert, G., 94
Hezekiah (King), 194
high priest 96-98, 109, 114, 116, 168, 170, 204, 242, 280, 290, 314, 429-31
Higher Criticism, 17
Hilary (of Poitiers), 297
history, 25-26, 65-66, 79, 175, 181, 188

Hittites, 18-19
holiness, 9, 68, 8, 100, 110, 134-39, 153, 161, 167, 256, 266, 303, 307, 311-17, 331, 375, 390-91, 428, 435, 440
hope, 16, 89, 92, 157, 162, 193, 204, 403, 408, 451-56
Hosea, 87, 108, 197
Huxley, J., 78
humility, 375, 456
hygiene, 315

I

idolatry, 66, 72-73, 83, 137, 153, 156, 162, 182-83, 185-90, 193, 256, 271, 339-41, 380, 390-91, 403-08
immorality, 66, 68, 137, 187, 256, 326
impartiality, 343-44
incest, 312-13, 380
intercession, 96, 159-63, 278, 337, 363, *see also prayer*
interest, 327
Isaac, 43-44, 79, 108
Islam, 67, 145
Issachar 464

J

Jacob, 44, 79, 108, 213, 268, 366, 412, 460
Jehoshaphat, 160
Jenkins, P., 448
Jericho, 201
Jerusalem, 191-92
Jesus, 17, 19, 22-23, 35, 41-42, 44, 57, 61-63, 68, 74, 78, 80, 85, 90-91, 96-98, 100-01, 104, 106, 110, 112, 113-14, 116-17, 119-20, 131, 134, 136, 147, 150-51, 166, 168-70, 174, 192, 204, 207-08, 212-13, 217-19, 222-23, 230, 233, 237-39, 241-45, 256, 257, 263-64, 266, 267-68, 272, 279-80, 286, 297-98, 303, 307, 313-14, 320, 322-24, 333, 334-35, 341, 345-46, 348, 351, 357-58, 361, 372, 374, 378-79, 381-2, 393, 401, 412-14, 416-19, 431-32, 435-38, 448, 452-54, 460, 461-64, 469, *see also Messiah*

Jethro, 27, 262
Jezebel, 252, 282-83
Job, 437
Jocebed, 38
John (the Baptist), 46, 150, 168, 207, 379
John Knox's House, 100
Johnson, T.L., 236
Jonah, 136
Jones, E. M., 67
Joseph, 143, 198, 322, 334, 366, 428, 463
Josephus, 392
Joshua, 33, 56, 61, 63, 95, 137, 186, 282, 326, 395, 421, 471
joy, 195, 211, 238, 243-44, 272, 288-89, 308, 319, 327, 333
Jubilee, 210, 219-20
Judah, 461-62
judgment, 174, 195, 199, 230, 252, 253, 256, 291, 340, 362, 386, 393, 405-06, 409, 427, 446, 451, 459, *see also chastisement*
justice, 250-53, 261-66

K

Kadesh-barnea, 60
Kennedy, D.J., 103-04
Kenya, 188, 360-61
kidnapping, 334-35
Kingship (in Israel), 267-73
Kipling, R., 153-54
Koran, 67
Korea, 50-51

L

Lady Justice (statue), 29
Lamb of God, 168, 189, 193, 207, 235, 237-8, 469-70
landmarkers, 281-83, 380
Law, W., 125-26
Law (of Moses), 137, 169, 262
law (ceremonial), 100-01, 211-12, 218, 263

law (civil),   100-01, 218
law (moral),   99-106, 211-13
leaven,   235-36
Lee, R.G.,   447
legalism,   104, 114
Levi,   462-63
levirate law,   348, 360-61
Levites,   95-96, 160, 169, 179, 192, 195, 207, 210-11, 217, 277-78, 377, 379, 436
Lewis (island),   111, 177
Lewis, C.S.,   267, 356-57
lex talionis,   283-86, 306
light,   10-11, 102, 134-35, 177, 204, 265, 288, 320, 375-76, 419, 430, 459
livestock,   299-300
Livingston, J.,   384-85
Lloyd-Jones, D. M.,   53
Lord's Supper,   79, 127, 234, 237-38, 473
Lot,   45, 50, 313
love (for God),   9, 102, 105, 109, 114, 117, 119, 139, 141-45, 169, 256, 368
love (of God),   10, 106, 109, 126, 136, 141, 216, 288, 307, 314, 333, 351, 366-67, 384, 390-91, 400, 411, 418-19, 442, 462

M

Mackintosh, H.R.,   74
Maimonides, M.,   205
manslaughter,   95
Marcellus,   84
marriage,   136, 138-39, 295, 305-09, 332-33, 371, 373, 390-91, 427-28
Mary (mother of Jesus),   460, 462, 464
Massachusetts Bay Colony   50-51
Massah,   129-30
materialism,   138, 157, 185
Mather, C.,   339-40, 430
Mayflower Compact,   395-96
McCheyne, R.M.,   331, 387
Mediator,   9-10, 80, 110, 112, 379

mercy, *see forgiveness and grace*
mercy seat,   168, 189, 429-31
Messiah,   44, 63, 97, 397, 413, 425, 448, *see also Jesus*
Micah,   63
Micaiah (ben Imlah),   279
millstone,   334
Milton, J.,   94, 288
Miriam,   337
Moabites,   45, 50, 313
Modernism,   67, 73, 77-78, 145, 206, 234, 276, 320, 356, 390, 406, 428
modesty,   301, 316
Molech,   193
Moravians,   424
Mordecai,   363
Morgan, G. Campbell,   37, 39
Moses,   17-21, 23, 37-38, 41, 59-64, 67, 110, 166, 278, 337-38, 375, 421-22, 433-34, 451-52, 467-73
Muhammad,   67
murder,   192, 287-92, 293-97
Murray, A.,   157, 461
mutilation,   312

N

Naaman,   417
Naboth,   252, 283
name (of God),   21, 197-202, 393
Naomi,   348
Naphtali,   464
Nathanael,   268
National Covenant (of Scotland),   384, 396
Nebuchadnezzar,   128, 446
new birth – *see heart, new*
New England,   340, 430
Newman, J.H.,   175
Newton, J.,   130
Noah,   205

O

oath (covenant), 395-401
obedience, 133-39, 141-45, 147-51, 158, 169, 266, 371-74, 377, 379, 383-87, 460
occult, 188, 269, 275-77, 327
Og, 56, 421
Onesimus, 222
Orr, J. E., 382
Owen, J., 317

P

Palestine, 115, 144
Palmer, B. M., 63
parapets, 302
pardon – *see forgiveness*
parents, 93, 122-23, 129-31, 148, 251-52, 264, 355
partiality, 29
Passover, 79, 194, 229, 233-39
patience, 61
Patrick (St), 443
Pentecost, 241-43
persecution, 319-20
Peter, 46, 169-70, 207, 268, 279, 412
Philemon, 222
Philip (evangelist), 238
Philip, J., 62, 75, 92, 385, 423, 429-30, 446, 463
Philistines, 50, 447
Philo, 205
Pigott, J.S., 111
Pilate, Pontius, 294
Pink, A. W., 16, 50, 60, 85
polygamy, 222, 296
poor, the, 211-13, 215-19, 271, 282, 327, 329, 339, 343-51, 367-68
pornography, 316
prayer, 59-64, 80-81, 130, 145, 194, 208, 256, 258-60, 290, 412, 471 *see also intercession*
predestination, 148, 184, 387
pride, 103-04
primogeniture, 295-96

Promised Land, 23, 33, 40, 45, 49, 62, 85, 89, 108, 125, 133-39, 162, 167, 180-1, 183, 210, 246, 262, 282
prophet, 198-200, 278-80, 321, 340
psychotherapy, 356-57
punishment, 284-86, 353-58, 361, 390-91, *see also chastisement*
Puritans, 74-75, 103, 127, 176, 185, 213, 229, 288-89, 317, 378, 413, 430

R

Rebekah, 44
Reformers (Protestant), 185
refuge (city of), 9, 95-98, 104, 281
relativism, 415
remembrance, 85-86, 89-94, 145, 439-44
remnant, 183-84, 399-400
repentance, 150, 157, 182, 200, 256-58, 294-95, 314, 340, 373, 386-87, 396, 409-14, 456-57
resurrection, 242-44, 246, 297, 316, 323, 345, 375, 460, 467, 470
Reuben, 461
revival, 384-85, 441
Richard (of Saint Victor), 121
righteousness, 417
Robinson, G.W., 111
Roman Empire, 52, 138, 174-75, 193, 275, 291
Rossetti, C., 373
Rushdoony, R. J., 306
Ruth, 313, 348, 361
Rutherford, S., 269, 321, 462

S

Sabbath, 13, 209-29, 313, 328, 349, 398, 423, 444
salvation, 91, 102, 137, 189, 200-01, 322-24, 389, 417, 441
Samaritan woman, 98, 189, 237, 264, 436
Samson, 447
Samuel, 198, 268-69
sanctification, 53

sanitation, 315
Sarah, 43-44
Satan, 17, 71-72, 83, 90, 136, 149-50, 160, 166, 193, 198-200, 206, 257, 270, 275-76, 279, 287, 317, 320, 322, 351, 375, 411, 417, 428, 437, 453, 462, 465
Saul (King), 269, 363, 393, 462
Schlossberg, H., 84, 380
Schmeman, Alexander, 190
Scotland, 219, 384
Scripture, 15, 25-27, 66-68, 72, 78, 89-90, 92, 96, 103, 138, 182-83, 186, 188, 189-90, 199, 203, 215, 219, 236-37, 258, 265, 271-72, 276-80, 290, 327, 404-08, 425, 440
Secularism – *see atheism*
Shillito, E., 98
Shiloh, 189, 191, 233, 243
Sihon, 52, 421
Silving, H., 252
Simeon, 461
sin, 22, 40, 86, 96-97, 103, 115, 151, 411 *see also disobedience*
Sinai (Mount), 78, 108, 110, 278, 459-60, 472
slavery, 221-25, 326, 351
Socialism, 349-50
Solomon (King), 69, 138, 168, 191, 271, 289
sonship, 119, 134, 171
sovereignty (of God), 35, 49-52, 60, 129, 142, 145, 154, 161, 256, 455, 465
Spanish Armada, 50-51, 57
species, 302-03
spies, 33-34, 37-39
Spirit, Holy, 23, 27, 47, 56, 63, 66, 69, 72-75, 90-91, 97, 101, 104, 106, 108-09, 111-12, 114-16, 137-38, 143, 147, 151, 168, 169, 173-4, 187, 199, 204, 211, 213, 217-18, 225, 238-39, 241-43, 258-59, 266, 278-79, 285, 290, 303, 309, 322, 324, 335, 347, 350-51, 372-73, 381-82, 384-86, 396, 398, 400-01, 403, 412-13, 423, 433, 435-36, 445, 448, 454-55, 457, 464, 471
Spurgeon, C.H., 60, 348

Squanto, 51
St Giles Cathedral, 75
Stalin, J., 181-82
stealing, 325-29
Still, William, 15-16, 73, 112, 320
Sunday, 211-12

T
tabernacle, 168, 189, 210, 229, 321-22, 431
Tabernacles (festival), 245-47, 423
temple (at Jerusalem), 168, 191, 207, 210, 217, 229, 256, 264, 377
terrorism, 32-33, 160
thankfulness, 125-28, 208, 210, 213, 324, 366
Thornwell, J. H., 454
time, 227-28, 234
tithe, 195, 210-14, 278, 365-69
transfiguration, 62-63, 472
trials, 31-36, 129-30, 147-49, 320, 366, 443, 462
Trinity, 120-21, 197, 201, 238, 301, 333, 460, 472-73
trust – *see faith*

U
unbelief, 40-42
uncleanness, 194
Uriah, 305

V
von Hugel, Baron, 55
vow, 327-28

W
warfare 15, 53-54, 71, 136-38, 291
Warfield, B.B., 12
Watts, Isaac, 87
Wesley, Charles, 121, 201-02
Wesley, John, 253-54, 284-5, 424
Wesley, Susanna, 30-31
Westminster Assembly, 10

Westminster Confession of Faith 100, 211, 217-18, 224, 237, 263-64, 269, 321, 384, 454
Westminster Shorter Catechism, 250
Wilberforce, W., 221
witness, 283, 337-41, 380
Word of God – *see Scripture*
work, 349-50
workers, 93-94, 195

worship, 10-11, 71-75, 185-90, 191-95, 197-202, 236-37, 250-53, 317, 327
wrath (of God) – *see God as consuming fire*

Z

zeal (of God), 452-54
Zebulon, 464
Zedekiah, 279

Scripture Index

Genesis
2:17   379
4:10   192
9:3-4   192
9:6   192, 293
12:1   468
14:20   213
15:1   130
15:7   53
15:16   53-54, 137
17:7-8   60
27:38-40   44
28:22   213
35   311
41:52   143
49   311-12, 460-64
50:20   143, 322

Exodus
3   80
3:7   235
3:14   21
12:2   233-34
13   227
15:14-15   52
16:18   214
17:1-7   129
17:8-16   362
18   27
20:2   103
22:2   288
22:16-17   307
23   215-19
23:2   250
23:6   344
23:15   235
31   168

Leviticus
11   205
11:45   167
17:10-14   193
18   54
18:6-24   137
19   348
19:2   103
20:20   306
23   348

Numbers
6:24-26   109, 168, 277, 429, 431
11   27
12:1-2   337
12:13   337-38
15:37-41   303
18   227
20   61
20:7-13   37
23:7-8   322
25:1-9   65
35:25   96

Joshua
8   381
8:30   393

Judges
2-3   455
5:20   84, 434
7   289
16:20   447

1 Samuel
2:30   463
14-15   363
16:7   381

1 Kings
21   282
22   326
22:11-28   279

2 Chronicles
20:12   160
30:18-19   194

Nehemiah
8-9   423
8:9   384
8:10   195
9:25   126
10:39   423

Job
1:21   203
2:4   231
9:33   110
12:23   51
14:5   468-69
42:5-6   437

Psalms
1   272
1:1-2   407
2:11   237
5:7   237
14:1   84
16:8   122, 156, 250, 253, 266, 272, 460
17:8   442
18:2-3   436
19:7-8   90
22:1   314
23   423
23:1   23, 275
24:1   53, 137, 291, 311, 325
27:4   237, 276
31:2-3   436
34:7   460
34:9   424
34:15   130
37:20   57

40:6   116
40:8   119
51   305
51:4   411
51:6-7   341, 381
51:17   85
65   292
71:3   95
75:6-8   456
76:10   462
78:5-8   26, 46, 397, 455
78:22   397
78:31   397
78:34   104
81:6   289, 443, 446
81:10-16   389
81:13-16   142
86:7   166
90:17   176, 177
95   41, 211
95:6   237
95:8-11   34
103   127, 449
106:23   162
110:3   9, 413
111:4-10   157-58
119:9-11   90, 407
119:96   10, 249, 299, 331
119:97   112
119:117   85
119:130   26
121   20-21, 323
121:4   33
122:1   195
126   409-10
130:3   10
132:8-9   382
132:15-16   382
136   377
137:1-4   409
139:1-7   381
139:7-12   391
139:23-24   341, 381, 411
141:1-8   21
142:6-7   393
143:3-9   26
145:9   360
145:15-16   360
147:11   386
147:13-14   289
148:9   292
148:14   68
150   176, 289

Proverbs
1:23   401
3:11-12   148
3:17   28
4:23   71, 405
7:9   428
7:21   428
9:10   373
11:1-6   362
12:10   360
13:24   354
14:12   265
19:18   354
20:11   357
21:1   181
22:7   224-25, 463-64
23:10-11   283
23:26   119, 373
28:13-14   383, 411
29:15   354
30:7-9   128, 349
31:8-9   295
31:25-31   176

Ecclesiastes
5:4-5   328
8:11   354
12   246

Song of Solomon
5:16   176
6:1   176

Isaiah
1:9   399
1:27   157
6   398
6:3   134
8:18-19   277
9:9-11   456
10:20-22   399
26:8-9   156, 414
28:21   386
30:18   167, 214
30:21   10
40:15-17   456
40:27-31   34, 161
42:24-25   455
44:1-3   435
44:6   435
48:9-11   453
53   238
53:3   454
53:4-6   357
53:6   317
55:1   170
55:6   237
55:8-9   451
56:3-5   312
65:24   126

Jeremiah
2:5   188
29:12-14   85, 401
31   112
31:31-34   10, 105, 115, 169, 173, 184, 266, 372, 413
33:3   165-66

Lamentations
1:12   322
3:21   89
3:23   31
3:33   389, 400

Ezekiel
11:8-10   156-57
11:16   183, 393
18:4   379
18:20   172
20:8-9   453
22:30   162
36:25-27   115, 173, 413
36:37   166-67
37:1-3   21-22

Daniel
3   34
4:28-32   128, 399
6   34
11:32   34

Hosea
4   326
6:2-3   440
7:2-3   406
7:6-10   406
8:4   84
13:6   154

Joel
2:11-14   457
2:21-27   457

Amos
3:6   391
5:19   391
8:5   362

Jonah
2:9   136

Micah
1:7   327
6:8   172, 407
7:14   389, 400

Habakkuk
3:3-6   459-60

Zechariah

8:22-23   465
9:6   312
14:20-21   303

Malachi

1:9   229-30
3:10-11   214, 278, 369

Matthew

3:14-15   150, 379
4:3-10   17
5:3ff   383, 385
5:14-16   134
5:17   169
5:17-20   211
5:25-26   286
5:36   337
5:38-39   284
5:44-45   174
6:3-4   266
6:24   138
9:29   161
11:28-30   473
12:1-8   328
16:26   271, 345
18:17   258
19   332
19:8   222
21:28-31   46-47
22:34-39   113-14, 119, 172, 368
25   81, 101, 185
25:24-40   174
25:34-36   195
26:11   215
26:28   454
26:39   372, 379, 453
26:75   412
27:53   242
28:19-20   137, 263-64, 291, 314

Mark

7:15   207
8:36   138
9:20-24   22, 58
14:1   237

Luke

2:14   460
2:36-38   464-65
6:38   328
9:30-31   469
11:13   106, 401
12:32   399
18:27   363
19:1-10   143
20:28   18
23:39-43   86
23:42   121
24:26-27   425

John

1:1   90
1:14   74
1:29   168, 207, 237
1:46-51   168
3:3-5   173, 398
3:15   184
3:16   288, 331
3:16-17   324
4:19-26   189
4:32   453
4:34   119
6:14   279
6:57-58   398
6:63   90
6:65   398
7:17   401
7:40   279
8:1-11   98, 257, 308
8:12   102
8:29   130
10   276
11:35   204
12:8   347
12:24   242
14:8   74
14:9   452
14:15   139, 141, 365, 372, 374
14:19   244
14:21   102
14:21-23   142
15   104
15:2   244
15:5   156
15:9-14   167, 418-19
15:11   289
15:15   9
15:17-21   320
17:4   45
17:5   453
17:17   415
17:24   438
18:11   341
19:30   379
20:21-22   219, 351
21:15-17   169-70

Acts

3:19-23   279
4:12   192
5:31   412
8:27   238
10:9-21   207
10:33   236
10:34   343
15:19-21   137, 207-08
15:29   192
16   356
16:25-30   176
17:26-27   51, 53, 291
17:29   72
20:31   60
20:35   348

Romans

1:23-28   404-05
2   105
2:6-9   405
3:10   317
3:20   103, 384
3:23   317
4:23-25   104
5:5   216
5:8   141
5:12-21   151, 223
5:19   379
5:20   166, 167-68
6:23   379
7:15   389-90
7:17-21   390
7:21   373
8:14-17   69
8:22-23   206-07
8:28   290, 323
8:29   148
8:32   22, 235, 324
9:3   162
9:9-11   367
9:27   184
10:1-3   400
10:6-9   68, 91, 400, 416-17
10:9-10   119-20
10:19   448
11:4-7   441-42
11:5   184
11:7-8   397
11:11   448
11:25-26   448
11:30-33   442
12:1-2   53, 172, 187, 195, 230, 424, 436
12:13   217
12:15   204
12:19   284, 323
13:1-4   286
13:8   225

13:10 100
13:12-14 308
15:4 16, 20

1 Corinthians

1:25-29 367, 456
3:3-8 63
4:7 126
5:6-8 236-37
6:9-11 9, 308
7 332
7:14 401
7:21 222
9:9 360
10:5-6 40-41
10:11 133
10:31 204
12:26-27 294
13:5 121
14:24-25 239
15:23 242
15:55 467
16 195
16:1 212, 244

2 Corinthians

1:20 379
2:15-16 319
3 162
3:13-18 398
3:17 120
3:18 112, 438
4:17-18 144
5:2 59
5:7 144, 422
5:16-17 174
6:14-18 139
7:1 440
7:10 412
8:9 166
8:12-15 212
9:6 214
9:8 214
10:3-5 54, 138, 194-95, 291
11:24 356

Galatians

3:13 297, 393
3:24 103
3:27-28 222
4:4 379, 468
5:1 335
5:22-23 169
6:7 429

Ephesians

1:3-6 92, 386-87
1:4 147
1:11 35, 39, 51
1:16-19 74
1:20-23 375
1:23 242-43
2:1 243
2:1-3 136
2:1-6 180
2:4-6 375
2:5-7 243
2:6 151, 346
2:8-9 34
2:10 147
2:11 85-86
2:11-13 92
2:12-16 314
2:13 68
3:14-15 109
3:20 130, 145
4:21-24 266
4:28 112, 218-19, 266, 329
4:29 338
5:21-33 106, 307
6:1-4 93
6:5-9 93
6:12 71, 290
6:17-18 138

Philippians

1:21 470
2:12-13 413
2:15 135
3:7-8 472
4:4 319
4:8 v79
4:11-13 123, 128, 345

Colossians

1:27 169
3:1-5 345-46
3:1-14 308-09

1 Thessalonians

4:3-8 309
4:13 204
5:18 128, 324

1 Timothy

2:1-4 256, 272-73
2:5 110, 192
3:6 27
4:4-5 194, 208
6:6-8 345
6:17 289

2 Timothy

2:19 386
3:12 319
3:16 15, 66, 203, 287

Titus

1:15 208

Philemon

15-19 223

Hebrews

1:2-3 452
1:14 460
3:1-6 280
3:15-19 41
4-8 381-82
4:1-2 34
4:9-10 41
4:11 52
4:14-16 41-42, 86, 97, 167, 204, 237
5:6 170
5:7-9 151
7:22-25 96, 162
8 112
8:5 168
8:6 110, 168
9:6-10 218
9:11-12 97, 218
9:14 110
9:22 114, 168, 172, 192, 379
10:9 218
10:11-12 97
10:14-20 189
10:16 105
10:25 423-24
11:1 38, 49
11:10 366
11:25 38
11:26 63
11:39-40 64
12:2 422
12:5-11 354, 449
12:11 148
12:17 412
12:19 80
12:25-29 218
13:8 50
13:14 64, 77
13:16 218
13:20-21 168

James

1:8 446
1:22 183
2:1-4 344
2:15-16 195, 213
2:19 121
3:8-10 338
4:1 287
4:3 166
4:7 465
4:8-10 237
4:13-15 407

1 Peter

1:2   147
1:7-8   195
1:16   103, 167
1:18-19   131, 351
2:5   114
2:9-10   91
2:13-17   251
2:21-24   358
2:24   297
3:1-4   285
3:8-11   285
3:18   110, 315-16
4:1-3   316

2 Peter

1:20-21   27, 66-67, 278-79
2:9   91
3:13   292

1 John

1:4   289
1:5   288, 437
1:7   419
1:8   373
1:9   98, 266
2:1-2   98
2:15   138
4:4   309
4:8   102, 109, 121, 288, 324, 333, 389
4:19   141
4:20   368
5:3   112, 191
5:4   38, 53
5:21   120

3 John

2   143
4   419

Jude

5   45
9   469
20-21   47

Revelation

1:10   212
2:5   46
3:18   398
8   80-81
12:10   469
12:11   231
13:8   168, 238, 323
15:3-4   433, 437
19:20   81
21:3   69
21:27   378
22:19   66

Christian Focus Publications

Our mission statement —

STAYING FAITHFUL

In dependence upon God we seek to impact the world through literature faithful to His infallible Word, the Bible. Our aim is to ensure that the Lord Jesus Christ is presented as the only hope to obtain forgiveness of sin, live a useful life and look forward to heaven with Him.

Our books are published in four imprints:

CHRISTIAN FOCUS

Popular works including biographies, commentaries, basic doctrine and Christian living.

CHRISTIAN HERITAGE

Books representing some of the best material from the rich heritage of the church.

MENTOR

Books written at a level suitable for Bible College and seminary students, pastors, and other serious readers. The imprint includes commentaries, doctrinal studies, examination of current issues and church history.

CF4·K

Children's books for quality Bible teaching and for all age groups: Sunday school curriculum, puzzle and activity books; personal and family devotional titles, biographies and inspirational stories — because you are never too young to know Jesus!

Christian Focus Publications Ltd,
Geanies House, Fearn, Ross-shire,
IV20 1TW, Scotland, United Kingdom.
www.christianfocus.com